FRIENDS OF FREEDOM

From the Sons of Liberty to British reformers, Irish patriots, French Jacobins, Haitian revolutionaries and American Democrats, the greatest social movements of the Age of Atlantic Revolutions grew as part of a common, interrelated pattern. In this new transnational history, Micah Alpaugh demonstrates the connections between the most prominent causes of the era, as they drew upon each other's models to seek unprecedented changes in government. As Friends of Freedom, activists shared ideas and strategies internationally, creating a chain of broad-based campaigns that mobilized the American Revolution, British Parliamentary Reform, Irish nationalism, movements for religious freedom, abolitionism, the French Revolution, the Haitian Revolution, and American party politics. Rather than a series of distinct national histories, Alpaugh shows how these movements jointly responded to the Atlantic trends of their era to create a new way to alter or overthrow governments: mobilizing massive social movements.

Micah Alpaugh is Associate Professor of History at the University of Central Missouri. His previous publications include *Non-Violence and the French Revolution: Political Demonstrations in Paris, 1787–1795* (2015), *The French Revolution: A History in Documents* (2021), and articles in *European History Quarterly, Journal of Social History*, and *French Historical Studies*.

FRIENDS OF FREEDOM

The Rise of Social Movements in the Age of Atlantic Revolutions

MICAH ALPAUGH

University of Central Missouri

CAMBRIDGE
UNIVERSITY PRESS

CAMBRIDGE
UNIVERSITY PRESS

University Printing House, Cambridge CB2 8BS, United Kingdom

One Liberty Plaza, 20th Floor, New York, NY 10006, USA

477 Williamstown Road, Port Melbourne, VIC 3207, Australia

314–321, 3rd Floor, Plot 3, Splendor Forum, Jasola District Centre,
New Delhi – 110025, India

103 Penang Road, #05–06/07, Visioncrest Commercial, Singapore 238467

Cambridge University Press is part of the University of Cambridge.

It furthers the University's mission by disseminating knowledge in the pursuit of
education, learning, and research at the highest international levels of excellence.

www.cambridge.org
Information on this title: www.cambridge.org/9781316515617
DOI: 10.1017/9781009026116

First published 2022

A catalogue record for this publication is available from the British Library.

Library of Congress Cataloging-in-Publication Data
Names: Alpaugh, Micah, author.
Title: Friends of freedom : the rise of social movements in the age of Atlantic revolutions / Micah
Alpaugh, University of Central Missouri.
Other titles: Rise of social movements in the age of Atlantic revolutions
Description: Cambridge, United Kingdom ; New York : Cambridge University Press, 2022. | Includes
bibliographical references and index.
Identifiers: LCCN 2021027004 (print) | LCCN 2021027005 (ebook) | ISBN 9781316515617 (hardback) |
ISBN 9781009012553 (paperback) | ISBN 9781009026116 (ebook)
Subjects: LCSH: United States – History – Revolution, 1775–1783 – Influence. | United States – History –
Revolution, 1775–1783 – Social aspects. | France – History – Revolution, 1789–1799 – Influence. |
Jacobins – History. | Political clubs – History. | Social movements – History. | Social movements –
International cooperation. | Liberty – History – 18th century. | Atlantic Ocean Region – Politics and
government – History. | Europe – Politics and government – 1789–1900. | BISAC: HISTORY / General
Classification: LCC E209 .A45 2022 (print) | LCC E209 (ebook) | DDC 303.48/409–dc23
LC record available at https://lccn.loc.gov/2021027004
LC ebook record available at https://lccn.loc.gov/2021027005

ISBN 978-1-316-51561-7 Hardback

CONTENTS

ACKNOWLEDGMENTS

This project began on a sunny spring afternoon in 2010 as light shone into the otherwise inhospitable Bibliothèque nationale de France's Salle L. Casting around for future project ideas in the weeks after finishing a dissertation about Parisian revolutionary protest, I came across a pamphlet I had never heard of: *The Correspondence of the London Revolution Society in London, with the National Assembly, with Various Societies of the Friends of Liberty in France and England* (1792). In it, I found an untold history of the origins of France's Jacobin Club, founded in emulation of Anglo-American models instead of by abstract Gallic design, as well as ongoing rich exchanges between French revolutionaries and British radicals. Immediately, I set aside other prospective projects and pursued the thread – ultimately finding that the British origins of the French Jacobins were only one in a long series of interconnected social movements that mobilized the Revolutionary Era.

Like all books, this one was shaped by its historical and historiographical moment, as old certainties about national histories faced new challenges. That winter, Ken Pomeranz had generously welcomed me to his World History Seminar at the University of California, Irvine, stimulating my interest in big history. During my graduate years there, professors like Daniel Schroeder, Vinayak Chaturvedi, Heidi Tinsman, Michelle Molina, and Jim Given pushed me to look beyond nation-states and find wider connections. Already, Atlantic history was becoming a growing field – unlike for prior generations of scholars, my first graduate seminar with Tim Tackett was on French colonial history, rather than that of the *métropole* by itself. My career has involved teaching more world history than European history courses, while even my upper-division European classes have become deeply infused by global approaches.

Ultimately spanning the United States, Britain, Ireland, France, and Haiti, this project has provided great opportunities to get to know new places and people. The University of Pennsylvania Humanities Forum (now Wolf Humanities Center) generously granted me a 2011–12 Postdoctoral Fellowship to pursue research, which enabled wonderful opportunities to learn about the Eastern Seaboard, its archives, and scholars. Subsequent summers featured months-long research tours, ultimately allowing me to visit nearly a hundred libraries and archives. Special thanks are due to the staffs of the places where I spent lengthy stints: the Bibliothèque nationale de France, British Library, Library of Congress (especially its exceptionally helpful manuscripts staff), and the Southern California oasis of the Huntington Library. Closer to home, this project could not have been completed without the rich collections of the University of Kansas, University of Missouri-Kansas City (particularly its digital subscriptions), and those the Interlibrary Loan desk of the University of Central Missouri could procure.

Working across many national histories also allowed me to present and collaborate with new groups of scholars. My thanks to audiences at meetings of the North American, Midwest, and Pacific Coast branches of the Conference on British Studies, Britain and the World, American Conference for Irish Studies, Society for French Historical Studies, Western Society for French History, Consortium on the Revolutionary Era, the Conference on Latin American History, and the Pacific Coast Branch of the American Historical Association. Jeff Horn generously invited me to present the Costello Distinguished Lecture at Manhattan College, Michael Goode and John Smolenski at their Specter of Peace in the History of Violence conference on colonial American History, Mathieu Ferradou at the Sorbonne's *L'Etranger en Révolution(s)*, my colleagues at the Mount Allison University Faculty Research Workshop and University of Central Missouri's Honors College, and Jeff Pasley and Ken Owen at the Missouri Regional Seminar on Early American History. A special thanks to Jeff for hosting many excellent scholarly gatherings through the University of Missouri's Kinder Institute on Constitutional Democracy and Ken for urging me to extend my project into the rise of the Democratic Party.

Many scholars and friends helped shape this book through their examples, suggestions, and encouragement. Suzanne Desan and Nathan Perl-Rosenthal read early drafts of my first Jacobin chapter in 2011 and helped convince me that I had something original to say. Penn's weekly seminar on "Adaptations," led by Warren Breckman and Jim English, wound up shaping my book's theoretical framing more than I could have predicted. Among many others, conversations with Matt Adkins, Bryan Banks, Katlyn Carter, Ian Coller, Manuel Covo, Matthew Rainbow Hale, Joe Krulder, Michelle Orihel, Julia Osman, Janet Polasky, Jeremy Popkin, Ben Park, Meghan Roberts, Noah Shusterman, Julian Swann, Catherine Tourangeau, Liana Vardi, Sophie Wahnich, and Philipp Zeische especially influenced my thinking. Tim Murtagh helped guide my Irish research at several Dublin pubs. Bill Kondrath and Chris Robb generously hosted me on multiple trips to Massachusetts. Tim Tackett and Helen Chenut remain valued mentors and friends. My parents Lee and Kathleen, sister Terra, and brother-in-law Peter Ianonne have been unfailingly supportive. Honors undergraduates and graduate students in my Atlantic World seminars at the University of Central Missouri read several chapters, and Kathleen Moore-Alpaugh, Heather

Alpaugh, and Erika Vause read the full manuscript. Many thanks to two anonymous peer readers who pushed me to extend my contextualization and conclusions further. Editor Liz Friend-Smith graciously helped guide the manuscript to completion, while Deepu Raghuthaman and Priyanka Durai kindly copy-edited it. My fellow historians at the University of Central Missouri have stayed supportive throughout this long project, and my thanks to Eric Tenbus, Jon Taylor, Josh Nygren, Stephanie Beers, and Wendy Geiger for arranging teaching schedules allowing me to usually keep writing in the mornings.

Angus McLoone (1978–2020) helped motivate me to take my first history class as an undergraduate, David Torrance (1951–2020) offered me my first teaching position, and this book bears the influence of Rose (1916–2002), Nick (1917–1999), and Diane Moore (1945–2010), Irish-American patriots.

Heather and Will came into my life just after the last major research trip for this project, but it would now be impossible to imagine my life without their presence and love. This book is dedicated to them.

~

Introduction

Into Charleston's sun-drenched harbor on April 8, 1793 sailed the French warship *L'Embuscade*. Crowds gathered by the dock, anxious to hear news of whether the French Republic had declared war on the British monarchy. Before them appeared Edmond-Charles Genêt, younger brother of Marie-Antoinette's best friend and prior French diplomat in Russia, who despite his upbringing had been expelled from the Court of St. Petersburg for revolutionary enthusiasm. Returning to Paris, Genêt spent the summer of 1792 imbibing the revolutionary atmosphere in the Jacobin Club, becoming friendly with the leaders of its Girondin faction. Taking appointment as French ambassador to the United States, Genêt's ship had been blown 600 miles off course from Philadelphia to a news-starved city passionately invested in the outcome of European events.

Not leaving the grand announcement of war between France and Britain (that had begun in late January) to a subordinate, Genêt orated the affirmative to loud applause. Charleston, sufferers of British siege, occupation, and atrocities during America's War of Independence, had become a hotbed of pro-French sentiment, boasting a French Patriotic Society by December 1792 becoming known as the "*Amis de la Constitution*," corresponding with the Paris Jacobins and affiliated with Bordeaux's Society of the Friends of Liberty and Equality.[1] Now, the port town extended Genêt the finest southern hospitality. The French ambassador spent eleven days participating in Charleston banquets, reviewing parades, arranging relief shipments for France's Caribbean islands, and commissioning pirating expeditions against British shipping. A new Charleston Republican Society formed during his stay.[2]

---

[1] Archives nationales de France, AF ET B(I) 372 439.
[2] "Correspondence of the French Ministers to the United States, 1791–1797," Frederick Jackson Turner, ed. *Annual Report of the American Historical Association 7* (1904), 212; Archives départementales de la Gironde, 12 L 30 207 and 209; Robert J. Alderson, *This Bright Era of Happy Revolutions: French Consul Michel-Ange-Bernard Mangourit and International Republicanism in Charleston, 1792–1794* (Columbia, SC: University of South Carolina Press, 2008), 43; Stanley Elkins and Eric McKitrick, *The Age of Federalism: The Early American Republic, 1788–1800* (Oxford: Oxford University Press, 1993), 335; National Archives (UK), FO 91/1 139.

Rather than taking *L'Embuscade – The Ambush* – north to the American capital in Philadelphia, Genêt instead made a weeks-long journey overland, where he "every where received the most flattering marks of attention" from the populace.[3] Genêt enthusiastically confirmed to the French government that Americans considered them "friends, allies, brothers" in the quest for freedom.[4] The citizens of Georgetown, in the under-construction Federal District, fêted Genêt and his nation for enacting "a government founded on the bases of equality and happiness."[5] Camden, New Jersey, presented Genêt with an address proclaiming Americans' "gratitude" for French aid in the War of Independence and celebrating the "noble example" France "now gives to the world, of hatred to tyrants and abhorrence of oppression." The French Revolution, they asserted, would make "man happy, by making him free."[6] With partisans having prepared festivities for his arrival in the City of Brotherly Love, the bells of Christ Church rang as Genêt crossed the Delaware by ferry. A Francophillic crowd met Genêt with tricolor ribbons on their hats and hair, carrying him in triumph over the last four miles to the capital and festivities at City Tavern.[7]

With Genêt embodying trans-Atlantic revolutionary possibilities, partisans capitalized on the effervescence to impact America's political order. With the country still lacking a Jacobin-style network of allied political societies, some believed the time ripe to promote a national network. Philadelphia's German Republican Society sought Genêt's allegiance, presenting an address asserting their hope that "the French nation will give an example to the European world" by fixing "the Rights of Man upon an immovable basis" for all people.[8] Genêt accepted their invitation to help plan a new political network. With "German Republican Society" too particular a name for the group's universal ambitions, club members initially suggested readopting the "Sons of Liberty" moniker, hearkening back to the revolutionary era's first integrated corresponding society network. Genêt, however, proposed a new name, reflecting the group's principles: "the Democratic Club."[9]

Thus, the renegade revolutionary French ambassador Genêt helped inspire – and personally named – a new club network, which laid the groundwork for America's Democratic Party. One in a chain of transnational inspirations that

---

[3] *General Advertiser*, May 17, 1793.
[4] Archives des affaires étrangères, P4666 425.
[5] NA FO 91/1 148.
[6] *City Gazette*, May 4, 1793.
[7] Turner, "Correspondence," 284; *Federal Gazette*, May 16, 1793.
[8] *Federal Gazette*, May 18, 1793.
[9] Philip S. Foner, *The Democratic-Republican Societies, 1790–1800: A Documentary Sourcebook of Constitutions, Declarations, Addresses, Resolutions and Toasts* (Westport, CT: Greenwood Press, 1976), 7; George Clinton Genet, *Washington, Jefferson and "Citizen" Genet, 1793* (New York, 1899), 34.

created modern social movements across the second half of the eighteenth century, American political parties arose through inseparable links with international – in this case, French Revolutionary – exemplars. Across the Revolutionary Atlantic, the era's most prominent social movements arose as part of an explicitly linked effort pursuing visions of liberty, as friends of freedom.

The Atlantic Creation of Modern Social Movements

As eighteenth-century historians have made the "global turn," portions of Atlantic history have received more attention than others. Studies of trade, empire, and state-building have proliferated, but the interconnected histories of resistance against that world's greatest concentrations of power remain disproportionally overlooked. This book aims to be the first to demonstrate the rich web of interrelations between the increasingly inclusive and cosmopolitan social movements of the Age of Revolution. Liberty and rights, concepts previously restricted to certain nations and privileged groups, became potentially applicable to anyone, anywhere. Only low barriers existed between movements and countries: indeed, many activists desired the reduction of borders, boundaries, and old hatreds to right past abuses. Exuberant hopes spread that the political, economic, class, religious, racial, national, and other Old Regime barriers could be abolished – perhaps quickly.

In the creative destruction of eighteenth-century empires, radical new possibilities seemed at hand. Old cultures and practices became suddenly vulnerable before waves of increasingly inclusive movements for greater freedom. Political crises loosened the hold of old elites, while growing strata of literate, prosperous, and aware citizens combined their efforts to advocate significant changes. If the public could be sufficiently aroused and instructed, virtually any enlightened change appeared possible. Embracing distant examples, organizers readily borrowed new methods and causes for regional and national mobilization. Whereas previously most politicized protest had been local, episodic, and loosely organized, now affiliated organizations arose on nationwide scales – winning wide swaths of the populace unprecedented political voice.

Mobilizing large groups across great distances was not new but had usually been undertaken in prior eras for religious rather than primarily political purposes. Reformation-era congregational networks and the confraternities of their Catholic counterparts brought together passionate adherents for acts of piety, advocacy, and community strengthening.[10] Especially when coordinating action across long distances – the Huguenots of sixteenth-century France

---

[10] David Garrioch, "'Man Is Born for Society': Confraternities and Civil Society in Eighteenth-Century Paris and Milan," *Social Science History* 41, no. 1 (2017), 103–19.

developed a tiered synod network on local, provincial, and national levels that mobilized their civil wars against the Catholic government – such organizations in many respects anticipated their revolutionary successors.[11] Yet, in these earlier contestations, civil politics remained subordinate to religious concerns, and such activism declined after the Wars of Religion. The first half of the eighteenth century largely lacked widespread, interconnected popular movements for political change.

Anglo-American political clubs developed from Reformation-era religious societies but expanded into sites for debate and learning that became the British Enlightenment's most emblematic organization.[12] Crossing into politics during the English Revolution of the 1640s, political clubs became generally tolerated by British authorities following the Glorious Revolution of 1688–1689. Profiting from broader British tavern and coffeehouse culture, it would be difficult to underestimate clubs' popularity across the eighteenth century. Aided in their "pub-assemblies" by "wine, beer, tea, pipes and tobacco," those united by "conformity of tastes, schemes of life, and ways of thinking" engaged in wide-ranging discussions.[13] Affection, fraternity, and common interests aided such groups' development.[14] Yet these clubs – usually composed exclusively of men – boasted of their independent and particular nature, limiting participation to those sharing their political, class, occupational, and local affiliations. Strangers without invitation were typically excluded.

By the mid-eighteenth century, the British developed clubs for an incredible variety of applications. Organizations spread from elite caucuses to local debating societies and a broad variety of other concerns at most only tangentially concerned with politics – from the Society for Promoting Christian Knowledge, to the Anti-Gallicans, Lunar Society, Poker Club, Hellfire Clubs, Medical Society, and the Society for the Discharge and Relief of Persons Imprisoned for Small Debts. As French *philosophe* Pierre-Jean Grosley wrote during his 1765 British tour, "public affairs generally furnish the subject of conversation; every Englishman gives as much attention to these matters, as if he were the prime minister: and this is the case even amongst the lowest class and country people."[15] These organizations profited from broader British free speech traditions, in which "Britons have a Right to complain as well as to be heard, whenever any Thing is in

[11] Mack P. Holt, *The French Wars of Religion, 1562–1629.* 2nd ed. (Cambridge: Cambridge University Press, 2005), 52.
[12] F. W. B. Bullock, *Voluntary Religious Societies, 1520–1799* (St. Leonard's on Sea: Budd & Gilatt, 1963), 3.
[13] Pierre-Jean Grosley, *A Tour of London, or New Observations on England and Its Inhabitants.* (London: Lockyer Davis, 1772), Vol. 1, 146–47, 260.
[14] Adam Ferguson, *An Essay on the History of Civil Society* (Edinburgh, 1767), 3.
[15] Grosley, *Tour*, Vol. 1, 148–49.

Question," as one pamphlet asserted.[16] Historian Peter Clark has estimated more than twenty-five thousand varied clubs formed across the English-speaking world during the eighteenth century.[17] In the American colonies, organizers like Benjamin Franklin founded a dizzying array of organizations, from artisan clubs to literary societies to political caucuses to scientific organizations to firefighting and other pragmatic civic concerns.[18] Britons came to believe they had a rightful voice in politics and made their opinions known. Yet, their pride in reputably being Europe's freest people may have deterred them from combining their efforts against the elite coteries still controlling British politics. No integrated networks of political clubs arose before 1765.

Euro-Americans in the eighteenth century increasingly felt part of an interconnected world, and many of their social practices deeply influenced the forms revolutionary social networks took. Mercantile trade and colonial administrative networks already produced a dense Atlantic web of exchange and correspondence across five continents, while many colonists kept in regular contact with their European counterparts.[19] Freemasons, though cloaking their actions in allegory, by mid-century constructed a formidable trans-Atlantic network of secret societies, while promoting egalitarianism among their members.[20] In an era of falling postal rates and growing print circulation that inspired a communication revolution, scientific societies, literary correspondence networks, the growing newspaper trade, and broadly inclusive spirit of the "Republic of Letters" multiplied long-distance interactions and accustomed participants to socializing in virtual communities.[21]

---

[16] *The Right of British Subjects to Petition and Apply to Their Representatives, Asserted and Vindicated* (London: Smith, 1733), 3, 6, 13.

[17] Peter Clark, *British Clubs and Societies, 1580–1800: The Origins of an Associational World* (Oxford: Oxford University Press, 2000), 2.

[18] Jessica C. Roney, *Governed by a Spirit of Opposition: The Origins of American Political Practice in Colonial Philadelphia* (Baltimore: Johns Hopkins University Press, 2014).

[19] Peter A. Coclanis, ed. *The Atlantic Economy during the Seventeenth and Eighteenth Centuries: Organization, Operation, Practice and Personnel* (Columbia, SC: University of South Carolina Press, 2005); John Brewer, *The Sinews of Power; War, Money and the English State, 1688–1783* (London: Routledge, 1989).

[20] Margaret Jacob, *Living the Enlightenment: Freemasonry and Politics in Eighteenth-Century Europe* (Oxford: Oxford University Press, 1991); Kenneth Loiselle, *Brotherly Love: Freemasonry and Male Friendship in Enlightenment France* (Ithaca: Cornell University Press, 2016).

[21] Brewer, *The Pleasures of the Imagination: English Culture in the Eighteenth Century* (Chicago: University of Chicago Press, 2000); Roy Porter, *The Creation of the Modern World: The Untold Story of the British Enlightenment* (New York: Norton, 2001); Dena Goodman, *The Republic of Letters: A Cultural History of the French Enlightenment* (Ithaca: Cornell University Press, 1993); Jacob, *Strangers Nowhere in the World: The Rise of Cosmopolitanism in Early Modern Europe* (Philadelphia: University of Pennsylvania Press, 2006).

Eighteenth-century literature furthered interest in foreign examples, making many increasingly receptive to new ideas, often from faraway places.[22] Indeed, the Early Modern Atlantic world has been conceptualized as a "continuous interplay" between groups – from local to global in scale.[23] All these processes influenced the forms revolutionary societies took.

The chief innovation of the Age of Revolutions' social movements lay in connecting and radicalizing recognizable Anglo-American organizations to more effectively pressure authorities. American Sons of Liberty in 1765–1766 revolutionized movement organizing, affiliating hundreds of clubs across the colonies to enunciate their grievances, embolden local direct action, and develop a mutual defense network in case British authorities attempted to repress the budding Patriot movement. Though local meetings could resemble older clubs, the broader organization's methods substantially diverged. Coordination through correspondence, deputations, and common activities created a powerful model surpassing what local, divided debating societies and social circles could accomplish. To be successful, the new organizations needed to minimize disagreements between members and differences across regions, while crafting common messages to inspire broad coalitions. Only by working together in unprecedented ways could they challenge entrenched political regimes.

Each of the social movements examined here took fundamental inspiration from their predecessors. The corresponding society model innovated by America's Sons of Liberty and Committees of Correspondence from British origins over the decade preceding 1775 sparked a first wave of social movements. In Britain, the Wilkes and Liberty cause borrowed American tactics to pursue greater liberties and soon sympathizers organized petitioning movements for peace and reconciliation with the colonies. Amid the war's reversals, activists redirected their efforts into the first organized push for British Parliamentary reform mobilized around American-style organizations. Concurrently, British imperial weakness encouraged Irish nationalists to develop a nationwide militia network similar to their American brethren that won Ireland parliamentary independence. Debates over American freedom's meaning motivated the rise of organized abolitionist movements first in revolutionary America and then in postwar Britain. Minority churches' agitation for religious freedom in America led British Protestant Dissenters into comparable campaigns.

The French Revolution – with its Jacobins taking explicit inspiration from recent Anglo-American movements – ignited a second wave of unprecedentedly dense, radical, and universalistic organizing both in their own country

---

[22] Lynn Hunt, *Inventing Human Rights: A History* (New York: Norton, 2008).

[23] J. H. Elliott, *Empires of the Atlantic World: Britain and Spain in America, 1492–1830* (New Haven: Yale University Press, 2006), xiv.

and around much of the Atlantic basin. The United Irishmen applied French universalism to overcome religious divides and pursue national independence. The "British Jacobins" sought Parliamentary reform to open their political system. Free-black and mixed race *Gens de couleur* in the French colony of Saint-Domingue organized to demand voting rights and helped spark the Haitian Revolution. The American Democratic Party developed as activists borrowed French models to more effectively oppose ruling Federalists. Each cause, recognizing their international origins, adapted preexisting examples for their national political purposes, bringing prior methods together in unprecedented and dynamic ways. Atlantic conversations led these movements to innovations they would likely not have discovered on their own. Through exploring such connections, we can better understand how – via precedent, impersonation, invention, adaptation, and evolution – the revolutionary era's most influential movements functioned as a totality.

Corresponding societies benefitted from both their simplicity of design and potential complexity in practice. As first developed by America's Sons of Liberty in late 1765, the network model brought together autonomous local branches to develop common messaging, tactics, lobbying, and public protests. While some proved more influential (with larger city branches becoming regional centers for their hinterlands), no local was dependent on another, and could freely correspond across the network. Repressing such a hydra-like organization appeared nearly impossible. This New World mutation on older British club life shocked Europe: political organizing would never be limited to small, elite coteries again. While some Sons of Liberty successors tried to centralize power more than others, all depended on their local affiliates' vitality. Though in some respects a family of movements – some revolutionary, some reformist, some special-interest and some (dialectically) conservative in scope, flexible in degree of inclusion across time, space, nationality, race, gender, and class – the model's inclusivity allowed the Age of Revolutions' grandest ambitions to be projected through and onto a common format.

In so doing, organizers forged new standards for pursuing enlightenment through activism. As "friends of humanity" and "friends of freedom," they commonly pledged to support their national and international brethren in sister movements against the era's worst excesses and participated in multiple campaigns themselves. An activist like Anglican antislavery stalwart Granville Sharp built connections with both London and Philadelphia Quakers, advocated for American political rights in the 1770s, participated in British Parliamentary reform movements, campaigned for English Protestant Dissenter civil rights, encouraged American action against slavery, and only then helped craft the British abolitionist societies that became the era's broadest and most inclusive cause. Soon, he also supported abolitionism and revolution in France. Frenchman Jacques-Pierre Brissot interacted with British abolitionists and reformers while living in London, and travelled across much of the United States (meeting revolutionary veterans and budding abolition-ists), before founding France's first abolition society, becoming a prominent Jacobin Club member, and leading its breakaway Girondin faction. Despite national pride, local particularity, and sometimes-selfish defense of their own interests, reformers and revolutionaries privileged models that stretched beyond their own causes, regularly cheering advancements elsewhere, pursu-ing distant interactions, and integrating useful international examples into their own movements.

While the product of a century of Enlightened liberal exchanges and reasoned discussion, the new societies' effects would be more radical still, encouraging democratization and the diffusion of political power. In an era before elite theorists became comfortable with the subject of democracy, activists succeeded in implementing largely democratic society networks in practice: commonly featuring elected leaders, open debating, participation across social classes, and a willingness to challenge the status quo.[24] By creating broadly based political forces more powerful than those governing elites possessed, revolutionary societies repeatedly captured political momentum to advocate for often-radical changes. As "democracy" advanced from an epithet, to an aspiration, to a governing system, activists modeled – and occasionally succeeded in enacting – their preferred modes of governance.

"Freedom" remained a contested concept throughout the era, as in our present day. The Sons of Liberty's conception rested predominantly upon their rights as freeborn Britons for self-rule, yet by the American War of Independence natural rights ideals had raised the thorny question of what it really meant for all men to be created equal.[25] Atlantic social movement networks would be founded for both abolitionism and the maintenance of slaveholder rights. Freedom in politics, however, became associated with collective action: few expected the elite cabals and intimate lobbying of prior eras to prevail indefinitely. As the extent and nature of freedom remained to be determined, the future seemed to belong to those who could shape associ-ational politics for their ambitions. The social movements of the late-eighteenth century were experiments in democratization, attempting to shape a new science of participation.

The Potential of Atlantic History

Amazingly, given their rich respective historiographies, this is the first time these movements have been the subject of a single book. Famed historian-

---

[24] Joanna Innes and Philp, eds. *Re-Imagining Democracy in the Age of Revolutions: America, France, Britain, Ireland, 1750–1850* (Oxford: Oxford University Press, 2015).

[25] See Eric Foner, *The Story of American Freedom* (New York: Norton, 1999); Annelin de Dijn, *Freedom: An Unruly History* (Cambridge, MA: Harvard University Press, 2020).

sociologist Charles Tilly, in his magisterial *Social Movements, 1768–2004*, claimed Wilkes' Society of Supporters of the Bill of Rights invented the social movement – overlooking preceding American Sons of Liberty agitation that had mobilized a far larger campaign, ignoring successive movements in Ireland and Haiti, and asserting French Revolutionary examples remained too episodic for his model.[26] Yet his core definition of a "social movement" – associated groups making a sustained public effort to convince authorities of their cause's (and their own) worthiness to advocate for legal and policy changes – applies to each movement analyzed in this book.[27] While William Warner has highlighted the innovations of American Revolutionary activism, David Brion Davis famously described an "Anti-Slavery International" among abolitionists, and scholars have broadly discussed French Revolutionary ideas' reception in Britain, Ireland, and (to a lesser extent) the United States, the transnational inspirations motivating social movement creativity across the full era have been overlooked.[28] Only by examining this broad range of cases together can we achieve an integrated understanding of the Age of Revolutions' development and the extent to which the era's most important movements functioned as an interconnected phenomenon.

As most historians are trained as specialists in a single national history, and much scholarly sociability and publishing remains organized around national distinctions, the Age of Revolutions' international dimensions have remained underserved. The most prominent early exception to this norm was R. R. Palmer's two-volume *The Age of the Democratic Revolution*, published in 1959 and 1964. With "Atlantic" having become a favored shorthand for shared Anglo- and European-American cultural and democratic traditions during the two world wars, Palmer employed such rhetoric to describe a common eighteenth-century "Revolution of Western Civilization," examining how Anglo-American and then French waves of democratic change swept across Europe and North America.[29] Written amid the Cold War, his book was celebrated in the United States and pilloried by the European left as a NATO

---

[26] Charles Tilly, *Social Movements, 1768–2004* (Boulder, CO: Paradigm Press, 2004), "Britain Creates the Social Movement," CRSO Working Paper No. 232 (Ann Arbor, 1981), and *Popular Contention in Great Britain, 1758–1834* (Cambridge, MA: Harvard University Press, 1995).

[27] Tilly, *Social Movements*, 3–4.

[28] William Warner, *Protocols of Liberty Communication Innovation and the American Revolution* (Chicago: University of Chicago Press, 2014); David Brion Davis, *The Problem of Slavery in the Age of Revolution, 1770–1823* (Ithaca: Cornell University Press, 1975), 213. Rich works in this vein include Seymour Drescher, *Abolition: A History of Slavery and Antislavery* (Cambridge: Cambridge University Press, 2009), and Robin Blackburn, *The American Crucible: Slavery, Emancipation and Human Rights* (London: Verso, 2013).

[29] R. R. Palmer, *The Age of the Democratic Revolution: A Political History of Europe and America, 1760–1800. I: The Challenge* (Princeton: Princeton University Press, 1959), Vol. 1, 5.

origins story.[30] Yet Palmer considered the revolutions (despite their overlapping Enlightenment origins) more simultaneous than interrelated and showed little interest in examining interconnections. Beyond his North Atlantic focus, Palmer's work now appears woefully incomplete for overlooking questions of colonialism and slavery – almost completely excluding the Haitian Revolution and subsequent Latin American independence movements.[31] Nevertheless, *Democratic Revolution* has retained a gravitational pull for younger generations of scholars through its erudition and daringness to work across national and thematic boundaries that many scholars still fear to tread.

Palmer's work inspired few followers until the 1990s, when "Atlantic" and "transnational" themes became among academic history's hottest topics. Responding to growing interest in – and concern about – globalization, Atlantic connections no longer seemed outliers to national histories, but rather forerunners of an increasingly borderless world.[32] Explaining modern capitalism and industrialization's development came to require oceanic and global foci.[33] Early Atlantic World studies tended to focus on trade and colonialism across broad areas – and those, especially Native Americans, enslaved Africans, and diasporas of marginalized Europeans, they displaced.[34] David Armitage, synthesizing the first decade of reinvigorated research in 2002, famously asserted, "We are all Atlanticists now," heralding that the approach could "supplement and even replace" national histories.[35]

---

[30] Marcel Reinhard, review of Robert R. Palmer, *The Age of the Democratic Revolution, Annales historiques de la Révolution française* 32 (1960) 220–23. More sympathetically, see Bernard Bailyn, *Atlantic History: Concepts and Contours*(Cambridge, MA: Harvard University Press, 2005).

[31] Palmer's rare Caribbean and Latin American missives were dismissive, including: "The hanging of numerous rebel slaves was regarded as a police action, of no political consequence; just as the desire of slaves for liberty, having nothing to do with American politics, was not even to be dignified by the epithet of Jacobinism." *The Age of the Democratic Revolution: A Political History of Europe and America, 1760–1800. II: The Struggle* (Princeton: Princeton University Press, 1964), 518.

[32] See, for example, Hunt, *Writing History in the Global Era* (New York: Norton, 2015).

[33] David Landes, *The Wealth and Poverty of Nations: Why Some Are So Rich and Some So Poor* (New York: Norton, 1998); Kenneth Pomeranz, *The Great Divergence: China, Europe and the Making of the Modern World Economy* (Princeton: Princeton University Press, 2000).

[34] Prominent works include Daniel K. Richter, *Facing East from Indian Country: A Native History of Early America* (Cambridge, MA: Harvard University Press, 2001); Paul Gilroy, *The Black Atlantic: Modernity and Double Consciousness* (Cambridge, MA: Harvard University Press, 1993); Peter Linebaugh and Marcus Rediker, *The Many-Headed Hydra: Sailors, Slaves and the Hidden History of the Revolutionary Atlantic* (Boston: Beacon, 2000).

[35] David Armitage, "Three Concepts of Atlantic History," in Armitage and Michael J. Braddick, eds. *The British Atlantic World, 1500–1800* (New York: Palgrave Macmillan, 2002), 11.

Yet, with longer-duration studies dominant, scholarship on "Atlantic Revolutions" has revivified more slowly. From the early 2000s, a British-Imperial turn in early American studies intensified, building on the classic work of Bernard Bailyn and Pauline Maier to show the extent to which American Revolutionaries interacted with British models both preceding and following independence, contesting parochial understandings of American and British politics and society.[36] Haitian revolutionary studies concurrently proliferated, as Laurent Dubois, Jeremy Popkin, and a host of other scholars examined history's only successful slave revolution as a mirror for the French Revolution's values and shortcomings, while calling attention to its manifold legacies for race relations across the Atlantic basin.[37] Other subjects, however, have been less transformed: although the Haitian Revolution has become an accepted dimension of French Revolutionary studies, still, as Suzanne Desan, Lynn Hunt, and William Max Nelson have noted, the Revolution within France's European hexagon remains predominantly "explained by reference to French factors," instead of Atlantic contexts.[38] Aside from studies of abolitionism, no major works in this new wave have focused on exploring transnational connections between social movements. Except for a small number of "comparative" studies, projects focused on interconnections between the British and French imperial systems during the revolutionary era have remained few.[39]

This study is greatly indebted to the proliferation of scholarly work on the "Atlantic World" over the past three decades, yet much of its inspiration came

[36] Bailyn, *The Ideological Origins of the American Revolution* (Cambridge, MA: Harvard University Press, 1967); Pauline Maier, *From Resistance to Revolution: Colonial Radicals and the Development of American Opposition to Britain, 1765–1776* (New York: Knopf, 1972); Eliga H. Gould, *The Persistence of Empire: British Political Culture in the Age of the American Revolution* (Chapel Hill: North Carolina University Press, 2000); Andrew Jackson O'Shaughnessy, *An Empire Divided: The American Revolution in the British Caribbean* (Philadelphia: University of Pennsylvania Press, 2000), Gould and Peter S. Onuf, eds. *Empire and Nation: The American Revolution in the Atlantic World* (Baltimore: Johns Hopkins University Press, 2005).

[37] Laurent Dubois, *A Colony of Citizens: Revolution and Slave Emancipation in the French Caribbean, 1787–1804* (Chapel Hill: University of North Carolina Press, 2004); Jeremy Popkin, *You Are All Free: The Haitian Revolution and the Abolition of Slavery* (Cambridge: Cambridge University Press, 2010); James Alexander Dun, *Dangerous Neighbors: Making the Haitian Revolution in Early America* (Philadelphia: University of Pennsylvania Press, 2016).

[38] Suzanne Desan, Lynn Hunt, and William Max Nelson, "Introduction," in *The French Revolution in Global Perspective*, Desan, Hunt and Nelson, eds. (Ithaca: Cornell University Press, 2013), 1, 11.

[39] Lester D. Langley, *The Americas in the Age of Revolution, 1750–1850* (New Haven: Yale University Press, 1998); Susan Dunn, *Sister Revolutions: French Lightning, American Light* (New York: Faber & Faber, 1999); Wim Kooster, *Revolutions in the Atlantic World: A Comparative History* (New York: NYU Press, 2009).

from the persistent sentiment (widespread even among scholarly specialists) that histories of the Atlantic World during the Age of Revolutions have not gone far enough. The prominent French Revolutionist Hunt has called attention to how "We still know so little" about the interplay between revolutionary movements, as most studies have dealt with such phenomena at most in passing.[40] David A. Bell argues, "we do not yet have a satisfying model for casting the French Revolution as part of a larger Atlantic or global process," asserting Atlantic origins have not yet been shown to have conclusively affected the shapes revolutionary politics finally took.[41] Grand declarations about France's Revolution being "Constitutively Atlantic" have not been adequately backed by detailed studies.[42] For the American Revolution as well, Bailyn, despite having spent much of his illustrious career explaining Atlantic connections, concluded his *Atlantic History: Concepts and Contours* by conceding "the full account of this story – which is not the aggregate of several national histories, but something shared by and encompassing them all – is a tale yet to be told."[43] Pathbreaking world historian William McNeil similarly considered that many of the most promising Transatlantic approaches "are yet to be successfully carried out."[44] Historians' Atlantic reach has often exceeded their empirical grasp – a lacunae still greater for the lesser-studied movements in this book.

The interplays between Atlantic revolutionary movements have remained under-examined. Most work to date – building from popular interest in America's core "Founding Fathers" and scholarly focus on European elite political culture – has centered on small coteries of trans-Atlantic intellectuals, garbled misunderstandings of events abroad, or else retreated into comparative history. Many studies, like their "global" history bedfellows, have been criticized for implicitly following neoliberal celebrations of economic integration, cosmopolitan elitism, and "disruptive" network construction[45] – while underserving the Age of Revolutions' transgressive potential, popular appeal, and social upheaval. After two decades as a hot concept, discussions of "Atlantic Revolutions" still focus more on the model's potential than its

---

[40] David A. Bell, "Questioning the Global Turn: The Case of the French Revolution," *French Historical Studies* 37, no. 1 (2014), 6.

[41] Ibid., 11.

[42] Dubois, "An Atlantic Revolution," *French Historical Studies* 32, no. 4 (2009), 655–61; Bell, ibid., 8.

[43] Bailyn, *Atlantic*, 111.

[44] William H. McNeill, "Transatlantic History in World Perspective," in *Transatlantic History*, Steven G. Reinhardt and Dennis Reinhartz, eds. (College Station: Texas A&M University Press, 2006), 4.

[45] Paul Cheney, "French Revolution's Global Turn and Capitalism's Spatial Fixes," *Journal of Social History* 52, no. 3 (2018), 575–83. See, for example, Niall Ferguson, *The Square and the Tower: Networks and Power, From the Freemasons to Facebook* (New York: Random House, 2018), esp. 9.

realization – increasingly, with a level of frustration that threatens the field's future.

Nevertheless, among recent Atlantic historiography's most inspiring trends has been the recapturing of revolutionary universalism. Whereas prior generations of national historians had typically dismissed eighteenth-century revolutionaries' international pretensions, scholars are now taking their inclusive rhetoric seriously for understanding their worldviews. Janet Polasky has alluringly traced such cosmopolitanism's power in *Revolutions without Borders*, by portraying revolutionaries' common enthusiasm (whether in person, through publication or correspondence) across national boundaries.[46] With passion for freedom and few hardened ideological distinctions, such movements' potential appeared virtually unlimited.[47] Seth Cotlar, studying the early United States, demonstrated the diffusion of "popular cosmopolitanism," informed by newspapers, orations, festive gatherings, and socialization.[48] This study explores how such adaptations inspired bourgeoning political groups to seek new connections across continents and mobilize in new ways.

More work is necessary on the application of animating examples across national boundaries, which repeatedly led to the genesis of new political combinations and movements.[49] Moving beyond elite intellectual history, this work highlights the vast number of individuals, groups, and interests working in concert to animate the era's national and international movements. Only those campaigns capturing popular grievances and/or the public imagination prospered. The Age of Revolutions consisted of people's revolutions challenging political, economic, and innumerable cultural constraints. The revolutionary era's social movements need a history as big as their ambitions.

Even in a manuscript as large as this one, some may consider it not expansive enough. Many groups examined here privileged male sociability, often

---

[46] Janet Polasky, *Revolutions without Borders: The Call to Liberty in the Atlantic World* (New Haven: Yale University Press, 2015).

[47] More controversially, see Jonathan Israel, including *Democratic Enlightenment: Philosophy, Revolution, and Human Rights, 1750–1790* (Oxford: Oxford University Press, 2011).

[48] Seth Cotlar, *Tom Paine's America: The Rise and Fall of Transatlantic Radicalism in the Early Republic* (Charlottesville: University of Virginia Press, 2011), esp. 49–81.

[49] Nathan Perl-Rosenthal's pathbreaking dissertation, "Corresponding Republics: Letter Writing and Patriot Organizing in the Atlantic Revolutions, circa 1760–1792" (PhD dissertation: Columbia University, 2011), fascinatingly explores eighteenth-century social networks, but whereas Perl-Rosenthal sees separate origins from different national prerevolutionary epistolary and associational traditions for each American, French, and Dutch network examined, my study foregrounds transnational connections and common inspirations. While in a recent article Perl-Rosenthal considers eighteenth-century cultures as "durable and slow to change," this work instead views the era's rapid shifts as indeed revolutionary. Perl-Rosenthal, "Atlantic Cultures and the Age of Revolution," *William and Mary Quarterly* 74, no. 4 (2017), 667–96.

admitting few female members (or none at all), while marginalizing the poor and refusing to admit slaves – though in subsequent eras suffragettes, socialists, and civil rights activists adopted social movement models largely inspired by eighteenth-century revolutionaries. A still-longer work could include movements for liberty in Switzerland, the Netherlands, Belgium, and Poland, each of which corresponded and shared personnel with those described in this book, and/or continue into Latin American independence movements.[50] Exchanges across the British and French imperial systems (creating the major movements examined here in the nascent nations of the United States, Britain, Ireland, France, and Haiti) appear the most extensive, diverse, and fertile, however, both in their direct political impact and as models for social change that continue being adapted by groups across the world.

Despite the vast historiographies dedicated to each campaign studied here, the direct connections between the age's principal social movements have been little pursued by scholars – partially due to the difficulty of conducting detailed primary-source research across so many locales. Jack P. Greene and Philip D. Morgan, in a sentiment shared by many historians, introduced an edited volume a decade ago by asserting that studying the Atlantic World, "even if some small share of it – will always be extraordinarily difficult to accomplish."[51] Twenty-first-century digital revolutions, however, are making geographically broader studies more feasible. Whereas few scholars in earlier eras could afford to conduct extensive research across several nations, now the broad digitalization of American and British newspapers, alongside vast numbers of pamphlets and political tracts for each movement examined, has made the present study achievable for even a full-time professor without sabbaticals. Historians, as Sarah Knott has described, now have "more information, from more places, than at any previous moment" before.[52] Even where digitization remains incomplete, pairing online-accessible materials with summertime archive tours permits strikingly new combinations of sources. The ability to study wide swaths of the Atlantic basin has come within reach.

---

[50] See especially Annie Jourdan, *La revolution batave entre la France et l'Amérique, 1795–1806* (Rennes: Presses universitaires de Rennes, 2014); Jane C. Judge, *The United States of Belgium: The Story of the First Belgian Revolution* (Leuven, Belgium: Leuven University Press, 2018); Marc Lerner, *A Laboratory of Liberty: The Transformation of Political Culture in Republican Switzerland, 1750–1848* (Leiden: Brill, 2014); Anna Maria Rao, *Folle controrivoluzionarie: le insorgenze populari nell'Italia giacobina et napoletana* (Roma: Carocci, 1999); Bogusław Leśnodorski, *Les Jacobins Polonais et leurs confrères en Europe* (Wroclaw: Ossolineum, 1964); Jaime E. Rodriguez O., *The Independence of Spanish Latin America* (Cambridge: Cambridge University Press, 1998).

[51] Philip D. Morgan and Jack P. Greene, "Introduction: The Present State of Atlantic History," in *Atlantic History: A Critical Appraisal*, Greene and Morgan, eds. (Oxford: Oxford University Press, 2009), 10.

[52] Sarah Knott, "Narrating the Age of Revolution," *William and Mary Quarterly* 73, no. 1 (2016), 6.

Movement by movement – on a large canvas attempting to recapture the era's grand ambitions – this work aims to rediscover the interconnected chain of social movements that inspired the Age of Revolutions. It attempts to recapture the internal dynamics of each campaign and the linkages that helped make the Age of Revolutions a Transatlantic event. Only in light of the accelerating flow of ideas, tactics, and events across international boundaries, challenging and often reconfiguring politics and society in each nation they touched, can the development of a common revolutionary era be understood.

PART I

The American Revolution Ignites Social Movements

1

The Sons of Liberty and the Creation of a Movement Model

On Christmas Day 1765, a new era in the history of protest began. On frozen Connecticut fields outside New London, Sons of Liberty from New York City met deputations from the surrounding region. Building from the escalating resistance to the Stamp Act across Britain's American colonies since news of the reviled legislation arrived several months earlier, the groups agreed "to associate, advise, protect and defend each other in the peaceable, full and just enjoyment of their inherent and accustomed rights as British subjects" – pledging to come "with their full force if required" to contest government incursions on their liberties. Even more importantly, all present pledged to spread the alliance to "perfect the like association with all the colonies on the continent" to reinforce their efforts.[1] Within weeks, their pact spread from New Hampshire to Georgia, enabling unprecedented coordination across the thirteen colonies.

The Sons of Liberty–centered opposition to the Stamp Act in 1765–66 created a fundamentally new kind of protest campaign. Utilizing correspondence and newspaper publicity, the colonists combined their efforts into an unprecedented political alliance, openly affiliating and coordinating their actions. In so doing, they created a model of allied corresponding societies with far-flung ramifications for both their standoff with British authorities and subsequent Atlantic movements over the decades to come.

The Rise of the Sons of Liberty

Word of the Stamp Act reached American shores in April 1765, though the legislation's start date and full contents were only published in late May.[2] Parliament passed the measure to service debts from the recent Seven Years' War, promoting austerity while exploiting the colonies' growing civil society and limiting their self-government. British authorities required various stamps on items from newspapers and pamphlets (though not books) to playing cards

---

[1] Connecticut Historical Society, American Revolution Collection, Box 11, Folder M; Edmund S. and Helen M. Morgan, *The Stamp Act Crisis: Prologue to Revolution* (Chapel Hill: University of North Carolina Press, 1953), 201.

[2] *Boston Evening-Post*, May 27, 1765.

and dice, to apprenticeship papers, professional licenses, and legal documents, even though "internal" taxes had previously been under the purview of colonial legislatures.[3] Colonists contemplated resistance. At an otherwise genteel Maryland planters gathering on a ship in Baltimore harbor that June, a French traveler described locals loudly, "Damning their souls if they would pay and Damn them but they would fight to the last Drop of their blood before they would Consent to any such slavery."[4] Elaborating an adequate method of protest, however – short of outright rebellion, which none yet endorsed – required innovations as unprecedented as the legislation itself.

The House of Burgesses, believing their unique right to levy internal taxes challenged by Parliament, galvanized an anti–Stamp Act campaign by passing the Virginia Resolves on May 30. Twenty-nine-year-old firebrand Patrick Henry's resolutions declared any British attempt to usurp taxation rights within the colony as "illegal, unconstitutional, and unjust," threatening "to destroy British, as well as American freedom." The Burgesses declined to pass even more radical resolves declaring their citizens "not bound to yield obedience to any law" violating their rights. Yet after rumors that the legislature would declare anyone enforcing the Stamp Act "an Enemy to his Country," Virginia's governor dissolved the assembly.[5] The resolves, immediately sent northward by courier, circulated broadly before being published in Boston (and then across the colonies), emboldening widespread opposition.[6] Protests against the unwelcome measures seemed certain: newspapers ran an anonymous July letter declaring "Associations are forming," with thousands subscribing to oppose the act, without describing how.[7] With enforcement to begin on November 1, papers printed several would-be stamp officers' names.[8]

Resistance to new British taxes had already begun two years earlier. In November 1763, reacting to growing British enforcement of long-dormant customs duties (some designed to quash virtually all trading with non-British colonies) during an acute postwar recession, Boston's merchants organized a "grand committee" to "open a correspondence with the principal merchants in all our sister colonies, endeavoring to promote a union, and a coalition of all

---

[3] Morgan and Morgan, *Stamp Act*, 96–97.
[4] "Journal of a French Traveler in the Colonies, 1765," *American Historical Review* 27, no. 1 (1921), 73.
[5] Jack P. Greene, *The Quest for Power: The Lower Houses of Assembly in the Southern Royal Colonies, 1689–1776* (Chapel Hill: University of North Carolina Press, 1963), 363; Mercy Otis Warren, *History of the Rise, Progress and Termination of the American Revolution* (Boston: Larkin, 1805), Vol. 1, 405–6; "Diary of a French Traveler," 745.
[6] NA CO 5/891 270; William Gordon, *The History of the Rise, Progress and Establishment of the Independence of the United States of America* (London, 1788), Vol. 1, 171.
[7] *New-York Gazette*, July 11, 1765; *Boston Gazette*, July 22, 1765.
[8] *New Hampshire Gazette*, June 28, 1765; *South-Carolina Gazette*, July 15, 1765.

their councils." New York passed a matching petition.[9] Officials responded by enlisting the British Navy to seize contraband cargo, even allowing crews to keep half the captured goods. Profitable (though illegal) trade with French and Spanish colonies was curtailed. The crackdowns affected most American importers, while favoring British and Caribbean interests over continental concerns.[10] Colonists observed a growing imperial consensus that excluded them. Only a significant show of colonial solidarity and resistance could derail Parliament's reorganization plans.

Massachusetts' House of Representatives urged other colonial assemblies to protest together for the restrictions' repeal – appointing a Committee of Correspondence to lead the campaign. Selected legislators would "acquaint" the other colonies with the instructions Massachusetts sent its London lobbyist, publicizing their "desire the several assemblies on the continent join with them in the same measures."[11] Legislatures from Rhode Island to South Carolina appointed similar committees, and nine petitioned Parliament in 1764 for redress.[12] Two hundred and fifty copies of committee resolutions reached London for the city's merchants.[13] Colonists nevertheless hoped to mitigate the worst British restrictions through presenting a powerful, united front. Parliament deciding American taxes seemed anathema. New York petitioned: "Without such a Right" to self-taxation, "there can be no Liberty, no Happiness, no Security."[14] Although the colonies competed for British favor and finance, and had previously been more concerned with imperial than "American" concerns, now, as dissenting minister William Gordon wrote in his early history of the era, "a new kind of correspondence was opened between the colonies, tending to unite them" against unwanted legislation.[15] The

[9] Charles Rappelye, *Sons of Providence: The Brown Brothers, the Slave Trade, and the American Revolution* (New York: Simon & Schuster, 2006), 43; Joseph S. Tiedemann, *Reluctant Revolutionaries: New York City and the Road to Independence, 1763–1776* (Ithaca: Cornell University Press, 1997), 62.

[10] Thomas P. Slaughter, *Independence: The Tangled Roots of the American Revolution* (New York: Hill and Wang, 2014), 250; O'Shaughnessy, *Empire*, 63–68; Edward Countryman, *The American Revolution*, rev. ed. (New York: Hill and Wang, 2003); 52–53.

[11] Gordon, *History of the Rise*, Vol. 1, 153; C. A. Weslager, *The Stamp Act Congress* (Newark: University of Delaware Press, 1976), 58.

[12] David Lee Russell, *The American Revolution in the Southern Colonies* (Jefferson, NC: Macfarland, 2000), 26; Les Standiford, *Desperate Sons: Samuel Adams, Patrick Henry, John Hancock, and the Secret Bands of Radicals Who Led the Colonies to War* (New York: Harper, 2012), 35; Robert Middlekauff, *The Glorious Cause: The American Revolution, 1763–1789* (Oxford: Oxford University Press, 1982), 68.

[13] Massachusetts Historical Society, Ezekiel Price Papers, 29.

[14] Edmund S. Morgan, *Prologue to Revolution: Sources and Documents on the Stamp Act Crisis, 1764–1766* (Chapel Hill: University of North Carolina Press, 1959), 9.

[15] Gordon, *History of the Rise*, Vol. 1, 153.

British Parliament, however, gave the 1764 petitions no formal consideration.[16]

The increasingly dysfunctional relationship between the colonies and Parliament contributed to the Stamp Act's disastrous rollout. Parliamentary authorities sent a preliminary proposal for colonial consultation in June 1764, with Prime Minister George Grenville asking for "the sense of the Colonies themselves upon the matter, and if they could point out any system or plan as effectual," he would entertain it. Colonial legislatures, seething after recent levies, nevertheless wanted more information. Massachusetts drafted an alternative tax plan, asking Parliament for "the particular sum expected from each province" in revenue.[17] Rather than continuing negotiations, Grenville pressed forward, impatient for funds and believing the prosperous colonies better able to shoulder new taxes than Britain itself.[18] London merchants petitioned against the measure due to colonial indebtedness (which new taxes would hinder their ability to collect), while addresses arrived from the West Indies, Virginia, and the Carolinas. They were dismissed unread with the ministry declaring the right to petition did not extend to "money bills."[19] No one during debates in Parliament spoke favorably of a colonial right to self-taxation.

The name "Sons of Liberty", and indeed much of the group's initial inspiration, came from abroad. An Irish Tory polemicist used the phrase in 1756 to rail against County Antrim's Patriot Club, likening such "Sons of Liberty" to "Cromwell's grim ghost" during an Irish Parliamentary financial dispute.[20] The term gained positive use during the British Parliament's Stamp Act debates. Colonel Isaac Barré, an Irish Protestant son of French Huguenots and veteran wounded in the recent conquest of Quebec, took a strong pro-American position, declaring the colonists "sons of liberty" and asserting early settlers "fled tyranny" to seek "true English liberties" in a harsh land.[21] By adopting a term from British and Irish debates, those colonists calling themselves Sons of Liberty sought Atlantic audiences.

More than most subsequent social movements, just who (or what) the Sons of Liberty initially were was only hazily defined. A secret organization to coordinate resistance in Boston known as the Loyal Nine developed by

---

[16] Bruce A. Ragsdale, *A Planters' Republic: The Search for Economic Independence in Revolutionary Virginia* (Madison, WI: Madison House, 1996), 50.

[17] Morgan, *Prologue*, 28.

[18] John L. Bullion, *A Great and Necessary Measure: George Grenville and the Genesis of the Stamp Act, 1763–1765* (Columbia: University of Missouri Press, 1982), 198.

[19] Gordon, *History of the Rise*, Vol. 1, 161; *Boston Gazette*, May 20, 1765.

[20] *Advice to the Patriot Club of the County of Antrim on the Present State of Affairs in Ireland, and Some Late Changes in the Administration of That Kingdom* (Dublin, 1756), 14; Vincent Morley, *Irish Opinion and the American Revolution, 1760–1783* (Cambridge: Cambridge University Press, 2002), 39.

[21] Peter Brown, *The Chathamites: A Study in the Relationship between Personalities and Ideas in the Second Half of the Eighteenth Century* (London: Macmillan, 1967), 190–97.

August 1765, featuring the outspoken Samuel Adams and *Boston Gazette* printer Benjamin Edes, though the extent of the group's linkage with the later organization is unclear. Keeping the Sons' composition and actions secret seemed prudent for an extralegal campaign. The movement appeared coordinated by well-placed figures, however: as early historian David Ramsay wrote, Stamp Act protests "were not ebullitions of a thoughtless mob, but for the most part, planned by leading men of character and influence" in the colonies. Believing "the bulk of mankind, are more led by their senses, than by their reason," organizers mobilized exemplary displays against stamp supporters.[22] Keeping the leadership secret made it easier to speak for the full populace, while crowds' apparent spontaneity made them all the more intimidating.

Boston initiated public protests, bringing the wrath and collective power of the townspeople against Stamp Act enforcers. On the Wednesday, August 14 market day, agitators allegedly organized by the Loyal Nine hung an effigy of prosperous merchant and would-be stamp collector Andrew Oliver from a well-placed tree and publicized an evening demonstration. Upon cutting the figure down, "some thousands" paraded the effigy past government headquarters on King Street, where the town council sat debating whether to repress the protest, giving "three huzzas" audible inside. The group continued to a new building Oliver was constructing, which they labeled a future "stamp office" and destroyed. Protesters proceeded with building beams to Fort Hill, used the tainted wood to build a pyre, and then incinerated the effigy. Hearing Oliver had returned home, protesters proceeded there, forcing the detested official to flee to Castle William.[23] Twelve days later, on August 26 a second mob after a bonfire rally marched on the residences of three prominent alleged Stamp Act supporters: the Admiralty court's Deputy Registrar, Comptroller of the Customs, and Lieutenant Governor. The crowd, "enflam'd with Rum & Wine," devastated their properties, "burnt & scattered the books & files," along with destroying windows, furniture, and personal effects, before promptly dispersing at midnight.[24] Though Boston's town meeting the next day would "vote their detestation" of such attacks on private property (offering £300 to "any one who shall discover the Leader, or Leaders of the

---

[22] David Ramsay, *History of the American Revolution* (Philadelphia: Aitken, 1789), Vol. 1, 69–70.

[23] *Providence Gazette*, August 24, 1765; *Pennsylvania Gazette*, August 29, 1765; *Parliamentary History*, Vol. 16, 126–27; Morgan and Morgan, *Stamp Act*, 123–24; Maier, *Resistance*, 85.

[24] *By His Excellency Francis Bernard, Esq. A Proclamation* (Boston, 1765); *New Hampshire Gazette*, September 6, 1765; *Boston Evening Gazette*, September 7, 1765; Harvard Business School Library, William Lloyd Letterbook, 151; MHS James Freeman Letterbook; NA CO 5/217 15; MHS John Tudor Papers.

Mob"), a denunciation assemblies down to Charleston echoed, a new paradigm of intimidating protest spread against Stamp Act supporters.[25]

The colonial press magnified Bostonians' actions, inspiring copycat protests
and a growing spirit of Stamp Act resistance. Norwich, Connecticut residents,
emulating the "noble patriotic fire" having "of late shown so conspicuous in
Boston," marched a stamp officer effigy through town before burning it on
a public square, where participants drank "very constitutional Healths" before
dispersing.[26] Newport, Rhode Island destroyed effigies of three suspect figures,
"burnt amid the acclamations of thousands," on August 27.[27] Southward,
protests erupted in Baltimore on August 28 and in Annapolis, Elk Ridge, and
Frederick Town, Maryland the next day, featuring effigies reading "Tyranny,"
"Oppression," and "Damn my Country I'll get money." The Annapolis effigy
met an ignominious end as protesters "whipped it at the whipping post, placed
it in the Pillory, afterwards hung it on a Gibbet and then burned it."[28] In
northern Virginia, Burgess and prominent landowner Richard Henry Lee even
enlisted his slaves to march an effigy of the local stamp officer to a nearby
courthouse, for having "endeavoured to fasten the chains of slavery on this my
native country," without apparent irony.[29] Across regions, the general British
attack on colonial privileges encouraged matching protests in response.

The symbolic violence's vehemence, so widely repeated, broadcast the
situation's seriousness. "Exhibitions of this sort are now very common in
this Province," the *Pennsylvania Gazette* described in mid-September.[30] Such
widespread agitation created a symphony of opposition, by which, as a Boston
letter informed *South-Carolina Gazette* readers, "we shall diffuse among his
Majesty's American subjects a general joy, equal to the resignation of
a STAMP-OFFICER, or even the repeal of the STAMP ACT itself."[31] Boston
Congregationalist minister Jonathan Mayhew found colonists "sanguine in the
expectation of a speedy repeal," with the measure becoming "pernicious to
Great Britain, by ruining the colonies." Though the colonies remained "very
far indeed, from desiring to be independent," he asserted, "this Act will never
be carried into execution, without the effusion of much blood."[32] Fellow
Boston reverend Samuel Mather asserted the Stamp Act encouraged

---

[25] *New London Gazette*, August 30, 1765; MHS James Freeman Letterbook.

[26] *New London Gazette*, August 23, 1765.

[27] *South-Carolina Gazette*, September 21, 1765; Gordon, *History of the Rise*, Vol. 1, 183.

[28] Library of Congress Peter Force Papers, American Stamp Act Papers, Box VIII B: 5–6;
Ramsay, Vol. 1, 69–70.

[29] J. Kent McGaughy, *Richard Henry Lee of Virginia* (London: Rowan & Littlefield, 2004),
78.

[30] *Pennsylvania Gazette*, September 12 and 19, 1765; *Boston Post-Boy*, September 23, 1765;
South-Carolina Gazette, September 28, 1765.

[31] *South-Carolina Gazette*, September 21, 1765.

[32] MHS Thomas Hollis Papers.

"alienation from the Mother Country: And any Methods to enforce it will only increase this alienation."[33] Governor Francis Bernard fretted, "if things do not take another turn before the 1st Novr, the very appearance of Government will cease."[34] British administrators would be unable to function in such a charged atmosphere.

As protests, breathlessly reported by the colonial press, spread across the colonies, soon too did stamp officer resignations. Oliver, three days after Boston's initial protest, resigned his commission on August 17. Bernard declared the government "utterly unable to oppose or correct an insurrection of this kind," given how protesters vastly outnumbered loyal forces.[35] "We doubt not," declared a New York letter published in the *Boston Gazette*, "the noble Example of our Brethren in Boston, as it is approved by all, will be unanimously followed by all the Colonies that boast the same Origin."[36] On September 16, rumors surfaced in Boston of a new stamp collector passing en route to New Hampshire, leading alarm bells to toll from local steeples. A large crowd met the ship, forcing the official's resignation. Celebrations followed around the recently consecrated Liberty Tree south of Boston Common into evening. Cambridge and Charlestown followed with nighttime bonfires.[37] By early autumn, every New England and New York stamp officer resigned his office. New Jersey's preemptively quit before any protests occurred.[38]

The Stamp Act's continental nature enabled an aggressive, trans-colonial response. In New Haven, on October 11, protesters forced a would-be replacement into a coffin under threat of being buried alive to renounce his office.[39] Eight days later in Charleston, protests erupted after rumors spread of an arriving ship holding "a stamp-officer, stamps, or stampt paper," while another crowd invaded a prominent merchant's house the next week searching for the dreaded stores.[40] Virginia's stamp officer was "ill-treated in effigy at some places," being "carted, whipped, caned, pilloried, crop'd, hanged & burnt," before he resigned on October 30.[41] Had protests died down, royal officials would have pressed ahead: Maryland's Deputy Governor Horatio Sharpe in September directed the vessel carrying stamped papers "to lye off from

---

[33] MHS Samuel Mather Papers.
[34] British Library, ADD MS 35911, Hardwicke Papers.
[35] NA CO 5/891 270.
[36] *Boston Gazette*, September 9, 1765.
[37] *Boston Gazette*, September 16, 1765; MHS James Freeman Letterbook.
[38] *London Evening Post*, November 7, 1765; BL ADD MS 35911.
[39] *Massachusetts Gazette*, November 17, 1765.
[40] LC James Grant of Balindalloch Papers, MSS 89460, Vol. 8; *South Carolina Gazette*, October 31, 1765.
[41] LC Peter Force Papers, Virginia Reports to British Secretary of State, Box VII E: 17–18 and American Stamp Act Papers, Box VII B: 5–6.

shore ... till the People shew a better Disposition."[42] Only the extent and intensity of the anti–Stamp Act protests prevented implementation.

Protesters performed for a British audience as much as for colonial ones. Boston merchant Ezekiel Price wrote to an overseas correspondent in September how New World events "will probably make a great noise on your side of the water," and fearing their being "very differently represented," he enclosed "Sundry Newspapers" giving "The Minds of the People" on the Stamp Act.[43] Colonial governors regularly wrote to London authorities in tones of exasperation and futility: "it is impossible for me to point out, or even to Conceive," New Hampshire Governor Benning Wentworth complained in October, "what is Necessary to be done to cure the Insania, which runs through the Continent."[44] American collective performances needed to broadcast their resolve but remained within British rhetorical traditions to appeal to audiences there.

British shows of force failed to deter the colonists. The stamped papers for Pennsylvania, New Jersey, and Maryland arrived at Philadelphia on October 5 "under the protection of a man of war." Although the port had been less unified in Stamp Act opposition than others, partisans mobilized. At the first sight of the battleship, "all the Colours in the Harbour were hoisted half Mast high," while church bells tolled all day. Agitated crowds gathered on the waterfront. But short of shelling North America's largest city, which would have been an unprecedented atrocity in a British political standoff, the naval show of force remained symbolic. The captain refused to dock, fearing "some violence" to ship or crew. That Saturday night, crowds forced the local stamp officer's resignation after marching to his home and threatening to destroy his "Person and Property" should he not resign.[45] No easy solutions existed for the British.

The campaign exhibited unprecedented unity across the social spectrum. Sara Franklin wrote to her famous father in London of how "The Subject is now the Stamp act and nothing else is talked of" regardless of gender, nationality, or race: "the Dutch talk of the stomp tack the Negroes of the tamp, in short every body has something to say."[46] North American British Army commander Thomas Gage reported to London in September with perhaps

---

[42] NA CO 5/217 23.

[43] MHS Ezekiel Price Papers, 58.

[44] NA CO 5/934 52.

[45] LC Peter Force Papers, American Stamp Act Papers, Box VIII B: 5–6; American Philosophical Society, Mss. 973.2.M31, Pennsylvania Stamp Act and Nonimportation Resolutions Collection, Vol. 1, 9 and 12.

[46] Benjamin Franklin, *The Papers of Benjamin Franklin*, Leonard W. Labaree et. al., eds. (New Haven: Yale University Press, 1959–2017), Vol. 12, 317–18; Mary Beth Norton, *Liberty's Daughters: The Revolutionary Experience of American Women, 1750–1850* (Boston: Little, Brown & Co., 1980), 170.

greater surprise that American protesters had succeeded "by Menace or Force to oblige the Stamp Officers to resign" and then pressure authorities to continue business without them. Gage realized, however, that his opponents used altered tactics: protest leaders worked "to prevent Insurrections, of the People, as before to excite them." Gage did not elaborate a clear plan to counter colonial actions, fearing in November that militants "wou'd immediately fly to Arms," while "the Clamour has been so general" that government allies would be scarce.[47] Stamp Act opponents succeeded through developing unanimity and intimidation.

Town meetings, though sometimes denouncing protesters' most violent and destructive actions, encouraged resistance. Weymouth, Massachusetts, found "distress is heard not only from every part of this Province, but from the continent in general," as "we behold poverty rushing in on us like an armed man." Declaring Parliament "mistaken," the small town asserted their "natural Rights," particularly "freedom of Speech & of the Press," to agitate for recompense. Pembroke, Massachusetts, similarly sought to block implementation, intending to "postpone the introduction of said Act until the united cries of the whole continent have reached the ears of our most gracious King and Parliament," expecting redress.[48] While presenting themselves as more respectable alternatives to street protests, town meetings nevertheless joined the movement.

Protesters' success in framing their campaign in terms of "liberty" kept their aggressive tactics largely unchecked by authorities. Maryland's Deputy Governor Horatio Sharpe wrote to London of how the populace "with one Voice" denounced the Stamp Act, while publications "inflame the People & persuade them that Obedience to such an Act was a Surrender of all the Rights they had hitherto enjoyed as British Subjects."[49] Colonial civil society's most influential sectors – newspapermen, lawyers, judges, merchants, and legislators – felt collectively aggrieved. Nor were the still-small urban areas isolated: Gage reported "Country-People who are flocking in" to join the protests.[50] With "the Ministry's giving no instructions" on implementation, Sharpe complained that enforcement appeared impossible without gravely escalating the crisis.[51]

As news of the colonial disturbances spread, authorities in London remained uncertain about how to counter the anti–Stamp Act campaign. Secretary of State Henry Conway wrote to Gage and each colonial governor, not offering "positive instructions," but urging them to navigate between

---

[47] Thomas Gage, *The Correspondence of General Gage* (New Haven: Yale University Press, 1931), Vol. 1, 67–68, 71.
[48] LC Peter Force Papers, Massachusetts Town Records, Box VII E: 39–41.
[49] LC Horatio Sharpe Papers, MSS 1722.
[50] NA CO 5/1098 8.
[51] LC Horatio Sharpe Papers, MSS 1722.

"caution" and the "vigour necessary to suppress outrage and violence" as necessary.[52] Following early disturbances, no high-profile protester prosecutions occurred, perhaps due to their usually avoiding physical violence despite engaging in intimidation and destroying property. The newspaper press, meanwhile, despite being the campaign's most influential facilitator and directly violating the Stamp laws, remained unpunished. Given "the present temper of the people," New York's Lieutenant Governor wrote to British authorities, "this is not a proper time to prosecute the Printers and Publishers of the seditious Papers."[53] Already afoul of colonial opinion, many officials favored tolerating protests to endure the controversy.

While volatile street-protests provided important events for galvanizing common citizens, consensus grew for a "Stamp Act Congress" for continental legislatures to issue a common rebuttal against the act. Though congresses had only previously convened to discuss military defense, Massachusetts issued invitations to "consider a general Address" to British authorities demonstrating colonial opposition.[54] Samuel Adams believed a "Union of Comtees from the several Colonys" could "collect the whole Strength of Reason & Argument" to make common cause.[55] Twenty-seven deputies from nine colonial legislatures met in New York from October 7 to 25, resolving "no Taxes be imposed on them, but with their own Consent, given personally, or by their representatives," considering their right under British precedent.[56] The Congress presented an imposing front: "The Spirit of Democracy is strong among 'em," Gage considered.[57] With the formal protest lodged, the body did not discuss further resistance, but neither did it discourage popular campaigning.

The trans-colonial congress' implications were not lost on Parliament when the American petition arrived. Maryland's colonial agent in London, Charles Garth, wrote of how Members of Parliament he consulted considered it "bespoke too much of a Federal Union," carrying "great Danger to his Majesty's Authority and Government." Parliament refused to formally consider the American address, not wanting to legitimate the Congress.[58] Americans moved boldly and British authorities recognized the risks.

Colonists increased pressure through an organized withdrawal from overseas trade by adopting nonimportation agreements. Particularly fitting since

[52] *Parliamentary History*, Vol. 16, 113–7; LC Peter Force Papers, Ezra Stiles Diary.
[53] Henry Dawson, *The Sons of Liberty in New York* (Poughkeepsie: Platt & Schram, 1859), 78.
[54] Walter H. Conser, Jr., "Stamp Act Resistance," in *Resistance, Politics, and the American Struggle for Independence, 1765–1775*, in Conser, Ronald M. McCarthy, David J. Toscano and Gene Sharp, eds. (Boulder, CO: Lynne Reinner, 1986), 48; Weslager, 50.
[55] Samuel Adams, *Writings*, Vol. 1, 57.
[56] Ibid., 106; LC Peter Force Papers, American Stamp Act Papers, Box VIII B: 5–6.
[57] NA CO 5/219 18.
[58] Maryland Historical Society, Revolutionary War Collection, MSS 1814.

authorities demanded customs duties be paid on stamped paper, nonimportation deprived the government of revenue while pressuring British manufacturing constituencies to join the repeal campaign. The American colonies, though having consumed only 5 percent of English exports in 1700, by the late-colonial crises purchased 25 percent.[59] Disrupting American Atlantic trade could trigger an Empire-wide recession. Mather in Boston that August already described resistance spreading "thro all the Colonies" and believed redress would come once colonists "endeavour less & less to be beholden to Great Britain for its Manufactures," so the British "will certainly lose more than they will ever gain by oppressive Measures."[60] Repeal ought to follow once the Stamp Act became economically unfeasible and politically damaging in Britain.

Organizing such a trans-colonial American effort required a significantly more concerted effort than scattered effigy-burnings, necessitating near-comprehensive adherence across the colonies to be effective. The compacts spread quickly, with Maryland planter Charles Carroll on October 5 describing a tense climate in which "no business will be done after the first of November," when the boycott would take effect alongside the Stamp Act.[61] In New York, Stamp Act opponents advertised their intention "to form an ASSOCIATION of ALL who are not already SLAVES, in OPPOSITION to all ATTEMPTS to make them so."[62] On October 31, a merchants' meeting of more than two hundred agreed to cease transatlantic exporting after January 1 for the Act's duration, depriving Britain of raw materials as well as markets for manufactured products. Widespread coordination remained essential: the merchants appointed a five-man "Committee of Correspondence" for broader mobilization and enforcement.[63] Albany followed suit. Philadelphia adopted a matching agreement on November 14 signed by four hundred.[64] Despite the economic risk, many grasped the movement's potential, through which resistance, the *Boston Gazette* wrote, "will ketch from Town to Town, and Province to Province, than which nothing can more contribute to a speedy Redress of our Grievances."[65] Boston merchants (belatedly) joined on December 9.[66] The movement's size and ramifications became unparalleled.

[59] Laurel Thatcher Ulrich, "Political Protest and the World of Goods," in *The Oxford Handbook of the American Revolution*, Edward G. Gray and Jane Kamensky, eds. (Oxford: Oxford University Press, 2013), 67.

[60] MHS Samuel Mather Papers.

[61] Charles Carroll, *Dear Papa, Dear Charley: The Peregrinations of a Revolutionary Aristocrat* (Chapel Hill: University of North Carolina Press, 2001), Vol. 1, 383.

[62] *Newport Mercury*, October 28, 1765.

[63] Dawson, *Sons*, 84–86; *New-York Gazette*, October 31, 1765.

[64] Tiedemann, *Reluctant*, 71; LC Galloway-Maxcy-Markoe Papers MSS 21857, Vol. 8; *Pennsylvania Gazette*, November 7, 1765.

[65] *Boston Gazette*, November 25, 1765.

[66] Gordon, *History of the Rise*, Vol. 1, 194.

The boycott effort entailed both risk and opportunity for the colonies. Some, especially in the imperial administration, expected economic catastrophe: Virginia's Lieutenant Governor prophesized to the Board of Trade in London in early November, "the distress the country will feel on a total stagnation of business, will open their eyes and pave the way for the Acts' executing its self."[67] Gage predicted that with a "Stop to Business, the people idle, and exasperated," would lose patience.[68] The British Navy increased patrols, deterring colonists' rampant smuggling with French and Spanish ports.[69] Yet as Boston merchant James Murray described, such restrictions could give domestic industry a "necessary Spur" with long-term benefits for the colonial balance of trade.[70] Other merchants favored nonimportation as a way to clear a glutted market, with Philadelphian John Chew estimating "there will be no want of goods for a Twelve month," while prognosticating that "the riotous Spirit of the Manufacturers of Great Britain," feeling the contraction worse than the colonists, "will work our Cure."[71]

If American merchants had departed from the nonimportation agreements, popular reprisals appeared almost certain. Philadelphia merchants' form letter to those of British ports on November 7 warned if goods arrived after the measure took effect, "and the Stamp-Act not be repealed, I shall not dare to dispose any Part of them, without a forfeiture of my Honour; nor indeed can I engage for their or my own safety."[72] Popular control of streets and wharves extended to the flow of commerce – and perhaps of politics. Expressing support for the Stamp Act or the ruling ministry in the colonies became anathema, with reprisals likely to follow.[73]

British preparations to enforce the Stamp Act met popular reprisals. Stamp Officer George Saxby's late-October arrival in Charleston sparked unrest led by "people who called themselves Sons of Liberty," likely the first combination taking that name.[74] A dual effigy procession of Saxby and Lord Bute began once his ship came into view, with townspeople crowding the docks to demand his resignation. The stamp man agreed, given popular dissatisfaction, that he "would not act in that office till his Majesty's further pleasure was known," satisfying those assembled. To "shouts of joy," the official entered town in triumph to ringing church bells and beating drums. Following "the laudable example of the northern Provinces," one Charlestonian described the campaign as "opening their Eyes and communicating a noble sense and spirit of

[67] LC Peter Force Papers, Virginia Reports to British Secretary of State, Box VII E: 17–18.
[68] Gage, *Correspondence*, Vol. 1, 71.
[69] "Journal of a French Traveler," 82.
[70] MHS James Murray Papers, P-141.
[71] LC Galloway-Maxcy-Markoe Papers, MSS 21857 Vol. 8.
[72] APS MSS 973.2.M31 Vol. 2, 2.
[73] Virginia Historical Society, Mercier Correspondence, MSS 5345 a124.
[74] South Carolina Historical Society, Robert Raper Papers, 34/0511.

Freedom." A trans-colonial movement coalesced even before the Stamp Act began.[75]

Colonists organized dramatic public demonstrations for the day the Stamp Act took effect. On November 1 in Boston, radicals again hung two effigies from the Liberty Tree and made an evening march through town culminating in the figures' destruction. Unlike in August, however, no property was attacked.[76] Later that week on Pope's Day, the North and South Ends renounced their annual brawl to make a unified procession, ending with incinerating not just the Pope and devil, but figures representing "tyranny, oppression, slavery, &c."[77] Portsmouth, New Hampshire protesters, the day after extracting a loyalty oath from a suspected stamp distributor, mournfully marched a casket marked "LIBERTY, aged 145, STAMPED," from the state-house to burial outside town.[78] In New York, with crowds "composed of great numbers of Sailors headed by Captains of Privateers" calling themselves "The Sons of Neptune" – a nickname long predating "Sons of Liberty" – together with thousands of locals, engaged in five days of disorder stretching from the Act's promulgation (that evening burning two effigies representing the Lieutenant Governor and the Devil) to Guy Fawkes Day. At their culmination, crowds gathered to storm the Battery fort where royal troops held stamped paper, only relenting after the governor released the hated cargo for incineration.[79] In Philadelphia a crowd menaced the house of Franklin, who as a colonial lobbyist in London seemingly acquiesced to the legislation.[80] Savannah, allegedly "occasioned by the inflammatory Papers & Messages sent by the Liberty Boys" from Charleston, conducted an effigy march and burning to the "acclamations of a great concourse of people of all ranks and denominations," declaring any stamp collector would meet "the sentiments of the people" on arrival.[81] A Fairfield, Connecticut, group, calling itself "true Sons of Liberty," performed the same ritual on November 12.[82] Such widespread, ostentatious demonstrations broadcast the depth and breadth of American anger.

---

[75] Ibid., Richard Hutson Papers, 34/0559, 3.

[76] *Boston Evening Gazette*, November 7, 1765; *Pennsylvania Gazette*, November 7, 1765.

[77] MHS James Freeman Diary.

[78] *Newport Mercury*, November 11, 1765; *Pennsylvania Gazette*, November 21, 1765; *Boston Gazette*, November 11, 1765.

[79] Gage, *Correspondence*, Vol. 1, 71; Jesse Lemisch, *Jack Tar vs. John Bull: The Role of New York's Seamen in Precipitating the Revolution* (New York: Garland, 1997), 84–86; Mike Rapport, *The Unruly City: Paris, London and New York in the Age of Revolution* (New York: Basic Books, 2017), 11; NA CO 5/217 26.

[80] Standiford, *Desperate*, 84.

[81] NA CO 5/218 26; *New-York Gazette*, January 16, 1766; *Pennsylvania Gazette*, January 2, 1766; *Boston Post-Boy*, January 27, 1766; *Boston Gazette*, January 27, 1766.

[82] *Pennsylvania Gazette*, December 12, 1765.

Alongside the boycotts, colonists engaged in civil disobedience, defiantly continuing to use stamp-designated items without paying the new tax. Many newspapers, some proudly boasting of appearing on unstamped paper, continued after November 1 uninterrupted, while others resumed after brief hiatuses. Publishers proclaimed themselves obliged to continue, as otherwise "their Offices would be in Danger from the enraged People."[83] Though many courts closed, rather than directly defy Parliamentary legislation (which many commoners favored as it suspended debt cases), elsewhere the populace successfully pressured their reopening. A town meeting in Norwich, Connecticut, asked "the Clerk Proceed in all Matter Relating to his office as Usual; And that the Town will save him harmless from all Damages that he may sustain thereby."[84] Boston's port resumed full operations by New Year, granting "Clearances with a Certificate that no Stampt Papers are to be had," while local courts resumed sessions.[85] In Providence the following March, reportedly "all business, public and private, is prosecuted in this colony without any regard to the Stamp Act, which is considered as a mere nullity."[86] Americans, resorting to their own interpretations of natural rights and the British constitution's fundamental precepts, found the law illegitimate.

Through a combination of coordinated efforts and copycat tactics, a common movement coalesced against the Stamp Act. Despite scattered property damage and threats of violent resistance, however, the campaign – increasingly directed by those calling themselves Sons of Liberty – almost entirely avoided physical violence, while innovating a broader coordinated campaign of public displays, civil disobedience, and reciprocal communication than any preceding Anglo-American movement.

The Sons of Liberty Alliance

By the Stamp Act's November 1 implementation, the Sons of Liberty moved beyond being a metaphor or temporary combination into a full-fledged association and social movement. Initially, diverse groups galvanized the anti-Stamp Act agitation, from colonial legislatures to town meetings, social clubs, commercial associations, and temporary combinations of townspeople, farmers, and sailors. From this tumultuous mix, by the year's end the movement developed a degree of structure, coordination, and endurance unmatched by any predecessors.

On November 6, New York's Sons met outside city limits on Manhattan Island fields and proposed appointing their own committee of correspondence

---

[83] *Newport Mercury*, November 4, 1765.
[84] LC Peter Force Collection MSS 20990, Norwich Town Papers, Box VII E:58.
[85] HBSL William Lloyd Letterbook, 263.
[86] MHS Portsmouth Sons of Liberty Papers.

to exchange intelligence with fellow continental branches. Whereas earlier corresponding committees were extensions of governmentally recognized organizations (legislative or mercantile), the Sons taking such an established, legally traceable form worried many. Though approving the design, over half an hour passed before any New York Son volunteered to participate. Only after prominent merchant Isaac Sears agreed did four others follow. They planned to "open a correspondence with all the colonies," while requesting Boston and Philadelphia serve as regional hubs.[87]

Sons of Liberty gloried in intimidation, using exemplary acts to recruit new members and raise their public standing. New York's branch publicized their plans against Maryland stamp collector Zachariah Hood, who had fled to Long Island. On December 2, two hundred men crossed the East River to Flushing, located Hood, and forced his resignation. The group combined paramilitary action with fraternal proceedings, holding a banquet afterward in which "Many constitutional Toasts were drank" amid "good Humour and Joy."[88] Similar actions followed elsewhere. Sons in Wyndham, Connecticut forcibly searched a prominent resident's house for letters written to London and then publicized their contents.[89] At Boston on December 17, "true-born Sons of Liberty" organized a two-thousand-person gathering to successfully extract Oliver's resignation.[90] Colonial newspapers increasingly described the Sons as a coherent group with central organizing principles, strategies, and forms of action.

Exemplary effigy displays maintained pressure on authorities. Philadelphia protesters in December hung a stamped newspaper "suspended by an Iron Chain, to which was affixed a Pair of Handcuffs." New York mobilized an effigy procession of Grenville, naval commander Lord Colville, and Quebec's governor for their respective roles in executing the Stamp Act, ending with the mannequins being "carried to the fields and burned." When British sailors attempted to covertly land stamped papers in January, a band of armed men stormed the ship and burnt the hated cargo at the dock.[91] Vehement rhetoric and reprisals against the British administration proliferated.

Anti–Stamp Act agitation spread beyond the Thirteen Colonies, across British domains northward and southward, but local responses varied. On October 31, rioters in the Caribbean port of Basseterre on St. Kitts, aided by American sailors, forced the stamp master and his deputy's resignation and torched their houses after they fled. At the nearby isle of Nevis on Guy Fawkes Day, protesters "totally destroyed the Stamps" and burned the stamp officers in

---

[87] Gordon, *History of the Rise*, Vol. 1, 186–87.
[88] *Pennsylvania Gazette,* December 5 and 12, 1765; *Massachusetts Gazette,* December 12, 1765.
[89] *Boston Evening Gazette,* December 16, 1765.
[90] Ibid., December 23, 1765.
[91] LC Peter Force Papers, American Stamp Act Papers, Box VIII B: 5–6.

effigy. Neither island enforced the Stamp Act.[92] Similar protests occurred in Halifax, though Nova Scotia soon submitted. Kingston, Jamaica, while avoiding such confrontations, continued processing ships without stamps. In some areas, however, authorities remained unyielding: though protesters compelled Antigua's stamp officer to resign, officials kept the stamps under strict military guard and appointed a replacement, who, as one merchant apologetically wrote to Philadelphia, "distributes them to the People who are Obliged to receive them, if very much against their wills."[93] The rest of Jamaica and all Barbados followed.[94] Strategically vulnerable areas, wanting stronger military garrisons to guard against potential French Canadian rebellions or slave uprisings on Caribbean sugar islands, ultimately acquiesced, leading to a near-equal split among Britain's twenty-six American possessions.

The Stamp Act's broad purview encouraged mobilizations across both class and gender divides. Much as merchants became expected to lead boycotts and common men to enforce nonimportation, women altered family consumption habits and promoted "homespun" cloth. Virtuous household consumption embodied American dedication, contrasting favorably with the moral corruption associated with aristocratic Britain. The "fairer sex" could thus promote more peaceful resistance methods; one letter noted, "when such examples are inforced by the tender persuasions of amiable women they cannot fail to produce wonderful effects."[95] Already during 1764's Sugar Act agitation, localities began resolving "not to buy any clothing (they could do without) which was not of their own manufacturing," to hurt the British economy and encourage manufacturers to pressure for repeal.[96] The 1765 movement encouraged families to produce for the home market. The *Newport Mercury* hoped market conditions "will animate the country people to make plenty of linens and woollens, as they may be assured of quick sale, and good prices."[97] Nonconsumption, more often than dangerous street protests, directly involved the populace in the campaign. Colonists adopted further boycotts against eating lamb to maximize wool supply.[98] Resistance spread into colonists' lifestyles as consumer choices became politicized.

Colonial citizens, as consumers and arbiters of taste, created a new radical chic of simplicity to support the boycott. Maryland's governor wrote of how "to encourage the Inferior Class to do so, many Gentlemen will this winter

---

[92] O'Shaughnessy, *Empire*, 89–91.
[93] Historical Society of Pennsylvania, Clifford Correspondence MSS 0136 Vol. 4 209.
[94] Gordon, *History of the Rise*, Vol. 1, 190.
[95] APS MSS 973.2.M31 Vol. 1, 2; T. H. Breen, *The Marketplace of Revolution: How Consumer Politics Shaped American Independence* (Oxford: Oxford University Press, 2004), esp. 263–65.
[96] APS MSS 973.2.M31, Vol. 1, 156.
[97] *Newport Mercury*, November 4, 1765.
[98] Ramsay, *History*, Vol. 1, 70–71.

cloath themselves with the Manufactures of Maryland."[99] The fashion revolution occurred rapidly: on November 28, a Philadelphian reported the "manufactures of this province are now daily coming to town."[100] Women, as household buyers and wool-spinners, played an outsized role: by winter, respectable young "Daughters of Liberty" hosted spinning bees to promote "a laudable Zeal for introducing Home Manufactures."[101] Many previously imitating high British fashions now embraced colonial homespun. Franklin, testifying before Parliament in early 1766, asserted that whereas American "pride" had previously been to "indulge in the fashions and manufactures of Great Britain," now they "wear their old clothes over again, until they can make new ones."[102]

The Stamp Act would be overturned not only via intercontinental resistance, but through transatlantic campaigning. In December, news of the boycotts arrived in Britain with adjoining cancellations of colonial orders. By February, resulting British losses estimated £120,000.[103] Franklin diffused American accounts into the British press, writing home he "reprinted everything from America that I thought might be of help for a common cause."[104] Many Britons, distrusting their government and hoping to economically rebound, became motivated to help secure repeal.

Influential colonists prodded potential British allies, drawing attention to the precedents coercion in America could set. Samuel Adams wrote to London in December, "The British Constitution makes no Distinction between good Subjects with Regard to Liberty," and thus rights abridged in the colonies could be denied to Britons. The system, he argued, "admits of no more Power over the Subject than is necessary for the Purpose of Government, which was originally designed for the Preservation of the unalienated Rights of Nature." America's cause necessarily was Britain's, since suppressing colonial autonomy could create precedents to abridge British rights.

Such campaigning spurred British repeal lobbying: London merchants formed a Committee of Correspondence to solicit protestations. Reportedly, "Petitions came from every trading and manufacturing Town" doing business with America.[105] Colonial protesters needed to influence the British to achieve changes. Ideological and economic sympathies intertwined with advocates on both sides of the Atlantic working together. "PERSEVERANCE TO THE SONS OF LIBERTY IN AMERICA" became

---

[99] LC Horatio Sharpe Papers, MSS 1722.

[100] *New Hampshire Gazette*, December 13, 1765.

[101] *Providence Gazette*, March 12, 1766; *Boston Post-Boy*, March 31, 1766.

[102] Standiford, *Desperate*, 100–101.

[103] *London Evening Post*, December 12, 1765; Morley, *Irish*, 52.

[104] LC Peter Force Papers, American Stamp Act Papers, Box VII B: 5–6.

[105] *Maryland Gazette*, March 6, 1766; Richard Champion, *The American Correspondence of a Bristol Merchant, 1766–1776* (Berkeley: University of California Press, 1934), 11.

a common toast across England and Scotland, while Irish allies pledged, "Destruction to the Stamp Act, and Success to the free Sons of Liberty in America."[106] The cause of liberty, and resistance against unprecedented governmental incursions, became a transatlantic effort.

Nonimportation, placing significant economic pressure on both the boycotters and boycotted, made rapidly reversing the Stamp Act essential. Royally appointed Massachusetts Lieutenant Governor Thomas Hutchinson wrote to Franklin on November 18, reporting New England "depend[s] upon the repeal of the stamp act as soon as the Parliament meets."[107] Economic interests might not be restrained much longer. In New Hampshire, Manchester's merchants and manufacturers brought a petition before their colonial assembly reminding them "home Consumption . . . is very small in Comparison of the Export Trade" and imploring relief for their plight.[108] Many colonials became increasingly unenthusiastic about sacrificing their financial well-being for abstract constitutional principles.

As 1765 drew to a close, colonists remarked on the unprecedented "spirit" of American unity. "The people," wrote Braintree, Massachusetts, lawyer John Adams, "even to the lowest ranks, have become more attentive to their liberties, more inquisitive about them, and more determined to defend them, than they were ever before known or had occasion to be." Indeed, "so universal has been the resentment of the people" that none dared defend the Stamp Act in public.[109] The *New-York Gazette* recapped the year by considering, "we are still free," though everything depended "upon our Firmness and Unanimity."[110] Particularly as word arrived of Quebec, Nova Scotia, and most of the West Indies submitting to the Act, a unified front became essential.[111]

In New London, Connecticut, on Christmas Day in 1765, Sons of Liberty representatives from across the state met those of New York. Militia associations had long been common across the colonies and Britain itself, but now the Sons mobilized against imperial commands.[112] Going beyond the corresponding connections established in recent months, the groups composed a full mutual aid agreement. The Sons would remain "vigilant" against officials who "from the Nature of their Offices, Vocations or Dispositions, may be the most

---

[106] *Maryland Gazette*, February 20, 1766; *Boston Gazette*, February 17, 1766; *Boston Post-Boy*, March 17, 1766.
[107] Franklin, *Papers*, Vol. 12, 380.
[108] *New Hampshire Gazette*, December 6, 1765.
[109] John Adams, *The Works of John Adams* (Boston: Little, Brown, 1852–1865), Vol. 2, 154.
[110] *New-York Gazette*, January 2, 1766.
[111] *New London Gazette*, December 20, 1765; *Boston Post-Boy*, December 23, 1765; *Pennsylvania Gazette*, January 9, 1766,
[112] Matthew McCormack, *Embodying the Militia in Georgian England* (Oxford: Oxford University Press, 2015); Joseph Seymour, *The Pennsylvania Associators, 1747–1777* (Yardley, PA: Westholme, 2012).

likely to introduce the use of Stamp'd Paper" and pursue violators. Meanwhile, they offered protection to all resisting officials, while resolving "to defend the liberty of the press" and all British rights. To accomplish this, the groups planned to spread their allied model across the colonies, strengthening connections to reinforce their efforts.[113]

The Sons of Liberty compact appeared highly aggressive, even paramilitary. The committees diffused their alliance across adjoining colonies with the Sons asking correspondents "to assemble as many of the true Sons of Liberty as you possibly can" to "form an Union of the Colonies" to resist British enforcement. The circular made clear the group would "not to be enslaved by any Power on Earth, without opposing force to force."[114] Within a week of the Christmas gathering, rumors flew of British military enforcement, and in mid-January protesters seized and burned stamped papers arriving at New York.[115] The group asserted they would physically contest Stamp Act enforcement, perhaps on a continental scale.

Sons of Liberty affiliations led to a new upsurge in collective action. Connecticut Sons set the confrontational tone, at the December 25 meeting resolving to demand "satisfaction" from their stamp collector, Jared Ingersoll. Wondering if he "Read the Late Papers of N. York and Boston," they threatened he would "Know by sad Experience all the horrors of falling away into the hands of A free & Enraged people whose bosoms Glowe with A True Spirit of British Liberty" should he not resign.[116] In early January, a crowd confronted Ingersoll near Hartford and pressured him into renouncing his office. Protests forced a stamp man's resignation in Savannah, while in Albany protesters sacked the accused's dwelling.[117] Crowds forced another recantation in Portsmouth, seizing the official instructions which they "stuck on the Point of a sword & carried all around the Town in Triumph, with Drums & loud acclamations," before delivering them to a ship's captain "who swore faithfull to deliver them in London" to the officials from whence they came.[118] As affiliation spread, the organization remained firm, with New York City's Sons on January 2 printing resolutions reiterating the need to "go to the last Extremity" against Stamp Act enforcement, but "maintain the Peace and good Order of this City, so far as it can be done consistently with the Preservation and Security of our Rights and

---

[113] Morgan and Morgan, *Stamp Act*, 201; CHS, American Revolution Collection, Box 11, Folder M.

[114] APS MSS 973.2.M31, Vol. 1, 17; Standiford, *Desperate*, 91.

[115] BL Henry Moore Papers, ADD MS 22679; NA CO 5/1098 35.

[116] American Antiquarian Society, United States Revolution Collection, Box 1.

[117] *Pennsylvania Gazette*, January 16 and February 14, 1766; *Pennsylvania Journal*, January 2, 1766; *Boston Post-Boy*, January 6 and 27, 1766; *Boston Gazette*, January 13, 1766; *New-York Gazette*, January 9, 1766; *Newport Mercury*, February 3, 1766.

[118] MHS Jeremy Belknap Diaries, P-363.

Privileges."[119] Utilizing measured force, in keeping with the movement's principles, gave the Sons an unequalled power.

The New York-Connecticut alliance wrote to Boston, seeking formal affiliation. Boston not only allied but sent a circular letter to nearby communities for local branches to gather the "dispositions of the people" there.[120] Not just a union of colonial capitals, but dense networks within colonies took shape. A Providence Son of Liberty attending Boston's meeting in mid-February reported the organization was "fast as Fate in their opposition to the Stamp Act & all its Abbetters, that they can at two Hours Notice Bring 3000 Men under the Tree of Liberty who would go anywhere for the preservation of the constitution," while possessing 40,000 affiliated across Massachusetts and New Hampshire.[121] With such power in numbers, the Sons' influence could not be ignored.

Ceremonies of affiliation and solidarity became increasingly public. The Sons of Liberty of New York, Connecticut, and Boston jointly wrote to Portsmouth's in early February, recommending, in the king's name, they "join in every laudable Measure to support his Crown and Dignity; and their own Liberties and Property, which are inseparably connected with his Authority." The letter was read outdoors amid a "great Concourse of the Inhabitants of this and the neighbouring Towns" and approved, after which "the Parade clear'd in Ten Minutes."[122] The Sons portrayed themselves as principled men, upholding the British constitution's highest principles. Portsmouth's branch pledged "to venture our lives and fortunes" against "fatal & ruinous measures," vowing united resistance.[123] Such resolutions promoted the Sons as more than a violent extralegal body – rather, an organization speaking for their community.

The Sons planned a February 20 day of action across the colonies, in which "the united Free-born Sons of Liberty" conducted effigy and stamped paper burnings before large crowds. Boston's members, after incinerating Grenville and Bute figures before a crowd of thousands, returned to their meetinghouse, toasting "Long Life, Health and Prosperity to all the Sons of Liberty on the Continent," exulting in the growing alliance.[124] Four days later, the Sons published their Christmas alliance.[125] With no officials daring to challenge them, the organization's ascendance continued.

---

[119] *Pennsylvania Gazette*, January 16, 1766; *Virginia Gazette*, March 7, 1766.
[120] John Adams, *Papers of John Adams*, Robert J. Taylor, ed. (Cambridge, MA: Belknap Press, 1977), Vol. 1, 170; Maier, *Resistance*, 79.
[121] New-York Historical Society, John Lamb Papers, reel 1.
[122] *New Hampshire Gazette*, February 14, 1766; *New-York Gazette*, March 6, 1766; *Boston Gazette*, February 17, 1766.
[123] MHS Portsmouth Sons of Liberty Records.
[124] *Boston Evening Gazette*, February 24, 1766; *Freeman's Journal*, April 22, 1766.
[125] *New-York Mercury*, February 24, 1766.

The Sons of Liberty network spread with New York's Sons sending circular letters as far as South Carolina, requesting trans-colonial affiliations.[126] New York's committee asked affiliates "to enter into a firm Union for the Preservation of our inestimable and undoubted rights." Branches received orders to "assemble as many of the true born Sons of Liberty as you possibly can," propose "an Association in order to form an Union of the Colonies, in Imitation of our Brethren in Connecticut, Boston &c.," and maintain correspondence with affiliates. The Sons pursued an "everlasting" colonial alliance to "not to be enslav'd, by any Power on Earth, without Opposing force to force."[127]

The circular received broad acclamations and growing Sons of Liberty affiliations. A February 24 meeting in Baltimore, displaying the New York letters, sought to recruit "subscribers" and spread the movement throughout Maryland. Building from Massachusetts' example, organizers requested each county form an association and send a dozen delegates to an Annapolis gathering on March 31.[128] Within a week, Baltimore reported "the whole Province seem unanimous in prosecuting the same design."[129] Sons in New London, Connecticut, in late February advertised a "general congress" of Sons from across the colony at Hartford the last Tuesday in March.[130] Each New Jersey branch the same month appointed a five-man committee to "act in Conjunction" with neighboring areas and "be in actual Readiness on any Emergency," while Maryland established committee coordination on township, county, and colony levels.[131] Colony-wide and trans-colonial organizations consolidated, creating solidarity and significant paramilitary manpower.

Organizers responded to the multiplying affiliations with great enthusiasm. "The whole Continent breaths the same patriotic Spirit with you," the Boston Sons' committee wrote to Portsmouth's on March 14, "we have the most sanguine hopes of being a united body, from South Carolina to New-Hampshire in a few Weeks," to "remain in perpetuity as a Barrier against the unconstitutionall schemes of designing Ministers."[132] Congregationalist minister Ezra Stiles reported from the Sons' Newport branch two weeks later, "the Resolves of the Sons of Liberty in different provinces, pour in upon us."[133] Only Philadelphia, among urban centers, remained outside the Sons' alliance.

In the uncertainty, many feared the British might send soldiers to uphold the Stamp Act by force. The Sons readied to oppose them. Norfolk's took a new

---

[126] Gordon, *History of the Rise*, Vol. 1, 199.
[127] MHS Portsmouth Sons of Liberty Records, 119.
[128] *Maryland Gazette*, March 6, 1766; *Pennsylvania Gazette*, March 20, 1766; Carroll, *Dear*, Vol. 1, 391.
[129] NYHS John Lamb Papers, reel 1.
[130] *Pennsylvania Gazette*, March 13, 1766; *Connecticut Courant*, March 24, 1766.
[131] *Pennsylvania Gazette*, March 13, 1766; Maier, *Resistance*, 80.
[132] MHS Portsmouth Sons of Liberty Records, 119.
[133] LC Peter Force Papers, Ezra Stiles Diary.

oath in April that should the Stamp Act "be inforced, that they will stand by each other in order to oppose it with all their might."[134] New York wrote to Boston on April 3, asking if they should prepare a "general plan" together for such an extremity.[135] Gage complained in February, "There seems throughout the Provinces to be a Dissolution of all legal Authority," whereby "all coercive Powers in Government are annihilated."[136] Rebellion neared with British influence at a frightening ebb.

Uprisings threatened in the American interior as the Stamp Act controversy broadened grievances against the ruling strata. In April 1766, Dutchess and Westchester County, New York tenant farmers seized areas belonging to rich landowners and discussed marching on Manhattan to free neighbors from debt prison. Though taking the name "Sons of Liberty," word that "hundreds of Tenants are also turned Levellers and are in arms to dispossess some and maintain others in their own, without rent or taxation" shocked New York City's Sons, who prepared for their town's defense. Neither side risked attack, however, with insurgent control continuing through summer. In Connecticut, too, four thousand people "signed to make an equal dividend of property there."[137] Though outside the Sons' network, agrarian rebels built from its growing associational culture, making British repression against any American movement still more problematic.

The Sons of Liberty movement's ascendance only ended with news of Parliament repealing the Stamp Act. George III dismissed Grenville as prime minister in July 1765, appointing the Marquis of Rockingham, who did not defend the hated legislation once colonial opposition's extent became clear.[138] Though the king officially assented to repeal on March 18, ships carrying official news only simultaneously arrived in Boston and Philadelphia harbors on May 19. The Sons, who had ratcheted down their activities the previous two months as intelligence from Britain gave hope of repeal, led the celebrations. To the sounds of ringing church bells and discharging cannons, Boston's Sons participated in the "firing of Guns, drinking loyal Toasts, and other decent Expressions of Joy." The organization undertook no reprisals with groups seeking "to demonstrate our Affection to Great-Britain."[139] Rural residents of both sexes joined the festivities, which continued into the night with fireworks and illuminations (including respectful animations of the royal

---

[134] LC Peter Force Papers, "Virginia Reports to British Secretary of State," Box VII E: 17–18.
[135] NYHS John Lamb Papers, reel 1.
[136] Gage, *Correspondence*, Vol. 1, 84.
[137] Irving Mark, *Agrarian Conflicts in Colonial New York, 1711–1775* (New York: Columbia University Press, 1965), 131–63.
[138] Slaughter, *Independence*, 240.
[139] *Pennsylvania Gazette*, May 29, 1766; *Boston Gazette*, June 2, 1766.

family) and spilled into the next day in Cambridge.[140] When word arrived the next day at New York, the Sons led "liberal Rejoicings" featuring banqueting, dancing, and bonfires, where "25 barrels of strong Beer, Also Rum, with Sugar, Bread, &c were given to the populace." The group adopted and published a proclamation congratulating their allies.[141] At Charleston, glasses rose to "all the true Sons of Liberty on the Continent," alongside toasts to "our worthy friends in England."[142] Colonists celebrated their associational success.

Amazingly, the movement had triumphed over a few short months. One British letter to a Philadelphia merchant reported the government now sought "to promote harmony, and an agreeable intercourse between the Mother Country and her Colonies," reversing their prior demands.[143] A London merchant related, "the Continual Account we had of the Sons of Liberty through All North America had its proper weight & Effect." Congratulations arrived from across the empire: one Antigua merchant reported the news "rejoicing the heart of every subject of Great Britain," bringing "immortal honor to the Americans."[144] British movements soon followed the Americans' model.

The new legislation's details, however, occasioned less joy. A Declaratory Act accompanied repeal, precedented on Ireland's subordination, considering the colonies "dependent upon the imperial crown and parliament of *Great Britain*," granting British authorities unrestricted purview to make laws for the colonies.[145] Virginia's Lieutenant Governor wrote in September, "the people are sour, partly occasioned by their private distresses, and partly by being spirited up by the newspapers." Still, "a spirit of discontent" ran against what "the late indulgencies, received from their Mother Country, ought to inspire them with."[146] Virginia's House of Burgesses, unlike other assemblies, refused to thank the king for the new legislation.[147] Long months of opposition instilled a conspiratorial view of British politics, and many colonists refused to view restoring long-held rights as benevolent charity.

Late 1766 brought an uncertain pause rather than resolution to the imperial crisis. As Rhode Island Son of Liberty Silas Downer prophesized in a letter to

[140] AAS Priscilla Holyoke Diary; HBSL William Lloyd Letterbook, 362; MHS John Tudor Papers.
[141] *Pennsylvania Gazette*, May 29, 1766.
[142] *Pennsylvania Gazette*, June 12, 1766; Basil Williams, *The Life of William Pitt, Earl of Chatham* (New York: Longmans, 1913), 202.
[143] LC Stephen Collins Records, MSS 16436 Vol. 5; LC Silas Deane Papers, 8B reel 11.
[144] NYHS John Lamb Papers, reel 1.
[145] *An Act for Securing the Dependency of His Majesty's Dominions in America upon the Crown and Parliament of Great-Britain* (London, 1766); Patrick Griffin, *The Townshend Moment: The Making of Empire and Revolution in the Eighteenth Century* (New Haven: Yale University Press, 2017), 97.
[146] LC Peter Force Papers, Virginia Reports to British Secretary of State, Box VII E: 17–18.
[147] Middlekauff, *Glorious*, 137.

New York's Sons, "What could not be brought to pass by an undisguised and open attack upon our liberties is intended to be done by secret machinations, by artifice and cunning."[148] Yet should a new assault on American liberties occur, a precedent for united action had been forged. As Samuel Adams wrote to a Charleston correspondent in December:

> When the Colnys saw the common Danger they at the same time saw their mutual Dependence & naturally called in the Assistance of each other, & I dare say such Friendships & Connections are establish'd between them, as shall for the future deter the most virulent Enemy from making another open Attempt upon their Rights as Men & Subjects.

Adams asserted colonial liberties would now be "infring'd upon in a less observable manner."[149] The new model appeared too powerful for direct assault.

The Sons of Liberty model's potential became clear even to opponents. Annapolis' former mayor wrote to Lord Baltimore in England of how though the colonies had long been "Different in Religion, and Polity, of dissimilar Manners and Habitudes, all for the most part extremely tenacious of their own, clashing Interests," the "Sharpest Oppression" had brought them into a unified design. At any future crisis, the "Unruly Democrative Sprit of our Northern Brethren" would lead a "general Union" of aggrieved colonies into "Concerted schemes of revolt."[150] Only the wisest British governance could prevent such a course.

In the interior, where the Stamp Act remained a secondary issue, mobilizations continued. A new association in Orange County, North Carolina, in August 1766 circulated a proposal to "Let each Neighbourhood throughout the County meet together, and appoint one or more Men to attend a general Meeting ... where there is no Liquor," to discuss "Abuses of Power" in government.[151] Such organizations created new ways to resist British authority. Showing their own worldliness, one group even claimed, "Every one of our Enemies here are utter Enemies to WILKES, and the Cause of Liberty." Associators claimed vigilance would bring authorities "under a better and honester regulation," contesting debt enforcement, protesting settlement restrictions, and more generally resisting tax enforcement.[152]

---

[148] Rhode Island Historical Society, Sons of Liberty Papers, MSS 9005.

[149] Samuel Adams Papers, LOC MSS 10223 Vol. 1.

[150] Maryland Historical Society, Revolutionary War Collection, MS 1814; NA PRO 39/8/97, 51.

[151] "An Impartial Relation of the First Rise and Cause of the Recent Differences in Publick Affairs, in the Province of North Carolina; and the Past Tumults and Riots That Happened in the Province," in *Some Eighteenth-Century Tracts on North Carolina*, William K. Boyd, ed. (Raleigh, NC: Edwards & Broughton, 1927), 257–58; Marjolene Kars, *Breaking Loose Together: The Regulator Rebellion in Pre-Revolutionary North Carolina* (Chapel Hill: University of North Carolina Press, 2002), 112.

[152] A. Roger Ekirch, *"Poor Carolina": Politics and Society in Colonial North Carolina* (Chapel Hill: University of North Carolina Press, 1981), 164, 187.

In the absence of new imperial crises, the Sons of Liberty took the guise of a commemorative organization. Though occasionally remobilizing, as in a New York confrontation with British soldiers cutting down the Sons' liberty pole in August, no active trans-colonial alliance endured.[153] On March 18, 1767, the Stamp Act repeal's first anniversary, local organizations held festivities featuring illuminations, gunfire, and banquets. In Boston, celebrations drew "as great a Concourse of People in the Streets as scarce ever was seen." Toasts that evening included to the king, "His Majesty's Ministry," Parliament, "The Extension of Traded Commerce," and "The United & Inseparable Interest of Great Britain & Her Colonies" for prosperity. Nevertheless, they asserted recent events ought to "be ever held in memory by all True Britons & Americans."[154] Any similar affront would likely bring a commensurate response.

Conclusion

Despite the geographic obstacles and cultural diversity of colonial America, the British legislation's ramifications encouraged colonists to forge a common political movement across a thousand miles with great intensity. While alternately building through long-standing legislative governing networks, merchant connections, consumer sociability, work solidarities, and crowd traditions, the colonists created something new: widespread, affiliated associations primed for either peaceful debate or forceful action. Warner in his influential book *Protocols of Liberty* has conceptualized American Patriots as effecting a communication revolution, bringing "decentralized and self-organized" groups under the umbrella of a common cause, yet his emphasis on the Committees of Correspondence of 1772–1775 (see Chapter 2) minimizes how the Sons of Liberty achieved much the same effect in 1765–1766.[155] As Sons of Liberty affiliations grew, the unified front they projected created a model for future movements to emulate, innovating a trans-regional campaign of interlocking organizations without precedent.

Through the Sons of Liberty's alliance-building, strenuous assertion, some property destruction, many threats, and yet minimal physical violence, the Stamp Act was defeated. As the colonies learnt the power of coordinated action, discontented groups across the British Empire observed and soon emulated the Sons' model. While the new American organization dissipated at the end of the Stamp Act crisis, their precedent would soon be called on again.

[153] Countryman, *A People in Revolution: The American Revolution and Political Society in New York, 1760–1790* (Baltimore: Johns Hopkins University Press, 1981), 41–43.

[154] *Boston Evening-Post*, March 23, 1767; John Rowe, *Letters and Diary of John Rowe, Boston Merchant, 1759–1762, 1764–1779* (Boston: Clarke, 1903), 125–26.

[155] Warner, *Protocols*, 1–2.

2

From Boycott Mobilization to the American Revolution

American patriots increasingly believed trans-colonial collective action could reset British imperial politics on a just basis. Over the decade preceding the War of Independence, boycotting remained colonial protesters' principal method. Burgess George Mason wrote to George Washington in early 1769 that if Americans could "confine ourselves to Linnens Wollens," this would "distress the various Traders & Manufacturers in Great Britain" and "awaken their attention [to] procure our redress."[1] Colonial lobbyist Dennys de Berdt similarly recommended colonists "persevere in your scheme of œconomy with silence & steadiness until the Enemies of America feel their error and alter their Conduct."[2] The movement against imported finery extended to luxury's highest reaches: at a 1770 Virginia House of Burgesses ball, the nearly one hundred women attending wore homespun gowns, displaying their "Concurrence in whatever may be the true and essential Interest of their Country."[3] Political direct action became stylishness itself.

Only a year after overturning the Stamp Act, Americans mobilized again to oppose the Townshend Acts, which Parliament passed to raise colonial customs revenue on imported paper, paint, glass, lead, and tea. Encountering hardened British opposition, colonists faced a tougher campaign, necessitating more diverse methods over a longer time period than in 1765–1766. Nonimportation boycotts, connected by corresponding committees across participating colonies, organized to pressure British authorities between 1767 and 1770. Yet colonial participation remained incomplete, resulting in only partial Parliamentary repeal. Facing adversity, patriots adapted their tactics to the complex political situation at hand. It took the Boston Tea Party of 1773 and the resultant 1774 Coercive Acts for Americans to reestablish the continental cooperation of 1766. Committees of correspondence only then took local power, mobilizing militias and forming a substitute government that enabled the break with Britain. Whereas the Sons of Liberty appeared a temporary effervescence to their opponents, the boycotting

[1] Washington, *The Papers of George Washington* (Charlottesville: University of Virginia Press, 1983), Colonial Series, Vol. 8, 182.
[2] Library of Congress, Dennys de Berdt Papers, MMC-0298.
[3] *Pennsylvania Gazette*, February 1, 1770.

associations and committees of correspondence showed the new model's endurance, and by 1775 inspired regime-changing applications.

Boycotting the Townshend Acts

The Townshend Acts of 1767 seemed designed to raise colonial ire. British officials did not seek American opinions on the legislation, even barring colonial agents from the House of Commons visitors gallery during discussions. With dissenting voices excluded, the measure passed Parliament without concerted opposition.[4] Though technically an "external" trade duty, preserving colonial legislatures' "internal" tax prerogatives, the plan appeared onerous. Parliament extracted revenue not just through customs taxes but by increasing port enforcement, deterring smuggling and thus raising Americans' cost of living. In response, colonists sought a new nonimportation compact. As confrontation deepened, effectiveness hinged on a coordinated American response.

Across fall 1767, new associations readied in several colonies, though initially to lessen imports rather than adopt a full boycott or incapacitate enforcement. New York sent an agent to Boston in September to discuss "acting in concert" again.[5] Both favored nonimportation, boycotting on local and then colony-wide levels. Boston's Town Meeting on October 26, days after incendiary placards beseeched the Sons of Liberty to force the new revenue officers' resignation, petitioned the governor to convene the legislature to develop "effectual measures to promote industry, œconomy, and manufactures, thereby to prevent the unnecessary importation" of foreign goods.[6] In Newport and Providence, November town meetings endorsed colonial "frugality," while other areas approved manufacturing plans for import substitution, while encouraging renunciation of "Superfluities."[7] Still, the movement spread slower than had the anti–Stamp Act campaign. Enthusiasm remained regionalized with the *Georgia Gazette* in October speaking of measures the "northern Colonies" took.[8]

The Stamp Act's repeal suggested an adequately dialogical relationship existed between colonists and British authorities to persuade Parliament to change course. Boston's town meeting on November 20 declared that if the colonies adopted reasonable measures and showed "abhorrence of all tumults," their "remonstrances would sooner or later be heard, and meet

---

[4] New York Public Library, Bancroft Collection, Connecticut Papers, 139; Griffin, *Townshend*, 130.

[5] NA CO 5/756 118.

[6] NA CO 5/757 3; *Boston Evening-Post*, October 26, 1767; *Pennsylvania Gazette*, November 5, 1767.

[7] *Boston Evening-Post*, December 7, 1767; *Pennsylvania Gazette*, December 10, 1767.

[8] *Georgia Gazette*, October 21, 1767.

with success, if supported by justice and reason." Citing the Glorious Revolution of 1689, in which they claimed no "disorder" occurred, Bostonians suggested political change could happen without violence should public opinion become clear.[9] Only by rejecting reconciliation, colonists implied, would Parliament force a different course.

Despite the intimidation, early boycott participation remained voluntary with organizers believing the colonists motivated to participate. Boston organizers in December 1767 encouraged "persons of all ranks" to subscribe.[10] If revenue lost clearly superseded what the new measures produced, it would be illogical for British authorities not to renegotiate.[11] Reports asserted British exporters had so "glutted this Country with Goods" that American merchants welcomed the adjustment. With most colonial shopkeepers deeply indebted to British merchants, who often predatorily "extended their Credit beyond all bounds of Prudence," suspending payments more than offset supply problems.[12] Economic tensions could become more powerful than even physical force.

The spreading boycotts alarmed many in Britain. Unlike in the anti–Stamp Act campaign, this time colonists did not win widespread British support. Merchants complained they had not received "the remittances they expected" from colonials since the Stamp Act's repeal, nor "proper gratitude" for helping overturn the legislation.[13] Franklin noted that colonists' nonimportation subscriptions incited "a great clamour here against America in general."[14] By March 1768, the *Boston Evening-Post* reported British "NewsPapers are in full cry against America."[15] British industries reportedly laid off workers due to canceled colonial orders and falling demand, while rumors spread of American agents fostering "Tumults and Insurrections" for Wilkes & Liberty.[16] Rather than collaborating with colonists on new legislation, many Britons now favored confrontation.

In the colonies, radicals fostered broader support by promoting boycotting and import-substitution across gender lines, extending the efforts women made during the Stamp Act crisis. Notices of patriotic spinning bees making homespun cloth appeared in newspapers by January 1768, praising women as "An Example of Industry to the young Men."[17] A town meeting conducted in Watertown, Connecticut, that month denounced "all foreign Teas as

---

[9] *Pennsylvania Gazette*, December 3, 1767.
[10] Ibid., December 10, 1767.
[11] *Boston Evening-Post*, December 23, 1767.
[12] NA CO 5/766 164.
[13] NYPL Bancroft Collection, Connecticut Papers, 125.
[14] Franklin, *Papers*, Vol. 15, 52.
[15] *Boston Evening-Post*, March 28, 1768.
[16] Gage, *Correspondence*, Vol. 1, 197.
[17] *Boston Evening-Post*, January 4, 1768.

Expensive & pernicious."[18] A general reformation of morals seemed necessary: "our present Luxury must inevitably destroy us," a printed New York letter declared.[19] With the nonimportation agreement modeling virtuous abstention and moral regeneration, the movement could succeed.

Alongside peaceable measures, intimidation and violent incidents rose, especially in Boston. On the March 1768 anniversary of the Stamp Act repeal, a crowd of "disorderly persons" menaced the inspector general's home but dispersed peaceably.[20] On June 10, following inspectors' seizure of John Hancock's ship *Liberty*, angry sailors and townsmen armed with clubs threw stones and assaulted authorities. The crowd advanced on the comptroller's house, breaking its windows to mock the Townshend Acts' glass duty. Returning to the port, they dragged another official's "Pleasure-Boat" ashore and burnt it on Boston Common.[21] "All real Power is in the hands of People of the lowest Class," Governor Bernard complained to Gage.[22] In mid-August, the Sons of Liberty organized a demonstration celebrating the third anniversary of the first Stamp Act protests of 1765. Nonimportation committees maintained their distance from such incidents, with ninety-six towns' representatives gathering at Boston in September to develop plans to "steadily persevere in orderly and constitutional applications" to British authorities.[23]

Trans-colonial support for nonimportation developed over 1768–1769. Within a dozen days of Boston's opening subscriptions on August 1, 1768, agreements arrived from localities across the colonies. Compliance proved more difficult: with subscriptions incomplete (including some prominent merchants' refusal), all remained suspicious, and none wanted to surrender market share to nonsubscribers. Nevertheless, the pact advanced. New York passed a nearly general nonimportation agreement – with the proviso it would only be enforced if the other colonies did likewise. Philadelphia's merchants belatedly joined in March 1769. Virginia associated in May, Maryland in June, South Carolina in July, Georgia in September, and North Carolina in November. Newport, joining that October after being boycotted by several colonies, described the growing compact as "the true American System."[24] Despite economic challenges, the movement approached critical mass.

---

[18] AAS United States Revolution Collection, Box 1.

[19] *Pennsylvania Gazette*, January 14, 1768.

[20] Ibid., October 20, 1768.

[21] *Boston Evening-Post*, June 20, 1768; Benjamin H. Irvin, *Samuel Adams: Son of Liberty, Father of Revolution* (Oxford: Oxford University Press, 2002), 75–76; NA CO 5/766 191.

[22] NA CO 5/757 353.

[23] Ibid., NA CO 5/757, *Pennsylvania Gazette*, October 13, 1768.

[24] Gordon, Vol. 1, 243, 256; *Boston Evening-Gazette*, January 2, 1769; Larry R. Gerlach, *Prologue to Independence: New Jersey in the Coming of the American Revolution* (New Brunswick, NJ: Rutgers University Press, 1976), 152; Leslie J. Thomas, "The Nonconsumption and Nonimportation Movement against the Townshend Acts,

Following the towns' example, support grew from the colonies' legislative assemblies. Massachusetts' House of Representatives in February 1768, under Samuel Adams' pen, sent a circular asking that colonial "Assemblies upon so delicate a point should harmonize with each other" to most effectively oppose the Townshend Act.[25] Coordination advanced between previously proudly separate colonies. By the end of 1769, only Georgia's legislature remained outside the alliance.[26]

The colonial compact developed despite British merchant objections. Some investment houses terminated their North American partnerships, redirecting money to more stable investments in the East or West Indies. Liverpool's Haliday & Dunbar in January 1769 declared themselves "uncertain" if they would accept American business again.[27] That December, Virginian William Lee wrote from London, "there is not at present the least murmur of any application for redress of American grievances," instructing colonists "your relief must spring from yourselves, little is to be expected from the goodwill of anyone here."[28] The American cause appeared abandoned.

Yet the boycott movement dovetailed with broader radical Whig contestations in British politics, leading colonists to hope for revived British interest. Wilkes wrote to Boston's Sons of Liberty in March 1769, denouncing the acts as a "direct violation of the great fundamental principles of British liberty," while complimenting colonists on having "prevented the effusion of blood" – more successfully than his English supporters.[29] The *Pennsylvania Gazette* printed a British letter in June 1769, asserting "Great Dissatisfaction prevails in this Kingdom, on Account of Wilkes' Expulsion, and the Restraints on the American Trade."[30] Additional correspondence crossed the Atlantic from Midlands manufacturing districts, declaring local opinion complained not of colonial resistance but rather of Parliamentary overreach. By early 1770, word spread of "petitions from all parts of England" for repeal.[31] Whereas prior to the Wilkes upsurge the ministry had considered outlawing nonimportation associations, now the "violence of party" deterred authorities.[32] Though merchant associations would not help the colonists, a broader radical coalition could.

1767–1770," in *Resistance*, 151–56; Middlekauff, *Glorious*, 182; *Pennsylvania Gazette*, November 9, 1769.

[25] LC Samuel Adams Papers, MSS 10223, Vol. 1.

[26] *Pennsylvania Gazette*, August 2, 1770.

[27] LC MSS 16436, Stephen Collins Records, Vol. 8.

[28] University of Virginia Special Collections, William Lee Papers.

[29] LC MSS 10223, Samuel Adams Papers, Vol. 2.

[30] *Pennsylvania Gazette*, June 8, 1769.

[31] Ibid., December 28, 1769 and January 4, 1770.

[32] Gordon, *History of the Rise*, Vol. 1, 280.

Colonists cultivated relations with their allies in the Wilkes & Liberty movement. Charleston's Sons of Liberty enthusiastically wrote to Boston's, "Our Countrymen in Great-Britain are equally engaged in the Defence of the Constitution," deserving "our Admiration and Imitation."[33] In December 1769, South Carolina's legislature voted £1500 to the Society of Supporters of the Bill of Rights, sending the money despite the Royal Governor and then British Parliament's attempts to block disbursement. Though colonists' support for Wilkes alienated British moderates, Americans found transatlantic allies for pursuing imperial changes.[34]

Enforcing such agreements required broad mobilization and intimidation. The press publicized female spinners with the *Boston Evening-Post* between May and December 1769 printing twenty-four articles about them.[35] Defending the cause from violators took more effort: In May 1769, the Boston enforcement committee's early inquiries found numerous subscribers, "some of them violent sons of liberty," had imported illicit goods, but allowed "the pretence of their orders having been misunderstood or miscarried," if they surrendered the contraband.[36] Should traders continue with impunity, municipal leadership that summer determined the community should "cease all Correspondence and Dealings with them."[37] Boston committee meetings handled grievances against those who "audaciously counteract the whole Continent," before audiences approaching a thousand, including many underemployed during the economic slowdown.[38] One merchant in January 1770 described such crowds mobilized "to Intimidate the Importers in that hall."[39] Concurrently, crowds occasionally "employ'd themselves in the Tar and feathering Way" against violators.[40] New York and Charleston's Sons of Liberty revived as nonimportation enforcers.[41] As years of lost revenue continued, colonists stressed the need for a common effort.

Increased British troop deployments sparked confrontations with colonists. Samuel Adams in November 1769 cited international examples of how whereas British troops had traditionally been "the Terror of the Enemies of

---

[33] LC Samuel Adams Papers, MSS 10223, Vol. 2.

[34] Greene, "Bridge to Revolution"; O'Shaughnessy, *Empire*, 127; NYPL Bancroft Collection, Connecticut Papers, 305.

[35] Norton, *Liberty's*, 166.

[36] NA CO 5/758 116.

[37] *Pennsylvania Gazette*, August 24, 1769.

[38] Dirk Hoerder, *Crowd Action in Revolutionary Massachusetts, 1765–1780* (New York: Academic Press, 1977), 217; *Pennsylvania Gazette*, February 1, 1770.

[39] AAS Jonathan Sayward Diary.

[40] Lawrence Shaw Mayo, *John Langdon of New Hampshire* (Port Washington, NY: Kennikat Press, 1937), 37; Benjamin H. Irvin, "Tar, Feathers and the Enemies of American Liberties, 1768–1776," *New England Quarterly* 76, no. 2 (2003), 207–8.

[41] Maier, *Resistance*, 116.

Liberty," now redcoats became "objects of contempt" for colonials.[42] The dislike remained mutual as a royal regiment again cut down New York's Liberty Pole in January 1770, though a subscription raised another replacement.[43] The "Boston Massacre" occurred amid a March 5 disturbance in which North and South End crowds converged to menace British troops with sticks and snowballs, while some pillaged Dock Square market stalls. In the murky incident that evening, troops (after protester provocations) fired, leaving five dead. The event intensified protester activity: The next morning, large crowds gathered while Boston's town meeting convened to petition for the troops' immediate removal, asserting the "Inhabitants & Soldiery can no longer live together in Safety."[44] At Salem, the populace became so enraged at the "late horrid Massacre" that 1,500 men prepared to "revenge the Murderers" if called upon.[45] Though patriots did not undertake reprisals, the victims' funeral drew crowds approaching the city's population of 13,000.[46]

In the backcountry, rural Regulator rebellions flared in the Carolinas, Pennsylvania, and New York. One such group described itself "Regulating publick Grievances and Abuses of Power," expelling authorities and governing themselves.[47] Such associations contested recent tax levies, court-enforced debt collection and local officials' corruption, while sanctioning settlement claims against both rich Eastern speculators and Indian treaties. In affected areas, at least one government agent found intelligence "impossible to obtain," with the populace "generally disaffected to government."[48] Rural Regulators grew formidable, with North Carolinians mobilizing several thousands in 1771, but failed to create a corresponding alliance beyond their immediate regions.[49] Even as Western rebels remained aloof from (and sometimes antagonistic toward) coastal ports, they spread a similar spirit of resistance.

As the boycott dragged on, a siege mentality deepened among radicals. Franklin advised from London, "if we do not now persist in this Measure till it has had its full Effect, it can never again be used on any future Occasion with the least prospect of Success."[50] Colonial Tories sought to undermine them with a "Real Merchants" meeting in Boston for boycott modifications drawing

---

[42] Samuel Adams, *Writings*, Vol. I, 446.

[43] *Pennsylvania Gazette*, January 25 and February 8, 1770.

[44] Gordon, *History of the Rise*, Vol. 1, 283; MHS John Tudor Papers; Eric Hinderaker, *Boston's Massacre* (Cambridge, MA: Cambridge University Press, 2017), 18.

[45] *Pennsylvania Gazette*, March 29, 1770.

[46] *Boston Evening-Gazette*, March 12, 1770; Slaughter, 301.

[47] William K. Boyd, *Some Eighteenth-Century Tracts Concerning North Carolina* (Raleigh: Edwards & Broughton, 1927), 263.

[48] Ekrich, *"Poor Carolina,"* 165.

[49] Ibid.; Kars, *Breaking*, 192–205.

[50] Franklin, *Papers*, Vol. 17, 112.

fifty in May.[51] Reports flew of Philadelphian and New Yorker noncompliance. New York radicals hung an effigy of a visiting Bostonian non-complier in response, which thousands paraded through the streets. Across the colonies, Sons of Liberty contingents pursued enforcement.[52] Despite such intensity, the threat of disunion remained.

The Townshend Acts' partial repeal, ironically passed the day of the Boston Massacre on March 5, divided the non-importers. Though eliminating all measures except the tea duty, the precedent to directly tax the colonists remained. To British administrators, the repeal eliminated the duties running "contrary to the true principles of commerce," without sacrificing their own legitimacy.[53] American debate raged over whether the boycott ought to continue until the tea tax's repeal or whether the movement had gone far enough (and gone on long enough). Rumors and innuendo of nonadherence by individual merchants and deviant ports threatened the alliance. Philadelphia, declaring "Our Sons of Liberty make up of almost the whole of our people," achieved "near-unanimity" – but not unanimity – in renewing its nonimportation agreements that June.[54] Boston similarly extended its boycott by a vote of 99 to 1.[55] Yet both ports rejected New York calls for a continental congress to craft a uniform nonimportation agreement. Despite this setback, New York gained local approval for even its toughest provisions, demanding illicitly imported goods be re-shipped abroad instead of warehoused until the boycott's end. Boston appointed a new Committee of Inspection, surveilling suspect merchants and confiscating contraband.[56]

Rhode Island deflections brought political and economic reprisals. Newport's ending their nonimportation agreements in May 1770 led Boston, New York, and Philadelphia to forbid all commerce with the town. Hartford, meanwhile, denounced the "present little SORDID VIEWS of self INTEREST" they blamed for the decision. Newport recanted and rejoined the movement. Providence's town meeting, keen to avoid pariah status, overrode the town merchants' decision.[57] For merchants, however, economic expediency trumped colonial politics.

[51] John W. Tyler, *Smugglers and Patriots: Boston Merchants and the Advent of the American Revolution* (Boston: Northeastern University Press, 1986), 154.

[52] *Boston Evening-Gazette*, May 21, 1770; *Pennsylvania Gazette*, May 17, 1770; Charles McLean Andrews, *The Boston Merchants and the Non-Importation Movement* (Cambridge, MA: John Wilson & Son, 1917), 241.

[53] Kent Archives, Pratt Papers, U840/O136/3.

[54] *Pennsylvania Gazette*, June 6, 1770; *Massachusetts Gazette*, June 14, 1770.

[55] *Pennsylvania Gazette*, June 6, 1770; *Newport Mercury*, June 4, 1770.

[56] Tiedemann, *Reluctant*, 162; *Pennsylvania Gazette*, June 7, 1770; *Boston Evening-Gazette*, June 11, 1770.

[57] *Pennsylvania Gazette*, June 14, 1770; *Massachusetts Gazette*, June 7, 14, and 28, 1770.

Despite formal reapproval, controversy over boycotting spread in New York City. General Gage, residing there, the previous December noted, "New-York has kept up to the Agreement with the most punctuality, and is consequently the greatest Sufferer by it," while "Country People begin to complain of the dearness of the Commodities" at markets.[58] The Sons of Liberty – which remained unusually active in the city – split, with the breakoff "Sons of Liberty and Trade" drawing merchants wanting nonimportation ended.[59] Others favored continuing the boycott with the merchants association on June 12 resolving full repeal "absolutely necessary for the Salvation of American Liberty."[60] At a late-June open meeting, after hearing letters from Boston, Philadelphia, and Connecticut towns favoring continued boycotting, New York's town meeting upheld the ban. A celebratory June 30 demonstration marched behind the banner "Liberty and no Importation, in Union with the other Colonies."[61]

Breaking the pact, New York's Merchants Association, fearful of accruing further debts, overturned their boycott on July 5. All items could now be imported except tea. The city's town meeting condemned the change, though the merchants countered by demanding a full town vote. With association members exerting substantial local influence, on July 9, a 794–465 vote gutted the agreements, despite the Sons' vociferous opposition. That night angry patriots marched "with colours flying and music playing" but met a comparable pro-repeal crowd. An indecisive skirmish ensued with each side wielding clubs and throwing stones.[62] No more nonimportation votes occurred in New York. While the boycott movement had survived smaller areas' defections, the city's abandoning the agreements dealt a decisive blow.

New Yorkers wrote to Philadelphia, encouraging them to end nonimportation too, subverting the coalition. Philadelphia's association initially denounced the undertaking, declaring its smaller northern counterpart had "deserted the cause of Liberty" and extended their boycott against New York.[63] Yet with offending merchants unrepentant, the financial advantage from lifting nonimportation appeared too great for other cities to refuse. Two months later on September 20 with British merchants already shipping goods with orders to continue to New York if refused elsewhere,

[58] Gage, *Correspondence*, Vol. 1, 242.
[59] Lemisch, *Jack Tar*, 150.
[60] NYHS McDougall Papers, Vol. 1.
[61] *Massachusetts Gazette*, July 19, 1770.
[62] Carl Becker, *The History of Political Parties in the State of New York, 1760–1776* (Madison: University of Wisconsin, 1909), 92–93; Tiedemann, *Reluctant*, 47; LC Silas Deane Papers, Series 8B Reel 11, 19.
[63] *Massachusetts Gazette*, July 26, 1770.

Philadelphia's merchants abandoned nonimportation. Boston in October sanctioned importation of all goods but tea.[64]

With the nonimportation movement crushed, perhaps permanently, merchants rushed back into the Atlantic market. Baltimore businessman Samuel Galloway condemned New York's "scandalous behavior," but now that "we are all at liberty to Import Goods," he decided to "set my Eldest son ... up in Annapolis."[65] The economic forecast brightened. William Lee reported from London that as boycotting "'tis over now," the "Merchts here and the Ministry are quite easy."[66] Sanctioned trade flourished, as did smuggling. While merchants maintained their agreements not to import British tea, many trafficked from Dutch and French sources. Smugglers, one official described, serviced New York and Philadelphia by landing tea on the Jersey shore, "and half the Navy could not prevent this trade." The contraband flow became so efficient it made "Tea cheaper than they had it from England." Particularly in the middle and southern colonies, tea drinking continued uninterrupted.[67] The political lull would not long endure.

A movement imperfectly adopted, meeting only partial success over a timetable several times longer than the anti–Stamp Act agitation, the nonimportation campaigns resulted only in imperfect gains. Radicals' intimidation and threats lost effect, as they undertook few reprisals against violators. Yet over the years of boycotting, colonists gained skill in organization, enforcement, and deploying collective strength. If offenses to the colonies still appeared too slight for outright rebellion, associational power would be reapplied amid the growing crisis of 1773–1775.

Developing Committees of Correspondence

The next step in network building found inspiration through corresponding with the latest British radical movement, Wilkes' Society of Supporters of the Bill of Rights, which affiliated corresponding societies across Britain on a model adapted from the Sons of Liberty (see Chapter 3). Virginian planter Arthur Lee, Richard Henry's brother, arrived in Britain in 1767 for information gathering, lobbying, and alliance-building between British and American radicals. Seeing Wilkes as "the atlas of popular opposition," advocating for British liberties and reform of government abuses, in 1770 Lee became the secretary of the Society of Supporters. With the Virginian considering Wilkes's partisans the opposition's "most active" branch, he helped convince the

---

[64] LC Samuel Collins Records MSS 16436, Vol. 11; *Pennsylvania Gazette*, October 4, 1770.
[65] LC Galloway-Maxcy-Markoe Papers MSS 21857 75.
[66] UVSC William Lee Papers.
[67] NYHS Andrew Elliot Papers, 35; Ian Christie, *Crisis of Empire: Great Britain and the American Colonies, 1754–1783* (New York: Norton, 1966), 73.

organization to endorse the principle of "no taxation, without representation."[68] Experiencing the power of the first British national reform society in the Wilkes movement, Arthur Lee began a correspondence with Samuel Adams in Boston totaling fifty-six letters between 1770 and 1775.[69] Lee repeatedly encouraged a new, integrated colonial network, which under Adams's influence in 1772 moved from concept to reality. Developing beyond the occasional exchanges of Sons of Liberty, town meetings, and merchant organizations, new Committees of Correspondence fostered broader communication and more powerful associational ties.

Such organizing sought to counter British ministerial designs. As Arthur Lee wrote Adams in December 1770, "It would be peculiarly unfortunate, if when the foes of Liberty & Virtue, are conspiring together, manifestly to subvert the Constitution the friends of freedom should stand single & ununited." Government actions provided "an example of secrecy, unison & perseverance which highly deserves imitation." Lee proposed, "Would it not be useful, to establish a correspondence between the leading men of the provinces, that you might harmonize in moving any measure in the different Assemblies, for the general good?" This could build internal unity and external influence, as Lee considered that in London such organizing would "render you formidable & respected here."[70] American patriots needed collective designs that could influence faraway authorities.

Taking Arthur Lee's advice, Samuel Adams proposed a tighter American corresponding network in September 1771, asking "the colonists, more frequently to correspond with, and to be more attentive to the particular circumstances of each other." Since the Sons of Liberty's network had atrophied and boycott associations declined through mistrust, a fresh and better-integrated colonial network appeared essential. Echoing Lee's language, Adams declared the colonial cause could not effectively function if less coordinated than their governmental opponents: "a dreadful stroke is aimed at the liberty of these Colonies: For the cause of one is the cause of all."[71] Massachusetts' House of Representatives, under Adams's influence, on July 14, 1772, asked fellow colonists to

---

[68] Richard Henry Lee, *Life of Arthur Lee* (Boston: Wells and Lilly, 1829), Vol. 1, 244; Wilkes later declared Arthur Lee his "*first* and *best* friend." John Sainsbury, *Disaffected Patriots: London Supporters of Revolutionary America, 1769-1782* (Montreal: McGill-Queen's University Press, 1987), 34–50.

[69] Louis W. Potts, *Arthur Lee: A Virtuous Revolutionary* (Baton Rouge: Louisiana State University Press, 1981), 92.

[70] LC Samuel Adams Papers, MSS 10223, Vol. 2.

[71] Samuel Adams, *Writings*, Vol. 2, 220; *Boston Gazette*, September 16, 1771; David Ammerman, *In the Common Cause: American Response to the Coercive Acts of 1774* (Charlottesville: University Press of Virginia, 1974), 20–21.

calmly look around us and consider what is best to be done. Let us converse together upon this most interesting Subject and open our minds freely to each other. Let it be the topic of conversation in every social Club. Let every Town assemble. Let Associations & Combinations be everywhere set up to consult and recover our just rights.

The legislature ended by quoting James Thomson's epic poem *Britannia*: "let us roam; & where we find a Spark / Of public Virtue, blow it into Flame."[72] The popular movement's disparate arms needed to collaborate to head off the coordinated advances feared from the British government.

Though Adams's proposal did not initially win over other colonies, Boston began recruiting a Massachusetts-wide network in November 1772. Despite fears of mobilization creating "a new ferment" that "nothing will satisfy but absolute independence," as Congregationalist minister Andrew Elliot described, the precipitating crisis erupted when the Crown in September announced it would pay the salaries of the Massachusetts Supreme Court, Attorney General, and Solicitor General (having recently assumed the governor's) directly via customs revenue rather than through the colony's legislature. Most believed direct payment would make the officials beholden to imperial interests and reduce colonial influence.[73] Samuel Adams, under the pseudonym Valerius Poplicola in the *Boston Gazette*, called for "Associations and Combinations [to] be everywhere set up to consult and recover our just Rights."[74] On November 2, after Governor Hutchinson refused a second time to send the controversial measure through the legislature, Adams successfully motioned in Boston's town meeting for a twenty-one-man Committee of Correspondence "to state the Rights of the Colonists" and "publish the same to the Several Towns in this Province and to the World" on pressing issues.[75]

The resulting Committee of Correspondence report to the Boston town meeting was radical, moving beyond British precedent to assert that the colonists possessed natural freedoms. "All men have a right to remain in a state of nature as long as they please," they asserted, "and in case of intolerable oppression, civil or religious, to leave the society they belong to, and enter into another." Bostonians defined "natural liberty" as being "free from any superior power on earth" with individuals only subject to "the law of nature for his rule." As no British law denied colonists the right to freely associate, the report – which the town meeting approved and sent its copies to six hundred towns – asked fellow colonists to appoint committees and defend their rights.[76]

[72] Samuel Adams, *Writings*, Vol. 2, 336.
[73] MHS Thomas Hollis Papers; Slaughter, *Independence*, 320–21.
[74] *Boston Gazette*, October 5, 1772.
[75] MHS MS N-1876, Vol. 1; Gordon, *History of the Rise*, Vol. 1, 314.
[76] *Old South Leaflets*, Vol. 7 (Boston: Directors of the Old South Work, 1906), 417–19.

Towns enthusiastically named corresponding committees and deliberated in league with Boston. Plymouth's town meeting on December 1 affiliated to "prevent if possible this Country from being overwhelmed by that torrent of tyranny" they considered had almost "destroyed" their rights. Cambridge joined Boston to "render her a Terror to Tyrants." Thirteen more towns affiliated in January.[77] Consensus spread, as Lexington declared on January 12, "that this Town has a Right to correspond with other Towns upon Matter of common Concern."[78] Sheffield asserted that such organizations would defend "those rights & privileges wherewith God & Nature have made us free."[79] By September 1773, 144 towns associated with Boston's Committee of Correspondence (almost half of them maintaining standing committees). The new institutions, recording their resolutions but not deliberations, spoke in their communities' name, seeking both local unanimity and regional alignment as a counterforce to royal authority.[80]

Though other colonies did not initially publicize their efforts like Massachusetts, organizing accelerated. Richard Henry Lee had already begun lobbying in Virginia's House of Burgesses for new "committees of Correspondence and enquiry" between the colonies in mid-1772, writing to Samuel Adams and Philadelphia's John Dickinson.[81] However, a youthful contingent of Virginia representatives including Henry and twenty-nine-year-old planter Thomas Jefferson spearheaded the cause. "Not thinking our old & leading members up to the point of forwardness & zeal which the times required," Jefferson recalled, they pursued "an understanding with all the other colonies" for "unity of action." In March 1773, the Burgesses approved a twelve-man Committee of Correspondence.[82] Whereas the legislature legally required the royal governor's convocation, the correspondence committee remained in permanent session. Although the governor ordered their dissolution, the committee continued beseeching other colonies to unify their efforts, "disturbed, by various rumors" of new measures afoot. They reiterated the need to diffuse "early and authentic intelligence" on any issue rendering "a Communication of Sentiments necessary."[83]

With the Virginia Committee of Correspondence's legal standing problematic, their example needed to be quickly emulated by other colonies. In soon-published letters to Massachusetts, Virginians declared their intentions "to

---

[77] MHS MS N-1876, Vol. 1, 6, 15, 77–364.

[78] Ibid. 77; AAS Lexington Town Meeting records, 25.

[79] LC Peter Force Papers, Ezra Stiles Diary MSS 20990.

[80] Warner, *Protocols*, 48, 76, 86; Ray Raphael, *The First American Revolution: Before Lexington and Concord* (New York: New Press, 2002), 35.

[81] McGaughy, *Richard Henry Lee*, 102.

[82] Thomas Jefferson, *Autobiography* (New York: Putnam, 1821), 9–10.

[83] APS Filippo Mazzei Papers; *Virginia Gazette*, March 18, 1773; *Pennsylvania Gazette*, April 7, 1773.

bring our sister colonies into the strictest union with us, that we may RESENT IN ONE BODY" future British incursions.[84] Samuel Adams soon encouraged "the Friends of American Independence and Freedom" to "open every Channel of Communication." As the "Liberties of all are alike invaded by the same haughty power," each colony should be "acquainted with the particular Circumstances of Each [other], in order that the wisdom and strength of the whole" be deployed. Doing so would revolutionize a heretofore poor continental communication system, in which "the best intelligence we have had … has been brought to us from England!"[85] Changes appeared essential, with the Patriot movement needing to out-mobilize a coordinated empire, and achievable, given the powerful colonial coalition forming.

Over the following year, each colonial legislature appointed Committees of Correspondence to create an integrated network. Rhode Island affiliated first in May "to obtain the most early and authentick Intelligence," while New York and New Jersey adhered last in January and February 1774.[86] Virginia-residing Italian merchant Filippo Mazzei described how via the committees "upon the first intelligence received," couriers "immediately bring the news to all the other Colonies." Each colonial affiliate spread information via local and regional committees, all sixty Virginia counties organizing by 1775, creating clear channels for passing information.[87] Geography, long seen as dividing the colonies, became an American advantage, with the movement's breadth making rapid British repression of the Patriot cause prohibitively difficult.

The agitation sparking the Boston Tea Party grew from Massachusetts' Committee of Correspondence network. By August 1773, word arrived of the East India Company's orders to ship six hundred chests of tea to Boston, Philadelphia, and New York. Such a direct affront to the nonimportation agreements stoked colonial ire, with Boston's committee receiving letters from eighty towns encouraging resistance to a tea landing. Particularly after the 1770 failure of broader boycotts, a growing sense pervaded that another setback would doom the movement. With Massachusetts merchants having imported far more tea over the prior five years (reportedly 2,714 chests) than others, it fell to Bostonians to "pledge their honor" to Philadelphia and New York to prevent importation.[88] Unless partisans abandoned the colonial cause, the tea could not land without incident.

With the tea ships en route, patriots prepared to confront their opponents. Boston's Committee of Correspondence the night of November 2 held a public

---

[84] *Massachusetts Gazette*, April 16, 1773.

[85] UVSC Lee Family Papers, Vol. 2.

[86] *Journals of the House of Burgesses of Virginia, 1773–1776, Including the Records of the Committee of Correspondence*, John Pendleton Kennedy, ed. (Richmond, 1905), 48, 59, 143–45.

[87] APS Filippo Mazzei Papers.

[88] Gordon, *History of the Rise*, Vol. 1, 314, 331–32; Warner, *Protocols*, 115.

meeting at North End Tavern, while multiple Sons of Liberty contingents gathered around town.[89] Word spread to meet at the Liberty Tree on November 3 to "hear the persons to whom the tea shipped by the East India Company is consigned make a public resignation of their offices" before the crowd. The officials did not show, and word arrived that they refused to resign. Protesters, though irate, dispersed. A Faneuil Hall mass meeting on the fifth declared it "the duty of every American to oppose" the landing and beseeched customs officials to desist.[90] Though protesters smashed one consignee's windows on November 17, he remained unharmed and still refused to resign the next day.[91]

Resistance to rumored tea landings heightened along the seaboard. In Philadelphia in late October, handbills circulated declaring a "large quantity of TEA ... hourly expected," which if landed would "change your present invaluable title of American freemen to that of slaves."[92] The city's Committee of Correspondence boasted the ship would "meet a warm reception here, as we are determined the Captain shall not land one chest of it."[93] New York merchants by November 3 claimed "complete victory over the opposition here," writing to Philadelphia, "We shall now be as glad to see the Tea arrived here first, as we heretofore wished it might be with you."[94] Anticipation led to radicalization as the principal ports tried to top each other's resolutions.

Dramatic action, of course, came first in Boston. Following rumors of an impending arrival, on November 20, patriots solicited participation from across the region for a Faneuil Hall meeting on how "to prevent the impending evil."[95] Surrounding towns sent militiamen to Boston to contest "the Importation of that Bane to America."[96] On November 28, the *Dartmouth* tea ship arrived and Boston mass meetings continued over the next two days, incorporating residents too poor for town meetings and partisans from nearby communities. The gathering remained "desirous of preserving the Tea untouch'd, for the E. India Company" but refused to see it landed and taxed, unanimously resolving to defy the governor's dispersion order. Protesters alternately approached the governor, customs officers, naval officials, the

[89] Benjamin Woods Labaree, *The Boston Tea Party* (New York: Oxford University Press, 1964), 109.

[90] William V. Wells, *The Life and Public Services of Samuel Adams, Being a Narrative of His Acts and Opinions* (Boston: Little, Brown, 1865), Vol. 2, 104; *Newport Mercury*, November 15, 1773.

[91] MHS Diary of Thomas Newell, 1773–1774, MS N-584; LC Peter Force Papers, Ezra Stiles Papers MSS 20990.

[92] *Newport Mercury*, November 1, 1773.

[93] *New-York Journal*, December 9, 1773.

[94] HSP James & Drinker Papers MSS 30795.

[95] MHS MS N-1876 Vol. 2, 458.

[96] *Virginia Gazette*, January 6, 1774.

ship's owner, and the tea consignees to negotiate, though without agreement.[97] Placards declared a tea landing would "accelerate Confusion and Civil War," with perpetrators "treated as Wretches unworthy to live."[98] A new committee communicated Bostonian designs to New York and Philadelphia.[99]

As two additional tea ships arrived on December 13, Boston's Committee of Correspondence met with five surrounding towns' representatives and summoned a new mass meeting. On December 16, more than 5,000 gathered at Old South Church, including 2,000 non-Bostonians. The meeting called forth the ship's owner, local merchant Joseph Roch, beseeching him to sail away to preserve the peace. He agreed, but on condition of receiving regulatory permission from the governor. Roch returned at dusk and announced Hutchinson had refused him a pass. Samuel Adams responded, "this meeting can do nothing more to save the country." After a "War Whoop," men disguised as Indians appeared in the doorway. Under the cover of near darkness, the famed Boston Tea Party commenced. Hutchinson reported a "vast body of people" from the meeting followed and gathered in solidarity around the faux Indians as they carried out the destruction.[100]

The Tea Party spiked mobilization across both the Massachusetts and transcolonial network. Samuel Adams considered the "Destruction of the Tea" merely "pretence," as "the real Cause is the opposition to Tyranny for which the people of that Town have always made themselves remarkable."[101] Some excused the incident, undertaken after "finding all methods fail'd," as merchant John Tudor described.[102] The affront seemed a tipping-point: according to John Adams, "This destruction of the tea is so bold, so daring, so firm, intrepid and inflexible, and it must have so important consequences, and so lasting, that I cannot but consider it an epocha in history."[103] Patriots repeatedly burnt captured tea thereafter on Boston Common, while area Committees of Correspondence maintained a night watch to prevent landings.[104]

Boston, with the town's committee of correspondence instructing fellow Patriots to prevent tea landing elsewhere, emboldened solidarity protests down the Atlantic seaboard. New York celebrated, as "every class of people" beneath

[97] Franklin, *Papers*, Vol. 20, 500; Mary Beth Norton, *1774: The Long Year of Revolution* (New York: Knopf, 2020), 27.

[98] NA CO 5/763 18.

[99] Peter D. G. Thomas, *Tea Party to Independence: The Third Stage of the American Revolution* (Oxford: Oxford University Press, 1991), 18; MHS Tea Party Meeting Minutes.

[100] Labaree, *Boston*, 127–41; Benjamin L. Carp, *Defiance of the Patriots: The Boston Tea Party and the Making of America* (New Haven: Yale University Press, 2010), 116–40; LC Samuel Adams Papers, MSS 10223, Vol. 4; Slaughter, 342; NA CO 5/769 42.

[101] LC Samuel Adams Papers, MSS 10223 Vol. 5.

[102] MHS John Tudor Papers.

[103] John Adams, *Works*, Vol. 2, 323.

[104] MHS Tea Party Meeting Minutes; NA CO 5/763 25.

ringing church bells demonstrated their approbation.[105] New York's Sons of Liberty resolved to shun anyone involved in tea importation, which they communicated via the city's correspondence committee across the colonies and to British merchants.[106] Philadelphia heard of Boston's Tea Party the same day the tea ship *Polly* arrived. With the captain coerced into abiding by "the opinion of the inhabitants," an outdoor mass meeting of eight thousand Philadelphians three days later forced the vessel's withdrawal and voted approval of Bostonian actions.[107] Charleston's meeting extracted new merchant oaths not to land such cargo. On their ship's arrival, officials confiscated the tea and left it to rot in a damp warehouse.[108] Any attempted landing in a major American port faced serious threats.

Patriots pursued unity in the imperial crisis. As Boston's tea merchants declared in December 1773, "congruity of action at this important crisis, is as necessary as a unanimity of sentiment" with Boston leading boycott measures to "stimulate [other areas] to adopt similar measures to ours." Other merchants moved even faster with Charleston merchants splitting their inventories' cost and incinerating remaining supplies.[109] Boston's merchants burnt theirs only a month later, using the occasion to report full New England adherence, asserting, "every British colony on the continent will concur" in the boycott.[110] Word spread outside the port-cities to "totally decline the use of all East India Tea" to prevent smuggling.[111]

Attempts to land tea at New York brought the threatened reprisals. When the *Nancy* finally arrived after being blown off course, men stormed aboard the evening of April 22, 1774, and dumped eighteen chests into the harbor. Protesters paraded the empty boxes to a bonfire outside the Merchants Coffee House. Within five days, New York's Sons of Liberty forced the ship's departure with its remaining cargo unsold.[112] With the committee movement dominating the ports, British authority seemed eclipsed.

Tea Parties radicalized the colonial standoff, deepening retrenchment on both sides. The "general dissatisfaction ... so eminently displayed," one published Philadelphia letter argued, demonstrated the seriousness of the patriot cause.[113] Over the following months, Committee of Correspondence

[105] *Newport Mercury*, January 31, 1774.
[106] *Pennsylvania Gazette*, December 22, 1773; *Virginia Gazette*, June 13, 1774.
[107] Thomas, *Tea Party*, 23; LC Peter Force Papers, Ezra Stiles Diary MSS 20990.
[108] NA CO 5/396 3; *Pennsylvania Gazette*, December 22, 1773; Slaughter, *Independence*, 344–45.
[109] *Boston Evening-Gazette*, December 27, 1773.
[110] *New-York Journal*, February 10, 1774.
[111] *Virginia Gazette*, January 13, 1774.
[112] Bernard Mason, *The Road to Independence: The Revolutionary Movement in New York, 1773–1777* (Lexington: University Press of Kentucky, 2014), 19; Carp, *Defiance*, 165.
[113] *New-York Journal*, January 6, 1774.

networks grew denser. Boston in March 1774 requested New York write to the principal towns southward, seeking cohesion "so the sense of the People may be known and measures taken effectually to establish a safe and constitutional method of conveying Letters and all necessary Intelligence from one part of the Continent to the other."[114] In May, a Philadelphia committee member wrote to Samuel Adams to confirm Boston's latest letter was "received from n York" and forwarded "to Baltimore, Annapolis, Williamsburgh, & Charlestown, S. Carolina."[115] Through participation, New York's Gouverneur Morris boasted, "The mob begin to think and to reason."[116] A colonial union readied.

The Tea Parties' sympathizers in Britain, however, remained few in number outside the radical fringe. Franklin reported Londoners' disapprobation, while "the Bill now brought into Parliament for shutting up Boston as a Port till Satisfaction is made, meets with no Opposition."[117] Many authorities still doubted colonial cohesiveness: Gage predicted in June 1774 that, given non-importation's collapse three years earlier, serious opposition appeared unlikely. Believing neither New York nor Philadelphia would reintroduce serious boycotts, he prognosticated, "Boston may get little more than fair words."[118] The new committee network would have to prove its effectiveness.

Committees of Correspondence and the Coming of the American Revolution

The British Parliament passed the Coercive Acts between March and June 1774: revoking Massachusetts' colonial charter, closing Boston's harbor until the town paid for the destroyed tea, deploying additional troops, and limiting town meetings to once a year, rendering correspondence committees essentially illegal. Prime Minister Lord North, friend of the king and opponent of colonial autonomy, during debates claimed Boston made a "declaration of their own independence," which threatened the empire.[119] Only submission or open defiance became ready American options as the crisis radicalized the committees into revolutionary governing bodies.

Outrage grew as the Acts' contents became known, motivating further alliance-building. On May 13, Boston's town meeting beseeched "the other Colonies [to] come into a Joint Resolution to stop all Importations from Gt. Britain and every part of the West Indies" until repeal. Samuel Adams wrote to Philadelphia's Committee of Correspondence the same day that the legislation could only by "joynt efforts" be frustrated. As Boston "singly will not be able to

---

[114] MHS MS N-1876, Vol. 2, 738; Ammerman, *Common*, 21.
[115] LC Samuel Adams Papers, MSS 10223 Vol. 5.
[116] Jared Sparks, *The Life of Gouverneur Morris* (Boston: Grey & Bowen, 1832), 25.
[117] Franklin, *Papers*, Vol. 21, 152.
[118] *Parliamentary History*, Vol. 18, 86.
[119] Slaughter, *Independence*, 354.

support the Cause under so severe a Tryal," broader coordinated action became essential.[120] British overreach, Philadelphia physician Benjamin Rush wrote to British abolitionist-reformer Sharp, could "unite us, and hasten the subscriptions to such associations."[121] Resistance radicalized as British authorities left little room for negotiation.

Public solidarity displays roused support. Patriots organized a "solemn pause" across the colonies on June 1 at noon as Boston's port closure began. A Philadelphian reported "sorrow mixed with indignation" as "the whole City wore the Aspect of deep distress, being a Melancholy Occasion."[122] Reports followed on the Coercive Acts' sharp effects with even the "necessaries of life" being forbidden.[123] By June 27, when Savannah residents gathered beneath their Liberty Pole to hear letters from six different colonies, and then formed their own committee, the principal ports across all thirteen colonies entered the compact against overseas trading.[124]

The general trade boycott, aided by the growing committee structures, took aggressive effect, with the committee network enforcing nonimportation, nonconsumption, and nonexportation. Boston circulated a model pledge, finding "no alternative between the horrors of slavery, or the carnage & desolation of civil war, but a suspension of all intercourse with the Island of Great Britain" until their grievances' resolution.[125] Not just merchants, but also farmers exporting to the Caribbean, were directly affected.[126] Boston's town meeting declared themselves "one essential Link in that vast Chain of Commerce" that "raised New England to be what it is, the Southern Provinces to be what they are, the West India Islands to their Wealth, and, in one Word, the British Empire to that Heighth of Opulence, Power, Pride and Splendor, at which it now stands."[127] Colonists' withdrawal could seriously affect the entire chain.

As 1774 advanced, Committees of Correspondence took broader functions first as Committees of Inspection and then assumed expansive military powers as Committees of Safety. With Boston blockaded, Massachusetts took the initiative. In military preparations, already in August Gage reported those involved "purchasing Arms, preparing them, casting Ball, and providing

---

[120] MDHS Purviance Papers MSS 1394.

[121] Rush, "The Correspondence of Benjamin Rush and Granville Sharp, 1773–1809," John A. Woods, ed. *Journal of American Studies* 1, no. 1 (1967), 8.

[122] HSP James Marshall Papers, MSS 0395; Richard Alan Ryerson, "Leadership in Crisis: The Radical Committees of Philadelphia and the Coming of the Revolution in Pennsylvania, 1765–1776. A Study in the Revolutionary Process." (PhD thesis, Johns Hopkins University, 1973), 43.

[123] MHS Boston Committee of Correspondence, 2, 6, 853.

[124] UVSC Berkeley Family Papers, Vol. 4; *Georgia Gazette*, July 14, 1774.

[125] LC Peter Force Papers, Ezra Stiles Papers, MSS 20990.

[126] NA CO 5/1139 91.

[127] *Pennsylvania Gazette*, June 1, 1774.

Powder, and threaten to attack any Troops who dare to oppose them."[128] The clergyman Gordon in September considered the "people at large have been for sometime preparing to defend their rights with the point of the sword," believing the British intended either they "be terrified, or driven into submission by an armed force."[129] Committee and militia activity multiplied.

Boston facilitated correspondence between surrounding Massachusetts towns, accelerating the committee network's radicalization. Gage in August prognosticated widening conflict with partisans having "contrived, while Boston affects Quiet and Tranquility, to raise a Flame not only throughout this Province" but across the colonies.[130] That September, Massachusetts' committees broadly recognized the Suffolk Resolves, which refused submission to the "voluntary slavery" of the Coercive Acts and recognized no royal authority until repeal.[131]

Need for coordination led to the calling of a general Continental Congress. Massachusetts' House of Representatives on June 17 resolved "a meeting of Committees from the several Colonies on this Continent is highly expedient" to find methods for recovering their liberties.[132] Philadelphia's town meeting on June 18 endorsed hosting the meeting for "obtaining redress" while "re-establishing peace" with Britain.[133] The coordinating Congress proved popular, Philadelphia committeeman Thomas Mifflin explained, for regularizing nonimportation to "prevent Jealousies & Infractions" that ruined the anti-Townshend boycott.[134] Some colonial legislatures wrested control from the Committees of Correspondence, with Massachusetts appointing congressmen as delegates. Nevertheless, other areas elected deputies through combinations of local meetings, committees, and conventions.[135]

The resulting Continental Congress of September–October 1774 endorsed the Suffolk Resolves and composed Articles of Association, including a general boycott beginning December 1 against all goods from Britain, Ireland, or the West Indies, while threatening to ban all exports if their demands were not met by September 1775. The measures showed vacillators little patience. With Georgia, the Canadian and Caribbean colonies declining to participate, the body made clear they would have to pick sides. Congress legislated "no trade, commerce, dealings or intercourse whatsoever" could continue with

---

[128] Gage, *Correspondence*, Vol. 1, 366–67, 374.
[129] Gordon, *History of the Rise*, Vol. 1, 380.
[130] Gage, *Correspondence*, Vol. 1, 366.
[131] Suffolk Resolves, http://www.masshist.org/database/viewer.php?item_id=696&pid=2.
[132] LC John Hancock Papers.
[133] *Pennsylvania Gazette*, June 18, 1774.
[134] LC Samuel Adams Papers, MSS 10223, Vol. 5.
[135] *Pennsylvania Gazette*, June 29, 1774; Countryman, *The American Revolution* (New York: Hill and Wang, 1985), 107.

abstaining areas.[136] Patriots instructed Bostonians to "persevere" despite the port closure, accepting heavy restrictions themselves.[137] Behind growing solidarity and coordination, the trans-continental movement consolidated.

Hope remained that collective resistance could resolve the conflict without bloodshed. As Samuel Adams wrote to Richard Henry Lee, "Should America hold up her own Importance," the matter could "be settled and the Principles of Equity & Harmony restored between Britain and the Colonies."[138] Together with legal and philosophical claims, many hoped the association would be effective with Gordon prognosticating in February, "Great Britain will not fight with her best customers, but will relax and accommodate."[139] Franklin asserted that "faithful Adherence to the Non-Consumption Agreement" would "lead Parliament into reasonable Measures."[140] Peaceful reconciliation remained the preferred method of resolution.

Many fretted at the nonimportation agreements' implications for America. New York merchant prodigy Alexander Hamilton predicted that "Goods are extremely scarce and I dare say before six months are past, there will be none to sell," by which "the poor people will suffer extremely this winter," and the country would "be in the Greatest Distress next year, in such, as this country never before saw."[141] Committees confronted profiteering merchants and some set price-ceilings, yet supply and demand problems remained.[142] Such measures' full ramifications, for both Britain and the colonies, could not be accurately prognosticated.

The Continental Congress empowered the committee system to enforce its decrees. As Philadelphia's Committee described, "By interesting people in every township, in the most remote as well as adjoining parts of the county, in the execution of the resolves of the Congress, they apprehend that intelligence, firmness and unanimity, will be more generally promoted." The committees asserted authority to surveil local merchants, arbitrate local complaints, examine account books, and detain suspects for interrogation. Those deemed violators were pressured to recant or face community retribution.[143] Decentralizing enforcement enabled broader popular activity.

Rough local enforcement undermined peaceable nonimportation rhetoric with the committee system thriving on intimidation. The committee in Bute

[136] John C. Miller, *Origins of the American Revolution* (Stanford: Stanford University Press, 1943), 386; Gordon, Vol. 1, 394.
[137] LC Peter Force Papers, Ezra Stiles Diary MSS 20990.
[138] LC Samuel Adams Papers, MSS 10223, Vol. 6.
[139] Gordon, *History of the Rise*, Vol. 1, 425.
[140] LC Charles Thomson Papers MSS 42861.
[141] LC John Glassford Papers, MSS 22939, Reel 16.
[142] Middlekauff, *Glorious*, 259.
[143] Christie, *Crises*, 93; Holger Hoock, *Scars of Independence: America's Violent Birth* (New York: Crown, 2017), 31–32.

County, North Carolina, swore to "Religiously observe" the association and have "no Dealings" with opponents.[144] Any violations over the coming year, Congress declared, would result in offenders being "universally condemned as the enemies of American liberty; and thenceforth we respectively will break off all dealings with him or her."[145] New York vetoed a suggestion "not to offer any insult or violence" to nonimportation violators, fearing "This would effectually destroy it as all terror will be removed."[146] Penalties could range from ostracization to tarring and feathering and/or rail-riding. Dissent from community agreements became intolerable.

The boycott of British goods this time generally held. Philadelphia's Committee of Correspondence in July considered that if nonimportation was only "partially observed like the last," it would only "expose all the Colonies to further injuries."[147] All violators were subject to intimidation and public humiliation, followed by their names' publication in the newspapers. Enforcement advanced even in politically mixed areas. New York City elected a Committee of Inspection despite their colonial legislature's refusal to associate. Radicals cemented a near-monopoly over public space, which Loyalists (though perhaps as numerous) lacked.[148]

The organizations grew powerful enough to ward off authorities' attempts at repression. Gordon described Massachusetts' "Assemblies, conventions, congresses, towns, cities, private clubs and circles" as "animated by one great, wise, active and noble spirit – one masterly soul, enlivening one vigorous body."[149] In Salem, Massachusetts, in August, Gage summoned the local Committee of Correspondence to cancel their planned session, declaring town meetings' broad freedoms inapplicable to them. British troops with loaded weapons moved within an eighth of a mile of city hall. Those assembled hurriedly chose delegates for a county meeting and adjourned. Committeemen faced arrest for organizing an "unlawful, seditious meeting."[150] Nevertheless, the wider movement remained undeterred.

The governing crisis grew. The "People here have taken the Government into their own Hands," a Worcester report asserted, with "a new Form of Government" under "Contemplation."[151] Growing confidence furthered

[144] *Bute County Committee of Safety Minutes, 1775–1776* (Warrenton, NC: Bicentennial Committee, 1977), 14.

[145] Richard R. Beeman, *Our Lives, Our Fortunes, and Our Sacred Honor: The Forging of American Independence, 1774–1776* (New York: Basic Books, 2013), 185–86.

[146] LC New York Committee of Observation Papers MSS 85783. My thanks to the Library of Congress' Julie Miller for this reference.

[147] *Pennsylvania Gazette*, July 27, 1774.

[148] Ammerman, *Common*, 103; T. H. Breen, *American Insurgents, American Patriots: The Revolution of the People* (New York: Hill and Wang 2010), 162.

[149] Gordon, *History of the Rise*, Vol. 1, 426.

[150] *Pennsylvania Gazette*, September 7, 1774.

[151] NA CO 5/763 323.

radicalization: Massachusetts' committees on September 27 denied royal troops labor and weaponry, with violators deemed "most inveterate enemies" of the movement.[152] Militias shut down local courts, making committees the chief instruments of justice.[153] With little recourse but to war, royal authorities stepped aside. New York's Lieutenant Governor Cadwallader Colden in August considered present British forces "cannot prevent the frequent meetings of the people, which have become common every where," while "the most violent men would have gained the great advantage" if they tried.[154]

Committees of Safety spearheaded local mobilization, creating a more extensive coercive apparatus than prior authorities possessed. Declaring their power legitimated by the Continental Congress, the committees created patrols and built militias to protect themselves from Salem-style prosecution.[155] Militias, though institutionally as old as the colonies, had long fallen into disuse but now became a way to rapidly expand the armed forces. In September 1774, a Massachusetts convention in Worcester organized a colony-wide reconstructed militia, while "recommending" local tax collectors redirect proceeds to them instead of the British.[156] Gage that month noted the "country people are daily exercising in arms" and even procured artillery as did five other colonies by early 1775.[157] Virginia in September 1774 began forming new volunteer regiments to prepare for "hostile Invasion" of their communities.[158] Groups of women, many of whom "surpassed the men for Eagerness & Spirit in the Defence of Liberty by Arms," began assembling cartridges.[159] The militias and committees built an army.

The rejection of British authority deepened as militia mobilization progressed. Portsmouth militiamen in December – after Paul Revere rode north from Boston to warn their committee of coming redcoat reinforcements – attacked Fort William and Mary soon after news arrived of a British ban on arms and ammunition imports, pillaging a hundred barrels of gunpowder. The governor reported participants "threatening still greater violence in Case of any Attempts to bring them to justice."[160] Elsewhere, regime change became nearly a *fait accompli*: Albany's Committee of Correspondence, belatedly

[152] *Pennsylvania Gazette*, October 12, 1774.
[153] Nash, *Unknown*, 181.
[154] *Parliamentary History*, Vol. 18, 123–24.
[155] Griffin, *America's*, 112.
[156] Raphael, *First*, 160–62.
[157] *Parliamentary History*, Vol. 18, 87; John Ferling, *Almost a Miracle: The American Victory in the War of Independence* (Oxford: Oxford University Press, 2007), 27.
[158] Michael A. McDonnell, *The Politics of War: Race, Class and Conflict in Revolutionary Virginia* (Chapel Hill: University of North Carolina Press, 2007), 41.
[159] *Boston Gazette*, September 5, 1774.
[160] NA CO 5/939 42, 44, 75, 89; Norton, *1774*, 247.

formed in January 1775, declared its presence necessary for "preventing the Anarchy and Confusion, which attend a Dissolution of the Powers of Government."[161] Even the pretense of obeying Britain increasingly ceased.

Nearly one thousand committees of all types were launched by summer 1775 with more than seven thousand men (nearly 2 percent of the free adult male population) participating.[162] Such groups served a democratizing function: as seen in a study of Philadelphia's committees, the average wealth of members fell as humbler men joined between 1774 and 1776, while the share of artisans on committees grew from 5 percent to 40 percent.[163] Opportunities widened as opposition radicalized. For all the colonies' differences, the commonality of threats facing them seemed most salient. British (though soon Continental) army officer Charles Lee wrote to Burke in December 1774 describing how

> I have now run through almost the whole Colonies from the North to the South; I have conversed with every order of men, from the first estated gentlemen to the poorest Planters, & cannot express my astonishment at the unanimous ardent sprit reigning through the whole. They are determined to sacrifice every thing, their prosperity, their wives, children & blood, rather than cede a little of what they conceive to be their rights.[164]

From fear grew greater unanimity, and expanding mobilization enabled the cause's further radicalization.

The militias' defensive posture (or pretense) sought to resolve the crisis through strength. Gordon in February 1775 rapturously described how in Massachusetts, "Some hundred thousand people are in a state of nature, and yet as still and peaceable, at present, as ever they were when government was in full vigor."[165] Showing their political maturity and capacity for self-control helped legitimate their demands and bolster their confidence. Samuel Adams described the formation "in every Part of the Province" of "Minute Men . . . well disciplind & well provided" who on "very short Notice" could "assemble a formidable Army."[166] Leaders counseled patience: New York merchant and committee member Alexander McDougall wrote to Boston discouraging "martial Measures," as "Adherence to the Association," ought to bring Parliamentary action. The Coercive Acts could still be repealed or reduced

---

[161] *Minutes of the Albany Committee of Correspondence, 1775–1778* (Albany: University of the State of New York, 1923), Vol. 1, 3.

[162] Nash, *Unknown*, 157; Kevin Phillips, *1775: A Good Year for Revolution* (New York: Viking, 2012), 14.

[163] Ryerson, *The Revolution is Now Begun: The Radical Committees of Philadelphia, 1765–1776* (Philadelphia: University of Pennsylvania Press, 1978), 181.

[164] NYPL Bancroft Papers, Letters to Burke.

[165] Gordon, *History of the Rise*, Vol. 1, 427.

[166] Samuel Adams, *Writings*, Vol. 3, 170.

like the Stamp and Townshend Acts. Only an "Attack of the Troops" would stimulate New York into war.[167]

British redcoats' offensive against local militia units at Lexington and Concord on April 19 led the committee network to mobilize onto full war footing. Gage had called for reinforcements the previous October, believing "Small Numbers will encourage Resistance and not terrify," leading British authorities to send several regiments.[168] Concord, where Massachusetts' Provincial Congress had stockpiled muskets and ammunition since autumn, made an appealing first target, but militiamen successfully repulsed the British forces.[169] Following the first skirmishes, Boston's Committee of Correspondence called for "all assistance possible in forming the army," warning "Death and devastation are the certain consequences of delay."[170] Adequately prepared, colonial militia units moved into rebellion.

Committees took full local governing powers with the collapse of British authority and commencing war. New York's Orange County committee claimed the "necessity of preventing the anarchy and confusion which attend a dissolution of the powers of Government."[171] Following the violence over its northern border, Rhode Island's legislature raised 1,500 men on April 22 to march into Massachusetts, though nominally as an "army of observation."[172] New York City's Committee of Observation mandated all to report their weapons and ammunition for authorities to dispense.[173] A Baltimore merchant on May 11 considered "the spirit of freedom spreads fast," as even "all the Southern provinces are getting under Arms."[174] The colonies lurched toward war.

The Second Continental Congress' decision to create a Continental Army on June 14 regularized the militia-expansion process and pursued war. By July 1, the congress brought under its command those forces the committees had mobilized and ordered all able-bodied men into militia service.[175] The logics of popular mobilization, continental interconnection, self-government, and martial preparations – following a long string of British provocations – found powerful application.

[167] NYHS Alexander McDougall Papers, Vol. 1.
[168] Raphael, *First*, 163–64, 192.
[169] Slaughter, *Independence*, 393.
[170] Gordon, *History of the Rise*, Vol. 2, 17.
[171] *Calendar of Historical Manuscripts Relating to the War of the Revolution in the Office of the Secretary of State* (Albany, NY: Weed, Parsons & Co., 1868), 5.
[172] *Newport Mercury*, May 22, 1775.
[173] LC Peter Force Papers 8D 109, New York Committee of Observation Papers, 15.
[174] LC Peter Force Papers 8D 194–4, Woolsey and Salmon Letterbook.
[175] Hock, *Scars*, 41; *Minutes of the Albany Committee*, 76.

Conclusion

"So generally are the principles of liberty disseminated," declared one letter to the press in February 1775 that "nothing but arms" could suppress the colonial movement.[176] Committees of correspondence developed from patriot ambitions: via unprecedentedly broad mobilizations over a decade – incorporating colonists across divisions of region, class, and gender – utilizing new interconnected organizations and corresponding tactics for purposes from nonviolent boycotting to wartime mobilization, the patriot movement spread so comprehensively that an infrastructure developed for a lengthy conflict. Appeals to the broad populace, brought together by town organizations affiliated into a dense network for correspondence and mutual aid, built the resistance movement that enabled the War of Independence. While the subject possesses a rich national historiography detailing these events' significance for the future United States, little attention has been paid to how the committees provided an international template for the most prominent social movements to follow over the rest of the eighteenth century. Corresponding networks became a substitute for government itself, creating a new model for revolutionary changes.

[176] *Pennsylvania Gazette*, February 22, 1775.

3

Wilkes, Liberty, and the Anglo-American Crisis

Across the 1760s and 1770s, budding British and American activists considered themselves engaged in a common struggle against the same illiberal forces influencing Crown and Parliament. Controversies galvanized supporters on both sides of the Atlantic. In 1769, the South Carolina legislature, despite the ongoing boycott against the Townshend Acts, disbursed £1,500 to the Wilkes-backing Society of Supporters of the Bill of Rights in London "for the support of the just and constitutional Rights and Liberties of the People of Great Britain and America."[1] The assembly sent the money without the royal governor's approval, leading to a constitutional crisis lasting until the War of Independence. The Society of Supporters returned effusive praise, declaring "We shall ever consider the Rights of all our fellow subjects throughout the British Empire in England, Scotland, Ireland and America, as stones of the one arch on which the Happiness and Security of the whole are founded." As an "Attack has been made by the same men, at the same Time, on both together," the society promised, "In this, and in every other constitutional Struggle on either side of the Atlantic, we are as ready to give as receive Assistance."[2] Wilkes himself declared liberty "the birthright of every subject of the British empire, and I hold Magna Charta to be as full force in America as in Europe."[3] British and American movements used each other to demonstrate how their grievances formed a pattern of government incursions against liberty and built from each other's examples in social movement organizing.

The years of imperial crisis following the Seven Years' War became a politically pivotal era for Britain as well as America. Over the preceding decades, the British government largely functioned as a placid, corrupt oligarchy, in which questions of principle paled before personal office-seeking or

---

[1] *Gazetteer*, February 9, 1770; Greene, "Bridge to Revolution."

[2] *Public Advertiser*, June 29, 1770; Pauline Maier, "John Wilkes and American Disillusionment with Britain," *William and Mary Quarterly* 20, no. 3 (1963), 373–95.

[3] David Bromwich, *The Intellectual Life of Edmund Burke: From the Sublime and the Beautiful to American Independence* (Cambridge, MA: Harvard University Press, 2014), 140.

were deterred by royal bribery.[4] The American controversies of the 1760s–1770s helped inspire the early British push for Parliamentary reform. British policy for America provided the most striking examples of what abuses the government might be capable of, while American responses offered new methods of collective mobilization and resistance. British national campaigns for Wilkes and Liberty and against the coming American war borrowed Sons of Liberty tactics, adapting the American national corresponding society model to contest British politics.

Wilkes and Liberty in an Atlantic Crisis

Few individuals could have been as undeserving of the support John Wilkes received as he, but no other personality so advanced Anglo-American debates on liberties and associational rights. Elected to Parliament in 1757, Wilkes remained a minor figure until 1762, when he began publishing the *North Briton* – a satirical newspaper criticizing the predominance of Scotsmen in Prime Minister Lord Bute's administration. Refusing government efforts to buy his silence in exchange for appointments as Governor of Canada or an East India Company director, Wilkes radicalized.[5] Following the treaty ending the Seven Years' War, Wilkes in the famous April 1763 issue no. 45 wrote a thinly veiled critique of the king's speech before Parliament that nearly accused the sovereign of lying about peace terms. The government prosecuted Wilkes for "seditious libel," claiming parliamentary immunity did not apply for such charges and soon added obscenity counts for his pornographic *Essay on Woman*. Years of legal battles ensued, in which Wilkes ingeniously deflected attention onto broader political principles. As a result of his case, legal reforms abolished "general warrants" for unlimited search and seizure (which in Wilkes's case had led to the pornography charge) while the attention Wilkes brought to government censorship fostered greater press freedom. Wilkes's affairs became an ongoing *cause célèbre*, as between 1764 and 1770 he progressed from Member of Parliament to alternately a declared outlaw, exile, political candidate, and state prisoner.

At nearly every stage, Wilkes gained support from popular demonstrations and campaigns for "Wilkes and Liberty," galvanizing dissatisfaction for "true revolution principles" against the combined powers of king, courts, and Parliament.[6] Returning from four years' exile in France in 1768, where he became the toast of radical salons, Wilkes again sought political office. Still an outlaw from British justice, Wilkes lost his first bid to become a London

---

[4] Lewis Namier, *The Structure of Politics at the Accession of George III* (London: Macmillan, 1929).

[5] Bromwich, *Intellectual*, 132.

[6] Horace Bleackley, *Life of John Wilkes* (New York: Lane, 1917), 112.

alderman. Wilkes's partisans next advanced his Parliamentary candidacy for Middlesex County (a suburban constituency abutting the capital) in April. Though only an elite few could vote, electors declared their choice in public as the community observed and sometimes pressured participants.[7] As the first morning of the two-day election dawned, Wilkes supporters seized the streets, assaulting opponents riding through Hyde Park, and any refusing to yell "Wilkes and Liberty!" faced having their carriage windows smashed. Nocturnal marchers demanded residents illuminate their dwellings in Wilkes's support or face the same penalty. More genteel supporters passed out handbills in which Wilkes asked "all possible measures" be "used to preserve peace and good order," to "convince the world that liberty was not joined with licentiousness."[8] Agents canvassed for votes and offered free carriage rides to the polls for supporters.[9] Wilkes won.

Not even their protagonist's subsequent arrest on outstanding obscenity and seditious libel charges diminished public enthusiasm. Wilkes, convicted in absentia four years earlier, surrendered himself and entered King's Bench Prison. From May 8 to 10, large crowds held a vigil outside in protest. On the third day, authorities intervened, confronting an estimated 43,000. After an officer ordering the crowds to disperse was hit in the head with a brick, troops fired on the crowd, killing seven. Wilkites reproduced the "Massacre of St. George's Fields" across hundreds of stories, illustrations, and broadsides. Cast as victims of governmental brutality, sympathy for the movement grew.[10] Protests spread, with more convinced of government malevolence. Franklin on May 14 wrote of London being "a daily scene of riot and confusion," describing how outside his window "a great mob of coal porters fills the street" protesting for higher wages.[11] Indeed, the word "strike" was first applied to labor agitation that year as sailors struck sails to pressure shipowners to address their grievances.[12] Protesters asserted that the Wilkes moment augured a fulcrum shift of political (and perhaps social) change for the kingdom.

From behind bars, Wilkes publicized his movement in the broadest possible terms as a showdown between liberty and despotism – not just for his own fate but Britain's and America's. To friends of freedom, each controversy's grievances resulted from the increasingly authoritarian pronouncements of

---

[7] Frank O'Gorman, "Campaign Rituals and Ceremonies: The Social Meaning of Elections in England, 1780–1860," *Past & Present* 135 (1992), 93–94.

[8] Arthur Cash, *John Wilkes: The Scandalous Father of Civil Liberty* (New Haven: Yale University Press, 2006), 210; John Wilkes, *English Liberty: Being a Collection of Interesting Tracts, from the Year 1762 to 1769* (London: Baldwin, 1769), 163–64.

[9] Cash, *John Wilkes*, 210.

[10] Wilkes, *English Liberty*, Vol. 1, 169–70; Cash, *John Wilkes*, 224.

[11] Franklin, *Works*, Vol. 7, 401.

[12] Sidney Tarrow, *The Language of Contention: Revolutions in Words, 1688–2012* (Cambridge: Cambridge University Press, 2013), 62.

a restrictive ruling class. "In proving yourselves enemies to ministerial persecution," Wilkes wrote to Middlesex's voters, "the eyes of the whole kingdom, of the
whole world, are upon you, as the first and firmest defenders of public liberty."[13]
Wilkites too referred to themselves as "Sons of Liberty" with Middlesex partisans using the term in 1768, "the Sons of Liberty at York" doing so in
October 1769, and a London banquet self-defining as "true Sons of Liberty"
that November.[14] Wilkes told his followers in 1770, "You have petitioned, you
have remonstrated, in the Spirit of true Sons of Liberty, but in vain."[15] Growing
radical frustrations on both sides of the Atlantic with the British governing
system led to increasing identification and borrowing between movements.

New organizational methods appeared necessary to counter threats to British
liberties. Two and a half weeks after the Commons expelled Wilkes from
membership and three days after declaring him ineligible to run again, radical
Anglican clergyman John Horne founded a new British corresponding organization, the Society of Supporters of the Bill of Rights. Founded at the London
Tavern on February 20, 1769, the Supporters borrowed from recent American
methods to create a corresponding organization supporting those whose rights
had been violated.[16] Attendees included "independent gentlemen, members of
parliament, eminent merchants, considerable traders, and other persons of
property" backing Wilkes's cause. American Patriot Arthur Lee became the
organization's first secretary. Lee had already lived many years in Britain,
attended Eton, earned a Medical Doctorate from the University of Edinburgh
and Judicial Doctorate from London's Middle Temple, and then became an
American political lobbyist while pursuing British investments.[17] The Virginian
became a vital link between the British and American movements.

The Society of Supporters' goals seemed more modest than America's Sons
of Liberty. The organization declared "the most effectual barrier against such
oppression" by the government, given the movement's charismatic protagonist, would be through enabling Wilkes to maintain his independence. The
organization named five bankers to collect subscriptions. Within two weeks
the organization raised £10,000, then nearly £10,000 more by Wilkes's April
release from prison. The Society sent circulars "to all the cities and borough
towns in England" for donations, while encouraging members to fund-raise.[18]

---

[13] Wilkes, *English Liberty*, Vol. 1, 162.

[14] *Public Advertiser*, March 28, 1768; *Freeman's Journal*, March 29, 1768; *Lloyd's Evening Post*, October 30, 1768; *Public Advertiser*, November 7, 1769.

[15] *St. James's Chronicle*, April 17, 1770.

[16] George Rudé, *Wilkes and Liberty* (Oxford: Oxford University Press, 1962), 61.

[17] Louis W. Potts, *Arthur Lee: A Virtuous Revolutionary* (Baton Rouge: Louisiana State University Press, 1981), 13.

[18] London Metropolitan Archives MS 3332, "English Liberty" Vol. 1, 333; *Lloyd's Evening Post*, February 24, 1769; *St. James's Chronicle*, March 7, 1769; Christina and David Bewley, *Gentleman Radical: A Life of John Horne Tooke, 1736–1812* (London: Tauris, 1998), 21.

"It seems reasonable to us," the society declared, "that the man who suffers for the public good should be supported by the public."[19] Provincial branches followed. Whereas earlier Wilkite agitation centered on London, now mobilization spread across England (though the movement's anti-Scottish sentiment kept North Britons away).[20] The committee of correspondence model – innovated by the Sons of Liberty four years earlier – gained enthusiastic British use.

Aid arrived from the American colonies. Though Franklin argued from London that Wilkes remained "an outlaw and an exile, of bad personal character, not worth a farthing," and never joined the movement, many colonists rushed to associate.[21] Not only influential individuals and political clubs but even Virginia, Maryland, and South Carolina's legislatures contributed. Such measures advanced through pragmatism as much as ideological sympathy: "it is now plain," Boston minister Elliot asserted, that if the British government "not had their hands full at home, they would have crushed the Colonies."[22] Radical cooperation, movement organizing, and publicity developed as the best remedies to imperial ills. "To sensible men," Arthur Lee wrote, "the combining of the complaints of the people of America and England, appeared just and politic."[23] No scope for the movement seemed too large.

Wilkes's financial solvency, however, served only as the organization's most immediate goal; the society endorsed an almost revolutionary expansion of popular sovereignty in British politics. The Society of Supporters required members "to aim at a full and equal representation of the people in Parliament," to overturn arcane election rules allowing only a small portion of adult males to vote, while calling for annual elections instead of seven-year terms. Equally, the organization sought aggressive anti-corruption measures to exclude royal pension recipients from the Commons and require Members of Parliament to take anti-bribery oaths. Moreover, they called for the present ministers' impeachment for their conduct against Wilkes. In colonial policy, the society required adherents to support "redress of the grievances of Ireland, and the restoration of the sole right of self-taxation to America."[24] Utilizing personal connections and newspaper publicity, radical consciousness and confidence flourished. The Wilkes cause animated a broad array of grievances.

Controversy only grew with Middlesex's April 13, 1769 election, called to name Wilkes's replacement. Wilkites again organized demonstrations to the

---

[19] George Stead Veitch, *The Genesis of Parliamentary Reform* (Hamden, CT: Archon, 1965) 30.

[20] H. W. Meikle, *Scotland and the Age of Revolution* (Glasgow, Maclehose, 1912), xvii.

[21] Julie Flavell, *When London Was Capital of America* (New Haven: Yale University Press, 2010), 224; Potts, *Arthur Lee*, 60.

[22] MHS Thomas Hollis Papers.

[23] Lee, *Life*, Vol. 1, 245.

[24] William Edward Hartpole Lecky, *England in the Eighteenth Century* (London: Longmans, Green, and Co., 1879), Vol. 3, 374.

election sites with some proclaiming themselves "SONS OF LIBERTY."[25] The opposing candidate was "pelted by the Mob" near Hyde Park Corner, and the Wilkite faction dominated with Wilkes gaining reelection 1143–1296.[26] In London, a celebratory march formed featuring flags reading "Bill of Rights" and "Magna Charta" alongside supporting clubs' insignias, moving along Pall Mall, the Strand, and over London Bridge to parade before Wilkes's prison window.[27] Two days after the election, however, the Commons upheld Wilkes's expulsion, seating the distant second-place finisher. Over fifteen hundred Middlesex electors – more than all who voted – petitioned the king (a tactic only used on rare occasions when Parliament appeared to violate the people's will) that with their "free choice having been repeatedly rejected," they were thus "reduced to the most abject slavery" by Parliament. Explicitly blaming "evil and pernicious counsellors" for violating their electoral rights, petitioners beseeched the king to intervene.[28] But with the seat awarded, authorities considered the matter closed.

Such governmental insouciance led to a national petition-campaign adapting recent American models. Whereas petitioning in Britain, one movement pamphlet noted, had been "a method seldom practised by them, except in extraordinary cases," now radicals stoked an unprecedentedly national campaign.[29] The *Middlesex Journal* alluded to New World contention: "Let the sons of liberty associate, and unite strongly in defence of their laws."[30] The next issue printed a Philadelphia Merchants Committee letter explaining that as "all the American colonies were equally affected, it was thought that their joint petitions would have more weight" and thus "assemblies communicated their sentiments to one another."[31] British activists, increasing coordination, sought the same effect.

Wilkes activists borrowed from American models not only for promoting changes in policy but also changes in consciousness. Arthur Lee wrote to his brother Richard Henry in Virginia in August 1769, describing British Wilkite petitions as "the most proper method of informing the people of the constitutional power they possess, and rousing them against the unconstitutional measures of the court." Through "appealing to the people at large," they

---

[25] *Middlesex Journal*, April 13, 1769.
[26] George Rudé, "The Middlesex Electors of 1768–1769," *English Historical Review* 75, 297 (1960), 602.
[27] London Metropolitan Archives, MS 3332 Vol. 1, 319; Wilkes, *English Liberty*, Vol. 2, 317.
[28] Walter Harrison, *A New and Universal History, Description and Survey of the Boroughs of London and Westminster, the Borough of Southwark, and Their Adjacent Parts* (London: Cooke, 1775), 660–65.
[29] *The Rights of the People to Petition, and the Reasonableness of Complying with Such Petitions: In a Letter to a Leading Great Man* (London: Williams, 1769), 17.
[30] *Middlesex Journal*, June 6, 1769.
[31] Ibid., June 8, 1769.

could effect "a change of measures as well as of men."[32] In dialogue with America's Sons, the Wilkes and Liberty movement developed a new type of British campaign, bringing nonvoters together with enfranchised citizens to defend political freedoms, monitor suspect authorities, and seek reforms.

The Society of Supporters developed corresponding committees to stoke the national petitioning movement. Though circular letters had previously been employed to solicit money for Wilkes, now they encouraged active dialogue as partisans worked to mobilize far-flung regions. The central committee urged areas to pursue "the best means to redress the grievances of the electors" to "restore" their threatened rights.[33] In June, the supporters extended recruiting across the imperial realm, "inviting the Friends of Liberty throughout the whole British Empire to concur in promoting the Constitutional purposes for which this Society was established."[34] Only by showing the extent of opposition could the movement demonstrate public opinion was on their side. "Let public meetings be called in every part of the kingdom," Wilkes wrote under the alias John Freeman in August, asserting the king "will graciously hear and redress our grievances and oppressions." Their efforts paid off first in areas closest to them. The City of London in July adopted a royal petition along the same lines as Middlesex.[35]

Parliamentary opposition leaders joined Wilkes's cause. On May 9, the day after the supporters' meeting, seventy-seven opposition Members of Parliament met at London's Thatched House Tavern, allying with the radical group so long as they did not simultaneously agitate for Parliamentary reform. With the campaign now focused on voters' rights, notables recruited petitions from distant areas. Whig opposition stalwart Rockingham helped mobilize Yorkshire, where eleven thousand freeholders signed a petition Arthur Lee coauthored. Burke helped procure signatures in Stowe, former Prime Minister the Duke of Portland lobbied in Liverpool, and numerous other opposition MPs mobilized their districts.[36] The Wilkes cause's potential – through American-style mobilization techniques – became apparent to even establishment politicians.

A petition wave from across England (though not Scotland or Wales) coalesced in 1769. In May, 5,413 Westminster electors signed to express their discontent at both the Wilkes decision and the ignoring of prior petitions, declaring government threatened the "speedy annihilation of our excellent constitution itself."[37] At Norwich in June, "A great Number of Gentlemen"

---

[32] Lee, *Life*, Vol. 1, 196.

[33] Rudé, *Wilkes*, 108.

[34] LMA MS 3332 Vol. 1, 436.

[35] *Middlesex Journal*, August 19, 1769.

[36] O'Gorman, *The Rise of Party in England: The Rockingham Whigs, 1760–1782* (London: George Allen, 1975), 243–61.

[37] Harrison, *New*, ibid.; John Almon, *Memoirs of a Late Eminent Bookseller* (London, 1790), 54.

formed a Society of Correspondence to work with the supporters.[38] Eighteen provincial centers sent addresses, including York, Liverpool, and Bristol, some calling for Parliament's dissolution and new elections. York asserted that the "Commons derives its existence from the election of the people, who have never entrusted that House with the authority to supersede its choice of electors." Sixty thousand petitioners – a quarter the number of Britain's electorate – signed in Wilkes's support, declaring Parliament violated the public trust by expelling him.[39] The government attempted to stoke counter-petitions, but with only limited success: the City of London gathering opposing Wilkes drew "not above thirty persons," while provincial loyal petitions remained few.[40] The Wilkes movement successfully out-mobilized their opponents and forced government allies to play the opposition's game. The previously London-centered Wilkes movement increasingly sparked national agitation.

Nevertheless, no exoneration of Wilkes followed, as the king refused to respond to the petitions. As signing in many places had not been restricted to enfranchised voters, the political establishment dismissed them as eman-ating from the "lowest sort."[41] Opponents accused Wilkes supporters of using the worst British electoral practices with one hostile account claiming the signatures procured after "bribing largely with Beer" groups of "itinerant sturdy Beggars."[42] On January 9–10, 1770, the Commons discussed the petitions but debated if the signers represented "popular opinion," whether signatories understood the documents, and if their concern for Wilkes was real or manipulated. Whig stalwart George Saville denounced skeptics by mockingly asking, "are these petitions the acts of a most audacious crimin-ality, or the awfull voice of our Constituents delivered in the most advisable, & authorized manner?" before warning, "If this House loses the dignity of the people, we lose our Constitution."[43] Parliamentary inaction carried a political price. British authorities appeared to violate not only individual liberty but the basic consultative links between populace and government. The Wilkes movement's virulent accusations of British governmental des-potism seemed justified.

Wilkes's supporters considered the right to petition the throne an important check on state power, and the king's ignoring of their pleas created a crisis of confidence in the regime. Conspiratorial thinking spread: "when bad men combine," wrote Burke in *Thoughts on the Present Discontents*, "the good

---

[38] *St. James's Chronicle*, June 6, 1769.
[39] *Public Advertiser*, April 4, 1770.
[40] Horace Walpole, *Memoirs of the Reign of George III* (London: Lawrence and Bullen, 1894), Vol. 3, 227.
[41] Rudé, *Wilkes*, 135.
[42] *Public Advertiser*, August 1, 1769.
[43] BL Edgerton ADD MS 3711, 6–68.

must associate." Only then could they "speedily communicate the alarm of any evil design."[44] The City of London's Common Council on March 5 admonished how "Subjects of the most despotic Prince on Earth, when they humbly petition their Sovereign on the Score of Grievances, though they cannot promise themselves Redress, at least expect an Answer."[45] Middlesex County's freeholders published their petition in April, "that right itself has been indirectly attacked, under pretence of censuring a supposed abuse of it." This resulted in a "most dangerous attempt to cut off the Communication between your Majesty and your People."[46] Numerous provincial petitions followed with total signatures surpassing thirty-five thousand.[47] Government unresponsiveness augured the campaign's growing radicalization.

Wilkes was released later in April 1770 to celebrations with at least fifty-eight towns throughout England holding public festivities. In Derby, supporters roasted sheep in the streets for a feast, where attendees were "plentifully supplied with liquor from the houses of entertainment" gratis. In York, forty-five prestigious Wilkes supporters met for a banquet of forty-five dishes, with forty-five bottles of wine, and drank forty-five toasts, before sponsoring a gathering for the general public. Despite the heady mixture of politics and alcohol, events remained peaceful: newspapers described York's festivities as the "greatest demonstration of Joy," Derby's "the greatest rejoicings that were ever known in this town," and London's "carried on with such decency, order, unanimity, and patriotic and grateful sentiments" as to disappoint opponents.[48] Charleston and Boston parties followed once news crossed the Atlantic. Nor were such acclamations a transient phenomenon – in 1771, Wilkes became London's sheriff.

Despite the organization's promising beginning, the supporters split in April 1771 between those focused on Wilkes and others more interested in building a broader movement. Although originally a fund-raising organization for Wilkes, the society promised protection "to every man, who by asserting the Rights of the people, shall become obnoxious to administration, or suffer from the hand of power."[49] From early on, rumors spread of supporters' infighting over money.[50] Horne, the society's founding organizer, sought aid for other dissidents, including a publisher facing charges for printing Wilkes's works. Wilkes refused, however, and the funding motion failed by two votes

---

[44] Edmund Burke, *Thoughts on the Present Discontents* (London: Dodsley, 1770), 105–6.

[45] *Public Advertiser*, March 5, 1770.

[46] Ibid., April 6, 1770.

[47] Brewer, *Party Ideology and Popular Politics at the Accession of George III* (Cambridge: Cambridge University Press, 1976), 179.

[48] Ibid., 178–79; *London Evening Post*, April 19, 1770; *Independent Chronicle*, April 20, 1770.

[49] LMA MSS 3332, Vol. 1, 449.

[50] William Strahan and David Hall, "Correspondence between William Strahan and David Hall, 1763–1777," *Pennsylvania Magazine of History and Biography* 11, no. 1 (1887), 103.

after two Horne supporters quit the club.[51] Horne's faction withdrew to form their own Constitutional Society. In the contentious aftermath, the rump supporters decreed no member who decided to "strike his Name out of the Books" could rejoin without being reelected. The following meeting consisted of "the Pot-companions of Mr. Wilkes."[52] The society's infighting ended their effective ability to aid either Wilkes's or Horne's factions.[53] Plans for a vigorous British association to keep pace with American patriots floundered.

The Virginia Lees, in a political misstep, remained with Wilkes's Society of Supporters. Arthur Lee bemoaned the "dissentions & division," as promoting any measure with "one party" became impossible "without incurring the ill-will and enmity of the other." Yet, as he considered the elder network "still the most popular Society," Lee stuck with Wilkes.[54] Arthur's brother William Lee condemned the new organization, asserting "Horne is offended because Wilkes is a greater man than himself," and thus "attempted, tho' pretty much in vain, to ruin him with the Public."[55] In 1773, Samuel Adams with "hearty thanks" accepted honorary Supporter membership even as the organization became moribund.[56] Wilkes's cause, despite its early promise as a movement promoting the "cause of freedom" for all British subjects, wound up a selfish cult of little use to its partisans or even Wilkes himself.[57]

On April 30, 1771, despite reformers' disorder, the Duke of Richmond and former Prime Minister William Pitt (now the Earl of Chatham) introduced Parliamentary reform in the Commons. Pitt, having denounced governmental corruption and waste for decades, allegedly commented in private, "either the Parliament will reform itself from within, or be reformed with a vengeance from without."[58] The motion – alongside a call to expunge Parliament's decision on Wilkes – failed overwhelmingly. Yet the question of reform, never taken seriously before, would never be absent thereafter.

Particularly as American resistance seemed broken after the anti-Townshend boycott movement collapsed, some reasonably believed that a radical change could come to Britain before America. In April 1771, William Lee wrote from London, "things must now very shortly come to a crisis, either absolute Tyranny in the Crown, or some popular revolution" – he counseled American correspondents to prepare "to live without the

---

[51] Veitch, *Genesis*, 30; Bewley, *Gentleman*, 40.
[52] *Middlesex Journal*, April 23 and May 16, 1771.
[53] George Albemarle, *Memoirs of the Marquis of Rockingham and His Contemporaries* (London: Bentley, 1852), Vol. 1, 209.
[54] LC Samuel Adams Papers, MSS 10223, Vol. 3.
[55] UVSC William Lee Papers.
[56] LC Samuel Adams Papers, MSS 10223, Vol. 4.
[57] BL John Wilkes Papers, ADD MS 30875.
[58] Francis Thackeray, *A History of the Right Hon. William Pitt* (London: Rivington, 1826), Vol. 2, 243–45.

assistance of this Country."[59] Revolution remained a British tradition, while few believed the present order secure.

Shorn of their Wilkes commitments, Horne's breakaway Constitutional Society revivified their radical program. Beyond "restoring to the Electors of Middlesex their Right of Election," society members pledged to "reserve to the people their constitutional right of an annual, or if that cannot be maintained, at least a triennial choice of representatives," instead of septennial elections.[60] The *Middlesex Journal* concurred, arguing that while Wilkes's friends focused on "circulation of the bottle," the Constitutional Society "frames a noble declaration of patriotism" for systemic change. Though not deserting Wilkes, the *Journal* celebrated reform groups' proliferation, asking, "shall there not be Patriots enough to furnish both SUPPORTERS and Constitutionalists?"[61] Wilkes's partisans ratified a similarly radical manifesto on July 23 to "restore annual parliaments," but its time leading reform efforts had ended.[62]

The Constitutional Society in June began asking Parliamentary candidates to explicitly adhere to their reform proposals. Anyone seeking their support had to pledge to "vote for, and use his utmost endeavours to procure a bill to shorten the duration of Parliaments," "reduce the numbers of placemen and pensioners in the House of Commons," and "obtain a more fair and equal representation of the people."[63] Most MPs resisted such demands, however, and no popular upsurge for legislative restructuring developed. Still, the dissatisfaction Wilkes encouraged began to germinate plans for reform.

With Wilkes's more principled supporters defecting and Wilkes himself ensconced in a comfortable London position, no grand transatlantic movement for reform or revolution developed in the early 1770s. Nevertheless, the American model of mobilization had diffused among Britain's prominent reformers and uncertainty over ministerial intentions made new campaigns seem probable. The new methods of mobilization opened the way for a multitude of movements challenging the British establishment.

The American War and British Liberty

With the Wilkes movement's grievances remaining unaddressed, Parliamentary escalations in America galled British activists. British merchants mobilized unprecedentedly broad resistance against the Stamp Act and the subsequent American crises remained integral parts of the campaigns to restore and ensure British liberty. Though radical factions'

---

[59] UVSC William Lee Papers.
[60] *Middlesex Journal*, May 16, 1771.
[61] Ibid., May 10, 1771.
[62] *The Letters of Junius*, John Cannon, ed. (Oxford: Oxford University Press, 1978), 404.
[63] *Middlesex Journal*, June 11, 1771.

influence fluctuated and their support for American causes could waver, for many Britons American patriots remained exemplars – extending British political possibilities and challenging the government's authoritarian pretensions. In lobbying for the patriot cause, Britons learnt the use of American-style mobilizational methods, which they subsequently applied to their own domestic campaigns.

During the Stamp Act crisis, British merchants mobilized for the colonial cause. Although America's Parliamentary lobby only consisted of a few part-time "agents" without considerable influence, British trade interests could hardly be ignored.[64] Though a Committee of North American Merchants already existed, headed by Quaker financier David Barclay, once word of American resistance reached Britain, a newly inclusive American Merchants Committee formed in London in December 1765. Having heard of the intensifying colonial discontent, the committee placed a public advertisement calling all North American merchants to come discuss "Affairs of great Importance," which drew several hundred. They appointed a twenty-eight-man committee, "of principal merchants trading to each colony," to counteract the "great Decay" the crisis caused.[65] Similarly to the alliance-building advancing across the colonies, traders mobilized an unprecedentedly national effort "to apply to the Outports and to the Manufacturing Cities and Towns for their concurrence and Assistance" in pressuring repeal. The committee sent circulars to thirty British commercial centers, urging petitions to Parliament.[66] Asserting "every other maritime and manufacturing part of these Kingdoms must be affected by the distresses of North American commerce," the movement stoked a national outcry. Twenty-six petitions arrived from Birmingham, Bristol, Liverpool, Manchester, and elsewhere, conveying an economically catastrophic forecast of manufacturing decline, rising unemployment, and investor losses.[67] The Stamp Act spiked a potent cocktail of transatlantic discontent for paltry New World revenue.

American pressure exacerbated British anti–Stamp Act agitation. By February 1766, colonists canceled virtually all orders or made fulfillment conditional upon repeal, while postponing payments on nearly £5 million owed to British creditors.[68] Bristol's petition argued the act caused "the

---

[64] Slaughter, *Independence*, 214.

[65] Thomas, *British Politics and the Stamp Act Crisis: The First Phase of the American Revolution, 1763–1767* (Oxford: Clarendon Press, 1975) 30, 146; *Public Ledger*, December 4, 1765; *London Chronicle*, December 5, 1765; SCHC Committee of Correspondence Papers, 1034.00.

[66] Thomas, *George*, 130; Bryce E. Withrow, "A Biographical Study of Barlow Trecothick, 1720–1775" (Master's Thesis, Emporia State University, 1979), 25.

[67] Thomas, *British Politics*, 146–47; Bourke, *Empire* 300.

[68] Thomas, ibid., 218–19.

interruption of commerce, and the stagnation of trade in this kingdom."[69] Threatening a fragile postwar economic recovery, such measures alienated merchants of all political hues. American partisans believed they constituted a compelling repeal coalition: As de Berdt wrote to Boston, "Both City & County as well as our own petitions" surpassed "any party opposition that can be made against us."[70] The British and colonial sectors' unprecedented solidarity formed an imposing counterweight to government policy.

Though British merchants had long been active lobbyists, they entered uncharted oppositional waters to press contentious American claims. Since 1734, London merchants trading to the mainland colonies associated to lobby together. They worked closely with each prime minister: gathering reports, offering information, and circulating petitions when necessary.[71] Now, merchant associations risked alienating the government whose armed forces and diplomatic support had fostered their prosperity. Yet, threatened by the postwar economic downturn, the lobby sacrificed Parliamentary goodwill to support the Americans. Townshend in April 1766 denounced the "Club of North American Merchants at the King's-Arms Tavern" who he "hoped, would never be suffered to give Law" to the country.[72]

As the American crisis grew, colonial grievances emphasized British political shortcomings. Pitt in January 1766 declared to Parliament, "The Americans are the sons, not the bastards of England," making them "entitled to the common right of representation" and taxable only by their own representatives. Dismissing arguments for virtual representation, Pitt considered such claims "the rotten part of the constitution," asserting they "cannot endure the century." Underrepresented British areas could sympathize with and build precedent via the American cause. "I rejoice," Pitt continued, "that America has resisted."[73] Through contesting injustice in America, British political change became more thinkable. By February, sympathy for Americans, enhanced by nonimportation's effects, made many Britons active partisans. The new Rockingham ministry initiated repeal proceedings in the Commons, with more than forty colonial agents and concerned merchants testifying of the Act's detrimental effects.[74] Through also passing the controversial Declaratory Act, ensuring full ruling prerogatives, Parliament temporarily defused political mobilization in both America and Britain.

---

[69] *Owen's Weekly Chronicle*, January 11, 1766.

[70] LC Dennys de Berdt Papers, MMC-0298.

[71] Alison Gilbert Olson, *Making the Empire Work: London and American Interest Groups, 1690–1790* (Cambridge, MA: Harvard University Press, 1992), 98–102.

[72] Jack M. Sosin, *Agents and Merchants: British Colonial Policy and the Origins of the American Revolution* (Lincoln: University of Nebraska Press, 1965), 84.

[73] Williams, *Pitt*, Vol. 2, 191–92.

[74] Sosin, *Agents*, 79.

After Stamp Act repeal passed the Commons in February 1766, celebrations spread across Britain. In Bristol, reportedly "Never was joy more general," with bells ringing "incessantly" all day, followed by "uncommon bonfires" that evening. Birmingham residents made "demonstrations of joy," while Leeds partisans illuminated their town.[75] George III's procession to Westminster to sign the repeal on March 18 met "infinite crowds" whose "acclamations ... pierced the skies," congratulating the monarch on striking a measure "grievous to one part of his subjects, and fatal to the wealth and prosperity of the rest."[76] The political crisis ended, but a new protest paradigm had formed.

Pro-American consensus did not last. During the Townshend crisis, Franklin reported colonial support became "one of the distinctions of party here" with the opposition "called by way of reproach *Americans*."[77] Middlesex's freeholders, after detailing in their 1769 royal petition a litany of abuses relating to the Wilkes affair and government corruption, blamed "the same evil Counsellors" for American "Grievances and Apprehensions similar to those of which we complain at Home."[78] Though radical Whig disdain for violations of British rights remained strong, many moderates stayed quiet. The broad British coalition achieved in the anti–Stamp Act campaign never rallied with such unanimity again.

A hard line against America helped conservatives fight British political battles by proxy and criticize opposition tactics.[79] Some asserted that British Wilkite agitation helped push Americans further. "We ought not much to wonder at the impatience of the people in America," Pennsylvania's proprietor Thomas Penn wrote from London in 1770, "when people in general here seem to have lost any decency in speaking and writing upon every political matter."[80] The moment appeared ripe to combat agitation on both sides of the Atlantic. To royal stationer William Strahan, the Americans took "advantage of our own Dissentions at home; else they would not surely venture on committing such great Outrages." Only by correcting governmental "Timidity and Indecision" toward dissidents, he argued, would disorder cease.[81]

British merchants reacted unfavorably to the next round of colonial non-importation agreements, which targeted 1768's Townshend Acts but affected them first. Mercantile bodies delayed reproaching Parliament, waiting to gauge

---

[75] *London Evening Post*, March 1, 1766; *New Hampshire Gazette*, April 25, 1766; *Lloyd's Evening Post*, February 28, 1766.

[76] *London Evening Post*, March 20, 1766.

[77] Thomas, *The Townshend Duties Crisis: The Second Phase of the American Revolution, 1767–1773* (Oxford: Clarendon Press, 1987), 2.

[78] *A Petition of the Freeholders of the County of Middlesex, Presented to His Majesty, the 24th of May, 1769* (London: Fenwick, 1769), 9–10.

[79] NYPL Bancroft Collection, Connecticut Papers, 139.

[80] LC Peter Force Papers, Thomas Penn Correspondence, Box VII E:59.

[81] Strahan and Hall, "Correspondence," 347.

colonial responses.[82] Americans' withdrawal from most transatlantic commerce, though injurious, no longer produced a crisis, as British trade grew on the European continent. Despite an attempt by MP Barlow Trecothick – a Boston native and absentee Jamaican planter who chaired the American Merchants Committee during the Stamp Act crisis – to raise London, Bristol, and Liverpool petitions for the duties' repeal, commercial associations remained reticent. London merchants addressed Parliament in 1770, declaring themselves divided between fully repealing, amending, or continuing the duties, noting colonial trade's importance but only requesting the relief the House thought proper.[83] Without merchant pressure, and with North denouncing American nonimportation agreements as "illegal combinations," Parliament only partially repealed the Townshend Acts.[84]

Americans' political prospects with British authorities and the general public waxed and waned. Arthur Lee gave contrasting views of British public opinion in his letters home to Virginia. In 1767, he found the political atmosphere "Very melancholy," and though Wilkes "speaks warmly of America," Lee felt the colonies had lost opposition leaders' patronage. By 1769, however, with the Wilkes movement spreading, Lee considered "the spirit of liberty now so truly and universally diffused, that I do not think it possible to suppress it."[85] The London Society of Supporters' May 1769 petition endorsed American efforts, asserting "the same evil councillors" aggravated colonial "grievances and apprehensions similar to those of which we complain at home."[86] The American nonimportation agreements' collapse in 1770, however, exacerbated already-declining radical British support. Lee described the news acting "like an opiate on all but the enemies of America," depressing supporters while emboldening the government.[87] Yet even as British sympathizers equivocated, the nation's readers remained interested in American controversies: of eighty-four pamphlets published on Anglo-American relations in the thirteen colonies between 1764 and 1770, thirty-seven were reprinted in England.[88] The American political drama played to a wide, if ambivalent, British audience.

The American controversies' potency became such that British radicals vied to associate with the cause over the early mid-1770s. Despite the Lees remaining in Wilkes's supporters, the Constitutional Society resolved to "endeavour to restore to America the essential right of taxation, by representation," while

[82] Olson, *Making*, 146.
[83] Thomas, *Townshend*, 14, 123, 171.
[84] Olson, *Making*, 125–26.
[85] Lee, *Life*, Vol. 1, 186–89, 196.
[86] Thomas, *Townshend*, 142.
[87] Lee, *Life*, Vol. 1, 249.
[88] Brewer, *Party Ideology*, 202.

declaring the Townshend duties "notoriously incompatible with every principle of British Liberty."[89] In the City of London, Trecothick, still a New Hampshire agent, became Lord Mayor in 1770 and Americans William Lee and Stephen Sayre were elected sheriffs in 1773, subsequently using their positions to raise petitions against the Coercive Acts. Arthur Lee placed 170 anonymous essays and fifty letters in British newspapers blistering government policies between 1769 and 1775.[90] American contention remained a touchstone and exemplar for British radical opposition across the pre-Revolutionary decade.

The 1774 Coercive Acts gave further evidence of British ministerial intentions and brought American support back into Britain's political mainstream. Despite general British disapprobation of the tea parties, one letter to Connecticut from a Pall Mall informant noted his "astonishment at the awfull power of tyranny" the government wielded.[91] New fund-raising began for blockaded Bostonians.[92] Many encouraged the colonists, with one Glasgow letter to Maryland predicting, "Nothing can save you but a Generall agreement over the whole Continent among the common People."[93] The New England minister Stiles noted British papers abounded with "a Spirit of Liberty ... rekindled with new Ardour."[94] Given the distrust of centralizing state power, many Britons needed little convincing that each new American confrontation resulted from royal and ministerial machinations.

The worsening American crisis neither politically nor economically escaped Britons' notice. Colonial nonimportation agreements showed how volatile trade could be. Customhouse tallies suggest exports to America rose from £1,325,000 in 1769 to around £4,200,000 in 1771 and then fell to about £2,000,000 in 1773 before crashing in 1774–1775. Colonial debts increasingly went uncollected.[95] With instability worsening, British interests could not remain unconcerned, uninvolved, or uncritical of Americans' proposed solutions. British merchants divided over colonial issues, however, while Americans showed decreasing interest in traditional Parliamentary lobbying, in some cases declining to appoint new London agents.[96]

---

[89] UVSC William Lee Papers; Alexander Stephens, *Memoirs of John Horne Tooke: Interspersed with Original Documents* (London: Johnson, 1813), Vol. 1, 166.

[90] Potts, *Arthur Lee*, 71; Michael G. Kammen, *A Rope of Sand: The Colonial Agents, British Politics and the American Revolution* (Ithaca: Cornell University Press, 1968), 291–92.

[91] CHS American Revolution Collection, Box 11, Folder A.

[92] Robert E. Toohey, *Liberty and Empire: British Radical Solutions to the American Problem, 1774–1776* (Lexington, KY: University Press of Kentucky, 1978), 11.

[93] MHS Revolutionary War Collection MS 1814.

[94] LC Peter Force Papers, Ezra Stiles Diary.

[95] Dora Mae Clark, *British Opinion and the American Revolution* (New Haven: Yale University Press, 1930), 57, 65, 92.

[96] Thomas, *Tea Party*, 7.

With participation in traditional mediatory groups declining, radical intellectuals stepped forward with plans to resolve the American crisis. James Burgh, a dissenting religious and political thinker, met fortnightly with Franklin, Priestley, and Price for several years to discuss philosophy and politics in the Club of Honest Whigs. In the late-1774 volume of his influential *Political Disquisitions*, Burgh endorsed bringing a comprehensive associational movement to Britain:

> there must be established a GRAND NATIONAL ASSOCIATION FOR RESTORING THE CONSTITUTION. Into this must be invited all men of property, all friends of liberty, all able commanders, &c. There must be a copy of the ASSOCIATION for every parish, and a parochial committee to procure subscriptions from all persons whose names are in any tax-book, and who are willing to join the Association. And there must be a grand committee for every county in the three kingdoms, and in the colonies of America.[97]

Burgh promoted an unprecedented expansion of popular sovereignty with associations representing the people better than their narrowly elected legislature. Parliament's claim to represent the British people could be superseded. British proponents sent complimentary copies of *Political Disquisitions* to influential colonists like John Adams and an American edition followed in 1775.[98] Many viewed the American crisis as a crucial experiment in popular organizing with wide ramifications for Britain's future.

For radical Britons, the American crisis remained a troubling case of state coercion and pivotal moment for asserting political liberty. *The Crisis*, a periodical marketed not only in London but also around Britain and the American colonies, began in January 1775, declaring, "the Altar of Despotism erected in America, and we shall be the next victims to Lawless Power" that would make Members of Parliament "mere Creatures of the King." The second issue declared "a powerful Opposition forming in every Part of England" through "ASSOCIATIONS" to preserve "RIGHTS and LIBERTIES."[99] The American cause could be saved through British collective action. Parliament ordered the publication seized and burned by London's hangman.[100]

American radicalization made peaceful resolution of the imperial crisis increasingly unlikely. Alongside an extensive nonimportation agreement, the Continental Congress in late 1774 instructed colonial agents to secure publication of American grievances, circulate news nationwide, obtain British

---

[97] James Burgh *Political Disquisitions: Or, an Inquiry into Public Errors, Defects and Abuses* (London: Dilly, 1774), Vol. 3, 429.

[98] Burgh, *Political Disquisitions* (Philadelphia: Bell, 1775); Carla H. Hay, "The Making of a Radical: The Case of James Burgh," *Journal of British Studies* 18, no. 2 (1979), 114.

[99] *The Crisis*, January 20 and 27, 1775.

[100] Lutnick, *American*, 3.

merchant support, and present their plan to the king. They did not, however, authorize negotiations with the British government. Only full repeal of the Townshend and Coercive Acts would end the boycott. Though Arthur Lee still hoped American controversies could embolden a Whig union between the Rockingham and Chatham factions, believing an "opposition, which supported by the popular voice" united with a strong merchant lobby could be "irresistible," such a plan required a nearly perfect storm of coinciding interests.[101]

Moderates' hopes for crisis resolution focused on mobilizing mercantile interests to deter a destructive conflict. London's Merchant Association, likely the best-positioned group to contest military action in America, drew more than 350 on January 4, 1775. They heard letters from Bristol, Liverpool, Manchester, and Leeds merchants endorsing collective action.[102] The London body, however, remained leery of alienating the ministry. Burke described merchant "apprehensions of taking any Steps displeasing to the authors of their grievances," and although considering American commerce "threatened with irretrievable Ruin," adopted a petition only mildly criticizing armed intervention.[103] Nevertheless, London's merchants coordinated a national campaign in the Americans' favor, meeting regularly over the next three months to encourage provincial addresses to Parliament.[104]

British merchant groups sent petitions declaring the American controversy dire, reengaging to mediate the crisis despite their prior apathy during the Townshend Acts controversy. Petitions reportedly arrived from "every trading and manufacturing town, which has the least Connexion with American Commerce," supporting the patriots.[105] Bristol and London merchants presented theirs to the Commons on January 23, which, though avoiding Americans' most radical claims, predicted economic ruin should war occur. Bristol's declared "several thousand persons depend for their daily support" on American trade there, while the Caribbean islands "essentially depends on the continent of America" for goods and markets. Twenty-six areas including Liverpool, Manchester, Glasgow, and four Yorkshire manufacturing towns petitioned that winter. Caribbean planters, while "exceedingly alarmed" by the Continental Congress, petitioned that they needed American crops and

---

[101] Sosin, *Agents*, 192–96.

[102] James E. Bradley, *Popular Politics and the American Revolution in England: Petitions, the Crown and Public Opinion* (Macon, GA: Mercer University Press, 1986), 20.

[103] Burke, *Correspondence* (Chicago: University of Chicago Press, 1958–1978), Vol. 3, 95; *Public Advertiser*, October 16, 1775.

[104] Kammen, *Rope*, 304.

[105] Richard Champion, *The American Correspondence of a Bristol Merchant, 1766–1776* (Berkeley: University of California Press, 1964), 11.

would be "reduced to the utmost distress" during a conflict.[106] Jamaica's assembly claimed that with the "incumbrance of 200,000 slaves," war would bring "the most dreadful calamities to this island and the inevitable destruction of the small sugar colonies involved."[107] The American cause had many friends who, from self-interest even if not ideology, had reason to favor reconciliation.

Yet amid growing splits between pro-Americans and loyalists, attempts to cultivate an overwhelming petition wave for peace from commercial centers did not coalesce. British opinions diverged, leading Rockingham to assert to Burke in February, "If the whole body of American and West India Merchants thought it a proper measure, it would come with force, but if a part only petition his Majesty I think it would do harm."[108] Birmingham and Leeds merchants adopted separate addresses after their municipalities approved petitions endorsing coercion.[109] Burke reported to Rockingham seven months later, "The Business of Petitions has hitherto proved so ineffectual that they altogether dispaird" with the addresses sent to a Parliamentary "committee of oblivion."[110] Burke noted many businessmen began to "snuff out the cadaverous *haut gout* of lucrative war" through profiteering.[111] With mixed motives, beset by internal divisions, merchant lobbying faltered.

Lacking merchant consensus, radical Whigs turned to raising petitions from across the nation to build consensus for colonial reconciliation. Amid a failed February 1775 call for reconciliation, Chatham declared "the cause of America is allied to every true whig," envisioning an imperial anti-war coalition: "The whole Irish nation, all true English whigs, the whole Nation of America, these combined make millions of whigs averse to the system."[112] On April 10, a demonstration by Wilkes and fellow City of London petitioners brought a royal address asserting they "plainly perceive, that the real purpose is to establish Arbitrary Power over all America." They predicted pernicious measures would concurrently advance in Britain with war bringing "more burthensome taxes, the increase of an enormous national debt," alongside "the loss of the most valuable branch of our commerce" in the new world.[113] The crisis typified the authoritarian governing tendencies Wilkes and his followers warned of. Directly petitioning the crown – bypassing Parliament, as during the Wilkes crisis – more than two hundred royal petitions arrived from across

---

[106] *Parliamentary History*, Vol. 18, 180, 219; Clark, *British Opinion*, 85; Thomas, *Tea Party*, 184; Kammen, *Rope*, 304.

[107] *Parliamentary History*, Vol. 18, 401.

[108] Burke, *Correspondence*, Vol. 3, 114.

[109] Bradley, *Popular Politics*, 22.

[110] Burke, *Correspondence*, Vol. 3, 208; Bradley, *Popular Politics*, 17–20.

[111] Albemarle, *Memoirs*, Vol. 2, 276–77.

[112] R. B. McDowell, *Ireland in the Age of Imperialism and Revolution, 1760–1801* (Oxford: Clarendon Press, 1979), 240.

[113] Sainsbury, *Disaffected*, 84; *Parliamentary History*, Vol. 18, 698.

England, Wales, Scotland, and Ireland. Indeed, in several municipal centers including Bristol and Newcastle, those circulating pro-American petitions did the same for Wilkes.[114] A radicalizing opposition questioned Parliament's representativeness and authority.

Authorities, however, mobilized a larger wave of loyal petitions backing military force. Though previous attempts to counter-petition against the Wilkes movement failed, war rallied conservatives. An Oxford University petition accused Americans of daring to "violate the laws, to resist authority, and at length to rebel against the sovereignty of the British legislature." Devonshire electors in October mocked "the Miseries which our deluded Fellow subjects in America have brought upon themselves." Connecting American Patriots with Wilkes's movement, the electors declared their "Disapprobation of these Associations," encouraged "by Circular Letters and Factious Emissaries dispersed throughout the Kingdom," urging their ringleaders "be brought to speedy and Condign Punishment."[115] Across Britain, a third of coercive petitions explicitly blamed domestic factions for inflaming the American crisis. Yet given how government agents solicited such addresses, the opposition doubted their authenticity.[116]

Americans closely followed the British contestations. Boston Committee of Correspondence member Thomas Young wrote to Samuel Adams in August 1774 of his excitement at the committee receiving "a large bundle of British papers from which, the Printers are busily collecting the most interesting particulars" for colonial diffusion.[117] Many American radicals, even in 1775, hoped for an imperial solution. That July, the Continental Congress signed the "Olive Branch Petition," offering peace on their interpretation of British constitutional principles to avert "the impending calamities that threaten the British Empire."[118] The British government, however, refused mediation.

Radicals kept boldly supporting the American cause. Following the Coercive Acts, Horne's Constitutional Society began sending beleaguered Bostonians donations (£100 in both March and April 1775). On news of Lexington and Concord, the society publicly raised money for the widows of the American rebels, "who, faithful to the character of Englishmen, preferring death to slavery," they considered "inhumanely murdered by the king's troops," without justification. Franklin received the first funds before he left for Philadelphia.[119] The campaign angered government supporters, leading to

---

[114] Bradley, *Popular Politics*, 37–38, 59 and "The Religious Origins of Radical Politics," in *Religion and Politics in Enlightenment Europe*, Bradley and Dale K. Van Kley, eds. (Notre Dame, IN: Notre Dame University Press, 2001), 204.

[115] NA HO 55/11 32, 12.

[116] Bradley, *Popular Politics*, 70; Clark, *British Opinion*, 133.

[117] LC Samuel Adams Papers, MSS 10223 Vol. 6.

[118] "The Olive Branch Petition," http://ahp.gatech.edu/olive_branch_1775.html.

[119] Stephens, *Memoirs*, 435.

Horne's conviction for libel against the British forces and imprisonment until 1779.[120] Sympathy continued for the Americans' cause, including for armed rebellion.

Overt dissent became more difficult after George III issued a Proclamation of Rebellion on August 23, 1775. Though directed against American colonists, the measure had ramifications across the empire, ordering subjects to "withstand and suppress" the uprising and targeting everyone "carrying on correspondence with, or in any manner or degree aiding or abetting" the insurgents' cause.[121] Potential capital prosecution threatened those supporting the colonists, but such a measure could not prevent critiques couched in loyal terms.

War weakened, but did not stop, raucous debates over America in Britain. Petitioning continued, asking for de-escalation and negotiation with the rebels. Bristol's merchants, with a New Yorker chairing the meeting, adopted a royal petition on September 27 endorsing American trade's advantages for Britain, asserting war "would destroy the commercial Connection" they had built. The conflict deprived "many thousand" of work locally and in a manner disgracing "every friend of humanity ... spread the horrors of civil war over a very considerable part of the British Dominions." The merchants implored the king to "put a stop to a ruinous war" and restore commerce.[122] The City of London two weeks later predicted the conflict would encourage "more burdensome taxes," increase "an enormous national debt," and lose the colonies.[123] American advocates presented the conflict as a disastrous war of choice.

In August, a London Association formed in a local tavern, calling for greater national coordination among the opposition. By October, the group sent circular letters recommending branches, each featuring a "Committee of Correspondence," in all interested locales. Despite wartime restrictions, the association described their task as "not to weaken, but invigorate the laws," particularly "public liberty" to dissent.[124] Only vigilance could stop further incursions on British rights: another communiqué declared the "REVIVAL OF LETTERS" had delivered Britain from "Monkish Superstition," while "FREEDOM OF THE PRESS ALONE" maintained liberty.[125] Only Newcastle, however, formed a full-fledged association on London's model, and only they, Nottingham, and Worcester sent petitions urging a negotiated American peace.[126]

Reaction to the British government's war against American colonists proved sharp across Britain. "Addresses, Petitions, Counter-addresses and

---

[120] Bewley, *Gentleman*, 68–71.
[121] Maier, *Resistance*, 257.
[122] *Lloyd's Evening Post*, September 29, 1775.
[123] Ibid., October 26, 1775.
[124] Ibid.
[125] Ibid., October 5, 1775.
[126] Bradley, *Popular Politics*, 56.

Counter-petitions springing up from every Quarter," one October report described, spread throughout the nation.[127] Debate raged over coercion, with divided votes over whether to petition in over half the larger "freeman's boroughs" (those possessing an electorate over 1,000). Virtually every area with two or more newspapers polarized. Even as the number of loyal addresses dwarfed peace petitions, more favoring peace were gathered in 1775 than dissidents procured for Wilkes in 1770 or against the Stamp Act four years earlier.[128] Glasgow denounced an "unnecessary, unnatural and ruinous war."[129] In several other towns, royal peace petitions gained approval with little opposition. Though professing loyalty to the king, they urged recognition of American rights. In Devonshire, 80 percent of freeholders petitioned for reconciliation, while Nottingham's gained unanimous adoption.[130] Southampton's asked American "natural and chartered rights" be "preserved inviolate."[131] Many peace petitions were raised following the passage of loyal addresses, typically drawing more signatures.[132]

Some believed the American conflict, given the extent of British opposition, would be short. An anonymous November 1775 letter sent to Virginia (but intercepted en route) considered it "impracticable for the Ministers to prevail with the people of England to continue the War another year," given how "well disposed" to America the "Great Majority of the People of England" appeared, alongside direct military costs of £7 million pounds per annum, and the "distress ... Manufacturers are every where complaining," from lost markets. Particularly, as another intercepted February 1776 letter described, "America has many friends, and well wishers in this Country," including among the "worthiest Characters in the nation," reconciliation appeared pragmatic.[133] Merchants complained of further delays to colonial debt collection and Caribbean colonies prophesized "Famine" as American exports ceased.[134] The war appeared one of choice, allowing an intensifying opposition to impugn the government's motives.

Amid the escalating American war, Wilkes on March 21, 1776 made the first detailed motion in the Commons for broad Parliamentary reform. Noting how "Old Sarum, where there is not a second house," sent as many deputies to Parliament as his own Middlesex or rapidly expanding Yorkshire, he proposed

---

[127] *Westminster Journal*, October 21, 1775.

[128] Bradley, "The British Public and the American Revolution," in *Britain and the American Revolution*, H. T. Dickinson, ed. (London: Longman, 1998), 137, 153 and *Popular Politics*, 127.

[129] *Middlesex Journal*, October 19, 1775.

[130] *Gazetteer*, October 25, 1775; *Lloyd's Evening Post*, October 25, 1775.

[131] *Lloyd's Evening Post*, October 30, 1775; *London Evening Post*, November 2, 1775.

[132] Bradley, *Popular Politics*, 4.

[133] LC Great Britain Colonial Office, Class 5, Vol. 40, 343 and 35.

[134] NA CO 5/116 99 and CO 5/117 146.

redistributing seats to larger counties and growing manufacturing towns. Wilkes declared the cause imperative due to the "ministerial junto" that "plunged the nation into a cruel, bloody and unnatural Civil War" with America.[135] North responded that Wilkes was "not serious" and entered into "a physical, chirurgical, and political disquisition on the nature and effects of amputation in general," in "the body natural and body politic" of the nation. Asking small boroughs to sacrifice "so beneficial a species of property" was unconstitutional. Wilkes's motion for a committee to consider Parliamentary reform failed.[136] Reform proposals nevertheless proliferated, reacting to imperial abuses with increasingly radical solutions. The American Revolution destabilized British politics, threating a reformation of their political system.

Many Whigs considered their political struggles fought by proxy in America. Legislator Charles James Fox, while declaring himself "convinced" in June 1776 that Americans "will finally succeed, whether by victories or defeats," privately considered British victory would "give the completest triumph to Toryism that it ever had." After the British captured New York in October, Fox wrote to Rockingham considering it "more necessary than ever to produce some manifesto, petition, or public instrument" to get the colonists "offers of accommodation," though none resulted.[137] The ministry's offensive methods made systemic reform appear necessary.

Americans, meanwhile, during the early fighting believed their cause included the British Empire's liberation. Baltimore merchant and committeeman Samuel Purviance asked Samuel Adams in September 1775 to "trust that our Virtuous Struggles will secure the Liberties of the whole British Empire, and gradually teach our Brethren at home to reform the many Evils that have crept into the constitution" since 1689's Glorious Revolution. With the American example so prominent, "Our Union & Firmness will I hope soon embolden our Friends in England & Ireland to stand forth more boldly than hitherto, & convince a Despotic Administration of their Folly."[138] Only when declaring independence in 1776, and still not fully then, could America divorce its cause from broader imperial contestations.

British collective movements against the war ebbed during the early fighting, but many opposition Whigs continued American advocacy. London's sheriffs in February 1777 petitioned against suspending habeas corpus in America, predicting "measures so violent and unconstitutional" would "precipitate the

---

[135] *St. James's Chronicle*, March 21, 1776; *General Evening Post*, March 21, 1776; Stephen Conway, *The British Isles and the War of American Independence* (New York: Oxford University Press, 2002), 218–19.

[136] *Parliamentary History*, Vol. 18, 1297.

[137] Charles James Fox, *Memorials and Correspondence* (London: Bentley, 1853), Vol. 1, 143, 145.

[138] LC Samuel Adams Papers, MSS 10223, Vol. 7.

impending ruin of this country." Radical Whig legislator Lord Abingdon perceived "herein that system coming home to ourselves, and with hasty steps pointing its dangers even towards the heart of the kingdom."[139] Discontent with the war's principles, incompetent strategy, and military spending led Richmond in April 1778 to call for British withdrawal. The Whig stalwart criticized land forces as "totally inadequate," British trade as "most materially injured," Britain's other "dependencies" left in a "ruinous and defenceless condition," and its navy in decline. The war's tortured course reinforced many Whigs' ideological opposition, believing the conflict's intent "to enslave America" and abrogate Britain's constitution. Twenty-one members of Rockingham's faction signed a declaration denouncing the government's "continuing that plan of ignorance, concealment, deceit and delusion" that precipitated the conflict. Rockingham Whigs protested the British army's irregular warfare, declaring the military leadership revivified "barbarism in war, which a beneficent religion and enlightened manners, and military honour, had for a long time banished from the Christian world."[140] The American war presented the worst excesses British reformers had believed the government capable of.

Between 1775 and 1778, eleven English counties and forty-seven boroughs and towns sent petitions to Parliament or the king signed by approximately forty-four thousand in England, plus another six thousand from Ireland and Scotland, urging British authorities to negotiate peace with the rebels.[141] Britons of similar political persuasions had no difficulties identifying with the colonies and realized the interconnectedness of their battles against governmental abuses. Though the dictates of wartime loyalism limited dissent, unprecedentedly coordinated campaigns for Parliamentary reform in both Britain and Ireland would arise utilizing American-style organizations before the war's end.

Conclusion

American revolutionaries' principles were largely those of their British counterparts. Reacting against the coercive growth of ministerial power after the Seven Years' War in both Britain and the colonies, many patriots on both sides of the Atlantic considered themselves in a common battle for British liberty. Although many historians have attempted to explain this transatlantic moment predominantly via its British context – Tilly, indeed, considering the Wilkes campaign the first modern social movement – the American Sons of Liberty's example deeply influenced the form the Society of Supporters of

---

[139] *Parliamentary History*, Vol. 19, 20 and 52.
[140] Ibid., 1013, 1059; Vol. 20, 43.
[141] Bradley, *Popular Politics*, 3.

the Bill of Rights took.[142] British historians, from Ian Christie to John Brewer to Peter D. G. Thomas, have not adequately emphasized the extent of American organizing methods' impact on early British reform movements.[143] Whereas earlier British clubs celebrated their independence, now unified and concerted action appeared a necessary step to exert greater pressure against the strengthening British government.

Together with the mercantile forces favoring American peace, prosperity, and trade, radicals – and, in their more daring moments, much of the Parliamentary opposition – allied with the Americans. Though remaining smaller in size (mirroring Britain's more restrictive electorate), eschewing paramilitary organization, and not precipitating a similar revolutionary crisis – partially due to British loyal patriotism and partially from the state coercive apparatus being closer at hand – Britons developed a growing dissatisfaction with the status quo and interest in systemic political changes. Corresponding societies could now be employed as engines for reform as well as revolution. Yet as the American Revolutionary War worsened, Britons began applying more radical strategies at home.

[142] Tilly, *Social Movements*.
[143] Christie, *Wilkes*; Brewer, *Party*; Thomas, *Townshend* and *Tea Party*.

4

The British Association Movement
and Parliamentary Reform

The British continued learning from their American counterparts. Much as the Sons of Liberty movement inspired Wilkes and Liberty, so would the American Committees of Correspondence further stoke British reform efforts. As John Adams wrote to his cousin Samuel in 1780 from Paris amid the War of Independence, "Your Committee of Correspondence is making greater progress in the World and doing greater things in the political World than the Electrical Rod ever did in the Physical. England and Ireland have adopted it, but, mean Plagiaries as they are, they do not acknowledge who was the Inventor of it."[1] Profiting from preceding transatlantic coordination and American examples, in 1779 a nationally focused Association movement began in Yorkshire, channeling discontent over the American war into support for a Parliamentary "reformation." Through corresponding county meetings, the associations cultivated an interconnected movement on a far larger scale than the Wilkes and Liberty movement, making the first sustained push for Parliamentary reform.

The American Revolutionary War and the Making of British Parliamentary Reform

Despite potential treason charges for pro-American activities after the war's outbreak, American sentiment and suspicion of British authorities remained strong among the opposition. Facing American rebellion, domestic political dissatisfaction, and army ineffectiveness, hopes for a quick conflict dissipated. London socialite Hester Lynch Thrale in 1778 described the government as "Despised at home, ridiculed abroad," with the king's "Subjects on the point of Rebellion even in his Capital, his Navy out of Repair, his Army in Disgrace, Public Credit a Jest, and a National Bankruptcy talked on as necessary, & expected as irresistible."[2] Resentments against government decisions and suspicion of ministerial motives led to a new movement for systemic changes.

---

[1] John Adams, *Papers*, Vol. 9, 44.
[2] Hester Lynch Thrale, *Thraliana: The Diary of Mrs. Hester Lynch Thrale (Later Mrs. Piozzi), 1776–1809* (Oxford: Clarendon Press, 1951), Vol. 1, 241.

Opposition voices began calling for peace, even at the price of American independence. Scientist and Franklin confidant David Hartley, the MP who in 1776 introduced the first Parliamentary proposal to abolish the Atlantic slave trade, in 1777 called for George III to "bestow upon the Colonies an entire freedom of their legislative powers" as a basis for peace to keep America within the empire. In 1778, with Britain's recent defeat at Saratoga and French entry into the war validating opponents' worst predictions, the cause became mainstream. In April, the radical Richmond called for American self-determination, as "dependence of distant colonies on a free country, can have no just foundation, or any permanent continuance, but in the consent and good-will of such colonies." Hartley published an antiwar tract denouncing the conflict's "folly and impracticability," charging "coercion, and not conciliation, was, from the very first, the secret and adopted plan, and has been systematically and inflexibly pursued ever since." Those in power had awakened "The people of England," who "have already begun more than to suspect the concealments and deceptions which have been practiced."[3] Hartley asserted the government needed to answer for its conduct.

In 1779, wartime menaces, including a possible Franco-Spanish invasion threatening London, grew for Britain and Ireland. One hundred and four enemy warships, outnumbering the British fleet, massed on France's coast with a 20,000-soldier expeditionary force and sailed in August within sight of England before retreating due to shipborne disease. Lord North doubled Britain's militia, while Irish Volunteer forces (see Chapter 5) threatened political stability.[4] The outlook for an internationally isolated Britain became grim: Rockingham in November considered the "wealth of this country is exhausted, its resources are sinking apace, and its credit" nearly "annihilated by its apparent weakness."[5] The American breakdown placed the British government at existential risk.

The ministry not only brought Britain to the precipice of losing their middle American colonies, but to the brink of government breakdown in the home islands as well. The influence of American Revolutionary and Irish Volunteer models on British dissent grew. The *Public Advertiser* urged on November 2:

> Let us in our Turn, unite in some Manner as the Irish have done, something, however, short of their Rebellion; let us constitutionally commune together. The Constitution allows the Correspondence of one County with another ... Join as the Irish do, to prohibit your members

---

[3] David Hartley, *Letters on the American War*, 6th ed. (London: Almon, 1779), 1, 4, 40, 53, 100.

[4] John Hardman, *The Life of Louis XVI* (New Haven: Yale University Press, 2017), 140; Robert Tombs, *The English and Their History* (New York: Vintage, 2014), 357; Fox, *Memorials*, Vol. 1, 229.

[5] Albemarle, *Memoirs*, Vol. 2, 387.

to grant the Supplies till the Pilferers of the Empire are brought to account.[6]

The newspaper added the following month, "The Associations in America . . . have set an example before Freemen of how to act when oppressed."[7] Popular mobilization seemed capable of rendering the government accountable and inciting real change.

Dissatisfaction spread, even when united by little more than dislike and suspicion of the ruling ministry. Recurrent denunciations of government corruption and authoritarianism dated from the Wilkes crises with Parliamentary proposals in 1768–1769 urging reform of the king's civil list (including a large number of pensionary positions used to reward Parliamentary allies). Such accusations intensified with a new Wilkes-related controversy: after a special Middlesex election following Wilkes supporter Serjeant Glynn's death in September 1779, the North ministry faced accusations of election-fixing for invalidating radical favorite George Byng's candidacy. Wilkes's former constituency petitioned that only "abuse and a perversion" of English laws could explain the ministry's machinations.[8] An unsuccessful conflict exacerbated animosities for an already troubled political system.

With Middlesex's voters assembling for a special election, calls circulated for monthly county meetings to correspond with likeminded organizations across England in a manner similar to the Americans.[9] Radical John Jebb, addressing Middlesex freeholders at Free Mason's Tavern on December 20, proposed an associational model that – if taken to its logical conclusion – could substitute for the House of Commons itself. Jebb declared recent petitions "ill calculated": since "Men possessed of power are not disposed to part with it," it made no sense to address a king "you could not legally coerce." Rather, change would come via "all the Counties" forming associations and developing a common program, perhaps by sending representatives to a national congress. Such a powerful consensus, Jebb asserted, could not be ignored. If better representation be established, particularly given current Parliamentary abuses, Jebb argued Britons should "look forward to futurity" and embrace new methods to reanimate ancient systems.[10]

[6] *Public Advertiser*, November 2, 1779.
[7] Ibid., December 4, 1779.
[8] Edward Porritt, *The Unreformed House of Commons: Parliamentary Representation before 1832*, Vol. 1 (Cambridge: Cambridge University Press, 1909), 247–48.
[9] O'Gorman, *Rise*, 407.
[10] John Jebb, *An Address to the Freeholders of Middlesex, Assembled at Free Mason's Tavern, in Great Queen Street, Upon Monday the 20th of December 1779* (London: Dixwell, 1779), 10–13, 21; Albert Goodwin, *The Friends of the People: The English Democratic Movement in the Age of the French Revolution* (London: Hutchinson, 1979), 60–61.

Though the Middlesex radicals responded enthusiastically to Jebb's call for county associations, they did not ratify the proposal, believing provincial counties' appeals would carry greater weight than those from metropolitan radicals. Yorkshire, where organizing had begun, appeared an ideal leader. In 1775, opposing local manufacturers' support for the colonists' cause, Yorkshire's rural gentry (alongside their Birmingham and Nottingham peers) raised loyal petitions supporting the American war. York's city corporation politically split, only belatedly following suit in 1776.[11] British reversals in America by 1779, however, changed many minds. Though not as radical as Middlesex, refusing to endorse Jebb's more extreme proposals and keeping their association limited to "freeholders" with voting rights, Yorkshire organizers pursued a nationwide movement to bring pressure on authorities.

The movement became led by moderates without prior records of radical activity. Christopher Wyvill, an Anglican clergyman and influential member of the Yorkshire gentry, had not previously been a political leader: His only known agitation before 1779 was signing the "Feathers Tavern Petition" while studying at Cambridge, against requiring university students to swear to the Church of England's Articles of Faith.[12] Yet, increasingly dismayed with British politics, amid the American War Wyvill urged fellow electors to protest governmental corruption and pursue Parliamentary reform. Without soliciting local officeholders' support, Wyvill called a meeting of York's voters – "the Nobility, Gentlemen, Clergy, and Freeholders of this County" – for December 14, 1779, excusing not convening an official county meeting due to the High Sheriff's recent death. Its advertisement declared "the duty and interest of every independent person, in times of national distress especially, to exert his best endeavours," and carried signatures of 211 freeholders.[13] Yet the proposal was vague: it remained uncertain whether the movement would focus uniquely on economic reforms against waste and corruption or attempt a broader reformation of British politics.[14] Wyvill and fellow organizers sent freeholders handbills asking for pledges of support so they could "print your name with a larger list" in York's newspapers before the meeting.[15] Word of the movement spread. George III instructed North to take "every measure" to get government supporters to attend, "stop the violence of the Meeting," and derail opposition plans.[16]

---

[11] John M. Norris, *Shelburne and Reform* (New York: St. Martin's, 1963), 121–22; Champion, *American* 51; Bradley, *Popular*, 83.

[12] Christie, *Wilkes*, 70–71.

[13] Ibid., 75; *General Evening Post*, January 6, 1780; Christopher Wyvill, *Political Papers* (York: Blanchard, 1794), Vol. 1, 1.

[14] Norris, *Shelburne*, 123.

[15] Untitled handbill, Huntington Library Rare Books 281258.

[16] Herbert Butterfield, *George III, Lord North, and the People, 1779–1780* (London: Bell, 1949), 242.

At the first gathering, York's association appointed a sixty-one-member Correspondence Committee, borrowing the American model to demonstrate the movement's ambition to coordinate with each British county and all significant urban areas.[17] Though Wyvill claimed the movement was "totally divested of party," he initiated discussion of "the calamitous state of the nation, the immense extent of the present complicated war, the increase of the national debt, the stagnation of trade and manufactures, the decline of public credit, and the general fall of the land rents of the kingdom."[18] A national conversation became necessary to develop remedies for Britain's ills. Whig leaders Richmond and Rockingham, though only belatedly invited and told they would have no veto over decisions, attended and endorsed the proceedings. Richmond emphasized "drawing the Attention of the People to their own Concerns in Times of so much National Distress," while Rockingham complimented the Association's "anxious solicitude for the Welfare, Freedom, & Happiness of their Country."[19] With broad support and a model for expansion in a moment of intense political discontent, the new organization developed a potent cocktail for reform.

The Yorkshire movement assumed leadership over an increasingly national reform campaign. Their first meeting garnered attention in the capital with the *London Courant* predicting, "public spirit will be immediately followed by every independent borough, town, and county in England."[20] Wyvill publicized the associational format to "convince the World, that the proposed Mode of supporting the Petition, is as harmless and peaceable, as the Object of the Petition is desirable."[21] Yorkshire demanded the Commons "correct the gross abuses in the expenditure of public money," particularly "unmerited pensions" for those on George III's civil list. A December 30 resolution empowered the Correspondence Committee to "prepare a Plan of Association," to "restore the Freedom of Parliament."[22] The movement found Parliamentary supporters. Burke in early January highlighted association's useful innovations: given local petitions' failure to prevent the American War, if petitioners would "correspond with such other Counties, Cities, and Boroughs," future efforts could achieve unprecedented strength.[23] Corruption and bad policy augured the British political system's opening.

---

[17] BL ADD MS 27849 52.
[18] Butterfield, 202.
[19] Ibid.; York County Archives M 25 149 and 171; *General Evening Post*, January 6, 1780; O'Gorman, *Rise*, 410.
[20] *London Courant*, December 15, 1779; *General Evening Post*, January 6, 1780.; *Whitehall Evening Post*, January 6, 1780; *Gazetteer and New Daily Advertiser*, January 7, 1780.
[21] Alexander Hunter and Christopher Wyvill, *Original Letters* (York, 1780), 4–5.
[22] Wyvill, *Political*, Vol. 1, 4.
[23] Burke, *Correspondence*, Vol. 4, 179.

Canvassing commenced, targeting those with the greatest political influence. Ten copies of an anti-corruption petition circulated in Yorkshire with additional copies in London and Westminster pubs for electors residing in the capital. In all, nine thousand freeholders signed.[24] Only status restrictions kept the number that low: Hull wrote to York's leadership reporting many more had volunteered their support. Affixing only freeholders' names angered many, given the vagaries of voting rights even among the propertied.[25] The movement's leaders, seeking legitimacy, nevertheless confined petitioning to voters but began corresponding with committees in Manchester, Birmingham, Liverpool, and other growing, under-represented towns.[26] The *Leeds Mercury*, borrowing an American term, declared the committees aimed "to form a convention."[27] Options for expanding the movement readied.

The Association movement gained adherents across England. Middlesex responded on January 8 by declaring the "county of York has taken the lead in this business," before adopting a new petition denouncing the "expensive and unfortunate war," bringing "a large addition to the national debt, a heavy accumulation of taxes, a rapid decline of the trade, manufactures, and land-rents of the kingdom." Cumberland County approved a petition "similar to that of the county of York" on January 17. Over the following month, ten more areas petitioned likewise.[28] Some areas only partially subscribed, with four counties adopting petitions but declining to form committees, noting they "had produced such recent effects in America, and even in Ireland, that the very terms were suspicious."[29] Nevertheless, by February 10 the movement claimed thirty counties' and towns' support with the City of London (their meeting chaired by Wilkite and former Lord Mayor Brass Crosby) joining six days later.[30]

Beginning in February, a nascent Westminster Committee, working to mobilize Britain's largest urban voting constituency and attract prominent Parliamentary opposition stalwarts, vied to direct the movement. As a popular arm, the group sponsored a Westminster General Meeting, whose first gathering attracted three thousand. Wilkes addressed them, saying "pointed things against the people in power, and expressed his happiness at that spirit of Association" pervading the kingdom.[31] Fox next denounced Parliamentary "corruption," asserting "ten to one" MPs would with "a nod" from the king's

---

[24] Ibid., 7, 50; Clark, *British*, 146.

[25] YCA M 25 197.

[26] Wyvill, *Political*, Vol. 1, 71.

[27] *Leeds Mercury*, January 25, 1780.

[28] *London Courant*, January 8, 18, 20, 21, 25, 26, 30, and 31 and February 1, 2, and 5, 1780.

[29] Butterfield, 248.

[30] *Yorkshire Freeholder*, February 10, 1780.

[31] Wyvill, *Political*, Vol. 1, 91; Marc Baer, *The Rise and Fall of Radical Westminster, 1780–1890* (London: Palgrave, 2012), 3; Reid, *Charles*, 105.

ministers vote as instructed. Nothing but "popular exertion" by "legal and constitutional association" could save the system. The methods to right the political order, Fox continued, should be readapted from abroad: "Your brethren in America and Ireland show you how to act when bad men force you to feel. Are we not born from the same original?"[32] Following lengthy applause, those assembled approved a "NATIONAL ASSOCIATION, on constitutional grounds."[33] With Fox's faction vying to topple North's ministry, reformists might win over the Commons.[34]

Though working to develop consensus, the movement received partisan responses from Parliamentary conservatives. Prime Minister North in February claimed the movement would wind up "raising insurrections, and producing a rebellion."[35] Many considered the petitions partisan devices due to the Parliamentary figures participating.[36] Amid the American War and Irish uncertainty, British associators needed to avoid inflaming opponents' worst impressions. Recent concessions in Ireland emboldened British reformers with Fox mockingly asking Parliament on February 8, "Is there one law for the associations in Ireland, and another for those of England?"[37] Similar methods appeared useful for each movement. Fox in his inaugural Westminster Committee address confronted claims that "petitions lead to anarchy and confusion," arguing they could "prevent every sort of public mischief" by rallying adherents.[38] As associations multiplied across the British Isles, pressure grew on elites to consider concessions.

Burke, meanwhile, cultivated a moderate faction between North and Fox's coalitions: embracing reform in principle, but limiting his program to minor economic measures reducing royal patronage. For Burke, preserving the careful British system of checks and balances meant reforming its worst abuses to avoid more drastic changes. "Early reformations are amicable arrangements with a friend in power," he considered, "late reformations are terms imposed upon a conquered enemy." On February 11, Burke brought a bill for "the suppression of sundry useless, expensive, and inconvenient" positions, arguing that reducing the king's purse would increase Parliamentary autonomy and restore balance between government branches.[39] Former Wilkes partisan

---

[32] Ralph Fell, *Memoirs of the Public Life of the Late Rt. Hon. Charles James Fox* (London: Hughes, 1808), Vol. 1, 110, 117.

[33] *London Courant*, February 4, 1780.

[34] John Derry, *English Politics and the American Revolution* (New York: St. Martin's Press, 1976), 188.

[35] *London Courant*, February 2, 1780.

[36] Alan Valentine, *Lord North* (Norman: University of Oklahoma Press, 1967), Vol. 2, 194.

[37] Bromwich, *Intellectual*, 349.

[38] Fell, *Memoirs*, 113.

[39] Russell Kirk, *Edmund Burke: A Genius Reconsidered* (Peru, IL: Sugden, 1988), 96; Bourke, *Empire*, 7.

Barré seconded Burke's proposal, and even North endorsed "any plan" for "reducing the public expence."[40] Conservatives, however, reversed their position before late-March's final debates, assailing Burke for attempting to eliminate offices without proof of corruption. After the House removed that clause via amendment, Burke declared his "indifference" to the rest.[41] A moderated version passed, giving Parliament supervisory powers over royal expenditures – thus limiting the king's power to engage in unseen bribery – but few expected "reformation" to end there.[42]

Partisans clothed the new organizations in British traditions of free speech, debate, and associational life. Alongside the association network grew a proliferating number of debating clubs, particularly in the capital – increasing from seven to thirty-three over 1779 and 1780 with some new venues seating 400–1,200.[43] The Westminster Forum's early February debate, "Are the present county meetings likely to produce any salutary effects?" asserted such gatherings underlay British liberty's greatest achievements: "it was an association, which this kingdom owes its *magna charta*; it was *an association* which expelled the tyrannical bigot, Janus, and brought about the *glorious Revolution*."[44] Debating topics included, "Ought the right of electing Representatives to serve in Parliament to depend on the property, or to be considered as the personal privilege of every Englishman?" and "Is it true, that the people of Ireland have grounded their claims upon the example and conduct of America?" Universal manhood suffrage and the right of resistance gained discussion. When audiences voted a winner, radicals typically triumphed.[45] The right to associate became the guarantor of liberty.

In agitating for "Parliamentary reform," a phrase the associators made a popular slogan, the movement's purview appeared vast.[46] Wyvill called for debate on potential reforms instead of any specific program, asking in February for "honest proposals from whatever quarter they may come, supported with decency and temper ... conformable to law and the constitution."[47] Discussion could develop stronger arguments for change. In March, Westminster's committee pledged, "to enter into every question"

---

[40] APS Benjamin Vaughan Papers, Mss.B.V46p; *London Courant*, February 11, 1780.

[41] *Parliamentary History*, Vol. 21, 310.

[42] Kirk, *Edmund*, 98.

[43] Donna T. Andrew, "Popular Culture and Public Debate: London 1780," *Historical Journal* 39, no. 2 (1996), 405.

[44] *London Courant*, February 5, 1780.

[45] Andrew, "Popular," 414–15.

[46] Joanna Innes, "'Reform' in English Public Life: The Functions of a Word," in Arthur Burns and Innes, eds. *Rethinking the Age of Reform: Britain 1780–1850* (Cambridge: Cambridge University Press, 2007) 71–97.

[47] *General Evening Post*, February 17, 1780.

relating to the "Independency of Parliament," including representation.[48] The British governing system fell into question.

National coordination, however, remained difficult to achieve. The London common meeting in March decided to "not recommend a Plan of Association in any special form," instead encouraging local branches to take the most pragmatically useful steps.[49] Abolitionist and reform theorist Sharp distributed "large bundles of Copies" of his works to county committees, finding most imprecise in their program but receptive to new ideas.[50] Collective deliberation itself appeared most important: Wyvill argued the British associations' breadth in the eighteenth century, with groups for anything from "the detection of swindlers" to "the preservation of game," permitted organizations for "important" measures. Wyvill explained the new movement would not consist of armed militias with the association refusing to take "arms in support of our laws and liberties," like their American and Irish contemporaries.[51] Peaceful debate became the weapon, yet the organization lacked its paramilitary counterparts' discipline. The Association Movement never developed a regularized affiliate model, limiting the exchanges that made comparable movements abroad so successful.

The movement organized a national congress from thirteen English counties and five towns at a Westminster tavern on March 11–20. While evoking America's Continental Congress, the association sought to allay conservatives' fears, with Fox cautioning delegates to "avoid every word that has been used in the commotions in America," while employing similar techniques.[52] Those assembled crafted a "general union" and common platform. With Wyvill presiding, the meeting agreed on a "plan of political reformation," incorporating economic and structural changes, including further financial reforms to establish the Commons' independence from royal influence, make representation more equal, and shorten legislative terms. Adherents asked no support be lent to Parliamentary candidates not advocating their reforms and recommended petitioning bodies form a "general association" until attainment.[53] The movement refused party compromise. Despite the Westminster Committee's influence, Wyvill successfully motioned to exclude Members of Parliament from being deputies.[54] Only "a vigorous, compacted, and unshaken union of all independent men throughout the Kingdom," they resolved, could triumph.[55]

[48] *London Courant*, March 17, 1780.
[49] Wyvill, *Political*, Vol. 1, 123.
[50] Gloucestershire Record Office, D 3549 13/1/C1.
[51] Wyvill, *Political*, Vol. 1, 151.
[52] Phillips, "Edmund Burke," 271.
[53] Wyvill, *Political*, Vol. 1, 111 and 126–27; *London Courant*, March 22, 1780.
[54] Fox, *Memorials*, Vol. 1, 242.
[55] *Whitehall Evening Post*, March 21, 1780.

Movement branches developed strikingly pro-American rhetoric. Cambridge's committee, closely following recent American examples, asserted a "natural right to life, liberty and property," while considering British government "a mutual contract between the governors and the governed," and the people's consent the "only worthy end of civil government." Yorkshire's meeting declared "an offensive war in America" to threaten "the final ruin of the British Empire."[56] Though corruption remained the Association movement's largest grievance, the war seemingly resulted from the government's bad intentions and despotic methods.

The Commons resolved that real problems existed with the governing system. On April 6, Westminster's Committee held a public meeting attracting a "prodigious concourse" with Fox eliciting cheers as he attacked corrupt royal influence, while calling for reformed representation and annual parliaments.[57] Allies presented approximately forty petitions to Parliament that afternoon, as "Vast parchments subscribed by thousands of names, were heaped upon the table."[58] MP John Dunning introduced a resolution, in movement language, "that the influence of the Crown has increased, is increasing, and ought to be diminished." North objected, claiming opponents were "pursuing measures calculated to overturn the constitution" and undertake radical reform.[59] Nevertheless, the motion passed 233–215. A second resolution, to provide "immediate and effectual redress of the abuses complained of in the petitions," gained unanimous approval.[60] A potential political reformation approached, though its form remained uncertain.

Attempts to obtain "economical reforms" remained stymied by the British aristocracy and monarchy. Dunning on April 10 motioned to announce all royal pensions and salaries at each Parliamentary session's beginning. The measure passed the Commons unanimously, while a more contentious proposal barring royal beneficiaries from retaining Parliamentary seats narrowly won approval 215–213. The House of Lords quickly defeated the second bill, however, while ignoring the first. Dunning on April 24 introduced a contentious new motion requesting the king not to dissolve or prorogue Parliament "until proper measures have been taken to diminish the influence and correct the other abuses" the petitions described. With conservatives arguing the April 6 resolution referred to no specific measures, however, the motion lost by fifty-one votes. George III beseeched supporters "to resist what no one can deny is a plan of changing the constitution," after which support

[56] Wyvill, *Political*, Vol. 1, 135, 148.

[57] *Gazetteer*, April 7, 1780.

[58] Reid, *Charles*, 108.

[59] *General Evening Post*, April 6, 1780.

[60] Boyd Hilton, *A Mad, Bad and Dangerous People? England 1783–1846* (Oxford: Oxford University Press, 2006), 41; Christie, *The End of North's Ministry, 1780–1782* (London: Macmillan, 1958), 21.

evaporated.[61] The stasis resulting from the British system's checks-and-balances risked radicalizing the reform movement.

As moderates and radicals argued over how to respond to reversals, the reform movement's divisions grew apparent. Leeds' committee wrote to York's in April complaining of "the great difficulty of drawing up resolutions that do not run too far into Party," while asking they avoid the "absurd prejudices" of their opponents.[62] Some pushed the movement to go further: Sharp wrote angrily about the Yorkshire Committee's moderating their demands to triennial Parliaments (better than the seven-year system, but not the annual elections many desired), believing it "falls far short of the true spirit & ancient legal Constitution for representation" and the "People's unalienable Rights."[63] The lack of unity troubled an unstable movement.

Behind the growing petition wave, the association motivated the Commons to pursue the question of Parliamentary Reform. More than forty constituencies, including the majority of English counties, wrote to Parliament. While Wyvill conspicuously avoided party affiliation, Rockingham's Whig faction adopted the cause.[64] Rockingham endorsed "the idea of equitable reform, in regard to what are called rotten boroughs" and pursued concrete plans, believing otherwise "confusion and disagreement will ensue" from the ideas circulating.[65] Support for reform (in principle) coalesced.

The association, however, overlapped with a rapidly growing Protestant Association, which linked encroaching governmental authoritarianism with growing toleration of (and alleged alliance with) their Catholic subjects. Parliament passed a Catholic Relief Act in 1778, which removed restrictions on Catholic land ownership, property inheritance, and army service in Britain (while the Irish Parliament passed an identical measure later that year). Originally introduced by association stalwart George Saville, the legislation won reformers' support.[66] Whereas Wyvill began organizing among Yorkshire's elite, Lord George Gordon – a former New York resident who resigned a naval commission to protest the American War – went outside usual political channels to cultivate public backing. Across late 1778, eighty-five Scottish locals subscribed to a common Society of Friends to the Protestant Interest, collecting more than twenty thousand signatures. Anti-Catholic riots

---

[61] Brown, *Chathamites*, 307–10.

[62] YCA M 25 269.

[63] GRO D 3549 13/1/AI.

[64] Valentine, *Lord North*, Vol. 2, 196; Christie, *Wilkes*, 75.

[65] Albemarle, *Memoirs*, 399–400.

[66] Thomas Holcroft, *A Plain and Succinct Narrative of the Late Riots and Disturbances in the Cities of London and Westminster and in the Borough of Southwark* (London: Fielding and Walker, 1780), 16.

erupted in February 1779 in Glasgow and Edinburgh.[67] Turning attention to England, Gordon organized a petition campaign, opening his house each day and placing copies in several pubs for all "Protestants" to sign. Declaring he would not present the petitions without at least twenty thousand more English signatures, Gordon's movement collected forty-four thousand for repeal in the London region alone.[68] Mass mobilization, Gordon demonstrated, did not need to follow Whig principles of tolerance and inclusion; indeed, religious and ethnic divisions (particularly with Catholicism considered in league with despotism) were more easily invoked to mobilize common Britons than liberal reform principles.

Popular anti-Catholicism's ranks appeared virtually inexhaustible and presented legislators with a harrowing vision of a mobilized populace's potential. Encouraging provincial committees of correspondence's formation, exhorting "All the true friends of Great Britain, and of Civil and Religious Liberty" to "unite in support of the Protestant interest," Gordon delayed presenting the Protestant Association's petition several weeks, "to give time for similar petitions from other parts of England, Wales and Scotland," which arrived bearing tens of thousands of signatures.[69] Brimming with confidence, Gordon called a mass meeting at St. George's Fields on June 2 (the site of violence against Wilkes supporters in 1768), as "no hall in London can contain forty-thousand men." From there, perhaps sixty thousand marched on Parliament. As legislators arrived, protesters pulled the carriages of supporters (or those they hoped would be), while confronting North, his loyal supporters, and others favoring Catholic relief. A deputation entered the Commons, presenting the vast signed parchment that Gordon boasted at full length "would reach from Buckingham house to Whitehall."[70]

Amid the day's agitation, Richmond – pulled to the House of Lords by protesters – unadvisedly introduced the most comprehensive call yet for Parliamentary reform. Moving beyond the Association movement's measures, he proposed 558 identically sized districts across Britain with all adult males

[67] Tombs, *English*, 359; Richard Bourke, *Empire & Revolution: The Political Life of Edmund Burke* (Princeton: Princeton University Press, 2015), 413–14; William Mathieson, *The Awakening of Scotland: A History from 1747 to 1797* (Glasgow: Maclehose, 1910), 79.

[68] Rogers, "The Gordon Riots and the Politics of War," in *The Gordon Riots: Politics, Culture and Insurrection in Late Eighteenth-Century Britain*, Ian Haywood and John Seed, eds. (Cambridge: Cambridge University Press, 2012), 28; Mark Knights, "The 1780 Protestant Petitions and the Culture of Petitioning," ibid., 46.

[69] *London Courant*, March 6, 1780; *London Evening Post*, May 11, 1780; Adrian Randall, *Riotous Assemblies: Popular Protest in Hanoverian England* (Oxford: Oxford University Press, 2006), 200; Nigel Yates, *Eighteenth-Century Britain: Religion and Politics, 1714–1815* (London: Pearson, 2008), 42.

[70] *Whitehall Evening Post*, June 3, 1780; Bourke, *Empire*, 417; Rogers, "Gordon Riots," 29.

voting each June for annual Parliaments.[71] Promising "equal representation for the people in the House of Commons," Richmond declared the motion would "introduce a radical Reformation in the great legislative Parts of the constitution."[72] Gordon's movement saw no contradiction between religious exclusivism and expanded representation for common (Protestant) citizens, which many believed to further Reformation and Glorious Revolution principles. The Lords, however, refused to vote on any measures.

The anti-Catholic upsurge sparked the Gordon Riots, the most serious disturbances to convulse eighteenth-century London. Almost simultaneously with Richmond's measure, in the Commons chamber Gordon demanded the Relief Act's repeal. When the Commons instead voted 192–6 to adjourn, protesters began wreaking havoc. Gordon supporters attacked several Members of Parliament who refused to shout "No Popery!" on command. Despite Wilkes declaring martial law and leading militiamen against the rioters, disturbances widened. Gordon's partisans attacked symbols of government, with Newgate Prison set aflame and the Bank of England threatened, while targeting Catholics and prominent reformers' property – the Anglican Archbishop of York's residence included.[73] Legislators feared for their property and lives throughout the five-day uprising. Anti-reformers could have found no better example of how petitions from the "people" possessed no necessary wisdom and popular movements could incite mass violence. "London mob" behavior horrified elites, forfeiting their traditional influence in British politics.[74]

The riots discredited the Protestant Association in British politics but the Association Movement could not be as easily denounced in turn. Yorkshire associators distanced themselves from the Gordon excesses, blaming the government for letting the protests escalate. Fox derided the riots as "a most fortunate circumstance for ministers."[75] The Association Movement's orderliness, mobilized through peaceful meetings and reasoned appeals, contrasted markedly with the less responsible commotions likely to spread should respectable combinations be ignored.

Nevertheless, the Gordon Riots slowed the association's momentum, while opinions diverged on the movement's rightful future. Though the disturbances "cast a disgrace, however unjust, on the very name of Associations, for the present," one commentator noted in August, with their grievances still

---

[71] Alison Gilbert Olson, *The Radical Duke: The Career and Correspondence of Charles Lennox, Third Duke of Richmond* (Oxford: Oxford University Press, 1961), 48.

[72] *Public Advertiser*, June 3, 1780; *St. James's Chronicle*, June 1, 1780.

[73] Burke, *Correspondence*, Vol. 4, 246; Holcroft, *Plain*, 20; Palmer, *Age*, Vol. 1, 300.

[74] Robert Shoemaker, *The London Mob: Violence and Disorder in Eighteenth-Century England* (London: Hambledon, 2004), 149.

[75] L. G. Mitchell, *Charles James Fox* (Oxford: Oxford University Press, 1992), 37.

unaddressed the campaign rebounded by the year's end.[76] Given the Parliamentary stasis, many believed real reform would only advance through heightening pressure. Radical threats remained: the *Public Ledger* asserted there "will never be any effectual reformation in this country brought about by lordlings." Rather, "a committee of the people with musquets in their hands and spirit in their hearts, are the only means to redress public grievances." Both America and Ireland drew their strength though "associations of the PEOPLE."[77] Closing moderate reform options could lead to radicalization.

Profiting from the reaction against popular excesses, George III called a Parliamentary election in fall 1780, a year ahead of schedule. Recent military news from America favored the British, and the crown hoped the Gordon Riots would reenergize conservatives. Authorities kept the contest as closed as possible, with election day a guarded secret until the legally specified time. By then, the First Lord of the Treasury had devised a patronage and bribery plan (projecting £61,763), largely focused on small Parliamentary districts, to ensure Lord North's supporters a favorable majority. Though the Rockinghams and several other opposition Whig factions made a good showing, giving the North ministry a narrower victory than in 1774, the outcome was little in doubt. Radicals (despite the Gordon Riots reaction) did well in open metropolitan contests but failed to make sufficient inroads into smaller districts.[78] No reform consensus existed among incoming Members of Parliament.

Despite the previous year's reversals, Wyvill's association made a new push for Parliamentary reform in 1781. With frustration over the American War increasing, political volatility grew. Sharp noted "continual depredations on our very Coasts" from France and Spain's larger combined navy, with trade plummeting.[79] A January address from Yorkshire beseeched members to petition anew for reform. The association deputized Wyvill to London to "communicate with the delegates of the other petitioning or associating bodies" on strategy.[80] A national meeting of association representatives convened at London's Guildhall on March 3. Though seeking to bring "the full Weight and Authority of the whole Collective Body" upon Parliament, the assembly ended in acrimony; Westminster demanded annual Parliaments, while Yorkshire desired triennial elections.[81] Amid multitudinous proposals, consensus continued to elude the reform movement.

---

[76] LC Silas Deane Papers, 8B reel 5 303–97.

[77] *Public Ledger*, December 16, 1780.

[78] Christie, *End*, 45, 69, 102; Rogers, "Gordon Riots," 38–39.

[79] GRO D 3549 13/1/C1.

[80] *An Address from the Committee of Association of the County of York, to the Electors of Great-Britain.* (York: Blanchard, 1781), 7; *London Courant*, January 8, 1781.

[81] *St. James's Chronicle*, March 3, 1781.

With details unresolved, associators brought petitions to Parliament in April 1781, only to find their organizations' legitimacy questioned. MP Thomas Coke attacked the unprecedented associations as "dangerous and unconstitutional." Fox responded that no law prevented such gatherings.[82] Parliamentary hostility surprised association backers, as committee meetings and petition-signings reported little local opposition.[83] Yet the implication, alongside Gordon Riot memories, persisted. Encountering reaction from British elites, no Parliamentary reforms followed.

The Yorkshire Committee's next missive in October frustratingly tried to explain how a broad-based movement resulted in "repeated rejection of a National Petition by their own Representatives." Poor coordination between petitioning bodies drew blame: inability to maintain pressure led reformers into "acting without steadiness, without concert," compared to the "discipline of the Mercenaries of the Crown."[84] Still, the committee did not enact measures to increase uniformity. Moderate reform efforts failed to sufficiently pressure entrenched powers into renouncing their spoils.

The Society for Constitutional Information and Cross-Movement Coordinating

While the association campaigns sought to develop a moderate consensus for Parliamentary reform, more radical bodies concurrently advanced. From the Westminster Committee's ranks arose John Cartwright's Society for Constitutional Information (SCI), bringing dissidents from the Wilkes movement together with American supporters, religious rights advocates, and antislavery activists. The society formed a coterie of radical intellectuals dedicated to advancing ideals of democratization, human rights, and associational power that could be applied to many movements, while diffusing such knowledge across the British nation.

Cartwright, a former naval officer who served in the Seven Years' War, took a radical turn during the American crisis in 1774, publishing *American Independence the Glory and Interest of Britain*. Using techniques Thomas Paine soon employed in *Common Sense*, Cartwright asserted his arguments sprung from "the most well-known principles of the English Constitution," together with "plain maxims of the law of nature and the clearest doctrines of Christianity" even a "plain man" could understand. Asserting that Americans advanced "the principles of freedom," he argued their movement presaged the

---

[82] *Parliamentary History*, Vol. 22, 95–97.

[83] Wyvill, *Political*, Vol. 1, 351.

[84] *A Second Address from the Committee of Association of the County of York, to the Electors of the Counties, Cities, and Boroughs within the Kingdom of Great Britain* (York: Blanchard, 1781), 7–8.

"liberty of mankind." If emerging from English traditions, he prophesized future universal rights: "The child of a slave is as free-born, according to the law of nature, as he who could trace his ancestry up to the creation."[85] Cartwright integrated himself into elite opposition circles, corresponding with Burke. Nevertheless, still a Nottingham militia major and fearful of losing his position, he published his first pamphlets anonymously.[86]

As American fighting escalated, the fledgling nation increasingly presented a model to Britain. In *Take Your Choice*, published in 1776 and reprinted under his own name in 1780, Cartwright proposed a "grand national association for the restoration of the constitution." The organization would undertake "a reformation" of Parliament, making the legislature annually elected, equally districted, and elected by all males over eighteen. Only through such a radical shift, he argued, could a system be changed which had seen "all ministers and all Parliaments" become "inexcusably guilty" of corruption. Parliament had become "proverbial for making war without wisdom, and peace without policy." Only by holding representatives regularly accountable to their constituents, superseding common modes of electoral corruption by increasing eligible voters, could hope exist for more virtuous public policy. Cartwright asserted, "liberty, like learning, is best preserved by its being widely diffused throughout society."[87] The imperial crisis demanded real changes, and popular associations appeared the first concrete step toward improving government.

Cartwright enthusiastically joined the Association Movement, helping radicalize its demands. He contributed to a Nottingham petition supporting Wyvill's movement in February 1780, became a delegate to the national General Meeting in March, and joined Fox's Westminster Committee. The committee quickly radicalized, endorsing proposals for universal male suffrage for taxpayers, annual parliaments, equal electoral districts, secret balloting, and abolishing property qualifications for candidates. Nowhere in Europe possessed such extensive liberties. In early April 1780, a demonstration featuring Fox, Jebb, Cartwright, and an estimated three thousand more marched from the King's Arms Tavern to Parliament under a banner reading "Annual Parliaments and equal Representation."[88] Neither Wilkes's populist demagoguery nor Wyvill's piecemeal changes appeared adequate for addressing systemic British problems. Positioning themselves on the reform movement's

---

[85] John Cartwright, *American Independence the Glory and Interest of Britain* (London: Woodfall, 1774), 6–8.
[86] Bradley, *Religion*, 160; Cartwright, *The Life and Correspondence of Major Cartwright* (New York: AMS Press, 1969), Vol. 1, 53.
[87] Cartwright, *Take Your Choice!* (London: Almon, 1776), ix, xii, xx, 62, 89.
[88] *Morning Chronicle*, April 6, 1780; Butterfield, *George III*, 277; *St. James's Chronicle*, March 4, 1780.

radical cusp, the Westminster Committee and Society for Constitutional Information hoped to ride a rising wave of domestic discontent.

Building from the Westminster Committee's growing radicalness, Cartwright in 1780 published *The People's Barrier against Undue Influence and Corruption*, celebrating recent reformist advances, but calling for radical principles' full implementation. Major changes in political consciousness had already occurred: "three years ago," Cartwright wrote, the "idea of reforming the House of Commons was then treated as a ridiculous project."[89] Now, a "new and irresistible party" developed. Critical of association committee members, Cartwright denounced excessive moderation, which he feared could spoil the movement, believing no thinking person could "approve of any dregs being left" of old corruption.[90] Annual parliaments, to increase political accountability, became Cartwright's defining issue.

Uncertain of the Westminster Committee's future, Cartwright formed the Society for Constitutional Information in April 1780, bringing together prominent radicals from several social movements: Richmond and Horne Tooke from Parliamentary reform; Sharp, the most prominent antislavery activist; and the leading intellectual promoting full civil rights for Protestant Dissenters, Richard Price. All opposed deploying military forces to America and demanded reform in British politics. The SCI's founding documents declared "annual parliaments are the undoubted right of the people of England," considering the current seven-year system "subversive of the constitution."[91] The new organization sought to spread knowledge of liberty by distributing free tracts among Britain's broad reading public. "To diffuse this knowledge universally throughout the realm, to circulate it through every village and hamlet, and even to introduce it to the humble dwelling of the cottager, is the wish and hope of this society," the manifesto declared.[92] They published classic political, historical, and philosophical works alongside new reformist writings from their members, each of whom paid a guinea a year to participate.

Cartwright entreated prominent activists to participate in ways reflecting their broader humanitarian sentiments. In 1775, just two years after arguing the Somerset Case, which established the precedent of freeing slaves who reached the British Isles, Sharp wrote the radically reformist *Declaration of*

---

[89] Cartwright, *The People's Barrier against Undue Influence and Corruption* (London, 1780), iii.

[90] Cartwright, *An Address to the Gentlemen, forming the several Committees of the associated Counties, Cities, and Towns, for supporting the Petitions for Redress of Grievances, and against the Unconstitutional Influence of the Crown over Parliament* (London, 1780), i, v, xvi.

[91] Cartwright, *Life*, Vol. 1, 133.

[92] *An Address to the Public from the Society for Constitutional Information* (London, 1780), 2.

the People's Natural Right to a Share in the Legislature, arguing that as all are "equally free by the laws of nature," denying representation to any British subject constituted "the most fragrant and stimulating injustice."[93] Sharp sought "Home Rule" through independent legislatures for both the United States and Ireland.[94] Cartwright in late 1779 suggested to Sharp that to avoid the fate of "wretched Negroes in an African market," British opinion needed to turn against Parliamentary factions abridging "the very essence of freedom," asking him to use abolitionist connections to place Parliamentary reform articles in newspapers.[95] Though abolitionists previously presented their cause as a moral campaign distinct from political party, Sharp grew so disaffected with the British political establishment that he joined the society. Parliamentary reform could open the political path toward abolitionism.

Price, a leading advocate for Protestant Dissenter civil rights (see Chapter 6), embraced the broader American and reform causes. A long-time Franklin associate and neighbor of Burgh at Newington Green outside London, in early 1776, Price published *Observations on the Nature of Civil Liberty*, declaring government "the creature of the people."[96] Associating American Revolutionary politics with British Protestant Dissenters' striving for freedom of conscience, he predicted American advances presaged British reforms, asserting "an important revolution in the affairs of this kingdom seems to be approaching."[97] The pamphlet became a bestseller with fourteen editions and sixty thousand copies printed in London alone that year.[98] Nevertheless, Price warned Cartwright in April, "it would not be easy to get any number of great men" to support America, "till some calamity comes that shall make us feel more, and awaken us more to reflection."[99] By 1780, however, he pursued active organizing.

Cartwright found a ready Parliamentary ally in Richmond. Prior to the war, Richmond affiliated with the Rockingham Whigs (taking a leadership role alongside Rockingham and Burke). But thereafter, Richmond distanced himself, desiring more thorough reform. Cartwright had sent *Take Your Choice* to leading Parliamentary figures, and in 1776 Richmond met with the reformer, sparking a growing friendship.[100] Richmond's June 3, 1780 bill, despite its

---

[93] Granville Sharp, *A Declaration of the People's Right to a Share in the Legislature: Which is the Fundamental Principle of the British Constitution of State* (London: White, 1775), 1.

[94] Toohey, *Liberty*, 53–63.

[95] GRO D 3549 13–1-C26.

[96] Richard Price, *Observations on the Nature of Civil Liberty, the Principles of Government, and the Justice and Policy of the War with America* (London: Cadell, 1776), 1; Toohey, *Liberty*, 27.

[97] Price, *Observations*, 109.

[98] Brown, *Chathamites*, 148.

[99] Price, *Correspondence*, Vol. 1, 245.

[100] Olson, *Radical*, 14–47, 53.

disastrous pairing with Gordon's Protestant Association petition, represented SCI demands for annual parliaments and universal suffrage. While Richmond's influence faded, his efforts demonstrated the plausibility of bringing radical reform measures before Parliament.

In Horne (newly taking the name John Horne Tooke), Cartwright allied with the co-organizer of the Society of Supporters of the Bill of Rights and breakaway Constitutional Society. Though both groups floundered by the mid-1770s, and Horne served a yearlong prison sentence in 1777–1778 for sending aid to the enemy and libel against British soldiers in America, the well-connected radical participated in the SCI thereafter. In 1780, Horne Tooke and Price cowrote a pamphlet denouncing government malfeasance and corruption through royal patronage. Only through obliterating "the corrupt influence of the crown," they concluded, could the nation recover.[101] In a 1782 reform pamphlet, Horne Tooke reflected the "VIRTUAL voice of the people of England resembles too nearly the VIRTUAL representations of the people of America," considering Britain "at the eve of a peaceful revolution" itself.[102] The British regime's corruption, together with America's example and reformers' efforts, could incite major changes.

Though more radical than the Association movement, Cartwright retained warm relations with principal moderate reformers. Wyvill himself became a Society for Constitutional Information member. In 1781, the Yorkshire reformer sent Cartwright his latest pamphlet, writing that if it met his approval, little could bring him "higher satisfaction, or a better hope of success."[103] Cartwright indulged him: gradual change remained attractive if prospects for immediate change seemed remote.

The Society for Constitutional Information did not attempt to become an independent club movement but remained an intelligentsia working to spark wider agitation. The society held only a few meetings, focusing on disseminating printed materials, and the organization engaged in little recruiting beyond prominent intellectuals and political figures. After a year, the society had only forty-nine members.[104] Burke plausibly questioned, "Whether the books so charitably circulated" were "ever as

[101] John Horne Tooke and Richard Price, *Facts: Addressed to the Landholders, Stockholders, Merchants, Farmers, Manufacturers, Tradesmen, Proprietors of Every Description, and Generally to All the Subjects of Great Britain and Ireland* (London; Johnson, 1780), 21, 115.

[102] Tooke, *A Letter on Parliamentary Reform: Containing the Sketch of a Plan* (London: Ridgway, 1782), 2, 6.

[103] Cartwright, *Life*, Vol. 1, 142.

[104] Veitch, *Genesis*, 74; John W. Osborne, *John Cartwright* (Cambridge: Cambridge University Press, 1972), 25; Cartwright, *Life*, 134–35.

charitably read" as intended.[105] Yet there would be no difficulty tracing their impact on movements to follow.

With the Association movement declining, the Society for Constitutional Information further radicalized. In 1782, they endorsed all adult males' active participation in government, regardless of economic standing. In catechism-style response to why a humble farmer should "sign or set marks" on petitions rather than "leave what we cannot understand to King and Parliament," the pamphlet assured, "You comprehend more than you can possibly imagine." Associational life could represent society itself: "Did it ever occur to you," the author asked, "every state or nation was only a great *club*?" Why, then, did the British nation not run via simple rules, in which the "opinion of the greater number, as in our village-clubs, must be taken and prevail"?[106] Universal participation – advancing with the political education the society spread – could in time predominate.

Even as the SCI's first efforts produced few direct results, its prominent members worked to advance several major causes. British political, religious, and humanitarian reform movements, along with sister movements in America, Ireland, and France, profited from their writings. Movement leaders worked together, asserting a rising wave of freedom could lift all their efforts. Moderate reform's legislative failures in Britain across the American War era opened the way for thinkers advocating more radical possibilities.

Pitt the Younger and the Promise of Reform

Following Britain's 1781 defeat at Yorktown, hopes that they could win the war and retain America (which enabled North's 1780 election victory) evaporated. Regime change abroad became unavoidable, and systemic alterations at home increasingly possible. MP Gilbert Elliot considered that as the "grand principle of distinction and separation between parties (the American dispute) is now removed," new political combinations became achievable.[107] After news of Cornwallis's surrender arrived in December 1781, the North ministry's popularity cratered, and governmental obstinacy in continuing the war threatened the remaining empire. Twice in March 1782, the government survived no-confidence votes in the Commons by margins of only ten and nine. North, fearing impending removal, resigned. Parliamentary opponents Rockingham and Fox (two of the war's most vocal opponents) "stormed the closet" to form

---

[105] Edmund Burke, *Reflections on the Revolution in France, and on the Proceedings of Certain Societies in London Relative to that Event* (London: Dodsley, 1790), 3.
[106] *The Principles of Government, in a Dialogue between a Scholar and a Peasant. Written by a Member of the Society for Constitutional Information* (London, 1782), 304.
[107] Gilbert Elliot, *Life and Letters of Sir Gilbert Elliot* (London: Longmans, 1874), Vol. 1, 75.

a ministry without George III's initial assent.[108] Given the new ministers' prominence on the Westminster Committee, peace augured hopes for reform.

Twenty-three-year-old William Pitt the Younger, elected to Parliament the previous year, aimed to combine the Association Movement's efforts with goodwill from his father's unaccomplished reform agenda to reintroduce such legislation in 1782. Moderate and radical reformers – Wyvill caucusing with Jebb, Price, Horne Tooke, and other leaders within and outside the Society for Constitutional Information – worked together for practical reform.[109] Before the Commons May 7, Pitt declared Parliament's composition "had at all times excited the regard of men the most enlightened," and as current abuses threated "totally to destroy the most beautiful fabric of government in the world," he urged "moderate reform of the errors which had intruded themselves into the constitution." Pitt proposed a Parliamentary committee to consider the abolition of rotten boroughs, extension of voting rights, and more frequent elections. He asserted reform enjoyed "a spirit of unanimity in every part of the kingdom," making "the present day the fittest for undertaking this great task."[110] Parliament rebuked Pitt, however, with the committee motion losing by 141–161. The reversal, the *Morning Post* reported, "staggered their friends" with reformers' optimism not matched by parliamentary moderates.[111]

Following the narrow loss, with the prospect of real changes still tangible, many radicals moderated their messages to work with Pitt. A Westminster Committee deputation including Cartwright congratulated Pitt on his recent efforts. The May 7 vote appeared only an opening salvo, and many expected MPs to feel greater pressure from reform organizations. Reformist MPs met on radical grounds at the Thatched House Tavern, encouraging activists to gather new petitions.[112] Despite the distance of Pitt's proposals from Cartwright's own, he joined other SCI committee members in professing their hopes Pitt would continue working toward "a reform essentially necessary to the independence of Parliament, and the liberty of the People."[113] Richmond similarly wrote to Rockingham May 11, "unless some essential parliamentary reform takes place, all we do will be undone."[114] The opportunity to effect pragmatic changes beckoned but risked becoming ephemeral.

---

[108] Christie, *End*, xiii, 299; Hilton, *Mad*, 39.

[109] Bewley, *Gentleman*, 76.

[110] *Parliamentary History*, Vol. 22, 1416–17; *London Chronicle*, May 7, 1782.

[111] *Morning Post*, May 9, 1782; William Hague, *William Pitt the Younger* (New York: Knopf, 2005), 80.

[112] William Pitt, *The Speeches of the Honourable William Pitt in the House of Commons* (London: Longman, 1806), Vol. 1, 26–33; Bewley, *Gentleman*, 77.

[113] *London Courant*, May 10, 1782.

[114] Albemarle, *Memoirs*, Vol. 2, 482.

Scotland, quiet during preceding campaigns, mobilized its own distinct movement, calling for "Burgh Reform." Scotland's limited franchise had been further impaired by barons granting land trusts for their allies to create new (partisan) voters, swinging municipal and Parliamentary elections for their chosen candidates. Though a long-standing practice, agitation elsewhere led many to seek redress. By the decade's turn, one Scottish doctor declared, "the subject not only engaged the attention of public bodies of men, but became a principal object of conversation in every company, and often excited angry debates which impaired the pleasures of social life, and weakened the confidence of friendship."[115] Though initially separate from the Association movement, by 1782 multiple branches corresponded with Wyvill. In August, twenty-three counties' delegates attended a convention in Edinburgh, endorsing regularized representation. Responding to the growing agitation, Yorkshire's Committee in November sent a circular to towns across Scotland seeking joint reform agitation.[116] An allied movement now formed across Britain.

Reform agitation led to retrenchment among conservatives who, fearing for their own positions, opposed any changes. Lord Loughborough, though previously a Wilkes partisan, in August 1782 attacked reform in principle, asserting British politics "can only be quieted by a steady adherence to the old Constitution." Only "abhorrence of innovation" could stem the destabilizing wave. "If these advantages are betrayed ... he is a wise man who can foresee which project will most likely prevail."[117] Any changes could upset the British constitution's delicate balance. Britain was already arguably Europe's freest country, and the American Revolution had just demonstrated the dangers of British disunion and destabilization.

The Association Movement continued seeking moderate reform, but its influence remained uncertain. York's committee in December 1782 still garnered correspondence from fourteen counties, including six in Scotland, and twenty cities. Still, as bodies of upstanding, respectable voters, they showed little willingness to broaden their movement and did not spark fears of extralegal measures. With threats of coercion absent, and Parliamentary rejection not motivating a greater groundswell, attention shifted elsewhere. The association's moderate aims blunted popular support: they showed no interest in extending the franchise to the broader population and came to represent entrenched interests uninterested in major changes. Within their demographic, however, in 1783 the movement still drew 10,000 signatures across

---

[115] Meikle, *Scotland*, 1, 8; Mathieson, *Awakening*, 101.

[116] Bob Harris, *The Scottish People and the French Revolution* (London: Pickering & Chatto, 2008), 19; Meikle, 6–9.

[117] Lord Auckland, *The Journal and Correspondence of William Eden, Lord Auckland* (London: Bentley, 1861), Vol. 1, 20.

nine counties and twenty-three cities. Pitt corresponded with Wyvill before reintroducing legislation, with the reformer urging the most proportional representation possible.[118] Though many expected the controversy to pass as the American War reached a negotiated conclusion, the movement heightened instead.

On May 7, 1783, the first anniversary of his failed committee proposition, Pitt presented his own reform proposal to add a hundred new Members of Parliament to offset rotten boroughs. Though attacking universal suffrage as a "mere speculative proposition," Pitt sought to shift representation to the larger counties and growing cities, while planning bills to punish bribery and limit campaign spending.[119] An "immense concourse of people" gathered outside Parliament while London and Westminster presented petitions. Pitt rose, declaring his intention to "invigorate the spirit of the constitution," and now "a proper time to enter upon the business of a reformation" with the war over.[120] Conservatives attacked his proposal, noting petitions had not specified the method for reform and, as North declared, they were signed by "infinitely the minority of each county." If real consensus existed, "Why have not 82 petitions from as many different counties been presented?"[121] Claiming to speak for the people seemed to many an absurdity. Pitt's proposal lost by 293–149.[122] Parliament appeared easily divided: Fox in July described its moderate reformers as "totally unarrangeable" and in "hardly any communication," dooming hopes for passage.[123]

Despite his motion's reversal, Pitt gained such influence that George III appointed him prime minister in December 1783. Pitt called a new election (three years ahead of schedule) in spring 1784. Unlike in the 1780 election, when government-led bribery maintained the existing stasis, this time discontent at the Fox-North coalition's corruption and ineffectiveness led to approximately 165 coalition supporters losing their seats. Pitt's popularity became such that even the small and conservative British electorate returned him a Parliamentary majority of around 120. More than two hundred congratulatory addresses arrived from across Britain. York's, however, rebuked him to focus on "parliamentary reform of which the nation

---

[118] *Report of the Proceedings*, 53–54; Veitch, *Genesis*, 92; *Letters on Political Liberty*, 29; Wyvill and William Pitt, *The Correspondence of the Rev. C. Wyvill and the Right Honourable William Pitt* (London: Todd, 1796), Vol. 1, 1–2.

[119] Robin Reilly, *Pitt the Younger, 1759–1806* (London: Cassell, 1978), 80.

[120] *Parliamentary History*, Vol. 23, 829; Michael Duffy, *The Younger Pitt* (Harlow, England: Longman, 2000), 14.

[121] *Parliamentary History*, Vol. 23, 850.

[122] Duffy, *Younger*, 14.

[123] BL Charles James Fox Papers ADD MS 47567 12.

had heard so much, but at the same time concerning which this House had done so little."[124] Reform's moment seemed at hand.

Parliamentary leaders developed a Whig Club network across Britain to augment reform efforts. Westminster's Committee turned into a national clearinghouse, disseminating information to "a variety of other clubs in the provincial towns of the kingdom, [that] may be considered the offspring of this prolific parent."[125] Whig political organization centralized over the decade, developing party managers, a Pall Mall headquarters, national canvassing, and fund-raising.[126] Preceding 1784's elections, they asked "public spirited persons" contribute "towards the heavy expence necessarily attendant on this vexatious contest," to contest "Court Candidates" receiving crown support.[127] Association models pushed the British toward modern party politics.

Developing Parliamentary consensus for a specific reform program, however, proved difficult for the young prime minister with many supporters less interested in changes once elected. The association attempted to remobilize extra-parliamentary pressure. Wyvill declared Parliament's refusal to confront such "alarming abuse" would lead the network "to press with increasing vigour" for real reform.[128] In December 1784, Pitt called Wyvill to a Downing Street meeting and asked for his help mobilizing a new petition wave, to which Wyvill assented, re-endorsing Pitt as "a Friend to the Constitution" who could bring change.[129] The renewed effort excited some reformers: young MP William Wilberforce enthusiastically expected further Yorkshire campaigning, "to procure as general a concurrence of the county as possible" and pressure Parliament, but a substantial petition wave did not coalesce.[130] Reform's momentum diminished.

Scottish reformers did not hide their frustration at English reform's tepidness. In 1784, a new convention with delegates from thirty-three Royal Burghs (half the total) pledged to place Scottish representation on "a proper legal and constitutional footing."[131] Some voiced displeasure with their southern counterparts, with one representative declaring, "Scots expect little or no assistance from the English." Following Parliamentary politics, they reportedly observed "with contempt the desertion of the

[124] *General Evening Post*, January 15, 1784; Hilton, *Mad*, 44.
[125] Charles Pigott, *The Whig Club, or a Sketch of the Manners of the Age* (London, 1794), 3–4; O'Gorman, *The Whig Party and the French Revolution* (London: Macmillan, 1967), 13.
[126] Donald E. Ginter, "The Financing of the Whig Party Organization, 1783–1793," *American Historical Review* 71, no. 2 (1966), 421–24.
[127] *London Chronicle*, June 12, 1784; *Whitehall Evening Post*, June 12, 1784.
[128] Pitt and Wyvill, *Correspondence*, 7.
[129] Reilly, *Pitt*, 131; GRO D 3549 13/1/W37.
[130] William Wilberforce, *The Correspondence of William Wilberforce* (London: Murray, 1840), Vol. 1, 4.
[131] Mathieson, *Awakening*, 101–2.

Yorkshire Association and Mr. Wyvill," considering "Pitt and the Court system" to work together. Inspiration came from abroad: "The new situations of Ireland, America, and Holland, have determined the body of the people in Scotland, to look like wise men to their own peculiar interests, independent of all other nations."[132] By 1785, forty-nine of sixty-six Burghs sent reform convention delegates, requesting suffrage for all propertied men but did not find Parliamentary support.[133] Little hope remained for a common British reform movement.

In April 1785, Pitt reintroduced a reform bill utilizing much of the Association movement's program, calling for thirty-six rotten boroughs' abolition and their seats' transfer to growing population areas. Pitt appealed to "enlightened" minds, asserting, "there never was a moment when they were more prepared" for such debate. Wilberforce seconded Pitt, denouncing Tories' unwillingness to entertain "any new ground of argument."[134] However, the legislation was defeated by 248–174. Pitt, already uncomfortable with many association petitions' heterogeneous composition, abandoned Wyvill as an ally. Radical MP John Sawbridge annually reintroduced reform motions but only garnered token support. Minor electoral changes failed to pass in 1786 and 1788.[135] Although Pitt remained prime minister for much of the next two decades, he proposed no further reform legislation, and another popular upsurge for systemic changes did not occur until the radicalizations of the 1790s.

Conclusion

Parliamentary reform, still only on the fringes of British politics prior to the American War, during the conflict became a near reality – deterred only by corruption's beneficiaries. The abuses perpetrated by the unreformed British Parliament in the American crises made the governing system's shortcomings apparent to many. Though international influences have received little attention in the few modern studies devoted to the Association movement, their model developed through adapting American-style committees of correspondence: developing unprecedentedly broad networks to build national consensus, criticize existing abuses, and propose detailed alternatives.[136] Though these tactics did not prove directly successful across the early mid-1780s – as British reformers remained more divided than their American

---

[132] *Gazetteer*, November 6, 1784.
[133] Mathieson, *Awakening*, 106.
[134] *Parliamentary History*, Vol. 25, 432, 462.
[135] Mori, *Britain*, 62; Michael J. Turner, *Pitt the Younger: A Life* (London: Hambledon, 2003), 76.
[136] See most prominently Christie, *Wilkes*.

brethren, failing to develop a common program that could appeal across a broad coalition, and often remaining reticent to expand their movement beyond propertied elites to mobilize the nonvoting population – such methods to virtually all reformers seemed the chief route forward for future contestations.

5

The Irish Volunteers and Militant Reform

The contestations of the American Revolution led similar resentments to smolder in Ireland. According to one 1780s synthesis of the Irish reform movement, "It was America, which first resisted the Oppressions, and oppressive claims of the English parliament," where "the corner stone of Irish liberty was laid."[1] Another even asserted, "it was on the plains of America, that Ireland obtained her freedom."[2] During the War of Independence, the Irish reappropriated American and radical British techniques to their campaigns for liberty and autonomy. In the years after 1778, motivated by similar grievances as their Atlantic brethren, Irish partisans created a broad-based Volunteer militia movement connected via American-style committees of correspondence concerned not merely with defense but major economic and political reforms. By cultivating public opinion, Volunteer efforts proved more successful than the British Associations, pushing the boundaries of acceptable mobilization to fight for greater Irish independence, albeit within the British Empire.

Irish Politics and the American-Imperial Crisis

Irish political clubs and an expanding press industry rose in popularity during the Wilkes era to contest a nearly closed political system. Anglicans had long banned Catholics and Presbyterians from voting and office-holding for not swearing an oath to the Anglican-affiliated Church of Ireland. Catholics' status eroded further: Their land-ownership fell from 14 percent in 1714 to 5 percent by 1776, and they could not legally sign long leases, join guilds, or have their own schools.[3] Even for Anglicans at the heart of the "Protestant Ascendency," significant political restrictions remained. Under Ponying's Law of 1495 and the 1720 Declaratory Act, the Irish Parliament became legally subordinate to British authority, permitting the crown-appointed Lord Lieutenant of Ireland

---

[1] Thomas Drought, *Letters on Subjects Interesting to Ireland, and Addressed to the Irish Volunteers* (Dublin: Coles, 1783), 10.
[2] Francis Dobbs, *A History of Irish Affairs, from the 12th of October, 1779, to the 15th September, 1782, the Day of Lord Temple's Arrival* (Dublin: Mills, 1782), 5.
[3] James Livesey, *Civil Society and Empire: Ireland and Scotland in the Eighteenth-Century Atlantic World* (New Haven: Yale University Press, 2009), 55.

and British Parliament to nullify legislation – a measure not replicated for any British New World colony. Nor was the Irish House of Commons freely elected: 236 of 300 seats remained "closed" boroughs chosen by only a handful of electors, with voting for the few "open" seats limited to Anglicans owning significant property. Elections occurred infrequently: the first Parliament under George II served his entire rule (1727–1760), while only a third of seats changed hands in the contest following his death.[4] Agricultural development compounded pressures: the island's population (aided by potato monoculture) doubled between the mid-seventeenth and mid-eighteenth centuries, while Dublin grew from 60,000 residents in 1700 to 125,000 at mid-century to 180,000 by 1800: Europe's ninth biggest city in 1750 and the largest not a sovereign capital.[5] Resentment smoldered under the weight of Irish grievances, making Ireland an eager participant in British imperial crises.

Patriotic clubs spread directly prior to and during the Seven Years' War. Taking names like "Friends of Virtue and Their Country" and "Friends of Liberty and the Constitution," such organizations intervened in local political contests, claiming to embody popular interests against aristocratic control. One patriot notice declared their club established due to the rising "spirit of freedom and independence," resolving "to cooperate, as far as their influence could extend, with patriot clubs throughout the kingdom."[6] Partisan organizations abounded in the 1760s with Pitt Clubs, Wilkite Clubs, and Corsican Clubs multiplying.[7] After the war, a club petition campaign arose to limit Parliaments to eight years. Ireland's Parliament, which legislator Lord Charlemont mocked as "dreading a national agitation," in 1768, passed the session limits, with British authorities ratifying the change.[8]

Mobilization concerning economic issues advanced, surmounting even religious concerns. Catholic merchant and tradesmen committees successfully sued to overturn guild "quarterage" (in which Catholics had to pay fees without receiving full membership) in 1758 and lobbied Ireland's Commons

---

[4] Stephen Small, *Political Thought in Ireland, 1776–1798: Republicanism, Patriotism, and Radicalism* (Oxford: Clarendon Press, 2002), 36; Maurice J. Bric, "Ireland and the Atlantic World, 1690–1840," in *Oxford Handbook of Modern Irish History*, Alvin Jackson, ed. (Oxford: Oxford University Press, 2014), 462; David Dickson, *New Foundations: Ireland, 1660–1800* (Dublin: Irish Academic Press, 2000), 143.

[5] Dickson, *Ireland*, 109; and *Dublin: The Making of a Capital City* (Cambridge, MA: Harvard University Press, 2014), 152; Nini Rodgers, *Ireland, Slavery, and Anti-Slavery, 1612–1865* (New York: Palgrave, 2007), 159.

[6] Bob Harris, "The Patriot Clubs of the 1750s," *Clubs and Societies in Eighteenth-Century Ireland*, James Kelly and Martyn J. Powell, eds. (Dublin: Four Courts Press, 2010), 234–36; *Universal Advertiser*, January 21, 1755.

[7] Powell, "The Society of Free Citizens and Other Popular Political Clubs, 1749–1789," in *Clubs and Societies*, 245–46.

[8] Earl of Charlemont, *The Manuscripts and Correspondence of James, First Earl of Charlemont* (London Eyre and Spottiswoode, 1891), 25.

to prevent its reinstitution in 1767–1768.[9] In 1761 a standing merchant committee formed in Dublin to lobby "defence of trade against any illegal imposition" by authorities. Defying normal confessional segregation, non-Anglicans constituted the committee's majority with seven of twenty-one selected merchants Presbyterians, and four Catholics.[10] Such inclusion bespoke growing prosperity: Irish exports had increased nearly fivefold over the previous century, becoming 10 percent of national income. Yet this made Ireland as sensitive to imperial policy as their American counterparts.[11]

Many Irish reformers sympathized with the American cause. Colonial action reopened the possibility of final recourse to revolution should appeals to Britain fail: an April 1769 Belfast banquet celebrating Wilkes's release from prison toasted, "may oppression never be carried so far, as to make it necessary for the people to resume the powers delegated to the magistrate," but "if it should, may their efforts for the restoration of liberty, prove irresistible."[12] News of America's Tea Parties brought strong reactions. The *Hibernian Journal* described the ensuing crisis as "the most important Business that has come under Consideration since the Accession of the present King."[13] Indeed, Dublin had its own tea party in early March 1775. After revenue officers seized ten carriages loaded with illegally traded tea, "a Number of Bucaniers" broke into the Watch House, reloaded the cargo, "and carried it away in triumph."[14] Though no similar incidents followed, American examples and Irish disaffection made domestic unrest a real possibility.

The imperial crisis in early 1775 led to a groundswell of Irish support for America. In Dublin on April 24, the Merchants Guild proposed a petition "praying Relief for our suffering Brethren in America." Partisans sought similar addresses elsewhere: "If but a few Petitions are presented," one newspaper article asserted they would appear "from the Malevolence of a discontented Party," but widespread unanimity could bring "ample Amends to the injured Americans."[15] Collective action appeared the surest method for resolving imperial crises.

America's Continental Congress encouraged Irish resistance, sending an address "To the people of Ireland" in July 1775. They requested "the good offices of our fellow subjects beyond the Atlantic ... aware, as they must be, that they have nothing more to expect from the same common enemy, than the

---

[9] Dickson, *Ireland*, 152.

[10] Dickson, *Dublin*, 181.

[11] Dickson, *Ireland*, 109–10.

[12] Henry Joy, *Historical Collections Relative to the Town of Belfast: From the Earliest Period to the Union with Great Britain* (Belfast, 1817), 111.

[13] *Hibernian Journal*, February 4, 1774.

[14] Ibid., March 3, 1775.

[15] Ibid., April 17, 1775.

humble favour of being the last devoured."[16] The address, exciting Whig anti-government suspicions, broadcast a common British imperial crisis. Resistance, if not revolt, would work best as a trans-imperial effort.

After the American War began, Irish opposition continued but did not spark rebellion. The Society of Free Citizens in July still toasted, "Our fellow subjects in America, now suffering persecution for attempting to assert their rights and liberties."[17] In October, Dublin's citizens approved a royal address "lamenting the present civil war; and humbly entreating his Majesty's inter-position to heal the breach." A British Member of Parliament estimated the Irish sided three-to-one with the Americans.[18] By December, after additional coffeehouse signings, Dublin petitioners presented the Lord Lieutenant with three thousand signatures for conciliation.[19]

Amid escalating civil war in the New World, dissent carried more risk, but many continued pressuring for American and Irish rights. In early summer 1776, Cork's municipality petitioned the king to end the conflict. Two years later, a demonstration there against exporting foodstuffs for the armed forces – while the British banned all other foreign shipments for the conflict's dur-ation – turned to riot, destroying suppliers' houses and cellars.[20] In the north, Presbyterians crossing the Atlantic declared they headed "to aid their Dissenting brethren in America."[21] Catholic elites and clergy took the opposite approach, sponsoring a loyal October 1775 "Petition of the Catholics of Ireland," proclaiming themselves "unarmed indeed, but zealous, ready and desirous to exert themselves" for the crown. Far from a show of disinterested loyalty, soon Catholics cited the address to call for expanded civil rights.[22] Still, no systematic push for Irish political or civil rights arose: in June 1776, Dublin native Burke considered the war a missed opportunity, with opposition a "feeble party" lacking coordination instead of acting as a "mediatrix in the quarrels of a great empire."[23] Ireland's smoldering antagonisms, however, by the conflict's middle years led to new conflagrations.

Anglo-Irish controversies expanded as the war continued. In 1777, a petition of "Roman Catholic Noblemen and Gentlemen," citing their loyalty

[16] Worthington C. Ford, ed., *Journals of the Continental Congress* (Washington: Government Printing Office, 1905), Vol. 2, 215, 218.
[17] *Hibernian Journal*, July 19, 1775.
[18] Neil Longley York, *Neither Kingdom nor Nation: The Irish Quest for Constitutional Rights, 1698–1800* (Washington, DC: Catholic University of America Press, 1995), 94.
[19] Conway, *British*, 133; Dickson, *Dublin*, 194.
[20] Powell, *The Politics of Consumption in Eighteenth-Century Ireland* (London: Palgrave, 2005), 177.
[21] Neil Garnham, *The Militia in Eighteenth-Century Ireland: In Defence of the Protestant Interest* (Woodbridge, UK: Boydell & Brewer, 2012), 94.
[22] James Anthony Froude, *The English in Ireland in the Eighteenth Century* (London: Longmans, 1895), Vol. 2, 191.
[23] York, *Neither*, 100.

"at the approach of danger," requested anti-Catholic laws' repeal, as "the Motives upon which the penalties were imposed have obviously ceased to exist."[24] Early in 1778, amid a worsening recession, Britain's Parliament tried to regain favor by granting Ireland trading rights with all colonies (not in rebellion).[25] The loss of Britain's monopoly, however, led to angry petitioning efforts from across the Midlands. Irish discontent with remaining British-mandated commercial restrictions, meanwhile, led to campaigning for unrestricted free trade.[26] Ireland's place in the British empire felt increasingly precarious and its lack of self-determination angered many.

As a semi-colonized people, Irish discontent rose with the perceived British abuses in administering both the American colonies and Ireland itself. Ireland's subordinate status bred resentment, while imperial war often affected the Emerald Isle more severely than Britain itself. Though the early American Revolution did not lead to widespread movements for systemic change in Ireland, the increasingly precarious wartime situation soon would.

The Rise of the Volunteers

France's entry into the American war in February 1778 led many to fear fighting in Ireland as well. During the Seven Years' War in 1760, the French captured Carrickfergus (controlling Belfast's harbor) and French aid to the Jacobite Catholic uprising of 1688–1691 remained prominent in Irish memory. American Congressman Richard Henry Lee wrote to Jefferson exulting how the French alliance put "Canada, Nova Scotia, the West Indies, and even G. Britain and Ireland in danger."[27] The Irish found themselves between two empires in a situation of peril but also opportunity.

With the British navy split between the New World and defending the home island, Ireland's weak defenses appeared easy prey. The official Protestant Irish militia, whose origins dated to early English settlement in 1556, seemed small and overmatched. Although a 1757 Militia Act reorganized and expanded forces in England and Wales, no measures passed for Scotland or Ireland. Indeed, only with difficulty had units suppressed Irish Catholic "Whiteboy" agrarian rebels in the early 1760s. Militia reform became a Whig political cause in Ireland after the Seven Years' War but remained hypothetical. In 1775, Ireland's Parliament overwhelmingly approved redeploying four thousand troops to America and refused German replacements. By 1776, new extralegal militias formed in Wexford, Kilkenny, Limerick, Tipperary, and Queen's

---

24 KA Pratt Papers, U840/071.
25 R. F. Foster, *Modern Ireland, 1700–1972* (New York: Penguin, 1989), 242.
26 Kelly, *Prelude to Union: Anglo-Irish Politics in the 1780s* (Cork: Cork University Press, 1992), 23.
27 Jefferson, *Papers*, Julian P. Boyd, ed. (Princeton: Princeton University Press, 1957–2017), Vol. 2, 215.

counties against renewed Whiteboy disorders.[28] British control became precarious.

Authorities prevaricated on militia expansion for fear of aggravating acute social tensions of class and religion. Lord Lieutenant the Earl of Buckinghamshire wrote to British authorities in April 1778 that outside Ulster "the number of Protestants is so inconsiderable, that it would be difficult to form a militia" of adequate size. The force's loyalty could prove problematic, as "opposition to the payment of rents, tithes, and assessments" might revive among the less-propertied.[29] Concurrently in England, local militia units were successfully mustered.[30] Irish administrators, cash-strapped and lacking adequate troops, proposed no effective measures amid an imperial crisis.

By then, popular militias began coalescing into a new, nationwide organization known simply as the Volunteers. St. Patrick's Day 1778, Belfast citizens formed the first Volunteer company.[31] A week later, the Irish Parliament started discussing a new militia bill for "independent companies, raised and commanded by individuals who can raise them" due to the government's lack of resources.[32] Before the debates' outcome, the now-140 Belfast men agreed to "associate ourselves together to learn the military discipline, for defence of ourselves and this town and country." Against most available models, they asserted their organization would be democratic: to be governed "by the voice of the majority," though with Irish notables for officers.[33]

The Volunteer model rapidly spread that spring and summer with three Londonderry corps and one in Lisburn mobilizing in June, thirty-eight in counties Cork and Tipperary in July; and by September, Dublin formed thirty corps which elected the influential Duke of Leinster their commander. Dublin's forces reportedly consisted, in units often organized by profession, "of independent respectable citizens" who furnished their own rifle, ammunition, and costly uniform. Though initially limiting enrollment to better-off Protestant citizens, tens of thousands armed for Ireland's defense.[34] It became apparent such organizations would not only be defensive military units but also promote political agitation. Newry's first Volunteer company resolved to defend "the Country against Enemies, foreign or domestic, opened or

[28] Gould, *Persistence*, 73; Garnham, *Militia*, 5, 73, 245; Morley, *Irish Opinion*, 104, 154.

[29] Henry Grattan, *The Life and Times of the Right Honourable Henry Grattan* (London: Colborn, 1839), 300–2.

[30] Gould, *Persistence*, 162.

[31] I. R. McBride, *Scripture Politics: Ulster Presbyterians and Irish Radicalism in the Late Eighteenth Century* (Oxford: Clarendon, 1998), 123.

[32] John Beresford, *The Correspondence of the Right Hon. John Beresford* (London: Woodfall and Kinder, 1854), Vol. 1, 26.

[33] Richard Robert Madden, *The United Irishmen: Their Lives and Times* (London: Madden, 1842–1846), Vol. 2, 291.

[34] *Morning Chronicle*, October 23, 1778; National Library of Ireland, Ennis Volunteers Records and Accounts MS 838 1; Dickson, *Dublin*, 198; McDowell, *Ireland*, 255.

concealed – to resist usurpation and maintain the constitution."[35] This would not be a narrow organization for contesting the French, but one with broad ambitions to restore and redefine Irish politics.

Economic and political grievances coalesced into a common reform campaign, integrating recent American innovations. In county Lowth, halfway between Dublin and Belfast, "principal gentlemen" protested Britain's recent customs legislation with a March 1779 nonimportation agreement boycotting all non-Irish cloth manufactures for two years hence.[36] An April appeal to "manufacturers of every Denomination in Ireland" argued only "absolute exclusion of English goods" would bring new legislation, without which Irish industry would fail.[37] An optimistic May notice asked "every county, town and village" to follow, until the Irish became "UNITED IN THE RESOLUTION OF NOT IMPORTING, OR USING ANY OF THE MANUFACTURES of Great-Britain, until OUR TRADE BE LEFT AS FREE AND OPEN as the air we breathe."[38] Meetings in fifteen counties and five cities between spring and fall 1779 adopted resolutions to buy Irish and boycott British goods.[39] Though building from the Volunteers' patriotic ardor, the campaign extended beyond the militia's social strata. Indeed, any comprehensive boycott needed to transcend the usual "political nation": no nonimportation movement could succeed without Catholics, Presbyterians, the poor, and women participating.

Though not all boycotters were Volunteers (even within the militia's limitations of age, gender, religion, and class), the militia enthusiastically supported nonimportation to display unanimity, patriotic spirit, and resolve against British mandates. County Dublin, establishing its Volunteer corps at the same meeting, adopted resolutions to "give every possible Encouragement to our own Manufactures" while buying none foreign.[40] Members of Parliament threatened to reject new war taxes should trade issues remain unaddressed. Volunteers upon enlistment personally subscribed to the nonimportation agreements. Though several prior boycotts had been undertaken in eighteenth-century Ireland, now active societies enforced them.[41]

In 1779, rumors flew of a French force massing on Brittany's coast to invade Ireland via Cork or Galway. The Volunteers expanded exponentially, from

---

[35] Public Record Office of Northern Ireland, Minute Book of the First Newry Volunteers, T/3202/1a.

[36] *Hibernian Journal*, March 24, 1779.

[37] Ibid., April 22, 1779.

[38] *Freeman's Journal*, May 18, 1779.

[39] Maurice O'Connell, *Irish Politics and Social Conflict in the Age of the American Revolution* (Philadelphia: University of Pennsylvania, 1965), 135.

[40] *Freeman's Journal*, August 7, 1779.

[41] Froude, *English*, Vol. 2, 259; *Freeman's Journal*, August 7, 1779; Powell, *Politics*, 183.

approximately fifteen thousand in April 1779 to nearly thirty thousand in September, forty thousand in December, and sixty thousand by mid-1780. Numbers did not climb higher still due to the cost of uniforms and equipment, requiring £80 for horsemen and £20 for infantry.[42] "The country is arming from one end to the other," concerned Irish MP John Beresford wrote.[43] Despite the groups' extralegal nature, the Volunteers rapidly spread as a patriotic, respectable response to Ireland's plights.

British-appointed authorities at Dublin Castle reluctantly embraced the Volunteers. Despite denying earlier weaponry requests, Lord Lieutenant Buckinghamshire in May 1779 admitted "seizing their arms would have been a violent expedient," and "preventing them from assembling without a military force, impracticable" given the few available troops. Although the Volunteers' legality remained debatable, as Buckinghamshire noted a late-seventeenth-century statute allowed the Irish to "carry arms for their own defence" without specifying whether groups could lead "learning the use of them," their popularity made repression untenable.[44] The Lord Lieutenant hoped internal divisions would doom the movement, writing in June that he declined "any sanction or encouragement," while claiming it "seldom happened that I have known anything of the association, until I saw them in the public newspapers."[45] By October, however, invasion fears grew so great that Castle administrators decided to distribute sixteen thousand arms to the Volunteers. As many regiments already had weaponry, government estimates reached twenty-five thousand armed men.[46] Afterward, Dublin barrister and movement leader Francis Dobbs noted, "the illegality of the Volunteers was no longer talked of."[47]

The government's providing rifles significantly lowered Volunteers' expenses, allowing many of more humble status to join the movement. An Ulster correspondent described enlistees having "purchased a genteel uniform, but the expence of musketry is really too much for them." As enthusiastic Volunteers scrambled to acquire arms, supplies depleted with a Gilford missive claiming enthusiasm so great that some corps "cannot procure" weaponry. Elite participation also increased: In County Armagh, Governor Lord Charlemont (like many other Whig elites) became an honorary Volunteer colonel and distributed 745 muskets, going beyond the official allotment to issue militiamen weapons from county arsenals.[48]

---

[42] McDowell, *Ireland*, 262; David Smyth, "The Volunteer Movement in Ulster: Background and Development 1745–1785" (PhD thesis, Queen's University Belfast, 1974), 70; McBride, *Scripture*, 123.

[43] Beresford, *Correspondence*, Vol. 1, 44.

[44] Grattan, *Life*, Vol. 1, 347–49; BL Flood Papers ADD MS 22930 99.

[45] Grattan, *Life*, Vol. 1, 357.

[46] Beresford, *Correspondence*, Vol. 1, 71; Dobbs, *History*, 10.

[47] Dobbs, *History*, 10.

[48] Charlemont, *Manuscripts*, 362, 366, 377–78.

Irish patriots highlighted the strength and necessity of associations. "An Association of the People is the dernier Resource," the *Hibernian Journal* declared in June, "which though may be marked with some Disturbance, like a Fever in the Blood, tends to remove an Evil from the Public Body."[49] Authorities usually warned of the movement's violent potential rather than its present forms. Opposition leaders like Henry Grattan lampooned the government's position, responding to Attorney General John Scott's hostile presentation before the Irish House of Commons in November by asking in jest, "do they mean that the independent companies should be disarmed?"[50] Volunteer associations acquired such strength that suppression would risk a constitutional crisis.

Boycotts continued with popular enforcement. Though Belfast remained stubbornly outside the agreement, sixteen counties and four cities (including the capital) between March and September 1779 entered binding nonimportation agreements.[51] Late May in Dublin, shortly after local newspapers published violators' names, three thousand assembled to break non-adherers' windows. Volunteer units "drove the Mob up Grafton-street, soon after which they dispersed, without doing any further Mischief."[52] The *Hibernian Journal* denounced the disorders, declaring it "impossible that good Ends can ever be attained by Violence and Tumult."[53] While needing to maintain adherence, excessive enforcement could spoil the movement for Irish liberty.

Much Volunteer rhetoric overlapped with concurrent British Parliamentary reform movements. As dissenting Presbyterian Rev. James Crombie orated to Belfast Volunteers on August 1, to "struggle for the liberties of our country, is a virtuous emulation," after which he castigated authorities for their "expensive luxury." Britain's empire had seemingly "fallen with a rapidity almost unexampled in the history of the world."[54] While Volunteers broadcast a common imperial crisis, authorities saw an increasingly united opposition. With the movement well-versed in the same radical Whig rhetoric as their transatlantic brethren, conservative opponents like Scott complained of "a people mixed with Republicans, French and American emissaries," imbued

---

[49] *Hibernian Journal*, June 9, 1779.
[50] Grattan, *The Speeches of the Right Honourable Henry Grattan* (London: Longman, 1822), Vol. 1, 29.
[51] Danny Mansergh, *Grattan's Failure: Parliamentary Opposition and the People of Ireland, 1779–1800* (Dublin: Irish Academic Press, 2005), 34; David Lammey, "The Free Trade Crisis: A Reappraisal," in *Parliament, Politics and People: Essays in Eighteenth-Century Irish History*, Gerard O'Brien, ed. (Dublin: Irish Academic Press, 1989), 84.
[52] *Hibernian Journal*, May 31, 1779; *Public Advertiser*, June 11, 1779; Grattan, *Life*, Vol. 1, 353.
[53] *Hibernian Journal*, June 2, 1779.
[54] James Crombie, *A Sermon Preached before the United Companies of the Belfast Volunteers, on Sunday the First of August, 1779, in the Old Dissenting Meeting-House* (Belfast: Magee, 1779), 8, 15.

with the "principles of America" while armed.[55] Further Irish escalation beckoned.

Co-opting anniversary celebrations of key British Ascendency events led to the Volunteers' most impressive musters. Occasions previously used to legitimate a narrow political oligarchy now highlighted British liberty and the force of an armed people. The July anniversary of the Battle of the Boyne, "which rid these Kingdoms of the Slavery of Popery and arbitrary power," brought Dublin's Volunteers to assemble outside Leinster's mansion and fire a "Feu de Joy."[56] Another Dublin general review commemorating King William III's birthday on November 4 marched from St. Stephen's Green past Dublin Castle before assembling at College Green around the monarch's statue to fire muskets, cannon, and rockets celebrating their "great Deliverer ... from Popery and Tyranny" and display the "enthusiastic Patriotism which first gave rise to the Guardians of our Freedom."[57] Though such occasions reflected traditional anti-Catholicism – a reminder of how Volunteers still excluded the great majority of the Irish – within contemporary bounds, the marches' reformist stance was clear.

Idealized praise for long-dead British leaders mixed with contempt for current authorities. Admiral Giles Keppel's acquittal in February 1779, following government attempts to blame him for recent naval reversals, led to widespread Volunteer celebrations. Ulster particularly mobilized, with Belfast's Volunteers parading in celebration, while evening bonfires and illuminations followed there, at Newry, Dongaghadee, and Ballymena. Kildaire and Derry held effigy trials of Keppel's accuser with burnings following conviction. Dublin presented the admiral with the freedom of the city, and Keppel Clubs began by springtime.[58] Irish support for British authorities remained tenuous.

Despite the French alliance and wartime dangers, many Irish remained sympathetic toward America. Franklin had visited Dublin in 1771 and found his hosts "all friends of America," supporting colonial rights.[59] He wrote to Volunteer leaders from Paris in October 1778, congratulating the militias while denouncing British fighting in America as a "combination of rapine, treachery, and violence, as would have disgraced the Government, in the most arbitrary country in the world." Though coming from an enemy government's representative, the *Hibernian Journal* printed the letter.[60] Dublin's Volunteers in 1780 adopted a flag featuring a serpent cut into pieces with the motto

---

[55] Beresford, *Correspondence*, Vol. 1, 82.

[56] *Hibernian Journal*, June 30, 1779.

[57] *General Evening Post*, November 11, 1779; *Gazetteer*, November 10, 1779; *Hibernian Journal*, November 3, 1779.

[58] Padhraig Higgins, *A Nation of Politicians: Gender, Patriotism and Political Culture in Late Eighteenth-Century Ireland* (Madison: University of Wisconsin Press, 2010), 66–67.

[59] Dickson, *New Foundations*, 193.

[60] *Hibernian Journal*, November 9, 1778.

"UNITE or PERISH," adapted from Franklin's famous cartoon.[61] While necessarily stopping short of endorsing the American cause, Irish interest in and imitation of the American movement persisted.

British MPs began urging economic changes for Ireland as a necessary palliative. Irish native the Earl of Nugent proposed liberalizing the island's trade in January 1779, urging "the necessity, as we had lost our trade with our American colonies, of taking care we did not lose Ireland next, by a separation or invasion." Burke the following month denounced the trade restrictions, blaming such "narrow and illiberal policy" for having "lost us America" while causing such corrosive effects elsewhere as to "prove the destruction one day or another of the British empire." Parliamentary rhetoric became more alarmist than the Volunteer movement's. Rockingham, presenting several Irish county petitions in May, warned of "the danger of irritating the people," lest they "be forced into resistance."[62] Irish and American grievances' similarity led to growing calls for reform.

In Ireland, boasts flew about the effects of their withdrawal from British commerce. *Freeman's Journal* in September reported "four fifths of the looms stand idle" in Halifax, Yorkshire, while "murmurs are heard every where, and riots are daily expected" from the unemployed.[63] Meanwhile, Irish manufacturing now "more than equaled what it was in the most flourishing times."[64] Boycotting areas renewed and expanded nonimportation agreements that month. Within two weeks, reportedly "most of the seaports of this kingdom are forming associations, and paying subscriptions into a general purse" for a national effort.[65] Participation grew such that in October opposition leader Grattan endorsed the effort in the Commons, asserting the cause could only succeed by "the ultimate operation of the People ... upon both houses of parliament." The campaign needed such a crescendo that "it should not be agreeable or safe for any man to oppose any application for a free trade." Grattan's ensuing motion thanking the associations was quashed but evinced their growing power.[66] Even established figures like Edmond Pery, Speaker of the House of Commons, now declared the Irish needed equal opportunity to "reap the profits of their own industry" like British subjects.[67]

The Irish boycott campaign opposed their commercial interests to England's but still won significant concessions. Cheshire and Lancashire mobilized in late October 1779 against changes, calling a manufacturers meeting "to prevent what must inevitably ruin the Trade of this Kingdom, and of

---

[61] Ibid., August 25, 1780.
[62] *Parliamentary History*, Vol. 20, 111, 135, 639.
[63] *Freeman's Journal*, September 7, 1779.
[64] *Hibernian Journal*, October 4, 1779.
[65] *London Courant*, September 26, 1780; *Public Advertiser*, September 27, 1780.
[66] Mansergh, *Grattan's*, 29.
[67] Lammey, "Free," 73–74.

these counties in particular."[68] Nevertheless, the British Parliament in December granted Ireland equal merchant access to all American colonies, the East Indies, and African slave trade. Though still without equal commercial rights in Britain, Irish industry could now compete across the empire. Yorkshire rallied against the Volunteers. "Was it love of Ireland," a meeting asked, "that made Lord North anxious to hurry the Irish bills through Parliament? No. It was 64,000 bayonets planted at his breast."[69] Aggressive political activism brought results.

Many Volunteer corps, anticipating freer trade and Irish home rule, refused to celebrate British concessions but still recognized their gains.[70] By early 1780, Newry's municipality sent notices nationwide for the "speedy institution of committees of correspondence" to make the boycott general.[71] Peaceful yet forceful mobilization amazed many: "The people had risen from a political torpor," orated Grattan on December 24, yet "not proceeded to political violence, a phenomenon never before known." Now, a "brave spirited nation with arms in its hands had asserted the majesty of the people," demanding a governing role. Ireland's political importance, Grattan continued, grew commensurately: though previously a "distant extreme spot on the globe," now the country "stands in the centre, midway between the old world and the new." Crises on both sides of the Atlantic gave Ireland's position new prominence. The Volunteers, he concluded, "exerted more than human force with more than human discretion," through their restraint, pressuring but guiding resolution of pressing problems.[72] As British negotiators in 1778 had offered America's rebel colonies full autonomy (including the Declaratory Act's repeal), Grattan and other Irish patriots asserted they deserved nothing less.[73]

Ireland's authorities remained at best ambivalent about the Volunteers. Their Parliament equivocated, while English-appointed administrators, only several months after distributing the Volunteers arms, openly desired their downfall. A new mutiny bill potentially applicable to rebellious Volunteers won legislative approval. One regiment resolved not to "protect the property of any member that voted with the ministry."[74] Dublin's Volunteers threatened to "recall those men who have betrayed the confidence of their constituents to a sense of public virtue."[75] Rumors flew of government plans to prosecute printers for publishing Volunteer resolutions.[76] The Lord Lieutenant wrote to North on December 31,

[68] *Hibernian Journal*, November 3, 1779.
[69] McDowell, *Ireland*, 297; Higgins, *Nation*, 72.
[70] Higgins, *Nation*, 77.
[71] Grattan, *Life*, Vol. 2, 410.
[72] Stephen Gwynn, *Henry Grattan and His Times* (London: Harrap, 1939), 80.
[73] Brown, *Chathamites*, 83.
[74] *Hibernian Journal*, August 23, 1780.
[75] Grattan, *Life*, Vol. 2, 130.
[76] *Gazetteer*, September 5, 1780.

1779, asserting the "expediency of putting an end to the volunteer companies," though admitting "so desirable an end is equally difficult and delicate." While suggesting doing so "as soon as the other liberal favours intended to this kingdom have been confirmed by Parliament," he did not receive permission.[77] Nevertheless, should the Volunteers have adopted more radical rhetoric or ran afoul of popular opinion, suppression would be certain.

Across summer 1780, the Volunteers consolidated into a regularized force. Regional gatherings proliferated as the movement organized regiments as well as local companies.[78] Officers at a large Newry review in August resolved, "the Freedom of this Country can only be preserved by the Spirit of the People," expressing determination "to persevere in the Exercise of Arms" indefinitely.[79] Trade boycotts aroused deeper antagonisms against British rule, with Dobbs reporting that among Volunteers, the "simple doctrine, that we could not be free, if any power on earth could make laws to bind us, save our King, Lords and Commons, quickly prevailed."[80] Not entering into "political questions," Galway's Volunteers resolved, would only be "calculated to render those public spirited Associations useless to the Nation."[81] The Volunteers accepted conflict if necessary, adopting the same structures Americans utilized: naming "Committees of Correspondence" to build the "Co-operation of the Volunteer Corps" by coordinating campaigns.[82]

In some regions, the Volunteers even incorporated well-off Catholics. Already in May 1779, the Earl of Tyron reported Roman Catholics "forming themselves into Independent Companies," though he claimed to have persuaded local units to disband.[83] Catholics received mixed messages from authorities: In July 1779, *Freeman's Journal* called Catholics to "shew their loyalty and zeal by preparing, with their fellow citizens, for a day of danger." Despite Ireland's religious conflicts, the author questioned whether "without arms or discipline, could they be useful subjects?"[84] In January 1781, a mostly Catholic corps developed in Clonmel. Resolutions in Meath and Wexford later that year explicitly allowed enrollment, while Roscommon reported Catholics being invited to join. The *Dublin Evening Post* published suspicions that two-thirds of Munster and Connaught Volunteers were Catholics.[85] When the Irish

---

[77] Beresford, *Correspondence*, 122.

[78] Dobbs, *History*, 42.

[79] *At a Meeting of Officers present at the Newry Review, on the 21st and 22d of August* (S.l., 1780).

[80] Dobbs, *History*, 36.

[81] *Freeman's Journal*, October 9, 1780.

[82] *At a Meeting*; Froude, *English* 288.

[83] Grattan, *Life*, Vol. 1, 352.

[84] *Freeman's Journal*, July 22, 1779.

[85] O'Connell, *Irish*, 304; Charles O'Conor, *The Letters of Charles O'Conor of Belanagare* (Ann Arbor, MI: Irish American Cultural Institute, 1980), Vol. 2, 169–70.

Commons dared to discuss Catholics' right to bear arms that December in a broader Catholic rights bill, the motion wound up tabled for fear of the "inflammable passions" it might provoke.[86] Nevertheless, despite its marginal legality, the number of regiments admitting Catholics climbed in 1782.[87] Though antagonisms, fear, and mistrust across Ireland's religious divides continued, many Volunteers broke from past rivalries to present an increasingly united front.

America appeared a useful example of revolutionary unity's power, including for overcoming religious divides. A Seven Years' War veteran declared before the Irish Commons in February 1782,

> I could very little expect, when serving in the last war in America, that it could ever happen that the French and American Dissenters could be united; that extraordinary circumstance proves to us that it is interest, and not difference of sects that draws communities now-a-days together, and we find by fatal experience that though they say their prayers differently, their military operations seem to agree but too well.[88]

Confessional fighting, though central to Ireland's past, could be unnecessary for the future. Volunteers called for reducing the panoply of anti-Catholic discriminatory laws.[89]

Though English militia units also formed against French threats, they would not achieve a political orientation similar to the Irish force. Even Cartwright, a major in the English militia, when writing to an influential Volunteer in 1780 evinced only limited enthusiasm for the force's politicization, but as "our foreign enemies increase it is possible that external danger may yet give rise to them."[90] Sharp, despite encouraging the "ancient Common Law Right of Associating" and proclaiming Irish Volunteers "the saving of that Kingdom," spoke of British cooperation as a distant hypothetical. Nevertheless, "as a Citizen of the World," he pursued interactions with Irish leaders, sending reform pamphlets.[91] Correspondence passed freely across the Irish Sea and each country's newspapers published accounts of organizing abroad.

As word of Irish resistance trickled into the fledgling United States, patriots crowed at their movements' similarities. Several American newspapers published a March 1780 letter from Londonderry boasting, "Ireland is become at length a free country," while the British "do not chuse to refuse any thing asked

[86] *The Parliamentary Register, or History of the Proceedings and Debates of the House of Commons of Ireland* (Dublin: Byrne and Porter, 1784), Vol. 1, 175.
[87] O'Connell, *Irish*, 358.
[88] *Parliamentary Register*, Vol. 1, 264.
[89] Thomas Bartlett, *Ireland: A History* (Cambridge: Cambridge University Press, 2010), 187–88.
[90] Higgins, *Nation*, 133.
[91] GRO D 3549 13/1/C6 and 13/1/E9.

by the Irish nation." Describing the rise of "sixty thousand independent volunteers," the writer intimated, "you may have some guess from where we took the example."[92] The *Connecticut Journal* found both Irish and American movements to concur that "resistance to evil kings and governors, but truly constitutional, is the indispensable duty of free subjects," and "in the present crisis, committees of correspondency should be every where established, for the regulation of the different corps, and the more effectually to obtain the great national objects now in view."[93] The American and Irish patriot causes resembled sister movements.

Volunteer spirit continued expanding even as the American war wound down. Parades and rallies grew more elaborate in 1781. From afternoon maneuvers, the events expanded into two- and three-day celebrations of Volunteer martial ardor. At least thirteen large-scale gatherings occurred across the country, including at Dublin, Belfast, Cork, Limerick, and Londonderry.[94] Leaders desirous of turning the Volunteers into a broader political force cultivated popular enthusiasm. As Charlemont wrote in March, "by not pushing forward, we may hazard the ground we have gained." He called for expanded Irish autonomy within the empire, arguing for Ireland's right to control its internal defense, while recommending Ponying's Law be "modified."[95] With the nation so mobilized, the Irish developed unprecedented leverage for reform.

Irish patriots successfully adapted the committee of correspondence model for Irish needs, retaining the militia structure of pre-Revolutionary American organizations while remaining loyalist and conciliatory toward British authorities. Profiting from the international situation, in which Britain could scarcely afford to station more troops in Ireland, the Volunteers became an effective organization for pursuing Irish rights. Once the possibility of French invasion faded, however, the movement's political potential remained uncertain.

From Defense to Reform

The British surrender at Yorktown in October 1781 brought the Volunteers into a new phase, ending the pretense of defense to make the Volunteers a movement for Irish political reform. Many authorities hoped de-escalation abroad would decrease Volunteer activity. The Irish Parliament the same month, despite having censured the Volunteers the year before, unanimously thanked them "for taking up arms in such a critical period" with even Attorney

---

[92] *Connecticut Journal*, August 17, 1780; *Connecticut Courant*, August 22, 1780; *Independent Chronicle*, August 24, 1780; *New-Hampshire Gazette*, August 26, 1780.
[93] *Connecticut Journal*, May 25, 1780.
[94] O'Connell, *Irish Politics*, 93.
[95] Charlemont, *Manuscripts*, 379.

General Scott praising "A Virtuous Armed People."[96] Many moderate Volunteers withdrew, but those remaining pursued systemic changes in government.

Already, some Volunteers had developed reformist stances, asserting Irish home rule. Dublin's in June 1780 approved resolutions that, while loyal to the British crown, they nevertheless would only obey laws "enacted by the King, Lords and Commons of Ireland," displaying hostility to British administrative power. Volunteer officers gathering at Londonderry that August passed an identical resolution, exulting in "the grand and unexpected prospect" for political change.[97] Irish autonomy advanced through the Volunteers, with Dobbs declaring in a 1780 pamphlet, "what applies to War . . . is equally applicable to peace. To be prepared to resist, is the Way to prevent an Attack."[98] Dissolving the Volunteers might undermine recent gains or even restore the status quo.

American examples helped advance reform plans. *Freeman's Journal* in early 1782 listed American freedoms "which the oppressed people of this country have no chance of obtaining," including "annual election of their representatives," "universal representation in the legislature," "universal toleration of religion," and "No standing army." Each gained greater Irish discussion. The same journal in May remarked how "Great Britain, by the arbitrary and extravagant mode of conduct she pursued, has already lost America," implying a similar Irish crisis.[99] Reform could prevent catastrophe. With British power's dénouement in the thirteen colonies, the time appeared ripe for fundamentally reassessing the broader British imperial state.

Armagh's Volunteers organized an Ulster muster for February 15, 1782, to pursue Irish Parliamentary reform. Seeking "to restore the constitution to its original purity," they resolved to "root corruption and Court influence from the legislative body." Choosing Dungannon, the province's "most central town," Armagh asked all areas to send delegates to compose a reform program.[100] As Dobbs described, the meeting carried real risks: should the gathering be "small and insignificant," the cause would appear "deserted." Controversial debates, meanwhile, could create agitation beyond the Volunteers' control. One hundred and forty-three regiments sent representatives, though this constituted under half of Ulster's Volunteer forces.[101] Even the *Hibernian Journal* warned, "the worst Actions have sometimes been conceived with the best Design."[102] The Volunteers sacrificed unanimity to pursue controversial goals.

[96] *Parliamentary Register*, Vol. 1, 9–10.
[97] Grattan, *Life*, Vol. 2, 102 and 447.
[98] Dobbs, *Thoughts on Volunteers* (Dublin: Mills, 1781), 7.
[99] *Freeman's Journal*, January 15 and May 9, 1782.
[100] Ibid., January 10, 1782.
[101] Dobbs, *History*, 50; Morley, *Irish* 288–89; *General Advertiser*, February 26, 1782.
[102] *Hibernian Journal*, February 4, 1782.

Beginning cautiously, the first Dungannon assembly built structures and precedents for future gatherings. First asserting their right to deliberate, the assembly unanimously resolved, "a Citizen, by learning the use of arms, does not abandon any of his civil rights," and then passed resolutions against Privy Council influence. The body pledged "to support those only who have supported us" in future elections. Further expanding the correspondence committee model, a permanent National Committee, featuring four members from each Ulster county but desiring to incorporate "the sentiments of the Volunteers of every Province," was appointed. The committee became responsible for convoking general meetings, including before any future Parliamentary election. The existing committee of correspondence network distributed the resolves, which gained near-general adherence. Regional gatherings pledged support, including one at Dublin drawing 139 units from across Leinster. City governments in Belfast, Dublin, and several towns also adhered. The organizations supporting the Dungannon resolves numbered nearly hundred thousand armed men.[103] Such power, if effectively galvanized, could be irresistible.

Volunteers declared the time ripe for major political and economic reforms. A second Dungannon meeting on April 6 wrote to Ulster's electors, declaring politics had changed: "The spirit of Liberty is gone abroad," to be "embraced by the people at large, and every day brings with it an accession of strength." Now, "the virtuous Sons of Ireland" would combat "Undue influence" in politics, while beseeching electors to vote only for those supporting measures "the nation approve."[104] They discussed broad reforms including annual parliaments, the sole appointment of Irish natives to high offices, an absentee tax against landlords residing in Britain or elsewhere, and full legislative independence.[105] Freeman's Journal endorsed their efforts, asserting that "if England had triumphed over America," Ireland would "have enjoyed hardly the shadow of a constitution." As a result, Ireland should press its "right to demand a freedom of trade and constitution" over British objections.[106] Only in a crisis of imperial weakness could such asymmetries be addressed.

In Britain, the Rockingham Whigs' taking power in spring 1782 led many to believe systemic change approached for both kingdoms. Many arguments for more equitable British Parliamentary representation suggested Ireland too needed reform. Grattan wrote to Fox in April declaring "the practical constitution of Ireland is diametrically opposite to the principles of British liberty,"

---

[103] General Advertiser, ibid.; Dobbs, History, 66; Froude, English, Vol. 2, 334; Morning Herald, March 15, 1782; London Courant, March 16, 1782; Hibernian Journal, April 5 and 17, 1782; Morley, Irish, 292; Mansergh, Grattan's, 75.
[104] Freeman's Journal, April 20, 1782.
[105] James Kelly, Henry Flood: Patriots and Politics in Eighteenth-Century Ireland (Notre Dame: University of Notre Dame Press, 1998), 343.
[106] Freeman's Journal, April 25, 1782.

while "you cannot reconcile us to your claim to power, without making us dangerous to your liberty."[107] The *Hibernian Journal* reported in early April of changes "intended in the political System here, similar to that of England."[108] Growing prospects abroad fused with increased Irish agitation: "nothing will satisfy the people," MP Charles Sherdian wrote, but "the total independence of the Irish legislature."[109] Lord Auckland in British Parliamentary debates warned, "if the motion before the House should be rejected," he would "not answer for the consequences."[110] Amid the American peace negotiations, activists sought a British empire of liberty.

Irish legislative independence, for the first time since the fifteenth century, gained approval through successive royal, Irish and British measures. George III on April 9 instructed the British Parliament that the Irish situation carried such "weight and importance," new measures needed to "give a mutual satisfaction to both kingdoms."[111] The Irish Parliament acted first, passing a Declaration of Rights on April 16 declaring legislative independence. Grattan that day praised the Volunteers having "united the Protestant with the Catholic and the landed proprietor with the people," building an organization "that was nothing less than society asserting her liberty" by demanding rights.[112] Only after the Volunteers pressured an Irish legislative assertion did the British Parliament repeal the Dependency Act and limit Ponying's Law in May. The changes ended the Lord Lieutenant's right to control the Irish parliamentary agenda and allowed only the king (not the British Parliament as since 1495) to veto legislation.[113] The Irish press reported Fox speaking "in Vindication of our illustrious armed Associations." The news arriving in Dublin sparked celebratory Volunteer marches amid "applauding thousands," bringing "universal joy and satisfaction to the people of Ireland."[114]

Legislative independence, however, did not promise an end to controversies, as economic and political inequality remained. Partisans promoted a new nationwide nonimportation agreement to gain more favorable British trade. The Volunteer National Committee concurrently turned to Parliamentary reform. The Volunteers now claimed 130,000 members, approximately a quarter of the total adult male population (both Protestant and Catholic).[115] Thirty volunteer corps gathered at Ballymoney on

[107] Grattan, *Life*, Vol. 2, 243.
[108] *Hibernian Journal*, April 5, 1782.
[109] Grattan, *Life*, Vol. 2, 215.
[110] *Parliamentary History*, Vol. 20, 1247.
[111] Ibid., 1264.
[112] Grattan, *Speeches*, Vol. 1, 121.
[113] Sean Connolly, "Patriotism and Nationalism" in *Oxford Handbook of Modern Irish History*, 33–34.
[114] *Hibernian Journal*, May 17, 1782; *Freeman's Journal*, May 21, 1782.
[115] *Hibernian Journal*, May 17, 1782; Froude, *English*, Vol. 2, 386.

September 19, seeking methods for "securing the freedom and independence of our constitution": "Those only are free," they resolved, "who are governed by laws to which they assent either in person or by their representatives freely chosen."[116] Irish legislative independence mattered little if a narrow Anglican squirarchy continued governing the country.

Freed from the yoke of British precedence, Volunteers pursued reforms befitting the era's full Atlantic possibilities. The prospect opened of Irish liberty advancing further than Britain's. Though many conservative Volunteer units disbanded after the Treaty of Paris signing in January 1783, those remaining redirected their campaigning, with one May report declaring, "Volunteering, instead of a decrease, is gaining additional Strength" from reform efforts.[117] In July, forty-five Ulster Volunteer companies met at Lisburn. The units, seeking "a more equal representation of the people in Parliament," appointed a new thirteen-man committee of correspondence gathering intelligence from "well-informed characters in Great-Britain and Ireland." The movement addition-ally contacted Franklin and French philosopher Guillaume-Thomas Raynal, while continuing correspondence with Association leaders.[118]

British reformers responded enthusiastically to the Volunteers' advances. Price complimented how, "after rescuing their trade and their legislature from the oppression of a sister kingdom," the organization combated "internal oppression, no less inconsistent with their liberty." Just as America made a "revolution in favour of the rights of mankind," so would the Irish show how the "blessings of legitimate government and a free constitution are inestimable." Wyvill congratulated "the noble spirit of reformation" among Volunteers, while pronouncing Britain's Associations ready in "any legal mode which can be devised, mutually to assist each other." Richmond highlighted the "equal rights of men to security from oppression," best preserved through extending the franchise, while Jebb declared "every restriction on the right of suffrage, as an infringement of the law of nature." Cartwright emphasized how "the friends of the constitution in both Ireland and England" should maintain "regular intercourse and consider a reform in their respective legislatures as a common cause."[119] Expanding Irish politicization opened new possibilities for both kingdoms. Prospects strengthened for a mutually beneficial alliance.

The Volunteers' correspondence committee tried to stoke British reform networks into coordinated action. A July 1783 circular asked for British clubs' help to achieve mutual reform. "The people of the two nations," the committee

---

[116] *Freeman's Journal*, September 24, 1782.
[117] *Hibernian Journal*, May 26, 1783.
[118] *Proceedings Relative to the Ulster Assembly of Volunteer Delegates: On the Subject of a More Equal Representation of the People in the Parliament of Ireland* (Belfast: Joy, 1783), 3–6; William Drennan, *The Drennan Letters, 1776–1819*, D.A. Chart, ed. (Belfast: HMSO, 1931), 18; Mansergh, *Grattan's*, 88.
[119] *Proceedings Relative*, 26–27, 33, 64, 83.

declared, "united in pursuit of the same important object, must not only be powerful, but irresistible." Inclosing "unanimous resolutions of about fifteen thousand volunteers" as evidence, the Irish sought a common front.[120] Yorkshire's committee in late September endorsed synchronized actions, as "the zeal of the two kingdoms operating at the same time" could restore full representation.[121] The Society for Constitutional Information, meanwhile, ordered Dungannon's resolves distributed to newspapers and "circulated gratis through the kingdom" as pamphlets.[122]

Volunteers superseded the association and committee of correspondence models to convene a legislative national convention not dissimilar to America's Continental Congress. "There will be shortly two parliaments in this kingdom, both appointed by the people," *Freeman's Journal* asserted in August, "one to meet at Dungannon, the other in Dublin; the former instituted to keep a steady eye on the latter, which otherwise might soon become the minister's parliament."[123] New measures to reduce corruption and increase popular input appeared necessary. Volunteer leader William Molyneaux, the week before the meeting, reminded delegates that without anti-corruption measures, "prostitute majorities" would predominate, sapping Irish liberty.[124] In holding an anti-Parliament, Volunteers embraced confrontation with Ireland's Parliament to pressure for significant changes in representation.

September's Dungannon convention adopted a radical reform program. Unanimously, delegates resolved "freedom is the indefeasible birth-right of Irishmen and Britons," and "they are only free, who are governed by no laws but those to which they assent" either individually or via directly chosen representatives. The Irish system denied this to almost everyone. Delegates declared the current order "Unconstitutional," urging "speedy and effectual redress" of their grievances.[125] Beyond the franchise, they demanded "total repeal of that infamous badge of slavery the Stamp Act, a comprehensive Bill of Rights, Equal Duties on the manufactures of Great Britain and Ireland, and an Absentee Tax" against nonresiding (typically British) landlords.[126] The accumulated grievances of centuries now required arbitration, as Irish patriots sought to reverse disparities of power.

Not seeing reform coming from established authorities, Volunteer plans coalesced for an extra-parliamentary National Convention, meeting mid-November in Dublin. Despite authorities' claims that the assembly would

[120] Ibid., 21–22.
[121] *Freeman's Journal*, September 11, 1783.
[122] *The History of the Proceedings and Debates of the Volunteer Delegates of Ireland, on the Subject of a Parliamentary Reform* (Dublin: Porter, 1784), 5.
[123] *Freeman's Journal*, August 19, 1783.
[124] Ibid., September 4, 1783.
[125] *Proceedings Relative*, 10–11.
[126] *Freeman's Journal*, September 11, 1783.

become a subversive anti-Parliament, Volunteers argued the Convention fell within their rights of assembly and free speech. If Volunteer agitation had been legal and constitutional when pressuring the British for home rule in 1782, many reformers argued, how could it not still be so in Irish politics – especially as they now discussed the new system's content? Many continued employing classical republican rhetoric glorifying citizen forces with one pamphlet arguing, "few nations have been safe or free, after they ceased to be martial," while militias in the Whig tradition provided a "power of ultimate resistance to their oppressors," if necessary.[127] Concurrently, new nonimportation agreements, protesting Irish industries' continued lack of protections, were adopted in Dublin, Cork, and Belfast, through club, trade association, and Volunteer pressure.[128]

Anglo-Irish authorities' concerns about the National Convention grew. General John Burgoyne, reassigned from the American War to be Britain's commander-in-chief in Ireland, wrote to Fox, recently appointed Foreign Affairs secretary, stating his "apprehensions" about the gathering.[129] Despite his prominent place in the British Association movement, Fox responded that the Convention would bring "Anarchy," in which "Government, and even the name of it, must be at an end" should the anti-Parliament succeed. Unless government rejected their demands, "Volunteers, and soon, possibly, volunteers without property, will be the only government in Ireland."[130] The Volunteers showed real prospects of becoming a revolutionary force.

The National Convention began debates as scheduled on November 10, 1783, after a procession through Volunteer-lined Dublin streets, hoping to reform Irish politics. The meeting moved to a larger venue to accommodate their 190 representatives. Yet despite consensus on reform's necessity, delegates sharply divided over whether to grant Roman Catholics suffrage.[131] As a result, Convention resolutions limited their demands to "every Protestant in every city, town, borough or manor" possessing a freehold gaining legislative voting rights with representatives facing reelection every three years. Current districting – and thus unequal representation – was retained, however, for being part of the constitution. Secret balloting, though promoted for lessening corruption, failed almost unanimously. Remaining issues were left to Irish Parliamentary "discretion." Reformer Henry Flood introduced the Convention's measures in the Commons on November 28. The bill met a cold reception, however. Members of Parliament, as Flood reported to the

---

[127] Small, *Political*, 118; *Thoughts on the Conduct and Continuation of the Volunteers of Ireland* (Dublin: Williams, 1783), 23.

[128] McDowell, *Ireland*, 311.

[129] Grattan, *Life*, Vol. 3, 99.

[130] BL ADD MS 47567 21.

[131] *History of the Proceedings*, 26; York, *Neither*, 176–77; PRONI T/2541/I.A. 1/13/231.

Convention, "opposed it on the pretext of allowing no ground for intimidation." The House rejected the reform bill, 159–85.[132]

Conservatives triumphantly broadcast reformers' growing disunity. The Lord Lieutenant of Ireland, the Earl of Northington, wrote to Fox after the Convention's dissolution of the delegates being "embarrassed by a multiplicity of plans, and are much alarmed by the Roman Catholics claiming a right to vote," which many opposed.[133] Though Catholic Volunteer participation became normalized, they remained a movement minority, whereas with universal manhood suffrage they could dominate the electoral process. Moderate reformers noted class distinctions: "The old, original Volunteers," Grattan orated the following year, "represented the property of the nation," whereas the expanded forces reflected "the poverty of the kingdom."[134] Irish Protestant landed elites would not abdicate political control.

Disaffection broadened following the Convention's failure. One January 1784 *Freeman's Journal* editorial declared reform's supposed friends in each parliament only "designing men" seeking personal gain. Reform became chimerical, "an object that will certainly elude our grasp when we think we are nearest possession."[135] Nevertheless, twenty-two petitions arrived before Parliament that winter seeking meaningful changes.[136] A radical break beckoned: "Custom," a February *Freeman's* editorial considered, "like the worst of tyrants often rules with uncontroulled despotism." Only by appealing "to the laws of nature and of God" could the system be righted.[137] Flood introduced a new reform bill in March, which failed by 159–85.[138]

Despite their inability to reunify the Volunteer movement, many continued promoting reform. New clubs like Dublin's Sons of the Shamrock expanded membership into the "burnishers of calves-skin" and "cobblers of High Street," a hostile notice described. A Constitution Society convoked to "diffuse throughout the kingdom, as universally as possible, a knowledge of the great principles of constitutional freedom."[139] Dublin's municipality on April 22, after adopting a new nonimportation agreement, pledged "to co-operate with all our virtuous Countrymen in every constitutional Exertion" for reform, "on which the Rights, Liberties and Happiness of Irishmen ultimately depend."[140] Belfast passed nonimportation measures two days later.[141] A shadowy

---

[132] McDowell, *Ireland*, 310.
[133] Gratan, *Life*, Vol. 3, 131.
[134] Ibid., 214.
[135] *Freeman's Journal*, January 8, 1784.
[136] McBride, *Scripture*, 143.
[137] *Freeman's Journal*, February 5, 1784.
[138] McBride, *Scripture*, 143.
[139] Powell, "Society of Free Citizens," 259, 276.
[140] *Hibernian Journal*, April 23, 1784.
[141] Ibid., April 26, 1784.

American-style "Tarring and Feathering Committee" formed in Dublin, carrying out several exemplary punishments.[142] Yet the Irish Parliament ignored the agitation.

Even as their immediate political prospects faded, continued musters helped enable the more radical conflicts to come. "We rejoice at the military ardour," Belfast's Volunteers resolved on July 14, 1784, "in which every man is either already enrolled a soldier" or "would in a few weeks be qualified to act in the army of the people." Interest varied regionally, with the *Hibernian Journal* by year's end proclaiming, "Volunteering is almost run out except in Belfast, Lisburn and Londonderry."[143] Yet the Volunteers did not disarm, publicizing their readiness to cooperate "in every measure directed to remedy the abuse of power, and the well-known defects in the Commons House of Parliament."[144] Only opportunity lacked.

Conclusion

The Irish Volunteer movement demonstrated the rich variety of possibilities for regime change during the American Revolutionary era as a common imperial crisis beset the British Empire. While Irish historians of the Volunteers have noted the international context (particularly the Franco-Spanish invasion threat) as an important factor in the movement's rise, they have not fully explored the deep commonalities and borrowings between the Irish and American patriot movements.[145] Although not set on promoting Irish independence, at least for the foreseeable future, Volunteers nevertheless effectively agitated for an imperial revolution, gaining significant autonomy for the Irish Parliament within the empire.[146] While centered on middle-class Protestants, the movement tentatively spread across class and religion, beckoning greater inclusion of the Catholic majority. Nationally linked, corresponding paramilitary organizations could – as American colonists had originally intended – be used to agitate for reform instead of revolution. Concessions by a British Parliament not desiring another American-style conflict forestalled the Irish paramilitary movement, depriving the cause of a consensus grievance. Though the Volunteer push for broader Parliamentary reform became divided by internal recriminations, a new round of crises in the 1790s would bring voices for radical reform and religious inclusion back to the fore.

---

[142] *Hibernian Chronicle*, August 25, 1784; NA PRO 30/8/329, 99–106.

[143] *Hibernian Chronicle.*, November 1, 1784.

[144] Grattan, *Life*, Vol. 3, 228.

[145] See most prominently McDowell, *Ireland* and Higgins, *Nation*.

[146] On the shortcomings of looking at the era solely from a national perspective, see Jeremy Adelman, "The Age of Imperial Revolutions," *American Historical Review* 113, no. 2 (2008), 319–40.

6

Religious Freedom, Political Liberty, and Protestant Dissenter Civil Rights

Freedom of religion, among the greatest conceptual and practical achievements of the revolutionary era, advanced via the social movements of British and American reformers and revolutionaries. Following a generation of upheaval, a 1794 Fourth of July address by South Carolina Senate President David Ramsay celebrated "universal equality" as the "most effectual method of preserving peace among contending sects." Whereas almost everywhere across the globe "fire and faggot await the man who presumes to exercise his reason in matters of faith," with established churches serving as "engines of oppression," the United States demonstrated how freedom of conscience could result in a "peaceable, orderly, virtuous and happy people."[1] Far from unraveling the social compact, religious freedom could confirm American exceptionalism and belief in freedom.

Such a change in mindset followed the campaigns of dissenting Protestant congregations – Puritans, Quakers, Unitarians, Baptists, and others – for broader religious freedom. Though such sects had been officially tolerated in Britain since 1689's Glorious Revolution, they remained excluded from many sectors of politics and society. Their push for civil rights in British and American political life regardless of confessional affiliation, demanding greater freedom of thought, speech, and spiritual expression, turned their cause into one of the era's most influential and enduring social movements. Religious Dissenters played an outsized role in creating political dissent as we know it.

British Dissenters and the Push for Civil Rights

Ever since 1689's Toleration Act, Protestant groups possessed the legal right to worship in congregations outside the Church of England. Enlightened travelers like Voltaire, in his famed 1733 *Letters Concerning the English Nation*, considered religious pluralism among England's great strengths:

> If one religion only were allowed in England, the government would very possibly become arbitrary; if there were but two, the people wou'd cut one

---

[1] National Archives of Ireland, Rebellion Papers 620/21/13.

another's throats; but as there are such a multitude, they all live happy and in peace.[2]

Voltaire, however, exaggerated.[3] Once Britons exercised nonconformity, they faced exclusion from many aspects of political life. Toleration did not supersede the Test and Corporation Acts of 1661 and 1673, which required an oath to thirty-nine articles of Church of England liturgy (some of which many dissenting sects repudiated, while Quakers refused to swear oaths at all) to take public office or attend university. An additional 1697 Blasphemy Act made it illegal to deny the Holy Trinity or Biblical teachings' divinity, with offenders stripped of office for the first offense and imprisoned for the second. In seventeenth-century context, such measures sought to contain the excesses of Puritanism that fueled the Civil War. But as focus during the eighteenth century shifted from controversies between denominations to fundamental disagreements with Deists and unbelievers, lessening Protestant tensions reduced enforcement and encouraged religious minorities to agitate for the restrictions' end.

Though dissenting congregations had many differences, in worship they commonly sought to empower lay congregants, establishing a "priesthood of all believers," more than the clergy-centered Church of England. Creating faith communities of "spiritual equals," dissenting Churches were often more open in structure and governance. Self-financing, as members paid for congregational upkeep while still contributing legally required Church of England tithes, the churches prided themselves on spiritual and intellectual autonomy. Dissenters, praising the British tradition of toleration even while suffering its shortcomings, continued advocating for expanded rights, in so doing often advancing broader British debates over liberty.[4] With Europe's Wars of Religion within popular memory, toleration represented hopes for peace, free thought, and perhaps even truth.

The Church of England concurrently faced internal pressure from the spread of Methodism, an evangelical movement that became a separate denomination only in 1795. From the 1730s onward, itinerant preaching rose in popularity. George Whitefield, the great firebrand, proclaimed religious reconversion a totalizing experience: "The new life imparts new principles, a new understanding, a new will, and new affections, a new conscience,

---

[2] Voltaire, *Letters Concerning the English Nation* (London: Davis, 1733), 45.

[3] On Voltaire's complex relationship with the British, see Dan Edelstein and Bilana Kassabova, "How England Fell off the Map of Voltaire's Enlightenment," *Modern Intellectual History* 17, no. 1 (2020), 29–53.

[4] Doreen Rosman, *The Evolution of the English Churches, 1500–2000* (Cambridge: Cambridge University Press, 2003), 119; J. C. D. Clark, *The Language of Liberty, 1660–1832: Political Discourse and Social Dynamics in the Anglo-American World* (Cambridge: Cambridge University Press, 1994), esp. xii.

a renewed memory, nay, a renewed body."[5] Seeking "new birth" in everyone, Whitefield disdained and preached across Protestant confessional boundaries. London crowds for his open-air sermons topped thirty thousand, and he personally preached eighteen thousand times across England, Scotland, Ireland, and America by his 1770 death in a Massachusetts town. These tours consolidated evangelical printing and letter-writing networks across the British Isles and Atlantic, with adherents holding a monthly "Letter Day" to read his latest sermons and testimonies of born-again conversions.[6] John Wesley, meanwhile, spearheaded the organizational effort, promoting small discussion groups (modeled on the "Holy Club" he cofounded while an Oxford student) visited by circuit-traveling ministers. Only by "voluntary association," wrote Wesley, employing the same term as contemporary political reformers, could "moral principles be guarded" against corruption.[7] Promoting free discussion, personal revelation, lay preaching, and empowerment like the Dissenting churches, such groups undercut Anglican authority – giving Methodists reason to fear establishment crackdowns.[8]

With Dissenters numerous in educated, urban circles (particularly among merchants), they were well-placed to pressure for expanding their rights. Many prosperous Dissenters had voting rights, legally retaining their ballots even while barred from holding office. Dissenters increasingly made political alliances with "Low Churchmen" supporting greater religious freedom. The Dissenting case appeared strong: already roughly equaling Anglicans per capita in wealth and influence, they judged the Anglican legal monopoly on government positions grossly unfair.[9]

The first organized push for repealing the Test and Corporation Acts began in 1732. Over the decades following 1707's Act of Union between England and Scotland, Anglican/Presbyterian divides seemed smaller, and patriotic rhetoric highlighted the empire's common Protestantism against international Catholic foes – motivating Dissenters to seek full rights.[10] Congregations of Presbyterians (lacking office-holding rights in England), Independents, and Baptists around London each appointed two lay delegates to a general assembly, who then elected representatives to "wait on leading men" in Parliament to advocate repeal. This Committee of Deputies of the Three Denominations, though distinct from the church hierarchy, in turn corresponded with the

[5] Stephen A. Marini, *Radical Sects of Revolutionary New England* (Cambridge, MA: Harvard University Press, 1982), 13.
[6] Frank Lambert, *"Pedlar in Divinity": George Whitefield and the Transatlantic Revivals, 1737–1770* (Princeton: Princeton University Press, 1994), 3, 21, 90–91.
[7] Rosman, *Evolution*, 147, 156–57; Andrews, *Methodists*, 17; Wilberforce, *Life*, Vol. 1, 131.
[8] Bernard Semmel, *The Methodist Revolution* (New York: Basic Books, 1973), 126–27.
[9] Bradley, *Religion*, 86.
[10] Linda Colley, *Britons: Forging the Nation, 1707–1837*, 3rd ed. (New Haven: Yale University Press, 2009), 54.

General Body of London Dissenting Ministers. Dissenters highlighted their loyalty, while emphasizing being "deny'd their natural Rights" as "free Britons" and good citizens. Nevertheless, the Commons' repeal vote failed by 251 to 123 in 1735 and by a similar margin in 1741.[11] Dissenters thereafter ceased repeal lobbying for decades.

British authorities sought to mollify Dissenter discontent by relaxing Test and Corporation Act enforcement. Authorities often suspended the statutes, tolerating Dissenters exercising "occasional conformity," taking the required Anglican oaths for universities, the civil service or government offices in England, but still worshipping in Dissenting congregations. Following the Occasional Conformity and Schism Acts' 1718 repeal, no legal penalties barred the practice.[12] Dissenters, however, still worried about renewed enforcement should they pursue wider changes.

Religious civil rights reignited as a movement in the 1760s among Rational Dissenters. English Presbyterianism's Unitarians theologically questioned Christ's divinity and sought to rationally interpret the Bible for themselves. While Dissenters could retain voting rights by swearing to thirty-five of thirty-nine articles, the Toleration Act accorded no such rights for those (like Unitarians) unwilling to agree that "in the unity of this Godhead there be three persons" instead of a supreme, undivided God.[13] Despite formal exclusion from British universities, the Unitarian clergy boasted some of the era's most prominent and best-connected thinkers. Minister Joseph Priestley divided time between his congregation and major accomplishments as a scientist (discovering pure oxygen), man of letters, and reformist political philosopher, believing social progress would follow free inquiry.[14] Politically allied with the Unitarians were Arians, who considered God supreme (rather than co-equal) in the trinity, with Jesus below the Father but above the Ghost.[15] Richard Price, their most influential minister, joined Priestley and fellow clergy in the era's most prominent political and religious campaigns. Socializing with fellow Dissenters in the "Club of Honest Whigs" at a London coffeehouse and corresponding with many others, their campaign became a crossroads of the revolutionary era.[16]

---

[11] Stuart Andrews, *Unitarian Radicalism: Political Rhetoric, 1770–1814* (New York: Palgrave Macmillan, 2003), 107; *The Case of the Dissenters of England, and of the Presbyterians of Scotland: Consid'd in a True and Fair Light* (London: Farmer, 1738), 11; *A Sketch of the History and Proceedings of the Deputies Appointed to Protect the Civil Rights of the Protestant Dissenters* (London: Burton, 1813), 3–10.

[12] Richard W. Vaudry, *Anglicans and the Atlantic World: High Churchmen, Evangelicals, and the Quebec Connection* (Montreal: McGill-Queen's University Press, 2003), 45–47; Bradley, *Religion*, 84; Yates, *Eighteenth-Century*, 53.

[13] Andrews, *Unitarian*, 3.

[14] W. R. Ward, *Religion and Society in England, 1790–1850* (London: Batsford, 1972), 21.

[15] Andrews, *Unitarian*, 14.

[16] J. C. D. Clark, *English Society, 1660–1832*, 2nd ed. (Cambridge: Cambridge University Press, 2000), 366.

The Dissenters' cause grew more strident alongside the rising Wilkes and Liberty movement. Wilkes came from a Dissenting family and helped reignite connections between religious and political reform.[17] Priestley's 1769 *View of the Principles and Conduct of the Protestant Dissenters* appealed to all free-thinking skeptics, describing nonconformists as congenitally independent: refusing to follow "the decisions of others, contrary to the convictions of our own minds," resisting spiritual coercion. In the two hundred years since the Church of England's establishment, Priestley argued, "an almost total revolution in the whole system of thinking in Europe" progressed favoring "free inquiry" over dogmatic reaction.[18] Basing the British state on questionable dogma seemed antithetical to promoting liberty, critical debate, and common rights.

Government measures against Wilkites and American patriots led to fears of similar religious crackdowns. In March 1769, rumors flew that the establishment sought to suppress Methodist and Dissenter congregations.[19] A resulting *Alarm to Dissenters and Methodists* pamphlet, stylistically similar to American patriot and Wilkes movement publications, declared "Liberty of Conscience" a "Birthright," denouncing "Spiritual Slavery being much more detestable and dreadful than corporeal Slavery, as the Concerns of an immortal transcend those of a mortal state."[20] Given recent British incursions against civil liberties and long-standing discriminatory measures against Catholics (not covered by the Toleration Act), fears arose that crackdowns against Protestant dissent would follow.

In 1770, Dissenters mobilized for the first time in almost four decades to push for the Test and Corporation Acts' repeal, directly lobbying Parliament. Rockingham ally and future Prime Minister Lord Shelburne reported many Parliamentary moderates desired to change the oath to confirming "the Old and New Testament to contain the mind and will of God," thus allowing free exercise of all forms of Christianity, while others fully embraced "Mr. Locke's general principles of toleration."[21] With the Church of England hierarchy unmoved, however, no changes resulted.

Frustrated by governmental inaction, Priestley politically radicalized with his movement. In 1771 he embraced the era's possibilities, publishing *An Essay on the First Principles of Government, and on the Nature of Political, Civil and Religious Liberties*. All freedoms remained vitally interconnected, Priestley declared, and "every man retains, and can never be deprived of his natural

---

[17] Ibid., 380.

[18] Priestley, *A View of the Principles and Conduct of the Protestant Dissenters* (S.l., 1769), 8, 25–26.

[19] *London Evening Post*, March 11, 1769.

[20] *An Alarm to Dissenters and Methodists* (London: Keith, 1769).

[21] William Pitt, *Correspondence of William Pitt, Earl of Chatham* (London: Murray, 1840), Vol. 4, 199–200.

right" to each. The era augured great opportunities to "free the minds of men" from prejudice and injustice. Though Dissenters were not large or powerful enough (even if united) to achieve radical changes themselves, Priestley considered, "This seems to be the time, when the minds of men are opening to large and generous views of things."[22] Hopes for change depended on convincing the British nation that freedom of thought deserved unconstrained exercise.

By 1772, a coalition of dissenting churches around the capital formed a fifteen-person committee to lobby Parliament. Moving beyond specific doctrinal fights, the organization focused on principles of free thought. Chairman Edward Pickard orated, "It is not for or against Anasianism or Arianism, it is not as Calvinists or Arminians, or Baxterians that we have applied," but rather for "Liberty of Conscience, the Right of Private Judgment" in determining belief.[23] The movement became known as "Latitudinarian": advocating for the right to interpret the Bible without penalty. Yet such universalist sentiments masked a divided reality with Methodists (siding with the Church of England) and Calvinists opposing them.[24]

Concurrently, sympathetic Anglicans sought to broaden acceptable dissent's boundaries within their own church. The 1772 "Feathers Tavern Petition," written by leading Unitarian minister Theophilus Lindsey and supported by Cambridge professors, called for abolishing the Acts for ordination and teaching. The petition declared all should "be restored to their undoubted rights as Protestants of interpreting Scripture" for themselves.[25] Two hundred Anglican clergymen (including future Association organizer the Rev. Wyvill and Westminster Committee stalwart the Rev. Jebb) and fifty laymen signed, while radical stalwarts including Cartwright and Saville lent support.[26] The Dissenter cause sought to identify with principles of free thought and conscience, making Anglican High-Church Tories seem out of step with their times.

Growing agitation led Parliament to pursue a relief act in April 1772. Dissenting ministers brought their own petition for relief from the incompatible Test and Corporation Act articles after the Feathers Tavern effort.

---

[22] Priestley, *An Essay on the First Principles of Government, and on the Nature of Political, Civil, and Religious Liberty*, 2nd ed. (London: Johnson, 1771), 12, 30, 296.

[23] Andrews, *Unitarian*, 107–8; Richard Price, *The Correspondence of Richard Price*, W. Bernard Peach and D. O. Thomas, eds. (Durham: Duke University Press, 1981–92), Vol. 1, 131.

[24] Ursula Henriques, *Religious Toleration in England, 1787–1833* (London: Routledge, 1961), 56.

[25] *Parliamentary History*, Vol. 17, 251–52.

[26] Colin Haydon, John Henry Williams (1747–1829), *"Political Clergyman": "John Henry Williams (1747-1829), Political Clergymen," "English," and "Empire" War, the French Revolution and Church of England* (Woodbridge, Suffolk: Boydell, 2007), 50; Clark, *English*, 410; Bourke, *Empire*, 275.

Opposition Whigs offered strong support, with Richmond writing to Rockingham beforehand, considering "the Bill a just one, founded on reason, good policy, and the true principles of Whiggism and toleration," while noting Dissenters "all over England are very powerful" and "stick pretty much together."[27] In Commons debates, relief proponents endorsed "liberty of conscience" with one MP even advocating "free and universal toleration," considering a "variety of opinions" as important in religion as in government.[28] Burke asserted toleration was a religious principle, arguing, "Christian charity consists in allowing others a latitude of opinion" to develop belief.[29] With fears of radical Puritanism outside living memory, conservatives only opposed the measure due to the Anglican Church's alleged weakness, offering continued temporary relief measures instead. Full repeal passed a divided Commons but lost overwhelmingly in the Lords after vigorous Anglican bishop lobbying, by 27–102.[30] Lord Lyttleton wrote to Price that even the bill's opponents made clear Dissenters had "no cause to fear" the "persecuting laws" being enforced.[31] Dissenters only gained their opponents' condescension.

After the 1772 defeat, ministers created the first nationally integrated social movement for Dissenter civil rights. London and Westminster's general meeting sought "correspondence with the country Ministers all through England and Wales," Lindsey described, "to procure their hands to a petition, which it is not doubted, will be signed almost universally."[32] Dissenters' adaptation of methods from radical politics did not pass unnoticed: one *General Evening Post* article advocated full toleration "as the most likely method to secure the peace of both Church and State."[33] As reform organizing advanced, Dissenters sought to keep their cause in the avant-garde.

Amid the polarizations preceding the American War, Dissenter reform met further reversals. In 1773's parliamentary session, Dissenters advocated altering the Test oath into a broader declaration of Christian principles, instead of seeking its abolition. Yet rather than win moderate votes, the Dissenters' cause receded, losing in the Commons by 761–90.[34] Dissenters found their opponents hypocritical: despite deeming nonconformist influence too destabilizing for the British system, in 1774 the House reversed its arguments to pass the

---

[27] Albemarle, *Memoirs*, Vol. 2, 225.

[28] *Parliamentary History*, Vol. 17, 434–35.

[29] *London Packet*, April 8, 1772.

[30] Henriques, *Religious*, 56; *Middlesex Journal*, May 19, 1772; *Parliamentary History,*Vol. 17, 432–33.

[31] Price, *Correspondence*, Vol. 1, 132.

[32] Theophilus Lindsey, *The Letters of Theophilus Lindsey* (Woodbridge, UK: Boydell Press, 2007), 141.

[33] *General Evening Post*, July 2, 1772.

[34] Lindsey, *Letters*, 155; *Parliamentary History*, Vol. 17, 435.

Quebec Act, removing any reference to Protestantism from the colony's allegiance oath and granting Catholicism full religious rights in the formerly French province. The compact, one critic argued, was "contrary to the spirit of the English constitution, and in violation of the King's coronation oath" to "oppose popery and all its horrid doctrines."[35] How could Dissenters be deprived rights at home, while the regime incorporated Protestantism's foe into the empire? Angered by governmental hypocrisy, some Dissenters radicalized.

Priestley, disillusioned with both British politics and increasing torpor in the Dissenter ranks, tried to turn movement energy toward the American cause. In 1774, he angrily wrote to a fellow minister that Dissenters had "disgraced themselves by not renewing their application to Parliament this session," letting the movement lapse. He published an *Address to Protestant Dissenters*, finding common cause with the Americans. Priestley asserted that as "Americans (particularly those of New-England) are chiefly dissenters and whigs," and "the chief abettors of Mr. Wilkes," they ran against the current ministry's designs. Warning the approaching parliamentary election necessitated "the last efforts of the friends of liberty in this country," Priestley denounced the administration's colonial conduct, declaring stated pretenses "too slight" to be their real motivation. American repression could be the first step in a general assault on British liberty. "In this situation," Priestley concluded, "the temptation of men to assert their natural rights, and seize the invaluable blessings of freedom, will be very great ... Enlightened as the world now is, with respect to the theory of government."[36] The principles of toleration and liberty needed to be defended, lest they be suppressed.

Smarting from recent reversals, Dissenters played a disproportionate role in the American controversies. Priestley, Price, and Lindsey became friends with Franklin and hosted him at the Club of Honest Whigs, discoursing on scientific, British, and increasingly colonial affairs.[37] Lindsey noted of a January 1775 gathering, "We began and ended with the Americans," with each attendee reading "4 or 5 long letters lately received from persons of worth and eminence in N. England – All of which concurred to assure us that our brethren on Ye other side the Atlantic will be free."[38] Priestley spent Franklin's last day in London with him "without any other company," examining the

---

[35] *London Evening Post*, June 14, 1774.

[36] Priestley, *An Address to Protestant Dissenters of All Denominations, on the Approaching Election of Members of Parliament, with Respect to the State of Public Liberty in General, and of American Affairs in Particular* (London: Johnson, 1774), 4–5, 9.

[37] Jack Fruchtman Jr., *Atlantic Cousins: Benjamin Franklin and His Visionary Friends* (New York: Thunder's Mouth Press, 2005), 16.

[38] Lindsey, *Letters*, Vol. 1, 204.

latest colonial newspapers and discussing the crisis.[39] After Franklin's departure, Priestley and Price remained two of America's most able British defenders.

Dissenters' political activities moved beyond operating as a special-interest group to become vocal supporters of civil rights and liberties not only for themselves but across the Empire. In Taunton and Nottingham in 1775, congregations signed peace petitions urging a negotiated peace.[40] Burke in a Parliamentary speech praised the prevalence of dissenting Americans, considering them "adverse to all implicit submission of mind," with their faiths "a refinement on the principle of resistance" embodying "the Protestantism of the Protestant religion."[41] Links between striving for religious and political liberty strengthened.

Domestic reaction loomed, however, against such enthusiastic support for American rebels. The "Dissenters agree in Doctrines; both religious and civil, with the Rebels in America; and no Man can doubt but they wish well to the same Cause," a hostile August 1775 *Public Advertiser* article asserted. Having "never done any thing here but sow the seeds of Rebellion," the author proposed letting them "migrate, like their Ancestors, to the Desarts of America."[42] Wesley denounced Price's *Observations on the Nature of Civil Liberty*, considering its system, "if practiced, would overturn all government and bring in universal anarchy."[43] Dissenters, nonconforming in English religious and (increasingly) political life, were vulnerable to charges of disloyalty.

Facing Tory denunciations, once the American War began the British dissenting cause limited itself to loyal opposition. Price declined the first attempt of Cartwright (himself a dissenting Unitarian who considered Jesus Christ "eminently distinguished as a reformer") to recruit him for Parliamentary reform campaigning in April 1776. The dissenting minister lacked "hope that any great reformation" in politics would occur until greater "calamity" opened the way.[44] Dissenters bided their time, waiting for future opportunities. In America across the same years, by contrast, Dissenters' co-religionists achieved gains British partisans had not even dared to ask for.

---

[39] Priestley, *Autobiography of Joseph Priestley* (Teaneck, NJ: Dickinson University Press, 1970), 117.

[40] James E. Bradley, *Religion, Revolution and English Radicalism: Nonconformity in Eighteenth-Century Politics and Society* (Cambridge: Cambridge University Press, 1990), 13.

[41] Gertrude Himmelfarb, *The Roads to Modernity: The British, French and American Enlightenments* (New York: Knopf, 2004), 82.

[42] *Public Advertiser*, August 11, 1775.

[43] Brown, *Chathamites*, 151.

[44] Price, *Correspondence*, Vol. 1, 245; Anthony Page, "Rational Dissent, Enlightenment, and the Abolition of the British Slave Trade," *Historical Journal* 54, 3 (2011), 750; Eileen Groth Lyon, *Politicians in the Pulpit: Christian Radicalism in Britain from the Fall of the Bastille to the Disintegration of Chartism* (London: Ashgate, 1999), 31.

Establishing Religious Liberty in America

America's religious old regime nominally looked much like Britain's, with most colonies supporting established churches, albeit of varying size and strength. Though most early colonies had recruited Protestant Dissenters, across the late-seventeenth and early-eighteenth century initially pluralistic colonies (New York, Maryland, North Carolina, and South Carolina) established the Church of England as their official faith.[45] Limited tolerance for private worship existed everywhere, as each colony followed England's 1689 Toleration Act, but so did restrictions. Dissenters typically had to acquire colonial authorities' approval for form parishes, while itinerant ministers could face jail time. Even Puritans who had faced repression in England still believed government deserved a religious basis, following their own faith's vision.[46]

Yet in the colonies promoting religious freedom, Rhode Island and Pennsylvania, a radically new paradigm of inclusive toleration arose that little resembled British traditions. Rhode Island, founded by Baptist Dissenter Roger Williams, included in its 1663 charter that no person should be disturbed "for any differences in matters of religion" not troubling public order.[47] In Pennsylvania, the 1682 Frame of Government guaranteed all believers willing to "live peacefully and justly in society" could follow their own creeds. Franklin celebrated the colony's distance from "slavish and arbitrary principles," noting Philadelphia possessed "half a Dozen, for aught I know half a Score, different sects." As the colony matured, "we should perhaps see a thousand Diversities more."[48] Freethinking and religious diversity seemed to advance together.

American separation from European religious mores developed through diverse immigration and irregular frontier religious practices. From the late seventeenth century onward, English arrivals were outnumbered by Scots, Irish, and continental Europeans bringing their own interpretations of Protestantism. Minority religious communities flourished almost everywhere. Whereas in 1690, 90 percent of churches followed their colony's established faith, in 1770 only 30 percent did. Moreover, by American independence only

---

[45] Jon Butler, "Coercion, Miracle, Reason: Rethinking the American Religious Experience in the Revolutionary Age," in *Religion in a Revolutionary Age*, Ronald Hoffman and Peter J. Albert, eds. (Charlottesville: University Press of Virginia, 1994), 5.

[46] Chris Beneke, *Beyond Toleration: The Religious Origins of American Pluralism* (Oxford: Oxford University Press, 2006), 6; John A. Ragosta, *Wellspring of Liberty: How Virginia's Religious Dissenters Helped Win the American Revolution and Secured Religious Liberty* (Oxford: Oxford University Press, 2010), 5; Steven Waldman, *Founding Faith: Providence, Politics, and the Birth of Religious Freedom in America* (New York: Random House, 2008), 9.

[47] Ahlstrom, *Religious*, 169–70.

[48] Beneke, *Beyond*, 45, 145.

12–17 percent of colonists were formal members of any church: the rest, especially in rural areas, receiving instruction from various (oftentimes outlaw) traveling preachers or developing lay ministries themselves.[49] Peopling and expanding settler colonies resulted in a degree of religious heterodoxy unmatched anywhere in Europe.

The transatlantic Great Awakening, from the 1730s onward, fueled evangelicalism's rise and further destabilized the colonial religious picture. Advancing both within and outside established churches, early evangelical religion highlighted individual conscience and choice, empowering fervor across social, racial, and gender divides. Whitefield, with printed word of his powerful preaching preceding him, drew hundreds of thousands over seven extensive colonial tours between 1739 and 1770. Thirty thousand gathered on Boston Common (perhaps ten times the town's population) to hear the farewell sermon ending his 1740 trip. Other itinerants followed – male preachers often accompanied by female "exhorters" urging repentance – regularly refusing compromise with existing religious "tyranny" and urging listeners to follow their own consciences. The multiplication of denominations and established churches' decline accelerated.[50] Through reestablishing their own faiths, believers learned to embrace change, work through upheaval, challenge authority, develop debating skills, dismantle and rebuild institutions, all skills readily adaptable for political campaigns.[51]

The push for spiritual independence predated and in certain respects inspired that for political independence. Solomon Paine, an evangelical Separate church minister, in 1748 brought a petition signed by more than three hundred followers to Connecticut's legislature. Describing freedom of religious conscience as an "unalienable right" from God, they called for "universal liberty" in worship. Their request was denied.[52] Dissenters, however, continued developing such arguments, while uncertainty over religious rights informed how many viewed other British edicts. By the American

---

[49] Patricia U. Bonomi, "Religious Dissent and the Case for American Exceptionalism," in Hoffman and Albert, 35 and *Under the Cope of Heaven: Religion, Society and Politics in Colonial America* (Oxford: Oxford University Press, 1986), 82; Waldman, *Founding*, 43–44.

[50] Sydney E. Ahlstrom, *A Religious History of the American People*, 2nd ed. (New Haven: Yale University Press, 2004), 284, 349–50; Bonomi, *Under*, 152–53, 168; Frank Lambert, *The Founding Fathers and the Place of Religion in America* (Princeton: Princeton University Press, 2003), esp. 127–58; Catherine A. Brekus, "The Revolution in the Churches: Women's Religious Activism in the Early American Republic," in *Religion and the New Republic: Faith in the Founding of America*, James H. Hutson, ed. (Lanham, MD: Rowan & Littlefield, 2000), 120.

[51] Susan Juster, "The Evangelical Ascendency in Revolutionary America," in *Oxford Handbook of the American Revolution*, 407.

[52] Kidd, *God of Liberty: A Religious History of the American Revolution* (New York: Basic Books, 2010), 46–47.

Revolution, three quarters of colonial Americans did not conform to the Church of England, considering their spiritual (and, increasingly, political) journeys distinct from the old country's norms.[53]

Amid the Stamp and Townshend Acts controversies, many believed a crackdown on religious toleration could follow. Boston's Town Meeting in May 1764 voiced concern over British authorities appointing an Anglican bishop for America, which could potentially obliterate "the civil Rights of this Province," beseeching colonial authorities to pursue "any suitable way to prevent it."[54] Some congregations endorsed Stamp Act resistance, hoping to undermine British authorities' pretentions.[55] Many considered a bishopric a first step toward trans-colonial tithing or limiting non-Anglican political participation. The powerful British-based missionary Society for the Propagation of the Gospel lobbied for strengthening colonial Anglicanism, and in December 1767 New York and New Jersey Anglican representatives met and requested "one or more Bishops be sent to America."[56] A highly impolitic proposal, the controversy drew the disparate colonies together as few other measures could.

Angry rebuttals followed against the feared bishopric, particularly from over-whelmingly non-Anglican New England. Editorials asserted that religious regulations augured a shift toward Catholic- or Islamic-style despotism.[57] Rumors flew that British authorities courted local Baptists as a counterweight against established Congregationalists. Others conjectured a bishop could "set up an ecclesiastical court to which all denominations will be equally subject," inciting religious persecution.[58] Boston Congregationalist minister Elliot warned a London correspondent in January 1768, "The people of New-England are greatly alarmed, the arrival of a Bishop would raise them as much as any one thing."[59] The 1770s could have featured a war of religion. An Anglican confessional state beckoned – perhaps not unlike that imposed on Ireland. Particularly given how, as fellow Congregationalist minister Stiles reasoned, "the Presbyterians & American Dissenters ... are collectively more than three Quarters of the Whites in America," while Anglicans "not the thirtieth Part" from Pennsylvania northward, the measure smacked of tyranny.[60]

[53] Bonomi, "Religious Dissent," 33.
[54] LOC Samuel Adams Papers, MSS 10023 Vol. 1.
[55] NA CO 5/217 17.
[56] *Newport Mercury*, December 28, 1767; Jewel L. Spangler, *Virginians Reborn: Anglican Monopoly, Evangelical Dissent, and the Rise of the Baptists in the Late Eighteenth Century* (Charlottesville: University of Virginia Press, 2008), 115.
[57] *Boston Chronicle*, January 18, 1768; *New-York Gazette*, June 8, 1768; BL Letters to the Rev. W. Butler, ADD MS 27578 81.
[58] *New-York Gazette*, April 18, 1768; LC Peter Force Papers, Ezra Stiles Diary.
[59] MHS Thomas Hollis Papers.
[60] LC Peter Force Papers, Ezra Stiles Diary.

Anglican ecclesiastical assertions advanced in tandem with Parliament's colonial incursions. Leading patriots throughout the crises denounced apparently intertwined conspiracies against colonial civil and religious liberty. Elbridge Gerry wrote to Samuel Adams, "in response to the word 'Christians' in your Resolves, I should be glad had that word been omitted," fearing its co-optation by "the establishment of those Tyrants in Religion, Bishops, which will probably take place."[61] The controversy led many to promote secularization. The *Virginia Gazette* prophesized a "mighty Torrent of spiritual Tyranny," which of "all Tyrannies . . . is the most to be dreaded."[62] Popular violence against Virginia Baptists, with preachers half-drowned by immersion and open-air meetings scattered by horsemen, exacerbated fears. Many Tories, meanwhile, hoped a strengthened establishment would reinforce the disintegrating colonial order.[63] Dissenters' efforts against threatened religious tyranny were consubstantial with the Revolutionary cause.

Fearing British assaults on their religious liberties, Dissenting denominations across several colonies formed a loose "confederacy" tied together via committees of correspondence. Preliminary organizing began in 1760 after rumors of the British assaulting "the chastity and order of our churches" by heightening restrictions. In 1766, the first interregional meeting in New Jersey drew representatives from across that colony, Pennsylvania, New York, and Connecticut. Corresponding broadly, subsequent annual gatherings drew five more colonies' delegates, while congregational committees from two more corresponded.[64] New York's representatives wrote "to all our brethren on the continent, to exhort them to form themselves into such societies, to correspond with each other," while initiating correspondence with the Dissenters' London committee and coreligionists in Scotland and Ireland.[65] Fearing a comprehensive British conspiracy attacking "Civil and Religious Liberty," the organization prospered until the war.[66]

Movements for greater toleration spread during the pre-Revolutionary controversies, largely through evangelical pressure. North Carolina Presbyterians petitioned to protest tithes supporting Anglican clergy and vehemently objected to 1767 legislation not recognizing future Presbyterian marriages, "a privilege granted even to the very Catholics in Ireland, and the Protestants in France."[67] In Virginia, where Jefferson estimated "two thirds of the people had become dissenters," Baptists responded to recent jailings of

---

[61] LC Samuel Adams Papers, MSS 10223 Vol. 3.

[62] Rhys Isaac, *The Transformation of Virginia, 1740–1790* (New York: Norton, 1988), 187.

[63] Ragosta, *Wellspring*, 3, 30, 194.

[64] Bonomi, *Under*, 206–7.

[65] *New-York Gazette*, July 24, 1769.

[66] *Public Advertiser*, January 2, 1775.

[67] Paul Conkin, "The Church Establishment in North Carolina, 1765–1776," *North Carolina Historical Review* 32 (1955), 14, 18.

unlicensed preachers by petitioning for relief.[68] Changes passed to the colony's Act of Toleration, but many Dissenters considered them insufficient. It took the War of Independence to enact a new order of religious liberty.

Moving beyond particularlist claims, Dissenters increasingly portrayed their cause as that of American liberty. "Liberty of conscience," declared a May 1774 *Virginia Gazette* editorial, "is so indisputably a right of every human being," that "the least invasion of it calls for the serious attention of all who wish well to their fellow creatures." As Virginia had been prominent "in opposing political oppression," they were now beseeched to "not be the last in abolishing religious persecution."[69] A new wave of dissenting petitions, with approximately ten thousand signatures, arrived urging greater tolerance.[70] Amherst County Presbyterians asked for a clean bill to "enjoy the full and free exercise of our religion, without molestation or danger of incurring any penalty whatsoever." They declared "American liberty" at stake.[71] No new measures, however, passed before war began in 1775. That August, Virginia Baptists petitioned the colony's revolutionary Convention, "alarmed at the oppression which hangs over America," declaring support for the new government.[72] The late-colonial controversies left Dissenters aggrieved and ready for revolutionary changes.

Many patriots by the mid-1770s believed an attack on American religious liberty would form part of Britain's authoritarian program. Stiles in 1773 considered the Bishops' plot a method "to confuse the Polity," to distract and divide them before Britain legislated further civil incursions.[73] Religious and political rights became seen as inseparable. A town meeting conducted in Braintree, Massachusetts, in March 1774 declared the recent Coercive Acts's "universality" suggested "our religious Rights are in danger as well as our civil," as "they must stand or fall together."[74] A June 1774 Boston handbill declared, "Religion can never be retained in its purity where tyranny has usurped the place of reason and justice."[75] Americans' radicalization over the next two years included an increasingly enthusiastic embrace of religious freedom.

Patriots on both sides of the Atlantic attacked religious restrictions as among Britain's most oppressive measures. "The people of England will soon have an opportunity of declaring their sentiments concerning our cause," one American letter in London's *General Evening Post* asserted in late 1774. If

---

[68] Lambert, *Founding*, 226.

[69] *Virginia Gazette*, May 12, 1774.

[70] Beneke, *Beyond*, 134.

[71] Thomas Cary Johnson, *Virginia Presbyterianism and Religious Liberty in Colonial and Revolutionary Times* (Richmond: Presbyterian Committee of Publication, 1907), 68–69.

[72] James, *Documentary*, 52.

[73] LC Peter Force Papers, Ezra Stiles Diary.

[74] LC Peter Force Papers, Massachusetts Town Records, reel 28.

[75] NA CO 5/763 216.

"Defenders of true Religion, and the Asserters of the Rights of Mankind," a government limiting (Protestant) religious choice appeared abhorrent.[76] American religious liberty captured the imagination of many even outside the Dissenting movement. London radicals at Fleet Street's Globe Tavern a year later toasted "Civil and religious liberty to every subject throughout the British empire."[77] Burke in March 1775 praised American religion as "a refinement on the principle of resistance," and amid the war orated before Parliament that the colonies had established "universal toleration."[78] Paine, of British Quaker origin, in *Common Sense* asserted America constituted "the asylum for the persecuted lovers of civil and religious liberty from every part of Europe," while "the cause of America is, in great measure, the cause of all mankind." He considered "diversity of religious opinions" among their greatest strengths.[79] Freedom of religion became an essential aspect of American liberty, including to Britons lacking the same freedoms.

Amid the War of Independence, breaking down colonial religious divides became a method of nation-building for American Patriots. The Continental Congress and army were necessarily religiously plural, only vaguely mentioning god in their proclamations. Dissenting churches lobbied for rights, while state governments touted ecumenism for recruiting.[80] When New Jersey's Provincial Congress in June 1775 called for a day of fasting, they appealed to "every religious denomination," seeking "divine Blessing on such measures as may be used for supporting our invaluable rights and privileges."[81] Among patriots even the words "dissent," "dissenter," and "toleration" grew unpopular as outmoded prejudicial terms, with religious freedom increasingly considered a right.[82]

Nowhere did the battle for religious liberty grow hotter than in Anglican-established Virginia. Dissenting congregations pressured the conformist gentry for structural changes. Jefferson recalled Virginia's legislature in 1776 "crowded with petitions to abolish this spiritual tyranny."[83] Anglicanism's troubles, meanwhile, were exacerbated by their clergy's loyalism. Approximately two-thirds of Virginia's established ministers, many originally British missionaries placed by the Society for the Propagation of the Gospel,

[76] *General Evening Post*, December 22, 1774.
[77] *Middlesex Journal*, November 9, 1775.
[78] Bonomi, *Under*, 187; *London Evening Post*, April 7, 1778.
[79] Thomas Paine, *Common Sense* (New York: Eckler, 1918), x, 22, 46.
[80] Spencer W. McBride, *Pulpit and Nation: Clergymen and the Politics of Revolutionary America* (Charlottesville: University of Virginia Press, 2016), 69.
[81] *Newport Mercury*, June 15, 1775.
[82] Beneke, *Beyond*, 114.
[83] Rhys Isaac, "Evangelical Revolt: The Nature of the Baptists' Challenge to the Traditional Order in Virginia, 1765 to 1775," *William and Mary Quarterly* 3rd Series, 31(1974), 345–68; Jefferson, *Autobiography*, 39.

abandoned their parishes during the war. After Wesley published his *Calm Address to Our Own American Colonies* in 1775, Methodism declined.[84] Facing such pressures, Virginia's Declaration of Rights passed in June 1776, making religion "directed only by reason and conviction, not by force or violence" and declaring all "equally entitled to the free exercise of religion, according to the dictates of conscience."[85] Though acrimonious debates followed over mandatory Anglican Church tithing in December, Jefferson noting "the majority of our citizens were dissenters" but "a majority of the legislators were churchmen," Dissenters were fully exempted from established church dues (in a bill also decriminalizing blasphemy).[86]

Decrees for broad religious freedom multiplied in the new republic. All seven Anglican colonies eliminated state support for their established churches by the Revolutionary War's end.[87] New Jersey's 1776 constitution specified "no establishment of any one religious sect in this Province in preference to any other." New York in 1777 granted "free exercise and enjoyment of religious profession and worship" to "all mankind."[88] Even where full religious freedom remained unadopted, many attempted to end Protestant confessional discrimination. Massachusetts' 1778 constitution guaranteed all Protestants free exercise, while South Carolina that year made "Protestant Christianity" as the state faith.[89] The wartime coalition's spiritual pluralism led to religious liberty's formalization. Ever responsive to his times, Franklin in 1776 proposed for the United States' seal an image of Pharaoh drowning in the Red Sea with the inscription "rebellion to tyrants is obedience to God."[90] To an extent unknown in Europe, principles of religious freedom flourished.

The push for full religious liberty extended beyond the pale of previously tolerated faiths. In Virginia, so hated did religious restrictions become that Chesterfield County petitioned in 1785, "Let Jews, Mehametans [Muslims], and Christians of every Denomination" practice freely.[91] After years of intermittent debate, in 1786 the Jefferson-composed Virginia Statute for Religious Freedom passed overwhelmingly, declaring civil restrictions enabled

[84] Ahlstrom, *Religious*, 368–71.

[85] Mason, *Papers*, Vol. 1, 289.

[86] Ibid., 318 and Vol. 2, 553-54; Jefferson, *Papers*, Vol. 1, 530; Daniel Dreisbach, "Church-State Debate in the Virginia Legislature: From the Declaration of Rights to the Statute for Establishing Religious Freedom," in *Religion and Political Culture in Jefferson's Virginia*, Garrett Ward and Dreisbach, eds. (Lanham, MD: Rowan and Littlefield, 2000), 142.

[87] Waldman, *Founding*, 110.

[88] Edwin S. Gaustad, "Religious Tests, Constitutions, and 'Christian Nation,'" in Hoffman and Albert, *Religion*, 218.

[89] *Continental Journal*, March 18, 1778; Miller, *First Liberty*, 19.

[90] Robert A. Ferguson, *The American Enlightenment, 1750–1820* (Cambridge, MA: Harvard University Press, 1994), 49.

[91] Thomas J. Curry, *The First Freedoms: Church and State in America to the Passage of the First Amendment* (Oxford: Oxford University Press, 1986), 145.

"hypocrisy and meanness," and making all men "free to possess, and by argument to maintain, their opinions in matters of religion" without restriction.[92] Any attempt to reimpose state religion, the Act declared, would "be an infringement of natural right."[93] Church and state, under the stress of revolutionary controversies, separated. Jefferson believed the measure the "standard of reason," glorified in its being translated and published widely in Europe, and later as president continued advocating a "wall of separation between church and state."[94]

Despite independence, British-American Dissenter conversations continued, pushing each other further in pursuit of religious liberty. Price in 1785 wrote for American publication a letter calling for the full repeal of Pennsylvania test laws requiring officeholders to swear to the Bible's divine inspiration, a measure passed during the American Revolution to exclude Quakers but also barring Deists and Jews. Repeal passed the following year, after which officials needed only to "acknowledge the being of God, and a future state of rewards and punishments."[95] Rush wrote to Price, praising his "excellent letter," hoping for "a revolution in favour of reason, justice and humanity" to continue unfolding. Noting the Quakers' antislavery efforts, he encouraged "the friends of humanity" to "persevere in their attempts to enlighten and reform the world."[96] With transatlantic correspondence rebounding after the American war, opportunities spread for renewed collaboration and inspiration.

Federalists, realizing America's religious plurality, embraced confessional diversity and avoided theological entanglements. James Madison in *Federalist* 10 declared religious freedom would prevent sectarian troubles: "A religious sect may degenerate into a political faction in a part of the confederacy; but the variety of sects dispersed over the entire face of it" would secure the government from danger.[97] Religious diversity became a strength. The United States Constitution, forbidding a national established creed, encouraged a pluralistic society. The document (unlike the Declaration of Independence's invocation of "Nature's God") claimed no divine providence, did not declare America a Christian society, and banned religious tests for national offices. Though not

---

[92] Merrill D. Peterson & Robert C. Vaughan, eds. *The Virginia Statute for Religious Freedom: Its Evolution and Consequences in American History* (Cambridge: Cambridge University Press, 1988).

[93] Curry, *First*, 146.

[94] Thomas E. Buckley, *Establishing Religious Freedom: Jefferson's Statute in Virginia* (Charlottesville: University of Virginia Press, 2013), 1, 82.

[95] Steven K. Green, *The Second Disestablishment: Church and State in Nineteenth-Century America* (Oxford: Oxford University Press, 2010), 82.

[96] Rush, *Correspondence*, Vol. 1, 371, 385.

[97] Alexander Hamilton, John Jay and James Madison, *The Federalist* (New York: Co-Operative Publishing Company, 1901), 51.

forbidding state churches – which persisted for decades in Massachusetts and Connecticut, while Catholic restrictions remained in four states, and three more excluded non-Christians from office – such restrictions eventually fell. Even for the many Americans who remained religiously devout and considered the new nation founded through God's providential design, forced religion and state-supported churches became anathema.[98]

Through dissenting sects' activism amid revolutionary upheavals, Americans developed unprecedentedly broad freedoms of religion. The Age of Revolutions included subjecting religious as well as civil leadership to close scrutiny. In so doing, religious choice became inseparable from Americans' conception of freedom. British nonconforming groups, with their island no longer the beacon of Enlightened religious progress, pursued increased activism. Against Britain's unmoved old regime, Dissenters concluded that their own rights would most likely expand through broader reformations of political liberties.

The British Dissenting Social Movement amid Atlantic Revolutions

Learning of American successes, British Dissenters revivified their own organizations for religious reform. Having staffed sister organizations calling for British political reform, Irish autonomy, reconciliation with America, and (increasingly) abolition of the slave trade, the era augured an unprecedentedly fertile moment for activism. As the American War encouraged a broadening of British citizenship and political participation, Protestant religious freedom beckoned.

Amid the dissatisfaction of the American War's middle years, piecemeal reforms passed for religious minorities. Ireland's Parliament granted Protestant Dissenters, largely with Scotch-Irish Presbyterians in mind, full civil rights in 1779 through exempting them from the Test Laws – which the British Parliament let stand.[99] Minor measures concurrently passed for British Dissenters. In March 1779, the Anglican Church signaled unprecedented support for reform with their bishops approving a measure releasing Dissenting ministers from thirty of the thirty-five articles of faith required to legally lead a congregation.[100] Reform legislation passed in Parliament requiring ministers only to swear belief in "the Holy Scriptures of the Old and New Testaments as commonly received in Protestant churches" as their doctrinal basis.[101] Burke, favoring both Catholic and Dissenter relief, praised the

---

[98] Waldman, *Founding*, 110–11, 129; Carl H. Esbeck and Jonathan J. Den Hartog, eds. *Disestablishment and Religious Dissent: Church-State Relations in the New American States, 1776–1833* (Columbia: University of Missouri Press, 2019).

[99] David Bromwich, *The Intellectual Life of Edmund Burke: From the Sublime and Beautiful to American Independence* (Cambridge, MA: Harvard University Press, 2014), 324.

[100] Lindsey, *Letters*, Vol. 1, 278.

[101] Henriques, *Religious Toleration*, 57.

measures as "Victories not over our Enemies, but over our own passions and prejudices."[102] Dissenter organizations, however, remained unsatisfied with partial reforms; Lindsey reported many ministers believed they would only "give more indulgence to Papists."[103] The movement pressured MPs to go farther.

Growing relief measures seemed to augur a new era of expanded religious liberty. Parliamentary debates began with Sir Henry Houghton critiquing how, despite Britain being "a liberal and enlightened nation," its "established church still retained the prejudices of barbarous times" against other denominations. Wilkes declared the Test and Corporation Acts "a direct invasion of the natural rights of the laity" and endorsed "unlimited toleration" toward "all sects and all religions." Free religious practice was not only practicable, Wilkes argued, but would "pour fresh vigour into a weak and feeble nation nearly exhausted, and almost sinking under a variety of oppressions." By contrast, Sweden's Diet had recently granted "full toleration," while France's crown reappointed a Protestant finance minister, Jacques Necker.[104] The repeal of restrictions on dissenting ministers passed, though Unitarians were still excluded for being "antitrinitarians," and the statutes forbidding Dissenter public office-holding remained.

The cause receded after the Gordon Riots of June 1780, which demonstrated many Britons' fierce reaction against an attempt to weaken the Establishment, intimidated many politicians from supporting the Dissenters. "Could a general toleration be established," a skeptical Duke of Manchester wrote to Rockingham, "I should be ready to go as far as any writings of Mr. Locke ever suggested, to all religions, consistent with public safety," but in present circumstances sectarian differences seemed best left alone.[105] There remained much more to lose by reopening religious debate than politicians could gain from Dissenter favor.

Contrasting with British intolerance, the growth of American religious freedom gained reformers' notice. Hector Saint-Jean de Crèvecoeur's 1782 *Letters from an American Farmer* (first published in London) asserted religious pluralism led not to sectarian conflict, but rather peace. Encouraging Americans "to follow the dictates of their consciences," diversity bred understanding, and even extreme sects, "if they are mixed with other denominations, their zeal will cool for want of fuel, and will be extinguished in little time."[106] Religious pluralism in practice appeared the inverse of what British naysayers prognosticated. Price, in his 1784 *Observations on the Importance of the*

---

[102] Burke, *Correspondence*, Vol. 4, 87.
[103] Lindsey, *Letters*, Vol. 1, 274.
[104] *Parliamentary History*, Vol. 20, 239–42; Vol. 29, 309–21.
[105] Albemarle, *Memoirs*, Vol. 2, 417.
[106] Hector Saint-Jean de Crèvecoeur, *Letters from an American Farmer and Sketches of Eighteenth-Century America* (New York: Penguin, 1986), 73–74.

American Revolution, declared "next to the introduction of Christianity among mankind, the American Revolution may prove the next most important step in the progressive course of human improvement." Celebrating "perfect liberty, *religious* as well as *civil*," Price prophesized a new "Liberty of Discussion" with no unassailable dogmas. Britons could now "catch the flame of virtuous liberty" from America.[107] Despite the British dissenting movement's political sophistication, New World advancements carried them farther.

This push for civil liberty placed the dissenting leadership in political opposition to the Church of England and even Methodists, who opposed the American War and generally discouraged British reform. Whitefield had advocated the American position against the Stamp Act, accompanying Franklin when he testified before Parliament in 1766, yet after his 1770 death prominent Methodists turned to loyalism.[108] Wesley rejected greater political participation in the name of "natural rights," declaring such supposedly inalienable freedoms did not correspond with any known society's. He denounced the American rebellion, though questioning the "law, equity or prudence" of British policy.[109] Such loyalism did not endear him to leading Dissenters: Lindsey called him a "prevaricating, time-serving wretch" in December 1775 for supporting the American war.[110] Otherwise, Wesley encouraged "no politics," aiming to keep the Methodists above factions to focus on religious instead of political concerns.[111] Indeed, given Methodism's tenuous toleration within the Church of England, preventing schism remained a great concern. Only on antislavery (together with many fellow Dissenters and Anglicans) would Methodists depart from their political conservatism.

By the mid-1780s, Dissenters' organizations featured many reform movement veterans ready for a new civil rights campaign. London's branch included at least ten Society for Constitutional Information members, eight from the Whig Club, and seventeen from the Revolution Society. Although the Dissenter rank-and-file remained more moderate, rhetoric crossed movements.[112] In 1786, the common meeting resolved, "Every man hath an inalienable right ... to judge for himself in matters of religion."[113] A January 1787 motion to petition Parliament for Test and Corporation Act

---

[107] Price, *Observations on the Importance of the American Revolution: And the Means of Making It a Benefit to the World* (London: Johnson, 1785), 1, 7, 18, 20.

[108] Lambert, *'Pedlar,'* 222.

[109] David Hempton, *Methodism in British Politics, 1750–1850* (Stanford: Stanford University Press, 1984), 45–47.

[110] Lindsey, *Letters*, Vol. 1, 219.

[111] Hempton, *Methodism*, 45–47.

[112] Thomas W. Davis, *Committees for the Repeal of the Test and Corporation Acts: Minutes 1786–1790 and 1827–1828* (London: London Record Society, 1978), xiii.

[113] Richard Burgess Barlow, *Citizenship and Conscience: A Study in the Theory and Practice of Religious Toleration in England during the Eighteenth Century* (Philadelphia: University of Pennsylvania Press, 1962), 221.

repeal passed unanimously. Dissenters remained ecumenically integrated around the capital with each Presbyterian, Independent, and Baptist congregation within ten miles of London appointing two deputies to an annual general meeting, preparing a campaign.[114]

Many believed the Dissenters' timing fortuitous but underestimated the Anglican establishment's strength and determination to preserve their privileges. A February 1787 report asserted Dissenters now "entertain good hopes of success" with Fox and his allies, while "Pitt owes so much to the dissenters, that he cannot oppose the measure."[115] The movement obtained a meeting with the prime minister, who promised "serious consideration" but withheld an "immediate opinion" on the issue.[116] Pitt met with fourteen Anglican bishops, declaring he would not support the bill without their consent. Twelve opposed toleration, with the Archbishop of Canterbury additionally wanting all Parliamentary discussion prevented. George III pressured against the bill.[117] Pitt could no longer hold both the support of the Anglican church and reformers. He chose the establishment.

Henry Beaufoy, a Dissenter holding his Parliamentary seat only through Occasional Conformity, introduced a new motion to repeal the Test and Corporation Acts in March 1787. Since Dissenters already "have a right as men to think for themselves in matters of religion," Beaufoy argued, they "naturally" ought to possess the right to hold office. Such was already granted in "most of the enlightened nations of Europe," including British possessions except England. North, now in opposition, denounced removing "a great bulwark of the constitution," particularly without an alternative religious test. Pitt took the conservative position, rhetorically asking "whether or not it was expedient to deprive the legislature of a discretionary power now vested in them?" He distinguished "between political and civil liberty," as "there must be some restriction of rights in all societies" including qualifications for office. Despite Fox retorting that religion is "not a proper Test for a political institution," the motion lost by 100–178.[118]

Dissenters' Parliamentary alliances frayed. Priestley published a blistering letter to Pitt that spring, declaring the young leader "misled by your education and connections" with Anglican clergy to "support every system that is once established, be it ever so absurd." Priestley beseeched the prime minister to

[114] *The Parliamentary Register, or History of the Proceedings and Debates of the House of Commons* (London: Debrett, 1787), Vol. 21, 529.
[115] George Wilson and James Trail to Jeremy Bentham, February 26, 1787, Electronic Enlightenment online, accessed June 29, 2014.
[116] Davis, *Committees*, 17.
[117] Earl Stanhope, *Life of the Right Honourable William Pitt* (London: Murray, 1861), Vol. 1, 337; Auckland, *Journal*, Vol. 1, 406; Jennifer Mori, *Britain in the Age of the French Revolution* (London: Longman, 2000), 3.
[118] *Parliamentary Register*, Vol. 21, 540–68.

encourage "the gradual spread of truth," rather than revivifying reaction. Though Priestley's letter did not conciliate Pitt, it stoked Dissenter opposition networks. In the Parliamentary vote's aftermath, the Dissenters' Committee for Repeal in mid-April resolved unanimously to continue their movement until obtaining relief.[119]

Responding to adversity, Dissenters sought to mobilize their congregations' collective strength. Beaufoy before Parliament earlier boasted how Dissenters "did not chuse to crowd your table with petitions," wanting to "owe their success, not to the number of claimants, but to the equity of a claim." This brought insufficient pressure, however, and led detractors to assert that "the Dissenters in general do not desire relief."[120] A national petitioning campaign seemed necessary to demonstrate consensus. Dissenters needed to bring their collective power to bear on discussions.

Many hoped that 1788, the Glorious Revolution's centenary, would be the year of repeal. But King George III's mental health crisis led Dissenters to postpone petitioning until the following year and focus on campaign building. Dissenters asked their "brethren in every part of England and Wales" to remonstrate. The Committee for Repeal directed all Dissenting congregations to write letters testifying their commitment to the cause. Equally, Dissenter voters were instructed to support candidates "well affected to civil and religious liberty," who "proved themselves friends to the rights of Protestant Dissenters."[121] Becoming single-issue voters, Dissenters leveraged their collective power.

To sway the broader public, Dissenters turned to pamphleteering. The Committee for Repeal targeted Anglican opponents in late 1788 with a *Letter to the Bishops of the Application of the Protestant Dissenters*, which they sent to Anglican authorities, and a more general *Right of Protestant Dissenters to a Compleat Toleration Asserted*, printing three thousand copies.[122] They endorsed an aggressive approach: If the Dissenters' case was worthy, "redress, in duty, ought to be granted at the instant in which it was asked." Anglican stalling tactics, meanwhile, appeared laughable: "it never can seem a proper time to give up any of its powers."[123] Seeking continuity of message, the London committee sent *Right* copies to every Dissenting parish in the kingdom.[124]

---

[119] Priestley, *A Letter to the Right Honourable William Pitt, First Lord of the Treasury, and Chancellor of the Exchequer; On the Subject of Toleration and Church Establishments* (London: Debrett, 1787), 1–30; Davis, *Committees*, 16.

[120] *Parliamentary Register*, Vol. 21, 530.

[121] Ibid., 26–27.

[122] Ibid., 26.

[123] *The Right of Protestant Dissenters to a Compleat Toleration, Asserted* (London: Johnson, 1787), 200–1.

[124] Davis, *Committees*, 27.

In May 1789, Dissenters' efforts brought another Parliamentary repeal vote. The cause fell into both old and new traps: preceding debates, a "Humble Petition of Catholic Dissenters of England" declared the restrictions "totally repugnant to political and civil liberty." Opponents surmised where increased Protestant toleration might lead. Beaufoy reintroduced the motion, asking MPs relinquish "the prejudice which misinformation had led them to adopt" against Dissenters. Pitt, however, argued repeal "would open the door again to all the abuse and danger which it had been designed to guard against." Though the Dissenters gained new votes, the motion still lost by 102–122.[125]

Amid growing enthusiasm over the French Revolution's outbreak and recent edicts of religious toleration, Dissenters by fall 1789 cloaked their campaigns in broad enlightenment principles. One provincial assembly denounced the Test Acts for violating "liberty, good sense, and humanity," neglecting "the spiritual advantage of mankind."[126] A Dissenter pamphlet from Birmingham beseeched Britons, as "citizens of the world" to follow France's recent example by establishing the "equal liberties of Christians" at home.[127] A Scottish pamphlet considered religious establishments "inconsistent with the reason of things, the rights of man, and the principles of true and equal liberty."[128] Lindsey similarly hoped revolutionary change would become "the speedy means of putting an end to tyranny every where."[129] Dissenters sought to channel the upsurge in radical egalitarian thinking to their century-old cause.

Having come close the previous year, Dissenters heightened activity as they pushed for a third Parliamentary vote. No fewer than fifteen provincial assemblies across England pledged to lobby their representatives for repeal.[130] Priestley in a sermon on the "Conduct to be Observed by Dissenters" asserted they needed to show authorities' "intolerance in their treatment of us, and that they really do persecute us." Persecution meant not just death or ruin, he argued, but lack of "civil respect" in their communities.[131] Dissenter influence remained strong over many Members of Parliament. Burke wrote to Fox, "the

[125] *Parliamentary Register*, Vol. 26, 90, 93, 106, 126.

[126] George Isaac Huntingford, *Letter the First Addressed to the Delegates from the Several Congregations of Protestant Dissenters Who Met at Devizes on September 14, 1789*, 2nd ed. (Salisbury: Easton, 1790), 33–34.

[127] *Public Documents Declaratory of the Principles of the Protestant Dissenters, and Proving That the Repeal of the Corporation and Test Acts, Was Earnestly Desired by King William III and King George I* (Birmingham, 1790), vi.

[128] William Christie, *An Essay, on Ecclesiastical Establishments in Religion* (Montrose, 1791), 12.

[129] Lindsey, *Letters*, Vol. 2, 26.

[130] Davis, *Committees*, 37–38; Henriques, *Religious Toleration*, 63.

[131] Priestley, *The Conduct to Be Observed by Dissenters in order to Procure the Repeal of the Corporation and Test Acts* (Birmingham: Thompson, 1789), 4–11.

honour of these men will be sensibly felt at the general election," and thus encouraged repeal.[132]

Some Dissenters sought to change not just British politics but develop a paradigm for the world. The London Revolution Society, largely composed of Dissenters, had formed to mark the Glorious Revolution's centennial in 1788, leading a national network of affiliates to celebrate British liberty.[133] The group reconvened for a banquet in November 1789, where those assembled – along with approving a congratulatory address to France's National Assembly (see Chapter 9) – heard Price deliver his *Discourse on the Love of Our Country*. Despite its title, the speech developed a universal model for liberty. Price urged full religious equality, asserting "An enlightened and virtuous country must be a free country." Only by openness and education could society advance, while ignorance and superstition would retard its progress. He concluded:

> Tremble all ye oppressors of the world! Take warning all ye supporters of slavish governments, and slavish hierarchies! Call no more (absurdly and wickedly) REFORMATION, innovation. You cannot now hold the world in darkness. Struggle no longer against increasing light and liberality. Restore to mankind their rights; and consent to the correction of abuses, before they and you are destroyed together.[134]

It fell to the present generation to solidify the rights of 1688: religious freedom, resistance against abusive power, and political participation.

British conservatives' reaction against Revolutionary French principles, however, complicated the Dissenters' campaign. Anglican clergy increasingly lobbied for maintaining the restrictions, and many apologists defended the established church. Some denounced the Dissenters' international connections, reminding Britons of their American advocacy. Opponents portrayed permissive tolerance as a conduit to violence, instability, and new forms of persecution. With the rise of revolutions abroad, the Test Acts represented "stability" to supporters.[135]

The Dissenters' challenge led to an Anglican counter-campaign directed by the missionary Society for Promoting Christian Knowledge. They declared the Test Acts necessary for the "Security of the Civil and Ecclesiastical Constitution," insinuating Dissenters' inclinations for political opposition movements.[136] The

---

[132] Fox, *Memorials*, Vol. 2, 360.

[133] Nicholas Rogers, *Crowds, Culture, and Politics in Georgian Britain* (Oxford: Clarendon Press, 1998), 178.

[134] Price, *A Discourse on the Love of Our Country* (London: Cadell, 1789), 19, 50–51.

[135] George Isaac Huntingford, *A Second Letter Addressed to the Delegates from the Several Congregations of Protestant Dissenters Who Met at Devizes on September 14, 1789* (Salisbury: Easton, 1789), 4–5, 40; Ward, *Religion*, 22.

[136] *General Evening Post*, February 4, 1790; *Corporation and Test Acts, December 30, 1789. By the Committee of Protestant Dissenting Laymen and Ministers of the Three Denominations for the West-Riding of the County of York* (Wakefield, 1790).

organization sparked a conservative petition-campaign defending the acts, featuring five diocesan clergy meetings (including York and London), four county meetings, and ten municipalities. The counter-movement built strange alliances with the otherwise often-radical City of London, declaring that removing such "bulwarks of our sacred constitution" would produce "civil anarchy," while the libertine Prince of Wales led donations to the SPCK's cause.[137] The Church of Scotland in February 1790 (though the Acts did not apply there) also denounced repeal.[138] Dissenters' belief in the goodwill of the British populace, including former allies, was shaken.

Negative publicity, from lampooning to condemnations, harmed the repeal movement. One pamphlet mocked Dissenters "appearing for the third time, before the same parliament, with a petition twice debated, and twice disapproved."[139] Burke – turning against his liberal allies from the American, reform, and Dissenter causes – denounced the Revolution Society and Price's *Discourse* in *Reflections on the Revolution in France*, describing a "literary cabal" allied for "destruction of the Christian religion," on the model of disestablished France. The Dissenters' campaign became portrayed as alien to British law and traditions: foreign in inspiration and dangerously attempting to institute a new order.[140]

Dissenters persisted despite growing Anglican opposition, taking continued inspiration from international examples. Priestley responded to Burke in soon-published letters, displaying "sensible regret" they were no longer allies, but found it "unaccountable" that an "avowed friend of the American revolution" now opposed the French. The United States flourished "without any civil establishment of religion at all."[141] One pamphlet compared the Dissenters' cause with American patriots': As "the actors in both scenes are in great part the same," pitting established churches against advocates for tolerance, conservative "obstinate rejection of every appeal to reason" had failed before.[142] Burke and his ilk appeared unenlightened, against reasoned reform.

Fox reintroduced the repeal motion for its third Parliamentary vote in March 1790, presenting the Dissenters' case as "of truth and liberty," and America's peaceful religious plurality as the vindication of their principles.

---

[137] *A Collection of the Resolutions Passed at the Meetings of the Clergy of the Church of England, of the Counties, Corporations, Cities, and Towns, and of the Society for Promoting Christian Knowledge, Assembled to Take into Consideration the Late Application of the Dissenters to Parliament, for the Repeal of the Corporation and Test Acts* (London: Rivington, 1790); *World*, February 1, 1790.

[138] *World*, February 26, 1790.

[139] Horsley, Samuel. *A Review of the Case of the Protestant Dissenters* (London: Robson, 1790), iv.

[140] Burke, *Reflections*, 15, 165, 12.

[141] Priestley, *Letters to the Right Honourable Edmund Burke, Occasioned by his Reflections on the Revolution in France* (Birmingham: Pearson, 1791), iii–v.

[142] *An Address to the Dissidents of England on Their Late Defeat* (London, 1790), 6–7.

Burke responded by denouncing the "abstract principles of natural right," claiming such innovations would break "asunder all those bonds that had formed the happiness of mankind for ages." North and Pitt also spoke against the measure, which failed again.[143] With the movement now stymied, Priestley counseled calm, asserting they would "patiently wait till the nation shall coolly reconsider the question."[144] Dissenters still sought broader mobilization, organizing a national Standing Committee of Protestant Dissenters in England and Wales, but campaigning subsequently declined.[145]

In 1791, removing the last major exception to their advocacy for religious liberty, Dissenters allied with Catholics. That February, Dissenters' lobbying committee carried a resolution wishing Catholic success in applying to Parliament for further relief. Catholic activists thanked them, and Lindsey saw the potential for an integrated movement, so "Catholics and their friends will in turn assist the Dissenters in their next application to the legislature."[146] With universal toleration achieved that year in Poland, reformers like Benjamin Vaughan found their opponents "stick by prejudices," maintaining power by "fomenting hatreds, instead of setting the example of getting rid of them."[147] Yet as British opinion turned against Revolutionary France's perceived excesses, the Dissenters' cause remained unremedied, and many of its more radical opponents like Priestley hounded into silence and/or exile (see Chapter 12).

Conclusion

Radicals, pursuing greater separation of church and state across the Age of Revolution, attempted to revivify individual conscience and freedom of thought. In advancing such ideals, it should be no surprise Dissenters politically mobilized and contributed stalwarts to several of the age's most influential campaigns. Deploying their existing congregational strength via methods borrowed from political reform campaigns, reaching and radicalizing portions of the population prior movements had not, the Dissenters pushed for and often achieved revolutionary changes in the laws governing religion. In America, the success of movements for religious freedom was almost complete, winning pluralism without sacrificing religion's influence. Embracing competition, American religion became as dynamic as the new nation's

---

[143] *The Debate in the House of Commons, on the Repeal of the Corporation and Test Acts: March 2, 1790* (London: Stockdale, 1790), 4–17; *The Writings and Speeches of Edmund Burke*, Vol. 4, Peter James Marshall, ed. (Oxford: Oxford University Press, 2015), 309–10.

[144] G. M. Ditchfield, "The Parliamentary Struggle over the Repeal of the Test and Corporation Acts, 1787–1790," *English Historical Review* 89, no. 1 (1974), 571.

[145] Andrews, *Unitarian*, 110.

[146] Lindsey, *Letters*, Vol. 2, 99.

[147] APS Benjamin Vaughan Papers.

politics. The British Dissenting cause, meanwhile, marked by its risky alliances with radical movements, did not attain full political rights for decades longer. The transatlantic links between these movements have been unduly minimized by American historians focusing on exceptionalist retellings of their nation's religious history, yet Dissenters' development of broad alliances repeatedly offered new mobilization techniques and real-life examples of the possibilities of both liberty and despotism. Soon, Price and fellow British Dissenters helped spark more radical change across the channel in Revolutionary France.

7

The Rise of American Abolitionism

From mid-eighteenth-century perspective, the Atlantic slave system's position appeared virtually impregnable. The transoceanic trade of the sugar and coffee that the enslaved produced enabled British and French ascendancy over the Spanish and Portuguese empires and unleashed a European consumer revolution. The cities of most dynamic growth – Liverpool, London, Bristol, Philadelphia, Bordeaux, and Nantes – could trace their fortunes to such voyages. Indeed, the slave system continued expanding exponentially: three quarters of all captives forced across the Atlantic arrived after 1750.[1] Each European empire permitted enslavement, and perhaps 2.5 million by the mid-eighteenth century toiled in New World bondage. All established churches upheld Old and New Testament justifications of slavery. Every authority, through precedent, laws, and military support, aided and encouraged the traffic.

The subsequent decades, however, recast the slave trade as a diabolical perversion of human rights. Quaker and Enlightened dissent over the inhumanity of slavery practices in the 1760s produced the first activists to contest the trade in the northern American colonies and Britain. Over the next twenty years, antislavery became tied to the American Revolution's most radical elements. The thirteen colonies ended the slave trade (some thought forever) with 1774's Continental Association. Vermont became the first place to formally abolish slavery in 1777 and measures for at least gradual abolition progressed across northern states. Prominent southern slaveholders including Washington, Mason, Jefferson, and Henry endorsed slavery's gradual elimination. Only closed-door Constitutional Convention dealings preserved the slave trade for another generation, indefinitely postponed southern slavery's abolition, and raised a strong dividing line between north and south.

The American Revolution's contribution to the rise of international antislavery has not been adequately recognized by existing studies. American historians, often seeking to place the revolution within long struggles over slavery and racism, have minimized the extent to which patriots' (partially successful)

---

[1] David Eltis, "Was Abolition of the U.S. and British Slave Trade Significant in Broader Atlantic Context?" *William and Mary Quarterly* 66, no. 4 (2009), 720.

attempts to dismantle the slave system represented the first systemic reforms in what became a humanitarian revolution in liberal conscience. A decade ahead of their European counterparts, Americans made abolition a reality – though not nearly as widespread as their highest ideals encouraged.

While American antislavery activists during the revolutionary era did not broadly organize as an autonomous mass movement, as their late-eighteenth-century British or Antebellum successors would, and although forms of passive (and sometimes active) slave resistance had long been universal, abolitionist organizing first emerged from the patriot movement. Slavery drew colonists' attention and concern, many of whom pushed for (and sometimes enacted) abolishing the slave trade or even slavery itself. Radical consciousness expanded with human rights for the poorest of society's members becoming an integral part of subsequent Atlantic campaigns.

Quakers, Enlightenment, and the Origins of Abolitionist Action

By the American Revolution, the Society of Friends, or Quakers, had functioned as a transatlantic community for over a century. Prominent in Britain's merchant community, Quakers from the 1650s onward spread across the empire. Slavery had been a contentious issue from the movement's inception. Despite the Bible's justifications for slavery, Quaker founder George Fox, personally taking his ministry to Barbados, voiced his unease with the practice, stressing humankind's equality before God and urging humane treatment of slaves. Critiques mounted that slavery prevented blacks from exercising free will (central to Quaker faith and salvation), forced Friends to violate their commitment to nonviolence, encouraged owners' sloth, and tempted lechery. Yet throughout the seventeenth and much of the eighteenth centuries, members continued buying and owning human beings. William Penn founded Pennsylvania in 1681, like every other British New World possession, as a slave colony. In many respects, the Quakers were egalitarian without a formal ministry, believing all regardless of race or gender could receive revelations and directly experience god. Yet male Quakers dominated most congregations, which did not allow blacks as equal members.[2]

Mobilizing Quakers to follow their teachings' higher dictates, given the involvement of many in slavery and the slave trade, was not easy. Despite their emphasis on spiritual equality, members had to maintain public unanimity on religious questions outside their meetinghouses. All Quakers, on threat of excommunication, could not make public pronouncements without their congregation's approval. Consensus had to build through Quaker governing

---

[2] Jean R. Soderlund, *Quakers & Slavery: A Divided Spirit* (Princeton: Princeton University Press, 1985), 3, 18, 148; Claire Midgley, *Women against Slavery: The British Campaigns, 1780–1870* (New York: Routledge, 1992), 14; Brekus, "Revoution," 120.

networks. All branches corresponded with one another through local monthly, regional quarterly, and continental yearly meetings, with the Philadelphia and London Yearly Meetings corresponding as autonomous equals.[3] Asymmetries multiplied between the British and American branches, including over slavery.

Quaker antislavery activism grew slowly and unevenly. Germantown, Pennsylvania, Friends founded the first antislavery society in 1688 outside their church's formal confines. Debates soon permeated the church and its corresponding networks: in 1696 Philadelphia's yearly meeting advised its members against slave trading, in 1700 asked their Barbados counterparts to cease shipping Pennsylvania slaves, and in 1719 barred members from trafficking. London progressed decades later, advising against slaving in 1727 and forbidding participation in 1761. Radical dissenting Pennsylvania members began denouncing slavery itself in the 1730s, and the church (more slowly) pressed the issue. Philadelphia's Friends in 1758 disallowed Church business with any slave-trading merchants, establishing a committee for enforcement and urging members to free their slaves. Yet even thereafter, most Quaker merchants dealt slave-produced products: tobacco, rum, molasses, sugar, and rice especially.[4]

Abolishing slaveholding itself, however, proved difficult within the Quaker community. Still in 1760, 70 percent of longtime Pennsylvania Quaker slave owners had not freed their slaves. Despite Quakers encouraging "gradual emancipation" to integrate free slaves into society, owners often made slaves sign labor contracts guaranteeing ten years' additional service before manumission.[5] Nevertheless, Friends increasingly believed massive changes approached. A School for Black People, run by prominent activist Anthony Benezet, began in 1770 to demonstrate their intellectual equality with whites.[6] A growing emphasis on humanitarianism, while pressuring coreligionists to uphold high moral standards, pushed the Quakers further.

American Quakers banned slaveholding in 1774. Even then, American Friends justified emancipation for their own spiritual reasons without advocating broader colonial reforms. Emphasizing withdrawal from the world's sins rather than creating an earthly utopia, Quaker leadership did not mobilize

---

[3] Soderlund, *Quakers*, 17; Roger Anstey, *The Atlantic Slave Trade and British Abolition, 1760–1810* (Atlantic Highlands, NJ: Humanities Press, 1975), 200–1.

[4] Wayne J. Eberly, "The Pennsylvania Abolition Society, 1775–1830" (PhD Thesis, Pennsylvania State University, 1973), 5; Soderlund, *Quakers*, 87, 148; Marcus Rediker, *The Fearless Benjamin Lay: The Quaker Dwarf Who Became the First Revolutionary Abolitionist* (Boston: Beacon Press, 2017); Anstey, *Atlantic*, 204 and 211; David Brion Davis, *The Problem of Slavery in Western Culture* (Ithaca: Cornell University Press, 1966), 305.

[5] Brycchan Carey and Geoffrey Plank, "Introduction," in *Quakers and Abolition*, Carey and Plank, eds. (Urbana, IL: University of Illinois Press, 2014), 4.

[6] Maurice Jackson, *Let This Voice Be Heard: Anthony Benezet, Father of American Abolitionism* (Philadelphia: University of Pennsylvania Press, 2009), 23.

a broader antislavery social movement. Amid a worsening imperial crisis, the colonial press ignored Quaker abolition.[7] Nevertheless, many Friends soon helped launch a campaign bringing abolition of the slave trade and even slavery itself into the revolutionary mainstream.

Before 1765's Stamp Act crisis, few non-Quakers openly considered ending slavery. Yet critiques of slavery's brutality had multiplied over recent decades. A growing number of British writers condemned slavery as a barbaric practice affronting their own freedom. Across Anglican, Presbyterian, and dissenting faiths, a growing emphasis on benevolence led many to hope Britain and Christian civilization in general would outgrow slavery, while wondering whether divine retribution would come against enslavers. Turning disgust into action against powerful mercantile slaving interests, however, remained another matter. Benezet corresponded not only with evangelicals like Whitefield and Wesley – hoping for dramatic conversion and enlightenment on the slave question – but with Canterbury's Archbishop, sending exposés on the traffic and urging the Church of England to consider the "great inhumanity and wickedness" exercised by Anglican parishioners. Still, Benezet proposed no specific measures and the church took no action.[8]

Much Enlightened opinion across Europe already held slavery in contempt. Though most seventeenth- and early-eighteenth century thinkers believed inequality a part of society more than equality a part of nature, and often justified slavery as saving Africans from indigenous war and irreligion, by the mid-eighteenth century new critiques of European practices advanced.[9] As one early antislavery pamphlet quoted Baron de Montesquieu, slavery is "neither useful to the master nor Slave," with the former's tyranny sapping "all moral virtues" and making practitioners "haughty, hasty, hard-hearted, passionate, voluptuous and cruel."[10] The French clergyman Raynal, in a multivolume history of European colonialism garnering fifty-five eighteenth-century editions in five languages beginning in 1770, secretly cowritten with leading *philosophe* Denis Diderot, considered slavery contrary to human nature and thus universally wrong. They asserted such injustice would end

[7] Christopher Leslie Brown, *Moral Capital: Foundations of British Abolitionism* (Chapel Hill: University of North Carolina Press, 2006), 91; keyword-searching "Quakers" and "slavery" in the Early American Newspapers database produces no items relating to their abolition of slavery. Accessed April 7, 2018.
[8] Robert Vaux, *Memoirs of the Life of Anthony Benezet* (Philadelphia: Parke, 1817), 32–34; Clarkson, *History*, 171; Nicholas Hudson, "'Britons Never Will Be Slaves': National Myth, Conservatism, and the Beginnings of British Antislavery," *Eighteenth-Century Studies* 34, no. 4 (2001), 559–76; James Walvin, *England, Slaves and Freedom, 1776–1838* (Jackson, MS: University Press of Mississippi, 1986), 99.
[9] Davis, *Problem of Slavery in Western Culture*, 391–94.
[10] Sharp, *A Representation of the Injustice and Dangerous Tendency of Tolerating Slavery in England* (London: White, 1769), 79.

via insurrection: "the negroes lack only a chief courageous enough to lead them to vengeance and slaughter."[11] To some radicals, slavery provided the clearest evidence for humankind's fall from nature into the corruption of society. Yet despite such Enlightened humanitarian invective, *philosophes* remained divided about slavery, with apologists alternately emphasizing African brutality, pseudoscientific racial difference, and the colonial system's utility.[12]

British writers had long considered "slavery" the antithesis of their own freedom, even while profiting from the slave system. John Locke began his *First Treatise of Government* in 1689 by declaring, "Slavery is so vile and miserable an estate of man, and so directly opposite to the generous temper and courage of our nation, that it is hardly to be conceived that an Englishman, much less a gentleman, should plead for it."[13] Yet Locke himself cofounded new slave-trading companies and helped write the nascent Carolina colony's constitution.[14] The popular mid-century anthem *Rule Britannia* ironically proclaimed, "Britons never shall be slaves," as they became the world leader in trafficking. Only slowly did the hypocrisy of men proudly boasting of their freedom while enslaving others lead to attempts at ameliorating the system.

A new generation of economists arose after mid-century questioning slave trafficking's necessity, claiming free labor's superiority over slave work. Authors including Franklin, the Marquis de Mirabeau, David Hume, and Adam Smith argued the cost of acquiring, housing, and feeding the enslaved, together with the slaves' disincentive to work more than necessary to avoid punishment, retarded rather than stimulated economic growth.[15] Slavery became the most dramatic example of an institution stifling individual initiative. For many reformers, utilitarian objections to slavery coalesced with humanitarian ones.

In moral terms, many Americans – even slaveholders – spoke of slavery's injustice, despite lacking comprehensive abolition plans. Arthur Lee, future London Society of Supporters of the Bill of Rights secretary, in 1764 responded to Smith's *Theory of Moral Sentiments*, beginning his argument in "vindication" of colonial practices, but concluded by condemning the slave system.

[11] Abbé Raynal, *Histoire philosophique et politique des établissemens & du commerce des Européens dans les deux Indes* (La Haye, 1774) Vol. 4, 226; Davis, *Problem of Slavery in Western Culture*, 14; Palmer, *Age*, Vol. 1, 239.

[12] Davis, *Problem of Slavery in Western Culture*, 419; Emmanuel Chukwudi Eze, ed. *Race and the Enlightenment: A Reader* (Oxford: Blackwell, 1997).

[13] Peter Gay, *The Enlightenment: An Interpretation: The Science of Freedom* (New York: Norton, 1969), 409.

[14] Robin Bernasconi and Anika Maaza Mann, "The Contradictions of Racism: Locke, Slavery and the Two Treatises, in *Race and Racism in Modern Philosophy*, Andrew Valls, ed. (Ithaca: Cornell University Press, 2005), 89.

[15] Robin Blackburn, *The Overthrow of Colonial Slavery, 1776–1848* (London: Verso, 1988), 52; Adam Smith, *An Inquiry into the Nature and Causes of the Wealth of Nations* (Edinburgh: Nelson, 1843), 159.

Showing his caste's prejudices, Lee considered black "understandings are generally shallow, and their hearts cruel," while admitting slavery's usefulness for plantations. Yet Lee found slavery "absolutely repugnant to justice" and "abhorrent utterly from the Christian religion." As "Life and liberty were both the gifts of God," Lee asserted, he refused to believe "necessity is a plea for injustice." Examining slave societies' histories, Virginia's freemen faced "fearful odds" against a major revolt.[16] Slaves constituted about 40 percent of Virginia's population, though significantly more in the Tidewater region, with their strength enhanced by new arrivals of captured African warriors.[17]

By the American Revolution, a diverse array of arguments – moral, economic, and pragmatic – developed against slavery and the slave trade. Still, there seemed little prospect of discontent turning into concerted action, particularly given the lack of precedent or models for such monumental changes. The examples of the Sons of Liberty and Committees of Correspondence, however, changed that. Challenging the slave system, opposing the powerful mercantile and plantation interests profiting from the slave order, advanced amid the upheavals and inspirations of Americans' broader push for liberty.

Abolitionism and the Coming of the American Revolution

Though not yet itself a distinct social movement, abolitionist sentiment became deeply entwined with the push for American independence. Motivated by their belief in natural rights and evolving moral standards, American abolitionism grew through a synthesis between patriot and Quaker/evangelical thinking. As patriots conceptualized their struggle against Britain as resistance to "tyranny" or even "slavery," while rethinking American government and society, growing Christian condemnations turned slavery from an accepted colonial arrangement to a scourge needing reform. Antislavery became an important aspect of revolutionary America's social movements.

Amid the Stamp Act crisis came the first calls to abolish the Atlantic slave trade. Benezet, already author of multiple exposés on the treatment of slaves, in 1766 published an antislavery manifesto, *A Caution and Warning to Great Britain and Her Colonies.* "At a time when the general rights and liberties of mankind," brought "universal consideration," the slave trade's injustice became profound. The current system, enslaving "our fellow-creatures, as

---

[16] Arthur Lee, *An Essay in Vindication of the Continental Colonies of America, from a Censure of Mr. Adam Smith, in His Theory of Moral Sentiments* (London: Becket, 1764), 13, 32, 37, 40–44.

[17] Alan Taylor, *The Internal Enemy: Slavery and War in Virginia, 1772–1832* (New York: Norton, 2013).

free as ourselves by nature, and equally with us the subjects of Christ's redeeming grace," appeared unjustifiable, while abolition deserved "the most serious consideration of all who are concerned for the civil or religious welfare of their country." Not only was the trade hypocritical, Benezet argued, but it debased free society, destroying "the bonds of natural affection and interest, whereby mankind in general are united." The pamphlet asked slavers to justify their practices, via "reason, equity and humanity," or cease operations.[18] From early in the prerevolutionary crises, Americans were encouraged to apply their principles of liberty against international slave trafficking.

American patriots, rhetorically adopting British Whig fears of decline into the metaphorical despotism of slavery, began developing empathy for actual slaves. In May 1766, the same month news of the Stamp Act's repeal arrived, Boston's town meeting instructed its representatives to consider outlawing the trade and even slavery itself in Massachusetts. "Oh! Ye sons of liberty," a 1767 pamphlet asked, "Can you review our late struggles for liberty, and think of the slave-trade at the same time, and not blush?"[19] Though some faulted slaves for not resisting oppression like "freeborn Britons," others began considering slavery as one of British rule's worst depredations. Boston's Joseph Warren in 1766 declared, "Freedom and equality is the state of nature, but slavery is the most unnatural and violent state that can be conceived of."[20] Particularly where economically unessential, slavery became a brutal and unjust exception to the society patriots sought to build.

Amid the prerevolutionary controversies, Massachusetts' legislature considered dismantling their slave system. In early 1767, the lower chamber debated a bill "to prevent the unwarrantable & unusual Practice . . . of inslaving Mankind," considering the practice "no real advantage" to the colony. The body tabled the measure, however, approving new taxes to deter slave importations instead.[21] Nevertheless, slavery debates multiplied. The *Boston Gazette* in March condemned traditional Christian justifications of enslavement to save African souls, considering the trade "a vile, detestable, hypocritical Artifice to smooth over their antichristian, diabolical Covetousness, Cruelty and Murder."[22] A 1768 Anglican sermon excerpted in the *Boston Evening-Post*

---

[18] Anthony Benezet, *A Caution and Warning to Great Britain and Her Colonies in a Short Representation of the Calamitous State of the Enslaved Negroes in the British Dominions* (Philadelphia: Miller, 1766), 3, 4, 34.

[19] Nathaniel Appleton, *Considerations on Slavery* (Boston: Edes and Gill, 1767), 19.

[20] Peter A. Dorsey, *Common Bondage: Slavery as Metaphor in Revolutionary America* (Knoxville: University of Tennessee Press, 2009), 13.

[21] John K. Alexander, *Samuel Adams: The Life of an American Revolutionary* (Lanham, MD: Rowan & Littlefield, 2011), 56–57; Gary B. Nash, *Race and Revolution* (Madison: Madison House, 1980), 9; Douglas R. Egerton, *Death or Liberty: African Americans and Revolutionary America* (Oxford: Oxford University Press, 2009), 56; NA CO 5/760 169.

[22] *Boston Gazette*, March 27, 1767.

declared enslavement "directly contrary to sacred scripture and solid reason," asserting, "Every man that is born into this world, is born free, and cannot justly be made a slave."[23] In 1771, a bill to abolish trafficking passed the legislature, only to be vetoed by Governor Hutchinson. Following Samuel Adams's personally presenting a petition from Massachusetts blacks, the measure passed the legislature again in 1774.[24] Without executive approval, however, no major changes occurred before the revolution.

Concurrently, Massachusetts blacks used the courts to sue for their freedom. In 1766's *Slew v. Whipple*, Jenny Slew, daughter of a white mother and slave father, won liberation after being kept four years as a slave. The Essex Superior Court considered the "contest between liberty and property" with "liberty of most importance of the two." In 1768, John Adams successfully argued an illegal enslavement case in *Margaret v. Muzzy* and later declared he "never knew a Jury by a verdict to determine a negro to be a slave – and they always found them free." Though subsequent studies have shown this to be an exaggeration (including of Adams's own record), regular emancipations demonstrated growing antislavery sentiment.[25]

Such a revolution in perceptions of slavery benefitted from a growing number of religious leaders adopting antislavery stances. Benezet targeted British imperial religious networks to spread his ideas, sending copies to the missionary Society for Propagating the Gospel and meeting with Whitefield.[26] Whereas previously opposition to slavery was left to individual conscience, across New England and increasing swaths of the mid-Atlantic colonies, ministers now circulated calls for collective abolitionist efforts. "For shame," Connecticut Congregationalist minister Nathaniel Niles orated, "let us either cease to enslave our fellow-men, or else let us cease to complain of those that would enslave us."[27] As American patriots' political action intensified, they became more willing to broaden debates into great moral questions as well.

The American controversies helped push pro-abolition agendas in Britain as well as America. Obscure customs clerk Granville Sharp began his rise to abolitionist prominence in 1768 by publishing *A Representation of the Injustice and Dangerous Tendency of Tolerating Slavery*, declaring involuntary servitude unconstitutional under British common law. Any slave brought to Great Britain itself, Sharp argued, should be confiscated like "contraband

---

[23] *Boston Evening-Post*, May 2, 1768.

[24] Egerton, *Death*, 56; Alexander, *Samuel Adams*, 57; LC Samuel Adams Papers, MSS 10223 Vol. 4.

[25] Steven M. Wise, *Though the Heavens May Fall: The Landmark Trial That Led to the End of Human Slavery* (Cambridge, MA: Da Capo Press, 2005), 131; Catherine Adams and Elizabeh H. Pleck, *Love of Freedom: Black Women in Colonial and Revolutionary New England* (Oxford: Oxford University Press, 2010), 242.

[26] Haverford College, Anthony Benezet Papers, MSS 852.

[27] Egerton, *Death*, 47.

goods" and set free. As a captive could only be enslaved if "divested of his humanity," Sharp sought to defend the highest conceptions of British liberty.[28] While publicly advocating American liberty, Sharp made clear support was conditional, denouncing the "enormous Wickednesses which are openly avowed & practiced throughout the British Empire."[29] He urged Americans to develop a new system as "men, who do not scruple to detain others in slavery, have but a very partial and unjust claim to the protection of the laws of liberty."[30] The expansiveness of evolving concepts of freedom led interested Britons to push American activists farther.

The first British assault on the slave trade did not occur through Parliament, but instead via the judiciary. James Somerset, born a slave in Virginia, was taken by his master to Britain. Keeping black servants remained fashionable in London, where 2–3 percent of the population by 1771 was of African descent.[31] That December, authorities found Somerset shackled in a ship's hull at the East London docks. Though captured Africans' legal status in Britain had long been ambiguous, Sharp - aided by Parliamentary radical and Bill of Rights society stalwart Serjeant Glynn - took Somerset's case, alleging unlawful detainment against a West Indian planter-merchant consortium demanding reenslavement. Chief Justice the Earl of Mansfield (who in 1768 liberated John Wilkes), citing precedents against serfdom in England, declared slavery "so odious" and antithetical to British liberty; "nothing can be suffered to support it but positive law."[32] The decision had limitations: only Somerset was initially freed, and the ruling only applied to owners trying to export their slaves back to the colonies against their will. The case did not provide a legal model for New World abolition, where colonial legislatures enacted detailed slave regulations. Nevertheless, a powerful precedent was established, judging slavery and British liberty incompatible. When planters asked Parliament for a "positive law" guaranteeing their property, the Commons refused.[33]

In the Somerset Case's aftermath, many prominent intellectuals increasingly supported antislavery causes. Franklin in London witnessed a shift among his British connections and American correspondents, writing to Benezet in 1772, the "People of the Northern colonies begin to be sensible of the evil tendency" of slavery. At Benezet's encouragement, Franklin (though a slave owner

---

[28] Sharp, *Representation*, 12, 15.

[29] GRO D 3549 13/1/R10.

[30] Sharp, *Representation*, 81.

[31] Wise, *Though*, 8.

[32] Gerald Horne, *The Counter-Revolution of 1776: Slave Resistance and the Origins of the United States of America* (New York: New York University Press, 2014), 210; Wise, *Though*, 183.

[33] Betty Fladeland, *Men and Brothers: Anglo-American Antislavery Cooperation* (Urbana, IL: University of Illinois Press, 1973), 21; James Walvin, *Black and White: The Negro in English Society, 1555–1945* (London: Allen Lane, 1973).

himself) began meeting with Sharp. The two agreed to "act in concert on the Affair of Slavery" and Franklin commenced circulating antislavery tracts among his reformist friends.[34] Though still writing anonymously, Franklin advocated abolishing the slave trade and a more gradual end to slavery in the *London Chronicle* the following year, using the Somerset Case to beseech "that the same humanity may extend itself" to America, including "declaring the children of present slaves free after they become of age." Thereby, slavery would end within a lifetime. Citing yearly slave importation figures of 100,000, Franklin bitingly asked, "Can sweetening our tea, &c. with sugar, be a circumstance of such absolute necessity?"[35] Even as Franklin continued doing Georgia's bidding (alongside several northern colonies) as a colonial agent, fundamental changes beckoned.[36]

Even in certain slave societies, especially Virginia, many sought to limit slavery's growth. Though most still considered enslavement an economic necessity for tobacco plantations, many began arguing for international trafficking's abolition. In 1767 and 1769, Virginia's House of Burgesses passed bills doubling slave importation duties.[37] As part of their June 1769 nonimportation agreement protesting the Townshend Acts, the House resolved to not allow "into the Colony, either by Sea or Land, any Slaves" who had not spent twelve months on the mainland.[38] As Virginia Governor Lord Dunmore explained, "the people with great reason tremble at the facility that an enemy would find in procuring such a body of men" with "no ties to their masters or to the Country."[39] Georgia and the Carolinas banned the Atlantic slave trade in their own nonimportation agreements. Though this led to speculation in slave prices (Maryland did not follow), the Atlantic trade's future fell into question – as more slowly did slavery itself. Word of Somerset's liberation spread among the enslaved, with at least one attempting to stowaway on a ship to England to gain freedom.[40] As late colonial politics destabilized, many Americans feared racial tumult.

Though colonists boycotted other items as a temporary expedient to deprive Britain of revenue, patriots debated permanently abolishing the Atlantic slave trade. Indeed, with plantation production remaining robust over the two years since nonimportation began, Virginia's House of Burgesses in April 1772 adopted a royal petition calling for trafficking's permanent abolition.

[34] Franklin, *Papers*, Vol. 19, 114; Fladeland, *Men*, 19; Vaux, *Memoirs*, 42; Jackson, *Let*, 114.
[35] Franklin, *Papers*, Vol. 19, 187; for claiming authorship, see letter to Benezet: ibid., 269.
[36] David Waldstreicher, *Runaway America: Benjamin Franklin, Slavery and the American Revolution* (New York: Hill and Wang, 2004), 201.
[37] Woody Holton, *Forced Founders: Indians, Debtors, Slaves and the Making of the American Revolution in Virginia* (Chapel Hill: University of North Carolina Press, 1999), 67.
[38] *Pennsylvania Gazette*, July 12, 1770.
[39] NA CO 5/219 101.
[40] UVSC William Lee Papers; Middlekauff, *Glorious* 182–83; Wise, *Though* 200.

Rationales were both humanitarian and pragmatic with the House denouncing the trade's "inhumanity," while asserting, "we have too much reason to fear" potential slave revolts that could "endanger the very existence of your Majesty's American Dominions."[41] Tacky's Revolt in 1760 British Jamaica killed four hundred whites and ninety-three blacks. Others plotted worse: Jamaican officials in 1765 uncovered a seventeen plantation-wide conspiracy, while insurrections were foiled at Montserrat in 1768 and Antigua in 1769. Slave uprisings at St. Vincent in 1772–1773 and Tobago in 1771, 1772, and 1774 required military suppression.[42] Particularly as American political controversies grew, dividing the oftentimes-small white communities, social revolution loomed. Abolishing the slave trade and improving present slaves' lot could serve colonial needs.

With the British refusing action against the slave trade, prominent Virginians claimed the moral high ground. From plantation owners' pens came unlikely denunciations of slavery. Henry in 1773, after reading Benezet's work, wrote in horror that such "a species of violence and tyranny" had "been introduced in the most enlightened times." Despite noting, "I am the master of slaves, of my own purchase!" he continued, "I will not, I cannot justify it." While refusing to manumit his own, for no better reason than the "general inconvenience of living here without them," he declared, "a time will come when an opportunity will be offered to abolish this lamentable evil."[43] Such sentiments spread among the planter elite. "The abolition of domestic slavery," Jefferson wrote in 1774, "is the great object of desire in these colonies, where it was unhappily introduced."[44] Even if accomplished gradually, this would be a revolutionary step.

Patriot consensus widened against the slave trade. Philadelphia Quakers in March 1773 reported Virginia, North Carolina, and South Carolina authorities "well-inclined" toward further slave importation restrictions.[45] Pennsylvania in April, following petitions from Quaker meetings and "Clergy both of the Church of England & Dissenters," doubled slave import duties from £10 to £20, which Benezet asserted would "effectually prevent" trafficking.[46] Public pressure grew with Rush asserting, "now three-fourths of the province as well as the city cry out" for the trade's abolition.[47] Philadelphia Friends reported slavery of "increasing Concern in the minds of many, not in religious

---

[41] *Pennsylvania Gazette*, January 13, 1773.
[42] O'Shaughnessy, *Empire*, 38, 52–53.
[43] Patrick Henry, *Life, Correspondence and Speeches* (New York: Scribner's, 1891), Vol. 1, 152–53.
[44] Brown, *Moral Capital*, 143.
[45] Swarthmore College, Philadelphia Meeting for Sufferings, MR-PH507.
[46] HC Quaker MS, MICRO BX 7619.L88 reel 7, 91 and Benezet Papers, MSS 852.
[47] Benjamin Rush, *Letters of Benjamin Rush* (Philadelphia: American Philosophical Society, 1951), 80.

Fellowship with us."[48] In 1774, petitions against the trade reached the North Carolina, Maryland, Pennsylvania, and New Jersey legislatures. New York and Massachusetts passed slave importation duties, though each colony's royal governor vetoed the measure.[49] The prerevolutionary crises fundamentally challenged slavery's place in the American colonies.

Antislavery activism represented the flower of American political idealism. Benezet asserted in 1773, "the cause we plead is so good it must in the end be an honour to those who will have appeared the first promoters of it."[50] Rush wrote glowingly in 1774 that American "benevolence and liberality are unbounded" and no cause could better show patriots' seriousness than grappling with slavery.[51] With the anti-tax campaigns controversial in Britain, antislavery provided a useful issue for building transatlantic connections. Benezet brought Rush into correspondence with Sharp and other British reformers. Rush publicized a rising "spirit of humanity and religion" against the trade, and his "hopes of living to see it abolished or put upon another footing in America."[52] Writing for an international as well as domestic audience, Rush published a pamphlet calling slavery a "national crime" inviting "national punishment." Even as colonists' actions lagged behind their rhetoric – Rush did not free his own slave for another fifteen years – collective changes increasingly seemed possible.[53]

Agitating against slavery allowed patriots to deploy natural rights arguments more easily. As Sharp wrote to a New Jersey Quaker in June 1774, shortly after Franklin sent two hundred copies of Sharp's *The People's Natural Right to a Share in the Legislature* to America, "if they hope to maintain their own natural rights and to have Justice on their side they ought not to deny the same Rights to others."[54] Colonists' rhetoric made slavery's continuation seem absurd to many – especially as they sought support abroad in their standoff with British authorities. Rush wrote to Sharp of "bringing about some great revolution in behalf of our oppressed Negro brethren," to add "blow to blow to the monster of British tyranny in America."[55] Abolitionist action could also answer Tory detractors: Samuel Johnson, in the *coup de grâce* of his 1775 *Taxation No Tyranny*, written at the North administration's request, famously mocked, "how is it that we hear the loudest yelps for liberty among the drivers

---

[48] HC Quaker MS, MICRO BX 7619.L88 reel 7, 91.
[49] *Newport Mercury*, June 13, 1774.
[50] HC Anthony Benezet Papers, MSS 852.
[51] Fruchtman, *Atlantic*, 35.
[52] Rush, *Letters*, 80.
[53] Nash, *Race*, 9.
[54] GRO D 3549 13–1-A8.
[55] Rush, *Correspondence*, 3.

of negroes?"[56] Though such Tory reposts sought to sink Americans' natural rights rhetoric, the provocations pushed patriots to apply their ideas. Long-avoided questions of morality became immediate concerns.[57]

African-Americans advanced their own cause. In Massachusetts, a "humble Petition of many Slaves, living in the Town of Boston, and other Towns in the Province" arrived before the House of Representatives in January 1773, pro-testing their "unhappy state" and asking for slavery's full and immediate abolition. The pamphlet version's preface asked for resolutions from Massachusetts' growing Committee of Correspondence network, while pres-suring authorities to pass abolition to demonstrate that "instead of being pretended Friends to Liberty, we are really hearty for the general and unalien-able Rights of Mankind." An afterword, signed "THE SONS OF AFRICA," the same name London's black activists used, praised local men who recently emancipated their slaves.[58] Several petitions followed over the next two years, including a phonetic one in 1774 asking "that we may obtain our Natural right our freedoms and our children may be set at lebety."[59] Lack of white redress, however, led to rumors of a Boston slave revolt that September.[60] Natural rights became self-evident and revolutionary rhetoric's applications readily comprehensible.

Antislavery's inroads into the transatlantic Christian evangelical revival deepened. In 1774, Wesley published *Thoughts on Slavery*. Recalling experi-ences in Georgia, the minister took inspiration from Benezet's *Some Historical Account of Guinea*, denouncing "that execrable sum of all villainies, commonly called the Slave trade." Indeed, Wesley's pamphlet lifted whole sections of Benezet's text, and more generally adapted both Quaker Biblical interpret-ations and natural rights philosophy to make a damning moral case.[61] He dismissed traditional arguments justifying enslaving non-Christians, arguing it "impossible" for "any reasonable creature to violate all the laws of Justice and Mercy, and Truth." Enslavers could only act immorally, as "No circumstances can make it necessary for a man to burst in sunder all the ties of humanity." Economic arguments seemed even more illegitimate: "Wealth is not necessary to the Glory of any Nation; but Wisdom, Virtue, Justice, Mercy, Generosity,

[56] Samuel Johnson, *Taxation No Tyranny: An Answer to the Resolutions and Address of the American Congress* (London: Cadell, 1775), 89; Bromwich, *Intellectual*, 228.

[57] Brown, *Moral*, 129, 134.

[58] *The Appendix: Or, Some Observations on the Expediency of the Petitions of the Africans, Living in Boston, &c.* (Boston: Russell, 1773), 9–10, 6–7, 12.

[59] Howard Zinn and Anthony Arnove, *Voices from a People's History of the United States*, 2nd ed. (New York: Seven Stories Press, 2014), 56–57.

[60] Gary B. Nash, *The Unknown American Revolution: The Unruly Birth of Democracy and the Struggle to Create America* (New York: Viking, 2005), 158.

[61] Jackson, *Let*, 154.

Public Spirit, Love of our Country ... Better no Trade, than trade produced by villainy."[62] Slavery's place in Christian thought came under attack.

The rise in prerevolutionary antislavery fervor – including for abolishing slavery itself – continued as the colonies moved onto war footing. Providence's May 17, 1774 town meeting, in the first motion passed for a Continental Congress, directed their deputies to obtain "an act of the General Assembly [of Rhode Island] prohibiting the importation of Negro slaves into this colony; and that all Negroes born in the colony, should be free, after obtaining to a certain age."[63] A growing number of patriots considered liberty and emancipation consubstantial.

Gradual emancipation, ending the slave trade while slowly implementing slavery's abolition, appeared most practical. A January 1775 *New-York Journal* editorial considered slaves' immediate emancipation would expose them "suddenly to poverty and distress, without properly preparing them for supporting themselves." Responsible reform required providing black youths with marketable skills.[64] Benezet prophesized bringing "reason & humanity & religion," together in a new system wherein work "would be better and more profitably done" by free laborers than slaves.[65] The slave system's economic and social power required a multi-tiered approach.

The desire for immediate action against the slave trade spread into Virginia's political mainstream. July 1774's Fairfax County Resolves, largely written by Mason and approved with Washington presiding, recommended that "during our present Difficulties and Distress, no Slaves ought to be imported into any of the British Colonies on this Continent," asserting "our most earnest Wishes to see an entire Stop for ever put to such a wicked cruel and unnatural Trade."[66] Indeed, a draft of Virginia's instructions to their Continental Congress representatives in August declared slavery "unhappily introduced in their infant state" and "so shameful an abuse of power" that they wished "to exclude all further importations from Africa."[67] Though the paragraph was deleted from the final version, such opinions – in the Virginian center of the American slave system – reflected major changes in consciousness. The colony suspended Atlantic slave trading in August as part of their nonimportation agreement against Britain, as did North Carolina the same month.[68]

[62] John Wesley, *Thoughts upon Slavery*, 4th ed. (Dublin: Whitestone, 1775), 19–21.
[63] Rappleye, *Sons* 144.
[64] *New-York Journal*, January 12, 1775.
[65] HC Anthony Benezet Letters, MSS 852.
[66] George Mason, *The Papers of George Mason, 1725–1792*, Vol. 1 (Chapel Hill: University of North Carolina Press, 1970), 207.
[67] Jefferson, *Papers*, Vol. 1, 130.
[68] Benjamin Quarles, *The Negro in the American Revolution* (Chapel Hill: University of North Carolina Press, 1961), 41.

Among the first measures the Continental Congress passed in September 1774, after Benezet personally lobbied delegates, was a comprehensive slave importation ban as part of their broader nonimportation agreement against British shipping.[69] In December the colonies together pledged to "wholly discontinue" trafficking and boycott non-adhering areas.[70] Despite enforcement difficulties, partisans considered the measure a principled stand. One *Pennsylvania Gazette* letter boasted how liberty-seeking colonists realized "the impropriety of demanding" from British authorities what "they have not been willing to grant to their fellow men."[71] Rush exclaimed to Sharp, "we have now turned from our wickedness," predicting "there will not be a Negro slave in North America in 40 years."[72] Though pragmatism mixed with principle – Benezet worried of the "dreadfull danger" slaves posed amid imperial destabilization – a revolutionary cocktail mixed.[73]

Quaker collaboration with budding American revolutionaries was badly injured, however, by their November 1774 withdrawal from the patriot coalition. Though their creative nonviolence had deeply influenced the recent boycotts, Friends could not abide by the militia mobilizations that tempted war. Pernicious British influence seemed to lurk behind the sect's decision with the Pennsylvania and New Jersey meeting in January 1775 resolving that American actions "threaten the subversion of constitutional government" for their Peaceable Kingdom.[74] Stiles did not understand why Friends could not continue in auxiliary roles, send "Petitions to the King & Parliament & pple. of England," or motivate London's meeting to lobby for the Americans.[75] The Quakers persisted in neutrality, sacrificing their standing in revolutionary slavery debates.

Despite Quaker withdrawal, American patriots innovated new forms of antislavery organization. Five days after Lexington and Concord, the Society for the Relief of Negroes Unlawfully Held in Bondage, the first organization specifically formed to advocate for black rights, held its first meeting at Philadelphia's Rising Sun Tavern. Though only about a dozen men attended, they included Benezet and Paine.[76] Rather than openly advocating abolition,

[69] J. Franklin Jameson, *The American Revolution Considered as a Social Movement* (Boston: Beacon Press, 1956), 24; Fladeland, *Men*, 26.
[70] *Massachusetts Gazette*, October 31, 1774.
[71] *Pennsylvania Gazette*, January 25, 1775.
[72] Rush, *Correspondence*, 13.
[73] HC Anthony Benezet Letters, MSS 852.
[74] NA CO 5/1286 41.
[75] LC Peter Force Papers, Ezra Stiles Diary.
[76] Richard Newman, "The Pennsylvania Abolition Society and the Struggle for Racial Justice," in *Antislavery and Abolition in Philadelphia: Emancipation and the Long Struggle for Racial Justice in the City of Brotherly Love*, Newman and James Meuller, eds (Baton Rouge: Louisiana State University Press, 2011), 49.

the group (as its name suggested) took up illegal enslavement cases: the first being "that Benjamin Bamerman Holds Contrary to Law an Indian Woman Named Dinah Nevill with 3 of his Children." The organization only met for six weeks, however, as wartime limited patriot involvement.[77]

Some colonists, however, felt no need to reform slavery. In 1774, eighty-one Perth Amboy, New Jersey residents – where rumors spread of nighttime slave meetings presaging a revolt – petitioned royally appointed governor William Franklin, warning of the "dismal consequences" of abolition schemes, claiming they would stimulate revolts to "bring the white people into the same state that the Negroes are now in." In the name of "preserving the liberty of the white people of this province," the petitioners pressured Franklin against changes.[78] Throughout the colonies, sentiment favoring slavery's full abolition remained largely limited to non-slaveholders. Communities reacted harshly to the pro-spect of black violence.

During the war, many British authorities attempted – often successfully – to embolden the slaves. Most famously, Virginia Governor Dunmore in November 1775 offered freedom to any slave willing to fight for the British. Patriots like Henry denounced the edict as "fatal to public safety" and declared it their most intolerable grievance, making Imperial reconciliation impossible.[79] Mason drafted an oath requiring all patriots to denounce how Dunmore made their "Slaves free," while "arming them to assassinate their Masters, our innocent Wifes and helpless Children."[80] From Britain, Sharp prophesized, "Britain & her colonies seem to be preparing themselves for mutual destruction," reaping the "monstrous oppression" they sowed.[81]

Slave passivity was clearly a white lie, as resistance intensified in wartime. In the months preceding July 1776, small slave disturbances and rumors of insurrections rocked Georgia, the Carolinas, Virginia, Pennsylvania, New Jersey, and New York. Virginia, fearing further provocations, passed a 1777 bill freeing all slaves brought into the state once they took a loyalty oath. Somewhere between twenty thousand and a hundred thousand slaves fled across enemy lines, including 20 percent of Georgia and South Carolina's, especially after a 1778 British proclamation accepted all regardless of age or gender, to take arms or do auxiliary work.[82] Continental Army and militia

---

[77] HSP Pennsylvania Abolition Society Records MICRO 572:1.

[78] James J. Gigantino II, *The Ragged Road to Abolition: Slavery and Freedom in New Jersey, 1775–1865* (Philadelphia: University of Pennsylvania Press, 2015), 25, 47.

[79] Horne, *Counter-Revolution*, 222–25; Robert G. Parkinson, *The Common Cause: Creating Race and Nation in the American Revolution* (Chapel Hill: University of North Carolina Press, 2016), 168–73.

[80] Mason, *Papers*, Vol. 1, 246–47.

[81] GRO D 3549 13/1/D3.

[82] Horne, *Counter-Revolution*, 240; Jefferson, *Papers*, Vol. 2, 22; Nash, "The African Americans' Revolution," in Gray and Kamensky, *Oxford Handbook of the American Revolution*, 261.

units patrolled against slaves as well as British forces, motivating northern states beginning in 1778 to match the British offer of freedom for service, leading to over six thousand African-Americans serving in the Continental forces (often in integrated units) by the war's end.[83]

The wartime need for unity partially eclipsed prewar humanitarianism in the patriot coalition, leading to hedging, contradictions, and silences in the Revolution's most important documents. Mason's May 1776 clause in the Virginia Declaration of Rights that "all men are by nature equally free and independent" elicited angry rebuttals in Virginia's Convention for allegedly extending rights to slaves, forcing the amendment "when they enter into a state of society," denying the enslaved legal rights.[84] The Declaration of Independence, without explanation, pronounced "all men created equal," while substituting the "pursuit of happiness" into the "life, liberty and property" triad slave owners often preferred.[85] Yet the Continental Congress struck a complaint against the slave trade from the declaration's final draft, while denouncing how the British "excited insurrections among us" with Dunmore's proclamation. Jefferson blamed the delegates of "South Carolina and Georgia, who had never attempted to restrain the importation of slaves" there.[86] Already, Americans became a house divided on slavery, adopting awkward compromises to preserve their coalition.

Quakers, despite their wartime neutrality, radicalized on abolitionism. Philadelphia's yearly meeting in 1776 began excommunicating Friends refusing to free their slaves.[87] They sought international Quaker adhesion, asserting to British Friends that slavery violated the "natural and Christian Right to Freedom" all humans possessed. Religion and politics converged, with Philadelphia describing changes "gradually taking place in the minds of many, who do not make religious Profession with us," encouraging united action. American Quakers urged coreligionists against "furnishing the means for carrying on this iniquitous Traffic, either by making, or vending Goods made for it, or by hiring their Ships," beseeching them to fully divest. Quakers, they urged, should "neither directly or indirectly, manifest a Fellowship with this work of darkness," but fully oppose it.[88] Amid an era of great upheaval, American Quakers risked their economic prosperity and transatlantic connections over the slave question.

[83] Jane G. Landers, *Atlantic Creoles in the Age of Revolutions* (Cambridge, MA: Harvard University Press, 2010), 24–25; Manisha Sinha, *The Slave's Cause: A History of Abolition* (New Haven: Yale University Press, 2016), 49–50.
[84] Egerton, *Death*, 134.
[85] Blackburn, *Overthrow*, 111.
[86] Jefferson, *Autobiography*, 33.
[87] Eberly, "Pennsylvania," 17.
[88] HC MICRO BX 7619.L88 reel 7, 145.

Evangelicals also reappropriated the era's rhetoric in the slaves' favor. Congregationalist minister Samuel Hopkins, in his 1776 *Dialogue Concerning the Slavery of the Africans*, sent to all Continental Congress members, highlighted the hypocrisy of enslaving those "who have an equal right to freedom" by the new compact's very language. Opportunity for "establishing universal Liberty to white and black" arrived. Gradualism had no place alongside principle: "If the slave-trade is unjustifiable and wrong; then our holding the Africans and their children in bondage, is unjustifiable and wrong."[89] As the founders rebuilt an independent American society, many found no rightful place for slavery.

Amid the war, northern states began abolishing slavery. Independent Vermont's 1777 Constitution, in its Declaration of Rights' first article, extended the logic that Virginia's Declaration of Rights and the Declaration of Independence refused to. Finding "all men are born equally free and independent," with "certain natural, inherent and unalienable rights," they freed all slaves upon reaching adulthood.[90] Pennsylvania (despite Quakers' expulsion from the state assembly for their pacifism) that year banned the trade and slowly began slavery's abolition, freeing all born beginning in March 1780 on their twenty-eighth birthday, but not affecting slaves then alive. The *Pennsylvania Packet* considered the measure aimed as much at international opinion as domestic, opining, "From Europe the intention must certainly receive the highest honours," as it addressed the contradiction "that a people so enlightened to their own rights, as we are, should remain blind to the case of the poor Africans, whom we hold in servitude."[91] Connecticut passed gradual abolition in 1784, while Madison in Virginia unsuccessfully introduced a similar bill in 1785. Massachusetts' Supreme Court ruled slavery illegal due to the state's constitution declaring "all men equal" in 1783. Rhode Island, after debates denouncing slavery as a "national evil," adopted rapid abolition in 1784. In all northern states except New York and New Jersey, immediate or gradual abolition plans passed by the mid-1780s.[92]

By the war's end, at least north of Maryland, abolition appeared a promising but uncompleted branch of the American project. A Boston banquet for

---

[89] Samuel Hopkins, *A Dialogue Concerning the Slavery of the Africans* (Norwich, CT, 1776), in Nash, *Race*, 100–111.

[90] "Constitution of Vermont – July 8, 1777," http://avalon.law.yale.edu/18th_century/vt01 .asp. Accessed January 19, 2015.

[91] *Pennsylvania Packet*, December 25, 1779; Eberly, "Pennsylvania," 26; Egerton, *Death*, 100–101.

[92] David Menschel, "Abolition without Deliverance: The Law of Connecticut Slavery, 1784–1848," *Yale Law Journal* 111 (2001), 183–222; Jefferson, *Papers*, Vol. 2, 470–73; James Oliver Horton and Lois E. Horton, *Slavery and the Making of America* (Oxford: Oxford University Press, 2005), 66; Egerton, *Death*, 110; Arthur Zilversmit, *The First Emancipation: The Abolition of Slavery in the North* (Chicago: University of Chicago Press, 1967), 137.

Washington's birthday in February 1783, after toasting "May tyranny and oppression be blown from the earth by the breath of liberty," raised another for "Freedom to the slave."[93] A Rhode Island newspaper, shortly before slavery's abolition there, celebrated "the rapid Progress of the Sentiment against domestic Slavery for Ten years past; not among any particular Denomination of Christians, or in America only," as humanitarian efforts expanded.[94] Indeed, a New York paper conjectured the London Quakers' 1783 Parliamentary petition for their slave trade's abolition might lead to "liberty, that common inheritance of all men," restoring "the humanity of every part of the world where it is practiced."[95] New empires of freedom beckoned nationally and internationally.

With the slave trade suspended since 1774's Continental Association, many Americans wanted to make the ban permanent. Seven states during the war, including Virginia, North Carolina, and Georgia, passed supplementary embargos against the Atlantic trade.[96] Given the threats of rebellion, trafficking African warriors seemed foolhardy. In spring 1782, French general the Marquis de Chastelleux reported Virginians "grieved at having slaves, and are constantly talking about abolishing slavery and of seeking other means of exploiting their lands."[97] Quakers petitioned the Continental Congress in 1783 for permanent abolition. Congress left such measures at state discretion, leading to a massive Southern postwar influx raising the nation's slave population from 500,000 in 1776 to 700,000 in 1787, but by the Confederation era's end only Georgia had not passed slave-trade restrictions.[98] No outstanding economic necessity demanded the trade's perpetuation, no philosophy now justified its continuance, and many whites' fears augured against it.

Abolition societies spread across much of the fledgling United States in the mid-1780s. Philadelphia's Society for the Relief of Negroes Unlawfully Held in Bondage reemerged in May 1784, faulting "National commotions" for their inactivity. Though initially advocating for illegally held free blacks, by September they appointed a Committee on the Slave Trade, a year after the London branch had done the same, to publicize "the good Effects of Manumission" and encourage further action.[99] The New York Society for Promoting the Manumission of Slaves organized in 1785, featuring powerful

[93] *Continental Journal*, February 13, 1783.
[94] *United States Chronicle*, January 29, 1784.
[95] *Independent Journal*, February 18, 1784.
[96] Fladeland, *Men*, 29.
[97] Nash, *Race*, 12.
[98] Howard A. Ohline, "Slavery, Economics and Congressional Politics, 1790," *Journal of Southern History* 46, no. 3 (1980), 336; Don E. Fehrenbacher, *The Slaveholding Republic: An Account of the United States Government's Relations to Slavery* (Oxford: Oxford University Press, 2001), 18.
[99] HSP Pennsylvania Abolition Society Papers, 572:1.

men including United States Secretary of Foreign Affairs John Jay and soon-to-be Federalist leader Hamilton. The slaves' cause remained stylish among American political elites. Before the decade's end, Rhode Island, Connecticut, New Jersey, Maryland, and Virginia formed affiliates.[100]

Evangelical organizations – even in the upper South – joined the antislavery agitation. A 1784 Methodist leadership meeting in Baltimore denounced slavery as "contrary to the golden law of God ... and the unalienable rights of mankind, as well as the principle of the Revolution." Promoting spiritual rebirth in anyone, whether white or black, by 1790 more than 20 percent of Methodists were African-American, rising to 33 percent by 1800.[101] All American Methodist church members became required to free their slaves on pain of excommunication (with the same penalty for slave trading). The following spring, Virginia Methodists petitioned their legislature for slavery's gradual abolition. This sparked reaction within the Methodists' own ranks, however, leading to a church repeal of mandatory emancipation or even recommending such in the lower South. Nevertheless, evangelicals continued bearing testimony. Virginia Baptists' General Committee in 1785 declared slavery "contrary to the word of God" and five years later asserted it was "a violent deprivation of the rights of man and inconsistent with a republican government."[102] Though southern revivalism's decentralized nature lessened such pronouncements' force, such testimony appealed to many. With manumission laws liberalized after the war's end, more slaves were voluntarily freed in southern states than by northern abolition acts.[103]

Northern abolition long remained incomplete. New York's manumission society in 1784 began petitioning for a gradual state abolition bill, arguing "the good Example set by others, of more Enlarged and liberal Principles, and the face of true Religion, will, in time, dispel the mist which Prejudice, self Interest and long habit" established.[104] Abolishing slavery remained controversial: New York citizens owned approximately twenty thousand slaves, the most north of Maryland, and stood to lose considerable wealth. Charles Adams wrote to his vice president father in 1796 that as many asserted "it will be best to let the evil work its own remedy" through voluntary manumission,

---

[100] Jameson, *American*, 23–25.

[101] Dee E. Andrews, *The Methodists and Revolutionary America, 1760–1800: The Shaping of an Evangelical Culture* (Princeton: Princeton University Press, 2000), 123; Carla Gardina Pestana, *Protestant Empire: Religion and the Making of the British Atlantic World* (Philadelphia: University of Pennsylvania Press, 2009), 208; Marilyn J. Westerkamp, *Women and Religion in Early America, 1600–1850* (New York: Routledge, 1999), 122.

[102] Davis, *Problem of Slavery in the Age of Revolution*, 204; Kidd, *God*, 158–59; Nash, *Race*, 15.

[103] Blackburn, *Overthrow*, 121.

[104] David N. Gellman, *Emancipating New York: The Politics of Slavery and Freedom, 1777–1827* (Baton Rouge: Louisiana State University Press, 2006), 60.

considering "people do not like to be forced to be generous."[105] With a gradual law freeing unborn slaves once they reached adulthood finally passed the Empire State's legislature in 1799, mandatory manumissions only began in the 1820s, by which point many owners had sold their slaves southward.[106] No "Northern" free state bloc quickly emerged. A 1784 Congressional proposal to ban slavery in the Western territories failed only by a New Jersey swing-voter's absence – while 1787's Northwest Ordinance paradoxically banned slavery in the upper Midwest but, after northern abolitionist posturing that slaves' "stepping over the line will ensure them their Liberty," decreed runaway slaves' capture and return.[107] Only amid the 1820 Missouri statehood controversy did the "North" consider itself (not entirely accurately) a free area.

Antislavery activists hoped for federal abolition of the slave trade at the 1787 Constitutional Convention. A Quaker antislavery petition arrived before the preceding Confederation Conference in October 1786, declaring, "national Guilt is daily accumulating," despite all that "has been spiritedly said in favour of Universal Liberty & the common Rights of Man."[108] Many saw the Constitutional Convention as a radical event capable of enacting real change with abolitionists considering it a potential new beginning for America with the excesses of slavery excised.

Philadelphia abolitionists reorganized in April 1787 as the Pennsylvania Abolition Society, the month before the Constitutional Convention met in the same city. Franklin now served (if ceremonially in old age) as president, and many well-connected patriots, including Paine, lobbied for major antislavery reforms as part of the Constitutional settlement.[109] The organization highlighted how "the rights of human nature" and "obligations of Christianity" required activists to help free blacks and promote abolitionism. The organization distributed a thousand copies of Pennsylvania's legislation for gradually abolishing slavery.[110] Rush, the society's secretary, confidently asserted in May that they expected "suppression of the African trade in the United States" would be "an essential article of the new confederation."[111] Abolishing trafficking gained broad support everywhere except Georgia and the Carolinas, but given their vulnerability to future Spanish and/or British invasion, they were the least plausible states to break from the union.[112]

[105] MHS John Adams Papers, reel 381.
[106] Gellman, *Emancipating*, 1–2.
[107] Nash, *Race*, 19; Paul Finkelman, *Slavery and the Founders: Dilemmas of Jefferson and His Contemporaries* (New York: Routledge, 1995), 37–57; GRO D 3549 13/1/M5.
[108] SC Philadelphia Meeting for Sufferings, MR-PH508.
[109] Nash and Soderlund, *Freedom*, 124.
[110] HSP Pennsylvania Abolition Society Minutes, 572:1; *Pennsylvania Gazette*, May 23, 1787, AN AD XVIIIc 117.
[111] Rush, *Correspondence*, Vol. 1, 417.
[112] Nash, *Race*, 6.

The Constitutional Convention, however, behind closed doors proceeded differently. Franklin declined to present the Pennsylvania society's petition against the trade, while Hamilton set aside the New York society's.[113] Though the finished Constitution never explicitly uses the word "slavery," which some believe helped pave the way for future abolition, six clauses directly concerned slaves – five upholding enslavement, while the sixth only permitted international trafficking's abolition twenty years hence.[114] Franklin, who in 1776 helped procure slaves' full (passive) representation in the Continental Congress, in committee likely engineered the three-fifths compromise, granting partial representation but not rights for the unfree. Though anti-Federalists objected to the trade's perpetuation and how the three-fifths compromise gave southern states greater influence, the better-organized Federalists secured ratification. Indeed, Federalists used abolitionists' gradualist rhetoric against them, claiming the Constitution would be the first step toward reform.[115]

The slave-trade compromise pleased some moderate abolitionists. New York's *Daily Advertiser* asserted, "the emancipation of slaves should be gradual," so by the "mild diffusion" of light, Americans would slowly "perceive and correct the enormities which folly, or wickedness, or accident, have introduced into their public establishments."[116] Many early abolitionists were enthusiastic gradualists, believing they could slowly sap the institution of strength, while converting slaveholders to more humanitarian and capitalistic thinking. Rush wrote ecstatically of how "In one-and-twenty years the new government will probably put an end to the African trade forever in America. O! Virtue, Virtue, who would not follow thee blindfold!"[117] In the gulf between American independence and the French Revolution, gradualism seemed adequately reformist.

Many anti-Federalists denounced the closed-door concessions to slavery as one of the Constitution's worst excesses. In Massachusetts' ratification convention, Washington himself drew criticism for how "he holds those in slavery who have as good a right to be free as he has," leading to the speaker's estimation that "his character has sunk 50 per cent." Another denounced how the compact contained "not even a provision that the negroes shall ever be free."[118] In claiming an "unalienable right to liberty" while oppressing

[113] David Waldstreicher, *Slavery's Constitution: From Revolution to Ratification* (New York: Hill and Wang, 2009), 104.

[114] Waldstreicher, *Slavery's*, 3; Sean Wilentz, *No Property in Man: Slavery and Antislavery at the Nation's Founding* (Cambridge, MA: Harvard University Press, 2018).

[115] Waldstreicher, *Runaway*, 214, 233 and *Slavery's*, 132–33.

[116] *Daily Advertiser*, December 20, 1787.

[117] Rush, *Correspondence*, Vol. 1, 446; Richard S. Newman, *The Transformation of American Abolitionism: Fighting Slavery in the Early Republic* (Chapel Hill: University of North Carolina Press, 2002), 23.

[118] *Independent Chronicle*, February 21, 1788.

Africans, the *Newport Mercury* editorialized, "we are guilty of a ridiculous, wicked contradiction and inconsistency; and practically authorize any nation or people, who have power to do it, to make us their slaves."[119] Maryland's Attorney General asserted slavery lessened "the sense of the equal rights of mankind, and habituates us to tyranny and oppression." Prohibiting government from restricting the slave trade appeared insidious, as "nothing could so materially affect both our national honour and interest."[120] The Constitution restrained a growing abolitionist cause and gave hated institutions new legitimacy.

Reports arrived from Britain of their growing movement against the slave trade. Sharp's February 1788 letter to the Pennsylvania Abolition Society, however, was condemnatory. "Remembering the declarations of the American Congress" during the war, Sharp expressed disappointment that American "consistence of character" faltered.[121] Nevertheless, European antislavery activists still hoped to convince the United States to join an international effort to persuade the British and French empires to abolish slave trading together.[122] America could be left behind, losing its status as a beacon of liberty, should it fail to keep step with Europe's preeminent empires.

Many northern states forbade their citizens from trafficking. Rhode Island's statute, finding the slave trade "inconsistent with justice, and the principles of humanity, as well as the laws of nature, and that more enlightened and civilized sense of freedom which has of late prevailed," levied serious fines of $100 per slave and $1,000 per vessel.[123] Massachusetts' resolution declared the slave trade violated "the rights of human kind" and thus constituted "unrighteous commerce."[124] Such laws' enforceability in international trafficking remained limited, however.

Under the new federal order, most American abolitionists settled into a longer game, promoting northern slaves' freedom and more gradual reforms in the south. Many expected such changes to be a continuing revolution. Jay, while president of New York's antislavery society, wrote to British abolitionists of how at the Revolution's beginning only an "inconsiderable" few opposed slavery and now debates grew widespread. Reformers "have good reason to hope and to believe that if the natural operations of truth" persist, "that end we all aim at will finally be achieved in this country."[125] Though achingly slow, paths opened toward emancipation.

---

[119] *Newport Mercury*, March 31, 1788.

[120] *Maryland Gazette*, January 22, 1788.

[121] *New-York Journal*, May 24, 1788.

[122] *Carlisle Gazette*, May 7, 1788; *Connecticut Gazette*, May 23, 1788,

[123] *Newport Herald*, November 11, 1787; Davis, *The Problem of Slavery in the Age of Revolution*, 27.

[124] *Cumberland Gazette*, May 1, 1788.

[125] John Jay, *The Life of John Jay: With Selections from His Correspondence and Miscellaneous Papers* (New York: Harper, 1833), Vol. 1, 232.

With the French Revolution's coming and votes to abolish the slave trade in Britain, more rapid radical changes beckoned, potentially repudiating the Constitutional compromise. Virginia Quaker abolitionist Robert Pleasants wrote in September 1789 of "the greatest probability that a total prohibition of the Slave trade" could occur in Britain, "a prelude to Emancipations in the W.I. [West India] Islands, and indeed the World over," especially as "the spirit of liberty in France was not to be restrain'd by all the Efforts of those in Power."[126] The North Atlantic could conceivably be closed to the traffic. Virginia Quakers wrote to London's that the "understandings of the people here have of late been so opened into the Nature of this iniquitous Trade," that "total abolition" came under congressional consideration.[127]

New antislavery societies developed, some expecting a continued upswing in public opinion. The Maryland Society for Promoting the Abolition of Slavery, and the Relief of Free Negroes, and Others, Unlawfully Held in Bondage first met in December 1789. Citing "the present attention of Europe and America to slavery," and a common "crisis in the minds of men," they pledged to "bear our testimony against slavery in all its forms, to spread it abroad as far as the sphere of our influence may extend."[128] Such organizations spread southward with a society founded in Richmond the following month. Emancipated blacks, unable to join the Pennsylvania Abolition Society, New York Manumission Society, or most others, organized mutual aid societies sponsoring political lobbying – with Philadelphia's Free African Society joined by similar organizations in Boston, Charleston, Richmond, and elsewhere.[129]

Those believing radical measures could succeed nationally, especially before 1808, were disappointed. February 11–12, 1790, petitions arrived at the U.S. Congress against the trade, similar to those flowing to Britain's House of Commons. Quaker meetings of Pennsylvania, New Jersey, Maryland, and Virginia resolutely called for the "final abolition of that pernicious traffic."[130] The next day the Pennsylvania Abolition Society's petition arrived, featuring Franklin's signature, considering slavery an "abomination of human nature" and asking Congress to "Step to the very verge of the Powers vested in you for discouraging every Species of Traffick in the Persons of our fellow Men."[131] Building from Henry's argument, they declared Congress empowered by the Constitutional preamble for "promoting the welfare and securing the blessings

---

[126] HC Robert Pleasants Collection, MSS 1116/168 155.
[127] HC Virginia Meeting Correspondence MSS 1116/159.
[128] *New-York Packet*, December 31, 1789; AN AD XVIIIc 117.
[129] *Gazette of the United States*, January 27, 1790; Newman, *Freedom's Prophet: Bishop Richard Allen, the AME Church, and the Black Founding Fathers* (New York: New York University Press, 2008), 60–62; Newman, *Transformation*, 5.
[130] *Gazette of the United States*, February 13, 1790.
[131] "Petition from Pennsylvania Abolition Society to Congress (1790)," in Nash, *Race*, 144–45.

of liberty for the people of the United States."[132] Fierce congressional debate arose over whether to give the bill a second reading, with Maryland representative Joshua Seney (though a plantation owner) asserting, "Congress should exert their constitutional authority to abate the horrors of slavery so far as they could," while Georgia's James Jackson predicted the measure would bring "revolt, insurrection, and devastation."[133] The petitions were sent to committee, whose ensuing March 8 report endorsed the Constitution's conventional interpretation, forbidding federal action on trafficking until 1808 or any overriding of state slave regulations.[134] No further restrictions of American slaveholder rights in territories already possessing such servitude came from Congress until 1865.

An American compromise developed: while the Atlantic slave trade perished, slavery itself became seemingly perpetual. In 1794 nine societies gathered in an American Convention of Abolition Societies seeking to end "domestic slavery in this country," as France's National Convention had recently done across the French empire. Nevertheless, attempts to coordinate an intense national movement on the recent British antislavery model (see Chapter 8) fizzled, while news of the Haitian Revolution emboldened some activists but led many to shun even cautious abolitionists.[135] Congress retained a moderate course, passing legislation forbidding American merchants to supply slaves to other nations. Virginia Congressman Anthony New, writing to his constituents, considered the legislation "not leveled in the remotest degree, against the rights of private property."[136] America's abolitionist limits became clear. Slavery expanded as the cotton trade ignited explosive southern growth with only the proviso that it would be undertaken in approved areas.

Facing a legislative stalemate, abolitionism atrophied. The small antislavery societies did not push for massive expansion or sponsor any giant petition-wave to match the British movement.[137] Northern free blacks by social customs and legal restrictions were forced into second-class citizenship. Growing racism, meanwhile, led many to consider slavery "natural" and part of the American compact. Southerners would not revisit their revolutionary crises of conscience. Though slavery never again existed unchallenged, another

---

[132] Fladeland, *Men*, 55.
[133] *Connecticut Courant*, February 25, 1790.
[134] *Gazette of the United States*, March 10, 1790.
[135] Sinha, *Slave's*, 110.
[136] HC Robert Pleasants Collection 1116/168 221; Cunningham, ed. *Circular Letters of Congressmen to Their Constituents, 1789–1829*, Vol. 1 (Chapel Hill: University of North Carolina Press, 1978), 19.
[137] J. R. Oldfield, *Transatlantic Abolitionism in the Age of Revolution: An International History of Anti-Slavery, c. 1787–1820* (Cambridge: Cambridge University Press, 2013), 72.

groundswell did not occur until American abolitionism developed its more famous "second wave" of the 1820s–1860s.[138]

Conclusion

Though early American abolitionism has (often with good reason) been harshly criticized for its partialness, hypocrisy, and backsliding, in broader Atlantic context it was of vital importance for the broadening of late-eighteenth century social movements. Whereas scholars since the time of David Brion Davis have acknowledged an "Antislavery International" of activists trying to reform, restrict, and/or abolish slavery, historians have not sufficiently explored abolitionists' deep connections with the era's revolutionary political movements.[139] Anti–Stamp Act activists, per British traditions, had begun protesting for propertied citizens' rights, yet among American patriots a movement developed in favor of the dispossessed. Slavery's existence became anomalous in a new world of political freedoms.

Before the American Revolution, despite slave resistance and growing moral uncertainty about the institution, nowhere around the Atlantic basin had there been hope of practical, government-led action against slavery (or virtually any other social ill).[140] In the early United States, abolition, based upon the same human rights rhetoric fueling the patriot cause, through the work of their enthusiastic proponents quickly appeared a natural extension of the broader drive for liberty. Such growing public opinion was directed into political action through adapting the patriot movement's organizing tactics. Although American abolitionism did not form a distinct and autonomous social movement like the others in this study, with early abolition societies remaining small, its proponents' ability to influence the mainstream patriot cause to such ends achieved much the same collective effect. The American Revolution did not free most slaves, but it did make ending slavery appear possible. Enthusiastic fellow sympathizers in Britain would soon adapt American political innovations to enable a mass movement with a nationally integrated movement to abolish the slave trade.

---

[138] Nicholas Guyatt, *Bind Us Apart: How Enlightened Americans Invented Racial Segregation* (New York: Basic Books, 2016); Matthew Mason, *Slavery and Politics in the Early American Republic* (Chapel Hill: University of North Carolina Press, 2006).

[139] Davis, *Age of Revolution*.

[140] On the importance of slave resistance, see Sinha, *Slave's*.

8

British Abolitionism and the Broadening
of Social Movements

Abolitionism arose in Britain amid fundamental debates over the British Empire's nature and the freedoms their citizens possessed. Whereas the prospect of abolishing the Atlantic slave trade seemed virtually nonexistent in early 1787, by late 1788 it came to appear (at least to many) almost inevitable. To "awaken the feelings of a generous nation," the Committee for Effecting the Abolition of the Slave Trade declared that August, "nothing more was necessary than to unfold the true state of the slave trade, and expose to public view the cruelties practiced in it." Over one hundred petitions arrived before the House of Commons from across the country, while other electors instructed their Members of Parliament to "promote at least, a fair enquiry concerning this traffick."[1] A growing belief in enlightened progress, that society could be improved and even rapidly changed, propelled the radical paradigm shift.

Only in the context of the recent American War of Independence, attempts for British Parliamentary reform, and pushes for religious civil rights can the massive 1787–1792 upsurge against the slave trade be understood. Despite long-standing unease about and resistance to slavery across the empire, British antislavery movements organized and spread for the first time by adapting the social movement tactics of American rebels, Irish nationalists, Dissenters, and early Parliamentary reformers to apply them on a greater scale than any preceding movement. Proponents, adopting the cause of the empire's most oppressed members – rather than, as in earlier movements, fighting for their own rights – reappropriated preceding social movements' structures, arguments, and personnel to promote an unprecedentedly broad vision of liberty.

Building Antislavery Feeling in Britain

British reformers became increasingly versed in antislavery arguments during the American crises as they defended natural rights theories and their conceptions of liberty. Their empathy toward Americans, often described as in danger of becoming "slaves" to British authorities, helped develop compassion toward New World slaves. Yet in their next campaigns, even with the outspoken Sharp

---

[1] *Bristol Journal*, September 13, 1788.

taking a leadership role in the Association movement and Society for Constitutional Information, friends of freedom did not prioritize antislavery issues, instead agitating for general political reform in the 1770s and early 1780s. Interest grew in abolition, but at no point during American controversies did slavery mobilize British collective action.

For decades, British Quakers equivocated on abolitionist measures, wary of their American counterparts' fervor and only slowly following them into activism. Quakers founded the Lloyd's and Barclay's financial empires, making fortunes from financing and insuring the slave trade.[2] While advocating reforms to make trafficking more humane, Quaker merchants long avoided confrontation with authorities and trading partners. Finally, in 1773, British Quakers lobbied Parliament to reform slaving practices, writing to their Philadelphia brethren, "such a Temper of Humanity is gradually prevailing amongst some here in Power."[3] Only a broader confluence of religious and political pressures, slowly superseding the financial advantages of silence, led British Friends toward sustained activism.

Throughout the American War, British Quakers avoided popular agitation, disapproving of their New World counterparts' activism. London's branch in 1780 urged Pennsylvania's to moderation, particularly warning them to be "circumspect" in imposing their views on North Carolina's branch. "We are with you on the necessity of such a liberation," the meeting counseled, but suggested slaves "might be nominally retained as Servants" in the same households.[4] Quaker spiritual conscience conflicted with deep social conservatism, and few sought to upend the communal order. Delaying out of wartime loyalty, only at the fighting's end in 1782 did British Quakers commit to campaigning against the slave trade.[5]

Despite the Somerset Case, support for changing imperial slaving practices grew slowly among British political elites. Contesting slavery itself still appeared impossible, as Mansfield's Somerset decision explicitly protected "positive" colonial slave law. The American War made further incursions against colonial (planter) rights in the New World unadvisable. But as slave trafficking remained a matter of imperial policy-making and limiting importations the most likely way to lessen colonial abuses and slave mortality, British abolitionists focused on the slave trade more than their American counterparts.

British popular opposition to slave trading rose with the infamous *Zong* case, in which traders, for lack of freshwater, threw 132 slaves overboard to drown during an autumn 1781 voyage. The Liverpool syndicate financing

---

[2] Davis, *Problem of Slavery in the Age of Revolution*, 233.
[3] HC Quaker MS, MICRO BX 7619.L88 reel 7, 97.
[4] HC Quaker MS, MICRO BX 7619.L88 reel 7 180.
[5] Blackburn, *Crucible*, 162.

the voyage, nonplussed by the outcome, sued their insurer to reimburse them for lost cargo. The case became a *cause célèbre* with newspapers printing the ghastly details. Sharp, already well known in reformist circles for his pro-American activism, demanded the slavers' arrest for murder. Courts, however, repeatedly ruled in the syndicate's favor. Chief Justice Mansfield in March 1783 ruled on final appeal, "just as if horses were kill'd they are paid for in the gross," slave cargo too must be reimbursed.[6] The affront to many reformers' sensibilities was profound. Whereas attention previously focused on New World slavery's horrors, now greater emphasis fell on the slave trade's brutality. Benezet urged London's Quakers to action, as "now appears a favourable Crisis" for reforms to win "the approbation of every reasonable feeling heart."[7] Enlightened humanitarian impulses drew reformers to the slave trade.

Coinciding with a bill increasing slave trade regulation, the Society of Friends in June 1783 brought their first Parliamentary petition to abolish the traffic. British Quaker thought had progressed in light of recent American abolitions. Now they worked to spread their testimony into the British mainstream, lobbying the powerful and stoking broader public opinion. The Friends beseeched the legislature's "humane interposition," expressing their "regret that a nation, professing the Christian faith, should counteract the principles of humanity and justice, as by the cruel treatment of this oppressed race" in their dominions. Finding slaves "entitled to the natural rights of mankind," they called for slave trading's entire abolition. Parliamentary speakers praised the petition but dismissed it as impractical. Though North expressed hopes "humane sentiments would have a proper weight in the House in dear time," he and other politicians reverted to pragmatic arguments that "a commercial view [has] become necessary to almost every nation of Europe," and thus the British could not uniquely disengage from trafficking.[8] Though many considered the Quakers' cause admirable, they needed a realizable plan for what would replace the slave trade.

Petitioning became effective only when supported by broader activist networks. After the *Zong* case, pro-slavery pamphlets typically conceded slavery's brutality but argued it remained a national necessity. For abolitionists, arguments for plausibly abolishing the trade without sinking the British Empire or economy needed to be refined and popularized. The Society for Constitutional Information endorsed the Quaker petition, while Friends began borrowing

---

[6] James Walvin, *The Zong: A Massacre, the Law, and the End of Slavery* (New Haven: Yale University Press, 2011), 1–2, 153.

[7] HC Anthony Benezet Letters, MSS 852.

[8] HC Letters from British Friends, MSS 681, Box 3; Thomas Clarkson, *The History of the Rise, Progress, and Accomplishment of the Abolition of the Slave Trade* (London: Longman, 1808), Vol. 1, 118–20; Adam Hochschild, *Bury the Chains: Prophets and Rebels in the Fight to Free an Empire's Slaves* (New York: Mariner, 2005), 78.

reformers' tactics.[9] In later 1783, the Quakers formed a twenty-three-person "standing Committee on the Slave Trade" on the political committee of correspondence model. Largely composed of businessmen, some of them traffickers until recently, the committee urged abolition on the grounds of economic inexpediency, publishing Adam Smith's recent reflections on wage labor's superior efficiency and morality.[10] Advancing American abolitionist connections, they pledged to their Philadelphia brethren to "awaken the Legislature and the Publick to a sense of the Evil."[11] The committee's first collective declaration, *The Case of Our Fellow-Creatures, the Oppressed Africans*, asserted this "national evil" could be resolved through "the humane interposition of the legislature." As "true friends of civil and religious liberty," it seemed contradictory for any legislator to back reform or Dissenter causes without supporting those denied even basic human rights.[12]

The organization initially printed two thousand copies of the *Case*, hoping to influence Britain's political elites. Each Member of Parliament received the pamphlet with Quaker deputations visiting key officials. When granting meetings, politicians endorsed the cause's morality, suggesting significant antislavery sentiment. Courtiers reported George III accepted his "very graciously." Nevertheless, most MPs considered legislation premature, even while promising "to promote it when opportunity offers."[13] Further groundwork remained necessary to motivate government action.

Cultivating public opinion against slave trafficking became at least as important for abolitionists as lobbying authorities. In July 1784, the committee resolved to distribute more *Case* copies "throughout the nation & particularly to Justices of the Peace, Clergymen & the Members of Corporations & merchants concerned in the West India and Guinea Trades."[14] Appealing beyond politicians, the movement sought the broader reading public, with the committee appointing members to write newspaper articles. Thomas Clarkson, a recent Cambridge graduate who composed an award-winning college essay against the trade, pursued "enlightening the public mind" against trafficking.[15]

---

[9] Brown, *Moral*, 369; Davis, *Problem of Slavery in the Age of Revolution*, 373.

[10] Simon Schama, *Rough Crossings: Britain, the Slaves, and the American Revolution* (New York: Ecco, 2006), 173; Walvin, "The Slave Trade, Quakers, and British Abolition," in Carey and Plank, 171.

[11] SC Philadelphia Meeting for Sufferings, MR-PH508; *Massachusetts Sentinel*, January 18, 1786.

[12] *The Case of Our Fellow-Creatures, the Oppressed Africans, Respectfully Recommended to the Serious Consideration of the Legislature of Great Britain, by the People Called Quakers* (London: Phillips, 1784) 3, 4, 14.

[13] Clarkson, *History*, Vol. 1, 120–21; Library of the Society of Friends, Minute Book of the Meeting for Sufferings Committee on the Slave Trade, MSS F 1/7.

[14] LSF, ibid.

[15] Clarkson, *History*, Vol. 1, 215.

Enlightenment appeared communicable and public opinion ripe for new possibilities.

Anglican liberals also turned against slavery's abuses. Rev. James Ramsay published *An Essay on the Treatment and Conversion of African Slaves* in 1784, denouncing how the "unnatural state of mankind" in the British colonies had "sunk human nature down to the lowest depth of wretchedness." No equivalent of the French Code Noir (granting, though not in practice guaranteeing, slaves basic rights) existed in British possessions, and owners oppressed their chattel without restrictions. Only by expanding slave liberties, curtailing brutal abuse, beginning individual manumissions, and more generally recognizing slaves' "humanity" could the system improve. Even if changes limited owners' privileges, "Liberty will think no concession too great that is to extend her empire."[16] Though the Church of England officially remained outside the movement – despite the repeated lobbying efforts of Sharp, grandson of the Archbishop of York – Anglicans thickened the antislavery ranks.[17]

A growing consensus on the slave trade's human trauma, religious evil, philosophical unreasonableness, and economic needlessness made antislavery modish by the mid-1780s. William Wilberforce, an Anglican evangelical and MP for Yorkshire (elected by many of the Freeholders who led the Association Movement) became the cause's Parliamentary leader. A close friend of the younger Pitt, the two Cambridge graduates had traveled together to France in 1783, meeting Franklin, Lafayette, and other *philosophes* with Pitt declining a marriage offer to Jacques Necker's daughter, the future Madame de Stael.[18] But not long after returning to England, Wilberforce fell under Evangelical religion's sway. He became "born again" in 1785, considered quitting politics, but instead became a voice for moral change. After sponsoring piecemeal Parliamentary reform measures in 1786 that passed the Commons but failed in the Lords, he combined forces with radicals seeking the slave trade's abolition. Groundwork coalesced to rapidly expand the British abolitionist movement.

Creating a Popular Antislavery Movement

Concurrently hoping the United States would abolish the slave trade in 1787's Constitutional Convention, British abolitionists attempted a broad-based popular campaign to rally not just political elites but the British people to their cause. As they explained to the Pennsylvania Abolition Society, their

---

[16] James Ramsay, *An Essay on the Treatment and Conversion of African Slaves in the British Colonies* (London: Phillips, 1784), 103, 263, 295.

[17] Brown, *Moral*, 192–95.

[18] William Hague, *William Wilberforce: The Life of the Great Anti-Slave Trade Campaigner* (Boston: Harcourt, 2007), 54–55.

"immediate aim is, by diffusing a knowledge of the Subject, and particularly the Modes of procuring and treating Slaves, to interest men of every description in the Abolition of the Traffic; but especially those from whom any alteration must proceed – the members of our Legislature."[19] Only by popular pressure could they compel Parliament to break with powerful slaveholding interests.

An expanded Committee for Effecting the Abolition of the Slave Trade began meeting in May 1787, to stoke a national, multi-denominational effort against trafficking. Wilberforce met with now-Prime Minister Pitt to solicit support. Pitt, stymied on political reform and seeking a new rallying cause, in March publicly declared his "disapprobation of the slave trade" and "hearty inclination to favour any practicable scheme for discouraging it."[20] While the onus fell on reformers to demonstrate workable alternatives, a popular movement could help convince skeptical legislators. Though Wilberforce declined to directly participate in popular organizing, he pushed reform allies to join the cause. Activists Sharp and Clarkson anchored the effort, while the twelve-man committee's majority were well-connected men of commerce, including two bankers, four merchants, and two manufacturers – the two radicals tempered by practical businessmen interested in building an effective movement.[21]

The committee built interconnected local, national, and international advocacy networks. Sending five hundred circulars to sympathetic reformers across Britain to publicize in their communities, the activists declared hope for the slave trade gaining discussion in the next Parliamentary session and urged "the general sense of the nation (which we are persuaded is in favour of liberty, justice and humanity) may be expressed by petitions to Parliament" supporting abolition.[22] Waves of pamphlets followed. Committeemen built connections with popular organizers and print distributors across the country (securing affiliates in thirty-nine counties) and by July initiated transatlantic communication with American abolition societies. The Pennsylvania Abolition Society encouraged their campaign, enclosing materials on liberated slaves' successes.[23]

Dissenting religious movements joined the cause. Though nine founding committee members were Quakers, the organization mobilized reformers of all persuasions. As dissenting congregations renewed their Test and

[19] *Daily Advertiser*, October 16, 1787.

[20] Letter from London of March 22, 1787, printed in the *Pennsylvania Packet*, May 18, 1787; *Salem Mercury*, June 5, 1787; *Massachusetts Gazette*, June 8, 1787.

[21] J. R. Oldfield, *Popular Politics and British Anti-Slavery: The Mobilization of Public Opinion against the Slave Trade, 1787–1807* (Manchester: Manchester University Press, 1995), 42, 72; Bodleian Library MS Wilberforce c.46 30.

[22] Oldfield, "The London Committee and Mobilization of Public Opinion against the Slave Trade," *Historical Journal* 35, no. 2 (1992), 334.

[23] Clarkson, *History*, 442, 461; BL Minute Books of the London Abolition Committee, ADD MS 21254 6.

Corporation Acts repeal campaign, championing liberty and natural rights while denouncing despotic slavery, in June 1787 Baptists' general meeting endorsed the abolitionist movement.[24] Priestley crafted an influential *Sermon on the Subject of the Slave Trade*, highlighting the cause's ecumenical nature, declaring antislavery "not the cause of Unitarianism, or Arianism, or of trinitarianism, but that of *humanity*, and our common *christianity*." He emphasized the moral duty "to do justice, and shew mercy, let what will become of the superfluities, or even the necessities of life."[25] In solidarity with Priestley, each Birmingham's congregation – Anglican and Dissenter – gave antislavery sermons the same Sunday.[26] Dissenting ministers of London and Yorkshire brought petitions to abolish the trade in February 1788 and the Association of Baptist Churches endorsed abolishing "a Traffic so unjust, inhuman, and disgraceful" in May.[27] Wesley, after meeting with Clarkson while each sought converts in Manchester, threw Methodism's weight behind the cause. Most MPs supporting Test and Corporation Act repeal came to support abolishing the slave trade.[28] The expanding rhetoric of freedom across religious, political, and international spheres deluged social movement boundaries.

Experienced radicals advised that broad coordination would bring success. With Sharp's prodding, supportive letters arrived from prominent radical circles, including Cartwright and Price's endorsement, with Price sending the committee American correspondence and movement literature. Cartwright warned the London committee of national coordination's difficulties: "Where Society is widely dispersed and thinly scattered, none but efforts of great vigour can put it in action to advantage."[29] Undaunted, antislavery activists continued recruiting: Manchester's Thomas Cooper, a leading Parliamentary reform proponent, published a pamphlet advocating a multi-pronged drive against the slave trade through coordinating religious organizations (congratulating Quaker, Presbyterian, and Methodist efforts) and every "man of common honesty, of any, or of no religion" supporting human dignity. He asserted Manchester's residents, reputed "for their spirited exertions against political oppression, will not want spirit in such a cause as this, merely because their peculiar interest is not concerned."[30] Manchester soon built perhaps the most active antislavery society.

---

[24] Clarkson, *History*, 446–53; Page, "Rational," 772.
[25] Joseph Priestley, *A Sermon on the Subject of the Slave Trade, Delivered to a Society of Protestant Dissenters, at the New Meeting, in Birmingham, and Published at Their Request* (Birmingham: Pearson and Rollasson, 1788), 33; *Massachusetts Centinel*, April 30, 1788.
[26] Jackson, *Let*, 118.
[27] *Public Advertiser*, February 13, 1788; *Independent Gazetteer*, March 31, 1789.
[28] Drescher, *Capitalism*, 117; Page, "Rational," 755.
[29] BL Minute Books, ADD MS 21254 17; Huntington Library, Clarkson-Wilberforce Letters HM 813.
[30] Thomas Cooper, *Letters on the Slave Trade* (Manchester: Wheeler, 1787), 28.

Transatlantic correspondence accelerated to develop plans for reforming slavery. Finding practical alternatives to African slave importation was key: as one British committee member told an American correspondent, "Commerce is now the grand spring of politics, and every thing which tends to check or to decrease the revenue, is certain of a vigorous opposition."[31] The United States demonstrated alternatives: despite having forbid importations during the war, its slave population nevertheless increased. Philadelphia's society, under Franklin's signature, sent the London committee a "large pacquet," displaying Benezet's successes in African-American education, testimonials from freed slaves, and proposed alternative labor systems.[32] In contemporary context, American models offered comparatively palatable alternatives to slaves' short, brutal lives on most Caribbean plantations.

Damning reports on the slave trade proliferated from British presses. Less than a month after the committee's founding, Clarkson began a research tour of slaving ports at the organization's expense. Despite his initial resolution that "no Treatment from the Inhabitants, should they know my business, be too horrid to deter me," Clarkson found many interlocutors willing to discuss trafficking in grisly detail. Beginning in Bristol, "There were facts, in short, in every body's mouth, concerning it; and every body seemed to excrete it, though no one thought of its abolition."[33] Clarkson, though derided by fellow abolitionists for insufficient "caution," pressed sailors, captains, merchants, and overseers for information, gathering evidence for confronting the slaving establishment.[34] Many slavers participated voluntarily, with London's committee already boasting in summer 1787 of corresponding with "principal persons at the out-ports, where the ships employed in this trade, are fitted out, so that a free, and fair discussion is expected."[35] Clarkson concurrently built the abolitionist network along the coasts, establishing committees in many towns he visited. By October 1787, he announced several prominent ports prepared petitions against slave trading.[36]

Pro-slaving interests counter-organized, defending trafficking on economic and pseudo-biological grounds. The commerce, proponents claimed, functioned for the captives' own good, with one London *World* apologia claiming they would otherwise be "put to death by the victors" in African wars. Additionally, the author questioned slaves' "reasoning faculty," doubting whether they experienced oppression. In the same issue, an address from Liverpool, the "metropolis of slavery" conducting 80 percent of British

---

[31] *Daily Advertiser*, October 19, 1787.

[32] Liverpool Record Office 920 ROS/252.

[33] Clarkson, *History*, 296; St John's College Library, Thomas Clarkson Papers, 1 1 7; BL ADD MS 21254, 5.

[34] LRO 920 ROS/247.

[35] *American Mercury*, October 22, 1787.

[36] BL Minute Books, ADD MS 21254, 15.

overseas trafficking during the 1780s, defended trafficking on economic grounds. The municipality reminded readers Liverpool "is still increasing, with more rapidity than London ever did," with profits spurring nearby Manchester's growth.[37] While controversy ensued – one local merchant considered the debate between "interest & humanity," producing "great havock in the happiness of many families" – pro-slavery arguments swayed some.[38] The *Public Advertiser* declared articles presenting religious proofs of slavery's beneficence so convincing, "the foolish Quakers ought to be very much ashamed of having opposed so Holy and Christian a branch of commerce."[39] Pro-slavery views, if increasingly challenged, remained widespread.

Traditional Christian defenses of slavery were further undercut by growing abolitionist advocacy within the Church of England. The Dean of Middleham in Yorkshire wrote a widely circulated call to religious conscience in October 1787. "For though Christianity," he argued, "at its first promulgation, for obvious reasons, did not affect to introduce any alteration in the civil rights of men, yet its genuine tendency is friendly to civil liberty."[40] Religion's moral teachings contained the seeds of human improvement. By January 1788, Oxford and Cambridge universities petitioned to abolish the trade, the latter arguing "Divine goodness" must oppose "treachery and violence."[41] By mid-1789, reports circulated that Anglican Bishops unanimously favored the traffic's abolition.[42]

Antislavery campaigning developed rapidly across much of the country. Wilberforce, writing to Wyvill (also an antislavery convert) in January 1788, considered it "highly desirable that the public voice should be exerted in our support as loudly and universally as possible." The committee convened fifty-one times between May 1787 and July 1788 in meetings typically lasting five hours. Members distributed letters and seventy-seven thousand antislavery books, pamphlets, and broadsheets across Great Britain.[43] Abolitionist sentiment spread in conjunction with an unprecedentedly integrated political machine.

Blacks living in England – numbering five to ten thousand in London alone, many of whom had experienced trafficking and/or slavery firsthand – allied for the cause. Already mobilized to combat reenslavement and achieve fuller civil

---

[37] Kenneth Morgan, "Liverpool's Dominance in the British Slave Trade, 1740–1807," in *Liverpool and Transatlantic Slavery*, David Richardson, Suzanne Schwarz and Anthony Tibbles, eds. (Liverpool: Liverpool University Press, 2007), 15.

[38] LRO 920 CUR/108.

[39] *Public Advertiser*, August 17, 1787.

[40] *Bristol Journal*, December 22, 1787.

[41] *London Chronicle*, January 29, 1788; *General Evening Post*, January 10 and February 7, 1788.

[42] *General Evening Post*, June 28, 1788.

[43] Clarkson, *History*, 571.

rights, several became among abolition's most able advocates.[44] Publishing first-person slave narratives furthered public empathy. Ottobah Cuguano's 1787 *Thoughts and Sentiments on the Evils of Slavery* gave an unvarnished glimpse of its horrors, asserting "nothing in history can equal the barbarity and cruelty" of the slave system. Cuguano encouraged slave resistance, considering pro-slavery defenses "the grossest perversion of reason, as well as an inconsistent and diabolical use of the sacred writings."[45] Africans participated in public debates: the Westminster Forum in 1788 promoted a "native of Africa" speaking on "remarkable circumstances respecting the Slave-Trade" to help determine "Can any political or commercial advantages justify a free people in continuing the slave trade?"[46] Some appealed to British magnanimity, with Gustavus Vasa (soon to write his memoirs as Olaudah Equiano) petitioning Parliament to intercede as "the dispensers of Light, Liberty, and Science to the uttermost parts of the earth."[47] Slavery's victims increasingly confronted the English.

Cuguano, Equiano, and others from London's black community formed their own pressure group, the "Sons of Africa." They represented a polyglot community largely composed of former slaves brought by their masters from New World plantations, Loyalist soldiers who fought in the American War, and sailors who experienced the Atlantic's depredations firsthand.[48] As their name suggests, they too sought to be sons of liberty. The organization suffered the planter community's disdain, which formed a Committee for Relief of the Black Poor seeking their deportation by Act of Parliament, arguing "nothing short of their removal" would avoid the "many inconveniencies" of their presence.[49] The Sons of Africa, while interacting with white-dominated abolition committees, remained an independent caucus for their own people. The group grew famous with a celebration of the Glorious Revolution's 1788 centenary in Plymouth toasting: "A speedy Revolution to the Sons of Africa; may they like us find a WILLIAM to redress their wrongs, and establish them in the rights of men."[50] Even in seaports, many Britons sympathized with their plight and desired to aid them.

Equiano published his *Interesting Narrative* in 1789. Unlike other slave memoirs, Equiano dared to describe the middle passage. British readers

[44] James Walvin, *An African's Life: The Life and Times of Olaudah Equiano, 1745–1797* (London: Cassell, 1998), 132.
[45] Quobna Ottobah Cuguano, *Thoughts and Sentiments on the Evils of Slavery* (New York: Penguin, 1999), xxi, 10, 76, 118.
[46] *World*, February 25, 1788.
[47] *Morning Post*, February 21, 1788,
[48] GRO D 3549 13/1/C1.
[49] Senate House Library, University College of London, West India Committee Papers, M915 reel 3.
[50] *Morning Chronicle*, November 14, 1788.

encountered "shrieks of the women, and the groans of the dying," rendering "a scene of horror almost inconceivable," leading many slaves to "preferring death to such a life of misery" in the ship's hold.[51] While his subsequent life story as a freed sailor was rare for a first-generation slave, Evangelical conversion helped him gain renown as a moral voice condemning the trade. Equiano spent years touring the British Isles on speaking tours promoting the abolitionist cause, bringing an eloquent former slave before diverse audiences. His *Narrative* remained a bestseller across the 1790s, spanning seven editions, including one each in Edinburgh and Dublin, unauthorized reprinting in the United States, and translation into Dutch, German, and Russian. Also supporting radical British and Irish reform societies, Equiano desired a coalition simultaneously agitating against the slave trade and broader British injustices.[52]

Abolitionists often mobilized through the municipal and county structures previously utilized for the Association and pro-American movements but developed followings beyond the political system's confines. Huntingdonshire in early January 1788 approved a petition calling trafficking "the scandal of these civilized, enlightened times" and asking their example "be followed, unanimously, by all the other counties throughout the kingdom."[53] Virtually all stalwarts of earlier campaigns participated. Middlesex petitioned, sending scrolls of signatures to Wilkes for Parliamentary presentation. York attracted over eighteen hundred, among the highest per capita. Unlike their reform predecessors, abolition societies solicited formal female participation, with women becoming 10 percent of all subscribers.[54] The cause drew an unprecedentedly national coalition, surmounting former barriers of religion, race, gender, and politics.

Already in January 1788, the London committee thanked the "spirited exertions of Manchester, Birmingham and other principal Manufacturing Towns," which together out-mobilized even the capital. Though industrializing towns remained underrepresented in Parliament, they participated in trade debates and now incited widespread pressure. Unlike in better-represented constituencies, there were no attempts to limit participation to "active" voters.[55] The previous December 29, in a general meeting at their Exchange Tavern, Manchester became the first to directly petition Parliament. The appeal declared slavery a "direct violation of the precepts of the true

---

[51] Olaudah Equiano, *The Interesting Narrative of the Life of Olaudah Equiano, or Gustavus Vasa, Told by Himself* (London, 1790), 51–53.

[52] Vincent Carretta, *Equiano, The African: Biography of a Self-Made Man* (New York: Penguin, 2005), 300; Walvin, *African's*, 161, 166.

[53] *Public Advertiser*, January 9, 1788.

[54] *Morning Chronicle*, March 6, 1788; Drescher, *Capitalism*, 75; Midgley, *Women*, 17–19.

[55] BL Minute Books, ADD MS 21254, 27; David Turley, *The Culture of English Antislavery, 1780–1860* (London: Routledge, 1991), 61.

Religion; in opposition to the principles of Liberty, Justice, and Humanity; and disgraceful in the extreme to every Country by which it is encouraged, or even tolerated." Religious, philosophical, and national ideals all condemned British participation. Those assembled thanked London organizers and "every other Friend to this cause of Humanity," resolving "to extend information on this important subject to every part of Europe."[56] In total, 10,639 citizens, an unprecedented number approximating two-thirds of Manchester's adult male population, soon signed.[57] Birmingham, Leeds, and Sheffield petitioned within a month.[58] Even though an Atlantic trade slowdown could injure their financial interests, most manufacturing cities backed abolition.

Ports' abolitionist advocacy proved even more surprising, particularly from some prominently involved in the slave trade. Bristol, the second leading British slaving center, at a municipal meeting featuring "many respectable merchants of this city," unanimously denounced trafficking as "inconsistent with humanity and justice, and abhorrent from the benevolent sprit of religion we profess."[59] Principle now could surmount even economic prosperity.

As political support for abolition intensified, many expected quick reform. The *General Evening Post* confidently asserted, "The general alacrity with which the proposition for abolishing the Slave Trade is adopted throughout every part of the kingdom, promises a happy issue of Mr. Wilberforce's motion on the subject."[60] Should "any man of humanity for a moment" consider abolition, the *London Packet* argued, "he will not have a doubt in his own mind, whether it ought to be abolished or not."[61] Over the first six months, 102 addresses bore over 60,000 signatures.[62] Trafficking's horrors violated all humanitarian values, and Britons pushed for principled action.

Popular mobilization, not confined to English centers, spread across the British Isles. In February 1788, petitions arrived from Scottish religious authorities with Aberdeen, Glasgow, and Edinburgh's Presbyteries supporting abolition.[63] Some spoke of ending slavery itself with the University of Aberdeen requesting Parliament "alleviate the rigours of Negro slavery and prepare the way for its final extirpation in every part of the British

---

[56] *World*, January 9, 1788.

[57] *General Evening Post*, February 9, 1788; Drescher, *Capitalism*, 70.

[58] *Lloyd's Evening Post*, January 23, 1788; *Morning Herald*, January 28, 1788.

[59] James A. Rawley with Stephen D. Behrendt, *The Transatlantic Slave Trade: A History*, Revised Edition (Lincoln: University of Nebraska Press, 2005), 198; *Morning Post*, February 12, 1788.

[60] *General Evening Post*, February 5, 1788.

[61] *London Packet*, February 4, 1788.

[62] Michael W. McCahill, *The Correspondence of Stephen Fuller, 1788-1795: Jamaica, the West India Interest, and the Campaign to Preserve the Slave Trade* (London: Wiley-Blackwell, 2014), 63.

[63] *St. James's Chronicle*, February 21 and March 11, 1788; *Public Advertiser*, March 8, 1788; *Whitehall Evening Post*, April 5, 1788; *General Evening Post*, April 8, 1788.

Empire."[64] In Ireland that March, following local Quaker lobbying, Dublin's Merchants Guild declared the trade "repugnant, not only to the principles of religion and humanity, but to the true interests of commerce," which would profit more from Africa's peaceful development. Though claiming Irish merchants did not directly participate in trafficking, each pledged support for imperial changes. With British abolitionists fearful that Liverpool and Bristol "slavemongers" might relocate across the Irish Sea, Irish merchants lobbied their Parliament to outlaw the trade as soon as Britain would.[65]

Liverpool merchants, seeing their city's economic livelihood threatened, built a counter-movement against abolition. Slaving interests claimed eliminating the trade would "destroy the honest tradesmen and merchant," badly injure overseas exchanges producing over 2 million pounds sterling annually, lessen naval readiness, and throw Britain's empire into precarity.[66] Prophesizing economic disaster, residents denounced the measure's unintended effects. With Manchester having innovated mass-petition signings, pro-slavers in Liverpool out-mobilized them. The anti-abolition petition collected 23,500 signatures, double Manchester's number. Separate petitions arrived from Liverpool's mayor, aldermen, corporation, planters' lobby, financiers, metal merchants, joiners, shipwrights, gun-makers, manufacturers, and even bakers.[67]

Pitt introduced antislavery legislation on May 9, 1788. Asserting public opinion "prevailed out of doors" against slave trafficking, Pitt declared either "the trade ought to be put a stop to," or "further regulations" strongly considered.[68] Though one committeeman described Pitt as "at best but a luke-warm Friend," Reformist Whigs made the antislavery cause their own.[69] Fox declared before Parliament, "the Slave Trade ought not to be regulated, but destroyed." Burke castigated trafficking as "so ruinous to the feelings and capacities of human nature, that it ought not to be suffered to exist."[70] The Commons approved a committee to consider abolishing the trade headed by Wilberforce.

Slaveholding interests made clear they would contest abolition. As witnessed during the American crises, merchant lobbies held significant Parliamentary sway. Since the early eighteenth century, the sugar colonies organized effective pressure groups, with the overlapping Society of West India Merchants and Society of West India Planters and Merchants in London, Bristol, and Liverpool

[64] Iain Whyte, *Scotland and the Abolition of Black Slavery, 1756–1838* (Edinburgh: Edinburgh University Press, 2006), 93.
[65] BL Minute Books of the London Abolition Committee, ADD MS 21255 10; GRO D 3549 13/1/L1; *Gazetteer*, April 12, 1788; *London Chronicle*, April 12, 1788; Rodgers, *Ireland*, 181.
[66] *Public Advertiser*, February 27, 1788.
[67] *Bath Chronicle*, March 20, 1788; *Pennsylvania Mercury*, August 13, 1789.
[68] *Parliamentary History*, Vol. 27, 495.
[69] LRO 920 ROS/253.
[70] *Parliamentary History*, Vol. 27, 501–2.

particularly influential.[71] Liverpool's representatives led the colonial cause in Parliament with Baron Richard Penrhyn responding to Pitt and Fox by asserting, "the merchants would be exonerated from that blame which has so profusely been thrown upon them." Caribbean planters declared themselves "ready to appear in vindication of their conduct" and defend their livelihoods.[72] Parliament, Penrhyn argued, had protected the trade for over a century, encouraging colonial investment predicated on a cheap, continuing flow of slave labor. Regulating imports, moreover, fell within colonial legislatures' traditional purview. Trampling on established colonial compacts, soon after the American War, could destabilize the remaining empire.[73]

Liverpool's pro-slaving committee extended their counter-campaign nationally. Allying with the West India Committee, Liverpool wrote to other slaving ports urging them to "contribute their proportion towards defraying the Expences attending the opposition to the slave bill," quickly gaining cooperation. The committee used funds to print pro-slavery justifications, circulate letters and model petitions, and pay traders' way to Westminster to testify and lobby for continued trafficking.[74] They beseeched associations to "be prepared" with new petitions should measures radicalize. Bristol's merchants asserted slavery and the colonial system's prosperity "must necessarily rise or fall together," while London's declared the colonies would "immediately decline" without fresh slaves.[75] Realizing the antislavery cause's appeal, its opponents to an extent unseen in previous counter-campaigns used activists' own tactics against them.

Though a final vote on abolishing the slave trade would not occur until a future session, legislators pressed ahead with reforming some of its worst abuses. A new bill sought to regulate the number of slaves aboard (relative to tonnage) to prevent overcrowding, while mandating sufficient provisions. Even this mild proposal incited slave traders' opposition with Liverpool and London merchants petitioning against "any sudden measure" upending their business. Pitt nevertheless pushed for passage, declaring, "if the trade could not be carried on from a manner different" than recent reports, he would support abolition.[76] Though abolitionist committees declined to endorse the reforms, fearing half-measures would derail their campaign, the regulations easily passed the Commons and, after the Lords granted merchant compensation to Liverpool lobbyists, took effect in July 1788.[77]

---

[71] Dale H. Porter, *The Abolition of the Slave Trade in England, 1784–1807* (Hamden, CT: Archon, 1970), 16–18.

[72] *Public Advertiser*, May 10, 1788.

[73] Davis, *The Problem of Slavery in the Age of Revolution*, 114.

[74] *Public Advertiser*, February 27, 1788; Bristol Archives SMV/7/2/1/15.

[75] BA SMV/7/2/1/15.

[76] *Parliamentary History*, 573–74, 598.

[77] *Times*, July 9, 1788; LSF, Mathews Papers MSS A 1/5 49.

The skirmish over regulations augured a difficult fight over abolishing the slave trade. Wilberforce in January claimed a "universal disposition in our favour in the House of Commons," but humanitarian reformers faced powerful opposition from many entrenched interests.[78] Abolitionist mobilization intensified: new county-level committees commenced in June to "procure fresh Subscriptions & Petitions," alongside firsthand trafficking testimonies. Cartwright joined a London subcommittee, while Clarkson traveled that summer to promote the new bodies.[79] Sharp welcomed the Parliamentary delay, so abolitionists could cultivate supporters.[80] Wilberforce's Parliamentary committee continued gathering evidence for the final debates, stoking public outrage by releasing some of the worst abuses found. One slave captain's testimony detailed the "intercourse between the Mariners and Female Slaves" with "sometimes violence" necessary for captors to fulfill their desires.[81] Moving beyond polite society's bounds, abolitionists exhibited the full range of abuses to demonstrate abolition's necessity.

As the movements for and against abolition intensified, however, it became impossible to maintain consensus in many communities. Abolitionist arguments that "no injury will accrue to the West-India islands – nor any diminution of the revenue" stretched credulity.[82] Merchants, fearing investment losses and recession, turned against the campaign. Together with Liverpool's anti-abolition petitions signed by fifteen thousand to the House of Lords, which had not received a similar deluge of antislavery petitions as the Commons did, Manchester merchants in June 1788 broke with the city's strong abolitionist movement to petition against changes. Bristol's slave merchants the following month caucused apart from their antislavery municipality, sending an anti-regulation petition. By April 1789, a merchant consensus against abolishing the lucrative traffic grew to the point that reportedly "every commercial town in Great-Britain" featured dedicated anti-abolitionists.[83]

Realizing the manpower and publicity the abolitionist effort generated, slaving groups marshaled their resources anew. In February the West India Merchants and Planters began their own research with colonial agent Stephen Fuller collecting materials "respecting the State of Slavery from the beginning of history to the present time," to argue "the impossibility of abolishing Slavery."[84] The group sponsored a London publicity committee, which at its first gathering in June 1788 prophesized "fatal Effects" for the colonies should

[78] Auckland, *Journal*, Vol. 1, 307.
[79] BL Minute Books, ADD MS 21255 28, 29, 44.
[80] *Bristol Journal*, September 13, 1788.
[81] *Public Advertiser*, March 25, 1789; *World*, June 14, 1788.
[82] *Independent Gazetteer*, April 16, 1788.
[83] *Morning Chronicle*, June 24, 1788; *World*, July 8, 1788; *St. James's Chronicle*, April 2, 1789.
[84] McCahill, *Correspondence*, 71.

trafficking be immediately abolished.[85] The group appealed to British self-interest in April 1789, asserting the "Manufactures, Trade and Revenue of Great Britain, must suffer" from abolition.[86] Slaving lobbyists printed pamphlets and planted newspaper articles like their abolitionist competitors, appealing to reason, good sense, and economic necessity.[87]

A campaign for continuing the slave trade could present itself as nearly as enlightened as one to abolish it. Anti-abolitionist appeals from the Caribbean prophesized panic, violence, and revolt should such legislation pass. In early July 1788, a Jamaican planter petition apprehended "an insurrection of the Slaves in consequence of passing such a Bill as the present, which would endanger the lives of 20,000 white inhabitants in the island of Jamaica alone."[88] Any reforms, they argued, would lead slaves to expect more, perhaps emancipation. Sacrificing colonial order threatened a great humanitarian disaster. Abolitionist agitation already made, one newspaper asserted, "Negroes, in many plantations ... restless, turbulent, and innovating."[89] Another, citing "a Gentleman in Jamaica," noted, "the Negroes begin already to talk of their being emancipated by the King."[90] Planter agitation spread with petitions from Nevis, St. Christopher's, Grenada, St. Vincent, and Dominica arriving in 1789.[91] As news and rumor echoed around the Caribbean, potential unintended consequences grew for the slave islands.

By August 1788, the London Committee for Effecting the Abolition of the Slave Trade procured over one hundred Parliamentary petitions from across the nation. Newspapers highlighted the movement's pan-British nature with petitions coming clear from "our wreck-watching friends to the north of Johnny Groat's house" in uppermost Scotland to "the west of Cornwall" at the opposite southern extremity.[92] A wider swathe of the British population participated than on any previous issue. Over half the petitions on any subject the British Parliament received in 1788 concerned the slave trade.[93]

Concurrently, Wilberforce sought international *détente* for Britain and France to simultaneously reform their slave trades, suspending or even abolishing them together. Doing so would disable the pro-slavery lobby's repeated argument that Britain's withdrawal from the trade would lead to their rivals' enrichment. Rumors grew of Franco-British joint abolition of the slave trade in 1787–1788, following the previous year's Eden Treaty mutually lowering trade

[85] *General Evening Post*, June 28, 1788; UCL M 915 reel 3.
[86] *World*, April 11, 1789.
[87] McCahill, *Correspondence*, 8.
[88] *Morning Chronicle*, July 5, 1788.
[89] *World*, July 5, 1788.
[90] *Morning Herald*, July 10, 1788.
[91] *Public Advertiser*, May 13, 1789.
[92] *Morning Chronicle*, June 20, 1788.
[93] Drescher, *Capitalism*, 76.

tariffs. Lord Auckland, author of a pamphlet proposing the trade's suspension, served as Britain's negotiator. Mutual distrust led both sides to demur, however, with a British Parliamentary committee arguing the Atlantic trade would not be the "least diminished" by British withdrawal.[94] Wilberforce countered by asserting such ardor could cross the channel. "The fire is kindled in various parts of the kingdom," Wilberforce wrote to Auckland in January 1788, "the flame every day spreads wider." He reported a society "set on foot in Paris."[95] The next month, word followed of organizations "forming on the plan of that of London" in Lyon, Reims, and Bordeaux.[96] Passionate proponents, both in government and fledgling popular organizations, promoted major changes for both countries.

Efforts concurrently advanced to implement alternative models for reformed Atlantic colonies. Realizing entrenched interests' strength in Britain, Sharp spent years promoting, and his personal savings to help found, a West African colony in Sierra Leone to produce similar products as the Caribbean islands without slavery.[97] With four hundred members in 1787 – including Loyalist veterans of the American War freed by Dunmore and impoverished London blacks, alongside East Indian and white minorities – Granville Town adopted a vision of race relations rooted in liberty and natural rights. Sharp, though not accompanying the settlers, composed a preliminary legal code. Asserting more strongly than Americans that on the basis of biblical, natural, and British common law "all men are created equal," Sharp extended to all settlers "of various nations, and various complexions, from the East and West Indies, from Europe, Asia, Africa and America" an "equal natural claim" to citizenship. Politically, all male householders possessed "equal voice in the 'common council'" governing the colony. Though retaining indentured servitude as a regrettable necessity to attract new immigrants, any slave arriving would be "deemed a free man" with equal "protection of the laws."[98] The settlers, however, quickly fell ill in the African climate, with 50 dying and another 150 sickened. An African attack torched the settlement in late 1789.[99] With their idealized colony annihilated, British activists rededicated themselves to ameliorating Britain's existing colonial system.

Wilberforce introduced his committee's legislation to abolish the slave trade on May 12, 1789. He presented the Commons with ample evidence of the

[94] BA Parliamentary Reports on the Slave Trade, 08527847.
[95] Auckland, *Journal*, Vol. 1, 305–6.
[96] *Bristol Journal*, February 9, 1788.
[97] Auckland, *Journal*, Vol. 1, 320–21.
[98] Sharp, *A Short Sketch of Temporary Regulations (Until Better Shall Be Proposed) for the Intended Settlement of the Grain Coast of Africa, near Sierra Leona* (London: Baldwin, 1788), viii, xxxvi, xxxix, 6, 22.
[99] Mary Louise Clifford, *From Slavery to Freetown: Black Loyalists after the American Revolution* (Jefferson, NC: McFarland, 2006), 73–79.

trade's horrors, declaring, "We are all guilty" of direct or indirect profit. Burke orated that no "necessity" could justify such trafficking. Capital, he asserted, would flow elsewhere in the British economy if the trade ended, while if the abolition effort now failed, traders would continue "with a redoubled attachment" and prevent future abolitionist efforts. Pitt also pressured for immediate abolition. The opposition, however, prophesized disastrous effects, with a City of London representative declaring abolition would render his entire constituency "one scene of bankruptcy and ruin." A Bristol MP defended the trade as "the practice of every civilized nation," while asserting changes required "public compensation." Wilberforce fell ill the following month, however, and the motion was tabled until the next Parliamentary session.[100]

Pro-slaving interests maintained a flood of petitions and publicity. Affected groups defended their livelihoods, with Caribbean colonists placing new levies on exports for legal fees and pamphlet printing. Bristol's meeting of merchants and manufacturers resolved to oppose all reforms, while intensively lobbying MPs. Liverpool brought a dozen more addresses from interested occupations with their "Merchants, Mortgagees, and other Creditors of the Sugar Colonies" declaring a colonial recession could ruin them.[101] London's West India Merchants and Planters meeting resolved, "a trade to Africa cannot be carried on to any great extent or national advantage, except in the article of slaves," while denouncing Pitt's refusal of merchant compensation. Parliament's deliberations became "of the most alarming nature to every one who feels himself interested in the commerce or prosperity of the kingdom."[102] African slave traders (hearing of uncertainty) reportedly raised prices along their coast so high British boats left for the Middle Passage half full. In August, false rumors arrived of a slave insurrection in French Saint-Domingue and more followed in March 1790.[103]

Little more than six years after the American War's end, using autonomist arguments like the thirteen colonies had, Jamaica's planters asserted they would resist any changes to their colonial compact. A plantation owner meeting in late 1789 resolved that as their charter granted the slave trade as a "temptation to settle," it was guaranteed by "the King of Jamaica." Having already (unsuccessfully) asserted their legislative independence amid the American controversies in 1774, they reintroduced arguments that the "Legislature of Great Britain" possessed "no right to legislate for Jamaica, nor

[100] *Parliamentary History*, Vol. 28, 42, 69–70, 76, 95, 100; Samuel Romilly, *The Life of Sir Samuel Romilly* (London: Murray, 1842), 263.
[101] *St. James's Chronicle*, May 19, 1789; Porter, *Creation*, 72, 86; BA SMV/8/3/2/5; *Whitehall Evening Post*, May 19, 1789.
[102] *Public Advertiser*, May 20, 1789.
[103] *Morning Star*, June 26 and July 3, 1789; *St. James's Chronicle*, August 25, 1789; *Whitehall Evening Post*, March 4, 1790.

to dispose any part of its trade."[104] Provoking American memories, declaring Jamaicans "able to defend" themselves, planters implied resistance and perhaps even war in Britain's largest Caribbean colony should Parliament proceed.[105] Rumors spread that in the French colonies "the leading Planters, rather than submit to [slave trade abolition] would solicit the protection of a foreign power."[106] The planters, and thus too their abolitionist opponents, played an increasingly dangerous game.

The abolitionist movement faltered: though meetings continued, the massive petitions of 1788 were not easily repeated. Parliament's slow pace confounded many supporters, one noting that with Pitt and Fox, "the two chiefs of the House of Commons seem to be unanimous," possessing unequalled "powers of argument and persuasion" the abolitionists could deploy.[107] The London abolitionist committee, explaining themselves in a July 1790 network communiqué, considered themselves "assailed from different quarters," needing to "repel evidence by evidence, and argument by argument." In urging Parliament to complete "the fullest investigation," however, they gave anti-abolitionists valuable time.[108] Newspapers increasingly published anti-abolitionist fear-mongering, dwarfing abolitionists' increasingly repetitive justifications. Clarkson's mission to revolutionary France failed to bring direct results. Abolitionists now faced a well-prepared opposition.

Anti-abolitionists increased pressure on their representatives. Merchant committees met with Pitt and the Privy Council to warn what abolishing the trade might cause.[109] Increasingly confident, anti-abolitionists called for voting in early 1791, declaring the sooner the question "is brought to a decision, one way or another, the better," to calm islanders' fears of colonial violence.[110] Short-circuiting debate, while spreading fear, seemed the best formula for preserving the status quo.

The early abolitionist hope that the trade could be abolished through British legislators' disinterested virtue increasingly appeared illusory. As the *Public Advertiser* mocked in June 1790, "here a candidate gains his election, because he supported the repeal of the Test Act – and there another, because he opposed it. Here a member is thrown out, because he voted for the Slave Trade – and here he is elected, because he voted against it."[111] While abolitionists like France-traveling writer Helen Maria Williams asserted, "Europe is hastening towards a period too enlightened for the perpetuation of such

---

[104] *General Evening Post*, February 11, 1790.
[105] *Public Advertiser*, March 17, 1790.
[106] *English Chronicle*, March 13, 1790.
[107] *Public Advertiser*, January 28, 1790; McCahill, *Correspondence* 22.
[108] *Woodfall's Register*, July 30, 1790.
[109] *St. James's Chronicle*, January 28, 1790; *Public Advertiser*, March 25, 1791.
[110] *Public Advertiser*, March 25, 1791.
[111] Ibid., June 26, 1790.

monstrous abuses," France's reconfirming the trade in mid-1790 denied abolitionists their desired international consensus.[112] Burke in his famed *Reflections on the Revolution in France* denounced "the rights of man" as a practical basis for a social order, predicting, "As the colonists rise" across France's colonies for autonomy, slaves would "rise on them," leading to "Massacre, torture, hanging!"[113] Autumn news arrived of the United States Congress confirming the slave trade's continuance until at least 1808.[114] If such human rights were refused amid revolution, how could a more cautious Britain declare them undeniable?

Parliamentary abolition debates recommenced on April 18, 1791. Presenting long proofs of the slave trade's needlessness and immorality, Wilberforce declared his confidence that "the people of Great Britain" would support immediate abolition now that its "injustice and cruelty" was demonstrated. Many MPs, however, sided with the slavers: Liverpool representative Banastre Tarleton asserted the slave trade employed 5,500 sailors and made £800,000 sterling a year, anchoring a West Indian trade annually topping £6,000,000. The next day William Young (a former colonial lobbyist and Caribbean governor's son) castigated abolitionists for wanting to wash Britain's hands "as Pontius Pilate," asserting it would lead rivals to "rush the coasts of Africa" for Britain's share. Though many reformists held firm, the motion failed by 88–163.[115] The news in Bristol and Liverpool sparked such rejoicing, officials declared a public holiday, with bonfires and fireworks.[116]

Such clashes of humanitarian principle with economic self-interest led many to despair at the resulting stasis. Auckland lamented, "Those who urge the immediate abolition know that it is impossible; those who propose the gradual abolition mean to baffle every species of abolition; and those who vote for the continuance of the trade, know well that it ought not to be continued."[117] Cold interest trumped sentiment. Dedicated abolitionists pronounced their disgust: Fox in the heat of Parliamentary debate declared, "no man who had either heart or understanding, could possibly vote against the motion for Abolition."[118] The traffic, clearly, would not die on its own: though slave prices reportedly rose both in coastal Africa and the Caribbean after the new regulations passed, massive importations continued.[119] Liberal reform did not persuade many.

---

[112] Helen Maria Williams, *Letters on the French Revolution: Written in France, in the Summer of 1790, to a Friend in England* (London, Cadell, 1790), 48; *World*, July 9, 1790.
[113] Burke, *Reflections*, 321.
[114] *World*, October 27, 1790.
[115] *Parliamentary History*, Vol. 29, 250, 281, 294, 296, 359.
[116] *Woodfall's Register*, April 26, 1791; *Morning Chronicle*, April 27, 1791.
[117] Auckland, *Journal*, Vol. 2, 400.
[118] *Lloyd's Evening Post*, April 22, 1791.
[119] *General Evening Post*, July 21, 1791.

The abolition bill's failure, however, led organizers to rekindle the popular abolitionist movement. The *Oracle* in April rhetorically asked whether the anti-slave trade bill would "have been inefficacious, provided the sentiments of the People of England could have been fairly collected on the occasion?"[120] Antislavery societies pledged continued agitation. Glasgow's branch in late April promised "never to abandon this cause until it shall be finally crowned with success," while London's central committee declared the vote "a delay rather than a defeat." As a "free and enlightened Nation" could not abandon "a subject in which its Justice, Humanity and its Wisdom are involved," the society would appeal "to the consciences of our countrymen" until convincing them.[121] To further synergize the cause's Parliamentary and popular branches, Wilberforce, Fox, and other antislavery legislators became formal London's Committee for Effecting the Abolition of the Slave Trade members.[122]

Combating the assertion that they spoke for only a British minority, abolition societies recommitted to the methods that fueled their prior upsurge. Manchester's committee in late May beseeched members to "renew the discussion of this great question both in and out of Parliament, upon every suitable occasion."[123] Edinburgh's society asserted that with Pitt and Fox's support, it would be foolish not to "persevere with unabated zeal" for another vote.[124] With so many accounts of trafficking atrocities, consenting to "the murder of thousands annually & the misery & slavery of still more," as Midlands coal mine owner Richard Reynolds considered, seemed abominable.[125]

A boycott movement against plantation-produced products arose to economically pressure slavers and raise personal antislavery commitment. The *Whitehall Evening Post* in June 1791 queried whether with

> The House of Commons having determined that our West India Islands cannot be cultivated without a continuance of the Slave Trade, is it not become the duty of every man of honour, justice, and humanity, to deny himself the use of the produce of those islands, viz. sugar, rum, &c till this abominable traffic is abolished?[126]

No slave-produced products were necessities and most were unhealthy. Without European profits, the triangle trade would collapse. Whereas only a small percentage of Britons had ever directly engaged in slaving, (non)

[120] *Oracle*, April 21, 1791.
[121] *Star*, April 29, 1791; *London Chronicle*, April 30, 1791.
[122] Oldfield, "London Committee," 332.
[123] *London Chronicle*, June 2, 1791.
[124] *General Evening Post*, June 4, 1791.
[125] University of Liverpool Sydney Jones Library Special Collections, Rathbone Family Papers, RP IV 1.1A 53.
[126] *Whitehall Evening Post*, June 21, 1791.

consumption provided a tangible interaction with the Atlantic trade. The abstention campaign, unlike most prior petition-signing, directly incorporated women into the abolitionist movement, as they did most household buying.

The antislavery movement profited from a broader upsurge in British radicalism as French Revolutionary principles gained strength. Radicals throughout the country gathered to celebrate the second anniversary of the Bastille's fall on July 14, 1791, and boasted of their antislavery activism. Toasts at Manchester's Constitutional Society banquet included "Abolition of the Slave Trade," "May the New World regenerate the old," and "the speedy overthrow of every Despotic Government."[127] Confrontations over liberty proliferated.

By autumn, word arrived of the slave insurrection that became the Haitian Revolution. To pro-slavery interests, the event represented the pernicious "doctrines of the Rights of Man" that led slaves to conjecture they were rightfully free.[128] To abolitionists, however, Saint-Domingue brought attention to how badly the colonies needed systematic reform. Leicester's municipality, petitioning in February 1792, described slavery's "fundamentally unjust, and enormously oppressive" features as "the great and radical cause of insurrections in the West-India Islands."[129] Ceasing imports largely consisting of African warriors became reasonable. Without the international trade, a November *Star* editorial argued, "no African strangers, rendered desperate by being dragged in chains from their native land, would arrive to blow up the flames of rebellion in the Colonies." Thereafter, the better treatment they would receive once they became less easily replaceable "would naturally abate their disposition to rebel."[130] The *Morning Chronicle* described abolitionists as "the best friends to the peace of the Colonies."[131] The Caribbean islands' status quo appeared unsustainable.

Nonconsumption – whether individual consumers should boycott slave-produced colonial products – became a national debate. Adapted from the American Patriot movement, boycotting promoted virtuous asceticism to prevent consumer money from supporting terrible abuses. Leading Baptist William Fox's pamphlet *An Address to the People of Great Britain, on the Propriety of Abstaining from West India Sugar and Rum* spurred the movement, claiming a family denying itself five pounds of sugar a week could in twenty-one months "prevent the slavery or murder of one fellow-creature," while eight families in a generation could save a hundred people. Each pound of sugar amounted to "consuming two ounces of human

---

[127] *Morning Post*, July 19, 1791.
[128] *Oracle*, October 29, 1791.
[129] *Star*, February 6, 1792.
[130] Ibid., November 3, 1791.
[131] *Morning Chronicle*, November 22, 1791.

flesh."[132] By December 1791, one London paper noted, "A great number of the inhabitants of this town abstain from sugar and rum, as the most likely means of abolishing the Slave Trade."[133] As the amount of sugar consumed in England likely equaled all of continental Europe, nonconsumption could have powerful effects.[134]

By January 1792, abstention reportedly became a "conversation in almost every family." The movement beseeched individuals to follow their principles and "in a moral light condemn all" still using such products, given the trade's iniquity.[135] A London public debate asked whether such produce "be stained with the blood of the enslaved Africans, and ought, on that account, to be viewed with horror, instead of being consumed as a luxury?" – with almost all six hundred attending favoring abstention.[136] A second event asked, "Which ought to be considered the most criminal, the Merchants and Planters, who carry on the Slave Trade, the British House of Commons who have refused to abolish it, or the People who encourage it by the consumption of Sugar and Rum?"[137] While the answer remained unpublished, many now considered nonconsumption their personal responsibility. By the boycott's height, Clarkson estimated three hundred thousand families participated. Even beyond petitioning areas, many in Wales and Ireland abstained.[138]

Many hoped the growing nonconsumption movement would revivify the stalled abolition campaign. One leader considered abstention "proves men's zeal more strongly than petitions," showing the depth of opposition.[139] Decreasing sales could spark an Atlantic economic crisis. A February 1792 Sheffield petition argued, "Revenue will be greatly injured if the trade is not soon annihilated."[140] As abolitionist literature routinely declared trafficking unnecessary for Atlantic profits, the "anti-saccharite" cause sought to make retaining the trade against plantation owners' economic self-interest. Though sugar prices nevertheless rose due to rising Continental demand on account of the Haitian Revolution, falling British consumption led many to believe a permanent shift in consumer patterns underway.

Nonconsumption and political direct action became complimentary tactics. The enthusiasm sugar boycotting engendered, together with popular anger at

[132] William Fox, *An Address to the People of Great Britain, on the Propriety of Abstaining from West India Sugar and Rum* (London: Gurney, 1791), 4–5.
[133] *Star*, December 26, 1791.
[134] Samuel Bradburn, *An Address to the People Called Methodists; Concerning the Evil of Encouraging the Slave Trade* (Manchester: Harper, 1792), 21–22.
[135] *Woodfall's Register*, January 3, 1792.
[136] Ibid., January 5, 1792, and January 18, 1792.
[137] *Morning Chronicle*, February 23, 1792.
[138] Drescher, *Capitalism*, 79.
[139] Romilly, *Life*, 350.
[140] *General Evening Post*, February 23, 1792.

earlier addresses being ignored, led to a February–April 1792 petition campaign far outstripping the 1788 wave. Whereas the prior effort focused on
active voters, mobilizing through electoral networks, the 1792 effort incorporated common Britons. Rather than jealously guarding the right to sign, to
avoid being associated with the disreputable, the campaign encouraged common men (though not women) to do so. A thousand signed at Bath, 1,500 at
Carlisle, 3,122 at Newcastle, 5,000 at Sheffield, 9,000 in Edinburgh, 13,000 at
Glasgow, and 15,000 at Manchester.[141] Far more people signed abolitionist
petitions than could vote in Parliamentary elections.

The new groundswell caught pro-slaving interests off-guard. The planters'
lobby belatedly met March 20, though only reiterated old exaggerations that
"the Abolition of the Slave-Trade would effect the immediate destruction of
the colonies."[142] Liverpool, Bristol, and other slaving ports stayed quiet. The
City of London rejected an abolitionist petition but did not petition to support
the trade either.[143] Increased commitment through boycott participation
altered the political dynamic, leading slaving interests to adopt a lower profile.

In contrast to abolitionists' earlier inability to coincide Parliamentary
debates with popular upsurges, now legislators seized the momentum.
Wilberforce announced on March 20 he would introduce a new motion to
ban the slave trade on April 2. Over that two-week interval, the massive
petition wave continued. The sixty-three petitions brought before Parliament
on March 27 took over two hours to present. March 29 featured more than
forty with the following days featuring twenty-three, seventy-nine, and forty-
nine petitions. In all, abolitionists brought 519 petitions – nearly five times
1788's total – with every English county and most in Scotland represented.[144]
Addresses arrived "from all parts of the country, and from almost every civil
and religious description of the inhabitants," creating a powerful concert of
opposition.[145]

Slaving interests, rather than keep opposing all changes, attempted to divide
the abolitionist movement. On April 2, Wilberforce again presented ending
the trade as a moral imperative, describing "a cruel system, unjust and tyrannical," before pursuing economic arguments for abolition. Yet Henry Dundas,
Home Secretary for colonial affairs, followed by successfully proposing an
amendment to the bill that the trade "ought to be gradually abolished," uniting
legislators friendly to the colonial lobby with moderates fearing destabilization.

---

[141] Midgley, *Women*, 23; *World*, February 29, 1792; *Gazetteer*, March 3, 1792; *Star*,
    March 21 and 23, 1792; *Woodfall's Register*, March 27, 1792.
[142] *Lloyd's Evening Post*, March 21, 1792.
[143] *General Evening Post*, March 20, 1792.
[144] *Times*, March 28, 1792; *General Evening Post*, March 29, 1792; *Star*, March 29, 1792;
    Woodfall's Register, March 30 and 31, 1792; *Lloyd's Evening Post*, April 2, 1792; Whyte,
    Scotland, 85.
[145] *Morning Chronicle*, March 6, 1792.

This tabled discussion until a revised motion could be drawn. Two days later, Wilberforce withdrew his support, repudiating gradual abolition because it would allow the detested traffic to continue. The legislation then fell to Dundas to direct, who submitted a gradual plan for Commons debate on April 25.[146]

Contemptuous of gradualism, abolitionists continued pressuring MPs to support immediate abolition. The London Committee resolved, "gradual Abolition of the Slave trade is not an adequate remedy for its injustice and cruelty" and violated "the general wishes of the People, expressed in their numerous and urgent Petitions to Parliament." Temporarily continuing the trade would bring "redoubled cruelties and ravages on the coast of Africa," and thus the committee called partisans to use "all constitutional means" to pressure the trade's immediate end instead.[147] Abolitionists encouraged another petition wave, needing to reach Parliament by April 25.[148]

New petitions arrived, some vehemently calling for the trade's immediate abolition, but their number remained few. Glasgow declared gradualist proponents ignored the "ardent Voice of the Nation, for a total Abolition of the Traffic." Darlington considered the measure "the sanctioning of robbery and murder for a limited time." Yet only "several petitions" arriving in the days preceding the final debate led some legislators to conclude most areas signaled consent through silence.[149]

With abolition's most vocal advocates quiet or opposed, gradualist plans floundered against special-interest subterfuge. The Commons on April 25 primarily debated abolition's proper speed. Dundas proposed ending the trade in 1800, but others prevailed for 1796. Gradual abolition passed the Commons but faced a House of Lords opposed to any changes. Lord Stormont moved to reject all the evidence of Wilberforce's committee on a technicality (it had not been collected under oath) and begin a fresh enquiry. Pro-slaving interests remobilized with the West India interest arranging petitions and meetings with key Lords.[150] Lobbyists claimed abolition petitions did not speak for Britain, that "three-fourths of the nation, understand nothing of it," and spread fear of colonial slave insurrections.[151] Abolition was stymied.

International events thereafter sidelined serious consideration of abolishing the slave trade for over a decade. Clarkson was denounced for his French Jacobin connections, while associational agitation was suppressed amid the

---

[146] *St. James's Chronicle*, March 31, 1792; *World*, April 5, 1792; *Woodfall's Register*, April 6, 1792.

[147] *General Evening Post*, April 7, 1792.

[148] *Woodfall's Register*, April 7, 1792.

[149] *London Chronicle*, April 14 and 19, 1792; *Star*, April 17, 1792; *Morning Chronicle*, April 24, 1792.

[150] *Evening Mail*, April 27, 1792; *St. James's Chronicle*, May 3, 1792; *Woodfall's Register*, May 12 and 15, 1792.

[151] *St. James's Chronicle*, June 2, 1792.

Revolutionary Wars.[152] George III made known privately he "did not like the measure" and "still less the manner in which it was asserted by addresses and petitions" constituting a "bad precedent to establish."[153] The Lords did not vote on gradual abolition in 1792, and after going to war with Revolutionary France in 1793, the issue gained only brief hearings and remained undecided. London's abolition committee declined, ceasing to meet entirely between 1797 and 1804. Though Wilberforce continued reintroducing his abolition bill in the Commons each year, for over a decade it remained a symbolic exercise. Only once Britain decisively ruled the seas after 1805's Battle of Trafalgar would abolitionists successfully pressure the slave trade's end – without the vast popular movement marking the agitation's earlier phases.[154] Yet, the traffic's final abolition in 1807 would have been unthinkable without the massive shift in public perceptions wrought by the campaigns of the 1780s and 1790s.

Conclusion

In the largest and in many respects most surprising social movement yet, the British campaign against the slave trade showed how rapidly expanding popular empathy, human rights rhetoric, and skilled social movement organizing could push activism in innovative new directions. Building from American examples, proponents – most of whom had never seen a sugar plantation themselves – militated for the rights of the British Empire's most oppressed members, in larger numbers than for any political reform campaign of the era. Though facing an extensive and an influential entrenched slaving lobby, abolitionists permanently altered British views about slavery.

The British campaign against the slave trade galvanized an unprecedented number of people for political direct action – and did so without militant intimidation, collective violence, or threatening regime change. Drawing adherents from the ranks of political reformers, the religiously devout, and common Britons newly emboldened to take action against the era's abuses, the movement developed a broad alliance unlike those of prior causes. Directing the political agenda no longer remained the prerogative of the privileged but became the responsibility of the public at large. The antislavery cause, though often discussed by historians in isolation, in broader political context provided a transition between the limited participation of the early reform campaigns and their more radical efforts to organize the broad populace in the 1790s. Moreover, starting in 1788, it mobilized like-minded activists across the channel in a France on the verge of precipitous change.

---

[152] *Morning Chronicle*, March 27, 1792.
[153] Earl of Malmesbury, *Diary and Correspondence of James Harris, First Earl of Malmesbury* (London: Bentley, 1844), Vol. 2, 463–64.
[154] Oldfield, *Popular*, 63.

PART II

The French Revolution Radicalizes
Social Movements

9

The Genesis of the French Jacobins

The London Revolution Society's intercession into French revolutionary politics helped inspire the creation of the Jacobin Club network. In the French National Assembly on November 25, 1789, the session's president read a letter from the British club, which, "disdaining National partialities," declared its approbation of France's revolution and "the prospect it gives to the two first Kingdoms in the World of a common participation in the blessings of Civil and Religious Liberty." Through asserting the "inalienable rights of mankind," revolution could make "the World free and happy." The address produced a "great sensation" and loud applause in the assembly, which replied to London that it had seen "the aurora of the beautiful day" where the two nations could set aside their differences and "contract an intimate liaison by the similarity of their opinions, and common enthusiasm for liberty."[1] Within a week, growing Anglophilia inspired the founding of Paris's own *Société de la Révolution*, which only in January 1790 adopted the better-known *Société des amis de la Constitution*, retaining the English-style nickname *Club des Jacobins*.[2]

Early French revolutionary clubs frequently and creatively built on international examples as they adapted revolutionary traditions to new ends. Alternately taking inspiration from British institutions, American forerunners, and the audacity of antislavery campaigns, the French used these models to launch a Jacobin movement that would eclipse all predecessors in size, scope, and radical ambitions.

French Discoveries of Social Movements

British and French associational life remained worlds apart during the period preceding the French Revolution, with the liberties enabling the British model

---

[1] *The Correspondence of the London Revolution Society in London, with the National Assembly, with Various Societies of the Friends of Liberty in France and England* (London, 1792), 3; M. L. Lacaste et. al., eds., *Les archives parlementaires: recueil complet des débats législatifs et politiques des chambres françaises* (Paris, 1867–), Vol. 10, 257.

[2] Alphonse Aulard, ed. *La Société des Jacobins: recueil de documents pour l'histoire du club des Jacobins de Paris* (Paris, 1889–1897), Vol. 1, xvi.

contrasting with French repressiveness. French lawyer Pierre-Jean Grosley, in London in 1765, wrote incredulously that compared to heavily policed Paris, "London has neither troops, patrol, nor any sort of regular watch; and is guarded at night only by old men chosen from the dregs of the people." Police did not "meddle with the management of public diversions," which took forms unmatched in France.[3] British clubs featured rowdy debates with few limits of politics or even good taste. By contrast, French salons – elite gatherings to foster consensus and build social connections – were infiltrated by legions of undercover police informants keen on rooting out sedition. Most Enlightenment-era salons remained patronized by important Old Regime state officials and direct political critique remained muted.[4] British club veteran and agronomist Arthur Young in July 1787 visited a French aristocratic salon and found the gathering "tame and elegant . . . uninteresting and polite," in which "All vigour of thought seems so excluded from expression, that characters of ability and inanity meet nearly on a par." Far removed from London's debating clubs, he wondered, "if you neither argue or discuss, what is conversation?"[5] The constraints of politeness and conformity blunted substantive critique.

A new French variety of explicitly political discussion groups, the "*musées*," described by a high police official as "imitated from the English," arose in 1779, and by 1783 it became fashionable in Paris to refer to philanthropic, artistic, and literary groups as "*clubs*."[6] Many made their way to London to study the British institutions. "The assemblies in London are overrun with the French," a correspondent of Lord Auckland complained in April 1786.[7] Despite a Paris police crackdown on clubs in 1787, some illicitly persisted.[8]

During France's prerevolutionary political crisis of 1787–1788, many existing salons became emboldened to discuss politics. Two months after his earlier encounter with insipid salons, Young in September 1787 visited another where the "conversation was entirely political." Among attendees, "One opinion pervaded the whole company, that they are on the eve of some great revolution in the government: that every thing points to it." If a minister of "superior talents" could not be found, "a strong leaven of liberty, increasing every hour since the American Revolution" might motivate "the government's total over-throw" in France. "All agree, that the states of the kingdom cannot assemble

---

[3] Grosley, *Tour*, Vol. 1, 48–50.

[4] Antoine Lilti, *Le monde des salons: sociabilité et mondanité à Paris au XVIIIe siècle* (Paris: Fayard, 2005).

[5] Arthur Young, *Travels during the Years 1787, 1788, & 1789* (London: Richardson, 1794), 26–27.

[6] Goodman, *Republic*, 233, 262; Josephine Grieder, *Anglomania in France, 1740–1789: Fact, Fiction and Political Discourse* (Geneva: Droz, 1985), 26–27.

[7] Auckland, *Journal*, Vol. 1, 369.

[8] Louis de Cardenal, *La Province pendant la Révolution: histoire des clubs jacobins, 1789-1795* (Paris: Payot, 1929), 113.

without more liberty being the consequence" – that mobilizing the nation would be incompatible with perpetuating absolutism.[9]

Early French antislavery agitation also grew from enlightened emulation of Anglo-American club life. In 1787, a year before liberal pamphleteer Jacques-Pierre Brissot and Genevan revolutionary-in-exile Etienne Clavière founded the *Société des amis des noirs*, the two began a *Société Gallo-américaine* in Paris to help the two countries "better understand each other" and build closer commercial relationships. Through "knowing what occurs in the United States," society members could "employ all their influence to adopt useful institutions."[10] Brissot, who had spent years in London, helped procure the club British newspapers, while famed member Crèvecoeur acquired from *"l'Amérique libre"* the best "gazettes, journals, books, acts of legislation, Congressional debates, etc."[11] Though the Gallo-American Club did not last long, it helped fund Brissot's desired American travels, and in May 1788 he departed on a seven-month tour of the United States. With letters of introduction from British abolitionists and the Marquis de Lafayette, from Boston to Philadelphia Brissot received "the most flattering welcome" from antislavery activists and older radicals like Samuel Adams.[12] After returning to France, even while editing the popular *Patriote français* newspaper, Brissot still published a three-volume travelogue in 1791, so the French could "observe men who conquered their liberty."[13]

Within three months of the British Committee for Effecting the Abolition of the Slave Trade's founding, the London leadership accepted Brissot and Clavière's offer to form a Paris-based *Société des amis des noirs* working to abolish the French traffic. Previously, during the American war, Benezet (a native Frenchman) had pursued an antislavery alliance with Raynal – enlisting Franklin as courier – but failed to spark a French movement.[14] Amid the growing political ferment of France's prerevolutionary crises, however, interest broadened in the humanitarian cause. The Gallo-American Society had begun corresponding with leading London Quaker abolitionist James Philips the previous year, "to capture the light which could be useful to France and the

[9] Young, *Travels*, 66–67.
[10] Etienne Clavière and Jacques-Pierre Brissot, "Prospectus de la Société Gallo-Américaine," in *De la France et des Etats-Unis* (London, 1787), 340–41.
[11] Brissot, *Correspondance et papiers* (Paris: Picard, 1912), 110, 115.
[12] Brissot, *Nouveau voyage dans les Etats-Unis de l'Amérique Septentrionale, fait en 1788* (Paris: Buisson 1791), Vol. 1, 51, Vol. 2, 10; Eloise Ellery, *Brissot de Warville: A Study in the History of the French Revolution* (Boston: Houghton Mifflin, 1915), 77–79.
[13] Brissot, *Nouveau*, Vol. 1, i.
[14] Maurice Jackson, "Anthony Benezet and the Dream of Freedom: Then and Now," in *The Atlantic World of Anthony Benezet (1713–1784): From French Reformation to North American Quaker Antislavery Activism*, Marie-Jeanne Rossignol and Bertrand Van Ruymbeke, eds. (Leiden: Brill, 2017), xvii.

United States."[15] Brissot there had promoted "the destruction of negro slavery" and, when passing through London on his American return, promoted a Franco-British alliance to abolish the slave trade across both empires.[16]

In late January 1788, the *Société* publicized the developing Franco-British entente. A letter from Sharp in the recently founded *Analyse des papiers anglois* newspaper (edited by the dissident Comte de Mirabeau, son of the antislavery economist) announced that although for "a long time the *Philosophes*" – naming Franklin, Raynal, and Paine – had denounced slaveholder abuses, now a "happy revolution in sentiments" spread in Britain. "From all over subscriptions and associations form to introduce legislation and formally suppress the trade and practice of black slavery." Proclaiming the British effort's imminent success, the journal invited "all friends of humanity" to participate. A second notice from Brissot and Clavière beseeched educated French society to "join to philosophical and political knowledge a true love of liberty and respect for the dignity of man" and "prepare this Revolution in France."[17] Proponents argued the French should join the British in a joint abolition "to advance the system of peace and fraternity which must unite all peoples."[18] France had surpassed Britain as Europe's leading slave-trading empire and, as Brissot wrote to Philips, the new society could inspire "all Europe" to renounce such spoils, pledging to "carry this generous resolution to the nations we interact with."[19] A year before the French Revolution began, many believed the greatest changes would come through international cooperation.

Brissot and Clavière's ambitions not only fit into British abolitionists' pragmatic diplomatic designs, but also both sides' universalist pretensions. Sharp told the *Société*, "we embarked on this cause, not simply as Englishmen, but as citizens of the universe" to stop the "rights of humanity" being violated "over all the globe." Yet this could only occur if Africans no longer found European buyers. The two leading empires, "instead of competing for Conquest," could embark on mutual "emulation, diffusing the Blessings of Peace, Freedom and Civilization thro' their extensive Possessions." Suzanne Necker, wife of the king's minister, joined a dinner party the *amis* hosted for a visiting London committeeman, and proclaimed "her intention of publishing

[15] Brissot, *Correspondance*, 107.

[16] Marcel Dorigny and Bernard Gainot, eds. *La Societe des amis des noirs, 1788–1799: contribution à l'histoire de l'abolition de l'esclavage* (Paris: UNESCO, 1998), 23; Popkin, "Saint-Domingue, Slavery and the Origins of the Haitian Revolution," in *From Deficit to Deluge: The Origins of the French Revolution*, Thomas E. Kaiser and Dale Van Kley, eds. (Stanford, CA: Stanford University Press, 2011), 223.

[17] *Analyse des papiers anglois*, January 31, 1788.

[18] *Discours sur la nécessité d'établir à Paris une Société pour concourir, avec celle de Londres, à l'abolition de la traite & de l'esclavage des Nègres* (Paris, 1788).

[19] Drescher, *Abolition*, 155; Brissot, *Correspondance*, 169.

some tracts on the subject, as soon as she could."[20] The London society, pleased with the French response, made Lafayette an honorary member. The *Société* repudiated Anglophobia, declaring themselves founded "after England and America's example," seeking to advance the "empire of reason" with their international brethren.[21] A rapid reconceptualization of empire appeared achievable.

Brissot hoped to inspire a popular French abolitionist movement, bringing antislavery conversations into growing debates over France's future during the months preceding the Estates General. "Enthusiasm is general in England," he orated at the *Société* meeting on March 4, 1789, "it will probably become so in France." To "enlighten spirits" they needed to "multiply writings," emulating the tactics working so well abroad: "What made the revolution in the United States? Its gazettes."[22] Alongside *Analyse* articles, the society distributed a Marquis de Condorcet-penned address to each of France's new electoral assemblies, asking for antislavery grievances' inclusion in their *Cahiers de Doléances*. Forty-nine constituencies obliged the *Société* – Metz' clergy declaring the slave trade "contrary to natural law and all the laws of humanity" – but the cause paled before France's vast domestic grievances.[23]

Despite France's rapid politicization, during the Revolution's early stages the French did not mobilize into extra-governmental political networks as recent American, British, and Irish movements had. The *Société*, while admiring Anglo-American antislavery models, remained an elite, Paris-dominated movement. In March 1788, Brissot advocated a wider campaign with increased distribution of antislavery writings and a newspaper creating "general enthusiasm," to be "devoured with avidity by artisans, farmers and men of all classes." The organization declined the venture, however, and in June 1789 still rejected taking "*la forme du club*."[24] Nevertheless, the *Société* lobbied the Estates General, and its members, including future Jacobins like Brissot, Mirabeau, Lafayette, Condorcet, Henri Grégoire, and Maximilien Robespierre, became increasingly aware of Anglo-American social movement strategies. *Amis des noirs* membership significantly overlapped with the shadowy Society of Thirty meeting in the Palais Royal (ultimately comprising fifty-five members including Lafayette, Mirabeau, and Condorcet) which, after deciding policy by a majority vote, composed and diffused radical political pamphlets. A faction of about twenty-five became known as "the Americans," seeking to limit monarchical authority. Though featuring over forty nobles

[20] LRO 920 ROS/257.
[21] Dorigny and Gainot, *Société*, 86–87, 156; Bibliothèque de l'Institut de France, Papiers de Condorcet, MS 857, Vol. 1, 29; AN AD XVIIIc 116 1 4; GRO D 3549 13–1-B35.
[22] Dorigny and Gainot, *Société*, 73, 77.
[23] Davis, *Problem of Slavery in the Age of Revolution*, 97–98; Popkin, "Saint-Domingue," 233.
[24] Doigny and Gainot, *Société*, 77–78, 230.

from France's finest lineages, this nascent "Patriot" party accelerated the radicalization of French political opinion over the months before the Estates General, agitating for doubled Third Estate representation.[25]

The prominent exception to the paucity of general-interest clubs in the early Revolution was the Breton Club deputies from Brittany organized as the Estates General began. The American War veteran Mazzei noted their forming "a sort of political academy in their own garden" welcoming "non-Bretons of a like mind" with membership growing to 150. The club sought to build consensus on legislative propositions, creating a powerful bloc of eloquent supporters. Differences were resolved by majority vote, after which all participants agreed to support the outcome in the legislature. Fusing efforts with the Society of Thirty, the club advanced the patriot movement that spring and summer, building consensus for Third Estate deputies to form a National Assembly and abolish feudalism.[26] Yet, the organization's influence seemed slight by September – Robespierre noted only a "*très petite* minority" siding with them against including a royal veto in the French constitution, and the organization reverted to being a provincial caucus by the October Days.[27] Indeed, the conservative *Monarchiens*, featuring elites from the National Assembly and Paris society, became the most powerful faction in summer and fall 1789.[28]

In spring 1789, gatherings at Paris's Palais Royal (freed from political surveillance by the princely privilege of its owner, the Duc d'Orléans) made political debate a mainstream activity. Estates General legislators arrived to "refresh themselves on public opinion" and cultivate popular support.[29] Young in June described "constant meetings" featuring "people of all descriptions" in the cafés, gardens, and apartments. "Not a word of any thing else is talked of" except the Estates General. By the Tennis Court Oath crisis' end, an apparent consensus developed among "all ranks of people" favoring "nothing less than a revolution in government, and the establishment of a free constitution."[30]

---

[25] Popkin, "Saint-Domingue"; Dorigny and Gainot, *Société*, 218; Daniel L. Wick, *A Conspiracy of Well-Intentioned Men: The Society of Thirty and the French Revolution* (New York: Garland, 1987) esp. 43–45, 294; Jonathan Israel, *Revolutionary Ideas: An Intellectual History of the French Revolution from the Rights of Man to Robespierre* (Princeton: Princeton University Press, 2014), 33–36.

[26] APS Filippo Mazzei Papers, Mss.Ms.Coll.47; Wick, *Conspiracy*, 312.

[27] Georges Michon, ed., *Correspondance de Maximilien et Augustin Robespierre* (Paris: Félix Alcan, 1926), 52; Timothy Tackett, *Becoming a Revolutionary: The Deputies of the First French National Assembly and the Emergence of a Revolutionary Culture (1789–1790)* (Princeton: Princeton University Press, 1996), 123–29, 206–7.

[28] Tackett, *Becoming*, 185–88.

[29] François-Louis d'Escherny, *Correspondance d'un habitant de Paris aver see amis en Suisse* (Paris: Gattey, 1791), 13.

[30] Young, *Travels*, 102, 119, 122.

The rites of a free society, still technically forbidden, became acts of resistance against absolutist authority.

Paris' General Assembly of the Third Estate, representing the capital's sixty districts recently established for electing Estates General deputies, amid the national crisis recommenced their sessions on June 25. Noble and ecclesiastical electors soon joined them, with the latter declaring the nation needed "a chain that, linking the people to the king, must save us simultaneously from anarchy and despotism." On July 10, Paris lawyer Jean-Henri Bancal argued that since the crown considered "measures of terror and violence" as it massed troops nearby, Parisians needed to restore its vestigial Bourgeois Militia to keep order themselves. Despite the old regime precedent, the militia more closely resembled recent American and Irish revolutionary organizations – a citizen force capable of contesting royal power. While the General Assembly left the Bourgeois Militia plan unadopted on the tenth, they ordered the districts to reassemble to "wreck the criminal projects of our enemies" threatening to subvert the revolution.[31]

Political ferment turned into revolutionary action with popular institutions forming in Paris amid the insurrection that captured the Bastille. The uprising began the afternoon of July 12 at the Palais Royal with "an infinite number of persons climbing atop lights, tables and chairs to harangue the people" into action.[32] After the king's troops suppressed the opening demonstration, the city's sixty voting districts began organizing the Bourgeois Militia (soon National Guard) that night – with militiamen reestablishing local government under a new municipal structure. The districts' actions became publicized as a "hearth of enlightenment [foyer de lumière]" with "two hundred thousand" mobilizing to defeat despotism.[33] The districts remained in session throughout the crisis, struggling to process all wishing to join. Louis XVI's capitulation following the Bastille's fall made the new structures the capital's government with men paying three days' labor in taxes gaining freedom of assembly as governing councils, controlling policing and local affairs in the capital's districts.[34]

The municipal revolution won in the Bastille insurrection and accompanying provincial uprisings that spread Paris's model across France took inspiration from their Atlantic revolutionary predecessors. As Brissot orated before Paris's District de Filles Saint-Thomas on July 21, all residents "have the right

---

[31] *Procès-verbal des séances et délibérations de l'assemblée générale des électeurs de Paris, réunis à l'Hôtel de Ville le 14 juillet 1789* (Paris: Baudouin, 1790), 90, 95, 134–40, 158.

[32] Bibliothèque nationale – Richelieu, "Journal des événements survenus à Paris, du 2 avril au 8 octobre 1789," FF 13713 36a.

[33] *Moniteur universel*, July 17–20, 1789.

[34] Micah Alpaugh, "A Self-Defining Bourgeoisie in the Early French Revolution: The *Milice bourgeoise*, the Bastille Days of 1789, and Their Aftermath," *Journal of Social History* 47, no. 3 (2014), 709.

to form a municipality," which "derives from that of all men uniting in society, assembling to advise ways to conserve their property." The multiplication of revolutionary authorities served as checks and balances, preventing "different powers from falling into the same hands; this is the principle constantly observed in the United States of America." Militias would guarantee French rights. Brissot cited "those American militias, who at Bunker Hill, and twenty other times, shocked the masters of the art" in fighting British redcoats.[35] "This is no longer Paris," the *Moniteur universel* exclaimed in August, "but a new city and a new people."[36] Regeneration occurred through participation.

Amid 1789's great expectations, revolutionaries believed they were establishing a new system for the world. One newspaper that summer considered "the French revolution advantageously distinguished from all others, by being consummated without any foreign nation's intervention," boasting, "Surrounding peoples and kings cannot stop watching us, some in admiration, some with shock."[37] Though rumors flew of foreign invasion (including the British burning the port of Brest) amid the Great Fear of late July and early August, optimism remained that France's revolutionary strength would set a powerful example to be emulated by its neighbors.[38] Condorcet, anonymously pamphleteering as an "American," asserted, "the more free people exist, the more the liberty of each is assured."[39] One newspaper that fall considered, "Paris, the author of this happy revolution, will be recognized in the universe as the capital of true liberty."[40] If Europe's greatest power could develop an enduring order for liberty, their example would be impossible to ignore.

Amid the early revolution's advances, many international reformers were greatly encouraged by the changes in France. As London Quaker abolitionist Daniel Rodgers wrote to Philadelphia:

> As Englishmen we are glad that the prospect opens for a general emancipation from Slavery & the overthrow of despotism. It is high time for Mankind to be free, to think & act for themselves: nor was it ever intended to be otherwise by the Great Creator of the Universe.[41]

Many experienced French changes as the latest in a great chain of events: Raynal told Young, "the American revolution had brought the French one in its train," to which Young replied, "if the result in France should be liberty, that

---

[35] Lacroix, *Actes*, Vol. 1, 292.

[36] *Moniteur universel*, August 8, 1789.

[37] *Journal des décrets de l'Assemblée nationale*, No. 1.

[38] Archives municipales de Lorient BB 14.

[39] Marquis de Condorcet, *Lettres d'un citoyen des Etats-Unis à un Français, sur les affaires presents, par Mr. le M** de C** (S.l., s.d.), 3.

[40] *Journal de la municipalité, du Département, des Districts & des Sections de Paris, et correspondance des départemens & des principales Municipalités du Royaume*, Prospectus.

[41] HC Letters from British Friends, MSS 681, Box 4.

revolution had proved a blessing to the world, but much more so to England than America."[42] Peace, prosperity, and liberty for the nations neared. Divisions appeared inundated by a revolutionary wave bringing solutions for all.

Not all forays toward international cooperation readily succeeded, however. Hoping to encourage Franco-British direct action on colonial slavery, British abolitionists sent Clarkson, their most successful organizer, to France that fall. Writing to Mirabeau, Clarkson declared antislavery inseparable from French Revolutionaries' cause of liberty, believing without colonial reforms, "very serious Revolutions (if they have not already happened) will take Place there." Advocating the slave trade's abolition and "amelioration" of colonial slavery, Clarkson approached the *Société des amis*.[43] The committee meeting was "thinly attended," however, with Brissot the only prominent figure present. The group planned to lobby Necker and introduce antislavery legislation into the National Assembly. Powerful *amis* in the legislature, however, proved unwilling to immediately push abolition. The group, rather than gathering French signatures, hoped Clarkson would mobilize a massive British petition beseeching French abolition (not as outlandish as it might seem given the utility of Anglo-French joint action). Clarkson declined but remained in France for six months, lobbying legislators and distributing publications on the slave trade's horrors and formation of antislavery societies.[44]

Popular gatherings multiplied in summer and fall 1789, alongside growing Anglophilia. Article II of August's Declaration of the Rights of Man and Citizen described the French revolutionary compact as a "political association" guaranteeing "liberty, property, security, and resistance to oppression."[45] English political examples gained influence in the National Assembly, as they sought to craft a new constitution sharing power between the king and legislature. Yet no extra-governmental club structure existed for revolutionaries across France, which became an increasingly acute problem. On August 30, Lafayette and the National Guard blocked a march on Versailles of 1,500 unarmed men to protest the royal veto's inclusion in the French constitution.[46] If the new revolutionary institutions – despite their creation through collective action – became forces for moderatism, radicals needed to develop alternative vehicles.

[42] Young, *Travels*, 179.
[43] HL HM CN 53.
[44] Clarkson, *History*, 123–64.
[45] Bernard Combes de Patris, ed. *Procès-verbaux des séances de la Société populaire de Rodez* (Rodez: Carrère, 1912), vii.
[46] Robert H. Blackman, *1789: The French Revolution Begins* (Cambridge: Cambridge University Press, 2019), 180–217; *Moniteur universel*, September 4, 1789; Bibliothèque historique de la ville de Paris, "Événements révolutionnaires," DP 736 40A.

The direct prompting for the Jacobin network's creation, however, came from a minor group in British reform politics, the London Revolution Society. The club, featuring prominent liberal intellectuals, sought support for Dissenter civil rights through mobilizing nationwide celebrations of the Glorious Revolution's centennial in 1788. George III's mental crisis, however, dampened celebrations.[47] Inspired by the early French Revolution, the Revolution Society sent congratulations. Having already greeted news of the Bastille's fall with a resolution to correspond with revolutionaries to help "the Sons of Freedom to assert their Rights," the club at a November 4, 1789 banquet adopted an address to the National Assembly. Writing as "Men, Britons, and Citizens of the World," the Revolution Society expressed their "ardent wishes that the influence of so glorious an example may be felt by all Mankind," until "Universal Liberty and Happiness prevail."[48] The address made the Revolution Society famous throughout France and sparked ongoing correspondence with the soon-multiplying French clubs.[49]

The early French Jacobin network did not emerge from a vacuum, but rather from the intellectual ferment and advances in social movement mobilization during the late 1780s. The new campaigns' cosmopolitan reach, speaking for broad human and/or political rights, encouraged inclusive methods for building support. Learning of club network models, in a time of growing interest in associational life's possibilities, early French Jacobins discovered adaptable methods for their own fledgling societies. The French developed revolutionary organizations through joining the Atlantic currents of their era.

Spreading the Jacobin Network

Though the early Jacobin network organized quietly in the months following the Revolution Society's address, remaining sources credit the British origins of the "Club." In a rare surviving founding document, Strasbourg's Jacobins in their January 1790 Act of Union described themselves as founded on the model of Paris's *Société de la Révolution*, created in turn "on the inspiration of that established in London."[50] The *Chronique de Strasbourg* elaborated how "America and England's examples prove their utility," making the "law respected" and royal ministers responsive to the populace.[51] Montpellier's

---

[47] Goodwin, *Friends*, 85; Price, *Discourse*, 41–44; J. E. Cookson, *The Friends of Peace: Anti-War Liberalism in England, 1793–1815* (Cambridge: Cambridge University Press, 1982), 14.

[48] *Correspondence of the London Revolution Society*, 42, 2.

[49] Burke, *Reflections; A Letter to the Right Honourable Edmund Burke, in Reply to His "Reflections on the Revolution in France, etc.," by a Member of the Revolution Society* (London, s.d.).

[50] Friedrich Karl Heitz, *Les sociétés politiques de Strasbourg pendant les années 1790 à 1795: extraits de leurs procès-verbaux* (Strasbourg: Heitz, 1863), 2.

[51] *Chronique de Strasbourg*, No. X.

Jacobins in February 1790 declared, "This town's citizens desire to form a *club*," specifying in their bylaws that "the word 'Club' in English signifies an equal-paying group; the first founding principle of a club is thus equality." Montauban's Jacobins, in their first writings, refer to themselves not as a *Société* but *Club des patriotes*, while Béziers' chose *club patriotique*.[52] Early Jacobins saw not just a common name, but a direct connection between French and British clubs: Vire's in their June 1790 founding bylaws accorded voting rights not just to local members, but all from "*Clubs patriotiques*, whether French or foreign, following the same principles."[53] The first Jacobin Clubs looked outward for inspiration and affiliation, considering themselves part of wider international trends.

Typically taking the formal name of *Société*, however, the organizations paid homage to the French salons, scientific and literary societies that also provided important inspirations. In many respects, such societies, like the new clubs, attempted to enlighten through diffusing specialized knowledge. The Jacobins' *Journal des clubs* highlighted their influence, considering "reason, philosophy, and the sciences let this beautiful day of liberty shine" in France. Political knowledge could be spread likewise: "A Patriotic Society is a school where one learns the science of free government." Sharing the results of experimentation in "*un commerce de pensées*" – "reassembling the dispersed rays to compose a mass capable of enlightening and vivifying all parts of the Empire" – appeared essential for the New Regime's success.[54]

The Jacobin Clubs' spread across the provinces was undoubtedly aided by the Paris branch's rapid development as a National Assembly caucus for like-minded legislators: "all of the democratic Party," according to one British report.[55] Renting space in the initially still-functioning Jacobin monastery on rue St. Honoré, just blocks from the new National Assembly hall by the Tuileries, the club developed a strong *esprit de corps*.[56] Young in January 1790, attending the "revolution club" less than two months after its founding, asserted, "all material business is there decided" in nightly meetings, "before it is discussed by the National Assembly." With annual club member-ship less than two days' pay for a legislator, the society became a social center for provincial representatives unfamiliar with the capital and a powerful tool for testing proposals and developing consensus.[57] The institution gave radical

[52] Archives départementales de la Tarn-et-Garonne, L 402 2; Archives départementales de l'Hérault L 5532.

[53] *Règlement pour la Société des amis de la Constitution, établie dans la ville de Vire le 6 juin 1790* (S.l., 1790), 5.

[54] *Journal des clubs*, Prospectus, 2–6.

[55] Oscar Browning, ed. *Despatches from Paris, 1784–1790* (London: Offices of the Society, 1910), 297.

[56] Rapport, *Unruly*, 185.

[57] Eric Hazan, *A People's History of the French Revolution* (London: Verso, 2014), 92.

legislators an advantage over less-organized rivals. Though Young worried the club resembled "a Paris junto governing the kingdom," partisans considered the organization "absolutely necessary," for if the Revolution did not consolidate quickly, "great opportunities would be lost, and the National Assembly left constantly exposed to the danger of a counter-revolution." Young witnessed a widespread "belief of plots," particularly concerning the king, and considered "the present devotion to liberty is a sort of rage" that "absorbs every other passion" among members.[58] The new organization's power became manifest.

The Paris Jacobin bylaws, adopted on February 8, 1790, promoted the organization as an unprecedented center for enlightened communication and consensus building. Those involved would "transmit the views resulting from the rapprochement of *lumières* and interests," dedicating themselves to "spreading truth, while defending liberty" and the revolutionary project. Rather than working outside government, as most preceding movements had, the organization sought the closest possible collaboration so constituents could share "their work, their views, their hopes" and help legislators transmit "the spirit of the National Assembly's decrees." All would collaborate for the "constitution's affirmation" and a regenerated France.[59]

Club movements spread the possibility of extending a virtual democracy across the nation. "We cannot all go to the Champ de Mars, as the early Romans did," the *Journal des clubs*' second issue noted, "we cannot, as in Athens, find one place capable of holding all citizens." The Jacobin model, however, could be the next best thing: "today we can move past this method. Since printing has been perfected, a thought can quickly be communicated to 200,000 men," to be "analyzed, discussed, and brought to a provisional judgment." Jacobin Clubs, with provincial branches often meeting twice a week to consider pivotal political issues, provided a format for "better understanding questions."[60] Unlike their British and American exemplars, the French Revolution could be completed without widespread violence: "this sagacious institution gives us the inestimable good of achieving total regeneration without a civil war," Vitry-le-François' Jacobins boasted.[61] Democratic input could be developed through combining real and virtual association.

Balancing foreign and domestic examples, club partisans elaborated justifications based on the French Declaration of Rights and agreed-on portions of the forthcoming constitution. On December 1, 1789 (just weeks after the

[58] Young, *Travels*, 268.

[59] Aulard, *Jacobins*, Vol. 1, xxviii–xxix.

[60] *Journal des clubs*, November 19, 1790; Christine Peyrard, *Les Jacobins de l'Ouest: sociabilité révolutionnaire et forms de politisation dans le Maine et la Basse-Normandie (1789–1799)* (Paris: Sorbonne, 1996), 47.

[61] *Procès-verbal de la séance de la Société des amis de la constitution de Vitry-le-François* (S.l., 1790), 10.

Jacobins' founding), a National Assembly deputy proposed outlawing meetings of over thirty people except for electoral proceedings. Mirabeau strongly opposed the motion: "Unarmed men have the right to gather in whatever number they want to communicate their *lumières*, wishes, interests; to stop them is to attack the Rights of Man."[62] Defeating the measure, the assembly two weeks later granted explicit permission for *"citoyens actifs"* (those men with sufficient property for voting rights) to participate. Clubs moved from the periphery to near the center of revolutionary politics.[63] Future Paris Mayor Jean-Nicolas Pache claimed Article XI of the Declaration, which guaranteed "free communication of thought," protected the clubs, reflecting Anglo-American free speech and association. The constitution explicitly assured the freedom to "assemble peacefully and without arms" for political discussions.[64] Clubs provided institutionalization. By summer 1790 over ninety Jacobin societies were established, climbing to over 300 by the year's end, 1,200 by late 1791, and cresting at 3,500 in the Year II.[65] Club restrictions, such as not organizing in the army or navy, or bringing petitions in all their members' names, remained few.[66]

Expanded political sociability through local societies, proponents held, would spread civic virtues and strengthen the revolutionary order. Through developing the "grandeur and pride belonging to a free nation," the *Journal des clubs* declared, associations would help members "avoid extremes" and develop more unamistic spirit.[67] "In the social order as in the state of nature," Saint-Affrique's Jacobins added, "the man who remains isolated remains weak," whereas sociability encouraged his potential.[68] Strasbourg's Jacobins asserted the revolution required "instructing the people," as preventing "arbitrary government" required citizens understanding political developments.[69] Building from knowledge of British and American examples, elaborating a denser civil society became imperative for educating active citizens. Yet early Jacobins went further: that *Journal des clubs* issue spoke not just of diffusing principles but of conducting "surveillance," particularly against municipal officials contesting Jacobin expansion.[70] The revolution needed to

---

[62] Aulard, *Société des Jacobins*, Vol. 1, vi.

[63] Serge Bonin, Jean Boutier, Philippe Boudry, and Claude Langlois, eds. *Atlas de la Révolution française, Vol. 6: Les sociétés politiques* (Paris: EHESS, 1992), 9.

[64] Jean-Nicolas Pache, *Observations sur les sociétés patriotiques* (S.l., 1790), 2.

[65] Bonin, *Atlas*, 34; Michael L. Kennedy, *The Jacobin Clubs in the French Revolution: The Early Years* (Princeton: Princeton University Press, 1982), 17.

[66] Combes, *Procès-verbaux*, vii.

[67] *Journal des clubs*, ibid.

[68] Abbé Raylet, "Procès-verbaux de la société des amis de la constitution de St. Affrique," *Mémoires de la société des lettres de l'Aveyron* (1942), 300.

[69] *Journal de correspondance de Paris à Nantes et du department de la Loire inférieure*, T. 6, no. 24 (September 1790).

[70] *Journal des clubs*, ibid.

be defended and propagated with both fraternity and vigilance remaining enduring Jacobin principles.

Anglo-American radical club and abolition organizations became studied as important precedents and models. The interconnected British antislavery, Parliamentary reform, and Dissenter movements received widespread press attention, with *Révolutions de Paris* in February 1790 detailing how activists "employed declarations, printed advices, public assemblies, to excite in all places and all spirits favorable opinions."[71] The *Patriote français* printed the Manchester Abolition Society's appeal for sister societies to pressure their Parliamentary representatives to abolish "this impious violation of humanity's rights."[72] The Society for Constitutional Information sent a soon-published address to France, celebrating "rapid progress of the principles and spirit of liberty" and asserting, "equal and pure representation will progressively establish itself in the great civil societies of Europe."[73] The confluence of movements and events across countries became remarkable.

Rapidly expanding across France from late 1789 through the first half of 1790, the Jacobin movement served as a virtual twin to the large Federation gatherings drawing hundreds of thousands across the provinces. "By such correspondence between Friends of the Constitution," wrote Carcassonne's Jacobins, "we can consolidate the bases of universal patriotism."[74] Each club communicated with nearby locals, as did larger centers with each other and all with Paris's *Comité de correspondance*. Regional issues could be resolved internally with each society possessing a potential national (sometimes international) reach. Cherbourg's Jacobins sought to build "the same principles, the same sentiments, by the uniformity of desires" to establish a new consensus.[75] "By rapid correspondence," Rouen's Jacobins wrote, "we can communicate inspirations and discoveries, mutually raising our patriotism, while guarding" against counterrevolutionaries.[76] The Jacobin network's strength relied as much on virtual relations through written exchanges as physical club meetings themselves.

Jacobins amplified their correspondence with printed circulars and, soon, newspapers publishing club communications. Part of the wider print revolution following censorship's 1789 collapse, clubs increasingly received printed letters from other societies, often hundreds of miles away. Even writers from small municipalities appeared well informed on national issues.[77] The first (unsuccessful) attempt at a common newspaper, the mid-1790 *Journal des*

---

[71] *Révolutions de Paris*, February 6, 1790.
[72] *Patriote français*, February 2, 1790.
[73] *Le Nouvelliste national, journal de Toulouse*, December 14, 1789.
[74] AD Hérault, L 5539.
[75] Archives municipales de Cherbourg 2 1 112 7.
[76] AD Tarn-et-Garonne, L 388.
[77] Kennedy, *Early Years*, 20–21.

sociétés-patriotiques françaises, argued isolated "patriotic societies cannot have the useful influence on opinion their patriotism merits."[78] A newspaper would facilitate exchanges. Later that year, the Jacobins' *Journal des clubs* began, embodying the network's idealistic hopes: Commercy's Jacobins asserted it could be "the organ of our patriotism: it can be a mirror bringing together all rays, reflecting their light and heat."[79] Information sharing, moving between the largest number of clubs with the greatest possible speed, could develop consensus and bring revolutionaries together. The Revolution could accelerate through circulating ideas faster. Never before in either France or Britain had a political club network acquired such scope or power.

French clubs corresponded with the London Revolution Society in growing numbers. The earliest communication, from Dijon's already-established *Club patriotique* on November 30, 1789, came only five days after the National Assembly read the Revolution Society's address. "Why do we worry about admitting," the letter began, "that the Revolution occurring in our country today is due above all to the example England offered us over the last century?" The Dijon club asserted, "English happiness has prepared that of the universe," by developing constitutional government. The Revolution Society responded by enunciating hopes for "fraternal union" between peoples, while congratulating French Revolutionaries on extending "principles of justice and reverence for human rights" through "common participation" in politics.[80] Early addresses did not focus on national particularities, but rather similarities in club principles.

Over the following year twenty-three addresses to the Revolution Society arrived from clubs across France, many thanking the Londoners for inspiring them. Strasbourg's Jacobins declared, "your honorable Society's example has given birth to all the *Amis de la Constitution*." Amiens' club described the Revolution Society as a "monument of English liberty," which led "our Revolution to form on your model a thousand societies animated by the same ardor and spirit." Aix-en-Provence's Jacobins credited them with "believing in the idea of establishing these societies multiplying in France today." The Jacobins of La Rochelle, a town with a long history of Catholic-Protestant conflict, declared the English and French would "follow the same principles ... carrying philosophy's flame into regions superstition and despotism still cover in shadows."[81] Consciously breaking with the past to establish broad fraternal alliances, local French clubs knew of their associations' Anglo origins and pursued further contact.

---

[78] AD Tarn-et-Garonne, L 236; *Journal des sociétés-patriotiques françaises*, prospectus.
[79] AD Tarn-et-Garonne, L 236.
[80] *Correspondence of the London Revolution Society*, 12, 16.
[81] Ibid., 60, 82, 87, 98.

Franco-American connections developed, though not as closely as with the British. Many revolutionary French took interest in American examples: Jefferson, Monroe and other Americans were fêted during their stays in France, while an American flag flew in Paris's Jacobin Club alongside the French and British, and Franklin's death in 1790 led to widespread public mourning. French legislators consulted translations of America's founding constitutions as they sought examples for a new French order.[82] However, there were more limitations to the Franco-American relationship than the Franco-British one. Despite limited correspondence between the *Société des amis* and Pennsylvania Abolition Society in 1790–1791, as well as Charleston's patriotic societies with Jacobin branches, the distance between countries did not allow for efficient epistolary exchange, whereas correspondence passed from Paris to London as quickly as to Marseille. Many early French revolutionaries also did not find America's example as applicable to their complex, old-world society as the British.[83] Moreover, American clubs' limited influence in the early Federalist era (see Chapter 14) offered the French fewer contemporary examples.

Beyond simple recognition, French clubs sought instruction from and collaboration with their British counterparts. Montpellier's Jacobins initiated correspondence with London less than a month after their founding, generating excitement across their region. "We can only applaud," Marseille's Jacobins wrote in October 1790, "your project of corresponding with the Revolution's friends in England, and with foreigners in Paris. We owe our union to these close-knit brothers who before us conquered their liberty. We have asked for affiliation and correspondence ourselves."[84] With the British exemplars for hundreds of French clubs, exchanging letters and ideas held great promise for the still-fledgling network. "We hope you can procure us," Nîmes' Jacobins wrote to Montpellier two weeks later, "a *mémoire* on the constitutional organization of patriotic societies" from London, asking for any correspondence received.[85] Though the relationship had limitations, with Jacobins' knowledge of how British club networks actually functioned remaining partial, early French clubs remained hungry for information on associational models and adapted aspects of British societies for themselves.

Despite Revolution Society members' exertions in the ongoing Dissenter, reform, and abolitionist movements, the club welcomed French correspondence, responding to each address. In July 1790, writing to Lille's Jacobins, the

---

[82] Zeiche, *Cosmopolitan*; *Patriote français*, February 21, 1792; Comte de Mirabeau, *Discours du comte de Mirabeau, dans la séance du 11 juin, sur la mort de Benjamin Francklin* (Paris, 1790); Denis Lacorne, *L'invention de la République: Le modele américaine* (Paris: Hachette, 1991), 78–79.

[83] HSP Pennsylvania Abolition Society Papers MICRO 572, Series 2, Reel 11, nos. 36, 62, 63.

[84] AD Hérault, L 5543 8.

[85] Ibid., L 5545.

Londoners declared themselves "pleased to feel the respect shown in the Addresses received" and solicited further exchanges, "Convinced the spirit of freedom is rapidly advancing across Europe[.]"[86] French clubs emulated British social movements' breadth: "The moment has come when everything abusive ought to be reformed," Clermont-Ferrand's Jacobins asserted.[87] With French clubs like Lorient's denouncing "religious differences" as among the Old Regime "prejudices which often divide nations," Dissenters accepted French financial contributions for their repeal effort.[88] With the Revolution Society publicizing French interactions, especially around their annual Bastille Day banquets, they declared the clubs' relationship mutually beneficial.

Following the Dissenters' failed 1790 campaign and intensifying attacks from British Francophobe conservatives and the Anglican Church, however, the Revolution Society became politically embattled. In April 1791, the Revolution Society chastised Jacobins for having "contemplated with more attention the excellencies of our Constitution than its deficits." Dissenters' formal exclusion from politics demonstrated the British system's limitations. With the French having "entirely emancipated yourselves . . . you will soon feel the superiority of *your* present government to *ours*."[89] Increasingly, French societies modeled themselves on clubs in their own network instead of foreign exemplars. Jacobins talked less of their British origins with some now omitting British precedents from club primers and bylaws altogether.[90]

Even among Anglophiles, the British example remained partial, and certain illiberal Jacobin aspects diverged from prior models. The Jacobins, one revolutionary newspaper boasted in April 1790, could "dispel from the earth the races of tyrants who for too long devoured human generations, and dishonored the name of man."[91] Entrenched interests would not voluntarily disperse. To protect and propagate the Revolution, Brissot's *Patriote français* asserted that June, a "holy confederation" of societies needed to "become the censors, the *surveillans libres*, of municipalities and departments to prevent the aristocracy" from subverting the government.[92] Robespierre similarly declared, "as long as there are vices and prejudices, liberty will have enemies."[93] Though British clubs traditionally guarded against royal encroachments, French clubs

---

[86] *Correspondence of the London Revolution Society*, 40.

[87] Archives départementales de Puy-de-Dôme, L 6375,

[88] *Correspondence of the London Revolution Society*, 52; *Révolutions de Paris*, February 6–13, 1790.

[89] *Correspondence of the London Revolution Society*, 86.

[90] *Qu'est-ce que les Cloubs, ou exposé simple & fidelle des principes & de la conduite de la Société des Amis de la Constitution établie à Tulle* (Brive, 1790); Archives départementales du Morbihan L 1530 1.

[91] *Annales patriotiques et littéraires*, April 11, 1790.

[92] *Patriote français*, June 19, 1790.

[93] AM Cherbourg 2 1 112 4.

developed defensive apparatuses to an extent unsuitable for Britain's relatively stable political environment. Vigilance became a central Jacobin function.

A second divergence from British precedents (though less so from their American predecessors) occurred in Jacobins' intolerance of rival clubs, compared to Britain's heterogeneous club scene. Counterrevolutionary clubs existed: Paris's *Club des impartiaux* recruited "all enemies of anarchy demanding legitimate authority's return," while so-called *Amis de la paix* established clubs in twenty-three towns over 1790–1791.[94] One provincial Jacobin club proposed sending twelve thousand men to petition the National Assembly to dissolve the conservative club taking the derivative name *Société des amis de la constitution monarchique*.[95] Though British clubs commonly remained private, Jacobins refused to countenance such practices. If "not open to all citizens," Confolens' Jacobins warned the assembly in April 1791, "shady conspiracies will form there."[96] The Jacobins also railed against the center-left *Société de 1789*, their first splinter faction, in early 1790. Featuring Lafayette, Bailly, and Sieyès, the society printed its own newspaper while seeking provincial satellites and foreign correspondents.[97] The *Cercle social* – a philosophical discussion group overlapping with the Jacobin membership, including Brissot, Camille Desmoulins, and Condorcet – began meeting in the Palais Royal's former circus in October 1790 with its first session attracting more than four thousand people (four times the Jacobins' Paris membership).[98] Jacobins viewed rival clubs with jealousy, asserting their goal was to "diminish their influence." Repeatedly, they warned provincial societies not to affiliate or correspond with such groups.[99] Across the provinces, Jacobins faced one or more competitors in at least 193 locales.[100] Free association, many Jacobins now declared, could be too destructive if applied for the wrong purposes.

The Anglo-French fraternal movement would be tested by the Nootka Sound crisis, which recurrently threatened to bring France and Britain to

[94] *Club des impartiaux*, Prospectus [ca. February 1790]; Paul R. Hanson, "The Monarchist Clubs and the Pamphlet Debate over Political Legitimacy in the Early Years of the French Revolution," *French Historical Studies* 21, no. 2 (1998), 301.

[95] Archives municipales de Nantes I2 C2; Earl Gower, *The Despatches of Earl Gower* (Cambridge: Cambridge University Press, 1885), 55.

[96] Bibliothèque municipal de Poitiers, Lettres recues par la Société des amis de la constitution, 142/1 S19.

[97] Philip Mazzei, *My Life & Wanderings*, S. Eugene Scalia, trans. (Morristown, NJ: American Institute of Italian Studies, 1980), 321; Kennedy, *Early Years*, 281.

[98] Gary Kates, *The Cercle Social, the Girondins, and the French Revolution* (Princeton: Princeton University Press, 1985), 77, 94.

[99] *Journal de la Société de 1789*, prospectus; Archives départementales du Haute-Vienne, L 822 21, 40 and 48; AD Puy de Dôme, L 6375.

[100] Kennedy, *The Jacobin Clubs in the French Revolution: The Middle Years* (Princeton: Princeton University Press, 1988), 45.

war in 1790 and 1791. Though National Assembly deputies of many persuasions (including some Jacobins) urged intervention to uphold French international "honor," the prospect of France fighting alongside Spain to uphold the
Bourbon "Family Compact" led radicals to denounce dynastic alliances and
agitate for peace.[101] Radical French publications increasingly distinguished
between British popular sentiments and their government's policies. "The
enlightened English," wrote *Révolutions de Paris*, "do not want war, on the
contrary they desire an alliance with [France], for the peace of Europe and the
universe."[102] Radicals declared they would not be swayed by past national
rivalries.

The Revolution Society pursued an enhanced relationship with France's
National Assembly but met mixed results. During the Nootka crisis on July 21,
1790, the assembly read a letter from the London club beseeching the two
nations to "learn to see each other as equals, and love each other as free men,
equals and brothers," inaugurating a new era of peace. Charles de Lameth
proposed the assembly send a favorable response, "to help Europe remain at
peace." Conservative Louis de Foucauld angrily replied, "a private society
cannot correspond with a National Assembly," and considered the "two
nations unfortunately rivals." He was drowned out, however, by cries of
"No!" The motion to correspond with the Revolution Society passed. The
legislature nevertheless maintained their prudence nine days later, after word
of a July 14 Revolution Society toast arrived, desiring "an alliance between the
world's two first kingdoms," and the "union of philosophy and politics which
honorably distinguishes our age." Lameth's request for a new response
failed.[103] Earlier eighteenth-century mistrust and Anglophobia could be
rekindled.

The Revolution Society's call for an alliance created a sensation across the
Jacobin network, however, and Limoges' club led a campaign for an international compact. In an October 1790 circular sent across France to "prove to
the whole world how the French want to unite all peoples," Limoges asked
fellow societies to petition Paris's Jacobins to open discussions with the
Revolution Society. Simultaneously, they published a proclamation "declaring
to all peoples our pacific intentions, and plans for the world's happiness."[104] At
least twenty-seven local clubs adhered, several asserting it would ensure
"universal peace" and counter court intrigues.[105] The "war the ministers
seem to have prepared could be adjourned indefinitely," Lorient's Jacobins

[101] Howard V. Evans, "The Nootka Sound Controversy in Anglo-French Diplomacy,"
Journal of Modern History 46 (1974), 635.
[102] *Révolutions de Paris*, July 24–31, 1790.
[103] *Archives parlementaires*, Vol 17, 229, 412.
[104] AD Hérault, L 5542; BM Poitiers, MSS 141 S18 39; AD Tarn-et-Garonne, L 236.
[105] Kennedy, *Early Years*, 237; AD Haute-Vienne, L 829, Archives départementales de la
Seine-Maritime L 828.

postulated.[106] Paris's Jacobins, fearing conservative reaction, nevertheless ignored the proposal.

Correspondence between Jacobin Clubs and the Revolution Society grew, with forty-seven addresses – more than twice as many as in 1790 – arriving from thirty-five French locals across 1791. This was not a one-time formality for many, as nine groups from the previous year wrote again, and the same number sent multiple addresses. Yet the letters, which in 1790 expressed fascination with the British model, increasingly fell into repetitive formulas of felicitation.[107] Still, hopes for an alliance continued. Tours' Jacobins wrote to London of how "humanity" would "make us Compatriots with all the earth's peoples."[108] With inaction in Paris, however, little progress occurred.

Coordination simultaneously augmented the antislavery effort. French newspapers, particularly Brissot's *Patriote français*, featured descriptions of abolitionist measures in northern American states and British Parliamentary debates on ending the slave trade, leading some to predict Atlantic trafficking's imminent demise.[109] Pro-slavery lobbyists worried such "poison infects public opinion more and more," and the *amis'* "hydra with a hundred heads" could inspire revolutionary action.[110] Though Jacobins did not develop British-style massive petition campaigns, in March and April 1791, fifteen affiliates brought abolitionist petitions before the National Assembly. Riom's Jacobins on March 24 asked slaves to be granted rights through "universal regeneration" to bring "tranquility to our colonies." Lyon's Jacobins on April 20 wrote to the *amis* proclaiming they "burn to unite our efforts together to ensure victory."[111] Even Jacobins from Nantes, France's leading slave-trading port, declared to Brissot, "your philanthropic principles are ours," pledging to help abolish trafficking.[112] Paris's branch continued lobbying legislators, believing slavery unsustainable while asserting, "free peoples make the most able merchants."[113] Only the late 1791 Saint-Domingue slave uprising halted momentum toward an alliance between Jacobins and the international antislavery campaign.

Revolutionary though the early Jacobins were, they remained interested in precedents, examples, and potential alliances. The integrated national networks of Anglo-American radical politics inspired French designs. While the

[106] Archives départementales du Morhiban L 2000 14.
[107] *Correspondence of the London Revolution Society*, 115–275.
[108] *Correspondence of the London Revolution Society*, 132. On broader French-British exchanges in 1791–1792, see Kennedy, *Middle Years*, 151–55.
[109] *Patriote français*, February 2, 1790, April 13, 1790, May 6, 1790; *Bulletin de Bordeaux*, January 30, 1790; *Révolutions de Paris*, February 6–13, 1790, February 12–19, 1791.
[110] AD Gironde C 4368 59; Archives départementales de la Loire-Atlantique C 628 155.
[111] *Adresse de la société des amis des noirs, à l'Assemblée nationale, à toutes les Villes du Commerce, à toutes les Manufactures, aux Colonies, à toutes les Sociétés des Amis de la Constitution* (Paris, 1791), 170, 231.
[112] Bibliothèque municipale de Nantes D-M 21 6 II 4.
[113] *Adresse de la société des amis des noirs*, 124.

French clubs' growth in many respects responded to the early-to-mid Revolution's unique conditions, British societies offered Jacobins important models for local, national, and international cohesion, demonstrating methods for applying egalitarian principles and cosmopolitan hopes to concrete political situations. As the French Revolution radicalized anew in 1792, the Jacobins possessed unmatched national strength.

Political Crises and Jacobin Radicalization

Jacobin ambitions outstripped any preceding Atlantic movement's. Building from international examples, Jacobins believed they were constructing a model that could be applied anywhere. "All the earth's peoples are watching us," Limoges' Jacobins declared in October 1790. "In vain will despots try to delay universal regeneration, in vain will they oppose the propagation of light" once other peoples learned.[114] As the Strasbourg club's president predicted that summer, after acknowledging the "fraternal salutations of several societies of friends in Ireland, Scotland and England," that "soon only tyrants and their slaves will be foreigners."[115] The example of free association and united action, so powerful and unprecedented in France, seemed exportable.

Facing so many challenges, French Jacobins envied the United States for their revolution's seeming ease. If Americans "had armies to combat," described a Rouen Jacobins orator in December 1790, France had "more difficult obstacles to surmount, many prejudices to destroy, a long rampart of privileges to demolish." Whereas Americans were "raised on sentiments of independence," the French "in a single step crossed the immense distance from slavery to liberty."[116] No ocean separated France from tyrants. Yet on hearing of the British reformer Price's death, Paris's Jacobins in May 1791 declared eight days' mourning, writing to the Revolution Society of their esteem for the American sympathizer, since "the revolution of the United States has so influenced our own."[117] Hope remained for a new order of stability and peace, alongside an open-eyed realization of the difficulties to surmount.

The Revolution would advance, proponents argued, through principle and emulation – not offensive war. Journalist Jean-Louis Carra, a European cosmopolitan who had traveled as far as Russia, before Paris's Jacobins asserted the

---

[114] *Le club des Jacobins de Limoges (1790–1795), d'après ses deliberations, sa correspondence et ses journaux*, A. Fray-Fournier, ed. (Limoges: Charles-Lavauzelle, 1903), 17.

[115] Heitz, *Sociétés*, 54.

[116] *Extrait de la délibération de la société des amis de la constitution à Rouen, du 18 décembre 1790* (Rouen, 1790), 11–12.

[117] *Journal de correspondence de Paris à Nantes et du department de la Loire inférieure*, T. 9, no. 15 (May 1791). Provincial societies including Bergerac also went into mourning. Henri Labroue, *La société populaire de Bergerac pendant la Révolution* (Paris: Au siège de la Société, 1915), 41, 119.

French "would not bring the flame of war or discord to our neighbors, but instead the genius of liberty. Our arts and our constitution, not our warriors, ought to cross the Rhine, the Alps and the Pyrenees." The National Assembly adopted a Declaration of Peace to the World in May 1790, renouncing all wars of conquest.[118] A Rodez Jacobins circular that summer asserted there would "be no more war, because France will not attack, and thenceforth no power dares attack a free people."[119] Many asserted Europe's crowned heads would face plenty of trouble at home. Louis-Antoine de Saint-Just, in his first published political writing in June 1791, asserted, "Europe marches quickly towards its revolution, which all despotism's efforts cannot stop."[120] Discussion and fraternity could bring peace and understanding, though how such revolutionary principles would spread across Europe remained uncertain.

Anglophilia continued despite intensifying conservative attacks. The *Société des amis de la constitution monarchique*'s newspaper in February 1791 described British societies "ridiculing each other, critiquing the court and city, criticizing the king and ministers who displease them," while "degenerating into the most intolerable licentiousness." French Jacobin adaptations created "fanatical factions of two opposing parties," making "neutrality a crime." The Friends of the Monarchical Constitution considered the Jacobins "instructed by Cromwell," spreading every "atrocious black calumny imaginable" to incite civil war.[121] Conservatives fanned exclusionary rhetoric beyond the language of the early Jacobins themselves.

For the Jacobins to achieve their lofty goals, local societies needed to prevent counterrevolutionaries from undermining French politics. One November 1790 orator in Montauban, where Catholic conservatives the previous May attacked Protestant revolutionaries, asserted patriots needed to form "a mass of enlightenment and force, to impose by terror" on the revolution's enemies.[122] Although it is tempting to see terror as consubstantial with the Jacobins' formation and the Revolution's development, they here described the need to deter conservatives from violence. In early 1791, Lyon's Jacobins warned of "shadowy plots against the friends of liberty," while Paris's branch declared the network "ought to inspire universal terror in the enemies of public good."[123] A moral revolution could not give free reign to purveyors of falsehoods and partisans of despotism. Still, for early Jacobins, "the force of reason," as a Strasbourg orator described in December 1790, developed

[118] David A. Bell, *The First Total War: Napoleon's Europe and the Birth of War as We Know It* (Boston: Houghton Mifflin, 2007).

[119] Combes, *Procès-verbaux*, 628.

[120] Louis-Antoine de Saint-Just, *Oeuvres complètes* (Paris: Gallimard, 2004), 363.

[121] *Journal de la Société des amis de la constitution monarchique*, February 12, 1791.

[122] François Galabert, "Le Club Jacobin de Montauban," *Revue d'histoire modern et contemporaine* 1 (1899–1900), 22.

[123] AD Hérault, 5542; AM Cherbourg 2 I 121 1.

through an "exchange of enlightenment advantageous for all," seemed the best method of combat.[124]

The Jacobins' alliance largely remained a defensive one. Paris's branch in January 1791 sent a circular to all affiliates warning of counterrevolutionary plots to "raise an army mutiny, stop tax collection, annihilate public credit" and make France ungovernable. All needed to "redouble their zealous vigilance" to disrupt attempted subversion.[125] Greater calamities approached: Strasbourg's Surveillance Committee received warnings of impending war with Austria. Rumors flew of Prussian, Dutch, and British spies infiltrating Jacobin societies.[126] In February, Artonne's Jacobins in the Massif Central swore to defend those willing to "denounce their country's traitors and conspirators against liberty."[127] Two years into the revolution, the only route appeared forward. Le Mans' Jacobins that March considered "fraternal reciprocity" necessary to stop "perfidious designs of the enemies of Public Good," taking new oaths as "fidelitous collaborators."[128] The months before the French constitution's completion seemed pivotal for maintaining unity and preventing backsliding.

Nevertheless, in winter 1791 the Jacobins remained France's most powerful organization, optimistically projecting peace and order ahead. Provincial clubs continued to multiply, securing affiliation once their members sent in references from two members of nearby clubs, three acquaintances in the Paris society, or five National Assembly members.[129] "Every day," a Paris circular declared in late January, "good citizens learn to oppose the Revolution's enemies with calmer and more powerful resistance" in their locals.[130] France, they proclaimed in March, had peacefully achieved "total regeneration without civil war," while "of twenty-six million, during two years of the greatest troubles, including insurrections and food crises, there were under four thousand" killed.[131] What great transformation ever occurred with so little bloodshed?

Popular associational activity grew in Paris's neighborhoods. Hoping to disperse radical factions, the National Assembly broke the sixty governing districts that organized the Bastille insurrection and controlled local policing

---

[124] Heitz, *Sociétés*, 75–76.

[125] Aulard, *Jacobins*, Vol. 2, 3.

[126] Heitz, *Sociétés*, 122; *Journal des amis de la constitution*, June 7, 1791.

[127] Fernand Martin, *La Révolution en Province: les Jacobins au village* (Clermont-Ferrand, 1902), 34.

[128] Archives départementales de la Sarthe L 270; *Adresse de la société des amis de la constitution du Mans, à toutes les sociétés patriotiques du royaume. Le Mans, 6 mars 1791,* (Le Mans: Pivron, 1791), 1–2.

[129] Kennedy, *1793–1795*, 5.

[130] Aulard, *Jacobins*, Vol. 2, 49–50.

[131] Ernest Jovy, *Documents sur la Société populaire de Vitry-le-François pendant la Révolution* (Vitry-le-François, Denis, 1892), 10.

into forty-eight redistricted sections in spring 1790. Many solidarities held, however: a Cordeliers district club (founded in April 1790) continued meeting and by early 1791 developed a network of "popular societies" across the capital, spreading democratic practices and vigilance against counterrevolutionaries. Whereas Paris's Jacobins remained an elite group with high membership fees (like their moderate and conservative opponents), the new network encouraged common Parisians' political participation. In May 1791, the bourgeoning popular societies federated with a coordinating Central Committee.[132]

Growing associational spirit in Paris also led to new organizations fostering women's participation. The Fraternal Society of the Two Sexes took residence in the rue St. Honoré monastery, meeting in a smaller hall the Jacobins had outgrown. Women became full members, gained voting rights, and were guaranteed at least two of six officer positions. The organization retained close relations with the Cordeliers Club, which allowed female speakers. Women also intervened in Jacobin debates from the spectator galleries, particularly when issues directly impacting them were discussed, and developed personality cults around favored leaders.[133] Though rhetoric of "Republican Motherhood" concurrently advanced, highlighting women's roles mothering male citizens instead of encouraging their own voices, avenues developed for expanding political participation. The Revolution's reach extended across class and gender to those excluded from every European representative system.

Clubs' popularity aroused opponents' ire, however, with the Jacobins by mid-1791 fighting for their existence amid French revolutionary politics' rapid shifts, facing dispersion or hostile takeover. Though encouraging discussion for consensus building, once the National Assembly had decided an issue, Jacobins as "Friends of the Constitution" considered themselves obligated to support its decisions.[134] Throughout the early revolution, many frowned on Jacobins' "excessive zeal" – while stories spread that Paris's Jacobin monastery had been the fanatical Holy League's stronghold during France's Wars of Religion.[135] Jacobins also engendered strong reactions in many provincial areas. The *Journal des clubs* in its inaugural December 1790 issue denounced how "nothing better proves the Societies' utility" than "the persecutions they endured in most municipalities," claiming accounts of repression arrived every day at the Paris society.[136] Rumors, meanwhile, spread that the Paris club's National Assembly members (approximately 250 strong, a quarter of the

---

[132] Albert Mathiez, *Le Club des Cordeliers pendant la crise de Varennes et le massacre du Champ de Mars* (Genève: Slatkine-Megariotis, 1975), 5, 30.

[133] Hazan, *People's*, 250; Noah C. Shusterman, "All His Power Lies in the Distaff: Robespierre, Women and the French Revolution," *Past & Present* 223, no. 1 (2014), 129–60.

[134] Kennedy, *Early Years*, 235.

[135] APS Filippo Mazzei Papers.Mss.Ms.Coll.47.

[136] *Journal des clubs*, prospectus.

legislature) were "oath-bound" to vote with them on important issues.[137] The Jacobins had to show they were not just another self-interested conspiratorial faction.

The King's Flight to Varennes on June 20–21 brought the Jacobins to their first existential crisis. Louis XVI's "Proclamation" to the French left in the Tuileries Palace blamed the Jacobins for the Revolution's radicalization, claiming they "form an immense corporation more dangerous than any existing before," and achieved "such preponderance that all administrative and judicial bodies, including the National Assembly, almost always obey their orders."[138] While the king exaggerated the Jacobins' influence, growing republican tendencies surfaced. Unlike the assembly, which propagated the fiction of the king being "kidnapped," Paris Jacobins' provincial circular (in stronger but still-measured terms) declared the king "misled by criminal suggestions" in fleeing.[139] On June 24, demonstrators supporting a "Petition of 30,000" from "almost all the members of Paris' political societies" marched to the National Assembly, asking them not to decide Louis XVI's fate until after consulting all provincial departments. Artonne's Jacobins asked France "be made a republic."[140] As National Guardsmen mobilized until the threat of counterrevolutionary invasion passed, Jacobin locals pronounced themselves "ready to go wherever patriots may be necessary."[141] One hostile National Assemblyman considered the Jacobins "misled by foreigners and the factious" and "in open rebellion against constituted authorities."[142] Civil war loomed.

Aristocratic moderates returned to the Jacobins to deter them from supporting the king's overthrow. Unable to stem tumultuous debates, however – which popular leaders sought to align with the radical Cordeliers Club's neighborhood network – on July 16 three hundred National Assembly deputies (including the club's president and secretaries) formally withdrew, reconvening at the nearby Feuillant monastery to found a more moderate club. The "Feuillants" sent an address across the provincial network, proclaiming themselves the legitimate "*Société des amis de la Constitution*," and asserting that "of the Jacobin Club even its name will not survive."[143] Meanwhile, they recruited assembly centrists, especially Society of 1789 members. Believing monarchist sentiment still strong nationally, the Feuillants promoted a strengthened executive monarch and

---

[137] APS Filippo Mazzei Papers, Mss.Ms.Coll.47.

[138] Louis XVI, *Déclaration du roi, à tous les François, à sa sortie de Paris* (Paris: Baudouin, 1791), 16.

[139] Aulard, *Jacobins*, Vol. 2, 538.

[140] Mathiez, *Club*, 48, 53–54.

[141] Labroue, *Société*, 145; Heitz, *Sociétés*, 157.

[142] Archives départementales de l'Indre L 110 49.

[143] Aulard, *Jacobins*, Vol. 2, 538.

reconciliation with counterrevolutionaries abroad.[144] Remaining Jacobins on July 17 joined the popular Republican movement, helping mobilize a petition-signing demanding Louis XVI's abdication and "a new executive power" should accusations against him prove true.[145] Moderates in the National Assembly and Paris Municipality, however, had no intention of overturning the nearly completed French constitution. Lafayette and Paris's National Guard violently suppressed the petition signing in what became the Massacre of the Champs de Mars, effectively ending the republican movement.

Radical Jacobins had to fight to retain their network in disadvantageous circumstances. Denouncing the "schism" in a July 17 circular, Paris's Jacobins claimed to maintain "a free arena open to all opinions," considering themselves the party of unity, telling affiliates "brothers who have only the same object cannot long stay divided." Loyal members like Brissot castigated the Feuillants as a "secret gathering of aristocrats" out to reentrench monarchy. The Jacobins reasserted their loyalty to the National Assembly three days later, asserting they dissented for "love of liberty" rather than from being "factious."[146]

The Jacobins slowly won back provincial Feuillant defectors.[147] Responses mixed shock, confusion, and indignation with Rouen's Jacobins denouncing "perfidious maneuvers" accomplishing "what force could never have obtained" in dividing them.[148] Most societies sought neutrality: during the first forty-five days, at least 243 clubs wrote to both the Jacobins and Feuillants urging reconciliation, refusing to take sides.[149] Some, like Honfleur, initially supported the Feuillants in July asserting Paris radicals were "making trouble and anarchy reign," only rejoining the Jacobins in October once the Feuillant network withered.[150] Factionalism went too much against club principles to easily succeed: "l'union fait la force," Caen's Jacobins asserted, "If France's patriotic societies have the misfortune to divide, French liberty would perish under the attacks of the aristocrats menacing it."[151] Revolutionary emphasis on unity corroded the Feuillants' position as the breakaway party, while the Jacobins retained greater legitimacy.

---

[144] Gower, *Despatches*, 297; David Andress, *The Terror: The Merciless War for Freedom in Revolutionary France* (New York: Farrar, Straus and Giroux, 2006), 52; BN-R Mathurin de Lescure, "Correspondance secrete," NAF 13278 270.

[145] Mathiez, *Club*, 136.

[146] Aulard, *Jacobins*, Vol. 3, 30–31, 60, 39.

[147] APS Filippo Mazzei Papers Mss.Ms.Coll.47.

[148] *Journal des amis de la constitution*, August 23, 1791.

[149] Kennedy, *Early Years*, 286.

[150] Michel Biard, ed. *Procès-verbaux de la société populaire de Honfleur (Calvados) (janvier 1791-février 1795)* (Paris: Éditions CTHS, 2011), 137, 766.

[151] *Adresse de la Société des amis de la constitution à Caen, à l'assemblée nationale* (S.l., 1791), 1–2.

By late July, feeling their position strengthening, Paris's Jacobins demanded new loyalty declarations from their members. All had to pledge "to remain a Member of the Society of the Friends of the Constitution" and submit to further "proofs" judged necessary. Having seen their network almost broken by internal divisions, Jacobins decided to monitor – and purge – their membership as the situation required.[152] Affiliated societies, Paris's Jacobins asserted, needed to "not be tepid, weak or corrupt."[153] Though both Paris and provincial societies reintegrated prodigal Feuillants, society policies thereafter grew more intolerant.

On the first National Assembly's second-to-last day in September, lame-duck moderates attempted to rid France of corresponding societies altogether. Jacobin opponents castigated them as harmful "corporations" unrepresentative of the French people or common interests.[154] Isaac Le Chapelier, who months earlier sponsored laws outlawing strikes and unions, successfully introduced legislation that "no society, club, association of citizens can have any political existence" or undertake "any action or inspection" against authorities. The assemblymen, having voted a "self-denying ordinance" preventing their own reelection, attempted to terminate early revolutionary political culture as well. With the assembly's "center" demanding a vote, the measure passed.[155] The law, however, never fully enforced, would soon be almost forgotten as French politics radicalized again.

Conclusion

In less than two years, political societies went from being a strange foreign import to the most popular (and contested) force in French politics. In the flourish of revolutionary enthusiasm from late 1789 to early 1791, Jacobin societies integrated themselves into urban life across France as rallying places for those seeking to defend the revolution and advance their own political ambitions. The early history of these clubs, particularly their interaction with British and other examples from abroad, has been nearly erased by historians with other foci, who have largely ignored early revolutionary universalism while focusing on preceding and subsequent Anglophobia. Whereas the leading historian of the Jacobin Clubs, Michael Kennedy, treats Jacobins' relationship with the London Revolution Society only in a chapter on foreign relations, the Franco-British exchanges proved integral to the Jacobins' development,

---

[152] *Journal de correspondence de Paris à Nantes et du department de la Loire inférieure,* July 31, 1791.
[153] Kennedy, *Early Years,* 19.
[154] Patrice Higonnet, *Goodness beyond Virtue: Jacobins during the French Revolution* (Harvard: Harvard University Press, 1998), 257.
[155] *Archives parlementaires,* Vol. 31, 624.

providing their corresponding model and ideal of enlightened political sociability through discussion and debate.[156]

The early fraternal emphasis of the Jacobins by 1791 was challenged, however, by an increasingly polarized French political scene. Manifold suspicions grew both within and against the movement: with the Flight to Varennes confirming many radical revolutionaries' worst suspicions of monarchy, the Jacobins were simultaneously challenged by moderates desperate to preserve the constitutional monarchy. The Feuillant split showed that the Jacobins could not necessarily trust even their own members. The network that emerged from the Feuillant crisis would be more guarded and suspicious, but still determined to achieve their revolutionary visions and well positioned for the crises ahead.

[156] Kennedy, *Early Years.*

10

The Coming of the Haitian Revolution

Understanding the Haitian Revolution's origins in an Atlantic context requires taking 1789's Declaration of the Rights of Man and Citizen and the abolitionist movements of the early French Revolution seriously. The Revolution's radical, universalist proclamations in favor of liberty and equality made the French empire's slave system appear untenable, removing all certainty from colonial society and placing all factions in competition. It is no coincidence the only successful slave insurrection in human history occurred amid the greatest revolution the world had yet seen.

The French Caribbean colony of Saint-Domingue developed a French Revolution in miniature with all the antagonisms of France itself, plus what would become a multisided race war. As such, the conflicts that within two years fueled the Haitian Revolution took not the form of a relatively straightforward revolutionary/counterrevolutionary dynamic, but rather involved numerous groups – French *amis des noirs*, colonial planters, merchants defending the slave system, poor whites, mulattoes, free blacks, and slaves – each mobilizing interconnected and opposing social movements using the era's tactics to turn the French Revolution to their own advantage. The great uprising followed a two-year revolutionary process of escalation, in which all groups sought to selectively deploy the latest conceptions of freedom to their advantage and co-opt the social movement mobilization methods honed around the revolutionary Atlantic.

The Coming of a Transatlantic Revolution

Before provocations from France, deep rifts divided not just the colony's rich planters from poor whites, but both from those mixed-race and black free persons known as the *gens de couleur* (free men of color). Descendants of slaves, often artisans or merchants and sometimes owning slaves themselves, the *gens* formed the society's "intermediary caste." Outnumbering whites, by the 1685 Code Noir's terms they possessed legal equality, including full ability to buy and sell land. With no democratic rights to contest, the communities largely coexisted with more prosperous *gens de couleur* intermarrying with whites and sending children to French schools.[1] Under the Old Regime government free blacks – considered by a 1780s writer "in some sense the bourgeoisie" – took significant roles, including militia service (remaining loyal amid slave revolts) and serving in *maréchaussée* policing forces.[2]

Nevertheless, the colony remained profoundly unequal with the extent of its racialization shocking visitors. The Westphalian Baron von Wimpffen, visiting in February 1789, described how whereas

> In Europe the knowledge of different degrees of regard, of consideration, of esteem more or less felt, of respect more or less profound, is a science requiring close study ... Here on the contrary, it is only necessary to have eyes to place each individual in their class.

Race overwhelmed more subtle gradations with "respect for color" constituting "the palladium on which the colonies' destiny is supposed to depend." In a slave society based on gradations between "masters and slaves," no free blacks regardless of wealth or skill could gain equal status with whites. Though an "absurdity in the eyes of reason," Wimpffen saw little prospect of change.[3]

All free persons had much to fear from the slaves constituting over 90 percent of the colony's population. Though slaves supposedly gained protection from inhumane treatment under the Code Noir, in practice owners had free reign to maintain control through atrocities and terror. Despite government absolutism that even "weighed heavily on the whites," royal Intendant the Marquis de Barbé-Marbois described, "despotism stopped religiously at their properties' gate."[4] Wimpffen found slave-owners at home "enjoy a degree of liberty and of power which sovereigns themselves might envy" with unrestrained use of their human property.[5] Colonists had reasons for unity, given their unparalleled powers. Nevertheless, the Revolution ruptured masters' solidarity, creating a power vacuum from which the French colony never recovered.

The colony's proprietors, notwithstanding the many absentee landowners residing in France, formed a tight-knit group. All who "are, or pretend to be,

[1] Stewart R. King, *Blue Coat or Powdered Whig: Free People of Color in Pre-Revolutionary Saint-Domingue* (Athens, GA: University of Georgia Press, 2001); Popkin, *You*, 33–34; Madison Smartt Bell, *Toussaint Louverture: A Biography* (New York: Pantheon, 2007), 10.

[2] Justin Girod-Chantrans, *Voyage d'un Suisse dans différentes colonies d'Amérique pendant la dernière guerre, avec une table d'observations météorologiques faites à Saint-Domingue* (Neuchâtel: Imprimerie de la Société typographique, 1785), 182; Samuel G. Perkins, *"On the Margin of Vesuvius": Sketches of St. Domingo, 1785–1793* (Lawrence: Institute of Haitian Studies, 1995), 308.

[3] Baron von Wimpffen, *A Voyage to Saint Domingo, in the Years 1788, 1789 and 1790* (London: Cadell, 1797), 41–43.

[4] Marquis de Barbé-Marbois, *Réflexions sur la colonie de Saint-Domingue, ou, Examen approfondi des causes de sa ruine, et des mesures adoptées pour la rétablir* (Paris: Garnery, 1796), 63.

[5] Wimpffen, *Voyage*, 299.

planters," Wimpffen described of colonial high society, socialized together, cultivating a shared outlook in which they "scarcely ceased to speak of their negroes, their cotton, their sugar, and their coffee," before recirculating the same topics.[6] Resentments grew, meanwhile, against the royally appointed governor who controlled troops and militias, deployed police, promulgated laws, distributed land grants, and enforced the *Exclusif* (preventing legal trade beyond France's empire).[7] Unlike British colonies, Saint-Domingue planters had no organized political assemblies. Despite many elite rivalries, their wealth, power, and connections positioned them to profit from France's growing administrative disorder.

Already in April 1788, planters and their allies associated to pressure for representation in future Estates General, which Louis XVI the previous November agreed to summon (though initially for 1792). Despite the lack of preceding political associations in the colony, regional committees followed American precedents to form and circulate petitions among propertied citizens in Saint-Domingue, French ports, and Paris, gaining four thousand signatures. After a July 15 meeting of "colonists residing in the capital," nine wealthy expatriate planters presented the petitions to Naval Minister the Comte de Luzerne, who endorsed an "analogous regime" to France's, insofar as "differences in climate, production and commerce permit," including the right to "send representatives to the assembly of a nation of which they are members."[8] However, in September 1788 the royal council denied colonists representation. Chamber of Commerce petitions for separate mercantile representatives were rebuffed to public ridicule.[9] Colonists had reason to fear if their interests would be well served.

By late 1788, word of the *amis des noirs* reached Saint-Domingue. Denunciations of slavery spread in French publications: one presented at Bordeaux's *Académie royale* declared "slavery contrary to the principles of natural morality" and a "public crime," announcing "numerous society forms

---

[6] Ibid., 107.

[7] Pierre Boissonnade, *Saint-Domingue à la veille de la revolution et la question de la représentation coloniale aux États generaux* (Paris: Geuthner, 1906), 6; Popkin, "Saint-Domingue," 222.

[8] Comte de Luzerne, *Mémoire envoyé le 18 juin 1790, au Comité des rapports de l'Assemblée nationale* (Paris: Imprimerie royale, 1790), 1; Mitchell B. Garrett, *The French Colonial Question, 1789–1791: Dealings of the Constituent Assembly with Problems Arising from the Revolution in the West Indies* (New York: Negro Universities Press, 1916), 7–8; Boissonnade, *Saint-Domingue*, 44, 110; Debien, *Les colons de Saint-Domingue et la Révolution* (Paris: Armand Colin, 1953), 63.

[9] Popkin, "Saint-Domingue," 230; AD Loire-Atlantique C 626 1 2 and 33; Pierre Bernadau, *Les débuts de la Révolution à Bordeaux, d'après les tablettes manuscrites de Pierre Bernadau* (Paris: Alcan, 1919), 33.

to annihilate slavery and the trade."[10] By mid-1789, colonial interests felt the need to speak "Against freeing the Blacks."[11] Within months, altering the colonial slave system went from the realm of fantasy to probability. New forms of colonial organizing appeared necessary to counter the changing political dynamics.

Seizing the initiative, Saint-Domingue elites illicitly formed an Estates General deputation via exclusive elections dominated by wealthy white planter families, heightening class and race antagonisms. Colonial administrators refused to legitimize such activities, declaring any gathering over five an "illicit assembly" meriting prosecution. The planters flouted the decree, in covert invitation-only meetings confirming eighteen deputies to send to France.[12] Private correspondence committees kept organizers abreast of the latest colonial and French developments.[13] Efforts to keep the meetings quiet failed, however: politics became the "unique subject of conversation" across social classes.[14]

Free blacks and mulattos, excluded from the planter assemblies and intimidated by authorities, organized illicit meetings to select their own deputies. "Clubs" allegedly formed in "every parish" with all sides having "caught the watchwords of the revolution" to promote their own interests.[15] Outnumbering whites by 24,000 to 6,000, *gens de couleur* highlighted their status as French citizens, their equal (or greater) paying of taxes, and as they could "see no difference between blacks and whites," asserted they "ought to be represented also." Not finding justice in the colony, they sent deputies to the National Assembly to appeal to French humanity.[16] More than mock-aristocratic planters, the *gens* believed they represented the colony's Third Estate.

The planters' delegation met unexpected complications in France from *Société des amis des noirs* supporters. A revolution became the ideal moment for action with Brissot publicizing how American antislavery campaigns advanced "when Americans developed a vigorous resistance against the

[10] André-Daniel Laffon de Ladebat, *Discours sur la nécessité et les moyens de détruire l'esclavage dans les colonies* (Bordeaux: Racli, 1788), 3–4.

[11] *Procès-verbal des séances de l'assemblée des colons électeurs de La Martinique, tenue à Paris* (Paris: Demonville, 1789), 1.

[12] Jean-Philippe Garran de Coulon, *Rapport sur les troubles de Saint-Domingue, fait au nom de la Commission des Colonies, des Comités de Salut public, de Législation et de Marine, réunis* (Paris, 1797), Vol. 1, 46–47; Boisonnade, *Saint-Domingue*, 150.

[13] H. E. Mills, *The Early Years of the French Revolution in Santo Domingo* (Poughkeepsie, NY: Haight, 1892), 41.

[14] Antoine Dalmas, *Histoire de la revolution de Saint-Domingue: depuis le commencement des troubles jusqu'à la prise de Jérémie et du Môle par les Anglais* (Paris: Mame, 1814) 30.

[15] Jonathan Brown, *The History and Present Condition of St. Domingo* (Philadelphia: Marshall, 1837), Vol. 1, 137.

[16] *St. James's Chronicle*, November 21, 1789.

English Government's auspicious tyranny," praising the young country's "northern and middle States outlawing forever the importation of Blacks."[17] The society sent circulars to many French electoral districts, "hoping the nation will see the trade and black slavery" as "among the evils of which it must prepare the destruction."[18] Antislavery opinions spread: nearly 50 of 520 surviving mainland French *Cahiers de doléances* grievance statements expressed disapprobation toward slavery and/or the trade.[19] While most favored gradual reforms, three demanded colonial slavery's immediate abolition – the Baillage of Senlis beseeching "the Estates General, in their wisdom, to reconcile political interest with the rights of nature."[20] As the Revolution turned against "despotism," no greater abuse existed than planters' ongoing colonial conduct.[21]

The French Revolution dawned favorably for antislavery interests. Necker mentioned their cause in his opening Estates General address, considering slaves "men like us in their thoughts and above all in their capacity to suffer."[22] The *Amis* followed up in early June, warning "moments are precious" for reforms, as "a total change in the colonial system" threatened. The king's minister ignored, however, their call for a committee of legislators, merchants, and planters to discuss abolishing the slave trade on the British model.[23] Many legislators nevertheless became partisans: Mirabeau believed three hundred deputies supported abolishing the trade, while another five hundred (constituting an absolute majority) would if Britain did so simultaneously.[24] As "the word 'liberty' is in all mouths and resounding in all hearts," one legislator asserted, while despotism crumbled, opportunities abounded to eliminate the Old Regime's worst excesses.[25] Amid August 4's euphoric Abolition of Privileges, planters were asked to voluntarily endorse abolishing slavery itself, but refused.[26] Each revolutionary lurch left threatened planter interests anew.

---

[17] Brissot, *Mémoire sur les noirs de l'amérique septenrionale* (Paris, 1789), 5.

[18] Bibiliothèque de l'Institut de France, Papiers de Condorcet 857, Vol. 1, 34.

[19] David Geggus, "Racial Equality, Slavery, and Colonial Secession during the Constituent Assembly," *American Historical Review* 94, no. 5 (1989), 1293.

[20] *Archives parlementaires*, Vol. 2, 144, 149, 324.

[21] Benjamin-Sigismond Frossard, *La cause des esclaves nègres, et habitans de la Guinée, porté au tribunal de la justice, de la religion et de la politique* (Lyon: Roche, 1789), Vol. 2, i.

[22] Laurent Dubois, *Avengers of the New World: The Story of the Haitian Revolution* (Cambridge, MA: Harvard University Press, 2004), 73.

[23] *Lettre de la Société des amis des noirs à M. Necker, avec la réponse de ce Ministre* (Paris, 1789), 5.

[24] Geggus, "Racial," 1294.

[25] David Duval de Sanadon, *Tableau de la situation actuelle des colonies, présenté à l'assemblée nationale* (S.l., 1789), 3.

[26] Louis-Marthe de Gouy d'Arsy, *Confession d'un député dans ses dernier momens, ou liste des péchés politiques* (S.l., 1791), 4. Deputy Leguen de Kerenval spoke of organizing "a code to exile slavery." *Archives parlementaires*, Vol. 8, 345; the Duc de la Rochefoucauld proposed "destroying servitude in all the kingdom and softening the fates of slaves in the

To combat the *amis des noirs*, planter interests in Paris – where many of the richest had long resided – in June 1789 formed Club Massiac, named after the Place des Victoires *hôtel particulier* where it met.[27] Formally known as the *Société correspondante des colons français*, it developed similar social movement models as its abolitionist opponents to deter National Assembly interference in colonial affairs. The organization recruited 435 members, including numerous noble families, wealthy merchant interests, powerful administrators, and National Assembly deputies. Indeed, at least 150 assemblymen held colonial investments. Taking a hard line against reform, Club Massiac opposed any changes to "property rights," and "no more wanted to admit the mulattos' pretensions than the blacks' to equality."[28] On no other contentious issue did nobles and prosperous commoners' financial interests so coincide, nor would practical and idealistic strains of French revolutionary thought clash so resoundingly.

Before learning of colonial elections, planters residing in Paris met at the Marquis de Gouy d'Arcy's home and chose several in attendance as National Assembly deputies for the colonies. Without a direct colonial mandate, planters sought to ensure their interests would be represented. Initially, they appointed thirty deputies (amounting to roughly a three-fifths slave representation similar to that recently enshrined in the United States Constitution). On July 4, the National Assembly instead confirmed six Saint-Domingue seats, proportionate to the free white population's size, with Martinique and Guadeloupe each receiving two representatives.[29] Monopolizing representation, planter interests showed little appetite for even the pretense of inclusion, instead expanding lobbying to profit from the revolutionary political crisis.

Club Massiac forced the *amis des noirs* onto the defensive. After Massiac calumnies, in August 1789, the *amis* had to deny in Brissot's influential *Patriote français* newspaper that they sought a Saint-Domingue slave uprising.[30] Slave-related questions remained sensitive for a new revolutionary order legitimating itself through the Rights of Man: that month Clarkson met with influential patriot deputies including Sieyès, Jerôme Pétion, the Duc de la Rochefoucauld, and Mirabeau. Though Clarkson reported the group ambivalent about whether France ought "to have colonies at all," while asserting the National Assembly "undoubtedly had the right to pursue this question," they

colonies," Alexandre de Lameth, *Histore de l'assemblée constituante* (Paris: Moutardier, 1828), Vol. 1, 98.

[27] Michel-Etienne Descourlitz, *Histoire des désastres de Saint-Domingue* (Paris: Gernery, 1795), 133.

[28] Lucien Leclerc, "La politique et l'influence du club de l'hôtel Massiac," *Annales historiques de la Révolution française* 14 (1937), 342–43; Garrett, *French*, 2.

[29] Popkin, *A Concise History of the Haitian Revolution* (Chichester, MA: Wiley-Blackwell, 2012), 27.

[30] *Patriote français*, August 18, 1789.

declined to pursue aggressive measures.[31] The dangers immediate action posed to the still-fragile revolution – and vibrant Atlantic economy amid France's financial crisis – remained apparent.

Club Massiac's corresponding network eclipsed the *amis des noirs*, becoming the most powerful in France prior to the Jacobins' rise. Like the later organization, Massiac branches pursued an "always active surveillance" of revolutionary politics, while pledging "constant" correspondence with provincial allies.[32] In August, Paris's club sent a circular to port cities' chambers of commerce seeking affiliation "to act in concert for our common interests," leading Bordeaux to found the first *Comité américain*. Nantes, La Rochelle, Saint-Malo, Marseille, Bayonne, Brest, and Calais established similar organizations in September.[33] Motivating mobilization, rumors grew that "motions will be made to abolish the slave trade," as La Rochelle's Chamber of Commerce warned.[34] Nantes and Le Havre each petitioned the National Assembly that autumn against "freeing the negroes," believing the measure imminent.[35] Although ports remained quiet on slavery during the early revolution, now many felt pressure to defend their financial interests. Massiac attempted to become an effective lobbying organization similar to the Liverpool-led effort opposing the British slave trade's abolition.

The nascent Massiac network appropriated revolutionary rhetoric for their program. They praised satellite organizations for having "viewed the merchants and the colonists as your brothers," promoting an "intimate relationship" between "all parts of the realm" for their mutual benefit. Counterproductive measures augured "commerce's ruin," while damaging "the state's riches."[36] True revolutionaries needed to avoid "excessive Philanthropy" ruinous to France.[37] Massiac sought to "proscribe forever the system of the *amis des noirs*," thereby "annihilating" them.[38] Across 1789's latter months, as revolutionaries (seeking a workable constitutional order) grew more pragmatic and compromising, the lobby's position strengthened.

Also inspired by the United States, though by the south rather than the north, Saint-Domingue's planters believed their moment for self-determination had come. Slaveholder interests remained too economically important to be treated otherwise. Gouy d'Arcy declared Saint-Domingue

---

[31] Clarkson, *History*, 139.
[32] AN W 14.
[33] AN D XXV 85 1 29; Garran de Coulon, *Inquiry* 54; Déborah Liébart, "Un groupe de pression contre-révolutionnaire: le Club Massiac sous la Constituante," *Annales historiques de la Révolution française* 354 (2009), 26.
[34] Archives départementales de la Charente-Maritime 41 ET P 69.
[35] Archives municipales du Havre F(2) 10 10 and 60.
[36] Cooper, *Letters on the Slave Trade*, 175.
[37] AD Gironde C 4364 36.
[38] AN D XXV 85 1 30.

presented to the "shocked eye" of the visitor, "sixty cities, 6,000 villages, that have become the richest, most powerful, most productive of our provinces," particularly valuable given "the disastrous state" of French finances.[39] Another pamphlet found the colonies' importance only matched by their differentness, as neither "the climate, nor the physical space, nor the morals, nor the nature of the properties, nor the commercial relationships, nor the type of industry, nor the population, nor the seasons" corresponded to French patterns.[40] Massiac lobbied for Saint-Domingue's own autonomous colonial assembly.[41]

Massiac's network realized colonial interests faced unprecedented threats to their legitimacy – with worry becoming particularly acute once the National Assembly passed the Declaration of the Rights of Man and Citizen in August. After reading from Brissot and Mirabeau's published explanations of the first article declaring "All men are born and remain free and equal in rights," a Paris Massiac speaker concluded that thereby "Saint-Domingue's negroes must be free." A letter to the club considered the measure adopted by deputies "expressly charged in their cahiers" to demand slaves' liberty without considering the "anarchy" and "rebellion" the decree would bring.[42] *Amis des noirs* writings radicalized to attack slavery in nearly absolute terms, one describing "an unhappy institution that nature and justice equally command to destroy."[43] With planters and their allies grasping the full possibilities of revolutionary rights – more than many revolutionaries yet did – the likelihood of American-style compromises receded, endangering the colonial order.

Gens de couleur merchants and artisans residing in Paris that August formed their own organization, *La société des colons américains* (also known as *La société des citoyens de couleur*), to colonial lobbyists' disdain. Members included influential pamphleteer Julien Raimond and future rebel leader Vincent Ogé. Though remaining allied with the *amis des noirs*, they composed their own *Cahier de Doléances* pushing for the Rights of Man to apply to nonwhites and contested planter representation of the colony in the National Assembly. Initially, the new organization sought accommodations with Paris's Club Massiac.[44] Some planters seemed willing to compromise: one letter to Saint-Domingue's regional committees in December described the *gens* as

[39] Louis-Marthe de Gouy, *Précis sur la position actuelle de la députation de Saint-Domingue, aux Etats-Généraux. Versailles, le 20 juin 1789* (Versailles, 1789), 6.

[40] P. J. Laborie, *Réflexions sommaires adressées à la France et à la colonie de S. Domingue* (Paris: Chardon, 1789), 5.

[41] Llébart, "Groupe," 26–27.

[42] AN D XXV 85 3 7, 822.

[43] *Réponse à l'écrit de M. Malouet, sur l'esclavage des nègres, dans lequel est exprimé le voeu formé par les colons d'avoir des représentants aux Etats-Généraux: Par un membre de la Société des amis des noirs* (S.l., 1789), 17.

[44] Armand de Brette, "Les gens de couleur libres et leurs deputes en 1789," *Révolution française* 29 (1895), 329–31; Florence Gauthier, *L'aristocratie de l'épiderme: Le combat de la Société des citoyens de Couleur, 1789–1791* (Paris: CNRS, 2007); Geggus, "Racial," 1298.

their "best defenders against the slaves," but Massiac's network refused their claims.[45] Indeed, port merchants enacted a travel ban preventing all *gens de couleur* from returning to the colony on their ships, asserting (on scant evidence) they would "excite a general uprising" against the whites.[46] Polarization advanced with politicization.

The *amis des noirs* increasingly promoted rights for free men of color. Grégoire, in an October National Assembly speech, considered the *gens de couleur* the colony's rampart, asserting that without them, "Whites would succumb by their inferiority" of numbers to the slaves. Should just demands not be redressed, "resistance to oppression is a right emanated from God, and recognized by the National Assembly." Men of color would unravel the colonial order through violence if necessary. The day approached when "living is nothing, living free is everything," and past degradations would no longer be tolerated.[47] Another address highlighted how while "Citizens of all classes have been called to the great work of public regeneration" the colony's "ambitious Aristocracy" blocked men of color from participating.[48] For the Revolution to establish universal rights, racial repression could not stand.

In early November, a *gens de couleur* deputation challenged planters' right to sit in the National Assembly. Claiming election by Saint-Domingue's free men of color, they asked for a just share of colonial representation. Admitted to the speaker's rostrum, they condemned the planters' excluding them from meetings and, more generally, flagrantly violating the Code Noir and Rights of Man.[49] The session president, liberal noble Emmanuel Fréteau de Saint-Just, responded that the body knew "no distinction between Blacks and Whites, but considers all men to have equal rights." Although he vaguely blamed "circumstances" for not discussing their claims immediately, the same excuse given for deferring debates on abolishing the slave trade, the assembly gave the deputies "provisional" seats.[50]

Seating African-American representatives was unprecedented among the era's Atlantic powers. London's *Woodfall's Register* pronounced their shock that the French "received into their National Assembly black Deputies," which they considered to "indicate that this infernal trade's destruction is at no great distance."[51] Yet the early Revolution's principles appeared too strong to avoid such issues with a November pamphlet declaring, "Citizens of color have in

---

[45] *Correspondance secrete*, 23.

[46] AD Charente-Maritime 41 ETP 175 4934.

[47] *Mémoire en faveur des gens de coueulur ou sang-mêlés de St.-Domingue, & autres îles françoises de l'Amérique, adressé à l'Assemblée nationale* (Paris: Belin, 1789), 31–32, 47.

[48] *Adresse à l'Assemblée nationale pour les Citoyens libres de couleur des Isles & colonies françaises* (S.l., 1789), 2.

[49] *Woodfall's Register*, October 30, 1789.

[50] *St. James's Chronicle*, November 21, 1789; *New-York Daily Gazette*, March 9, 1790.

[51] *Woodfall's Register*, January 8, 1790.

their favor Natural Right, the principles of Positive Law, the ancient Laws of the Colonies, the National Assembly's Decrees, Justice, Reason, and Humanity."[52] In radical times, legislators could hardly justify eluding the *gens'* pleas.

Mirabeau's efforts to abolish the slave trade excited panic along the Atlantic coast. Rouen merchants claimed it would "annihilate our maritime commerce," Nantes' prophesized "total commercial ruin," and colonial deputies demanded a resolution supporting the slave trade to prevent "a negro insurrection."[53] Abolishing the trade appeared only a first step toward attacking slavery, with Le Havre merchants asserting its suppression would increase English smuggling.[54] On March 1, 1790, Mirabeau attempted to sway the Jacobins, eloquently orating for three and a half hours that "the era of artifices and violence against good sense has ended." He even asserted, "freeing the slaves can only be a matter of time," endorsing gradualism only to "prepare the means" for elevating "all the peoples of the world under the pavilion of peace and brotherhood."[55] Despite strong support from Paris's districts, many deputies remained unconvinced. Mirabeau relented from proposing the slave trade's abolition in the assembly, as fellow deputies lacked enthusiasm for another destabilizing measure.[56] Still, as in Britain and the United States, the prospect of future legislation remained.

With Saint-Domingue's residents having little direct say in France's revolutionary proceedings, as ships took five weeks or more to traverse the Atlantic, the colonial order had already lost its inevitability.[57] Revolutionaries appeared "drunk on liberty," declared the colony's white deputies in August 1789, ready to "seize this occasion to propose freeing our blacks."[58] Since feudalism had fallen in weeks, what could be an adequate bulwark for literal slavery? As revolutionaries aggressively dismantled the Old Regime, there could be little certainty of colonial reform remaining moderate on American or (proposed) British models. The egalitarian pretentions becoming mainstream in France, together with powerful new club models for advocacy and agitation, were an obvious provocation against the repressive colonial system. The latent tensions within a brutal hierarchical order surfaced as all sides recognized

---

[52] *Dernières observations des citoyens de couleur des isles et colonies françoises* (S.l., 1789), 3.

[53] AD Loire-Atlantique C 626 2 246; AD Gironde C 4365 43; Anna Julia Cooper, *Slavery and the French Revolutionists, 1788–1805* (Lewiston, NY: Mellen Press, 1988), 169.

[54] AM Le Havre D(3) 38 76.

[55] AD Gironde 61 J 5.

[56] Dorigny, "Mirabeau and the Société des Amis des Noirs: Which Way to Abolish Slavery?" in *The Abolitions of Slavery: From L. F. Sonthonax to Victor Schoelcher, 1793, 1794, 1848* (Oxford: Berghahn, 2003), 128; AD Charente-Maritime 41 ETP 69 685.

[57] Archives nationales d'outre-mer, 213 MIOM 134.

[58] *Lettre des députés de Saint-Domingue à leurs commettans, en date du 12 aout 1789, intercepté par un mulâtre* (Paris, 1790), 4.

new possibilities to achieve their greatest ambitions, often at their opponents' expense.

The French Revolution and the Destabilization of Haiti

From its early stages, Saint-Domingue's Revolution unfolded on racial terms. Upon news crossing the Atlantic of the Bastille's fall, partisans distributed tricolor cockades "to everybody who had a white face" – with some refusing to wear it shot or knifed.[59] In Petit-Goave, a judge "long suspected of favoring the mix-blood caste" was lynched.[60] Anyone advocating mulatto rights risked the same. Without irony, colonial whites "haughtily spoke of liberty before the slaves, and bitterly declaimed against privileges, prejudices and despotism."[61] *Gens de couleur* were banned from wearing the cockade. François Raimond, the Paris activist's relative, watched white colonists with bemusement, noting "the blacks," who "understand that the cockade is for liberty and equality, wanted to rise up." Whites accused, arrested, and hanged several alleged conspirators of color.[62] Rumors (incorrectly) spread of deputy Moreau de Saint-Méry betraying the colonial cause by proposing slavery's abolition in the National Assembly.[63] The Revolution opened new, often terrifying possibilities for a strained and unequal colonial order.

Municipal revolutions commenced with white-dominated committees taking power in the largest cities. Once news arrived "that in France the people seized public authority by forming committees and municipalities" planter Jean-Félix Carteau described, colonists did likewise. Inspired by "the dissolution of chains that held our European brothers in oppression," another chronicler related, colonists confronted "the arbitrary power and tyranny with such deep roots here too."[64] Given the "popular authorities forming throughout France," propertied white men ignored laws against associations and formed new corresponding organizations across the colony.[65] Without irony, white colonists celebrated French revolutionary freedoms for themselves, while asserting unchanged prerogatives at home.

---

[59] Samuel G. Perkins, *On the Margins of Vesuvius: Sketches of St. Domingo, 1785-1793* (Lawrence, KS: Institute of Haitian Studies, 1995), 314; Dalmas, *Histoire*, 23; Garran de Coulon, *Rapport*, 74.

[60] Descourtliz, *Histoire*, 139–40.

[61] Dalmas, *Histoire*, 23.

[62] Garran de Coulon, *Rapport*, 74.

[63] AN D XXV 59 584.

[64] François-Raymond de Pons, *Observations sur la situation politique de Saint-Domingue* (Paris: Quillau, 1790), 15–16.

[65] Garran de Coulon, *Rapport*, 71; Pamphile Lacroix, *Mémoires pour server à l'histoire de la révolution de Saint-Domingue* (Paris: Pilles, 1819), Vol. 1, 14.

Men of color still served in the colonial militia, however. A traditional avenue for emancipation and social advancement through service, the forces reorganized as a National Guard under the committees' command.[66] Revolutionary disorders appeared as great as in France: one report considered "anarchy reigning" with "couriers, business and justice all suspended" amid regime change.[67] National Guard service, previously considered "a *corvée*, now became a mania," but the white population remained too small to fill its ranks.[68] Despite political antagonisms over civil and political rights, *gens de couleur* retained their military standing, accepting present arrangements for "the colony's prosperity."[69] Considering themselves legitimate men of property, free men of color still tried to join the colonial elite rather than overthrow them.

Not even the whites, however, maintained solidarity amid revolutionary politics' manifold possibilities and temptations. Sailors often outnumbered free citizens in Saint-Domingue's ports, dooming attempts to limit French news.[70] During an October 12 *Te Deum* in Saint-Marc celebrating the Abolition of Feudalism, "a crowd of young men" broke into the local debtors prison to release the white prisoners, after which *gens de couleur* liberated their own. The next night white mobs pillaged mansions. Fears of social breakdown appeared imminent: on October 21 in Le Cap, rumors of a slave rising kept regiments mobilized all night, anticipating twenty thousand slaves attacking the city.[71] Fear and opportunity coalesced.

Saint-Domingue politics grew more inflamed after increasingly desperate communications arrived from their representatives in France. After the National Assembly legitimated club meetings on August 12, planter deputies urged their colonial constituents to mobilize. As "every society has the right to assemble to freely consider communal affairs," the assemblymen urged colonists to "have open eyes about the effects the kingdom's reigning fermentation could produce," asking them to "maintain order, peace, and subordination."[72] Association appeared essential to preserve the colonial order. Rather than promoting free discussion, planters built from the Jacobins' more coercive features, attempting to monopolize the public sphere. They warned *amis des noirs* would "wait for a favorable moment to raise a storm against slavery,"

---

[66] Erica R. Johnson, *Philanthropy and Race in the Haitian Revolution* (New York: Palgrave Macmillan, 2018), 214.

[67] AN D XXV 59 584.

[68] Lacroix, *Mémoires*, Vol. 1, 12.

[69] *Woodfall's Register*, January 11, 1790.

[70] Julius Scott, *The Common Wind: Afro-American Currents in the Age of the Haitian Revolution* (London: Verso, 2018), 39.

[71] Garrett, *French*, 36; ANOM 213 MIOM 134.

[72] *Correspondance secrète des colons députés à l'Assemblée constituante: servant à faire connaitre l'esprit des colons en général, sur la Révolution* (Paris: Anjubault, s.d.), 6–10.

recommending colonists arrest dissidents and "seize writings in which the word 'Liberty' is mentioned." They warned of a *gens de couleur* influx from France, spreading news, ideas, and trouble.[73] Revolutionary ideas needed to be controlled, lest they render the colony ungovernable.

More revolutionary edicts arrived, with the Declaration of the Rights of Man and Citizen creating a colonial uproar. Word spread back to Europe that white citizens "regarded it as a dangerous and unpardonable blow, leveled at their power over the negroes and mulattoes."[74] *Gens de couleur* now had the explicit language of the French Revolution's most important document on which to base their claims. They drafted a new *Cahier de doléances*, demanding "the same rights, ranks, prerogatives, franchises, privileges" for all free men, "whether Free Blacks, Mulattoes, Quadroons [one-quarter black], or otherwise." They considered the situation degraded by the "pretensions" of "oppressor Citizens," alluding to the Declaration of Rights' guarantee of a right of resistance.[75] None knew if French revolutionaries would enact further changes – or, unbeknownst to them, already had. A letter arrived in Port-au-Prince erroneously reporting Paris's Assembly of Electors had pursued "freeing the negroes."[76] Whites wrote to France complaining of the colonial system's "reversal," prophesizing imminent catastrophe.[77]

Gens de couleur leveraged their corresponding society for lobbying, hoping the National Assembly would address their status. Clarkson arranged dinners for black lobbyists with legislators, describing them to Sharp as "well informed Gentlemen, much above the generality of the Parisians in point of Education & Learning," interacting on par with the legislators.[78] Seeking to sway public opinion, an October pamphlet denounced the planters as an "ambitious aristocracy," to whom "liberty is nothing but the unlimited right to dominate other men."[79] In November, they petitioned against the National Assembly's new Colonial Committee half composed of white planters and half of French maritime city representatives (excluding *amis des noirs* and themselves). Now "menaced with being forgotten," *gens* demanded the "same balance for whites and citizens of color."[80] Before the National Assembly, Raimond recalled the Declaration of Rights' definition that "all political association" sought "to

[73] Cooper, *Letters on the Slave Trade*, 172–73.
[74] Bryan Edwards, *The History, Civil and Commercial, of the British Colonies in the West Indies* (London: Stockdale, 1793), 331.
[75] *Cahier contenant les plaintes, doléances, & réclamations des citoyens-libres & propriétaires de couleur des isles & colonies françaises* (S.l., s.d.), 1–2.
[76] ANOM 213 MIOM 134.
[77] AM Le Havre F(2) 10.
[78] GRO D 3549 13/1/S9.
[79] *Adresse à l'assemblée-nationale, pour les citoyens-libres de couleur, des isles & colonies françoises. 12 octobre 1789* (Paris, 1789), 2; AN D XXV 85, dossier 824.
[80] *Supplique et pétition des citoyens de couleur des isles et colonies françoises* (Paris, 1789), 1–3, 10.

conserve the natural and imprescriptible rights of man."[81] *Gens* attempted to hold the French assembly to its highest principles.

As colonial whites and *gens de couleur* politically organized, so too (more surreptitiously) did groups of slaves. Word of northern abolitions in the United States spread, sometimes exaggeratedly, and many conjectured France would go further.[82] Colonial administrators worried slaves knew "everything being done and written in France for their liberty."[83] Slaves rebelled in France's next largest sugar islands, Martinique and Guadeloupe, with some believing the king had already granted them freedom. "If giving us our liberty be opposed," insurgents communicated to Martinique authorities, "we will spread fire and blood through all the colony."[84] Rumors also convulsed Saint-Domingue, while false reports reached France by late 1789 of open rebellion.[85] Far from the begging, submissive slave abolitionists placed on the *Société des amis* logo (copied from Wedgewood's British design), none could afford to discount slaves' latent power. From the Revolution's early days onward, all acknowledged the possibility of extreme bloodshed and a full colonial social breakdown.

In France, embattled planter interests attempted to block all reforms. Bordeaux's Massiac branch wrote to Paris's in late November that Martinique's slave uprising was only a "spark," heralding a broader colonial "explosion."[86] Finding revolutionary thinking contrary to their interests, on December 2, 1789, Paris's Club Massiac demanded the Rights of Man's colonial suspension. Propaganda funding expanded with the club distributing pamphlets in early 1790 promoting colonial autonomy and the racial system's retention. The organization raised petitions opposing slave-trade abolition, directing sympathetic municipalities and merchant groups to declare it "impolitic and dangerous."[87] Alienation led to desperation among colonial elites.

Across autumn 1789 in Saint-Domingue, a new General Assembly (disdaining the name Colonial Assembly for its subordinate implications) took shape. Meeting in the western town of Saint-Marc, the assembly painted on its walls "*Saint-Domingue, la Loi et le Roi*," implying its own nationalist course toward autonomy or perhaps even legislative independence.[88] Over its first months,

---

[81] *Réclamations adressées à l'Assemblée nationale, par les personnes de Couleur, Propriétaires & Cultivateurs de la Colonie Françoise de Saint-Domingue* (Paris, 1789), 3.

[82] Daniel Lescallier, *Réflexions sur le sort des nègres de nos colonies* (S.l., 1789), 8.

[83] Vertus Saint-Louis, *Mer et liberté: Haiti (1492–1794)* (Port au Prince: Bibliothèque nationale de Haiti, 2008), 164.

[84] *Daily Advertiser*, February 25, 1790.

[85] *Woodfall's Register*, December 12, 1789; *World*, January 7, 1790.

[86] AN D XXV 90 2 4.

[87] Leclerc, "Politique," 347, 348; AN D XXV 824 37; St. John's College Library, Clarkson 1 8; AM Besançon AA 36.

[88] Lothrop Stoddard, *The French Revolution in San Domingo* (Boston: Houghton Mifflin, 1914), 100.

the General Assembly declared itself permanent, seized control of finances, demanded military commanders' subordination, standardized revolutionary municipal structures, and composed a constitution "better adapted" for local conditions.[89] White colonists envisioned the French Revolution advancing their own liberty, but preserving the social hierarchy.

White colonial politics splintered: given Saint-Domingue's mountainous division into northern, western, and southern portions, three autonomous regional assemblies developed. Political differences remained pronounced. The northern province, where many representatives had close French merchant and administrative ties, favored the governor and French National Assembly. Radicals wanting colonial autonomy (or perhaps even independence) increasingly dominated the west and south.[90] The planters' National Assembly deputies, meanwhile, opposed sending additional French troops to the colony. Each faction pursued their political desires with little concern for compromise or maintaining order.

Despite white divisions, no colonial group sought *gens de couleur* as allies. Even the most moderate attempts to win token free black representation under the emerging order met brutal repression. Petit-Goave *gens* petitioned an electoral meeting for a single deputy of color in the Assembly of the West. Officials arrested the petitioners immediately, pressuring them into naming the petition's author. Blame fell on the local electoral committee's president, Ferrand de Baudières, for allegedly encouraging (and perhaps composing) their address. During his interrogation, a white lynch mob surrounded the jail, overwhelming the guard, dragging the old royal officer outside, beheading him, and placing his severed cranium on a pike.[91] Across the southern peninsula in Aquin, another crowd tried to lynch an elderly mulatto believed to possess a petition copy.[92] Though some northern parishes allowed *gens* to vote in primary assemblies, none dared to elect blacks. In most areas, lower-class *"petit blancs"* prevented black voter participation through intimidation and violence.[93]

Municipal revolutions further consolidated local whites' power at the central authority's expense. At Port-au-Prince in January 1790, the royal governor and high bureaucrats swore to make decisions in consultation with the city's revolutionary committee. Le Cap's municipal committee seized the treasury,

---

[89] Charles Tarbé, *Rapport sur les troubles de Saint-Domingue* (Paris: Imprimerie nationale, 1791), 10; *Relation authentique de tout ce qui s'est passé à Saint-Domingue avant et après le départ forcé de l'Assemblée coloniale* (Paris, s.d.), 4; Brown, *History and Present*, 144.

[90] Dubois, *Avengers*, 78–79.

[91] Lacroix, *Mémoires*, Vol. 1, 19.

[92] Carolyn E. Fick, *The Making of Haiti: The Saint Domingue Revolution from Below* (Knoxville: University of Tennessee Press, 1990), 79; Mills, *Early*, 48.

[93] Lacroix, *Mémoires*, Vol. 1, 23.

directing payments for work done in the king's name.[94] Such rapid developments scared many, exciting European press reports that Saint-Domingue
revolutionaries "stirred up citizen against citizen, formed cabals, excited
tumults and insurrections" along factional lines.[95] Free blacks could not join
on equal terms: those taking a civic oath to participate in Western Province
public functions, for instance, had to swear to "always respect the Whites."[96]
Racial despotism remained entrenched in Saint-Domingue.

Gens de couleur in the Western province, angered at their marginalization
under the new supposed system of liberty and equality, took arms. Near Saint-
Marc, where the General Assembly met and gens formed a particularly large
and influential artisan class, militiamen established a camp outside town,
raising white fears of an insurrection. Authorities only mobilized after armed
forces arrived over the mountains from Le Cap, dispersing the camp and
capturing its leaders. All free men of color were forbidden to publicly carry
arms, on pain of treason charges.[97] Amid political anarchy, the economy
imploded. By March a local report complained, "all payments are suspended,
business is dead, and currency entirely disappeared," with little hope of
improvement.[98] The colonial political crisis deepened.

In Paris, gens de couleur allies attempted to hold the National Assembly
accountable to its principles. As Paris municipal officer Étienne de Joly orated
on their behalf before the legislature in January 1790, extending the era's
totalizing rhetoric, it had become "impossible to retain in slavery a people
who want to be free." Freedom now seemed to "spread like light," and "no
power can suspend its course." Seeing this outcome as the era's culmination, he
argued, "Enlightenment, sciences, Philosophy have prepared the Revolution,"
compelling revolutionaries to apply its grand precepts.[99] Those opposing such
changes seemingly did so from selfish interests: in February, Brissot before
Paris's municipality accused colonial planters of "trying to incite, even lead
commercial towns into insurrection," believing a conspiracy underway for
colonial independence.[100] Rumors flew that planters refused to acknowledge
National Assembly legitimacy and plotted a royalist counteroffensive.[101] With
the planters increasingly acting like an aristocracy, powerful revolutionaries
now considered the gens' cause akin to their own.

---

[94] Federal Gazette, February 24, 1790.
[95] Woodfall's Register, September 28, 1790.
[96] Thomas Madiou, Histoire d'Haiti (Port-au-Prince, 1847), Vol. 1, 39.
[97] Descourtliz, Histoire, 145; AD Gironde, 61 J 71.
[98] Nouvelles de Saint-Domingue, March 9, 1790.
[99] Étienne de Joly, Adresse des citoyens de couleur des Isles & colonies françoises; à
     l'Assemblée générale des représentans de la Commune de Paris, Prononcée le premier
     Février 1790 (Paris, 1790), 2–3.
[100] AN D XXV 89 9 30.
[101] Browning, Despatches, 295.

Meanwhile, *amis des noirs* expanded their activities. Brissot in March 1790 sought to make the society "more Liberal & extensive," as mass politics and radicalization enabled new possibilities. International examples still inspired: Brissot reported an (overly optimistic) letter from New York "that a very considerable number of friends have applied to Congress for the abolition of slavery throughout the United States." Meanwhile, if "the trade is abolished in the House of Commons, their labors will revive enthusiasm in our National Assembly." French Revolutionaries would be too "ashamed" not to join such a grand humanitarian project.[102] Abolitionists' audacity advanced, despite manifold national and international obstacles.

Massiac allies continued denouncing the *amis des noirs*, claiming the abolitionists conspired with the British and presenting wild accounts of what their rivals might accomplish. Toulouse's *Nouvelliste national* in March 1790 printed "grave accusations against *les amis des noirs*" for "corresponding with the English," who "want at the price of their colonies to cost us ours," claiming French profits exceeded their rivals'. Old rivalries proved easy to reinflame, while fears that abolitionist dialogues could "spread amongst the negroes maxims of independence" outweighed most advantages.[103] Nevertheless, antislavery activists kept pursuing broad alliances.

With the March 8 Decree of 1790, the National Assembly – fearing the economic and strategic implications of destabilization – attempted to broker colonial compromise, albeit one favoring whites.[104] The decree excluded the colonies from the forthcoming French Constitution's full provisions. Each would form a Colonial Assembly to adapt French revolutionary principles to local contexts by composing a revised document. The Rights of Man would be abrogated with slavery and the slave trade continuing unimpeded. Colonial whites celebrated French respect for "their climate, their customs, their interests."[105] However, the assembly also granted the *gens* support, decreeing "all free persons" paying requisite taxes possessed voting rights, which colonial authorities refused to enforce.[106] In Saint-Domingue, there remained no prospect of a white assembly voluntarily sharing power with free blacks.

Atrocities multiplied in the uncertain atmosphere. In April, Le Cap authorities executed Augustin Lacombe, a free man of color arrested the previous fall for asserting the entire Declaration of Rights should apply in the colony. On

---

[102] SJCL Clarkson 1 11, 12.

[103] *Nouvelliste national*, March 8, 1790; Alan Forrest, *The Death of the French Atlantic: Trade, War and Slavery in the Age of Revolution* (Oxford: Oxford University Press, 2020), 121.

[104] Jeremy J. Whiteman, *Reform, Revolution and French Global Policy, 1787–1791* (London: Ashgate, 2003), 169–214.

[105] *Suite de la découverte d'une conspiration contre les intérêts de la France* (S.l., 1790), 51.

[106] Garran de Coulon, *An Inquiry into the Causes of the Insurrection of the Negroes in the Island of Santo Domingo* (London, 1792), 11–12.

June 3, white militias in Saint-Pierre, Martinique assembled for a religious procession that black militiamen attempted to join. After a fight erupted between a mulatto and a white man, a race riot ensued killing nineteen *gens de couleur* and three white officers.[107] The extreme brutality predicating the colonial order encouraged insecure whites to commit escalating atrocities.

White politics became intractably contentious. The General Assembly survived a June 1790 referendum, winning most support in the South and West provinces, but unwisely continued attempting to consolidate power thereafter.[108] A breach opened between those favoring French authority (strong in the Northern province) and those supporting the revolutionary General Assembly. Wimpffen, writing a final letter before departing for Europe from Port-au-Prince in July 1790, saw the colony's "political fever" reaching the "first convulsions of a delirium." Neither the governor nor assembly appeared able to weather the crisis. Despite the propertied classes having "equal interest in maintaining order," a "revolutionary vertigo" set in. The colony's political convulsions led whites to "indulge themselves in the most imprudent discussions on liberty," which reached slaves' ears and minds. Colonial "ruin" beckoned. Wimpffen left Saint-Domingue exclaiming, "the more I know the inhabitants, the more I felicitate myself on quitting it."[109]

Saint-Domingue became regionally divided. After the General Assembly declared internal autonomy, rumors spread of an American-style revolution for independence from France, while others feared the colony being "sold to the English," alleging 40 million *livres* distributed to assemblymen in bribes (made more plausible by a decree opening colonial ports to all nations' ships). Militias organized, adapting the model of America's Committees of Correspondence for defensive alliances, with each side accusing the other of subverting the French Revolution. Le Cap's provincial Assembly of the North, which unlike the General Assembly accepted subordination to the National Assembly, became a separate regime. Northern militiamen emptied arsenals to establish a six thousand–man force, abjuring loyalty to the General Assembly (accusing them of desiring colonial independence) and aligning with the governor.[110] The Provincial Assembly decreed they would not follow General Assembly decrees without the provincial assemblies', governor's, National Assembly's, and king's approval. After reconciliation attempts failed, provincial authorities ordered a General Assembly delegation to leave Le Cap,

[107] Geggus, *The Haitian Revolution: A Documentary History* (Indianapolis: Hackett, 2014), 60; Médéric Moreau de Saint-Méry, *Considérations présentées aux vrais amis de repos et du Bonheur de la France, à l'occasion des nouveaux mouvemens de quelques soi-disant Amis-des-noirs.* (Paris, 1791), 23.

[108] Mills, *Early*, 66.

[109] Wimpffen, *Voyage*, 333–36.

[110] Edwards, *History*, 338–39; Descourtliz, *Histoire*, 153; AD Gironde C 4369 1; *Cumberland Gazette*, May 3, 1790; *Rélation authentique*, 5; AD Loire-Atlantique E 691.

which responded by decreeing the Provincial Assembly traitors.[111] As competing authorities multiplied, colonial coordination disintegrated.

Royal governor the Comte de Penier attempted to suppress the General Assembly, proclaiming in Port-au-Prince on July 29 the assemblymen "traitors" themselves and issuing arrest orders.[112] With the capital increasingly divided, skirmishes that night killed five – Colonel Thomas-Antoine Maudit du Plessis justified opening fire by asserting "one part of the town would surely soon be massacred by the other" otherwise – after which the General Assembly invited "all good citizens to arm in defense."[113] Saint-Marc's municipality sent a deputation "swearing to shed the last drop of their blood to defend Saint-Domingue's representatives." Accounts reaching France described the colony as "prey to despotism's furors" with "cowardly assassinations militarily committed on peaceful citizens."[114] Western parish assemblies in August planned a "confederation" gathering to rally support but were dissuaded by authorities, while a similar pro-assembly muster occurred in the South.[115]

No authorities could alleviate escalating factional tensions. With civil war becoming probable, the assembly fled. Eighty-five members on August 10, 1790, embarked for France aboard the mutinous French warship *Léopard*, declaring they would take their case to the king and National Assembly. On arrival, they reported "open war" between Saint-Domingue's factions.[116] France's National Assembly, however, disdaining General Assembly pretensions to independence, declared the colonial assembly dissolved and its members ineligible for further office. Barnave, speaking for the National Assembly's Colonial Committee, reported the General Assembly acting as though French authorities were "devoid of any right to impose laws" there. Having "not only refused allegiance to the mother country, but even communication," they were blamed for the disorders and "stripped of all power as Deputies."[117] The National Assembly declared General Assembly laws null and charged the governor with enforcing the status quo ante until new elections.[118]

The colony the assemblymen left behind fell into "anarchy" with centralized power disintegrating and alliances uncertain.[119] In the crackdown against General Assembly supporters, an American consul described "an almost

[111] Tarbé, *Rapport*, 12; Brown, *History and Present*, Vol. 1, 149–50.
[112] Tarbé, *Rapport*, 13; *Affiches américaines*, August 14, 1790.
[113] Descourtliz, *Histoire*, 154; Stoddard, *French*, 107.
[114] *Rélation exacte des troubles de S. Domingue et les attentats commis par les agens du pouvoir exécutif, dans la nuit du 29 au 30 juillet 1790* (Paris: Caillot, 1790), 2–3.
[115] Tarbé, *Rapport*, 18; Lacroix, *Mémoires*, Vol. 1, 49.
[116] *London Chronicle*, September 18, 1790; Popkin, *You*, 71.
[117] *St. James's Chronicle*, October 16, 1790; James Franklin, *The Present State of Hayti* (London: Murray, 1828), 56–57.
[118] Garrett, *French*, 75.
[119] Descourtliz, *Histoire*, 158; *Nouvelles de Saint-Domingue*, No. 7.

total suspension of justice as well as government."[120] Dissention continued, with the government receiving little urban support in the South and West: Governor Penier's successor the Vicomte de Blanchelande, taking office in late 1790, found "the diversity of opinions divides everyone," especially dangerous as the colony "has no existence except through Slaves."[121] Defiance of central authority led a British correspondent to compare events "to nothing but the troubles at Boston" in the 1770s.[122] Despite a formal truce between factions after the General Assembly's departure, few expected peace to hold. Amid a metastasizing panoply of alliances, associations, and antagonisms, Saint-Domingue radicalized even faster than France itself.

The Arrival of the Haitian Revolution

Saint-Domingue whites, having warned since the Revolution's outbreak of French radicals infiltrating their colony and leading rebellions, found their fears confirmed with Vincent Ogé's insurrection. From a rich merchant and coffee plantation-owning family, Ogé lived in Bordeaux at the Revolution's outbreak. Traveling to Paris, he joined the *amis des noirs* but in September 1789 appeared before Club Massiac, offering to help lead a responsible revolution granting political rights to all men of property. However, he warned, "if we do not quickly bring together all our enlighten-ment, all our means, all our efforts ... blood will flow" thereafter. "Commerce would be annihilated, France receive a mortal blow, and a multitude of honest men impoverished, ruined; we would lose everything."[123] Taken aback by Ogé's prophecies, Club Massiac's majority, promoting racial hierarchy and disdainful of free men of color, refused to work with him. Ogé joined the pamphlet war, publishing his address and signing *gens de couleur* petitions.[124]

Disappointed by Parisian rejection, Ogé returned to Saint-Domingue to raise a rebellion. Taking an indirect route via London – with Brissot and Clarkson's knowledge, interacting with abolitionists – and Charleston, Ogé arrived in Saint-Domingue (possibly disguised as an American sailor) on October 12, 1790.[125] In his native Dondon, Ogé recruited nearly six hundred men, plus additional agents traveling across Saint-Domingue to spark a colony-wide insurrection. Seeking an exemplary victory to motivate *gens de couleur* to rebel en masse, Ogé attacked Grande-Rivière the night of

---

[120] AN 251 MI 1.

[121] Ibid.; ANOM Correspondance générale 213 MIOM 138 20; *Courrier politique et littéraire du Cap-Français*, April 21, 1791.

[122] *Public Advertiser*, September 30, 1790.

[123] Vincent Ogé, *Motion faite par M. Vincent Ogé, jeune, à l'assemblée des colons, habitans de S-Domingue, à l'hôtel de Massiac* (Paris, 1789), 5; Brown, *History and Present*, Vol. 1, 157.

[124] Garrigus, *Before*, 48–49.

[125] SJCL Clarkson 1, 11 and 15; Scott, *Common*, 116.

October 28, occupying the town and disarming whites without bloodshed. Ogé wrote to the Assembly of the North demanding full equality for *gens de couleur* per the National Assembly's decrees, while making clear "we will no longer rest under the yoke, as we have for two centuries." The northern legislature responded by declaring a state of emergency. Troops and militiamen departed from Le Cap to pursue the rebels, capturing many. The band's remnants fled over the border into Santo Domingo, where Ogé was arrested by Spanish forces no more interested than the French in seeing their colonial order destabilized.[126]

Ogé's actions spurred revolts in the West and South provinces. In the western town of Petite-Rivière, where authorities rebuffed *gens'* earlier voting rights petitions, an uprising began that was not defused until reinforcements arrived from Saint-Marc. Royal authorities met free black leaders, persuading them to disperse after promising concessions. In the South, authorities and rebels made a similar truce after a smaller standoff, arousing white suspicions. Nevertheless, the North's Provost wrote to the General Assembly, "Ogé would not have acted without being confident of support" from men of color.[127] Further uprisings became likely.

Despite negotiated truces and authorities' calls for "unity," Ogé's insurrection diminished what little trust existed between white and free black communities.[128] Planters could not ignore their parallels with the French aristocracy, nor revolutionary insurrection's potential for overthrowing white privilege. *Gens de couleur* at Le Cap, attempting to survive the reaction, felt obligated to "protest their fidelity," as rumors spread of whites vowing "vengeance upon the whole race" through massacres.[129] Back in France, the Massiac network received British reports of Ogé's meeting Clarkson, and asserted international abolitionists had sent Ogé "to operate by deed what they could not obtain by right."[130]

Rather than allowing the episode to die down, Le Cap's superior court instead sentenced Ogé to exemplary public punishment. Ogé and his chief lieutenant were publicly broken on the wheel and put to death, followed by two hundred rebels' execution. Rumors nevertheless flew that mulattoes would rise to "avenge" their fallen. Still more perniciously, authorities condemned others to death in absentia – many of whom hid until August's slave rising.[131] While

---

[126] Tarbé, *Rapport*, 21–22; Dalmas, *Histoire*, 70–72; Madiou, *Histoire*, 57–58; AN D XXV 86 829 3 and DXXV 89 9 65; AD Loire-Atlantique C 627 65.

[127] *Nouvelles de Saint-Domingue*, No. 27; Moreau, *Considérations*, 26; Edwards, *History*, 242.

[128] *Gazette du jour*, November 10, 1790; *Affiches américaines*, November 18, 1790.

[129] Descourtliz, *Histoire*, 163; Edwards, *History*, 343.

[130] AD DXXV 90 6 35.

[131] James Barskett, *History of the Island of St. Domingo: From Its First Discovery by Columbus to the Present* (S.l., 1818), 78; *Carlisle Gazette*, March 30, 1791; Dalmas,

the colonial press refused to carry updates on Ogé's uprising, they publicized the punishment, and little could be done to prevent sensational retellings across the colony and ocean.[132] In Paris, Saint-Domingue deputies denounced the *amis des noirs*, asserting the Ogé insurrection was just the network's first foray and they would "sacrifice 100,000 whites to establish their erroneous system."[133] In publicizing violence, planter interests heightened its likelihood.

The only commonality among the factions fighting for power was their antipathy toward Saint-Domingue's massive slave majority. Raimond, writing to colonial *gens de couleur*, advised letting the National Assembly "pronounce the slaves' future," after they "reconciled residents' properties and the home country's interests."[134] As free men, the *gens'* status would be addressed first. Slaves were told, "no alleviation of their miseries was ever to be expected from Europe," and their "humble interests had been equally sacrificed or forgotten by all parties."[135]

In metropolitan France, Ogé's insurrection moved public opinion in the free blacks' favor. Ogé became a martyr for liberty, fighting planter despotism. His torture and execution embodied colonial "cruelty" and "injustice."[136] After news arrived, the municipality of Bordeaux – a city with a significant mixed-race population, many of whom knew Ogé personally – endorsed full *gens de couleur* political rights.[137] With dissatisfaction growing toward the aristocracy and the limitations on voting rights within France, free black rights became politically resonant. The National Assembly remained embroiled in colonial controversies, discussing such issues fifty-one times between March 1790 and May 1791. Under pressure, the assembly increasingly rejected the colonial status quo. Although eleven National Assemblymen were members of both Club Massiac and the Jacobins, the latter began a petitioning campaign for *gens de couleur* voting rights.[138] The rich symbolism and high risks of colonial contestations over liberty enlivened French revolutionary debates.

Politics among colonial whites continued to destablize. In February, word arrived that the National Assembly would not reinstate the exiled General Assembly, leading to "delirious joy" at Le Cap.[139] The uncertainty of what

Histoire, 98; Benot, "The Insurgents of 1791, Their Leaders, and the Concept of Independence," in Geggus and Fiering, *World*, 100.

[132] Popkin, "A Colonial Media Revolution: The Press in Saint-Domingue, 1789–1793," *The Americas* 75, no. 1 (2018), 7.

[133] AD Loire-Atlantique C 628 156.

[134] Raimond, *Correspondance de Julien Raimond avec ses frères de Saint-Domingue* (Paris: Cercle sociale, 1793), 14.

[135] Garran de Coulon, *Inquiry*, 15.

[136] Dalmas, *Histoire*, 109.

[137] Geggus, "Racial," 1302; Debien, *Colons*, 107.

[138] Léon Deschamps, *La constituante et les colonies: la réforme colonial* (Paris: Perrin, 1898), 184; Gauthier, *L'aristocratie*, 151.

[139] Descourtliz, *Histoire*, 167.

order would emerge, however, led to new outbreaks of violence. Colonel Maudit, in retribution for firing on Port-au-Prince protesters the previous July, was confronted by his soldiers and, after refusing to repent, assassinated at the massacre site. The troops placed his dismembered head atop a bayonet, dragged his body through the streets "to the various spots where he had repulsed force with force," and leveled his house. Governor Blanchelande, fearing he would be the next target, abandoned the capital to hide.[140] With royalists cowed, fearing a wider massacre and "military despotism," the colony's political future remained fraught.[141] Le Cap's Assembly of the North held an honorary funeral for Maudit to display their disapprobation.[142] Governance remained lax: Caribbean pirates infested the coasts and few prospects remained for ending factionalism.[143]

Troops sent from France to Port-au-Prince to keep royal authority in place and supervise new General Assembly elections joined the municipal faction backing the exiled legislature. When the soldiers disembarked, "every house and cellar were thrown open" and they "feasted on the luxuries of the tropics."[144] Already nearly mutinous, the soldiers pledged loyalty to the municipal faction. Still, the victory remained incomplete: "we cannot hide," the new General Assembly wrote to allies in Le Havre, "that the peril is extreme and a prompt remedy must be applied."[145] French aid inflamed factionalism.

Saint-Domingue approached a political precipice. Despite a Port-au-Prince attempt to found a Jacobin Club calling colonists to "unite" for the "*cause commune*," divides worsened.[146] One letter viewed the colony as divided into two parties: the *pompons rouges* ("the late Colonial Assembly's friends") and *pompons blancs* ("the friends of the government, whom others call aristocrats"). The red faction held sway at Port-au-Prince and across the South, while the whites controlled Le Cap and the North. The "two parties are extremely violent against each other," and many feared "animosities will break into open civil war," especially as French troops favored the red faction. The General Assembly elections might "restore tranquility to the island, or increase the fermentation which at present too unhappily prevails."[147] With

---

[140] Tarbé, *Rapport*, 25–26; *Connecticut Journal*, April 13, 1791; Lacroix, *Mémoires*, Vol. 1, 75; Bibliothèque municipale de Nantes, "Lettre sur les désordres de Port-au-Prince (4 mars 1791)," MS 1810; *Moniteur colonial*, March 10, 1791.
[141] *Whitehall Evening Post*, May 3, 1791; Brown, *History and Present*, Vol. 1, 165; AM Le Havre F(2) 11.
[142] *Courrier politique et littéraire du Cap-Français*, May 12, 1791.
[143] *Gazette de Saint-Domingue*, January 12, 1790.
[144] Brown, *History and Present*, Vol. 1, 164.
[145] *Gazette du jour*, November 21, 1790.
[146] *Courrier politique et littéraire du Cap-Français*, June 5, 1791.
[147] *Daily Advertiser*, May 10, 1791.

civil war looming between whites, their ability to control the slave and free-black populations lessened.

In France the same month, domestic pressures led the National Assembly after five days' debate to a compromise with the May 15 Decree, which enfranchised *gens de couleur* born of free parents and possessing sufficient property – a small minority – to vote in General Assembly elections. Discussions grew heated "not just in the Assembly, but in the city," as many Parisians identified with the free blacks' cause, publicly insulting colonial representatives.[148] Planter deputies bitterly protested the decision, withdrawing from the assembly, while Nantes merchants envisaged "losing all our colonies."[149] When word reached Saint-Domingue, whites reacted with "fury," accusing the National Assembly of "treachery," for having "abandoned us" amid crisis.[150] The Assembly of the North considered severe boycotts, including an embargo on France-bound ships, suspending payments home, and refusing all arriving vessels, "even the *nègriers*," but adopted none.[151] White militiamen in Le Cap began forcibly disarming black and mixed-race counterparts, as fragile colonial compacts ruptured.[152]

French control over their most important colony fell into crisis. The General Assembly defiantly wore the counter-revolution's black cockades instead of revolutionary tricolors, while National Assemblyman and abolitionist Abbé Grégoire hung in effigy on a Le Cap street. Blanchelande declared he could not enforce the enfranchisement decree. Voting assemblies pledged only to follow the March 8 decree granting political autonomy.[153] The planters considered allowing *gens* to vote "the violation of the holiest promises, destroying the colony's foundation."[154] The divide between white colonists and free blacks appeared insurmountable. A new General Assembly was elected via predominantly white suffrage and even moderate reform proved unenforceable in Saint-Domingue's political cauldron.

Gens de couleur sought to force planter acceptance of their political aims. As the new assembly took power in May, free blacks began organizing armed militias. Rebel bands in July seized a military fortress in the south and a "powerful body surrounded Port-au-Prince," demanding full enforcement of the National Assembly's decree. When government troops fired on the

---

[148] AM Marseille 4 D 3 76.
[149] AD Gironde C 4371 49.
[150] *St. James's Chronicle*, August 30, 1791; Garrett, *French*, 98–101.
[151] AD Loire-Atlantique 1 ET A 28 79.
[152] Gower, *Despatches*, 116.
[153] John D. Garrigus, *Before Haiti: Race and Citizenship in French Saint-Domingue* (New York: Palgrave Macmillan, 2006), 259; *Woodfall's Register*, May 26, 1791; *Morning Chronicle*, September 6, 1791; Geggus, "Racial," 1303; Dalmas, *Histoire*, 113–14; Edwards, *History*, 347.
[154] Descourtliz, *Histoire*, 177.

rebels, "they spread over the country, and set fire indiscriminately to all the plantations" within reach.[155] The northern province, however, remained quiet and troops repressed the southern disturbances. Though executing 113 *gens de couleur*, some whites considered the "hangmen insufficient," as rebels lurked in the mountains.[156] The colony reached a "dangerous state of fermentation," alternately from free blacks and independence-seeking whites, while rumors spread of the National Assembly inciting troubles as a pretext for "the abolition of slavery."[157] The social order verged on disintegration.

As politics radicalized and inhibitions fell, virtually any change became thinkable, including ending slavery itself. National Assemblyman Jean-Louis de Viefville des Essarts on May 11, 1791, proposed abolishing colonial slavery. Describing the practice as "a violation of all social and humane laws," he asserted French revolutionaries needed to "efface ancient servitude's last traces" from all territories. Though wanting to "soften" the measure through gradual abolition, a new order became necessary as the old one crumbled.[158] The assembly's majority still collaborated with slaveholding whites, while potential compromises shrank, but none could discount the possibility of radical change.

All these destabilizations by August 1791 helped motivate slaves to revolt. Power became so diffuse and rivalries so bitter among the colony's free men that the moment seemed precipitous for an uprising. Despite localized slave rebellions' suppression near Port-au-Prince in June and July, north coast slaves planned a massive uprising to overwhelm the fragile colonial system. An abortive attempt occurred near the northern town of Limbé on August 11 that government troops crushed, inspiring white overconfidence.[159] Trusted slaves, permitted to socialize with others from nearby plantations on Sundays, coordinated a broad conspiracy. At Bois Caiman (Alligator Wood) between the Morne Rouge mountains and coastal plain, abutting the Lenormand de Mézy plantation, on August 14, 1791, two hundred elite slaves ("two deputies" per plantation) met to finalize plans for an uprising. They read a document purporting Louis XVI had granted slaves three days per week of liberty and abolished corporal punishment.[160] Garbled news of the king's flight to

---

[155] *An Inquiry into the Causes of the Insurrection of the Negroes in the Island of St. Domingo* (London: Johnson, 1792), 19–20; Barskett, *History*, 84.

[156] *Evening Mail*, July 27, 1791; Lacroix, *Mémoires*, Vol. 1, 88.

[157] *London Chronicle*, August 27, 1791; *Morning Post*, September 2, 1791; Rouvray, *Correspondance* 19.

[158] Jean-Louis de Viefville des Essarts, *Discours et projet de loi pour l'affranchissement des nègres, ou l'adoucissement de leur régime, et réponse aux objections des colons* (Paris: Imprimerie nationale, 1791) 1–2, 26.

[159] Brown, *History and Present*, Vol. 1, 172; Stoddard, *French*, 129.

[160] Landers, *Atlantic*, 60; Fick, *Making*, 91; Geggus, *Haitian*, 81; Antoine Métral, *Histoire de l'insurrection des esclaves dans le nord de Saint-Domingue* (Paris: Scherff, 1818), 15.

Varennes lent the story more plausibility. Slaves asserted they were rebelling for their rights.

Presiding at the August 14 ceremony was Boukman Dutty, trusted slave coach-driver and voodoo priest, who called the slaves to action. After a pig sacrifice, he rallied his compatriots to arms in the name of French revolutionary liberty and resistance to oppression:

> This is the first time, my dear comrades, that liberty unites us ... Every year the sea and the earth are watered with our tears and our blood ... only to enrich masters who live in abundance and laziness, while we lack everything necessary. There are none among us who are not sullied by tyranny's imprint ... They deflower our daughters barely out of childhood, profane our unions by adultery .... The past only presents unexampled crimes towards us and our race; as will the future. Children of the Sun, what is there between us and our masters? .... Oppression has only fallen too often on our heads .... Let us act with force; our population is innumerable, compared to our terrible enemies. ... Let's make these workshops, eternal instrument of our slavery, no more than ashes and ruins! ... comrades, let's take our liberty .... Destruction and carnage are inevitable passageways from servitude to freedom.[161]

Though only published in 1818, the speech's essentials bear marks of the revolutionary ferment visible to a well-placed slave. Revolutionary principles, together with political destabilization, opened the way for an unexampled slave insurrection.

Surreptitious planning meetings occurred on area plantations. At one, slave leaders asserted, "the moment of vengeance approaches; tomorrow, in the night, all the whites must be exterminated."[162] Authorities arrested several suspects the night of August 21, who under interrogation falsely said the conspiracy would unfold in Le Cap and did not specify whether it would be an insurrection of whites, free blacks, or slaves (each being plausible). With the town's vicinity quiet, authorities considered the rumors another of the many "false alarms" spread over the prior two years.[163]

The uprising began the night of August 22. In a ceremony on the Choiseuil plantation on the northern plain, plotters ceremonially sacrificed a second pig and then launched their attack, overwhelming several plantations, killing whites, smashing equipment, burning fields, and destroying sugar refineries. The flames signaled surrounding areas to rise in turn. Slaves from a hundred sugar plantations joined the conflagration.[164]

[161] Métral, *Histoire*, 16–19.
[162] Dalmas, *Histoire*, 117.
[163] Filbert-François de Blanchelande, *Supplément au Mémoire de M. Blanchelande, sur son administration à Saint-Domingue* (Paris, s.d.), 9.
[164] Madiou, *Histoire*, 70; Félix Carteau, *Soirées bermudiennes, ou Entretiens sur les événemens qui ont opéré la ruine de la partie française de l'Isle Saint-Domingue*

News of the insurrection reached Le Cap the morning of August 23, as did the first waves of white refugees fleeing the advancing rebels. Reportedly, "the revolters proceeded from parish to parish, murdering the men, and ravishing the unfortunate women who fell into their hands." Quickly, as became apparent from town, "the sword was exchanged for the torch, and the cane-fields blazed in every direction."[165] White planter families, with loyal slaves, poured in with "accounts of continued distress and destruction."[166] The insurrection spread alarmingly: 50,000–100,000 slaves rebelled and 453 plantations burned.[167] Captured leaders related the slaves' ambitions to "burn every thing in the plain, and even Cape François [Le Cap]."[168] The planter Carteau, observing from Le Cap, described "the whole horizon" in flames, producing a "rain of fire from burning cane-straw" that winds carried into town. "Such was their voracity that for nearly three weeks we could scarcely distinguish between night and day," as the city residents choked amid the destruction.[169]

Even in retreat, many whites reacted to the slave uprising with blind fury. One letter boasted of white militias having "killed an infinity of negroes" to contain the insurrection.[170] Rumors flew of the insurrection organizing through secret cabals in Le Cap that the rural uprising was just a first phase, as "the conspiracy must be general" across the colony.[171] Word spread that the most trusted slaves had planned the insurrection and, as one Le Cap resident related, suspicion fell on "our valets, our workers, our bakers, our cooks, our nurses," destroying local bonds of trust.[172] Urban mobs of *petits blancs* attacked the first men of color they saw" and murdered as indiscriminately as they believed rebel slaves did. Most *gens de couleur* took refuge in a religious house, surrounded by a military guard, hoping the populace's rage would subside. Some, despite owning slaves themselves and initially opposing the uprising, joined the rebels.[173] Only desperation brought on by the slaves' advance led to a truce between whites and free blacks (who had faced disarmament after the Ogé uprising) to reintegrate the latter into the National Guard

---

(Bordeaux: Pellier, 1802), 86; Geggus, *Haitian Revolutionary Studies* (Bloomington: Indiana University Press, 2002), 12.

[165] Edwards, *History*, 349; *Daily Advertiser*, October 10, 1791.

[166] *Independent Gazetteer*, October 8, 1791.

[167] *Daily Advertiser*, October 20, 1791; AN 252 MI 28; AD Charente-Maritime 41 ETP 175 5006.

[168] *Litchfield Monitor*, October 26, 1791.

[169] Stoddard, *French*, 131.

[170] AN D XXV 78 90.

[171] AD Charente-Maritime 41 ETP 175 4979.

[172] Ibid., 5006.

[173] Descourtliz, *Histoire*, 183; Dalmas, *Histoire*, 127; Tarbé, *Rapport*, 38; Garrigus, "Saint Domingue's Free People of Color and the Tools of Revolution," in Geggus and Fiering, 49.

on August 25.[174] Saint-Domingue's fractured social order lost important time against the slave uprising to a combination of rivalry, reprisal, and racial hatred.

Slave insurgents repulsed all militia attempts at suppression, despite possessing "no fire arms" and fighting with "procured daggers, knives, swords and other weapons."[175] Despite facing trained colonial militia, they persevered, as government forces "commonly put to death on the spot" slaves attempting to surrender, or seized them for torture. Despite killing an estimated thousand insurgents during the first days, Le Cap's militias could not venture far into the countryside. Slaves dominated the tropical hills, where white troops "tired quickly, from heat and fatigue."[176] Ignorant city-dwellers commonly massacred neutral slaves or even those defending their master's property, motivating more to become insurgents. Rebel slaves, likely 60–70 percent African-born, preyed on detachments with hit-and-run guerilla tactics likely borrowed from Congolese warfare. White-led forces became so preoccupied with massacring that they often neglected to press their military advantage.[177]

Violence spread, as insurrection flared in the western province. Eight days after the northern slave rising, two thousand gens de couleur formed an "armed camp" outside Port-au-Prince. Realizing themselves "almost as numerous as the whites" and more united, the movement sought political rights whites refused them.[178] The gens' insurrection burned an area extending ten leagues with Governor Blanchelande alleging their "committing the same excesses and cruelties on whites as in the North." Rumors spread of their burning Port-au-Prince or inciting area slaves to insurrection. White colonials' position became so untenable they negotiated a treaty with the free black insurgents, granting them voting rights on the National Assembly's compromise terms.[179] Even this served only as a temporary truce, however, as France's newly elected National

---

[174] *Copie de la lettre de M. Nicoleau, habitant de Saint-Domingue. Au Cap, le 3 septembre 1791* (S.l., 1791), 2; ANOM 213 MIOM 138 119; *Gazette de Saint-Domingue*, September 3, 1791.

[175] *Dunlap's American Daily Advertiser*, September 22, 1791.

[176] Tarbé, *Rapport*, 47; *Independent Gazetteer*, October 8, 1791.

[177] Thomas O. Ott, *The Haitian Revolution, 1789–1804* (Knoxville: University of Tennessee Press, 1973), 48; Lacroix, *Mémoires*, Vol. 1, 99; Dubois, *Avengers*, 109; Robin Law, "La cérémonie du Bois Caiman et le 'pacte de sang' dahoméen," in Lannec Hurbon, ed. *L'insurrection des esclaves de Saint-Domingue (22–23 août 1791): actes de la table ronde international de Port-au-Prince, 8 au 10 décembre 1997* (Paris: Karthala, 2000), 131; Carteau, *Soirées*, 99.

[178] Stoddard, *French*, 142–43.

[179] Blanchelande, *Supplément*, 15; AN D XXV 110 Fol. 872, no. 74; Henri de Grimouard, *L'amiral de Grimouard au Port-au-Prince: d'après sa correspondance et son journal de bord (mars 1791-juillet 1792)* (Paris: Larose, 1937), 39.

Assembly in September repealed the May 15 Decree after hearing of the colonies' reaction. When word of repeal arrived in October, colonial whites ended their truce, *gens de couleur* flew to arms, and in one brutal battle two thousand blacks perished against better-armed colonial militiamen.[180] Whites remained excessively confident, expecting outright victory, and maintained no alliances with free men of color.

Planters responded with a hard line against revolutionary principles and those spreading them. The General Assembly's president wrote to Jamaica's legislature, prophesizing, "In a short time, this delightful country will be but a heap of ashes." He blamed "Principles, destructive of our property," having "kindled a flame amongst us, and armed the hands of our own slaves. Philosophy, which is the consolation of mankind, has reduced us to despair."[181] Only stopping revolutionary ideas' spread, and suppressing uprisings, could restore the colony. In France, meanwhile, many blamed the *amis des noirs* for inciting such destruction. A December 1791 colonial petition to the king accused those who had, following Robespierre's heated words, "prophetically" called for "the colonies to perish rather than our principles."[182] The *amis des noirs* advocated the insurrection's repression, while blaming planter cruelty and promoting full equality among free men to restore peace.[183] French financial interests gained the planters a more sympathetic hearing, while the *amis* faded from revolutionary politics.

Over a dozen years of civil war followed. As late as December 1791, slaves only asked for abolishing whipping as a punishment, an extra day of rest per week, and three hundred leaders' manumission, but the General Assembly rejected those terms.[184] By 1794, facing worsening conditions including British and Spanish invasions alongside continuing slave rebellions, French authorities took the drastic step of abolishing colonial slavery, attempting to win rebel slaves back to the French Revolution's side. Though a new order emerged under Louverture's subsequent dictatorship, Napoleon's attempt to reestablish white control over the colony led to another lengthy round of warfare ending in Haiti's 1804 independence – making the Haitian Revolution history's only successful slave rebellion, but resulting in an impoverished and isolated independent nation.

---

[180] Edwards, *History*, 353–54.

[181] *General Advertiser*, October 8, 1791.

[182] *Adresse au roi et discours à Sa Majesté par les colons français de Saint-Domingue réunis à Paris* (Paris, 1791), 5–6.

[183] Dorigny, "Le movement abolitionniste français face à l'insurrection de Saint-Domingue ou la fin du mythe de l'abolition graduelle," in *L'insurrection des esclaves de Saint-Domingue (22–3 août 1791)*, Laennec Hurbon, ed. (Paris: Karthala, 2000), 106–7.

[184] Bell, *Toussaint*, 33.

Conclusion

In August 1791, more than fifty American ships, and an untold greater number flying the French tricolor, moored in Le Cap's harbor as the plantations burned.[185] Stories of the rebellion, and large numbers of planter refugees, spread throughout the Atlantic Basin (Philadelphia becoming nicknamed the "New Cape").[186] The shocking event, however, was by no means unthinkable – slave rebellion had been a constant fear throughout American societies. The methods used, moreover, by all political factions over the two years preceding the slave rebellion's outbreak – particularly meeting and correspondence-based social movements – were adapted from the associational models of their recent social movement predecessors. Contrary to widespread scholarly emphasis, the social movements that unleashed the Haitian Revolution closely followed recent international designs and humanitarian debates.[187] The slave meeting at Bois Caiman in its ambitious alliance-building around principles of liberty echoed its Atlantic predecessors. The spread of ideas and debates about radical equality, radicalizing from limited contestations over middle-class political participation into often-absolute proclamations of freedom that resonated with slaves themselves, in a matter of months turned the abolition of slavery from an impossibility to a legitimate hope and threat. The Haitian Revolution could not have occurred as it did or when it did without French revolutionary instigations. Though a repudiation of the French Revolution's shortcomings, the Haitian Revolution owed much of its form and radicalism to its Atlantic revolutionary brethren.

---

[185] Gordon S. Brown, *Toussaint's Clause: The Founding Fathers and the Haitian Revolution* (Jackson, MS: University Press of Mississippi, 2005), 49.

[186] White, *Encountering*, 11.

[187] Popkin, *You*, esp. 12–22; John K. Thornton, "I Am the Subject of the King of Congo": African Political Ideology and the Haitian Revolution," *Journal of World History* 4, no. 2 (1993) 181–214; Fick, *Making*.

11

The French Jacobin Network in Power

On March 11, 1792, Angers' Jacobins gathered for festivities celebrating not just France's revolution, but the "free peoples of the world": French, English, Americans, and Poles. In a ceremony repeated in numerous cities that winter, revolutionaries marched the four national flags across town before hanging them for permanent display in the Jacobins' hall. With international war on the horizon, cries along the parade route included *"Long live liberty! Equality or death! Peace to all peoples, war to all despots! Long live the nations, death to tyrants!"* Jacobin orators declared it time to "enlighten the universe with a new order" and end "slavery's reign." Hoping to "establish free communication of ideas," they sent their proceedings abroad to the Whig Club, American Congress, Polish Diet, and "all the kings of Europe opposed to our revolution," elaborating, "it is against despots, against tyrants that we mobilize."[1]

The Jacobins took their revolutionary role and radical rhetoric seriously. Believing peace near, perhaps a universal one to end all wars, Jacobins pushed their model further. Sensing the incredible power of coordinated revolutionary action, nothing seemed impossible. Operating in tandem with the early French Republic's radical governments, the Jacobins helped implement more radical changes than any prior social movement. Whereas the classic "thesis of circumstances" claims Jacobin-inspired revolutionaries led the French toward terror from fears of annihilation, Jacobin source records show hope and ambition remained at least as prominent for club activists across the early French Republic.

Such incredible possibilities for freedom and peace motivated the Jacobins to continue redoubling their efforts, especially against their growing legions of enemies. There appeared nowhere to go but further. With near-utopia seemingly close at hand, rooting out conspiracies perverting the natural progression toward liberty (and, in time, executing their ringleaders) became readily justifiable, pushing Jacobins to terrorist tactics. Incredible rigor seemed necessary to accomplish such designs. Only through their incredible ambitions for the world would the Jacobins lead the French toward terror.

[1] BM Poitiers S 26 146/1 8.

War for Freedom and the Fall of the Monarchy

Growing fears of counterrevolution piqued and intensified Jacobin network functions. On September 15, 1791, fifteen days before the new French Constitution's adoption, Paris's branch wrote a worried circular to fellow "friends of the constitution" on the need to intensify their activities. They called for greater educational outreach, to establish "points of reunion, where all fellow citizens can gather together on days off work, to hear the reading of public papers, good works, and explanations of them." More mobilization appeared necessary because of real threats from old elites and misguided commoners. The Jacobin network needed to remain vigilant, as "without the circulation of ideas ... liberty will soon be annihilated."[2] Comprehension of revolutionary concepts remained limited across France, and much light needed to be shone into the provinces' dark recesses.

While Jacobins continued believing in their revolutionary example's international power, un-liberated lands abroad harbored unknowably vast counterrevolutionary *émigré* factions. A Paris Jacobin address to "neighboring peoples" warned of counterrevolutionaries "making you instruments for their perfidious designs against our liberty." The Jacobins promised "just punishment" for enemy agents, while calling the "English, Belgians, Germans, Swiss, Savoyards, Piedmontese, Spanish" to become "a single people, a single family, of which disunion will hereafter be impossible."[3] If France, formerly Europe's most powerful absolutist monarchy, could be liberated, so could surrounding lands – despite contrary efforts from despotism's agents.

In the countryside, destabilized by religious conflicts, where the Jacobins often remained weak, counterrevolution threatened. Priests refusing to swear revolutionary oaths, hostile nobles, and conservative peasants militated against the new order. The southwestern small-town Lauzun Jacobins considered that "philosophical spirit has not made rapid progress," while many "women and men who are women" remained under priests' spells. Provincial branches feared infiltration with the Norman village of Condé-sur-Noireau in January 1792 calling "all patriotic societies to rally" against refractory agents, "whose number grows daily."[4] The club movement's overwhelmingly urban and middle-class composition left significant lacunae: Paris's Jacobins in February admitted they had "little penetrated the countryside" and endorsed rapid expansion into towns and villages.[5]

---

[2] AD Haute-Vienne L 822 89.
[3] *Adresse des sociétés des amis de la Constitution, établies en France, aux peuples voisins* (Paris: Imprimerie nationale, 1791), 2.
[4] *Journal des débats de la société des amis de la constitution*, nos. 3 and 1.
[5] Aulard, *Jacobins*, Vol. 3, 413–14.

Debates over declaring war on the Austrian Empire separated the offensive Girondins from the initially conflict-skeptical branch ultimately retaining the Jacobin name. First known as the "Brissotins," the pro-war group had grown friendly participating in the *amis des noirs, Cercle social*, and Jacobin Club. While still regularly attending Paris's branch, the core group also met for salons hosted by charismatic political wife Marie-Jeanne Roland (though future opponents like Robespierre also attended).[6] As the Legislative Assembly commenced, many newly elected provincial deputies, especially from Bordeaux and the Gironde region – often antislavery despite representing a slaving port – caucused with the well-connected activist and newspaperman-turned-assemblyman.[7] Brissot, invoking America's War of Independence, asserted a French revolutionary conflict could become a "crusade for universal liberty," which ally Maximin Isnard described as "a war of peoples against kings."[8] Many remained unconvinced, however, as prominent Jacobin (and future Committee of Public Safety member) Georges Couthon considered war rumblings the "vain cries of foolish emigrants."[9] Soon, legislators sat on the left, right, and center of the hall based on their political persuasions, as the previous National Assembly had. Together with the Feuillants, who initially held nearly half the Legislative Assembly's allegiance, but lost support as war fever progressed in late 1791, controlling the legislature became a contest between competing factions, all Jacobin descendants.[10]

Jacobins worried that prior allies would form new coalitions with the king and counterrevolutionaries. Paris's club warned their network in February that while "Feuillants no longer assemble," still "their spirit dominates the administration," and should they recruit "a National Assembly majority, counterrevolution will occur."[11] Indeed, a strange pro-war coalition formed across the political spectrum of radical Girondins, moderate Feuillants, and conservative ex-nobles.[12] With the Feuillants' attempted takeover of the Jacobin network having failed, radicals like Couthon feared they sought a new way to "annihilate the popular societies," potentially under wartime cover.[13] As Jacobins

---

[6] Kennedy, *Middle Years*, Vol. 2, 127; Sian Reynolds, *Marriage and Revolution: Monsieur and Madame Roland* (Oxford: Oxford University Press, 2012), 137.

[7] M. J. Sydenham, *The Girondins* (London: Athlone Press, 1961), 66, 90; Bette W. Oliver, *Jacques Pierre Brissot in America and France, 1788–1793: In Search of Better Worlds* (Lanham, MD: Lexington Books, 2016), 75; Reynolds, *Marriage* 162–63.

[8] Annie Jourdan, *La Révolution: une exception française?* (Paris: Flammarion, 2004), 218; Tackett, The *Coming of the Terror in the French Revolution* (Cambridge, MA: Harvard University Press, 2015), 168.

[9] Couthon, *Correspondance*, 26.

[10] Tackett, *Coming*, 149, 157; Andress, *Terror*, 56, 66.

[11] Aulard, *Jacobins*, Vol. 3, 377.

[12] Andress, *Terror*, 72.

[13] Couthon, *Correspondance*, 93.

ceased believing in their opponents' good faith, they increasingly saw themselves (in Strasbourg's formulation) as "lone ramparts of the constitution and people's rights, the only keepers of liberty and equality."[14] With conservatives, moderates, and divergent radicals combating them, Jacobins saw rivals on all sides.

The British, however, still remained outside the counterrevolutionary coalition forming on the Continent. Many French revolutionaries considered them historical exemplars: "the first to break the iron chains" of despotism," a Lorient Jacobin declared, proving "men could cease being slaves."[15] The London Revolution Society, responding to Bordeaux Jacobins' concern over British armaments, declared a landing in France impossible, "since you are troubled by interior enemies to your constitution, not at all prepared for war, and not provoking any."[16] Revolutionaries had far greater concerns than the British and believed positive change would come to the Isles. Birmingham rioters' destruction of Joseph Priestley's laboratory on Bastille Day 1791 brought Jacobin condolences, with Paris's considering "the people's ignorance is the patrimony of tyrants," but asserted reaction would pass and "humanity's cause" triumph.[17] Paris's society still held a civic festival celebrating Britain and America in December 1791 to cries of "Long live the three free peoples of the universe!"[18]

Despite initial skepticism, the Jacobin network wound up overwhelmingly endorsing war. Though Paris's Jacobins in a January 1792 circular warned since "the executive power [king] desires war, this is enough for us to fear it," club members developed their own rationales.[19] Despite opposition from leaders like Robespierre and Marat, on February 15, the capital's branch resolved that "our country's salvation depends" on offensive war, welcoming confrontation where "the soldiers of liberty will measure themselves against despotism's satellites" in a final conflict against the forces of old and evil.[20] By April 20, 1792, 141 of 154 club resolutions called for war.[21] Distrust of the French monarchy became the most common rationale. Saint-Flour's Jacobins asserted: "the disasters war could bring worry us much less than this deceptive, perfidious peace in which we have so long slept. Only war can save us and begin a second, necessary revolution."[22] Châlons-sur-Saône in late March

---

[14] *Journal des débats de la société des amis de la constitution*, March 1, 1792.

[15] BM Poitiers S 26 146/1 89.

[16] *Journal de correspondence de Paris à Nantes et du department de la Loire inférieure*, August 12, 1791.

[17] Ibid., August 28, 1791.

[18] Aulard, *Jacobins*, Vol. 3, 290.

[19] *Journal des débats de la société des amis de la constitution*, February 1, 1792.

[20] Aulard, *Jacobins*, Vol. 3, 376–81.

[21] Kennedy, *Middle Years*, 129.

[22] *Journal des débats de la société des amis de la constitution*, March 1, 1792.

declared if Europe's "tyrants" coalesced against the revolution, "we will exterminate their race."[23] Louis XVI, little recovered since Varennes, sat on
a teetering throne. Even at the price of war, Jacobins demanded the revolution
move forward.

Developing beyond debating societies, surveillance committees became
a larger part of Jacobin activity. Dijon established theirs on March 29, 1792,
three weeks before the war began. Considered "indispensable in the present
circumstances," the club appointed a twenty-eight-man surveillance committee (only two publicly known), charged to "unmask traitors" but "scrupulously
observe the law" themselves.[24] In a national circular, Paris Jacobin leader
Clavière declared his frustration that in the fourth year of liberty, their
"enemies still threaten," suggesting the network needed "new ardor."[25]
On April 2, the National Assembly's *Comité de surveillance* asked for the
Jacobins' help:

> You will not ignore, brothers and friends, the crisis the public good finds
> itself in; you will not ignore that some want to throw France into civil war,
> so that armies and rangers can carry out exterminations in our interior.
> Your love for the Constitution, your pure patriotism that enlightens us are
> the surest guarantee of the efforts you will make to uncover conspiracies,
> denounce traitors and cement the Revolution.[26]

Out of their love for the Revolution, the Jacobins – the nation's largest
organization, by some measures including the French government itself –
went into emergency action to prevent the Revolution's subversion.

The Jacobins greeted the Declaration of War on April 20, 1792, with
confidence. Robespierre, despite earlier opposition, orated at the society that
as the moment arrived where "liberty's enemies will deploy their audacious-
ness," revolutionaries needed to respond in kind, not just driving opponents
from France but "conquering Brabant, the Netherlands, Liège, Flanders, etc."
Now, "the French people must arm and rise together, for combat abroad and
surveillance against despotism at home."[27] Revolutionaries recognized the
enormous risk they took in internationalizing their revolution.

In wartime, political clubs appeared essential to the revolution's strength.
Jacobins would protect against suspect characters, while reaffirming high
principles: "All Europe sees the moral influence patriotic societies have on
the government," one Jacobin newspaper declared.[28] A Bordeaux Jacobin
circular asserted, "Never has nor will liberty exist without popular assemblies,"

---

[23] Ibid., March 29, 1792.
[24] BM Poitiers S 26 146/1 77.
[25] AD Puy de Dôme L 6374.
[26] Fray-Fournier, "Règlement," 46.
[27] Aulard, *Jacobins*, Vol. 3, 516, 547.
[28] *Journal des débats de la société des amis de la constitution*, April 26, 1792.

tracing their existence from Greek democratic assemblies through how "by them England and Holland formed two free nations." Popular societies served as "liberty's first school, the wisest and happiest voluntary institution."[29] Wartime manpower needs, together with the growing necessity of political allies, motivated Jacobins to promote collective participation and popular society models even more broadly.

Paris's Jacobins sought to mobilize their followers against royalist reaction, fearing imminent subversion. The central branch, in a June 6 circular, considered the French cause already in peril: many generals had abandoned the revolution, while others "stalled" as the enemy advanced. An "Austrian Committee" surrounding the royal family became the "cause of all our problems," undermining the war effort. They counseled their network to persist in "courage, union, surveillance" despite the crisis.[30] At least forty-nine Jacobin Clubs wrote to Louis XVI asking he withdraw his vetoes on legislation concerning émigrés, refractory clergymen, and the war effort by mid-June.[31] Facing royal refusal, prominent Paris Jacobins endorsed the thirty thousand–person Parisian demonstration of June 20, 1792, that marched through the Tuileries and confronted the king. The Jacobins that evening declared they "live to shock tyrants," ignoring conservatives angered by the royal humiliation.[32] The era of compromise, accommodating those wishing the revolutionaries' destruction, was over.

Disrespect for Louis XVI became endemic across the Jacobin network. Rodez' branch warned they would "no longer count on often-violated oaths" taken by the king. "If liberty perishes, we will perish with it."[33] Lorient believed Louis "wants to annihilate the constitution."[34] Nantes considered him "as much the King of Coblenz [where his counterrevolutionary brothers gathered their followers] as King of the French," as one would be "quite blind to refute the evidence" against him.[35] Strasbourg asserted he had "ceaselessly conspired since the revolution began against the people's rights."[36] The war made Jacobins sensitive to royal machinations and prepared for further political change.

In response, French army commanders began calling for the Jacobins' suppression. Lafayette, now a general, after demanding the Jacobins' "annihilation" by letter, left his forces to address the National Assembly on June 28, advocating "the instigators of the violence" during the (physically nonviolent)

---

[29] AM Bordeaux I 79 15.
[30] Aulard, *Jacobins*, Vol. 3, 665–67.
[31] Kennedy, *Middle Years*, 376.
[32] Aulard, *Jacobins*, Vol. 4, 28.
[33] Combes, *Procès-verbaux*, 165.
[34] *Journal des débats de la société des amis de la constitution*, July 5, 1792.
[35] BM Nantes D-M 21 6 VI 13.
[36] BM Poitiers S 26 146/2 61.

protest eight days earlier be punished, alongside the Jacobins' suppression: "to destroy a sect smothering sovereignty, tyrannizing the citizenry, and whose public debates leave no doubt of its leaders' atrocious plots."[37] Lafayette returned to the front lines without penalty and retained broad moderate support. General Nicolas Luckner soon pronounced, "clubs, undermining the wisest Constitution, have declared war," considering them a pernicious "corporation" responsible for revolutionary radicalization: "Jacobins or Feuillants, Republicans or Monarchists, all these associations are equally harmful, and bring the State the same misery."[38] Troops threatened to "exterminate" the Jacobins and other societies before deploying.[39] With military commanders against them, the Jacobins faced potential annihilation.

Outsiders' denunciations brought the Jacobins closer together. Bordeaux's branch now considered "popular societies the essence of liberty itself." If denied the right "to write, speak, and assemble," revolutionary demobilization would make "the constitution the legal code of despotism."[40] Clubs became the revolution's guarantor. Paris's Jacobins considered "peoples have the just right to gather," including to assemble "a popular congress to regulate in good faith the pretensions of monarchs who, blinded by authority, have been accustomed to regard peoples as their property."[41] Attacks on core rights, amid a desperate war, remained anathema.

Worries grew extreme. France faced "several thousand madmen's projects of fury and vengeance, preferring to turn their country into ruins than believe in equality," Orléans' Jacobins asserted.[42] Robespierre, at the Paris club on July 11, denounced "a conspiring general leading our armies," tying Lafayette to "a corrupt court ceaselessly machinating against our liberty and constitution."[43] Such a situation could not long endure. By August 6, a leading Jacobin newspaper considered the "Tuileries court, even more than the concert at Vienna and Berlin" inspired counterrevolutionary conspiracies.[44] Nevertheless, clubs proceeded carefully on the royal question: one study shows that while 150 Jacobin locals criticized Louis XVI between June 20 and August 10, some wanting his suspension, none dared demand his removal.[45]

---

[37] AD Puy-de-Dôme L 388 20; Laura Auricchio, *The Marquis: Lafayette Reconsidered* (New York: Knopf, 2014), 259.

[38] Heitz, *Sociétés*, 224.

[39] John Rylands Library, "Gazettes manuscrites sent to Breton René le Pretre de Châteaugiron, 1775–1793," French MSS 51 1.

[40] BM Poitiers S 26 146/1 41.

[41] *Journal des débats de la société des amis de la constitution*, July 22, 1792.

[42] BM Poitiers S 26 146/2 26.

[43] Aulard, *Jacobins*, Vol. 4, 89.

[44] *Journal des débats de la société des amis de la constitution*, August 6, 1792.

[45] Kennedy, *Middle Years*, 278; Planté, *Jacobins*, 31.

Frustrated by the National Assembly's inaction against the king and vote of confidence for Lafayette on August 8, Paris's sections created an "Insurrectional Commune" to confront the monarchy.[46] The new revolutionary organization gained Jacobin approbation: "In extreme danger, it is necessary to raise extreme energy," former legislator Jean-François Goupilleau orated to Paris Jacobin applause. Popular action became essential: "only a general insurrection" could save the nation.[47] When Feuillant administrators raised legal objections to the commune they were told, "when the people enter a state of insurrection, they regain all power for themselves."[48] With the Jacobins' unofficial approbation, the sections raised twenty thousand armed demonstrators on August 10, with the provocative but limited goal of searching the royal palace for weapons. Once arriving outside the Tuileries, the king's Swiss Guards ambushed them, leading to the palace's capture by revolutionary forces and, since Louis had not ordered his forces to stand down, the monarchy's suspension.

With the sections effectively controlling Paris during elections for the new National Convention, the Jacobins became at least complicit in the September Massacres. With the Prussians' capture of Verdun raising fears of the Revolution being annihilated by force, many accepted recourse to desperate measures. Like the rest of the lame-duck Legislative Assembly, the Jacobins made no attempt to dissuade Parisians from killing. A drafted circular on September 12 declared only that "the people of Paris have felt the necessity" of undertaking "severe surveillance on the tools and agents" of royalty.[49] Yet with the wartime situation soon improving, the Jacobins would gain new opportunities to implement some of their most ambitious plans.

The Jacobin Network and the Coming of the Terror

The French Republic's establishment in September 1792, coinciding with reduced foreign threats, brought a new rush of hopes for the revolutionary Jacobins. Despite the traumas surrounding the monarchy's fall and continued legislative rivalries spilling over from the prior National Assembly, the First Republic appeared a new beginning. However, political inflexibility and wartime stresses led to escalating infighting, regional civil war, and trust breakdowns between revolutionaries across the still-fragile republic.

As the National Convention began, revolutionaries could now implement their core principles without degrading compromises to king and aristocracy. "Our first legislators' great philosophical views prepared France's happiness,

---

[46] Tackett, *Coming*, 184–87.
[47] Aulard, *Jacobins*, Vol. 4, 187.
[48] Tackett, *Coming*, 187.
[49] Aulard, *Jacobins*, Vol. 4, 280.

but have not achieved it," Metz' Jacobins considered on the Convention's first day, "they created the light for us, we must create the movement."[50] Ideas needed to be applied to lead the Revolution onward: "Only real virtue, solid science, enlightened zeal can receive praise," Reims' Jacobins added.[51] Enlightened possibilities needed to be distilled into governing principles and enforced to create a new reality.

Hopes also grew in the international sphere. Rouen's Jacobin civic festival declared, even in July's worsening crisis, "*Il n'y a plus d'Océan* (There are no more oceans)": the world's peoples and their movements for freedom became too interconnected to be separated.[52] Given France's encirclement by Europe's crowned heads, Vannes' Jacobins on September 27 proposed an alliance not with the British government, but with the nation's people instead. In early October, Paris's Jacobins wrote to the "Patriotic Societies of England, Scotland and Ireland," declaring "despotism forever annihilated in France," and asking British subjects to follow them "for a liberty divorced from the vices of courts," toward a common republican future.[53] The United States Consul in Bordeaux co-led a march with the local Jacobin president to a banquet on October 8, where toasts included the "propagation of the rights of man over all the earth."[54] A Bordeaux Jacobin circular declared, "The aurora of the happiness of nations has risen," to be accomplished by "annihilating royalty, the natural enemy" of human rights.[55]

Despite France's grand ambitions abroad, however, the Convention failed to maintain fraternity among its own members. Factional infighting was consubstantial with the new republic. Jacobin Clubs operated in tandem with "the Mountain," the radical faction sitting atop the Convention's high left seats, which during the legislature's early months drew the regular support of 153 of more than 700 deputies. However, there is evidence of only eighty of them participating at Paris's Jacobins. The Girondins, meanwhile, taking opposite seats on the right, had as few as fifty-eight core supporters. Both vied for moderate deputy support to gain a legislative majority on any measure.[56] Two days after the Convention began, the Girondin leadership denounced Jacobin leaders Robespierre, Marat, and Danton for inciting Paris's September Massacres (that ended just two weeks before) and plotting a dictatorship. The Girondins failed to sway enough moderates for expulsion, but with their

---

[50] Auguste Mauger, *Discours prononcé dans la Société des amis de la Liberté et de l'Egalité de Metz, le 23 septembre 1792* (Metz, C. Lamort, 1792), 2.

[51] AM Reims FR 2I108 34.

[52] Kennedy, *Middle Years*, 152.

[53] Aulard, *Jacobins*, Vol. 4, 356, 359.

[54] BM Poitiers S 26 146/1 31.

[55] Ibid., 36.

[56] Allison Patrick, *The Men of the First French Republic: Political Alignments in the National Convention of 1792* (Baltimore: Johns Hopkins University Press, 1972), 15–19.

faction controlling many ministries, including the judiciary, threats of prosecution loomed. Paris's Jacobins expelled several Girondin members, though they had already ceased attending club meetings.[57] The split between former club compatriots became final.

Facing growing conflicts abroad and across France, the Jacobins increasingly accepted conflict as the price of real change. "Since the era began," declared Le Mans' Jacobins, "we have lived in this baneful disunion that the diversity of opinions, which inevitably follow a regeneration injuring so many interests" across France.[58] No revolutionary needed to look far for real, potentially dire, opposition: "The torches of fanaticism desolate the countryside; furors of civil war menace the towns," Bordeaux's Jacobins lamented in late September.[59] Rather than seeing repression as degrading the Revolution, Beaune's Jacobins asserted, "thwarting liberty-killing plots is always an honorable function of popular societies."[60] Spread across the nation, the Jacobins were the only extra-governmental organization with the power and reach to confront the counterrevolution's many forms.

If the Revolution needed to get ugly, that seemed a small price for establishing a new regime of liberty. "A revolution is always a hideous thing in its details," Convention deputy Claude Basire orated before Paris's Jacobins on November 4, "a man of state ought to envisage its totality and consequences for a generation" instead.[61] Perpetual peace would be deferred until revolutionaries created its necessary environment. Many accepted hard fights ahead: "The most dangerous moment for the liberty of peoples," a Strasbourg orator declared, "is the moment they acquire it," as the "government greatly surpasses the level of general enlightenment" in France.[62] A difficult adjustment period seemed unavoidable.

The Jacobin-Girondin split worsened in fall 1792. On October 15, Paris's Jacobins wrote a circular declaring "despotism reproduces itself under new forms" with opposition "serving only Brissot's faction." The club blamed Girondins for "brusquely declaring war, without any measures prepared to deter the Tyrant of the Tuileries," or conspiring officers. Counterrevolutionary collusion remained a real threat. The Girondins seemed a cabal, forming a rival Reunion Club holding closed sessions.[63] Girondins accused the Jacobins, meanwhile, of conspiring with Paris's sections to control French politics. Armand Gensonné, deputy from Bordeaux, in December denounced the Jacobins for "dominating the National Convention by terror, and by the

[57] Tackett, *Coming*, 230–31.
[58] BM Poitiers S 26 146/2 1.
[59] Ibid., 146/1 38.
[60] Ibid., 27.
[61] Aulard, *Jacobins*, Vol. 4, 453.
[62] *Journal des débats de la société des amis de la constitution*, November 5, 1792.
[63] Aulard, *Jacobins*, Vol. 4, 394.

Convention all of the Republic."[64] Some provincial Jacobins considered Girondins the voice of reason, with the ex-Feuillant society of Honfleur unable "to conceive how, in the Paris club, Marat and his sectarians find defenders."[65] Each side to their enemies represented menacing conspiracy.

Many provincial Jacobin societies sympathized with the Girondins, with at least 140 branches supporting some of their positions.[66] Angers' branch in November wrote to Paris's that "Marat, Robespierre and their accomplices cannot rest much longer amongst you," denouncing them as "Anarchists" seeking domination and encouraging violence. If the radicals remained, Angers declared, "we will not long be counted amongst your affiliated societies."[67] Rodez Jacobins blamed "the Paris Commune, the sections, the societies," who overwhelmingly backed Marat for coercing the Convention.[68] The Jacobin compact remained fragile. With unanimity and coordination cardinal virtues, Jacobins' failure to maintain cohesion was profound.

The Paris club and its allies demanded unity, while labeling opponents defectors and subversives. After Bordeaux's society (the Girondins' strong-hold) ceased corresponding with Paris on Christmas Eve, declaring Marat, Danton, and Robespierre's followers "anarchy's artisans" who "cannot be our brothers or true republicans," the central branch responded that they should "Remember the Club of 1789, the *Monarchiens* and the Feuillants," who fell into political oblivion.[69] Paris responded to Angers' Jacobins in early January, asserting they sought "everyone's happiness," but would not indulge "intriguers."[70] The same week, they threatened Troyes' vacillating branch that if "unity & indivisibility" were not their principles, "you can leave" and prepare to fight.[71] More moderate Jacobins sought to heal the split. Strasbourg's – across the Rhine from the counterrevolutionary coalition – sought conciliation, as "our enemies want to divide us and we want to remain united." The "true friends" were "those loving union."[72] For a network so concerned with unity, the split violated their central principles yet, under the era's stresses, proceeded anyway.

Bordeaux responded on January 8 by questioning the legitimacy of the Jacobins' existence. The club demanded the Convention cast out "this guilty minority." If nothing was done, "the Departments will not remain tranquil spectators." Asserting their "energy and rights," they threatened a Girondin

---

[64] Patrick, *Men*, 4.
[65] Biard, *Procès-verbaux*, 768.
[66] Kennedy, *1793–1795*, 9.
[67] BM Poitiers S 26 146/1 10.
[68] Combes, *Procès-verbaux*, 178.
[69] BM Poitiers S 26 147/2 2.
[70] *Journal des débats de la société des amis de la constitution*, January 5, 1793.
[71] BM Poitiers S 26 147/2 5.
[72] Heitz, *Sociétés*, 246.

coup.[73] Some societies backed the undertaking: Bayeux in mid-January asked "citizens to confederate, go to Paris and support our representatives' liberty," by guarding Girondins against Jacobin-supporting Parisian protesters. Though Bayeux recanted days later, had other areas joined them, civil war in the capital's streets could have resulted.[74]

Club membership expanded as the Jacobins' social reach grew. After initially gathering educated local notables, now clubs increasingly sought to mirror the First Republic's universal suffrage. "Sans-culottes have greatly expanded our numbers," noted Nîmes' Jacobins in October.[75] Even in Paris, where most artisans were sent to Paris section and popular society meetings, Augustin Robespierre considered the Jacobins "incorruptible" due to their "deliberating amidst four thousand people" judging their character.[76] Civic education remained the foundational goal. "Our most dangerous enemy is ignorance," Laval's Jacobins asserted.[77] But despite growing rhetoric celebrating sans-culotte virtue, Jacobin leaders still considered the bas peuple easy prey for counterrevolutionary manipulations.

The network rejoiced in the first "liberations" of neighboring peoples, recruiting new Jacobins there. Following Savoy's capture, Jacobin Clubs spread revolutionary doctrine. Annecy's club sent an early-November circular declaring its Alpine residents ready to "live free or die," as "the entire Universe hears" the revolutionary cry.[78] Word spread that Savoy would soon "be filled with clubs."[79] By the following October, one Savoyard local considered the Jacobins "an always-active center of patriotism, surveillance and enlightenment" to direct the "electrical fire" of revolution.[80] The expansion of both hopes and recognizable enemies in late 1792 and early 1793 offered little means of containing the revolutionary war: "War with the Universe, if it must be, and peace thereafter," Convention deputy Étienne Chatillon asserted.[81] The more striking the example of despotism's overthrow, the better: "their blood cements," Strasbourg's Jacobins declared, "universal liberty on earth and sea."[82] As borders expanded, so did revolutionary possibilities.

Such ecstatic hopes of an unchained Europe's potential became government policy. In November 1792, the Convention issued an "Edict of Fraternity,"

[73] BM Poitiers S 26 148/1 27.
[74] Journal des débats de la société des amis de la constitution, January 19 and 26, 1793.
[75] Ibid., October 29, 1792.
[76] Robespierre, Correspondance, 313.
[77] Journal des débats de la société des amis de la constitution, April 15, 1793.
[78] BM Poitiers S 26 146/1 12.
[79] Lloyd's Evening Post, October 22, 1792.
[80] François Mugnier, La Société populaire ou Club des Jacobins de Thonon (Paris: Champion, 1898), 62.
[81] BM Nantes Correspondance d'Etienne Chatillon, Tome 1, Vol. 44 (Mic B 48/44).
[82] BM Poitiers S 26 148/2 83.

promising "aid to all peoples wanting to recover their liberty," for the revolutionary armies to "proclaim in all languages, wherever their forces march."[83] Given their international friends in Paris and encouragement arriving from across Europe and America, many Jacobins believed the world not far behind them in their quest for liberty. As royal legitimacy collapsed, many believed French universalism could replace it.

In their largest territorial gains yet, after the Battle of Jemappes on November 6, revolutionary forces overran Belgium. The country in 1789–1790 had undertaken the Brabançon Revolution, mobilizing committees and militias (featuring at least one American Revolutionary War veteran) to force their Austrian overlords from the territory after Emperor Joseph II attacked their ancient privileges, declaring a republic of "United Belgian States." Divisions among local "Patriots" led to Austrian reoccupation, though underground activity continued through organizations like the Society of the Friends of Public Safety, while many leaders went to France to build Jacobin connections. French Revolutionaries believed Belgian apprenticeship could be short, and in late November over a thousand enthusiastic Brussels residents inaugurated their Jacobin branch, toasting the end of the "reign of error" and a new order of reason.[84] The organization, however, ran afoul of Belgian moderates by calling for religious reforms and the abolition of privileges, while the French-installed Provisional Government became unpopular. The broader Belgian populace proved overwhelmingly skeptical of French radicalism and few resisted when Austria reoccupied the territory after defeating French forces at Neerwinden in March 1793. Local politics proved less amenable to universal liberty than the French had hoped.

Revolutionary ardor encountered still less fertile soil as revolutionary armies advanced into the Rhineland. Three days after Mayence's capitulation in October 1792, German enthusiasts founded a Jacobin "Society of the German Friends of Liberty and Equality," asserting the French fought the war "so there would be no more to fight in the future," to "punish inequality," "make peoples understand they are born free," and spread the rights of man.[85] Jacobin Clubs cultivated popular support for their universalist program, but French authorities continued extracting wealth and manpower without local approval. Most Germans met French occupation with indifference that turned to resistance, while collaborators faced royalist retribution in areas recaptured during 1793's counteroffensives.[86] Though prepared for counterrevolutionary reprisals, the Jacobins struggled to understand opposition abroad.

[83] *Moniteur universel*, November 20, 1792.
[84] Polasky, *Revolution in Brussels, 1787–1793* (Brussels: Académie royale de Belgique, 1987), 102, 211, 218.
[85] Albert Sorel, *L'Europe et la Révolution française* (Paris: Plon, 1885), Vol. 3, 106.
[86] T. C. W. Blanning, *The French Revolution in Germany: Occupation and Resistance in the Rhineland, 1792–1802* (Oxford: Clarendon, 1983).

The only surprising lacunae in Jacobins' universalist rhetoric, tellingly, was the lack of discussion of France's Caribbean colonies after the 1791 slave insurrection. Early Jacobins (many of whom had colonial investments) divided over controversies surrounding voting rights for free men of color and abolishing the slave trade, considering the issue an excessive complication amid so many other conflicts. Many questioned whether counterrevolutionaries (perhaps British agents) had stoked the slave uprising. Perhaps to support Jacobin unity, the clubs remained remarkably silent on the revolt in the future Haiti. Most references to "slaves," meanwhile, remained abstract or directed at those serving counterrevolutionary monarchs ("loyal slaves of the House of Austria") than the oppressed under French rule.[87]

Soon after Louis XVI's execution, supported by the Jacobins and opposed by the Girondin leadership, the Convention preemptively declared war against George III on February 1. With British conservatives long accused of aiding the counterrevolutionary coalition, confrontation with the British aristocracy appeared necessary. Libourne's Jacobins smuggled a letter to the London Revolution Society, declaring, "tyrants, rightly intimidated, have seen the messenger of their destruction, and Peoples that of their manumission and happiness." Now, "liberty will be communicated to all Peoples."[88] Jacobins' fondest hope remained that British radicals would rise against their king and "corrupt Parliament," bringing the empire into the revolutionary camp.[89] The radical *Thermomètre du jour* newspaper translated Lord Stanhope's antiwar address to Parliament arguing France desired a "close friendship," and a "pacific system ought to be a wise, enlightened nation's first politics."[90] A new compact could undermine Britain's war machine. Yet the conflict would continue with only short truces, for twenty-two years – and a loyalist upsurge largely silenced British radical clubs. By March, Robespierre exhorted Jacobins to match "the concert of English authorities" in their national cause.[91] British and French clubs' animating relationship largely ceased amid wartime's disruptions. The isolation coincided with Jacobin radicalization.

Yet to focus only on fears and threats surrounding the Jacobins minimizes the ecstatic sense of possibility as the Revolution successfully combated its many enemies. While "this moment is terrible," Girondin deputy Jacques-Charles Bailleul argued, "it could be the most glorious for France."[92] The victorious French could "enlighten all the earth's peoples, returning their primitive rights," a Clermont-Ferrand festival welcoming war with Britain

[87] AD Bouches-du-Rhône L 2076.
[88] BM Poitiers S 26 148/1 75.
[89] AD Nord L 10248.
[90] *Thermomètre du jour*, February 26, 1793.
[91] Robespierre, *Oeuvres complètes* (Paris: Leroux, 1912–), Vol. 9, 311.
[92] AM Le Havre D(3) 41.

declared.[93] The sentiment remained, Rennes' Jacobins asserted, that "victory, followed by French liberty's affirmation, could be the work of a single campaign."[94] Robespierre at Paris's club on March 6 reiterated the need to "correspond with all virtuous men worthy of regenerating the world."[95] So successful in France, the Jacobin model held universal potential.

The Jacobin-Girondin split, however, worsened with the Girondin-sympathizing General Charles-François Dumouriez's April 5 defection to the enemy Austrians, after attempting to turn his army against the Convention in a conspiracy to restore the monarchy. Many wondered who would defect next, with Paris's Jacobins declaring, "Brissot is the civil La Fayette," waiting to strike.[96] Rumors spread of "Bordeaux Feuillants," among the most insulting anti-Girondin slurs, dissolving neighborhood assemblies there.[97] There seemed no underhanded tactics the Revolution's enemies would not attempt. Convention deputy Jean-Baptiste Soulignac before Paris's Jacobins on March 31 warned of "a great conspiracy against French liberty," in which counterrevolutionaries posed as good *sans-culottes*.[98] Now came "the terrible hour," Paris's Jacobins declared on April 5, "when the fatherland's defenders have to triumph or be enslaved," telling the network to "arrest all our revolution's enemies and suspects."[99] Jacobins realized the need "to electrify the people and show them the means of saving themselves."[100] Tolerance lessened amid the treacherous war's exigencies.

Girondin-Montagnard infighting led France to the precipice of a civil war. The Girondins indicted (but unsuccessfully prosecuted) firebrand journalist Marat for his role in the April 5 Jacobin declaration, claiming it incited treason.[101] Many affiliates sided with Marat and the Montagnards with the Provençal town of Riez sending a circular that, given Paris's troubles, "all are ready to rise up, if you do not end them." They demanded expulsion of "perfidious" Girondin deputies "who did not vote for the tyrant's death."[102] Many seemed primed for civil war: Marseille asserted Girondin elements had "profited from our brave sans-culottes' absence" at the front to dominate municipalities, creating "a system tending to oppress" the common people.[103] Paris also drew concern, with Robespierre denouncing "suspect

[93] AD Puy-de-Dôme L 657.
[94] Ibid., April 9, 1793.
[95] Robespierre, *Oeuvres*, Vol. 9, 296.
[96] Aulard, *Jacobins*, Vol. 5, 102.
[97] *Journal des débats de la société des amis de la constitution*, March 30, 1793.
[98] Fray-Fournier, "Règlement," 117.
[99] Aulard, *Jacobins*, Vol. 5, 126–27.
[100] *Annales de la République française*, 8 avril 1793.
[101] Hanson, *The Jacobin Republic under Fire: The Federalist Revolt in the French Revolution* (University Park, PA: Penn State University Press, 2003), 295.
[102] Archives départementales des Bouches-du-Rhône, L 2075.
[103] *Journal de la Montagne*, June 1, 1793.

men spreading trouble in the sections," as no one knew their influence's extent.[104] As the tightly knit Jacobin network cracked open, few loyalties remained clear, with subversion rife.

The Girondins responded in kind. On May 10, Bordeaux's society sent a circular instructing all to "Rise up! It's time." They declared the Convention "no longer at liberty" with "representatives harassed by factious intriguers" perverting the legislative process.[105] The Girondins appeared to recruit conspirators: rumors flew of Roland directing 40 million in embezzled funds. Paris's Jacobins mockingly responded that if Bordeaux wanted "to unite with Vendée counterrevolutionaries and reestablish the royalty, they can try it," calumniating that "Bordeaux negotiated with Pitt to be an independent city" – which seemed believable given Anglophiles' recent actions.[106] Each faction now believed the worst about each other.

Ignoring Girondin threats did not appear a viable option. If the Jacobins could not "annihilate these anarchists," Rouen's branch asked on May 26, how could they confront the Revolution's other enemies? Langres' Jacobins similarly called for Paris's branch to "Avenge liberty" with "terrible cry of the *Patrie en danger* ringing again," demanding stringent measures to punish the faction.[107] After the Girondins made arrests on May 24, including prominent radical newspaperman Jacques-René Hébert, Jacobin leadership plotted a new uprising to expel key Girondins.[108] The Convention's majority voted to investigate a rumored Parisian insurrection on May 28 but failed to diffuse the May 31–June 2 uprising, in which Paris's sections, at Jacobin urging, brought tens of thousands of demonstrators each day to the Convention's doors calling for the detested leaders' removal. On the third day, protesters blocked the assembly exits, intimidating moderate deputies to approve Girondin arrests.[109]

Given the sanguinary possibilities of the months-long standoff, in many respects the Girondins' expulsion appeared a measured (though partisan) response. Proscribed deputies were only placed under loose house arrest and authorities took no measures against dozens of others who commonly voted with them.[110] The Paris Jacobin circular afterward celebrated the events as a "third insurrection," the rightful successor to the Bastille's storming and

[104] Robespierre, *Oeuvres*, Vol. 9, 478.

[105] BM Poitiers S 26 148/1 28.

[106] *Annales de la République française*, 25 mai 1793; Aulard, *Jacobins*, Vol. 5, 235.

[107] AD Bouches-du-Rhône, L 2076.

[108] Georges Lefebvre, *The French Revolution, Volume II: From 1793 to 1799* (New York: Columbia University Press, 1964), 43–53.

[109] Peter McPhee, *Robespierre: A Revolutionary Life* (New Haven: Yale University Press, 2012), 149, 154; Micah Alpaugh, *Non-Violence and the French Revolution: Political Demonstrations in Paris, 1787–1795* (Cambridge: Cambridge University Press, 2015), 139–50.

[110] David P. Jordan, *The Revolutionary Career of Maximilien Robespierre* (New York: Free Press, 1985), 144.

monarchy's overthrow, removing "calumniating counterrevolutionaries" from power.[111] Purging the Girondin leadership effectively broke the faction – with most allies disengaging from debates thereafter, Montagnards controlled the Convention leadership for the following year.[112]

Many in the provinces celebrated the events. "Peoples of the universe," wrote the Jacobins of Robespierre's hometown of Arras, "you will learn from us the great art of insurrections." The events of May 31–June 2 would "make the enemies of our happiness tremble" alongside the "despots conjuring against us."[113] To Limoges' Jacobins, the coup tested revolutionaries' resiliency: despite betrayal by "a perjurous king, perfidious ministers, infamous generals, and infidelitous representatives," revolutionaries had persevered.[114] Pro-Jacobin papers celebrated the "Revolution of 1793" and predicted all "intriguers" would "fall into the same abyss" as the Girondin leadership.[115] Parisian radicals believed they had again defeated forces attempting to subvert the Revolution.

Girondins' expulsion brought immediate denunciations from across the nation. Sixty of eighty-three departmental administrations at least temporarily withdrew recognition of the Convention.[116] Chartres' Jacobins considered Parisians at "the point of losing, instantaneously, the fruit of four years' work" by annihilating deliberative freedom.[117] Jacobins in the Norman town of Falaise denounced "liberticide tribunes" directing the Convention, proclaiming themselves ready to "die as Frenchmen, or to live without a master."[118] The Jura department began convoking electoral assemblies and two others endorsed a new Convention (on a Girondin plan) to meet near France's geographic center at Bourges, over a hundred miles south of Paris. One study finds documented local Jacobin opposition in all but fifteen of France's eighty-nine departments.[119]

Several Girondin-favoring areas revolted. Lyon, anticipating the purge, already rose on May 29 to oust radical Jacobins from municipal politics.[120] In Marseille, where Jacobins similarly controlled the municipality, moderates incited an insurrection through local governing districts with Section de Bon

---

[111] Bibliothèque de l'Assemblée nationale, *La société des amis de la liberté et de l'Egalité, séante aux ci-devant Jacobins St.-Honoré, à Paris, aux citoyens des départemens, sur l'insurrection du 31 mai* (Paris: Imprimerie patriotique, 1793), C5, Ch5, 34.

[112] Tackett, *Coming*, 286.

[113] BM Poitiers S 26 148/1 13.

[114] Fray-Fournier, "Règlement," 134.

[115] *Annales de la République française*, 7 juin, 1793.

[116] McPhee, *Robespierre*, 158.

[117] *Journal de la montagne*, June 10, 1793.

[118] BM Poitiers S 26 148/1 63.

[119] *Annales de la République française*, 12 juin 1793; Kennedy, *The Jacobin Clubs in the French Revolution, 1793–1795* (New York: Berghahn, 2000), 25.

[120] Hanson, *Jacobin*, 57.

Pasteur asserting "National representation is violated, a great number of its members arrested," while "the Paris Commune decides laws for all France." Marseillais marched north but advanced no further than Avignon.[121] Bordeaux's administrators, after word arrived of the Girondins' ouster, created a Popular Committee of Public Safety to raise troops to march on Paris.[122] Rebel areas imitated the national government, forming ruling committees, closing rival clubs, and arresting suspects.[123] Though aiming to recapture national power by force, irresolution and military deployments deterred Federalist forces from marching on Paris, leading to regional fracturing and suppression.

Most of France remained neutral, fearful of disunion and a victorious faction's vengeance. Dunkirk, for example, lamented the "furors of parties," wanting reconciliation to avoid fulfilling "our enemies' prediction that we will destroy ourselves" through internal dissention.[124] Most locals not directly implicated in the uprisings continued meeting, with Valence's Jacobins blaming the Rhône valley disturbances on "disguised aristocracy," aided by "the calculus of mercantile avidity."[125] Valence hosted a September congress of loyal Jacobins from seventy-one societies across nine departments, while a purged Marseille branch hosted four hundred clubs in October.[126]

Many hoped the Federalist revolts' suppression would regenerate the network, while to others the events seemed only the first purge. Limoges' Jacobins considered the outcome "the despair of moderatism," as the network could now "coalesce" without further backsliding.[127] Saint-Just in the Convention demanded investigation not just of suspects but their associates, as "in revolutions, a traitor's friends are legitimate suspects."[128] Provincial Jacobins' autonomy remained shattered: disagreement with Paris's branch was no longer permissible.[129] Tarbes' Jacobins requested moderates' expulsion from the Convention: "It is finally time to drain the swamp ["marais" being slang for the center seats where the unaffiliated sat]; it's time to see only Montagnards compose the Convention."[130] Political pluralism, already difficult for revolutionaries to accept, seemed a present danger for the fragile Republic.

---

[121]   AD Bouches-du-Rhône L 1971; Hanson, *Jacobin*, 29, 90.
[122]   Hanson, *Jacobin*, 93.
[123]   Lefebvre, *French Revolution: Volume II*, 57.
[124]   AD Bouches-du-Rhône, L 2076.
[125]   BM Poitiers S 26 148/2 119.
[126]   Kennedy, *1793–1795*, 58.
[127]   *La Société populaire de Limoges, à la société populaire de Paris, dite des Jacobins* (Paris, 1793), 2.
[128]   Saint-Just, *Oeuvres*, 606, 617.
[129]   Kennedy, *1793–1795*, 3.
[130]   *Annales de la République française*, 4 septembre, 1793.

Fear of foreign agents stirring new revolts in France, together with British reformists' abject failure in deterring the war effort and widespread Anglo-American affinity for the Girondin faction, led the Convention on August 1 to a draconian decree arresting all foreigners from belligerent countries (not already residing in France on July 1, 1789) and confiscating their papers. Despite disbanding foreign regiments in the French army, revolutionaries had previously encouraged foreign civilian contact to help universalize the revolution.[131] Though in some respects a pragmatic measure, responding to wartime circumstances, exclusionary nationalism's ideological ramifications could not be ignored – with rising xenophobia replacing the cosmopolitanism previously characterizing the Jacobins.[132] While revolutionaries had approved restrictions that spring against foreign agents, this decree included revolutionary partisans. Hundreds of foreign nationals were arrested, and in late December 1793, even exemplary foreigners elected to the Convention – Anacharsis Cloots and Paine – were expelled with the first guillotined and the second imprisoned.[133] As the Year II dawned, no prior favor helped any group believed to run afoul of the French war machine.

The Jacobin network's greatest hopes did not survive summer 1793. As Paris's Jacobins came to political power, the legislative leadership increasingly dominated the network – while after the Federalist Revolts and German reversals, they had trouble trusting provincial satellites or international allies. As the Jacobins' worldview shrank, in self-defense network partisans turned from fraternity to terror.

Jacobin Terror and Its Eclipse

In the Year II, victory and defeat each appeared close for committed revolutionaries. Political exigency required every reasonable effort, perhaps more, to stop the Revolution's enemies. Despite the difficulties of disentangling Jacobin network views from both the Convention's "Montagnard" faction and Robespierrist leadership in the Committee of Public Safety, particularly in a political atmosphere demanding unanimity, the Jacobin network disseminated the Paris leadership's views across France's daunting political landscape. Amid an unprecedented revolution, Jacobin Clubs embodied the popular

---

[131] Sophie Wahnich, *L'impossible citoyen: L'étranger dans le discours de la Révolution française* (Paris: Albin Michel, 1997), 23; Mathiez, La *Révolution et les étrangers: cosmopolitisme et defense nationale* (Paris: Renaissance du livre, 1918), 46; Christopher J. Tozzi, *Nationalizing France's Army: Foreign, Black, and Jewish Troops in the French Military, 1715–1831* (Charlottesville: University of Virginia Press, 2016).

[132] See Rapport, *Nationality and Citizenship in Revolutionary France: The Treatment of Foreigners, 1789–1799* (Oxford: Clarendon Press, 2000).

[133] Wahnich, *L'impossible*, 117–22, 185; Rapport, *Nationality*, 200.

mobilization capable of creating a radical new reality – but also readily attracted opponents' fear and enmity.

Even at the start of the revolutionary Year II, Jacobins considered terror more the model of their enemies than the Jacobins themselves. "Tyranny no longer exists," declared Saint-Marcellin's society that autumn, with it relegated to "those centuries of terror and ignorance, when lords practiced it without restraint" on the people.[134] Revolutionaries thus had to prevent the old order's reestablishment. Robespierre orated on October 11, "we have reached the moment that must decide Europe's destinies," believing "fortune will follow the flags of justice, courage and humanity" for revolutionary victory.[135] Extreme measures became justifiable in extreme circumstances.

Only in the First Republic's treacherous circumstances did liberty and terror seem to work together. Convention deputy René Levasseur orated before Beauvais' Jacobins on November 1, 1793, "Popular societies must never forget they are liberty's safeguards; their surveillance must be active and continual." No freedom could be afforded to despotism's agents, particularly "false patriots," sowing anarchy and distrust from within.[136] Counterrevolutionary agitation would continue: "revolutions," Limoges' Jacobins considered, "cannot operate without producing malcontents."[137] Denunciation, even of one's friends, became seen as a revolutionary duty.[138] France could not win the war and free the universe, Robespierre argued, without strict unanimity. The incorruptible opposed "every measure of indulgence towards exterior or interior enemies."[139] The stakes seemed too great to do otherwise.

Nevertheless, weeding out potential subversives became a major revolutionary preoccupation. Twenty-one Girondins stood trial for abetting the Federalist Revolts (among other charges) between October 24 and 30 and, found guilty of "crimes against the unity of the republic," were executed the next day.[140] The Jacobins did not believe their troubles ended there. Starting in late November, Paris's Jacobins began their society's "purification," subjecting members to questions including "What have you done for the revolution?" "What was your fortune in '89? What is it now?" and "Has your quill and advice never served anything except liberty?"[141] The central branch directed

---

[134] Adresse de la Société républicaine de Saint-marcellin, Département de l'Isère, à la Convention Nationale (Saint-Marcellin: Beaumont, 1793), 3–5.
[135] Robespierre, Oeuvres, Vol. 10, 147.
[136] Léonard Thiot, Les sociétés populaires du Beauvais, 1793-1794 (Beauvais: Imprimerie départementale de l'Oise, 1910), 22.
[137] Fray-Fournier, "Règlement," 169.
[138] Marisa Linton, Choosing Terror: Virtue, Friendship, and Authenticity in the French Revolution (Oxford: Oxford University Press, 2013), 13.
[139] Robespierre, Oeuvres, Vol. 10, 171 and 241.
[140] Tackett, Coming, 308–11.
[141] Gérard Walter, Histoire des Jacobins (Paris, 1946), 330.

affiliates to "purge yourselves; we purge ourselves too, and hope all popular societies will follow our example."[142] Robespierre and other leaders subjected themselves to scrutiny, sending model transcripts to affiliates.[143] Some provincial societies expelled nearly half their members.[144] Jacobins were no longer safe through membership, now facing harsher scrutiny than most unaffiliated. Yet some Jacobins enthusiastically considered purification a method of renewing trust. Villeneuve's branch, after finishing investigations, encouraged fellow Jacobins to "correspond with us in all confidence."[145]

On October 30, the same day the Girondin trials ended, the Convention decreed, "clubs and popular societies of women, under whatever denomination, are forbidden." Jacobins had encouraged female attendance and sometimes even (nonvoting) membership in their clubs but remained opposed to political equality.[146] The Society of Revolutionary Republican Women had been founded in May 1793, encouraging "companies of Amazons" to fight against "enemies within." Though only 170 members strong, society detachments had participated in the May–June uprising against the Girondins, but thereafter took to patrolling the streets looking for women not wearing the patriotic tricolor cockade, fighting opponents in the streets. The organization's gender-bending militancy led to denunciations from both the Jacobins and the Convention under fears they would soon demand to vote, serve in the army, and attack other male bastions. The Committee of General Security, considering "Can women exercise political rights, and take an active role in government affairs?" responded negatively.[147] The radical revolution had opened the possibility of all adults participating in the democratic process, but the Jacobin leadership failed to pursue its most radical and inclusive rhetoric. Though elite women remained politicking behind the scenes as hosts and influencers while working women continued agitating on economic issues, paths to direct participation in the political process closed.[148]

Concurrently, the Jacobins limited participation by ordinary men, as reduced club membership became paired with fewer meetings. Paris's Jacobins endorsed restricting the capital's section meetings to six per month, declaring frequent sessions "favor the aristocracy, because *sans-culottes* cannot attend every day," while nonrepresentative meetings could "endanger public

[142] AM Reims FR 2I113.
[143] Jordan, *Revolutionary*, 190.
[144] Kennedy, *1793–1795*, 94.
[145] AM Reims FR 2I102.
[146] Kennedy, *1793–1795*, 105–6.
[147] Dominique Godineau, *The Women of Paris and their French Revolution*, Katherine Streip, trans. (Berkeley: University of California Press, 1998), 119, 165–66, 169, 170.
[148] Marisa Linton and Mette Harder, "'Come and Dine': The Dangers of Conspicuous Consumption in French Revolutionary Politics, 1789-1795," *European History Quarterly* 45, no. 4 (2015), 615–37.

tranquility."[149] The club called for similar policies in the provinces. Nevertheless, remaining meetings needed to retain their enthusiasm: one Jacobin Representative on Mission to Burgundy, Bernard de Saintes, declared popular societies remained in charge of "enlightening the people," while "surveilling public functionaries, denouncing abuses, and pursuing traitors" with still-greater zeal.[150]

The Jacobins increasingly abridged free speech. Before Paris's club on November 1, de-frocked monk and Convention deputy François Chabot argued that whereas English press liberty "counterbalanced despotism," now under the "French republican government, I argue liberty of the press must respect the government," while any author "speaking maliciously of democracy" deserved punishment.[151] Petition-campaigns to influence national policies nearly ceased during the Year II.[152] Jacobins, fearing excessive anarchy, wanted to direct discussion toward preferred issues but risked choking the movement's creative freedom.

The Jacobins, despite growing repressiveness, nevertheless believed they were propagating an unprecedentedly democratic system. Before the Convention on February 5, Robespierre declared the new regime both "democratic" and "republican." Though "democracy" since Ancient Greece had typically been a slur for mob politics and anarchic government, the Jacobin leader embraced the term, asserting, "democracy is a state where the sovereign people, guided by the laws which are their work, do all they can, and by delegates all they cannot do themselves." As "democracy is equality," it was the French Revolution's basis. Yet this address became known as the "Virtue and Terror" speech, asserting a "popular government in revolution" required a "despotism of liberty against tyranny" to triumph. The Convention ordered it "translated into all languages" for universal diffusion.[153] Terror became justified as a necessary step toward a better future. Full democratization would have to wait until the world was made safe for it.

Hopes rose, in vain, that Britain would overthrow its aristocracy and rejoin the cause of liberty. In early 1794 false reports spread that "Pitt is hanged" and "revolution is underway in London," though French Revolutionaries again were disappointed.[154] Robespierre thereafter orated the Revolution would "enlighten the English people" anew against a political order "wanting to retrograde a nation that has conquered its rights towards despotism and ignorance." From French perspective there seemed little reason that British

---

[149] Ibid., FR 2I113.
[150] Marcel Henriot, *Le club des jacobins de Semur* (Dijon: Rebourseau, 1933), 337.
[151] Aulard, *Jacobins*, Vol. 5, 492.
[152] Kennedy, *1793–1795*, 58.
[153] Robespierre, *Oeuvres*, Vol. 10, 352–66. On the uses of "democracy" in this era, see Philp and Innes, *Re-Imagining*.
[154] Couthon, *Correspondance*, 277.

reactionary loyalism, particularly among "a people previously the friends of philosophy and liberty," should succeed.[155]

Despite great fears of internal subversion, the Jacobins continued recruiting local branches (renamed *sociétés populaires*) across most French villages. They hoped to mobilize the broadest number against plots and encourage revolutionary participation. The Revolution's democratizing potential seemed nearly fulfilled. Convention deputy Marc-Antoine Julien, on mission in Saint-Malo, wrote to Robespierre on October 1 that he

> preached to the popular societies the need to rally to the Convention, through establishing popular societies in every commune. The people must be shown that the Revolution is made for them, that it is time the poor and the *sans-culottes* dominate because they are the majority; the good of the greatest number must be the social contract's goal.[156]

Club affiliates skyrocketed, tripling from two to six thousand from late 1793 to spring 1794. In some areas, repentant purged members were allowed to rejoin. Interest spread in including humble Frenchmen: even in the hyper-politicized Paris region, 80 percent of communes formed their Jacobin Club in the Year II (September 21, 1793).[157] The revolutionary alliance could solidify, with Paris's Jacobins declaring the clubs would hold the "Confidence of all good citizens and authorities," as revolutionaries worked to strengthen the new regime.[158]

Jacobin radicals believed they needed to act ruthlessly to ensure the Republic's survival. Saint-Just in February orated before the Convention, "Justice is not clemency: it is severity." Inflexibility became the method for avoiding backsliding: "Those who make revolutions halfway are only digging a grave." Amid foreign and civil war, the new order could only be established with force. Believing present instability could not continue, he asserted, "the generous violence of patriotism" would carry France forward.[159] Extreme circumstances encouraged unforgiving measures.

By March 1794, there was no lack of candidates on which Jacobin suspicion could fall. Hébert, "voice of the *sans-culottes*," at the Cordeliers called for a "sacred insurrection" against the Convention to expel Robespierre and his allies (like that against the Girondin leadership the year before), to which two Paris sections rallied – demonstrating wavering support even among the revolutionary avant-garde. Hébert and several followers were arrested the night of March 13 and executed the twenty-fourth.[160] Danton and

---

[155] Robespierre, *Oeuvres*, Vol. 10, 344–45.
[156] Robespierre, *Correspondance*, 190.
[157] Higonnet, *Goodness*, 49; Kennedy, *1793–1795*, 94; Monnier, "Sociétés," 358.
[158] AM Reims FR2I113.
[159] Saint-Just, *Oeuvres*, 662, 667, 682.
[160] Morris Slavin, *The Hébertistes to the Guillotine: Anatomy of a Conspiracy in Revolutionary France* (Baton Rouge: Louisiana State University Press, 1994).

Desmoulins, renowned for their revolutionary exploits, nevertheless fell afoul of the regime for speaking against the escalation of terror. Castigated as "Indulgents," they were arrested on March 29. Not just conspiracy but insufficient zeal became a revolutionary crime: "indulgence is ferocious," Saint-Just orated, "because it menaces the fatherland."[161] Both leaders were guillotined after speedy trials on April 5. Committee of Public Safety member Couthon encouraged "rigorous purification" of Jacobin Clubs, finding "no lack of candidates," even if proof remained rare. There could be little objection to "raising the mask of hypocrites" undermining the Republic.[162]

Festivals celebrating Jacobin humanitarianism proceeded apace. Although colonial slavery's abolition resulted from Saint-Domingue insurgencies rather than French charity, while Jacobins had remained quiet on colonial issues since the 1791 revolt, the club network nevertheless celebrated the first comprehensive abolition in any Atlantic empire. Limoges' Jacobins considered the revolution had again defeated "despotism and tyranny," while "regenerating nature" and extending virtue.[163] At *Commune-affranchie* (Lyon's imposed name after the Federalist Revolt), a Jacobin orator celebrated "Africans, Americans, and all peoples from one pole to the other" whom "no one has the right to oppress, to shackle a being born like themselves for liberty."[164] Even former slaving ports like Le Havre, renamed Havre-Marat, celebrated with a civic festival.[165] Though forced by colonial civil war's exigencies, the grand act captured the imagination of a club network founded to propagate freedom.

Culturally, the Jacobins seemed close yet far from their desired order. Robespierre in a May oration described the paradox by which "nature tells us man is born for liberty, and the experience of centuries shows us man as a slave."[166] How to break from recorded history's destructive patterns posed real challenges. Limoges' Jacobins in May called for "promptly organizing public education" to propagate "moral theory."[167] Still, it remained difficult not to consider, as Bergerac's Jacobins wrote to the Convention, that "fanaticism and superstition here take the place of reason," as Jacobin culture increasingly separated from the surrounding population's.[168] The cultural revolution remained incomplete.

Dual Jacobin emphases on liberty and terror could not hold. At Paris's club on 6 Thermidor (July 23, 1794, according to the old calendar), fighting

---

[161] Saint-Just, *Oeuvres*, 734.
[162] Couthon, *Correspondance*, 305, 307.
[163] Fray-Fournier, "Règlement," 259.
[164] BM Poitiers S26 150/1 77.
[165] AM Le Havre K 45.
[166] Robespierre, *Oeuvres*, Vol. 10, 443.
[167] Fray-Fournier, "Règlement," 301.
[168] Labroue, *Société*, 356.

recurring ill-health and possible mental breakdown, Robespierre revivified past divisions, claiming "Brissotins and Girondins recombine" to "mislead" the Convention and French people. On 8 Thermidor, in the Convention, he delivered a Manichean speech "Against New Factions and Corrupt Deputies," asserting, "There are two powers on earth: reason and tyranny." The next day, on 9 Thermidor, legislators drowned out Saint-Just, and when Robespierre appeared, Convention legislators chanted, "Down with the tyrant."[169] Retreating to City Hall, Robespierre called for a Parisian insurrection, but having had their deliberative powers reduced, few sections responded.[170] The Jacobin Club only belatedly voiced support for the Robespierrists, but when their deputation saw Convention-loyal soldiers surrounding the proscribed faction, they went home. The troops captured the Robespierrists, locked up the empty Jacobin Club, and guillotined selected leaders the next morning.[171]

Under the early Thermidorian order, the Jacobin Clubs' future was uncertain. The Paris club's session on 11 Thermidor, as Robespierre's allies continued being carted to the guillotine, remained "few in number." Yet the Jacobins expected to continue playing a significant role in national government, particularly once the anti-Robespierre reaction passed.[172] Marseille opened its sessions on 17 Thermidor with cries of "*Vive la République! Vive la Montagne! Vivent les Sociétés Populaires!*" Robespierrists were recast as "accomplices of the most execrable plots against our liberty."[173] Indeed, many clubs undertook further proscriptions with "moderates" still targeted. Jacobins took new oaths "to the National Convention and the one indivisible Republic."[174] Across France, only 4.4 percent of locals closed in Thermidor.[175]

Most clubs intended to carry Jacobin projects forward. To Marseille's Jacobins on 5 Fructidor (August 23), the "energy the Mountain has always deployed against the Revolution's enemies" needed to be redoubled.[176] Paris's Committee of Correspondence wrote to Poitiers two weeks later of how "Aristocracy never ceased to mask itself" and now "arrange themselves amongst tyranny's victims."[177] Many still demanded extra-constitutional "Revolutionary government until the Peace" and highlighted the Jacobin network's positive aspects: Brest sent a national circular encouraging club members to maintain "a concert of thoughts, opinions, and means to further

[169] Robespierre, *Oeuvres*, Vol. 10, 539, 542–76, 587–88.
[170] Colin Jones, "The Overthrow of Maximilien Robespierre and the 'Indifference' of the People," *American Historical Review* 119, no. 3 (2014), 689–713.
[171] Andress, *Terror*, 342.
[172] Aulard, *Jacobins*, Vol. 6, 295.
[173] AD Bouches-du-Rhône L 2076.
[174] Martin, *Révolution*, 193; Labroue, *Société*, 364; AD Puy-de-Dôme L 6372; Le Roy, 205.
[175] Kennedy, *1793–1795*, 263.
[176] AD Bouches-du-Rhône, L 2077.
[177] BM Poitiers S26 149/1 95.

the world's first democracy" through constant action.[178] With the fight for liberty ongoing, dedicated Jacobins considered their mission undiminished.

With the wartime situation improving, accomplishment of the Jacobins' grandest designs appeared close. "Our arms are everywhere victorious on the continent," Le Mans' Jacobins declared on 19 Fructidor. "Each theater of war has moved onto enemy territory." While advancing, they sought to "electrify inhabitants' hearts with flames of liberty" for universal victory.[179] In what still seemed to many Jacobins a moment of triumph, victory would be a terrible thing to waste.

The Thermidorian press, however, increasingly turned against the Jacobins. One pamphlet titled *Hang the Jacobins, They Are Evildoers* considered the organization by 1793 "infested with propagandists," while the "supreme arbiters of their fellow citizens' life and honor." Clubs "dissolved all social connections," arbitrarily judging which local citizens upheld their rapidly changing standards.[180] Another, its title declaring *The Jacobins Assassins of the People*, denounced them as "aristocracy's bastards," claiming superiority and undermining real democratization.[181] Jacobins' use of terror led many to demand their proscription.

The Jacobins were not prepared to go quietly. Though many "seek to destroy this fraternal union," Paris's Jacobins wrote in a circular the Second Complimentary Day of the Year II (September 19), they pledged to redouble efforts to "unmask intriguers" in the republic. The war continued, and Jacobins would "combat with the same energy and courage all internal enemies."[182] Provincial addresses adopted similar tones. Reims wrote to the Convention the same week, pledging to "not abandon to the furor of aristocrats or intriguers" their "frontier department" in wartime. Only by continuing could they establish "the harmony that must reign amongst all Republicans wanting to conserve their Liberty." Though denouncing "Robespierre the tyrant," they sought to maintain Jacobin practices.[183] "Annihilating popular societies means reversing the republic," Toulouse's Jacobins added, asserting Ancient Greece's fall began when Athenians ceased "meeting on the public square" and deferred to generals and demagogues.[184]

The Jacobin cause cratered due to actions of both their members and enemies. Some clubs began expelling "terrorists." Many less committed Jacobins, meanwhile, voted with their feet – attendance fell in many locals over Year II's last month. By 25 Vendémiaire Year III, the Convention began

[178] BM Poitiers S26 150/1 50.
[179] AD Sarthe L 270.
[180] *Pendez les Jacobins, ce sont des scélérats* (S.l., 1794), 4–5.
[181] Barthel, *Les Jacobins assassins du peuple* (Paris: Bonnes Gens, 1794), 7–8.
[182] Aulard, *Jacobins*, Vol. 6, 494–97.
[183] AM Reims FR 2I108 30.
[184] BM Poitiers S26 150/1 217.

punitive measures against the weakened network, banning clubs' collective correspondence, petitions, and interference with government work. The revised Declaration of the Rights of Man and Citizen, promulgated days later, eliminated the right to assemble. Thermidorian Representatives on Mission, meanwhile, purged provincial societies of radical members.[185]

As reactionary young Muscadins seized control of Paris's streets, aided by sympathetic legislators, the Jacobin Club became an attractive target. On 22 Brumaire (November 12, 1794), after rumors of Jacobins considering new "incendiary motions against national representation," a crowd gathered outside, throwing rocks through the windows. Muscadins beat those fleeing the shattering glass, forcing them to run a humiliating gauntlet through rue St. Honoré's open sewer, amid the jeers of three thousand opponents.[186] In the name of public order, the Convention decreed the Paris club's permanent closure two days later.

By Ventôse Year III (February 1795) 58.9 percent of Jacobin Clubs closed, increasing to 84.8 percent by Prairial (May).[187] Many clubs' participation had already declined: Honfleur's last session discussed low attendance, while disputing rumors that "the Convention wants to destroy popular societies."[188] While such organizations were permitted several months longer, on 6 Fructidor Year III (August 23, 1795), the day after the Convention approved the Constitution of the Year III, they ordered "assemblies known by the name of Club or Popular Society dissolved," closing halls and confiscating club papers.[189] Though the Convention initially proclaimed the measure temporary, pending new regulations, suppression proved permanent. Justifications included that the clubs had not respected national sovereignty – exercising influence as a "tumultuous minority" and forming "inquisitorial committees" to intimidate the government.[190] Authorities castigated clubs as a failed revolutionary experiment.

Though surreptitious neo-Jacobin Clubs formed over the following years, for a time threatening to recapture political power in Year V, the Jacobins never regained the influence they had during the early First Republic. Though surviving radical Jacobins were freed by the political amnesty the Convention

---

[185] Kennedy, *1793–1795*, 264–65; Aulard, *Jacobins*, Vol. 6, 584; Isser Woloch, *Jacobin Legacy: The Democratic Movement under the Directory* (Princeton: Princeton University Press, 1970), 16; Danièle Pingué, *Les mouvements jacobins en Normandie orientale: Les sociétés politiques dans l'Eure et la Seine-Inférieure, 1790–1795* (Paris: Editions CTHS, 2001), 333.

[186] *Gazette de France*, 21 Brumaire Year III; *Courrier républicain*, 21 Brumaire Year III; and *Mercure universel*, 23 Brumaire Year III.

[187] Kennedy, *1793–1795*, 263.

[188] Biard, *Procès-verbaux*, 684.

[189] Aulard, *Jacobins*, Vol. I, CI.

[190] Dupont de Nemours, *Avant-dernière chapitre de l'histoire du jacobinisme* (S.l.: Dupont, s. d.), 10, 13; Woloch, *Jacobin*, 16.

voted as its last act, ongoing state surveillance and repression prevented the reestablishment of a centralized corresponding network on their earlier model.[191] Aside from small, underground cells of dedicated conspirators, no associational networks reemerged in France for decades. Nowhere around the revolutionary Atlantic did clubs rise higher, or crash harder, than in revolutionary France.

Conclusion

Only in the context of an unprecedentedly heated war for liberation, together with revolutionaries' idealistic attempts to spread liberty abroad, did Jacobin radicalization take the forms it did. Rather than isolating Jacobin foreign policy from domestic concerns, this book considers international concerns integral to the French Jacobin Clubs' development.[192] Rather than a Jacobin network primarily propagating an exclusionary discourse of liberty, as François Furet argued in his famed *Interpreting the French Revolution*, we instead find a movement based on universalist inclusion fighting for its principles under extreme circumstances.[193] Revolutionary near-utopian hopes, as well as their commitment to do whatever necessary to assure liberty's final triumph, led the Jacobins to unprecedented measures. Only amid the frustrations and shortcomings of universalistic idealism did the Jacobins turn toward terror.

Despite the movement's disappointing endings, however, the Jacobin movement represented a great step forward in intensive social movement organizing, soon to be widely imitated around the Atlantic world. The campaigns dominated by privileged and middle-class activists that had typically preceded the Jacobins now paled before the imposing mass movements of the First Republic, creating an unprecedentedly dense network celebrating the participation of common townspeople and *sans-culotte* workers. They sought to mobilize whole communities to surveil the government and its enemies. Even after the Jacobin Clubs' extermination in France, the movement continued to represent the possibilities and risks of a new, democratic future.

---

[191] Peyrard, *Jacobins*, 307; Woloch, *Jacobin*, 149.
[192] See Kennedy's trilogy.
[193] François Furet, *Interpreting the French Revolution*, Elborg Foster, trans. (Cambridge: Cambridge University Press, 1981).

12

Radicalizing Club Life in 1790s Britain

The British, innumerable patriotic orations declared, prided themselves on being the world's freest people. Even though the early British Parliamentary reform movement borrowed heavily from American examples, this was soon forgotten, and British political chauvinism endured. As South Carolinian and future Congressman John Rutledge, Jr., wrote in his travel diary of London in 1788, "The English are great Politicians. People of all ranks and degrees talk Politics & wherever I went Politics were the topic. My feelings were frequently agonized at hearing the French abused, ridiculed & despised; & America whenever she was talked of pitied."[1] Whatever their system's shortcomings, before the French Revolution most Britons congratulated themselves on having forged the world's finest political compact.

As France's revolution radicalized, surpassing easy parallels with Britain's constitutional order, British and French clubs' relationship changed. Increasingly, France became the avant-garde and Britain the country adapting the other's examples. In 1792, a new British radical network arose, the London Corresponding Society (LCS), militating for widespread political reform through a French-style associational model. While the history of the "English Jacobins" has usually been characterized as a reception of French revolutionary ideas in Britain, this account highlights how the movement developed in active dialogue with their French counterparts, who considered the new British organization a potentially pivotal partner for international change. Only war's arrival in early 1793 halted growing convergence between British and French radical networks.

The French Revolution and British Reform Movements

The early French Revolution appeared a fantastic event in Great Britain, with the French – long-mired in absolutist government – embracing liberty on largely Anglo-American models. London's *Public Advertiser* considered the National Assembly's formation "achieved without bloodshed," resembling "the memorable British Revolution of 1688." Even after the Bastille's fall,

---

[1] Duke University Special Collections, John Rutledge, Jr. Papers.

St. James's Chronicle considered the "Revolution in France is remarkable for its mildness" with history providing no examples of such grand advancements occurring with so little carnage.[2] Still, French events' direct effect on British politics in 1789 remained small: with British liberty considered several centuries' accomplishment, France seemed only starting down a long road to freedom.

As the French Revolution rapidly consolidated, however, their advancements – achieving levels of democratic participation unknown in Britain – made recent British reform efforts' futility more pronounced. As "the science of government is now better understood," one 1790 reform pamphlet considered, the caution and conservatism blocking reform seemed unjustifiable. With the "idea of representation" further developed, "a whole community may concur in framing the laws by which it is governed, without being endangered by those tumults and commotions that are inseparable from large assemblies."[3] Prior constraints appeared outmoded as France's great leap made so much seem possible.

Dissenters, particularly through the Revolution Society, loudly publicized their relationships with French revolutionaries. Though declining an invitation to Paris's 1790 Fête de la Fédération, the organization spearheaded British July 14 celebrations.[4] Their London banquet, to "testify their common Joy at an Event so important in itself, and which is likely to promote the general Liberty and Happiness of the World," drew 652 participants to the Crown & Anchor Tavern, including a Nantes Jacobin deputation.[5] Toasts included "the glorious revolution of France," "the triumph of liberty and the destruction of the Bastille," and "Perpetual union between France and England; peace and happiness to the entire world." Emphasizing French liberty became a strategy for pressuring Parliament to expand British civil rights, with Stanhope thanking the French for establishing "liberty of conscience and religion which is the first birthright of man." Reformist speeches followed from Price and Horne Tooke.[6] "We can assure you," reported Nantes' deputation, "the people of London are at least as enthusiastic for the French Revolution as the people of France."[7] French influence grew in Britain at a moment when more liberty seemed won in weeks than across prior centuries.

Bastille Day became a British radical holiday. Travelers poured across the channel for Federation ceremonies with Williams finding the French "madly

[2] *Public Advertiser*, July 7, 1789; *St. James's Chronicle*, July 23, 1789.
[3] B. de Mons, *Reflections on the Causes and Probable Consequences of the Late Revolution in France with a View of the Ecclesiastical and Civil Constitution of Scotland* (Edinburgh: Hill and Cadell, 1790), 20–21.
[4] Price, *Correspondence*, Vol. 3, 306.
[5] *Anniversary of the Revolution in France* (London, 1790); AM Cherbourg 2 1 124.
[6] *Nouvelliste national*, July 25, 1790.
[7] *Journal de Bordeaux*, October 6, 1790.

fond of the English," having "imbibed, with the principles of liberty, the strongest sentiments of respect and friendship toward that people, whom they gratefully acknowledge to have been their masters in this science."[8] In the southern port of Seaford, the local Whig Club arranged tavern festivities expressing hope the French would "extend the ardour of Liberty over all the nations of the earth," making "religious, as well as civil liberty, be universal." They demanded substantive change: "May the decayed limbs be amputated from the body politic of Old England, that its excellent Constitution may regain its native vigour."[9] In Scotland, Dundee's Whig Club celebrated the "triumph of liberty and reason over despotism, ignorance and superstition," sending the National Assembly their "warmest wishes that liberty may be permanently established in France." The assembly replied to Dundee, asserting, "this great example ought to prepare the day when all men will regard themselves as brothers."[10] British reformers and French revolutionaries anticipated a closer relationship to help each other pursue greater freedoms.

The French Revolution did not appeal as broadly to Parliamentary Whigs as many had hoped. Friendly revolutionaries sought out Burke, an American sympathizer and sponsor of Parliamentary reform. Liberal noble Charles-Jean Depont wrote to him in November 1789, wishing to discuss "the Grand Principles of Government." Burke wrote back cautiously that he would gain "heartfelt pleasure when I hear, that, in France, the great publick assemblies, the natural securities for individual freedom, are perfectly free themselves." Depont responded affirmatively. Cloots, a German noble and prominent revolutionary, contacted Burke in May 1790 while helping plan Paris's Fête de la Fédération, suggesting, "Quit your island, my dear Burke, come to France, if you want to experience the most magnificent spectacle that philosophy has ever created."[11] French revolutionaries saw no contradiction between their principles and those of British liberty.

Only thereafter did Burke denounce the French Revolution and its British supporters, writing *Reflections on the Revolution in France*, which he published in November. Responding to the Revolution Society's address to the French National Assembly that sparked the Jacobins' rise, Burke mocked their small numbers – "The cabals here who take a sort of share in your transactions as yet consist but of a handful of people" but worried they would "smuggle" radicalized society models "into this country, manufactured after the newest Paris fashion of an improved liberty." Burke sought to defend England from French contagion, believing it foolhardy to fashion a new order, rather than rely on ancient institutions. "France," he predicted, "will be wholly governed by the

---

[8] Williams, *Letters*, 69.
[9] *English Chronicle*, July 15.
[10] Meikle, *Scotland*, 44–45.
[11] Burke, *Correspondence*, Vol. 6, 31–60, 116.

agitators in corporations, by societies in the towns" bent on "destruction of the crown, the church, the nobility, and the people."[12] Burke reinstilled pride in British institutions and traditions, fearing Francophillic enthusiasm could annihilate the existing order.

Allowing broad-based popular corresponding societies threatened moderate Whigs' very positions. As Burke's son, MP Richard Burke, wrote to House of Lords stalwart Earl Fitzwilliam:

> Suppose the Whig club was to meet the Revolution society, the Constitutional Society – (most of whom, by the way, are our most rancorous enemies) together with some other societies instituted for elections and other purposes – on both sides – do you not think they might form a body – on general principles – which for activity, members, correspondence – to say nothing of junctions and societies in other parts of the Kingdom – to say nothing of the contingencies which might happen to excite a popular ferment (no man can foresee it) do you not think all this, might form a body, which if it meant innovation and violence, it might not be so easy for your Lordship and other moderate men to resist.[13]

The prospect of an allied, unprecedentedly inclusive corresponding society was apparent to British political observers before any such organization existed. Many elites, however, worried about popular mobilization's dangers. "We are all agreed as to our own liberty," Boswell quoted Johnson in his famed 1791 biography, "but we are not agreed as to the liberty of others: for in proportion as we take, others must lose."[14] Interest in reform paled before many propertied men's desire to maintain hierarchy.

British reformers tied their political fate to the French Revolution's progress. A second Nantes deputation to England arrived in September 1790, staying with Stanhope, and was fêted by a Revolution Society meeting on November 4 marking the Glorious Revolution's anniversary, where Fox toasted "the establishment of liberty in all the world." The Nantais wrote home, "All announces to us the most complete success" in building British connections, except with the governing ministry. Though Pitt remained "impenetrable, we count on the opposition to dissuade him from making war."[15] The Revolution Society wrote to Cherbourg's Jacobins in March 1791 proclaiming their "desire that the same principles unite France and England," particularly in "retaking the natural rights which raise human beings out of the most vile oppression."[16] Hope for a future alliance between movements remained.

---

[12] Burke, *Reflections*, 36, 131, 283.

[13] Burke, *Correspondence*, Vol. 6, 128.

[14] Corey Robin, *The Reactionary Mind: Conservatism from Edmund Burke to Donald Trump*, 2nd ed. (Oxford: Oxford University Press, 2017), 8.

[15] *Journal de Bordeaux*, October 20, 1790; *Journal des clubs*, February 17 and March 5, 1791.

[16] AM Cherbourg 2 1 124 2.

Dissenters' campaign for political rights, however, faltered against increasing Anglican opposition – with many believing the reformers leagued with French Revolutionaries. Church of England clergy mounted an anti-disestablishmentarian counter-campaign opposing Test and Corporation Act repeal, declaring the church "in danger." Popular conservative appeals beseeched Britons to "guard" the Constitution "from being trampled on, or annihilated by ambitious democrats," helping spark unrest on July 14, 1791.[17] Fearing disorder, prominent reformers including Fox, Horne Tooke, and Stanhope declined to participate in the annual Revolution Society banquet. The ensuing festivities, including a toast to "Perfect Freedom, instead of Toleration, in Matters of Religion," gathered an evening crowd that paraded along the Strand, encouraging and intimidating inhabitants to burn candles in their windows – until a "corrective crowd" arrived to demand the lights be extinguished.[18] Rioting occurred in Birmingham, where conservatives forcibly dispersed the local Bastille Day banquet, destroyed four Dissenter churches and sacked twenty-seven revolutionary supporters' properties, including Priestley's house, library, and laboratory. Whereas "Religious and political distinctions" had decreased in recent years, one spectator noted, now "like a smothered fire, they burst forth with amazing fury."[19] Rioters shouted, "No philosophers – Church and King for ever!"[20] Priestley never returned to Birmingham and soon sailed to American exile.[21]

The French Revolution's first English enthusiasts were silenced through intimidation. The Revolution Society denounced the Birmingham riot, writing to Rennes' Jacobins, "it is shameful that such atrocities should have been committed by any people, under any denomination of Christians, at the end of the Eighteenth Century," especially being "countenanced in England! which boasts of its freedom, its knowledge and its humanity, is abominable."[22] Yet no groundswell of English support followed. Indeed, conservatives celebrated the

---

[17] Thomas Walker, *A Review of Some of the Political Events Which Have Occurred in Manchester, during the Last Five Years* (London: Boden, 1794), 11–15; Herbert S. Skeats, *History of the Free Churches of England, 1688–1891* (London: Alexander & Shepherd, 1891), 494–95; *Journal des clubs*, July 13, 1791; *Observateur provincial*, V. 7, no. 15; W. T. Laprade, *England and the French Revolution, 1789–1797* (Baltimore: Johns Hopkins University Press, 1909), 41.

[18] *Evening Mail*, July 13, 1791; *Woodfall's Register*, July 15, 1791; *General Evening Post*, July 12, 1791.

[19] HL W. Hutton, "A Narrative of the Dreadful Riots in Birmingham, July 14, 1791," HM 847; *Patriote français*, July 26 and 27, 1791; Robert and Isabelle Tombs, *That Sweet Enemy: Britain and France: History of a Love-Hate Relationship* (New York: Vintage, 2006), 198.

[20] Romilly, *Life*, 343.

[21] Birmingham Public Library, MS 3219/4/13.

[22] Archives municipales de Rennes I 74.

event: the socialite Thrale blamed the event on "Treasonable Toasts," while asserting the destruction "will cure the Taste these Madmen have gained for Revolutions better than any thing that could have happened."[23] As the Dissenters' movement withered, the Revolution Society – which never substantially expanded membership into the wider community – ceased being a major political force, not even organizing a Bastille Day banquet in 1792, creating opportunity for new associations to advance radical reforms.[24]

In Scotland, growing Francophilia merged with smoldering resentment over Parliamentary inaction on Burgh reform. In a May 1791 House of Commons debate, the conservative Dundas did not contest the petitioners' grievances – defending inaction only on the grounds that the Royal Burghs had existed since 1469, and English representation was often as bad.[25] Reformers organized Bastille Day banquets with Glasgow partisans on July 14, raising glasses to the rights of man and abolishing the slave trade, desiring "the dawn of liberty on the continent soon be followed by its meridian splendour" and "the French Revolution be the aera of universal liberty to mankind."[26] Edinburgh's gathering predicted "unexampled happiness to the human race" and warmly toasted Paine and Priestley.[27] The French Revolution inspired reformers to act more boldly than before.

Nevertheless, broad interest in the French Revolution remained in many British liberal and radical circles. The elite Whig Club in autumn 1791 wrote to France's legislature celebrating "the fundamental principles" of their new constitution. As "sons of liberty," they asserted, "should any attempt be made by any despotic power, or powers, to enslave the people of France," they would with their "lives, interest & fortunes, oppose all such measures, until the destruction of slavery, usurpation and tyranny is compleated." National Assembly President Bernard-Germain Lacepède responded, celebrating "the coming alliance between English and French liberty," and the legislature ordered the exchange distributed in English and French.[28] Another wave of letters from Jacobin societies followed; Lorient's celebrated how the "cause of humanity enflames all hearts," while Chartres' encouraged extinguishing "the spirit of rivalry" between the two nations.[29] A Friends of Liberty club

[23] Thrale, *Thraliana*, Vol. 2, 813.

[24] *World*, July 11, 1792.

[25] J. A. Lovat-Fraser, *Henry Dundas, Viscount Melville* (Cambridge: Cambridge University Press, 1916), 38.

[26] John D. Brims, "The Scottish Democratic Movement in the Age of the French Revolution" (PhD Thesis, University of Edinburgh, 1983), 83.

[27] Meikle, *Scotland*, 71.

[28] *Patriote français*, December 8, 1791; *Lettre de la Société des Whigs constitutionnels à l'Assemblée nationale avec la réponse de M. le Président* (Paris: Imprimerie nationale, 1791), 2–6.

[29] *Patriote français*, December 27, 1791.

organized among Whig elites in spring 1792.[30] Prospects for cooperation between the two nations strengthened.

The lack of a radical and socially inclusive British club network with the French Jacobins' power or scope, however, led to calls for a new, national British association. The Francophile *Argus* newspaper in November 1790 declared "frequency of communication" integral to Whigs' political networks, while lack of "unanimity" was "one of the principal reasons why the endeavors of former Oppositions have been ineffectual." Reformers needed closer affiliation to unite their efforts.[31] Paine's *Rights of Man*, selling two hundred thousand copies over 1791–1793 (nearly seven times Burke's *Reflections*), stimulated the idea that a national corresponding network could replace government itself.[32] "If we are asked, 'What is Governments?'" he orated at a radical London club that August, "we hold it to be nothing more than a National Association," for promoting the greatest possible liberty.[33] Given reformers' dissatisfaction with the British government, proposals for new associations moved forward.

Cartwright's Society for Constitutional Information by mid-1791 believed the time for such a moment close. "It is certain that if there are no reforms," their address in Paris's *Journal des clubs* declared, "this society will seize the first occasion to set into action the public spirit of a kingdom enlightened in its interests, to raise a terrible popular indignation." All ought to "voluntarily abandon all unconstitutional authority."[34] Action needed to come from outside the Parliamentary system, as political elites appeared too corrupt to sponsor thoroughgoing reforms. The society did not lead popular mobilization but soon allied with a new French-inspired organization.

The London Corresponding Society and British Radical Associating

The London Corresponding Society, founded in January 1792, attempted to adapt a Jacobin-style network to Britain. In the spirit of international cooperation, Covent Garden shoemaker Thomas Hardy and Maurice Margarot, a multinational radical just arrived from Paris, served as founders. Seeking radical Parliamentary reform to establish universal manhood suffrage, the movement incorporated the working classes to build a broad club network for elaborating reformist politics and educating common people. Though only eight attended the first meeting in a Strand tavern, and twenty-five the second, plans progressed for rapidly expanding the movement. Whereas earlier reform

[30] Laprade, *England*, 57.
[31] *Argus*, November 8, 1790.
[32] Palmer, *Age*, Vol. 2, 476.
[33] Paine, *Address and Declaration to the Friends of Universal Peace and Liberty* (London, s. d.), 5.
[34] *Journal des clubs*, June 22, 1791.

societies had been elite-centered, the Corresponding Society primarily featured artisans, laborers, and shopkeepers (though women remained
excluded).[35] Hardy denounced the "avaricious extortions of that haughty,
voluptuous and luxurious class of beings who wanted us to possess no more
knowledge than to believe all things were created for the use of that small
group of individuals."[36] He initially proposed making the organization open
only to the unenfranchised but reconsidered to build broader coalitions,
including an alliance with the Society for Constitutional Information.[37] The
movement widened political participation to pursue radical reform.

Following earlier networks' example of diffusion through correspondence,
the London Corresponding Society recruited affiliates throughout the British
Isles. "Several thousands of the first printed Address," Hardy recounted, "were
distributed *gratis* throughout the Nation" and printed in newspapers.[38] The
society's first circular declared humans "entitled to Liberty" and resolved "to
keep a watchful eye on the Government," echoing Jacobin vigilance. As
corresponding societies proliferated, branches split into autonomous cells of
20–30, splitting in two when growing further to deter repression. Locals met at
a public house each week, forbidding drunkenness but encouraging sociability
to further their grand designs. Each group sent a delegate for the society's
general committee meetings.[39] The society's Bastille Day banquet in London
boasted forty thousand adherents. By November the organization had twenty-
six divisions in the capital, increasing "much every week," while expanding
into fourteen cities.[40] The rise of a Jacobin-style network, primarily composed
of men excluded from formal participation in British political life, threatened
the political order.

The group drew militants from recent causes. The abolitionist Equiano
shared a residence with Hardy as the LCS formed, leveraged his abolitionist
connections for the new movement, and during book tours recruited

---

[35] Mary Thale, ed., *Selections from the Papers of the London Corresponding Society,
1792-1799* (Cambridge: Cambridge University Press. 1983), 5; BL ADD MS 27808 4;
H. T. Dickinson, *British Radicalism and the French Revolution, 1789-1815* (Oxford:
Blackwell, 1985), 9; George Woodcock, "The Meaning of Revolution in Britain," in *The
French Revolution and British Culture*, Ceri Crossley and Ian Small, eds. (Oxford: Oxford
University Press, 1989), 18.

[36] Palmer, *Age*, Vol. 2, 473.

[37] Clive Emsley, *Britain and the French Revolution* (London: Pearson, 2000), 30.

[38] Thale, *Selections*, 8; Lucyle Thomas Werkmeister, *A Newspaper History of England,
1792-1793* (Lincoln: University of Nebraska Press, 1967), 72.

[39] Michael T. Davis, "The Mob Club? The London Corresponding Society and the Politics of
Civility in the 1790s," in *Unrespectable Radicals? Popular Politics in the Age of Reform*,
Davis and Paul A. Pickering, eds. (London: Ashgate, 2008), 30–31; Thale, *Selections*, 9–10;
BL ADD MS 27808, 4; Walter Phelps Hall, *British Radicalism, 1791-1797* (New York:
Columbia University Press, 1912), 168–69.

[40] University of Reading Special Collections, Turner Collection, 263 90; NA TS 11/959.

provincial affiliates.[41] Others gained new "Subscriptions" to the corresponding societies "in the same way as they were obtained for the abolition of the Slave Trade," as the politically passionate again pulled friends into direct action.[42] Radical societies endorsed abolitionist goals: Sheffield's affiliated Society for Constitutional Information pledged, "That no Man who is an Advocate from Principle for the Liberty of a Black Man" would fail to "strenuously promote and support the Rights of a White Man, and vice versa."[43] British friends of freedom developed a common front.

Corresponding society agitation particularly rose in the underrepresented Midlands that had supported antislavery and reform with such fervor. One hostile paper noted a "great many associations on the same principles have been formed in the manufacturing towns," where "the labourers have been deluded into a belief that by a revolution their situation would be bettered."[44] Sheffield by May reported over two thousand members with surrounding towns forming associations "copying after us," and by September held celebrations drawing 5,000–6,000 for the French army's victory at Valmy.[45] Britain's political class expanded, promoting participation in ways frightening to the political establishment.

A great range of political possibilities lay before the corresponding societies. Paine, having thrice visited France between 1789 and 1791, asserted its essential similarity with what he witnessed in the New World: "The Revolutions of America and France have thrown a beam of light over the world," while the "opinion of the world is changing with respect to systems of Government," including in Britain.[46] A "general revolution in Europe" became increasingly possible. Paine anticipated an alliance of free peoples: America, France, and a liberated Britain. Through "connections and conventions," British "progress will be rapid, till despotism and corrupt government be totally expelled" from the isles.[47] No book gained broader discussion than Paine's, furthering debates on the British establishment's legitimacy.

The Corresponding Society network's first deputation to France came from Manchester, the growing industrial city already at the forefront of the parliamentary reform and antislavery movements. James Watt, Jr. (the steam engine

[41] Carretta, *Equiano*, 296, 348; David Featherstone, "Contested Relationalities of Political Activism: The Democratic Spatial Practices of the London Corresponding Society," *Cultural Dynamics* 22, no. 2 (2010), 89.

[42] National Archives of Scotland, Home GD 267/1/16/10.

[43] *Second Report of the Committee of Secrecy* (London: Debrett, 1794), Appendix D.

[44] *St. James's Chronicle*, December 8, 1792.

[45] *Second Report*, Appendix D; Gwyn A. Williams, *Artisans and Sans-Culottes: Popular Movements in France and Britain during the French Revolution* (New York: Norton, 1969), 58.

[46] Paine, *Rights of Man: Being an Answer to Mr. Burke's Attack on the French Revolution* (London: Jordan, 1791), Part I, 128; Rapport, *Unruly*, 216.

[47] Paine, *The Rights of Man* (London: Jordan, 1792), Part II, 166, 170.

innovator's son), and author-chemist Thomas Cooper arrived at Paris's Jacobin Club on April 13, 1792, a week before the Declaration of War against Austria. Assuring the Paris club "there are men all around who take a lively interest in your cause, the cause not only of the French, but of humankind," the Englishmen orated, "the time has come to abolish all national prejudice, and embrace as brothers all free men, no matter what country they come from."[48] Watt asserted the revolution would only continue forward: with the French becoming enlightened, a counterrevolution could only succeed if "you can make men unknow what they have once known."[49] Whereas the London Revolution Society had only written occasionally to the Paris leadership, the Watt-Cooper deputation requested "friendly correspondence" to "establish the important principles of universal liberty, the only means to establish an empire of peace and happiness for men on a solid and unshakable basis." Paris's Jacobins, in contrast to their coolness toward a Revolution Society alliance the previous year, erupted in applause, embraced the Englishmen, and took an "unbreakable oath" to support the Manchester club, considering them "the natural product of human reason's irreversible progress," and sent Manchester's address to all provincial affiliates. Two days later, Watt and Cooper carried the British flag in the Châteauvieux Festival, marching across Paris to shouts of "Long live the free nations! Long live the union of the English, Americans and French!"[50] A common transnational movement seemed attainable.

Many British conservatives, fearing Frenchified associational designs, believed the new network resulted from French intrigue and international conspiracy. "The Jacobin Club," the *World* newspaper asserted, "have emissaries in almost every city, endeavouring to create disturbances, and raise commotions among the people."[51] By summer, reports circulated detailing "dangerous associating of Jacobin Frenchmen who swarm about the Coffeehouses" in London, "reviling monarchical Government on every occasion."[52] British interactions with French Revolutionaries looked like guilt by association: "Their correspondence with France is another proof," *St. James's Chronicle* asserted, of a conspiracy "to bring about in this country all that has happened there."[53] As the revolution's offensive potential became clearer, few Britons remained neutral toward French models.

---

[48] *Discours de MM. Cooper et Watt, Députés de la société constitutionnelle de Manchester, prononcé à la société des amis de la Constitution, séante à Paris, le 13 avril 1792* (Paris, 1792), 2–5.

[49] BPL MS 3219/4/13/30.

[50] *Discours de MM. Cooper*, 2–5; Aulard, *Jacobins*, Vol. 3, 500; *Belfast Newsletter*, May 4, 1792.

[51] *World*, April 20, 1792.

[52] *Evening Mail*, September 17, 1792.

[53] *St. James's Chronicle*, December 8, 1792.

International war, to British and French radicals, provided opportunity. Watt breathlessly wrote to his father from Paris, "the whole nation has long impatiently desir'd" the conflict and could now combat counterrevolutionaries. Accusing British elites of having "a preconcerted plan to embroil us with the French," he argued French support needed to be voiced "by every other Society of a similar nature in England, as I have no doubt it will." The fights the French picked, Watt continued, improved the "Moral & Physical state of the nation," as the "vice & immorality of all ranks is diminished since the absence of the emigrants & the reform of the Court."[54] With the revolution's opponents uncovered, the time for establishing a new order arrived.

The Corresponding Society used French exchanges to bring its developing network together, generating publicity and support. Watt found the Manchester address "makes a great noise here," adding he "sent copies home which will probably be inserted in the English papers with the [Jacobin] President's answer." Such gestures inspired through demonstrating the palpable closeness between peoples and movements. Watt believed his deputation helped lay "the foundation of a general alliance amongst the patriotic Societies of Europe to fix a barrier against the intrigues of Ministers & Kings," while establishing "the peace & happiness of Nations upon a broad and durable basis, the will of the people."[55] Beyond symbolic exchanges, an integrated British-French club alliance could become an irresistible popular force.

To many, the French Revolution presented an opportunity for domestic change not to be wasted. "Four years of revolutions," wrote Irish native turned French General Arthur Dillon in mid-1792, "are worth more than fifty years of meditation." The time came to "turn attention to our internal government's abuses," and not be dissuaded by "timid spirits fearing the danger of innovation" who derailed prior efforts.[56] The king's birthday on June 4, traditionally for loyalist patriotic celebrations, incited rioting in Edinburgh, where the following week, crowds marched an effigy of anti-reform leader Dundas (mocked as "Harry the Ninth"), which they burnt outside his residence.[57] Yet many remained amenable to peaceful change instead of forcible overthrow: the 1792 Bastille Day toasts, after saluting "the glorious revolutions of France and America," asserted, "revolutions become unnecessary through radical reform."[58] Regardless of method, the present revolutionary moment appeared the time to act.

---

[54] BPL MS 3219/4/13/31, 32, 33.

[55] Ibid., 3219/4/13/31.

[56] Arthur Dillon, *Progrès de la Révolution française en Angleterre* (Paris: Gattey, 1792), 11–13.

[57] Kenneth J. Logue, *Popular Disturbances in Scotland, 1780–1815* (Edinburgh: John Donald Publishers, 1979), 136–38.

[58] URSC Turner Collection, 263 90.

Elite reformers, however, considered the new corresponding societies a threat rather than an ally. MP Gilbert Elliot in April believed the "association is in its infancy," but well-positioned to "excite a clamour and raise a flame" on Parliamentary reform. Through promoting "associations all over England," encouraging discussions among the broad populace, the movement became uncontrollable for elite purposes. At a "party of lords and great people" the following month, he found "all of a mind in condemning it."[59] Change had to be initiated from outside the political class.

The London Corresponding Society doubted the House of Commons would ever abridge its own power without great pressure. "A Reform in Parliament," Sheffield's branch declared, "is almost universally allowed to be essentially necessary," yet the "Enemies to a Reform are a very active, numerous, and powerful Body in almost every Neighbourhood and never fail to unite" against any threat. Confronting a "jealous, powerful, and well-disciplined Phalanx, long enured to every possible Mode of Attack" would not be easy.[60] Popular interest nevertheless spread: Sheffield alone gathered ten thousand signatures for manhood suffrage in May.[61] Yet how to proceed without incurring treason charges from an elite-dominated political order remained an enduring problem.

By summer 1792, British radical politics changed in Scotland as well. The Commons rejected a Burgh reform motion in April 1792 and refused to even hear supporters' petitions (including one signed by eleven thousand Edinburgh residents), effectively ending legislative hopes.[62] Scottish agitation's social composition widened: as one hostile Scotsman described, whereas previously "Reform took its rise from the Burrow Politicians that were out of power and wanted to get into it," now "poor tradesmen, manufacturers and laborers" mobilized.[63] Cotton mill workers in Partick formed a society of "the Sons of Liberty and the Friends of Man."[64] Following the French example, now "many People, and some of no mean ability, are determined to exert themselves to bring about a similar Revolution" at home. Regional gatherings increased with a "Generall Meeting of delegates from all the Revolution Societies" of Edinburgh (dubbed "the Paris of Scotland") asserting "the will only is wanting" to "overturn the present Government and set a new one in any form they think proper."[65] By autumn, Edinburgh's associated clubs cemented

---

[59] Elliot, *Life*, Vol. 2, 11, 20.

[60] *Second Report*, Appendix F, no. 1.

[61] Robert R. Dozier, *For King, Constitution and Country: The English Loyalists and the French Revolution* (Lexington: University of Kentucky Press, 1983), 27.

[62] Harris, *Scottish*, 77; Harris, "Political Protests in the Year of Liberty, 1792," in *Scotland in the Age of the French Revolution*, Harris, ed. (Edinburgh: Donald, 2005), 60.

[63] NAS Home GD 267/1/16/7.

[64] Brims, "Scottish," 204.

[65] NAS Home GD 267/1/16/7.

an alliance with the United Irishmen.[66] Britain now seemed awash in popular politics, threatening elite control.

The London Corresponding Society sought the closest possible alliance with revolutionary France. On October 11, 1792, the central committee, asserting the international situation required them to back "the French Nation's arduous struggle against despotism and Aristocracy," asked branches to fully endorse the French war cause by approving a proposed address to the National Convention or sending objections in writing.[67] The resulting document reached the Convention on November 7, pledging society support for "the defenders of the Rights of Man."[68] Endorsing the French Revolution became a prerequisite for inclusion in British radical politics. Margarot communicated to France the society's desire for a "triple alliance (not of crowns but) of the people of America, France, and Britain," to bring "freedom to Europe, and peace to the whole world.[69] The British movement tied its future to a favorable outcome of the French revolutionary wars.

A new London Corresponding Society deputation arrived at France's National Convention on November 28, publicizing the British movement's program and connections with French Revolutionaries. The culmination of a century of Enlightenment and decades of Revolution approached:

> A stronger light, image of the real Aurora, shone forth from the bosom of American Republic, but its distance prevented it from enlightening your hemisphere. It was necessary that the French Revolution, beaming forth in the full fervor of a meridian sun, should suddenly display in the midst of Europe the practical result of the principles which philosophy had sown in the shade of meditation, and which experience every where confirms.

As "parallel societies now form in all parts of England" the address concluded, "revolutions will become easy. It would not be extraordinary if in a short time you received greetings from a National Convention of England."[70] Considering France a shining example, the deputation broadcast the French origins of their radicalization and plans for British change.

French assemblymen responded enthusiastically, believing British radicals could spark regime change. Such "frequent testimonies of affection," deputy

---

[66] Mathieson, *Awakening*, 122; Alte L. Wold, *Scotland and the French Revolutionary War, 1792-1802* (Edinburgh: Edinburgh University Press, 2015), 14; E. W. McFarland, *Ireland and Scotland in the Age of Revolution: Planting the Green Bough* (Edinburgh: Edinburgh University Press, 1994), 73.

[67] NA TS 11/952 3496; Scott, 159–60.

[68] *Adresses, &c., &c., &c.* (London, 1792), 12–15.

[69] Peter Mackenzie, *The Life of Thomas Muir, Esq.* (London: Simpkin & Marshall, 1831), xiii.

[70] "Députation de la part de la Société constitutionnelle de Londres, admise à la Convention nationale de France, le 28ieme novembre, 1792," *A Collection of Addresses by Certain English Clubs and Societies to the National Convention of France* (London, 1793), 13–14.

Nicolas Marey-Monge considered, demonstrated real potential.[71] The Convention adopted an address urging British reformers to "filter useful information through all branches of the social tree," promoting an "eternal alliance" between free peoples.[72] Legislator Jean-Henri Bancal expected the societies to "lead England to a glorious revolution" by convoking a "National Convention." Thus, "Our example will be useful to the English, as we have profited from that they provided us."[73] The Jacobins circulated the LCS addresses, declaring revolution "will circle the earth."[74] Given the quick spread of prior reform, antislavery, and Jacobin networks, another groundswell seemed possible.

The deputation joined a formidable community of British expatriates in Paris pursuing the widest applications of universalist revolutionary possibility. Not far from the Palais-Égalité, White's Hotel, also known as *Hôtel de la Philadelphie*, hosted a twice-weekly "British Club" for Anglophones and on November 18 held a banquet "celebrating the victories of the French Republic's armies and the triumph of liberty," featuring Paine, Barlow, former British MP Robert Smyth, Irish MP Lord Fitzgerald, writer Helen Maria Williams, and (possibly) poet William Wordsworth. Toasts included to a "Convention of Britain and Ireland," "perpetual union of the peoples of England, France, America and the Netherlands," and a "democratic alliance" between the world's free peoples.[75] In the moment's elation, such possibilities beckoned.

Many French Jacobins, enamored with Britain's potential and seeking all available help to combat the Austrian invasion, pursued interactions with British clubs. "Generous Republicans," wrote Jacobins from the threatened northeastern town of Laon in December after receiving British arms and supplies, "the philanthropic gift you present France's warriors announces your enthusiasm for the sacred cause they defend." Soon, they declared, "France and England shall form a Treaty of Union as lasting as the course of the Seine and the Thames."[76] Less-threatened areas concurred: "How glorious will it be for France & England to confederate for the destruction of Tyrants?" asked Jacobins from the Provençal town of Apt. "[S]oon they will become our allies," asserted Mâcon's.[77] Though the Convention responded to a martial address received from a radical society at Newington (near Dover) on November 10 by urging English adherence to neutrality, the Society for Constitutional Information (SCI)'s shipping a thousand pairs of boots to

[71] AD Côte-d'Or L 3024 3.

[72] URSC Turner 263 195.

[73] BM Clermont-Ferrand, "Lettres de Jean-Henri Bancal, député de Puy-de-Dôme à la Convention," MSS 348.

[74] AD Hérault, L 5527.

[75] Israel, *Expanding*, 304–5; *Journal de Perlet*, November 21, 1792; Mathiez, *Révolution*, 37.

[76] NA TS 11/952 3496.

[77] Ibid.

Dunkirk led France's War Minister to thank them for helping "propagate Universal Liberty."[78] Londoners burnt Prussian commander the Duke of Brunswick in effigy on Guy Fawkes Day in Kensington Gardens. Glasgow protesters did likewise, chanting "liberty or death."[79] Throughout 1792, nationalism remained less salient than the Revolution's international potential.

In France, the British continued being celebrated as a people ripe for revolution. In the Convention, many like Couthon became convinced, "The English, our neighbors and our friends, are affected as if in a fever of liberty," with rumors spreading in November of the royal family fleeing the British capital in fear.[80] Recognizing British fervor, multiple French districts elected Paine a Convention deputy with the author (despite not speaking French) agreeing to represent Pas-de-Calais. Bordeaux's Jacobins, after telling "English People, one hundred years after your last revolution, the French march in your steps," suggested the French Revolution offered "the model of a wiser and truly free government, and we would be happy to see you imitate us."[81] After three years of revolution, British regime change remained no more implausible than many recent French changes.

Revolutionary influence altered British politics in unprecedented ways. French victories in fall 1792 elicited rapturous responses. The French press noted "festivals and illuminations" in "the principal cities," including caricatures of the defeated monarchs.[82] Workingmen's support spread: a hostile December report from Norwich noted the "discontented are a very numerous body, and chiefly manufacturing men."[83] Demonstrations in Perth, Dundee, and Aberdeen, Scotland, burnt Dundas effigies again, some chanting "liberty, equality and no king!"[84] Many Britons took revolutionary France's side, supporting even its most radical acts.

Mobilizing Loyalism and Repressing Radicalism

Despite 1792's radical upsurge, the British state and conservatives proved stronger still, mobilizing vast numbers of Britons to drown the revolutionary wave. Many considered the French Revolution an attack on hierarchy threatening all of virtually any standing.[85] Conservatives wound up adapting the revolutionary corresponding society to their own purposes, mobilizing new

---

[78] *A Collection of Addresses*, 3; Reading, Turner 263 194.
[79] *Patriote français*, November 16, 1792; *Public Advertiser*, November 26, 1792.
[80] Couthon, *Correspondance*, 208.
[81] BM Poitiers S 26 146/1 32.
[82] *Journal des débats de la société des amis de la constitution*, November 27, 1792.
[83] BL Crown & Anchor Association Papers, ADD MS 16920 2.
[84] Meikle, *Scotland*, 96; Emma Vincent, "The Responses of Scottish Churchmen to the French Revolution, 1789–1802," *Scottish Historical Review* 73, no. 2 (1994), 191.
[85] Robin, *Reactionary*, 13.

loyalist organizations to repress radical challengers, accepting mass politics on a scale no European Old Regime would countenance.

Reacting against growing discontent, authorities targeted radical publishing rings. The Crown on May 2, 1792, ordered "suppression of divers wicked and Seditious writings published and industriously dispersed with a view to Encite discontents, Tumults and disorders."[86] Seventy counties and three hundred town meetings, including reformist strongholds like Manchester, sent supportive loyal addresses.[87] On May 14, Paine's official publisher was indicted. Radical presses' proliferation continued, however, distributing to nearly a thousand booksellers and even more circulating libraries across England and Wales alone: the Marquess of Buckingham wrote to Grenville in November, "it is hopeless to endeavor to restrain them," as such publications' number and diversity made seditious libel charges ineffective.[88] Such radical industry, in tandem with French triumphs, shook British politics anew.

Many mainstream newspapers, to avoid growing repression, turned against the radical movements. *Woodfall's Register* in August saw a great coalition forming of "LEVELLERS – INNOVATERS, REFORMERS – ASSOCIATORS – FRIENDS OF THE PEOPLE – ENGLISH JACOBINES," combining against the throne.[89] *The World* mocked "the danger and the folly" of the French permitting "their country to be governed by a Club."[90] Through attempting to reduce French revolutionary governance to the Jacobins, the press condemned similar British organizations.

As French war became likely, the administration sought allies. Grenville in November, to "stop the clubs which are making, particularly in London, a most alarming progress," called "for counter associations," as "the peace of the country cannot otherwise be preserved."[91] Dundas wrote to Pitt that as "the Spirit of liberty and equality continues to spread," those "well affected to the Constitution" needed to take "an open and declared part to check the first appearance of Sedition."[92] Isolated elites could not maintain the British order alone – an active populace needed to contest radicals' broadening support.

---

[86] NAS RH2/4/66.

[87] Alan Booth, "Popular Loyalism and Public Violence in the North-West of England, 1790–1800," *Social History* 8, no. 3 (1983), 298; Evans, *Debating*, 56.

[88] J. B. Fortescue, *The Manuscripts of J.B. Fortescue, Esq., Preserved at Dropmore*, William Windham, ed. (London: Stationary Office, 1892), Vol. 2, 336; Evans, *Debating*, 34; Ray Hemmings, *Liberty or Death: Early Struggles for Parliamentary Democracy* (London: Lawrence and Wishart, 2000), 65.

[89] *Woodfall's* Register, August 27, 1792.

[90] *World*, July 6, 1792.

[91] Michael Duffy, "William Pitt and the Origins of the Loyalist Association Movement of 1792," *Historical Journal* 39, no. 4 (1996), 946; Austin Mitchell, "The Association Movement of 1792–1793," *Historical Journal* 4, no. 1 (1961), 59.

[92] Duffy, "William," 943.

The Association for Preserving Liberty and Property against Republicans and Levellers, founded that month by conservative judge and former Newfoundland governor John Reeves, rapidly created a nationwide association to rally patriotic opinion against radical societies and publishers. The association used London's Crown & Anchor Tavern as their headquarters, where the Revolution Society previously held Bastille Day banquets, a three-story public house with a great room seating two thousand and a prominent location on the Strand. Defending a conservative interpretation of British constitutional liberties, they sought to suppress those they believed to be licentiously undermining such freedoms. The association pledged loyal aid to the British government to "support the Laws, to suppress seditious Publications, and to defend our Persons and Property against the innovations and depredations" of their opponents.[93] The new organization pledged to use all legal measures, enhanced by recent repressive legislation and executive orders expanding treasonous offences, to defeat the radical movement through attrition.

For precedent, Reeves spoke glowingly of sister antihumanitarian movements, particularly the anti-abolitionist movement to preserve the slave trade. Whereas "a few months ago there was a general outcry against the Cruelty & Oppression of the Slave Trade, & hundreds of Petitions were presented from different places to abolish it," they asserted "proper steps were taken to inform the public all clamour subsided, and we hear no further complaints against it at the present."[94] The association received the powerful West-India Merchants and Planters lobby's aid, creating an alliance between the era's two most influential antireform groups. Slave traders denounced the radical societies as "tending to loosen the bonds of well-ordered society, destructive of Property," similarly to how they denounced abolitionists. Few groups had greater reason to "declare our firm attachment to the established Constitution of Great Britain" in all its peculiarity.[95] Organization branches reached out to corporate interests, as political upheaval "would so much concern their own Interest as well as the public tranquility."[96] Uniting to oppose expansive conceptions of human rights, loyalist defenses of British imperial exploitation became increasingly unapologetic. Conservative movements could converge like radical ones.

Endeavoring to defeat radical formations, the Society for the Preservation of Liberty and Property used many of their political opponents' strategies to

---

[93] *Association Papers*, 2. On the Crown and Anchor, see Christina Parolin, *Radical Spaces: Venues of Popular Politics in London, 1790–c.1845* (Canberra: Australian National University Press, 2010), 105–22 and Baer, "Political Dinners in Radical, Whig and Tory Westminster," *Parliamentary History* 24, no. 1 (2005), 189.

[94] BL Crown & Anchor Association Papers, ADD MS 16919 1.

[95] *World*, December 22, 1792.

[96] BL ADD MS 16920 84.

create a national club network.[97] Like the Corresponding Society, the new conservative organization employed meetings and "cheap Publications" for "undeceiving and informing those persons, who have been misled, and deluded by specious Reasonings" from their radical brethren.[98] Similar to France's Jacobins, the network promoted vigilance against those seeking to undermine British patriotism. A London suburban meeting in Peckham associated to combat "Factious Men, who may attempt a lawless Reformation of our present happy Constitution and Government," resolving to correspond with any group seeking "detection of all Treasonable or Seditious Practices."[99] In a country without extensive police forces, associators deemed citizen action necessary amid dire threats.

In other respects, radical and conservative club models diverged – with the latter considering popular mobilization a temporary expedient rather than a new political paradigm. Even though conservative societies drew their power from popular action, they specified most business "should be conducted by a committee," as "these are not open Societies for talk and debate," but rather practical organizations for suppressing dissent. Indeed, not all were freestanding clubs, as many affiliated with merchant associations, town or county bodies, local combinations of farmers or laborers, or even Freemason lodges.[100] Chester's branch described themselves as "unconnected with any Party," simply pursuing "wicked and interested Disturbers of the public Peace."[101] Crown & Anchor directives in late November declared,

> The object of such Societies should be to check the circulation of seditious publications of all kinds, whether newspapers or pamphlets, or the invitations to club-meetings, by discovering and bringing to justice not only the authors or printers of them, but those who keep them in shops, or hawk them in the streets for sale; or, what is much worse, are employed in circulating them from house to house in any manner whatever.

By preventing seditious materials' distribution – uncovering, intimidating, and disabling all steps of their supply chain – while becoming government collaborators, associators believed they could choke French principles' spread. Additionally, locals would "hold themselves in readiness to prevent or suppress tumults or riots, if necessary." While freedom of speech in clubs had been an "irregularity ... once permitted," now such opinions became "always

---

[97] *Association for Preserving Property against Republicans and Levelers / Crown and Anchor Tavern, Strand. November 10, 1795* (London, 1795).
[98] *Lloyd's Evening Post*, November 30, 1792.
[99] *Oracle*, November 30, 1792.
[100] Harris, *Scottish*, 128.
[101] *General Evening Post*, December 20, 1792.

seditious, and very often treasonable."[102] Conservatives co-opted the club model for illiberal and repressive designs.

Particularly around London, many association locals mobilized through Anglican parishes, leveraging congregations for direct political action as only Dissenters previously had. Reeves endorsed preserving the Anglican establishment, while disdaining "Poor Parishioners who are pleas'd, & flatter'd, by the levelling doctrine they hear" from Dissenting ministers.[103] London's St. Martin in the Fields appointed churchwardens to their committee, while Bloomsbury's multi-parish committee featured two rectors.[104] The upsurge became so effective that the central Crown & Anchor branch in December recommended, "Parishes which have not yet united, will immediately proceed to form themselves into Societies, after the Examples of those already instituted."[105] The society equally praised "the established Church" and "the established Constitution."[106] With the British system appearing a single compact, Middlesex' St. Luke parish considered, "We should be ungrateful to God, rebellious to our King, and forgetful of every domestic claim, if we did not stand forth upon the present occasion."[107] Adherence became so widespread that one Devonshire associator asserted, "there are very few parishes but have had meetings, and entered in resolutions."[108] The organization brought the most powerful institutions of British life together.

The new club network, raising ample funds, rewarded authorities for prosecuting radicals. Westminster's St. Anne's Church branch offered to "defray the expense of prosecuting all such offenders" and unstated sums to "reward the Constables, Beadles, Patroles, Watchmen and others" apprehending them.[109] Nevertheless, associations justified such methods for preserving "Peace, Order, and due subordination," with circumstances requiring their vigilance as patriotic citizens.[110] Unprecedented collusion between political organizations and policing forces developed.

To stop radical ideas' spread among the common people, the movement – like the radical corresponding societies – extended across classes, well beyond the British political nation's usual bounds. On December 6, the Crown & Anchor branch requested "all Masters of Families, all Master-Manufacturers, Traders and others" to "undeceive and inform their Servants, their

---

[102] *Public Advertiser*, November 28, 1792.
[103] BL Crown & Anchor Association Papers, ADD MS 16919, 1.
[104] *Oracle*, December 10, 1792.
[105] *Woodfall's Register*, December 13, 1792.
[106] *General Evening Post*, March 5, 1793; *Liberty and Property Preserved against Republicans and Levellers*. No. 1.
[107] *World*, December 13, 1792.
[108] Mitchell, "Association," 62.
[109] *World*, December 8, 1792.
[110] BL ADD MS 16929 1, 38.

Journeymen, their Apprentices, their Neighbours and all persons whom they find misled and corrupted," to encourage loyal opinions and warn of "treasonable" activities' risks.[111] Peers, high clergymen, and Members of Parliament, meanwhile, mostly distanced themselves from the movement.[112] Loyalists organized popular festivities, including over four hundred Paine effigy parades and burnings across Britain (often with his *Rights of Man*), while clergy officiated and bands played "God Save the King" and other patriotic songs.[113] Feeling their growing political potential, common people took increasingly active roles in British politics.

In response to their international opponents, the Preservation association glorified British nationalism and particularism. The Crown & Anchor branch warned that French innovation could annihilate British tradition, asserting the "lives and properties of all persons in this Island would be exposed to the arbitrary disposal of self-opinionated Philosophes, and a wild and needy Mob, deluded and instigated by them."[114] The City of London's "Merchants, Bankers, Traders, and other Inhabitants" argued revolutionary fervor risked Britain's prosperity, threatening "the flourishing State of Navigation and Commerce" of the empire.[115] Britain's advantages in economic development and personal freedom, together with fear of French innovations, provided powerful arguments for the status quo.

Patriotism offered a threatened elite ready refuge, with blind defense of the old order becoming the favored rhetorical method. Bath highlighted how the British constitution "stood for ages the envy and admiration of all Europe," administering "impartial justice" from which "the high-born and the low, the rich and poor" profited.[116] Middlesex' Hendon parish asserted the Constitution possessed "a degree of excellence and perfection to which ancient Legislators and Philosophers thought it impossible for any system of Government to attain."[117] Hackney's suburban London branch considered the Constitution the "pride and boast of Britons," possessing the "admiration of the World."[118] Also considering themselves "Friends to Freedom," associators faced down reformers' critiques and glorified the British system.[119] Loyalism's hitherto latent political power became manifest.

---

[111] *Woodfall's Register*, December 7, 1792.

[112] Philp, "Vulgar Conservatism, 1792–1793," *English Historical Review* 110, no. 435 (1995), 52.

[113] O'Gorman, "The Paine Burnings of 1792–1793," *Past & Present* 193 (2006), 111–55; Nicholas Rogers, "Burning Tom Paine: Loyalism and Counter-Revolution in Britain, 1792–1793," *Histoire sociale / Social History* 32, no. 64 (1999) 139–71.

[114] *General Evening Post*, November 27, 1792.

[115] *Evening Mail*, December 5, 1792.

[116] *Morning Herald*, December 19, 1792.

[117] *Oracle*, December 21, 1792.

[118] *London Chronicle*, December 4, 1792.

[119] BL Crown & Anchor Association Papers, ADD MS 16922.

Associators publicized the prospect of foreign subversion to scare compliance. The Crown & Anchor branch reported "considerable numbers of French lately arrived in the metropolis," associating "with various ill-disposed persons, in Clubs and other meetings" for subversive activities.[120] Westminster's St. Anne's Church branch collected the names and professions "of such Foreigners" residing there.[121] Others engaged in vandalism, pulling down liberty trees in Edinburgh and Dundee.[122] Aggressive measures did not raise ethical quandaries: "We exhibit to mankind," Kington's Association (near the Welsh border) described, "a happy combination of liberty and force."[123] Intimidation, prosecution, and nationalistic exclusion became the network's guiding tactics.

The Preservation society movement succeeded not just through minimizing radical dissent, but by coercing former reformers to join them. Associators drew lists not just of their own members, but those declining to join.[124] Reeves himself recommended keeping a book listing those who "propagate the new Doctrine of Liberty & Equality or such like evil Terrors."[125] Fox, only weeks after denouncing loyal associations at the Whig Club, joined a London local to remain in the political mainstream. Several former reform societies reorganized as association branches.[126] Protestant Dissenters belatedly followed Anglicans into congregation-based associations. Manchester's combined parishes, however, still endorsed a "Constitution so formed ... to redress every real grievance, and effect every necessary improvement."[127] The movement did not so much eliminate dissent as limit it to approved channels.

Conservative mobilization spread across Britain. Scottish loyalists also formed associations: Edinburgh's merchants on December 6 glorified "that happy Establishment, both in Church and State, which has so long been the glory and pride of this Nation."[128] In Aberdeen's Town Hall a week later, the new organization called for "peace and tranquility in this City," pledging to suppress sedition.[129] Allowing "Anarchy" to spread, Glasgow's city council considered, would "ruin our flourishing Commerce and Manufactures," leading Britain to "misery."[130] While moderate reformers influenced a few resolutions, Perth's calling for "a truer Representation of the People" in Parliament to

---

[120] *London Chronicle*, December 4, 1792.
[121] *World*, December 8, 1792.
[122] NAS RH2/4/66 254 and 258.
[123] *London Chronicle*, January 3, 1793.
[124] Dozier, *For*, 64.
[125] BL ADD MS 16919 3.
[126] O'Gorman, *Whig*, 112; *World*, December 20, 1792; Dozier, *For*, 59.
[127] *Courier*, January 1, 1793; BL ADD MS 16929 13.
[128] RAS RH2/4/66 231.
[129] *Morning Chronicle*, December 28, 1792.
[130] RAS RH2/4/66 280.

increase stability, they avoided radical proposals.[131] Only rare corresponding society strongholds, most notably Sheffield, deterred loyal associations from forming.[132] The club came to boast over 2,000 affiliates, including 150 London locals.[133]

Associators sought to limit public discussion of the impending Franco-British war by closing spaces for spreading dissent. Sunderland's branch on December 27 asserted, "the greatest management is necessary to keep off discussions, that will infallibly lead the people into too near and too hazardous an inspection of the mazes and hitherto inaccessible mysteries of wars and government."[134] Adherents threatened pub owners with revoking their licenses if they allowed radical gatherings, while a Manchester mob attacked a private residence where reform meetings had retreated. In some areas, publicans and innkeepers formed their own associations, one counting 680 subscribers in Sussex, to prevent meetings or discussions that might "disturb the public peace."[135] Debates over the French Revolution in Britain ended less through reason than coercion.

Conservatives increasingly portrayed a French war as inevitable and necessary for preserving the British way of life. The *Evening Mail* on January 21 considered "the tranquility of this country" impossible without "some sort of fixed government in France," which they considered impossible for the revolution to establish.[136] The association laid the groundwork to profit from a wartime loyalist upsurge. The conflict appeared "the most popular in which this country has ever been involved," with popular opinion wanting stability restored.[137] Loyalists promoted war as an unavoidable necessity to stop international Jacobinism's spread.

English radicals countered the association's designs ineffectively. A new "Friends of the Freedom of the Press" society in early December, daring to meet at the Crown and Anchor Tavern, denounced attempts "to deter the People of Great Britain from publishing their thoughts on subjects most interesting to their happiness," yet found minimal support. In January, the new Friends attacked Reeves' Association as "doubtful in law, and unconstitutional in principle – a sort of partnership of authority with the executive power," to squelch free speech.[138] Conservative opponents, however, denounced them as "the same persons who had lately obtruded themselves

---

[131] D. E. Ginter, "The Loyalist Association Movement of 1792–1793 and British Public Opinion," *Historical Journal* 9, no. 2 (1966), 186.
[132] Palmer, *Age*, Vol. 2, 486.
[133] Mitchell, "Association," 62.
[134] *Courier*, January 1, 1793.
[135] Dozier, *For*, 87; Goodwin, *Friends*, 237, 265.
[136] *Evening Mail*, January 21, 1793.
[137] *Public Advertiser*, January 22, 1793.
[138] Goodwin, *Friends*, 273; Parolin, *Radical*, 122.

upon the Public under the description of Friends of the People."[139] Although the new Friends emphasized "the liberties ... of an enlightened people," pragmatic considerations became more important in British politics.[140]

War between Britain and France, though long a possibility, followed Louis XVI's January 21, 1793 execution. The British government immediately expelled France's ambassador, and on February 1 the Convention preemptively declared war. While acknowledging strong support among the British "people," Brissot and other French legislators nevertheless declared their differences with George III and Parliamentary conservatives irreconcilable.[141] Despite Anglo-French fraternal sentiment, fears of international aristocratic conspiracy proved more salient. Some hoped revolutionary success could lead to British regime change: one French pamphlet viewed British popular societies' rise as presaging their monarchy's overthrow, anticipating "social happiness" and "eternal peace" between the nations.[142] Such rhetoric, however, placed British radicals in an untenable domestic position.

The British Parliament continued curtailing political dissidents' rights. As Elliot in December 1792 described the drift into repression, "I think it the peculiar duty of the present hour to support the government in measures right in themselves, though irregular in their forms." Defense became more important than constitutional stringency. Elliot feared "one year of confusion will entail more misery" than "any reform can compensate in half a century," given the possibilities of abject disaster.[143] Delineating between "liberty and anarchy," one pamphlet declared, became more important than distinctions between "liberty and tyranny" Britons traditionally emphasized.[144] Pitt considered banning all political meetings, but instead targeted his radical opponents. In April 1793, conservatives introduced a bill against "all Traitorous correspondence with, and aid to, His Majesty's enemies."[145] Parliament gave the bill overwhelming support. With "patriotic" opinion mounting against France, radical opposition proved ineffective.[146]

[139] *Sun*, January 18, 1793.

[140] *Morning Chronicle*, December 4, 1792; Philp, *Reforming Ideas in Britain: Politics and Language in the Shadow of the French Revolution, 1789–1815* (Cambridge: Cambridge University Press, 2014), 60.

[141] Brissot, *Exposé de la conduite de la nation française, envers le peuple anglais, et des motifs qui ont amené la rupture entre la République française & le Roi d'Angleterre* (Paris, 1793).

[142] *Exposé historique des motifs qui ont amené la rupture entre la République française et S.M. Britannique* (Paris, 1793).

[143] Elliot, *Life*, Vol. 2, 80–82.

[144] Thomas Somerville, *The Effects of the French Revolution, with Respect to the Interests of Humanity, Liberty, Etc.* (Edinburgh, 1793), 32.

[145] Wold, *Scotland*, 26; *Journals of the House of Commons*, Vol. 48, 609.

[146] E. P. Thompson, *The Making of the English Working Class* (New York: Pantheon, 1964), 119–22.

Though claiming to be a temporary response to the international crisis, the association prospered beyond the early fighting. In September 1793, 386 loyalist affiliates (several times any reform network's) remained active with members instructed to disrupt radical networks' meetings and correspondence.[147] By their second year, the organization claimed they had "saved the Nation at a time when nothing else could have saved it." With no loss of irony, one radical compared them to the French: "The affiliated Jacobin Clubs of the French Provinces have been made the model of the Reevesian Associations ... Every man is called upon, more palpably than in France, to declare the Constitution glorious and unreformable."[148] Despite networked clubs' initial development as a radical platform, they became useful regardless of their followers' political orientation, with strategic similarities abounding between radical and conservative organizations.

Many conservatives, however, still distrusted the association model, fearing it would rouse the British people to demand a regular say in politics. Pamphleteer Vicesimus Knox argued such bodies brought "tens of thousands, in all ranks, from their indolent repose, to the investigation of political subjects." Doing so "awakens them to political life, and prompts them to read forbidden books of which they had scarcely heard the name before." Once people could "feel their own weight," the author worried it "will teach them to throw it into the opposite scale" with reformers.[149] Elite enthusiasm for the associations cooled and their activity declined in late 1793.

Radical reformers now found formal British politics closed to them. "Where then are we to look for the remedy?" the London Corresponding Society asked their Norwich affiliate, "To that Parliament of which we complain? To the Executive Power, which is implicitly obeyed if not anticipated in that Parliament, or to ourselves, represented in some Meeting of Delegates" to develop their own plans.[150] Fox, observing conservative aggressiveness, in June 1794 found "parallel" between "the Jacobins of France and the Crown party here!"[151] Intolerance became endemic in mid-1790s politics.

Audaciously, Scottish and English radicals collaborated to establish a "British Convention" on the French model. Recruiting deputations from

---

[147] *Association Papers. Part 1* (London, 1793), 1–2; David Eastwood, "Patriotism and the English State in the 1790s," in *The French Revolution and British Popular Politics*, Philp, ed. (Cambridge: Cambridge University Press, 1991), 154; Kevin Gilmartin, "In the Theater of Counterrevolution: Loyalist Association and Conservative Association in the 1790s," *Journal of British Studies* 41, no. 3 (2002), 291–328.

[148] *Association Papers*, iii; Daniel Stuart, *Peace and Reform, against War and Corruption* (London, 1794), 18–19.

[149] Vicesimus Knox, *Personal Nobility: or, Letters to a Young Nobleman, on the Conduct of His Studies, and the Dignity of the Peerage* (London: Dilly, 1793) xxii.

[150] *First Report*, 6.

[151] Fox, *Memorials*, Vol. 3, 77.

across Britain, the assembly claimed to embody popular sovereignty, particularly given the British Parliament's unfair representation.[152] Building from a General Convention of 160 delegates from 80 Scottish clubs in fall 1792 and a second abortive spring 1793 meeting seeking peace petitions, radicals planned a national gathering. Yet, between the repressive atmosphere and strong Reevesian support, mobilizing a representative gathering became difficult. Organizers corresponded with the United Irishmen, encouraging them to "speak and vote in this Convention."[153]

British Convention support nevertheless remained lukewarm. The London Corresponding Society named delegates on October 28, only a day before Edinburgh proceedings began. Many locals sent only regrets that no member could attend. The Scottish societies, furnishing 160 delegates, did not wait – endorsing reform alongside an antiwar petition to the Crown before adjourning.[154] Cautiously, they declined to respond to an Irish address seeking cooperation toward "Universal Emancipation."[155] The body reconvened after the London deputies' November 6 arrival, declaring their "undoubted right to meet" and determination to pursue "a real representation of the people, and annual election, until compelled to desist by superior force."[156] Claiming the right to interpret the constitution themselves, in the "1st year of the British Convention," the assembly refused submission to authorities.[157] Hopes remained to establish precedents for grander future gatherings.

The British Convention's overreach led the Crown to dissolve the assembly on December 6, 1793, and begin prosecuting its leaders. Government spies infiltrated the radical networks and, after the London Corresponding Society proposed a new National Convention for spring 1794, authorities arraigned their leaders on treason charges, one judge openly pronouncing his fears that the societies could multiply "*ad infinitum*" to become "the most powerful combination that I think the world ever saw."[158] Scottish prosecutors gained convictions of ringleader Thomas Muir (also an inducted United Irishman) and LCS co-founder Margarot, deporting both to Australia, and executed Robert Watt for treason. English juries, however, acquitted Hardy and Horne Tooke after the prosecution failed to demonstrate any concerted treasonous conspiracy. Yet by suspending Habeas Corpus from May 1794 to

---

[152] Kenneth R. Johnston, "The First and Last British Convention," *Romanticism* 13, no. 2 (2007), 105.

[153] Brims, "Scottish," 514; NAI Rebellion Papers 620/20/83.

[154] *First Report*, 8; Meikle, *Scotland*, 139–40.

[155] "Report: The Fifteenth March 1799," in *Reports of the Committees of the House of Commons* (S.l., 1803), Vol. 10, 791.

[156] *Second Report*, 58.

[157] Mathieson, "Awakening," 135.

[158] NA TS11/952 3496; John Barrell, *The Spirit of Despotism: Invasions of Privacy in the 1790s* (Oxford: Oxford University Press, 2006) 48; Davis, *Mob*, 27.

July 1795, the government detained those considered significant threats, while intimidating the rest. Some radical societies were pressured into closing, others dwindled, and even after leaders' arrests, none dared forcibly resist. With fears growing of French invasion, authorities raised a national Volunteer militia in 1794, but unlike in Ireland it remained a loyalist stronghold.[159] Given loyalist fervor's extent, British politics did not permit a unified popular movement.

Strategically retreating, some radical societies continued meeting covertly. Angry resolutions multiplied against their governmental antagonists: "Law ceases to be an Object of Obedience," Norwich declared in January 1794, "whenever it becomes an Instrument of Oppression."[160] The LCS similarly wrote to Edinburgh that since their petitions "have all been unsuccessful," their "attention must now, therefore, be turned to some more effectual means."[161] A Sheffield meeting questioned, "What is the constitution to us if we are nothing to it?"[162] With resentments unaddressed, the clubs remained dangerous.

After over a year without significant public gatherings, a St. George's Fields mass meeting coalesced for June 29, 1795 in London, drawing tens of thousands for manhood suffrage and annual parliaments. Amid high bread prices, rising unemployment and a seemingly endless war against liberty, the potential for resurgent club movements remained. Again in October, the LCS organized an open-air mass meeting near Marylebone, renewing demands for peace, bread, reform, and a new ministry. A hostile crowd three days later pelted the king's carriage during the annual procession to open Parliament.[163] Loyalism remained only as popular as the regime, while elite intolerance carried real risks of radicalization.

Parliament responded to the renewed agitation with the Seditious Meetings Act of December 1795, declaring mass meetings a "great danger to the public peace," and any gathering over fifty persons for drawing a petition illegal. Popular politics became illegitimate: one Lord during debates asserted he did "not know what the bulk of the people in any country had to do with the laws but obey them."[164] With Parliament again suspending Habeas Corpus, ringleaders faced indefinite detention. Despite poor harvests and simmering

[159] Chris Evans, *Debating the Revolution: Britain in the 1790s* (London: I.B. Tauris, 2006), 20–21; Fehrenbacher, *Slaveholding*, 25; Emsley, "An Aspect of Pitt's 'Terror': Prosecutions for Sedition during the 1790s," *Social History* 6, no. 2 (1981), 175, and "Repression, 'Terror' and the Rule of Law in England during the Decade of the French Revolution," *English Historical Review* 100, no. 397 (1985), 807–8; Austin Gee, *The British Volunteer Movement, 1794–1814* (Oxford: Clarendon Press, 2003); "Report: The Fifteenth March," 791.

[160] *Second Report*, Appendix C.
[161] Ibid., 47.
[162] Palmer, *Age*, Vol. 1, 21.
[163] Goodwin, *Friends*, 372; NA PRO 30/8/121 263; Meikle, *Scotland*, 158.
[164] Mori, *Britain*, 41.

discontent, under such repression agitation stalled. Network organizers made a surreptitious August 1797 attempt for simultaneous gatherings nationally but were quickly dispersed.[165] The LCS continued in diminished form until 1799, when the Corresponding Societies Act banned it outright. Some diehards emigrated to America, while many others abandoned political agitation.[166] The Jacobin model, affiliating radicals in large networks for concerted reform campaigns, became too dangerous to be tolerated by British governing elites.

Conclusion

Moving beyond single-issue antislavery, repeal, and moderate reform efforts, applying new radical club models for a general French-style campaign for political change shocked the British system. Whereas prior generations of scholars explored the radical societies as a largely British phenomenon, influenced by the French but isolated from them, this study shows the importance of the vibrant British-French club exchanges that ended only with the arrival of war in early 1793.[167] Behind a strong egalitarian ethos, escaping the isolation that limited earlier club models, radical corresponding societies networked toward a collective power previously unmatched.

Despite possessing a more extensive groundwork for reform than any preceding British movement of their era, the London Corresponding Society and sister radical organizations of the 1790s floundered against an unprecedented wave of loyalism and anti-associational sentiment. In fall 1792, the associational model cultivated by reformers for decades was hijacked by their conservative opponents, who created a broad, socially inclusive network on a scale the radicals had only imagined. The British – ironically, in the name of their own traditions – repudiated their rich club traditions and social movement culture for fear of anarchy and social revolution. None of Britain's great eighteenth-century corresponding movements produced direct changes. However, the Association for the Preservation of Liberty and Property against Republicans and Levellers opened new avenues for the development of modern social movements. No one political perspective thereafter could (reasonably) claim to represent the full people. The development of modern democratic politics required mobilization across multiple political perspectives.

---

[165] Andress, *Terror*, 31; MHS John Adams Papers, reel 385.
[166] "Seditious Meetings Act," *English Historical Documents, 1783–1832*, David C. Douglas, ed. (Oxford: Oxford University Press, 1959), 320; Wil Verhoeven, *Americomania and the French Revolution Debate in Britain, 1789–1802* (Cambridge: Cambridge University Press, 2013), 8.
[167] Goodwin, *Friends*; Thompson, *Making*; Emsley, *Britain*.

13

The United Irishmen in an Atlantic Crosswind

The year 1791 proved a time of Irish radicalization, with Bastille Day celebrations becoming foundational events for popular mobilization. While the previous year some Volunteer units forsook July 12 anniversary centennial celebrations of the Protestants' triumph at 1690's Battle of the Boyne for July 14 festivities commemorating the French fortress' fall, now wider combinations coalesced to celebrate French universalism. Particularly across Ulster, banquets featured Volunteers alongside Whig Clubs and the broader populace.[1] Radical leader Theobald Wolfe Tone described the Irish watching France's "progress of freedom with the utmost anxiety," while "the public spirit of Ireland rose with utmost acceleration." Ireland "divided into two great parties, the Aristocrats and the Democrats (epithets borrowed from France)" with reformers' ambitions tied to popular agitation.[2] France's abolition of religious distinctions, made by what organizer William Drennan considered "its truly National Assembly where Protestants sit" alongside Catholics, led to hopes "the time may be accelerated when the rights of men and the rights of citizens may meet together in the name of Irishmen."[3] Irish Catholics and Protestants increasingly celebrated French progress together. The time appeared ripe for a new, inclusive network to agitate for systemic changes – the United Irishmen.

Despite the achievement of nominal legislative independence in 1782, Ireland's dependence on Britain remained profound. At the American war's end, elite interests succeeded in deterring reform plans, and much of the Volunteer movement's promise remained unfulfilled. In peacetime, the militia movement atrophied and political elites ignored 1783's reform program. It took a new revolution, led by Catholics in France, to revive reform campaigning and mobilize an unprecedentedly inclusive Catholic-Protestant social movement.

The United Irishmen embraced the radical possibilities of the 1790s as much as their American, British, and French counterparts. Passionately borrowing from Atlantic models, organizing a mass movement reaching into Western

---

[1] Thomas Bartlett, *The Fall and Rise of the Irish Nation: The Catholic Question, 1690–1830* (Savage, MD: Barnes & Noble Books, 1992), 124; McDowell, *Ireland*, 354.
[2] Tone, *Life*, 43.
[3] Drennan, *Drennan*, 58–59.

Europe's poorest population could show the new politics' reach, while over-coming sectarian divides would demonstrate Enlightened universalism's potential. Yet, the effects of foreign domination, enduring sectarianism, and political stasis by 1798 led the frustrated movement into the era's most disastrous uprising.

The French Revolution and the Rise of the United Irishmen

Across the mid-1780s lull in reform organizing, local rebel movements (alternately Catholic and Protestant) continued across the countryside. The tactics remained largely unchanged from earlier eras with gangs attacking their opponents' properties, cattle, and persons, or extorting protection payments. Protestant Peep-O'Day Boys forcibly entered Catholic homes to search for weapons (even of Volunteers).[4] Tensions grew. A new "act to prevent tumultuous risings and assemblies," drawn by the king's appointed Lord Lieutenant, passed the Irish Parliament in 1787, funding expanded policing.[5] The 1780s brought frustration and trepidation, more than relief, to many.

As the French Revolution commenced, Irish Parliamentary reformers remobilized for more dramatic changes – though initially kept their rhetoric within British political boundaries. In August 1789, Grattan recalled, "the opposition thought it expedient to form a society called the 'Whig Club,' similar to that in England, and upon the same liberal and constitutional principles." Two months before the Jacobins' founding, the Irish club's program called for an "unremitting watch" to contest Britain's "unconstitutional influence in her Parliament" and a "responsibility bill" to make the treasury accountable to the Irish instead of British legislature.[6] The extent of Whig interest in major Parliamentary reforms remained uncertain, with their club "reserved for the access of every gentleman, whether Senator or not, introduced by a member," but the institution nevertheless challenged the governing status quo.[7] Burke considered such "meetings prevent the evaporation of principle in individuals and give them joint force, and enliven their exertions by emulation." In the present international context, he argued, "Party is absolutely necessary at this time."[8]

Rather than remaining a Parliamentary drinking club, the Whig Club worked to expand into a national network. The Dublin branch established

---

[4] Richard Musgrave, *Memoirs of the Different Rebellions in Ireland from the Arrival of the English* (Dublin: Marchbank, 1802), Vol. 1, 32; Sean Farrell, *Rituals and Riots; Sectarian Violence and Political Culture in Ulster, 1784–1886* (Lexington: University Press of Kentucky, 2000), 18.

[5] Musgrave, *Memoirs*, 45.

[6] Grattan, *Life*, Vol. 3, 428, 434, and Nancy Curtin, *The United Irishmen: Popular Politics in Ulster and Dublin, 1791–1798* (Oxford: Oxford University Press, 1998), 39.

[7] *Belfast Newsletter*, November 24, 1789.

[8] Charlemont, *Manuscripts*, Vol. 1, 105.

a committee in December 1789 "to correspond with such Whig Clubs, as are or may be hereafter established in this kingdom" on the common model, desiring one in each county.[9] Burgeoning radicals like the young lawyer Wolfe Tone joined, considering the Whigs "the best constituted political body" for reform efforts.[10] In 1790's local Dublin elections, Whig partisans won control of municipal government for the first time since mid-century.[11]

Others attempted to resurrect the Volunteer militia's influence. A "Volunteer Association Secret Committee" in September 1790 declared they would "Hazard of our Lives & Properties" to support a "Plan of National Reform," calling for a new convention to seek redress through the organization. Most branches ignored the appeal, but Belfast reformers considered how, "as the former Emancipation of this Kingdom was owing to the Exertions of our volunteers," revivifying "this Glorious Phalanx" could advance the effort.[12] The Volunteers' latent potential remained considerable.

The most influential Irish reform group in 1790 was the General Catholic Committee, seeking voting rights for propertied Catholics and relaxation of other discrimination laws. Though a Catholic Association existed since 1756 and lobbied for 1782's Catholic Relief Act that restored the right to purchase land and lessened Catholic clergy restrictions, it now reorganized with new-found vigor.[13] The movement spread beyond Whig Club parameters, with Catholics assembling a national committee system.[14] Like British Dissenters before them, Catholics used their parishes as voting assemblies, electing a nationally representative central committee. In February 1791, the committee circulated a new petition citing their "fidelity in times the most perilous," beseeching Parliament to "unite them forever to their country by every tie of gratitude & interest."[15] Highlighting their loyalty and peaceable conduct, Catholics requested inclusion in national political life.

Irish reformers associated themselves with human rights and revolutionary possibility, cultivating international connections. One banner in Belfast's Bastille Day July 14, 1791, parade read, "Can the African slave trade, though morally wrong, be politically right?" Another asserted, "For a people to be free, it is sufficient that they will it."[16] Anglo-Irish politics' narrow confines lost their

[9] Grattan, *Life*, Vol. 3, 461; *Belfast Newsletter*, November 24, 1789.

[10] Tone, *Life*, 30.

[11] Marianne Elliott, *Wolfe Tone: Prophet of Irish Independence* (New Haven: Yale University Press, 1989), 87.

[12] NAI Rebellion Papers 620/19/11 and 12.

[13] Bartlett, *Ireland*, 50; "Minute Book of the Catholic Committee, 1773–92," *Archivium Hibernicum* 9 (1942), 116.

[14] Grattan, *Life*, Vol. 4, 44.

[15] "Minute Book of the Catholic Committee," 122.

[16] Curtin, "Symbols and Rituals of United Irish Mobilization," in *Ireland and the French Revolution*, Hugh Gough and Dickson, eds. (Dublin: Irish Academic Press, 1990), 69.

inevitability. Bordeaux's Jacobins sent encouragement in August as "France has given the signal of a bold insurrection against all prejudices, all abuses, all illegitimate authorities." They declared the day "will arrive; when the different parts of the civilized world shall raise together their eloquent voice" to assert common rights and develop "the empire of reason" through justice.[17] The French Old Regime's crumbling threatened the discriminatory Irish system.

As political possibilities expanded, the reforms the Volunteer movement achieved now appeared slight. Wolfe Tone described Ireland in 1791 as possessing "no National Government," asserting, "the Revolution of 1782 was the most bungling, imperfect business that ever threw ridicule" on the term. Instead of feeling pride in earlier advancements, "it is much better we should know and feel our real state than delude ourselves" at Irish freedom's extent. The prior revolution "left three-fourths of our countrymen slaves" in "wicked and contemptible hands" like before.[18] He and fellow radicals spurned the Whig Club as too moderate and corrupted by the Protestant Ascendancy. Radicals complained the Dublin branch did "nothing more than eat and drink," while lacking "fellow feeling with the people" for broader mobilization.[19] A new, more ambitious pressure group appeared necessary.

The United Irishmen secret society took shape, circumventing Irish formal politics' polite limits to pursue revolutionary possibilities. Drennan, a Dissenting Belfast physician, in spring 1791 circulated plans for a new society with "much of the secrecy and something of the ceremonial of freemasonry" to form a "benevolent conspiracy" for religious toleration, the rights of man, and Irish freedom.[20] Drennan asserted secrecy could "communicate curiosity, uncertainty, expectation to the minds of surrounding men," attracting friends while intimidating enemies. The United order would not be another faction, but

> a plot for the people – no Whig Club – no party title – the Brotherhood its name – the rights of man and the greatest happiness of the greatest number its end – its general end, real independence to Ireland and republicanism its particular purpose.[21]

Proponents discussed establishing a National Convention of the Irish People with equal representation for all Irishmen. To pursue such goals, the new organization opened correspondence with like-minded British, French, and American groups.[22]

---

[17] Francis Plowden, *An Historical Review of the State of Ireland* (London: Roworth, 1803), Vol. 4, 1–2.

[18] Tone, *Letters*, 25–26.

[19] Jean Agnew, ed. *The Drennan-McTier Letters, 1776–1793* (Belfast: Irish Manuscripts Collection, 1998), Vol. 1, 357.

[20] McDowell, *Ireland*, 383.

[21] Agnew, Drennan-McTier, Vol. 1, 357.

[22] McDowell, *Ireland*, 383.

The United Irishmen possessed features different from their Atlantic revolutionary predecessors. Britain's role in the future Irish nation, if any, remained uncertain. Secrecy could "confound and terrify its enemies" over the "extent, the direction, or the consequences" of the movement. As "Our Provinces are perfectly ignorant of each other," the organization could forge the Emerald Isle's "separate nations" together. Originally named the "Irish Brotherhood," such a union could make "pale and ineffectual light, converge," advancing political justice by working toward convoking a convention of the Irish people to decide proper reforms.[23]

A United Irish organization would extend across geographic and sectarian lines. An October planning meeting resolved, "the weight of English influence in the government of this country, is so great as to require a cordial union among all the people of Ireland." All groups needed to unite for "radical reform of the representation of the people in parliament," including "Irishmen of every religious description."[24] No previous social movement of the era had successfully mobilized significant percentages of both Catholics and Protestants. While disproportionately drawing Dissenters and Catholics over establishment Anglicans, solidarity across the divisions the British used to manipulate Irish society would be necessary to craft a strong and stable new order.

The United Irishmen considered themselves part of an international wave of regime change. "In the present great era of reform," Dublin's November founding communiqué declared, "when unjust Governments are falling in every quarter of Europe," and "all Government is acknowledged to originate from the People," the British system in Ireland became insupportable. The new societies throughout the nation would promote "constitutional knowledge, the abolition of bigotry in religion and politics, and the equal distribution of the Rights of Man through all the Sects and Denominations of Irishmen."[25] Bringing enlightened toleration together with revolutionary fraternity, the society's constitution sought "a brotherhood of affection, an identity of interests, a communion of rights, and an union of politics" for a revived nation.[26] The society in December asserted that whereas "ignorance has been the demon of discord," now "the Catholic and the Presbyterian are at this instant holding out their hands and opening their hearts to each other." The United Irishmen would model a new order for all the Irish.[27]

Despite its officially secret ways, the organization spread rapidly. In many areas, the Irishmen grew in partnership with the Volunteers, reviving

---

[23] NAI Rebellion Papers 620/19/24.
[24] Madden, *United*, Series 1, Vol. 1, 136.
[25] *Proceedings of the Society of United Irishmen, of Dublin* (Philadelphia: Stephens, 1795), 1–5.
[26] *The Report from the Secret Committee of the House of Commons* (Dublin: King, 1798), 5.
[27] Madden, *United*, Vol. 2, 315; NAI Westmoreland Papers, PRIV 1258 Box 1 31.

participation in the older association.[28] Wolfe Tone considered "affairs are going on swimmingly," with the new organization established not just in major cities but having "secured all Connaught," comprising western Ireland, while "fighting out the other two provinces."[29] Though numbers remained modest in many areas, in Ulster's counties Antrim and Down a denser parish-based network developed.[30] In October, Wolfe Tone met the central "Secret Committee, who are not known or suspected of co-operating, but who, in fact, direct the movements of Belfast." He asked committeeman Thomas Digges, an American War veteran who served as the Baltimore organization's secretary, "whether they any way resembled the Committees of America in 1775, and afterwards." Digges answered, "Precisely."[31] The organization avoided most government surveillance, with one report lamenting "the Catholics are so connected it is not easy to trace their progress."[32] Regularized Catholic committee communications provided an exemplar and possible vector for the new movement's spread.

Though still claiming to favor "an Equal, Full, and Adequate Representation of all the People of Ireland" within the British imperial system, as the Irishmen's membership oath declared, some considered a more radical break for Irish independence.[33] Digges postulated:

> France would most probably assist, from the pride of giving freedom to one kingdom more. So would all the enemies of England ... If Ireland were free, and well governed, being that she is unencumbered with debt, she would, in arts, commerce, and manufactures, spring up like an air balloon, and leave England behind her, at an immense distance. There is no computing the rapidity with which she would rise.[34]

Change, one proclamation argued, depended not on "external circumstances," but rather "the internal energy of the Irish nation."[35] Though Wolfe Tone wrote in his diary of a "furious" two-hour dinner debate on Catholic rights among Belfast's Protestant reform leadership, ending with many "doubting as to the expediency," the United Irish pressed onward.[36] In December 1791,

[28] Elliott, *Partners in Revolution: The United Irishmen and France* (New Haven: Yale University Press, 1982), 35.

[29] Theobald Wolfe Tone, *Life and Adventures of Theobald Wolfe Tone* (Glasgow: Cameron, 1898), 152; Curtin, *United*, 43.

[30] Thomas Graham, "'A Union of Power'? The United Irish Organization: 1795–1798," in Dickson, Keogh and Whelan, 244.

[31] Tone, *Life*, 141, 146.

[32] NAI Westmoreland PRIV 1258 Box 1 no. 24.

[33] *The Declaration, Resolutions and Constitution of the Societies of United Irishmen* (S.l., s. d.), 5.

[34] Tone, *Life*, 143.

[35] NAI Westmoreland PRIV 1258 Box 1 31.

[36] Tone, *Life*, 149.

Belfast's branch unanimously resolved, "the Catholic Committee should ask nothing short of total emancipation and full right of citizenship," as any movement for radical change would need the support of the nation's majority.[37]

The Catholic cause became a fruitful analogy for the depredations all Irish suffered from the British. *An Argument on Behalf of the Catholics of Ireland*, an August 1791 Belfast pamphlet anonymously written by Wolfe Tone as "a Protestant of the Church of Ireland," noted similarities between British anti-Catholic and anti-Irish prejudice. "The people here are despised or defied; their will does not weigh a feather in the balance, when English influence, or the interest of their rulers, is thrown into the opposite scale."[38] Only with reform achieved, the pamphlet argued, "and the three great sects [Anglican, Presbyterian, and Catholic] blended together, under the common and sacred title of Irishman," assuming "the common rights of man," would Ireland be justly governed.[39] The pamphlet quickly sold six thousand copies, and in 1792 United Irishmen distributed ten thousand copies in Ulster.[40] Protestant tyranny over Catholics seemed as unjustifiable as British administrative tyranny over the Irish.

The Volunteer movement maintained its distance from the United Irishmen but continued advocating toleration and moderate reform. In October 1791, Dublin's Volunteers passed a resolution denouncing the Castle's prosecution of Catholics owning firearms. Such measures being "enforced instead of being repealed, in these enlightened days, must be a matter of astonishment," particularly as "France, a country of Catholics, has opened its arms to the religious of all persuasion" and enacted equal rights, of which "bearing arms is the most essential." A second motion, from "the Protestant Members," asked if they "and our Roman Catholic brethren, would unite, like citizens, and CLAIM THE RIGHTS OF MAN."[41] Irish discrimination appeared unjust and unsustainable.

The growing reaction against the French Revolution in Britain led many to denounce its Irish sister movement. Secretary of State Dundas wrote to Dublin Castle expressing concern at attempts to "associate together different Descriptions of Persons in Ireland," believing they would endorse "leveling Principles ... incompatible with the Exercise of any regular government." Dundas asserted Catholics should maintain "that quiet and regular Demeanor, which has procured to them former Relaxations, and justly entices them to look for further Indulgences" from Protestant authorities.

[37] Drennan, *Drennan*, 102.
[38] *An Argument on Behalf of the Catholics of Ireland* (Belfast, 1791), 7, 14; Bartlett, 126.
[39] *Argument on Behalf*, 21, 26.
[40] Rosamond Jacob, *The Rise of the United Irishmen* (London: Harrap, 1937), 56; Elliott, *Wolfe*, 129.
[41] Grattan, *Life*, Vol. 4, 451–52.

Nevertheless, he called for Catholic access to all professions, intermarriage with Protestants, unrestricted education, jury service, and use of firearms. Authorities took a harder line, considering Catholic voting rights "an Abandonment of the Protestant Power & a sacrifice of it to Catholic Claims." Lord Lieutenant the Earl of Westmoreland endorsed raising a "Confederacy of the Protestants" to "resist every Concession to the Catholics."[42] United Irishmen faced the coercive power of the establishment, some amenable to tactical concessions, but none sympathetic to their program.

Catholic emancipation radicalized with the era's growing ambitions. The British Parliament passed a Catholic Relief Act in 1791, reforming civil rights by removing restrictions on practicing law and access to education. In an era when America and France had granted religious freedom, however, minor changes became insufficient. Wolfe Tone described the cause attaining "considerable magnitude, so much indeed as to absorb all other political discussion" in the country.[43] Drennan considered the campaign a prelude to radicalization, prognosticating that to "grant them liberties by piecemeal is but to whet their appetite."[44] Belfast's citizens met in January 1792 to discuss petitioning Parliament on the Catholics' behalf, which became the largest assembly "we ever recollect here, if we except the Celebration of the French Revolution, on the 14th of July last." They adopted an address demanding an end to Catholic "degradation and slavery," the repeal of confessional restrictions, and universal civil rights.[45]

In February 1792, however, the Irish Commons rejected Dublin and Belfast's pro-Catholic petitions with alacrity (208–25). Not even opposition Whigs dared support Catholic voting. Though the Irish Parliament passed civil rights legislation later that month, granting Catholics rights to teach, take apprentices, and marry Protestants, such concessions paled before suffrage questions.[46] According to Catholic Committee agent Richard Burke, anti-Catholic "publications paid for by, and written under the sanction of the Castle," containing "the vilest scurrility," undermined their cause.[47] Seeing bold advances elsewhere, the Irish grew impatient for major changes. Many beyond the Catholic Committee readied. One Belfast writer considered the United Irishmen could be "as terrible to Government, as the Hydra of Calamities," should significant changes not occur.[48]

---

[42] NAI Westmoreland PRIV 1258 Box 1 24, 41, 53.
[43] Theobald Wolfe Tone, *The Writings of Theobald Wolfe Tone, 1763–1798*, T. W. Moody, R. B. McDowell and C. J. Woods, eds. (Oxford: Clarendon, 2009), Vol. 1, 324.
[44] Agnew, *Drennan-McTier*, Vol. 1 383.
[45] Henry Joy, *Belfast Politics: Or, a Collection of the Debates, Resolutions, and Other Proceedings of That Town* (Belfast: Joy, 1794), 5–8.
[46] Elliott, *Wolfe*, 156–57.
[47] National Library of Scotland, Henry Dundas Papers, MS 16 35.
[48] NAI Rebellion Papers, 620/19/68.

With public opinion intensifying in their favor, the Catholic Committee, rather than accepting incremental reform, announced elections in May to expand into a Catholic Convention. Each parish, democratically and without property qualifications, nominated a representative to join a county electoral assembly sending two deputies to the Dublin national meeting.[49] The committee argued, "if the representatives of three millions of oppressed people were once suffered to meet, it would not afterwards be safe, or indeed possible, to refuse their just demands." Though Irish authorities, and even Catholic bishops, opposed the plan, elections proceeded.[50] Catholic mobilization, though remaining peaceful, frightened many in prominent positions. The committee in February spoke against those "wickedly and falsely" misleading Protestants about their efforts.[51] Yet if Catholics could be deemed worthy of liberty, an increasingly mainstream political opinion, little justification remained for an exclusionary Protestant Ascendency.

Full Catholic political and civil rights now became many reformers' goal. Grattan orated that without suffrage Catholics would "never be free" and subject to "everlasting slavery" at Protestant elites' hands. Yet he prophesized "reason and justice" would "liberate the Catholic and liberalize the Protestant."[52] The radical *Northern Star*, after Parliamentary rejection of Dublin and Belfast's petitions for Catholic political rights, beseeched readers to lay "aside all religious distinctions," to seek "Parliamentary reform, and equal liberty to all."[53] One Belfast United Irishman wrote to Wolfe Tone that suffrage became "the cause of suffering millions and the cause of reason."[54] The apparent injustice of Ireland's political order created a growing vacuum of illegitimacy.

Reformers pursued solidarity with abolitionists. Drennan in early February 1792, copying the antislavery tactic, drew up "a subscription paper about abstinence from sugar, and shall soon get many thousand signatures" for abstaining until the slave trade's abolition. Looking beyond national campaigning, Drennan asked adherents to "cast round the world an equal eye, and feel for all that suffer."[55] After the British House of Commons voted to abolish the trade in April, the *Northern Star* printed a letter from Stanhope to Condorcet, asserting, "We touch, at length, the glorious moment when philosophy and reason make justice triumph everywhere, and when the friends of the rights of men will overthrow all abuses and tyrannies." Condorcet

[49] James Gordon, *History of the Rebellion in Ireland, in the Year 1798* (Dublin: Porter, 1801), 10.

[50] Tone, *Life*, 65.

[51] "Minute Book of the Catholic Committee," 151.

[52] Grattan, *Life*, Vol. 4, 63.

[53] *Northern Star*, February 8, 1792.

[54] Tone, *Life*, 219.

[55] Agnew, *Drennan-McTier*, Vol. 1, 388.

responded, "the moment is come, when every year, every day will be marked by the destruction of a prejudice," until such "fatalities" ceased.[56] No injustice appeared too great. Though British abolition failed in the Lords, a general coalition across radical movements became tantalizingly close.

Festivities emphasizing reconciliation between Protestant and Catholic communities spread. St. Patrick's Day in 1792 occasioned Volunteer marches throughout the north, followed by banquets featuring patriotic toasts, including that the "spirit of liberty" might "extend from nation to nation till it covers the utmost corners of the earth."[57] The Irish nation, Belfast's United branch declared days later, needed to "open their eyes to the light, to that light which we have seen produce resistance in America and Freedom in France."[58] On May 3, banquets followed on "the day set apart by the King and People of Poland, for the commemoration of their newly acquired Constitution." Toasts wished "Philosophy enlighten all Nations, and form the whole into one vast family."[59] Bastille Day took weeks of planning with Drennan sending advice north to Belfast, "You should have four flags for France, America, Poland, and Ireland, borne by handsome boys in suitable dresses."[60] Wolfe Tone remarked on the British flag's striking absence, no longer in freedom's avant-garde.[61] Float banners proclaimed, "Where Liberty is, THERE is my country," and "Superstitious jealousy, the cause of the Irish Bastille: Let us unite and destroy it."[62] The concluding banquet took place "not at an expensive tavern," but rather included all interested outdoors.[63] Gatherings materialized across the nation, particularly in the North, with Ballymoney toasting "A speedy and eternal overthrow to all Tyranny, Civil and Ecclesiastical," while demanding, "Abolition of Slavery all the world over."[64] For enthusiastic participants, revolutionary fraternity flowered.

Belfast's Bastille Day gathering wrote to France's National Assembly, building international alongside national alliances. With war against central Europe's crowned heads underway, Ulster Irishmen wished France success in creating a new world order. The "imperishable spirit of freedom alone," they declared, "now animates the heart of Europe," to soon "communicate its energy throughout the world" beyond. As "the Almighty is dispersing the political clouds which have hitherto darkened our hemisphere," opportunity grew for "universal freedom, harmony and peace," in which "those who are

56 *Northern Star*, April 14, 1792.
57 Curtin, *United*, 230.
58 NAI Rebellion Papers 620/19/72.
59 *Northern Star*, April 25, 1792; Joy, *Belfast*, 47.
60 Agnew, *Drennan-McTier*, Vol. 1, 409.
61 Tone, *Life*, 161.
62 Madden, *United*, Series 1, Vol. 1, 185; Musgrave, *Memoirs*, Vol. 1, 110.
63 Agnew, *Drennan-McTier*, Vol. 1, 409.
64 *Northern Star*, July 18, 1792; Curtin, *United*, 230.

slaves be speedily free."[65] Old prejudices' eclipse and the rise of popular politics made fundamentally reorganizing power seem possible.

Such urban utopianism spread unevenly across the countryside, however, as violent attacks by Catholic "Defenders" multiplied. The organization started in County Armagh in the mid-1780s to defend Catholics from Protestant gangs. Roving nighttime bands maimed cattle, burned crops and homes, intimidated, and attacked hostile Protestants. An early 1792 pamphlet denounced "A RAGE among the ROMAN CATHOLICS for illegally arming themselves" with the disenfranchised considering "possession of arms is the distinction of a Free Man from a Slave."[66] Though the Catholic Committee denounced violence, revolutionary rhetoric meshed with old grievances. A catechism displayed on a man hanged alongside the road to Shannon asserted "the National Convention" would "quell all nations, dethrone all kings, and plant the true religion that was lost at the Reformation," an explosive combination of Irish resentments. From a northern lodge in an Armagh pub, the Defenders affiliated into a paramilitary league.[67] Protestants mobilized their own defensive organizations in kind. Westmoreland wrote to Pitt that the "Protestant Flame in this country grows hotter and hotter," making him "afraid we shall not be able to carry the smallest Concession" to the Catholics.[68] Pressure grew from all sides.

Debates over Catholics arming remained fraught. In July, the Catholic Committee, attempting to reduce tensions, resolved against "parading in large bodies, and with arms," pledging to oppose all "offenders against the public peace, be their party or religion what it might."[69] Yet mobilization continued. In August, Wolfe Tone (the committee's secretary) reported Northern Catholic offers to recruit Volunteers. He noted, in jest, "more volunteer companies springing up like mushrooms, nobody knows why."[70] Catholics remained interested in maintaining peace, but unwilling to remain subordinate to the Protestant minority.

France projected tantalizing revolutionary prospects, overthrowing monarchy and, little over a month later, expelling counterrevolutionary Austrian and Prussian forces from French territory. Belfast partisans illuminated the town in celebration, as "Everyone demonstrated sincere pleasure in the disgrace of two tyrannical courts" menacing France with "political bondage." Streets "presented a blaze of approbation," while revolutionary signage included:

[65] Joy, *Belfast*, 67–69.
[66] NAI Rebellion Papers, 620/19/50.
[67] KA Pratt Papers, U840/0147/14/1; Foster, *Modern*, 271.
[68] NAI Westmoreland Papers, PRIV 1258 Box 2 3.
[69] Tone, *Life*, 479.
[70] Ibid., 172–73.

Perfect union and equal liberty to the men of Ireland – Vive la Republique: Vive la Nation – Church and State Divorced – Liberty Triumphant – The Rights of Men established – Despotism prostrate – The Tyrants are fled; let the People rejoice ... France is free; so may we; let us will it – Awake O ye that sleep ... The Cause of Mankind triumphant – Irishmen rejoice – Union among Irishmen – Rights of Man – Irishmen! Look at France.[71]

Tories dared not appear. Across the north, "revolutionary societies" raised contributions for France's soldiers.[72] Political momentum advanced with the revolutionary armies.

Protestant Loyalist rituals, meanwhile, fell into disrepute. Wolfe Tone described how on November 4 in Dublin "the volunteers refused to parade round King William's statue" on his birthday and abolished orange cockades – symbol of the Protestant Ascendancy – for inclusive green ones, considering this "striking proof of the change in men's sentiments."[73] Lisburn's Volunteers hosted an alternative review celebrating French victories, imploring, "IRISHMEN UNITE." Ballynure (County Antrim) Volunteers built a bonfire, toasting, "the final aim of all learned Citizens, be to promote peace on Earth, EQUAL LIBERTY, and good will to all mankind."[74] A new universal vision eclipsed sectarian identifiers.

French inspirations led many United Irish to radicalize. Wolfe Tone in November advised "Catholics, at every refusal, to rise in their demands" for fuller rights. "Right or wrong," the French "are fighting our battles, and if they fail, adieu to liberty in Ireland, for one century!"[75] Dublin's United Irishmen wrote to Edinburgh's British Convention that month, agreeing only "a radical reform in the House of the People" would bring Ireland freedom: "without such a reform the Revolution itself [of 1782] was nominal and delusive." Over the decade, no internal reforms succeeded. The Volunteers alternately "resolved – they convened – they met with arms – they met without them – they petitioned. But all in vain," as the political establishment remained.[76] New efforts were required to profit from the international situation and achieve real change.

Catholic interests pressed their advantage. A new Catholic Convention assembled in Dublin on December 3. With delegates "from all the counties and the principal cities of Ireland," they declared themselves "the only power competent to speak the sense of the Catholics of Ireland" and approved a royal

---

[71] Curtin, *United*, 231–32; Joy, *Belfast*, 86.

[72] Musgrave, *Memoirs*, Vol. 1, 113.

[73] Tone, *Life*, 203.

[74] *Northern Star*, November 10, 1792.

[75] Tone, *Life*, 205.

[76] "Address from the Society of United Irishmen in Dublin, to the Delegates for Promoting a Reform in Scotland, November 23, 1792," in Drennan, *Letters*, 38.

petition for reform.[77] Westmoreland worried the committee would develop "such influence and authority as would be quite incompatible with the existence of any other Government."[78] Indeed, the elected Catholic body was far more directly representative of the Irish population than their Parliament. The new organization sought to leverage its numerical strength into political influence. Rather than projecting fear of a crackdown should Britain war with France, the Catholic leadership instead "perceived that Ireland could not be defended against a foreign enemy without their assistance." With their kind "originally enfeebled by being dissociated and disarmed," they "now acquired a consciousness of strength" through mobilization.[79] Not just a radical fringe, but elected Catholic representatives now favored resistance over suppression. The body adopted a petition that month declaring, "no measure short of an abolition of all distinctions, between them and their fellow subjects of other religious persuasions, would be either just or satisfactory."[80] Catholics made clear they would not back down.

War, Repression, and Resurgence

Imperial war against France drastically altered Ireland's political landscape as it did Britain's, but the early conflict's effect on broader contestations for Irish liberty remained uncertain. The American War had drastically increased political mobilization and many Irish patriots expected the French Revolutionary War to help them achieve greater freedom. Ireland's political situation became dire for both sides, with an aroused populace ready to advance their liberties.

In December 1792, the Lord Lieutenant formed a new Irish militia as Anglo-French war loomed, simultaneously ordering the suppression of the Volunteers and "all seditious associations." Privately to Pitt, Westmoreland declared his intention to limit "French Mania," while rallying loyal Protestant support.[81] Such measures, however, only worsened political discontent. The First Belfast Volunteer Company published a declaration in the *Northern Star* that "taxation without representation is OPPRESSION – that the People are NOT represented," and thus "neither Proclamations nor Threats shall deter us from the pursuit of our rights." They called Irishmen to "Unite," asserting an "armed Nation can NEVER be made Slaves."[82] Dublin's United Irishmen

---

[77] Grattan, *Life*, Vol. 4, 76; Elliott, *Wolfe*, 197.

[78] William Edward Hartpole Lecky, *A History of Ireland in the Eighteenth Century* (London: Longmans, 1892), Vol. 3, 90–91.

[79] *A Brief Account of the General Meeting of the Catholic Delegates Held in Dublin, December 1792* (Dublin: Fitzpatrick, 1792), 8.

[80] Tone, *Life*, 238.

[81] NA PRO 30/8/331 191.

[82] *Northern Star*, December 15, 1792.

urged Volunteers to remain mobilized, while advocating a "convention of the Protestant People" to negotiate an alliance with the Catholic Convention.[83] War, with Britain joining counterrevolutionary forces against France, threatened to radicalize Irish politics beyond mere reform.

To Irish activists, Britain's governing abuses flowed from a single system. Belfast's United Irishmen wrote to the British Convention that "violations" of the "constitution, the perversion of its principles, the abuse of its powers, and the avowed influence of venality and corruption, must be swept away together." They declared it "time to recognize and renovate the rights of the English, the Scotch, and the Irish Nations." Avoiding violence – "may Heaven avert the dreadful necessity!" – required "a voluntary, immediate and radical Reform" in government with representation necessary for a lasting compact.[84] Several weeks later, Dublin's United Irishmen wrote to London's Friends of the People, citing the "fraternity of feeling" between organizations, inspired by "all that has been done over the face of the globe for Liberty, and feeling all that can be suffered for the want of it."[85] Irish radicals in Paris, meanwhile, joined British expatriates in a Society of the Friends of the Rights of Man, gaining recognition from Paris's Commune and France's National Convention. Rumors flew of 130,000 French rifles massed at Liège for Irish distribution.[86] The time for moderate reform and half-measures seemed past, with a rising international tide lifting all movements.

The future hinged on the government's response to reformers' grievances. In Templepatrick (Antrim) on December 19, local United Irishmen resolved that all regimes "may become corrupt and oppressive; and when so, it is the Duty of the governed to interfere," believing "Reform is now absolutely necessary to secure the Peace" of the realm.[87] A Belfast town meeting proclaimed, "Reform MUST take place whenever the UNITED voice of the people shall call for it."[88] The reformist coalition became formidable. Grattan recalled the political geography of

> the Whig Club in Dublin and the Whigs of the north; the Catholic Convention and Committee; the Protestant Convention [Volunteer meetings] at Dungannon; the United Irishmen in Belfast and in Dublin; and the associations of the "Friends of the Constitution." All these various

[83] *Society of United Irishmen*, 44–46.
[84] Joy, *Belfast*, 102; Jacob, *Rise*, 196.
[85] *Morning Post*, January 3, 1793.
[86] Rachel Rogers, "The Society of the Friends of the Rights of Man, 1792–1794: British and Irish Radical Conjunctions in Republican Paris," *Révolution française* 11 (2016), 3–4; NAI Rebellion Papers 620/19/110.
[87] *Northern Star*, December 20, 1792.
[88] Ibid., December 22, 1792.

bodies shook the island from centre to circumference, and showed that some general measures of relief were indispensable.[89]

As one 1793 pamphleteer observed, Ireland possessed "either a vast deal too much, or a vast deal too little democracy."[90] Political elites risked isolation and violent opposition at an unprecedentedly fraught moment in foreign affairs.

Even war's outbreak in late January 1793 did not dampen Irish reformist zeal. Volunteers illicitly assembled once more at Dungannon in early February, proclaiming themselves an Ulster "Convention of Delegates" for reform. Their "very numerous" gathering, reportedly "democratic in its nature and organization," declared Irish House of Commons representation "inadequate, subversive of the Rights of the People, and an intolerable grievance." With the Commons having pledged an enquiry into representation, the Volunteer Convention declared "complete Parliamentary Reform essential."[91] Elsewhere, loyalist declarations ambiguously professed their constitutional allegiance and highlighted participation by "every religious persuasion" in the war effort.[92] War would not distract reformers from their goals. Many believed the present order could not last much longer.

Irish authorities responded to growing pressure with moderate reform. Dundas wrote to Irish authorities that "limited participation" posed fewer risks than Catholics' "total exclusion" from suffrage.[93] In April 1793, Catholics gained voting rights through Castle-sponsored legislation, but only in county constituencies accounting for under a fifth of seats. Still, no Catholic could become an Irish Member of Parliament.[94] The legislation remained far short of the "Compleat Catholick Emancipation" many sought.[95] Tone asserted, "If the Catholics deserved what has been granted, they deserved what has been withheld," but in wartime, most considered overt dissent unwise.[96] The Catholic Committee declared support for future Parliamentary reform but demobilized, keeping only a small subcommittee on education.[97] Moderate Catholics, from prudence, abandoned the United Irish cause.

[89] Grattan, *Life*, Vol. 4, 127.
[90] *Letters of an Impartial Observer, on the Affairs of Ireland* (Dublin: Clarke, 1793), Letter II, 3.
[91] Agnew, *Drennan-McTier*, Vol. 1, 462; *Northern Star*, February 13 and 16, 1793.
[92] Alan Blackstock, *Loyalism in Ireland, 1789–1829* (Woodbridge, UK: Boydell Press, 2007), 52.
[93] McDowell, *Ireland*, 397.
[94] Bartlett, *Ireland*, 147.
[95] NAI Rebellion Papers 620/20/56.
[96] Elliott, *Wolfe*, 207.
[97] S. J. Connolly, *Divided Kingdom: Ireland, 1630–1800* (Oxford: Oxford University Press, 2008), 446.

Meanwhile, wartime repression against radical reformers and militants accelerated in Ireland as in Britain. A Gunpowder Act, restricting munitions access, passed in February 1793, and a Convention Act severely limiting political meetings followed in August. The first measure declared popular societies "seditious and unlawful assemblies," banning all representative groups.[98] Authorities began forcibly disarming remaining Volunteers, raiding gun shops, and searching known members' homes to confiscate their weapons. A new Irish militia enrolled twenty thousand loyal to Dublin Castle.[99] Recent reforms seemed submerged by the government crackdown: Wolfe Tone incredulously noted "the same session which afforded a mutilated though important relief to the Catholics, carries on its records a militia bill, a gunpowder act, an act for the suppression of tumultuous assemblies."[100] The political scene, recently seeming to open, now clamped shut under wartime repression.

The United Irishmen turned to revolutionary militancy. Two weeks after Britain's war began, Dublin's branch denounced the conflict, considering its real goal to "produce a counter-revolution in France," check "republican sentiment in Great-Britain and Ireland," and "stop the progress of liberty throughout Europe."[101] The French conflict appeared a British war against them. A United Irish catechism to recruits instructed, using French rhetoric, "I believe in the Irish Union, the supreme majesty of the people, in the equality of man, in the lawfulness of insurrection and of resistance to oppression."[102] Wolfe Tone, deprived of his respectable Catholic Committee position, believed authorities were "goading the people to desperation and open insurrection, in order to color and justify the violence of their measures."[103] By July the United Irishmen declared "persecution of principles was the real object of the war," beseeching the Irish to assemble.[104]

The pulverization of Irish civil society became such that violence appeared the only remaining recourse for change. Drennan considered Ireland "sinking by a violence of bad measure in such a hurry of absurdity and tyrannick acts" that soon "nothing but arms is left." Moderate Catholic committees' power, meanwhile, had "gone out, like a candle in the socket."[105] Another United Irish leader, Thomas Emmet, declared the movement "despaired of obtaining a Reform in Parliament by peaceable means" and thus turned to

---

[98] Madden, *United*, Vol. 2, 294.
[99] *Northern Star*, February 27, 1793; Bartlett, *Ireland*, 215.
[100] Tone, *Life*, 91.
[101] *Society of United Irishmen*, 62.
[102] Curtin, *United*, 29.
[103] Tone, *Life*, 107.
[104] *Gazetteer*, August 9, 1793.
[105] Agnew, *Drennan-McTier*, Vol. 1, 562, Vol. 2, 93.

militancy.[106] Alliances became attractive, with Wolfe Tone prognosticating "Ten thousand French would accomplish a separation," by igniting an Irish insurrection.[107] Popular disorders rose with a Dublin anti-conscription riot in May and Defender incidents across at least twenty-one (of thirty-two) counties that summer, often countered by Protestant gangs.[108] The French Republic's Year II (September 1793–September 1794) became a political winter for Irish dissent.

British authorities, worried about losing the Irish political center, briefly appointed a moderate reformist, Earl Fitzwilliam, to the Lord Lieutenancy in late 1794. The hopeful believed greater Parliamentary reform and Catholic emancipation near. Fitzwilliam, indeed, wrote to the British administration that it would "not only be exceedingly impolitic but perhaps dangerous" to resist Catholic demands, while asserting the "Catholic business will be carried easily" through Ireland's Parliament.[109] In March 1795, however, two months after his Irish arrival, British authorities removed him. His successor, Lord Camden, arrived with directives to refuse further Catholic concessions, solidify Protestant support, and prevent the United Irish from coordinating an uprising with the French.[110] Now, as a Dublin bookseller described, instead of extending "rights of citizenship ... the old jobbers are to be reinstated and the same system of corruption and oppression pursued."[111] Dublin observed the day of Fitzwilliam's departure in mourning with businesses closed, black drapery hung, and Irish reformers pulling his coach to the docks.[112] Hopes for moderate reform seemed to sail with him.

Though massive petitions protesting Fitzwilliam's dismissal coalesced, County Wexford's reaching 22,251 signatures, authorities ignored them. Many lost hope for substantive change within the British system. Catholic Committee members entertained proposals for boycotts or mass refusal to enlist in the armed forces, but no movements emerged.[113] Trinity College students made a nighttime demonstration "damning the present Administration," but affected little.[114] Out of disillusionment came

---

[106] Alexander Knox, *Essay on the Political Circumstances of Ireland* (London: Plymsell, 1798), v.

[107] Tone, *Life*, 107.

[108] LC Pinckney Papers, Vol. 9; Musgrave, *Memoirs*, Vol. 1, 125.

[109] KA Pratt Papers, U840/C112/1A.

[110] Elliott, *Wolfe*, 250; NAI Rebellion Papers 620/22/8; Eric G. Tenbus, "Crisis in Ireland: The Tenure of Lord Fitzwilliam, 1794–1795," *The Consortium on the Revolutionary Era: Selected Papers, 1998* (1999), 47–56.

[111] Dickson, "The State of Ireland before 1798," in Cathal Póirtéir, ed. *The Great Irish Rebellion of 1798* (Boulder, CO: Mercier Press, 1998), 22.

[112] Lecky, *Ireland*, Vol. 3, 321.

[113] Edward Hay, *History of the Insurrection of the County of Wexford, A.D. 1798* (Dublin: Stockdale, 1803), vi, 34; KA Pratt Papers U840/0143/4.

[114] KA Pratt Papers U840/0143/2.

radicalization: many United Irishmen became "convinced, that it would be as easy to obtain a revolution as a reform, so obstinately was the later resisted" by the establishment.[115] An April meeting broadcast international communications, declaring "the coming of the French would save their cause and give freedom to Ireland."[116] Little except unconditional Irish submission or unexpected British concessions could prevent a revolutionary break.

The Convention Act's inability to stamp out illicit organizing remained apparent. A new Catholic bill in May 1795 failed after legislators noted how "Since the beginning of the French Revolution, a new power has been erected in this country by cabals, committees, councils and meetings," which persisted yet. With movements retreating from public gatherings, they became difficult to monitor, leading elites to fear them more. French-style organizing developed ambitions British imperial governing elites would not countenance. Little hope of reconciliation between authorities and the increasingly underground United Irish movement remained.

Toward Insurrection

For the societies to have practical effect, in their wartime context, paramilitary preparations seemed essential. Reconciliation with British-appointed officials had failed, and not just revolutionary possibilities but the basic guarantees of Anglo-Irish civil society diminished. With force but not influence on their side, together with French encouragements and Protestant incitements, temptations for a United Irish uprising grew, seeking to unite the vast majority of the Irish people across religious divides against the narrow Anglo-Irish squirarchy.

United Irish efforts to represent the people were contested by the Orange Order founded in September 1795. In Ulster's County Armagh, where a decade earlier the Catholic Defenders began, upstanding Protestants joining rural Peep-O'Day Boys to found the new organization, gaining thirty thousand members over the next two years.[117] Repudiating Catholic integration into militia forces, the Orange Order's bylaws explicitly regulated, "No Roman Catholic can be admitted," due to Ireland's history of sectarian fighting.[118] An estimated seven hundred Catholic families had their homes burned. Whereas annual commemorations of William of Orange's victory on July 12

---

[115] *Memoire, or Detailed Statement of the Origin and Progress of the Irish Union: Delivered to the Irish Government, by Messrs. Emmett, O'Connor and McNevin* (London: Robinson, 1802), 3.

[116] Francis Higgins, *Revolutionary Dublin, 1795–1801: The Letters of Francis Higgins to Dublin Castle*, Bartlett, ed. (Dublin: Four Courts Press, 2004), 79.

[117] Elliott, *Partners*, 72; Smyth, "Volunteer," 14.

[118] William Blacker and Robert H. Wallace, *The Formation of the Orange Order, 1795–1798* (Belfast: Grand Orange Lodge of Ireland, 1994), 67.

had declined in favor of Bastille Day celebrations, the Orangemen revivified marches venerating the Protestant king, "Who bravly Supported and freed us from Popish Slavery."[119] A 1796 intelligence letter described the festivities as intended for "Insulting, & intimidating the Roman Catholicks," with thousands flying orange flags and banners with "Inflammatory Devices & Mottoes."[120] Authorities encouraged the organization, sometimes participating in Orange events.[121] A revitalized, contentious marching tradition proliferated.

The Orange Order, a popular conservative force unlike any American loyalists or French counterrevolutionaries ever mustered, became an imposing counterweight to the United Irishmen. Whereas the British Preservation society collaborated with authorities to suppress radicals, the Orangemen extra-legally took matters into their own hands. Catholics running afoul of the Orangemen received notice of impending attack against their properties, often reading, "To hell or to Connaught with you, you bloody papists; and if you are not gone by [their chosen date] we will come and destroy yourselves and your properties: we hate papists here."[122] The *Northern Star* by 1796 considered "all the horrors of a CIVIL WAR" approaching.[123] That summer, an informant reported, "a general terror prevails amongst the Protestants" that "their throats are to be cut by the Papists" outnumbering them.[124] The Irish struggle exacerbated Catholic-Protestant rivalries, though many Protestants still supported the reformers.

Across 1795 and 1796, the United Irishmen restructured. With fears of infiltration rising, the organization broke into cells communicating only with the provincial committees above them.[125] A local consisted of thirty-six, and then only twelve men, "as nearly as possible of the same neighborhood," remaining in close contact. Each had a "committee of public safety" of the four longest-serving members to monitor its members and correspond with higher branches. The United hierarchy passed through "lower baronial," "upper baronial," and "county" levels, and then four "provincial committees," answerable to a single "general executive committee" in Belfast consisting of five members only known to provincial committee secretaries. The United Irishmen ascended "in gradation, like the component parts of a pyramid or cone, to a common apex or point of union."[126] The structure seemed the height

[119] Denis O'Bryen, *A View of the Present State of Ireland* (London: Jordon, 1797), 23, 68.
[120] NAI Rebellion Papers 620/24/20.
[121] KA Pratt Papers U840/0173/4.
[122] Hay, *History*, 38.
[123] *Northern Star*, January 18, 1796.
[124] NAI Rebellion Papers 620/24/46.
[125] Alvin Jackson, *Ireland 1798–1998: Politics and War* (London: Blackwell, 1999), 13.
[126] Gordon, *History of the Rebellion*, 31–32; Curtin, "The United Irish Organization in Ulster: 1795–1798," in Dickson, Kogh, and Whelan, *The United Irishmen:*

of Enlightened order – so long as links between different movement branches held.

Despite rural brutality, most United Irish remained dedicated to spreading reasoned thought and inclusive politics. Across counties Down and Antrim, "reading societies" flouted the Convention Act. Reportedly "formed after the model of the Jacobin Clubs in France," they discussed "inflammatory publications" including Paine's, early anarchist William Godwin's, United Irish manifestos, and American tracts, while discussing the movement's future.[127] Lord Camden in August 1796 denounced the "democratic Societies and Clubs upon the Principles of the French Revolution" that "revive their Committees & Assemblies" with new vigor.[128] In strongholds, branches met openly: some rural societies began discussing redistribution, asserting "a general division of land" could follow the movement's triumph.[129] Locals continued receiving correspondence from British groups, flouting authorities' attempts to isolate movement branches.[130] The United Irish commandeered the era's radical spirit, responding to British repression by seeking to harness revolutionary associational life's full potential.

Battles with Orangemen and other Protestant gangs remained endemic, as United Irishmen raided for weapons, undertook violent reprisals, and intimidated witnesses. Protestant authorities saw seditious threats everywhere, asserting the secret organization assembled "under pretence of saving corn, and digging potatoes" for arrested dissidents, while co-opting "Lottery Clubs," "funerals, foot-ball meetings, &c." Even when no direct actions resulted, the gatherings helped teach "the people the habit of assembling from great distances upon an order being issued, and making them more accustomed to shew themselves openly in support of the cause."[131] Those refusing to participate faced retribution as "Orangemen or informers."[132] Such tactics alienated many, including allies, with Drennan noting in Dublin, "We hear they are murdering each other in the North as usual, and here they are cursing United Irishmen."[133]

In autumn 1796, the United Irishmen joined forces with the Defenders, swearing new members into both simultaneously. The resulting organization became formidable. In Ulster alone, in October 1796 the combined movement boasted 38,000 members and by May 1797, 118,000. National strength may

Republicanism, Radicalism and Rebellion (Dublin: Lilliput Press, 1993), 212; KA Pratt Papers, U840/0147/13/2.

[127] Musgrave, *Memoirs*, Vol. 1, 155; KA Pratt Papers U840/0147/13/2.

[128] NAI Rebellion Papers 620/18/11/1.

[129] Ibid., 620/18/14/4; KA Pratt Papers U840/0146/3.

[130] NAI Rebellion Papers, 620/18/14/20.

[131] *Report of the Secret Committee*, 6, 8; NAI Rebellion Papers 620/18/14/37 and 620/26/16;

[132] McSkimin, *Annals*, 45.

[133] Agnew, *Drennan-McTier*, Vol. 2, 247.

have approached five hundred thousand.[134] Many possessed weapons training, with "a large part of them having been formerly Volunteers."[135] Whereas previously Defenders mobilized through loose local alliances, now they developed "methodized operations ... bound together by a secret and mysterious chain" not breached by authorities. The full network rising for a "democratick revolution" seemed plausible.[136] Drennan considered the societies to have created powerful divisions, "what may be called civil anarchy, and from that to civil war, where the contending powers will be too equally balanced to hope for a speedy termination or a happy one."[137] Disastrous conflict approached.

Hoping to break the standoff with forces from abroad, United Irishmen cultivated a French alliance. Though France's Jacobins had been suppressed and the Directory regime became known for corruption and exploitation, including in occupied Belgian, Dutch, German, and Italian territories, the revolutionary regime remained the power capable of aiding the Irish dissidents. One assessment found "landing places are innumerable" along the coasts, noted Brest being nautically twice as close as Plymouth, and considered British forces insufficient, believing success or failure rested on Irish people's response.[138] French authorities, influenced by Wolfe Tone and other Irish leaders now in Parisian exile, asserted Ireland could become a Vendée for Britain, forcing troops and resources away from the revolutionary war's other fronts.[139]

In late 1796, the French loaded fifteen thousand soldiers at Brest to land at Bantry Bay in County Cork and spark an Irish insurrection. The force sailed in December, but storms separated the fleet, and though peasants witnessed a seascape "crowded with foreign masts" for five days, unopposed by the British Navy, waves prevented their landing – necessitating a return to France. Still, the sortie's effects were profound: never, one Irishman recalled, "had Ireland experienced an hour of greater excitement" or was "her population more agitated with alternate hopes and fears."[140] Authorities seemed shocked they had not received intelligence on the French force, responding by arresting 500–600 suspected radicals and increasing weapons searches.[141]

---

[134] Elliott, *Partners*, 96; Connolly, *Divided*, 466; John Thomas Gilbert, *Documents Relating to Ireland, 1795-1804* (Shannon: Irish University Press, 1970), 152.

[135] NAI Rebellion Papers 620/18/11/1.

[136] Knox, *Essay*, 72.

[137] Drennan, *Drennan*, 235.

[138] *General Observations on the State of Affairs in Ireland, and Its Defence against an Invasion. By a Country Gentleman* (Dublin: Johnson, 1797), 5, 7, 43.

[139] Elliott, *Partners*, 87.

[140] Charles Hamilton Teeling, *Personal Narrative of the "Irish Rebellion" of 1798* (London: Teeling, 1828), 65–66; Lecky, *Ireland*, Vol. 3, 540.

[141] Jackson, *Ireland*, 15.

Indeed, much of the United Irish movement primed for an uprising. In rural County Down, already in September 1796 a thousand representatives met to consider an insurrection. In an open vote, seven hundred favored rebellion, but with the other three hundred strongly opposed, they postponed. In spring 1797, though Ulster newly endorsed pressing forward, Dublin's branch deferred, creating "coolness" between delegates.[142] Numbers nevertheless multiplied, with Dublin and surrounding counties exceeding 56,000 adherents, while Cork's strength reached 75,000–90,000.[143] Despite fierce government repression, four years after the Gunpowder and Convention Acts the British press reported Dublin Castle "so panic struck, that every one is alarmed lest a general Insurrection should take place."[144] The exodus of loyal Northern gentry from their country estates accelerated.[145] Authorities could not confidently ascertain the movement's potential.

The movement extended across the Irish Sea, affiliating United Englishmen and Scotsmen. Spy reports claimed Belfast "carried on correspondence to every public society in England, this Kingdom and Scotland," while developing American links.[146] The United movement gained affiliates, burnished by Irish expatriates and emissaries, in Scotland (reportedly over 9,600 at Dundee and Perth in 1797), Lancashire (eighty cells strong), Yorkshire, Manchester, Birmingham, London, and elsewhere. Allying with the underground British opposition, the Irish claimed formidable partners.[147] Illicit letters crossed the short sea on smuggling boats – leading British officials to recommend more "revenue cruizers" patrolling.[148] United Irishman Arthur O'Connor in late 1796 wrote to British reformer Fox, asserting, "a new order of things would force its way into the World," considering even the French not "so ripe as some other Countries in Europe" for revolution. The United movement provided a vector to "promote Brotherly Love" and build unprecedented coalitions, perhaps in both nations.[149] As potential French invasion loomed for Britain as well, none could know where political change would first occur.

Open conflict and the real prospect of revolutionary change seemed close. Intelligence presented before the Irish Commons noted "great joy expressed" among United Irishmen at the Bantry Bay episode with their forces "ordered to be ready" for a French landing. They asserted directives were given for "All the

---

[142] Musgrave, *Memoirs*, Vol. 1, 158; *Report of the Secret Committee*, 23.
[143] McDowell, *Ireland*, 477.
[144] *True Briton*, April 26, 1797.
[145] Fortescue, *Manuscripts*, Vol. 3, 314.
[146] Bartlett, *Revolutionary*, 125.
[147] Elliott, *Partners*, 174; NAI Rebellion Papers 620/18/14/36; Dickinson, *British Radicalism*, 50–51; Iain McCalman, *Radical Underworld: Prophets, Revolutionaries and Pornographers in London, 1795–1840* (Cambridge: Cambridge University Press, 1988).
[148] NAI Rebellion Papers, 620/31/11.
[149] Ibid., 620/15/3/7.

persons in government to be massacred" and a "republic and convention to be established." Moreover, if alliances held and "the Defenders join them they need not wait for the French."[150] Camden worried a "system of terror" advanced to intimidate government supporters.[151] Yet aside from raising military corps under aristocratic officers, whose regional popularity varied greatly, administrators avoided loyalist mobilization, believing "Parliamentary Reform and other questions would be apt to mix themselves in the discussion."[152] Camden tried to regain moderate support by offering pardons to United Irishmen while threatening repression of those persisting. Meanwhile, British informants infiltrated the organization.[153] A final crisis approached, yet each side spent the rest of the year biding time, not ready for battle.

The government accelerated arrests of United Irishmen, attempting to destroy their cell system. Authorities suspended Habeas Corpus, indefinitely detaining United Irish leaders. Communication breakdowns multiplied in the rebel ranks. Troop seizures of tens of thousands of illegal arms pushed rural cells into risky raids on Orangemen, leading to counter-reprisals responsible for perhaps hundreds of United Irish deaths, while others manufactured pikes. With the United Irishmen's effective power decreasing, desperate leaders pushed the rebel society toward action.[154] As conciliatory possibilities faded, United Irishmen declared "Parliamentary Reform" to be "Now the Watch Word for Revolution."[155] Growing repression made revolutionary change essential.

Coercion grew as areas consolidated for the United Irish or Orange camps. Intelligence from County Down accused the United movement of forcing "people into their associations with the most gross threats" of retribution. Groups of "night walkers," often hundreds strong, pillaged and burnt opposition dwellings. Fervor grew among the populace with one report finding, "Every Man and Woman are now United, I almost Doubt Whether there is One in Forty that is Not," with both sexes sporting green ribbons, handkerchiefs, and shoelaces. "Whenever the French land, this Country is gone,"

---

[150] Gilbert, *Documents*, 104.
[151] KA Pratt Papers, U840/O160/15.
[152] Ibid., U840/01/4/15; NAI Rebellion Papers, 620/26 14. Belfast, on forming a Yeoman Corps, used the occasion agitate for reform anyway: NAI Rebellion Papers, 620/26/177.
[153] *Oracle*, May 24, 1797; Elliott, *Partners*, 165.
[154] Kevin Whelan, *The Tree of Liberty: Radicalism, Catholicism and the Construction of Irish Identity, 1760–1830* (Notre Dame: University of Notre Dame Press, 1996), 113; Teeling, *Personal*, 204; Ruán O'Donnell, *The Rebellion in Wicklow, 1798* (Dublin: Irish Academic Press, 1998), 88; Joseph Holt, *Memoirs of Joseph Holt, General of the Irish Rebels, in 1798* (London: Colburn, 1838), 20; Lecky, *Ireland*, Vol. 4, 29, 100; NAI, Rebellion Papers, 620/25/150; Elliott, *Partners*, 189.
[155] NAI Rebellion Papers 620/18/14/28.

worried one Cork official.[156] Both sides expected imminent rebellion across 1797.

France, having reduced its continental enemies, possessed available forces to invade Ireland and an alluring opportunity. The United Irish beseeched the French to join them, claiming "universal disaffection" primed "millions" to "joyfully join the hero of Italy," Napoleone Buonaparte, rumored to be participating.[157] In February 1798, the network called "all United Men to be in a State of preparation," believing the moment close. Branches reportedly continued meeting twice a week, "under the pretence of dining," through which new intelligence spread "through the country like wild fire," despite government attempts at disruption.[158] Authorities declared martial law on March 2, taking particularly aggressive measures in Dublin. Likely over half a million United Irish readied. The government estimated nearly half that number armed and battle-ready with St. Patrick's Day slated "the first, and universal day of killing."[159] In a pregnant pause, throughout the winter the United network and French horizon remained quiet.

Despite the extensive preparatory efforts, the United Irish rebellion, finally undertaken across several counties for May 23, 1798, without the French, failed to become a unified, national uprising. Most notably, the rebels took County Wexford on Ireland's southeastern tip closest to France with an onlooker in Enniscorthy reporting "corn in flames in every direction" with United Irishmen "demolishing the houses of those called loyalists, Orangemen, &c."[160] But in broader perspective, United Irishmen lost time and energy in retributive violence against neighboring Orangemen and their property.[161] The uprising remained under-coordinated with communications weak since authorities had decimated the committee system. Despite United Irish calls for a universal insurrection – "Arise then, united sons of Ireland, arise like a great and powerful people, determined to live free, or die" – most areas stayed quiet.[162] Dublin's uprising was quickly extinguished, while Belfast and the north demurred, allegedly from "not being willing to riske their persons & their property until they see better hopes of success" to the south.[163] Suddenly disunited by movement stresses, political pragmatism, quick British responses, and fears of reprisal, United Irish partnerships faltered.

---

[156] Ibid., 620/28/143; 620/28/237; 620/35/130; 620/29/289; 620/29/277.
[157] *City Gazette*, May 2, 1798.
[158] NAI Rebellion Papers 620/18/14/72; 620/35/130.
[159] Lecky, *Ireland*, Vol. 4, 252; Curtin, *United*, 254–55; NAI Rebellion Papers 620/18/14/72.
[160] NAI 1576, Joseph Haughton Papers.
[161] John D. Beatty, ed. *Protestant Women's Narratives of the Irish Rebellion of 1798* (Dublin: Four Courts Press, 2001), 54, 119.
[162] Gordon, *History of the Rebellion*, 79.
[163] KA Pratt Papers, U840/0156A/39.

The government kept rebel areas isolated and overmatched. Hoping to avoid another "American war," Dublin Castle administrators responded with overwhelming force before United Irish forces consolidated.[164] Atrocities spread with a British officer describing his orders as "to treat the people with as much harshness as possible," to "excite terror, and by that means obtain our end speedily."[165] Rebels suffered 90 percent of the thirty thousand military casualties. After years of rifle confiscations, insurgents often fought with pikes or pitchforks.[166] Five different counties' rebellions were separately over-whelmed. Though County Wexford mobilized fifteen thousand, partially fueled by rumors that Orangemen would massacre Catholics, other areas did not match their ardor. British authorities incredulously noted that overwhelm-ingly Catholic western counties, where no Orange Lodges existed, had not risen. The United Irishmen's failure to seize cities, partially attributable to stronger police repression there, led provincial rebels to feel abandoned with Wexford insurgents considering Dublin to have "betrayed" their followers. Meanwhile, national communication lines remained open for government coordination even in the worst of the rebellion.[167]

Though rebels seized several seaports in May, they received only belated and inadequate French support. The Directory possessed less than half the naval ships Britain did and proved reluctant to risk them for an ill-timed Irish uprising. By July, only scattered rural guerilla forces remained in remote areas, though continued eluding government forces as they lacked heavy artillery and thus moved faster than British columns.[168] The French arrived in late August, unstrategically in quiet northwestern County Mayo, with barely a thousand troops and little surplus weaponry to arm Irish rebels. With Buonaparte successfully lobbying the Directory to divert expeditionary resources to an Egyptian invasion, Ireland remained a diversion. In October, the British navy dispersed French reinforcements off Donegal. The United Irish rebellion, never gaining full strength, suffered brutal suppression with around ten thousand killed.[169]

---

[164] Ibid., U840/0165A/36.

[165] John Moore, *The Diary of John Moore* (London, 1904), Vol. 1, 289.

[166] Evans, *Debating*, 25; McDowell, *Ireland*, 605, 616.

[167] Fortescue, *Manuscripts*, Vol. 4, 264; *Courier of New Hampshire*, August 14, 1798; Thomas Parkenham, *The Year of Liberty: The Story of the Great Irish Rebellion of 1798* (London: Thomas & Parkenham, 1969), 143; Bartlett, *Revolutionary*, 253; Teeling, *Personal*, 157.

[168] Hugh Gough, "France and the 1798 Rebellion," in Póirtéir, 40; O'Donnell, *Rebellion*, 2; Charles Cornwallis, *Correspondence of Charles, First Marquis of Cornwallis* (London: Murray, 1859), Vol. 2, 358.

[169] Jackson, *Ireland*, 20; Trinity College, Prior Notebooks MSS 3365 2–35; Bartlett, "Clemency and Compensation: The Treatment of Defeated Rebels and Suffering Loyalists after the 1798 Rebellion," in *Revolution, Counterrevolution and Union*, Jim Smyth, ed. (Cambridge: Cambridge University Press, 2000), 100.

Two decades of campaigns toward greater Irish national freedom led to a mismanaged rising, followed by brutal suppression. One British traveler in 1799 noted:

> In the capital, I observed the streets were crowded with the widows and orphans of those who had fallen in battle: In the country, I beheld the villages every where burnt and razed to the ground. Every thing I cast my eyes on, presented the melancholy features of ruin and desolation.[170]

Dublin's United Irishmen reorganized surviving shards of the organization in winter 1799, permitting only oral communication. Meetings and retributive violence continued across much of the country, while coordination persisted with United Britons. With movement leaders again seeking collaboration with the French, many hoped the 1803 breakdown of the Peace of Amiens between Britain and France would make Ireland again a theatre of war. A small Dublin insurrection, Emmet's Rebellion, was nevertheless quickly crushed in July.[171] Five years after 1798, there proved no national inclination for a new united rising.

Meanwhile, British authorities sought Irish political pacification, as even earlier 1780s gains were rolled back. Fearful of full Catholic Emancipation, future attempts at independence, or a French alliance, the Irish Parliament in 1800 passed the Act of Union, merging Ireland with Great Britain to form the United Kingdom. Catholics were again politically disenfranchised, and the political status quo restored. Popular mobilization resulted in disaster. The Age of Revolution would be remembered in Ireland for missed opportunities as universalist ambitions ceded to endemic and enduring sectarian divides. As across Europe, the 1790s ended in repression, division, and disappointment.

Conclusion

Liberation felt close at hand in late eighteenth century Ireland. Spreading ideals of freedom combined with a politically engaged populace and British imperial precarity to open the prospect of Irish self-determination. Combining the pragmatic examples of the American Committees of Correspondence and the Irish Volunteers with the radicalness of French revolutionary universalism, the United Irishmen created a paramilitary system incorporating half a million to seek major changes to Ireland's unequal and subservient political order. Unlike most other movements chronicled in this study, Irish historians have embraced the international dimension of United Irish developments, while

---

[170] George Cooper, *Letters on the Irish Nation, Written during a Visit to That Kingdom, in the Autumn of 1799* (London, 1800), 128.

[171] James G. Patterson, *In the Wake of the Great Rebellion: Republicanism, Agrarianism and Banditry in Ireland after 1798* (Manchester: Manchester University Press, 2008), 4.

placing blame for the uprising on France's insufficient and mistimed aid. As a result of political contingencies, Ireland's sectarian divide, rather than receding like elsewhere in Europe, endured as the symbol of an unequal British political settlement. In many respects, the United Irish movement fell victim to an Atlantic Thermidor, in which the French Directory's realpolitik weakened its support for the United Irish, while the repression of sister movements in the Anglophone world prevented extensive aid or an allied uprising. Divided and distracted by a continent at war, prospects for universal liberty were smashed as the British wartime government aggressively sought domestic pacification.

14

The French Revolution and the Making of the American Democratic Party

Despite the Sons of Liberty and Revolutionary Committees of Correspondence's centrality to modern social movements' creation, most Americans during the first decade after the War of Independence discouraged extra-governmental alliances. For responsible self-government, most Federalists and Anti-Federalists alike argued, debate should be limited to print, electoral, and legislative realms while "partial combinations," or parties, would undermine patriotic consensus and sap government support. The Bill of Rights' First Amendment ambiguously allows "the people peaceably to assemble, and to petition the government for a redress of grievances" but leaves broader associational rights uncertain and subject to restriction. Many founders did not consider such freedoms to extend to enduring political combinations and parties. Although organized special-interest politicking occurred across the early Republic, as this book chronicles for religious groups, merchant associations, abolitionists, and anti-abolitionists, such formations did not expand into general political coalitions. Educated Americans commonly blamed "party" for the ancient Roman Republic's fall and few before the mid-1790s endorsed such creations.

Consubstantial with the American party system's creation were the young nation's interactions with revolutionary France. Americans of all persuasions enthusiastically greeted news of 1789's grand events, as their ally seemingly followed their examples. Madison, for instance, considered "The light which is chasing darkness and despotism from the old world" to be "an emanation" from "the establishment of liberty in the new."[1] By 1793, however, American opinion divided: the French Republic held out a tempting model of greater equality and expanded rights for many, while representing political and social breakdown to others. A new club network encouraged by a renegade Jacobin French Ambassador calling itself the Democratic-Republican Society and derived from the Jacobin model, together with often-Francophillic dissident "Republican" legislators, overturned the Federalist consensus and inspired the rise of a new, more powerful association: the Democratic Party.

---

[1] Ralph Ketcham, *James Madison: A Biography* (New York: Macmillan, 1971), 316.

Citizen Genêt and the Rise of Democratic-Republican Societies

By 1791, a growing number of Americans considered French liberty – as promoted by widespread and aggressive club networks – to surpass their own. Analyzing French political clubs' spread, Philadelphia's *General Advertiser* that July considered, "A new light has risen upon the horizon of France," whereby "French Academies, uniting with English Clubs, have discovered a new mine of wisdom which our forefathers dreamed not of," sparking unprecedented popular mobilization. Nearly a generation after American independence, beyond many young partisans' living memory, French developments appeared revolutionary. Even if such organizations reportedly "excited the blaze of Liberty with the torch of Sedition," they nevertheless augured an imposing power.[2] The following year, Phillip Freneau's opposition *National Gazette* promoted "constitutional societies in every part of the United States, for the purpose of watching over the rights of the people, and giving an early alarm in case of governmental encroachments thereupon."[3] Though Americans remained reticent to undertake such radical designs, the option readied.

Though during Constitutional debates "party" and "faction" were synonymous insults, in the Federalist regime's first year a concerted political opposition developed.[4] The new order cracked first from within: Madison and Jefferson, the first an influential Congressman and the second becoming Secretary of State upon returning from Paris, objected to many Federalist measures. Jefferson described himself "daily pitted in the cabinet like two cocks" with Treasury Secretary Hamilton over policy differences.[5] Hamilton's plans to create a national bank and centralize states' war debt, while rewarding predominantly urban merchant debt speculators, passed despite Jefferson's objections and Madison-led Congressional resistance. The divide became regional: northern Congressmen voted 33–1 for the bank bill and southern representatives opposed it by 19–6.[6] A permanent rift resulted between dissidents taking the British name "Whigs" and then "Republicans" (ancestors of the Democratic Party) and establishment "Friends of Order," "Friends of Government," or "Federalists."[7] With Jefferson and Madison asserting every Federal decision created dangerous precedents, the bank bill sought to extend

[2] *General Advertiser*, July 16, 1791.

[3] Foner, *Democratic-Republican*, 3.

[4] Richard Hofstadter, *The Idea of a Party System: The Rise of Legitimate Opposition in the United States, 1780–1840* (Berkeley, CA: University of California Press, 1969), 64.

[5] John Ferling, *Jefferson and Hamilton: The Rivalry That Forged a Nation* (New York: Bloomsbury, 2013), 223; Terry Bouton, *Taming Democracy: "The People," the Founders, and the Troubled Ending of the American Revolution* (Oxford: Oxford University Press, 2009).

[6] Morton Borden, *Parties and Politics in the Early Republic, 1789–1815* (Arlington Heights, IL: Harlan Davidson, 1967), 44.

[7] Noble E. Cunningham, Jr., *In Pursuit of Reason: The Life of Thomas Jefferson* (Baton Rouge: Louisiana State University Press, 1987), 164; David Hackett Fischer, *The Revolution*

the federal government's powers.[8] Opposition organizing advanced, though remained unwilling to mobilize the broad populace.

Recruiting like-minded colleagues, Republicans sought to protect revolutionary liberty from governmental encroachment. Initially, Jefferson and Madison appealed to Southern representatives wanting more agricultural instead of merchant-favoring policies. Northern factional divides brought additional allies with New York's powerful anti-Hamiltonian faction led by Governor George Clinton and Senator Aaron Burr allying with the Congressional opposition. Careful not to identify with earlier Anti-Federalists, though working with them, the growing group considered themselves a "loyal opposition" maintaining constitutional principles.[9] With American newspapers overwhelmingly pro-Federalist, Madison and Jefferson recruited Freneau to found a partisan *National Gazette* in 1791, supporting his efforts with paid State Department translation work and finding subscribers.[10] With newspaper mailing subsidized by the federal postal service, the *Gazette* achieved a national following. Freneau elaborated a Republican perspective critical of the Federal government's motivations, undercutting officeholders' self-portrayal as independent arbiters above all parties. In subsequent elections, with Federalist-favoring newspapers responding likewise, voters became aware which candidates possessed "Federalist" or "Republican" persuasions.[11]

Madison reversed his arguments against political parties made during the Constitutional ratification to endorse their creation. Though previously a close Hamilton ally, writing the majority of the *Federalist Papers* – declaring "every appeal to the people would carry an implication of some defect in the government" and deprive elected representatives of "veneration" and "stability" – in early 1792 Madison declared political organizing part of a balanced government.[12] In the *National Gazette*, he argued in "every political society, parties are unavoidable," asserting their compatibility with the Constitution he helped write: "By making one party a check on the other," they could strengthen the government. Also, they might foil intrigue: Madison believed Hamilton's financial faction "the weaker in point of numbers," succeeding through the influence of "moneyed" men.[13] Party combinations became a pragmatic way to resist unrepresentative policies.

of American Conservatism: The Federalist Party in the Era of Jeffersonian Democracy (New York: Harper & Row, 1965), 51.

[8] Cunningham, *Pursuit*, 165.

[9] Ibid., 42; Saul Cornell, *The Other Founders: Anti-Federalism & The Dissenting Tradition in America, 1788–1828* (Chapel Hill: University of North Carolina Press, 1999), 172–94.

[10] Irving Bryant, *James Madison: Father of the Constitution, 1787–1800* (Indianapolis: Bobbs-Merrill, 1950), 334–36.

[11] Jeffrey L. Pasley, *"The Tyranny of Printers": Newspaper Politics in the Early American Republic* (Charlottesville: University Press of Virginia, 2001).

[12] James Roger Sharp, *American Politics in the Early Republic: The New Nation in Crisis* (New Haven: Yale University Press, 1993), 45.

[13] Elkins and McKittrick, *Age*, 266–68.

By 1792, Federalist-Republican divides appeared irreconcilable. Jefferson referred to his opponents as "stock jobbers and king-jobbers," as Hamilton's policies facilitated a wealth transfer to the privileged few. House clerk and opposition organizer John Beckley summarized national politics as "the struggle between the Treasury department and the republican Interest."[14] In the sixty-five-man Second Congress (1791–1792), seventeen Representatives voted with Madison at least two-thirds of the time, while a Federalist group of fifteen consistently opposed them, making nearly half members of conflicting factions.[15] Hamilton by May considered, "Mr. Madison cooperating with Mr. Jefferson is at the head of a faction decidedly hostile to me and my administration," with Madison betraying their earlier alliance to become "a political enemy."[16] Opposing views on the Federal government's rightful size and nature, spiked by personal conflicts, became the genesis of the American party system.

National electoral politics responded to the elite power struggle. New York, already possessing decades-old "Whig" and "Tory" factions, ramped up political mobilization for the 1792 election. Both Republican and Federalist-allied politicians organized correspondence committees and local canvassing operations, as the Republican Clinton won a close race over Federalist John Jay. Organizers entreated local activists, as one Federalist circular described "to call a meeting of such of our Friends in your town" and "unite their exertions" for the candidate. Once establishing local support, they encouraged "appointing a Committee with whom we may Correspond" for broader coordination.[17] The committees distributed "tickets" for candidates across the Empire State, resulting in a significant Republican state legislative majority. In Pennsylvania Congressional elections, Republicans (aided by similar committees) won nine of eleven districts. Virginia Republicans mobilized likewise to retain their stronghold.[18]

With the opposition's growing success, rising partisanship and the adaptation of revolutionary methods for elections worried many. Vice President John Adams denounced "Jacobins in this Country," now "pursuing objects as pernicious by means as unwarrantable as those of France," as party organizing's efficacy became clear.[19] In other states, the new group's structure remained loose, based on friendships and informal domestic gatherings rather

---

[14] VHS John Beckley Papers, MSS B3886.

[15] Cunningham, *The Jeffersonian Republicans: The Formation of Party Organization, 1789–1791* (Chapel Hill: University of North Carolina Press, 1957), 20–22.

[16] Hamilton, *Papers*, Vol. 11, 429.

[17] LC Peter Van Schaack Papers, MSS 4918.

[18] Ketcham, *James*, 335; Cunningham, *Jeffersonian*, 35–45.

[19] *Adams Family Correspondence*, L. H. Butterfield, ed. (Cambridge, MA: Harvard University Press, 1963–2015), Vol. 9, 338.

than clubs and caucuses.[20] Even New Yorkers did not keep their constituents mobilized after the brief election season. Fearful of being branded disloyal by Federalist elites, organizers continued encouraging deference to elected leaders. Despite Republicans' inclusive rhetoric, broader coalitions needed to develop beyond the Southern planter class and disaffected New York elites.

French republican politics' expanding possibilities led many to expect similar American developments. French, British, and Irish club resolutions multiplied in American newspapers and many gazed enviously across the Atlantic.[21] The *National Gazette* on July 4, 1792, proposed a society "for the discussion of Political knowledge called THE FRIENDS OF THE PEOPLE," on the Francophillic British reformers' model, though no such organization followed.[22] Word spread that the French organization outstripped in size and political reach even America's earlier Sons of Liberty or Committees of Correspondence. Baltimore's *Federal Gazette* in November, in a widely reprinted notice, described Paris's Jacobins leading "about 40,000 societies of a similar nature, dispersed over every part of the nation. All public and constitutional questions are here debated in the fullest, the most free, and open manner."[23] Freedoms of speech and assembly seemed greater in France than America.

Many Americans found new hopes in the French ferment, while conservatives saw the menace of mob politics or encroaching terror. Lafayette denouncing the Jacobins drew particular notice, given his American reputation and powerful friends. Writing to Washington in March, the General decried "the most violent popular party, the Jacobin club, a Jesuitic institution, more fit to make deserters from, than converts to our cause."[24] French politics' rapid factional changes gave American politicians pause, particularly once Lafayette unsuccessfully called for the Jacobins' suppression and defected to the enemy Austrians that summer. Still, the opposition focused on the revolution's potential. Even growing radicalization gained approbation, with Virginia Senator James Monroe suggesting the king's execution and other revolutionary violence "incidents to much greater" cause most Americans "wish to see accomplished."[25] News of the French army's victory at Valmy

[20] Cunningham, *Jeffersonian*.
[21] Albrecht Koschnik, "The Democratic Societies of Philadelphia and the Limits of the American Public Sphere, circa 1793–1795," *William and Mary Quarterly* 58, no. 3 (2001), 618.
[22] Pasley, *The First Presidential Contest: 1796 and the Founding of American Democracy* (Lawrence: University of Kansas Press, 2013), 83.
[23] *Federal Gazette*, November 26, 1792; *Connecticut Journal*, December 5, 1792; *Washington Spy*, December 7, 1792; *New-Hampshire Gazette*, December 19, 1792; *City Gazette*, December 27, 1792.
[24] Washington, *Papers*, Presidential Series, Vol. 10, 117.
[25] James Monroe, *The Writings of James Monroe* (New York: Putnam's Sons, 1898), 252.

sparked celebrations with Boston crowds in January 1793 marching from their Liberty Tree through town to a civic feast, singing *Ça ira*.[26] France's revolution could not fail to complicate politics for America's still-fledgling constitutional order, presenting a dramatic tableau for each side's hopes and fears.

The ardor to imitate French examples spiked with the new French ambassador Genêt's arrival. The thirty-year-old envoy, a charming conversationalist fluent since childhood in English and German, had already lived a complex life. After a childhood at Versailles, family connections won Genêt postings at London and Vienna and then a secretarial commission at the Russian court in 1788 at age twenty-five. Though absent during the French Revolution's formative years, Genêt embraced the New Regime with a convert's passion. After proselytizing universal liberation at St. Petersburg, Empress Catherine the Great expelled him in July 1792. Back in Paris, Genêt attended Jacobin Club meetings, building connections (particularly with the Brissotin/Girondin faction) and seeking a new assignment. The revolutionary leadership – possessing few professional diplomats with such enthusiasm – first appointed Genêt minister to the Netherlands, though war intervened, and then changed his posting in November to the United States.[27]

While such an assignment, far from the cauldron of European intrigues, at first perhaps seemed disappointing, the revolutionary leadership gave Genêt important missions. Keen to spread "wars of liberation," Genêt was ordered to develop pro-French ardor in the United States to "fortify the Americans in the Principles that engage them to unite with France," thus perpetuating the "Eternal Alliance" between the two republics. More directly, Genêt was to recruit seamen for French warships and mobilize invasions of Spanish Florida and Louisiana. Genêt on arrival commissioned five hundred men to march overland through Ohio and Kentucky to incite local Louisianans, "almost all French or Anglo-American," to revolt, promising them they could sack Spanish headquarters. A second commission would raise a southern force to incite Anglophone squatters south of the Florida-Georgia line to liberate the colony from the Spanish. Together, these forces could divert Spanish forces and weaken their empire.[28] Furthermore, Genêt armed pirate expeditions against British shipping, seeking to diminish their naval advantage.

---

[26] Simon P. Newman, *Parades and the Politics of the Street: Festive Culture in the Early American Republic* (Philadelphia: University of Pennsylvania Press, 1997), 1–2.

[27] Genet, *Washington*, 1–14; Henry Ammon, *The Genet Mission* (New York: Norton, 1973), 1–9; Frederick Jackson Turner, "The Origin of Genet's Projected Attack on Louisiana and the Floridas," *American Historical Review* 3, no. 4 (1898), 650–71.

[28] Douglas Bradburn, *The Citizenship Revolution: Politics and the Creation of the American Union, 1774–1804* (Charlottesville: University of Virginia Press, 2009), 115; "Correspondence of Clark and Genet," *Report of the Historical Manuscripts Commission of the American Historical Association* (1898), 946–47, 959.

Such unprecedented maneuvers caught American officials by surprise. The Minister Plenipotentiary to France, Gouverneur Morris, via Paine's introduction, reported Genêt "a man of good parts and very good Education," but of "ardent Temper and who, feeling Genius and Talents, may perhaps have rated himself a little too high" in the revolutionary world. Morris dismissed Genêt as an "Upstart" yet had no inkling of his instructions.[29]

Though sailing for the American capital of Philadelphia, Genêt's ship blew off course and arrived in Charleston on April 8 (three days before the German-Republican Society's pronouncement). Charleston – a city rich in French Huguenot heritage that endured a brutal six-week siege against the British in 1780 – already boasted corresponding links with French clubs, while sending aid to Saint-Domingue planters battling a slave insurrection commonly blamed on royalist agitations.[30] Now, the city became a showcase for pro-French displays. To Genêt, "exciting the Americans to second our views" was pivotal. He socialized with leading politicians and merchants, while participating in popular banquets.[31] Charleston's *City Gazette* described the young ambassador as "easy, affable and pleasing," fluent in English, German, and French, who "fascinates all" he met.[32] The new Charleston Republican Society was only his most public alliance.

Genêt pursued his instructions pertaining to France's Revolutionary War. The ambassador recruited privateers to raid British shipping, which sympathetic South Carolina Governor William Moultrie, after meeting with Genêt, did not oppose (even recommending leaders for the Florida expedition). At no loss for subtlety, the four pirating vessels were (de)christened *Le Républicain*, *le Sans-Culotte*, *l'anti-George*, and *le patriote Genêt*. Washington soon heard of the ambassador's actions.[33] With the spirit of audacity dear to French revolutionary politics, Genêt sought to destabilize America in France's favor.

Rather than sailing north to Philadelphia, Genêt traveled overland, stoking pro-French revolutionary fervor across the South. Over a twenty-eight-day voyage across the Carolinas and Tidewater states, Genêt met honorary deputations, banquets, and civic festivals celebrating the French Revolution. Tiny Statesburg, South Carolina, received Genêt outside town, leading him to

---

[29] Gouverneur Morris, *A Diary of the French Revolution, 1752–1816*, Beatrix Cory Davenport, ed. (Boston: Houghton-Mifflin, 1939), Vol. 2, 593–95.

[30] "Correspondence of the French Ministers," 212; AN AF ET B(I) 372 439.

[31] Robert J. Alderson, *This Bright Era of Happy Revolutions: French Consul Michel-Ange-Bernard Mangourit and International Republicanism in Charleston, 1792–1794* (Columbia, SC: University of South Carolina Press, 2008), 43; McKitrick, *Age*, 335; Edwin S. Gaustad and Leigh E. Schmidt, *The Religious History of America*, rev. ed. (New York: HarperOne, 2002), 104; "Correspondence of the French," 254.

[32] *City Gazette*, July 4, 1793.

[33] Hamilton, *The Papers of Alexander Hamilton*, Harold C. Syrett, ed. (New York: Columbia University Press, 1961–1987), Vol. 14, 454; "Correspondence of the French Ministers," 213; Ammon, *Genet*, 45.

festivities where a municipal address predicted "the ripening of the fruits of liberty and equality" for France. In Richmond, Genêt met the governor, war veteran Light-Horse Harry Lee (brother of the Wilkite Arthur Lee), who declared that if not for his recent marriage, he would have joined the French Revolutionary Army. Only Baltimore – "This town is rich and the English have a great influence," Genêt sniffed – snubbed him.[34]

Even his Southern travels little prepared Genêt for the scenes awaiting him as he entered the Delaware Valley. Citizens of Camden, New Jersey, greeted him with an effusive proclamation:

> Science and knowledge have not yet enlightened sufficiently any other nation in Europe, to emulate her glorious example: she stands alone in the noble contest, and bids defiance to the united despots of the world, who have combined against her; and we trust the invincible spirit of liberty will carry her through all her difficulties with honor and glory, to the confusion of her foes.[35]

The events became opportunities, the *National Gazette* described, "to shew our republicanism," the "degree of gratitude we feel for our French allies, and the interest we take in their conflicts for the rights of humanity."[36] Genêt, emboldened by the receptions, anticipated a new republican alliance.

Seeing Genêt's effect on public opinion, Washington as commander-in-chief issued a "Proclamation of Neutrality" on April 22. Drafted by Jay, it warned American citizens "carefully to avoid all acts" privileging a belligerent power, threatening prosecution of anyone aiding or abetting hostilities.[37] Faced with potentially ruinous intervention abroad and a worsening domestic political split (one Federalist congressman considering the measure a "triumph" over the "Sons of Faction in Philadelphia"), Washington defended an eroding political middle ground.[38] While claiming neutrality technically did not violate 1778's alliance with France due to their inability to protect the United States from British naval depredations, to many it betrayed an ally fighting for freedom against despotism. Washington ordered state militias to seize privateer vessels in port. Genêt responded by asserting the "voice of the People continues to neutralize President Washington's proclamation of neutrality. I live here in the midst of perpetual fêtes."[39] Though not expecting

---

[34] NA FO 91/1 139, 147, 141–42.

[35] *City Gazette*, May 4, 1793.

[36] *National Gazette*, April 24, 1793.

[37] Washington, *Papers*, Presidential Series, Vol. 12, 473; Norman K. Risjord, *Chesapeake Politics, 1781–1800* (New York: Columbia University Press, 1978), 424–25.

[38] George C. Rogers, Jr. *Evolution of a Federalist: William Loughton Smith of Charleston, 1758–1812* (Columbia, SC: University of South Carolina Press, 1962), 242.

[39] Furstenberg, *When the United States Spoke French: Five Refugees Who Shaped a Nation* (New York: Penguin, 2014), 50; John Marshall, *The Papers of John Marshall* (Chapel Hill: University of North Carolina Press, 1974), Vol. 2, 183–84.

America to become a formal belligerent, Genêt hoped for grain shipments to France and a blind eye to his anti-Spanish expeditions. The self-consciously elite and Anglophile Federalist government, meanwhile, seemed shaken by the Francophilic popular upsurge.

Though French support became increasingly partisan, much of Philadelphia keenly anticipated Genêt's entry. On May 2, the French warship that carried Genêt to Charleston arrived, firing a fifteen-gun salute returned by the city's defenses. A "vast collection of people," John Adams's son Thomas wrote to his mother, shouted "repeated huzza's" and welcomed the sailors, who "Sing Ci [Ça] Ira – and dance the Marselais, call each other Citizen and in short exhibit the true spirit of the Revolution."[40] Plans circulated before Genêt's arrival that a three-shot salute from the l'Embuscade would summon crowds to the Delaware River ferry crossing to greet him. Thousands responded on May 16, carrying Genêt the final four miles.[41] "My trip has been a succession of uninterrupted civic festivals and my entry to Philadelphia a triumph for liberty," Genêt enthused, "true Americans are filled with joy."[42] Federalists watched nervously, while Jefferson observed that with the Anglo-French war, "all the old spirit of 1776 is rekindling."[43] The French Revolution revivified American political spirit.

French fervor spread with Americans embracing the Revolution. Monroe, traveling in Virginia in early May, reported to Jefferson he found "scarcely a man unfriendly to the French revolution as now modified." Though many "regret the unhappy fate" of Lafayette and Louis XVI, "they seem to consider these events as incidents to a much greater one, & which they wish to see accomplished."[44] Even beyond Genêt's Southern tour, acclamations poured in with now-Massachusetts Lieutenant Governor Samuel Adams predicting the ambassador would extend "the universal cause of liberty and the rights of man."[45] Madison opposed the neutrality proclamation, arguing it "wounds the popular feelings by a seeming indifference to the cause and liberty," and "If France triumphs," abandoning the alliance would injure America in the new world order.[46] The revolutionary empowerment of France, already Western Europe's greatest force, could overwhelm its imperial competitors. Genêt embodied an overflowing, transatlantic revolutionary exuberance.

---

[40] *Adams Family*, Vol. 9, 425.
[41] *Federal Gazette*, May 13, 1793; Furstenberg, *When*, 49; "Correspondence of the French," 284.
[42] "Correspondence of the French," 214.
[43] Alfred F. Young, *The Democratic Republicans of New York: The Origins, 1763–1797* (Chapel Hill: University of North Carolina Press, 1967), 365.
[44] Monroe, *Writings*, Vol. 1, 252.
[45] William V. Wells, *The Life and Public Services of Samuel Adams* (Boston: Little, Brown and Co., 1865), Vol. 3, 321.
[46] Bryant, *James*, 375.

Anglophiles, despite the Proclamation of Neutrality's support among Federalist officeholders, appeared neutralized. The British consul in Philadelphia, Phineas Bond, noted that after Genêt's arrival "french seamen ranged the streets by night and by day, armed with cutlasses," committing "the most daring outrages, whenever they met any of our seamen," or those mistaken for them. When word spread of Genêt continuing to New York, partisans in early August superseded Federalist authorities by convoking a vast open-air gathering to approve an address to the French ambassador, winning acclamation over Anglophile objections.[47] Bond denounced American inability to "enforce any measures in opposition to the views of the French faction existing here," cautioning against pressing British issues.[48] The Genêt-inspired upsurge in pro-French feeling impacted local, national, and international considerations.

Club gatherings multiplied across early 1793, aiming to recapture American Revolutionary fervor, adapt French practices, and pursue wider alliances. A Philadelphia Société française des amis de la Liberté et de l'Egalité of French expatriates formed in December 1792 to spread patriotic ardor and surveil the French Republic's agents.[49] Philadelphia's German-Republican Society organized its first meeting in late February and on April 11 – just after news of Genêt's Charleston arrival and the day before Washington's Proclamation of Neutrality – advocated "political societies" being "established throughout the United States, as they would prove powerful instruments in support of the present system of equality, and formidable enemies to aristocracy in whatever shape it might present itself." Not vigilance alone but democratic sociability would promote the necessary effects, "for the spirit of liberty, like every virtue of the mind, is to be kept alive only by constant action."[50] Seizing an opportunity for publicity, the German-Republicans greeted Genêt with a congratulatory address.[51]

The month following Genêt's arrival, the Democratic Society of Philadelphia formed, superseding the German-Republican Society to become America's largest corresponding organization. With the "German" moniker seeming too ethnic for a network of left-leaning Francophiles, leaders sought a new name to stoke a nationwide cause. Initially, many supported calling the society the "Sons of Liberty," but Genêt personally intervened in favor of a name speaking to the group's principles: "the Democratic Club." Organization bylaws declared "The Rights of Man, the genuine objects of

[47] NA FO 91/1 176.

[48] Phineas Bond, "Letters of Phineas Bond, British Consul at Philadelphia, to the Foreign Office of Great Britain, 1790–1794," J. Franklin Jameson, ed. Annual Report of the American Historical Association 11 (1898), 529, 536.

[49] AN D XXV 59 582 8.

[50] Foner, Democratic-Republican, 6, 53.

[51] Elkins and McKitrick, Age, 342.

Society, and the legitimate principles of Government . . . clearly developed by the successive Revolutions in America and France," and urged citizens "to erect the Temple of LIBERTY on the ruins of Palaces and Thrones."[52] Though requiring dues, it nevertheless attracted members ranging from prosperous professionals to artisans. Women's attendance would also be encouraged at many society functions.[53] The society established a "Corresponding Committee," to affiliate with any chapter "established on similar principles in any other of the United States."[54] On July 3, the new alliance published its bylaws alongside a circular rallying Americans to "cultivate a just knowledge of rational liberty."[55] Genêt described the society "composed of the patriots of 76," supporting "liberty, equality, rights of man, country, French Republic."[56] There seemed no necessary contradiction between American and French principles.

The new network sought to strengthen the international republican cause against counterrevolutionary forces, spreading liberty's principles and resisting incursions on their rights. In late May, a Republican Society formed in Norfolk, "cherishing Republican sentiments, manners, morals and associations," while recognizing France's "virtuous exertions" against "the Tyrants of the world combined" in a war of extermination.[57] As the term "Democrat" rose in popularity, so too did "Aristocrat" as its contrary.[58] Philadelphia's Democratic Society on July 4 asserted the "European Confederacy, transcendent in power, and unparalleled in iniquity, menaces the very existence of freedom." Meanwhile in America, they found "the spirit of freedom and equality" threatened "by the pride of wealth and the arrogance of power." Only through "constant circulation of useful information, and a liberal communication of republican sentiments" could counterrevolution be contained and American principles solidify.[59]

Responding to the democratic societies' fervor, powerful Federalist-supporting groups adopted resolutions for governmental neutrality. Philadelphia's merchant association the day of Genêt's arrival resolved, "the happiness of the People of the United States" could be assured through

---

[52] Foner, *Democratic-Republican*, 7; Genet, *Washington*, 34.

[53] Koschnik, "Democratic," 620; Rosemary Zagarri, *Revolutionary Backlash: Women and Politics in the Early American Republic* (Philadelphia: University of Pennsylvania Press, 2011), 84.

[54] Foner, *Democratic-Republican*, 64.

[55] *Dunlap's Daily American Advertiser*, July 13, 1793; Eugene Perry Link, *Democratic-Republican Societies, 1790-1800* (New York: Columbia University Press, 1942), 12.

[56] NYHS Genet Family Papers.

[57] Link, *Democratic-Republican*, 9.

[58] Matthew Rainbow Hale, "Regenerating the World: The French Revolution, Civic Festivals, and the Forging of Modern American Democracy, 1793–1795," *Journal of American History* 103, no. 4 (2017), 891–920.

[59] Foner, *Democratic-Republican*, 66.

peace.[60] By late summer, town meetings, alarmed by Genêt's exertions, adopted pro-neutrality petitions. New York recommended "A conduct friendly and impartial towards all the powers at war," regardless of their internal politics.[61] "The Friends of Government," who previously desired political demobilization outside of elections, organized their own political displays.[62]

The Democratic Society's calls for a national network, meanwhile, in some quarters met denunciations as loud as their acclamations elsewhere. Richmond's Hanover County, Virginia, on July 27, declared their "apprehensions that political societies," regardless of how initially well intentioned, could "be perverted into clubs of faction" and then "Courts of inquisition." Clubs appeared "fatal precursors of anarchy, and its invariable follower – Despotism."[63] The controversy reached Congress, where Federalist Fischer Ames denounced the prospect that "every six miles square be formed into a club sovereignty," leading to "ten or twenty thousand democracies" producing "fires of discord" against the government.[64] To the many believing partisan groups produced faction, disunion, and likely civil war, the Democratic Societies embodied what needed to be prevented.

After the conservative reaction, Democratic Societies organized quietly over the second half of 1793 but continued drawing Federalists' ire. Vice President John Adams in December asked his son John Quincy for news of Boston's "Democratical Society" branch before sneering, "There ought to be another Society instituted according to my Principles, under the Title of Aristocratical Society."[65] Yet knowing the societies' extent, much less intentions, proved difficult. "A Democratic Club has been established here," Boston attorney Christopher Gore reported, but "there are very few men who do not deny their connection with such a Society."[66] Many suspected the new institution's methods with New York's *Daily Advertiser* claiming, "In imitation of their parents the Jacobins of Paris," the clubs aimed "to establish a tyrannical aristocracy on the ruins of liberty."[67] A partisan political club network conjured to its opponents all the horrors, but not achievements, of their revolutionary predecessors.

---

[60] Washington, *Papers*, Presidential Series, Vol. 12, 599.

[61] Ibid., 389 and 425.

[62] Lisle A. Rose, *Prologue to Democracy: The Federalists in the South, 1789–1800* (Lexington: University of Kentucky Press, 1968), 80–81.

[63] *General Advertiser*, August 8, 1793.

[64] Leutscher, *Early*, 60.

[65] *Adams Family*, Vol. 9, 469–70.

[66] Rufus King, *The Life and Correspondence of Rufus King* (New York: Putnam's Sons, 1894), Vol. 1, 509.

[67] *Daily Advertiser*, February 27, 1794.

Genêt, meanwhile, ran up against a Federalist elite firewall. Had he sailed north from Charleston and arrived in Philadelphia before the neutrality proclamation, while avoiding popular politicking, he might have negotiated diplomatic concessions for France from a country indebted for the War of Independence. But by Genêt's arrival, Washington, Hamilton, and their faction resisted all revolutionary designs. The Executive Branch outlawed French privateering as a violation of neutrality on June 5, rejected bulk payment on American debts to France a week later, and even deemed Genêt's proposal for compensation with foodstuffs insufficiently neutral. Indiscreetly, in Philadelphia's harbor Genêt led the reequipping of captured British vessel *Little Sarah* as a privateering *La Petite Démocrate* and partially staffed it with American crewmen, part of a thirteen-vessel fleet along the American coast including *L'Antigeorges* and *Le Ca-Ira*.[68] Growing rumors of Genêt commissioning anti-Spanish rebels, together with advocating an American referendum ("Appeal to the People") to repeal the Proclamation of Neutrality, led Washington to demand Genêt's recall in August. Genêt had already left the capital to commission more privateers in New York. Even Jefferson agreed the French ambassador possessed "most unfounded pretensions" of French rights.[69] Genêt's superiors, now from the Jacobin instead of Girondin faction, reprimanded him on July 30 for not acting as "the organ of the French Republic instead of the chief of an American party."[70] The Committee of Public Safety decommissioned Genêt, now an irritant to an important strategic partner, later that year.

In response to the Proclamation of Neutrality and Genêt's incursions, many cities and counties sent the president loyal addresses, mirroring recent British tactics, to bolster the administration. Kent County, Maryland, in late August praised the president's diplomatic "wisdom and moderation," while Annapolis lauded Washington for "averting the calamities of a war." Some asserted continued amity with France – Alexandria, Virginia, considering the French Revolution a "glorious contest" for liberty – but all concluded America's joining the war, as Virginia's Albemarle County wrote, would be too potentially "injurious to the welfare of this infant country."[71] Philadelphia celebrated Washington's birthday with "uncommon parade" in February 1794, even as Genêt discouraged the holiday for smacking of monarchism.[72] Yet the depth of support for Washington remained unclear: Madison found Americans "attached to the President," but also "to the French Nation and Revolution," while "averse to Monarchy and a political connection with that of Great

---

[68] Ammon, *Genet*, 65–86; Elkins and McKitrick, *Age*, 345; NA FO 91/1 178.
[69] Jefferson, *Papers*, Vol. 26, 696; Ammon, *Genet*, 111.
[70] "Correspondence of the French," 228.
[71] Washington, *Papers*, Presidential Series, Vol. 14, 3, 112, and 276.
[72] Duke University Special Collections, Ephraim Kirby Papers, Box 5 1.

Britain," desiring peace and a strong executive but not counterrevolutionary alliances or anti-French measures.[73]

Though record survives of only nine Democratic-Republican clubs in 1793, the network added twenty-three popular societies in 1794, pushed by radicalization in Europe and growing American political polarization. Meetings were often held in the evenings to encourage workingmen's support.[74] Many old American Revolutionaries found common cause, with Samuel Adams considering the European war one of "Nobles against the equal rights of Men" with the former trying to "crush the new formed Republick in its infancy."[75] For American Republicans, French revolutionary chic made stylish political statements. In October 1793, Paris's Jacobins granted the Genêt-inspired Republican Society of Charleston affiliation. Americans joined the world's most powerful organization for radical change.[76] An Atlantic republican alliance seemed imminent and, if not for the rapid changes still rocking France, might have solidified.

Democratic-Republican societies held open banquets, broadcasting their Francophilia. French military victories proved the most popular celebrations, alongside a summertime calendar of the Revolution's greatest triumphs (the Bastille's July 14 capture, the monarchy's overthrow on August 10, and the republic's proclamation on September 22).[77] New York's March 1794 toasts included, "May the allied Republics of America and France, be bound together by the indissoluble ties of Liberty, Friendship and Justice," and "the genius of philosophy and liberty extend her wings over all the world to bless the children of mankind." Believing themselves backed by the revolutionary era's highest principles, the clubs accused opponents of limiting (or subverting) the country's democratic structure.[78] "That government must be unfit for free men which cannot bear investigation," a Philadelphia circular declared, whereas "that administration must be corrupt which hides itself in darkness."[79] A Savannah banquet organized by "Friends of Genet" found participants "ripe for revolution & War."[80] Only citizen inquiries could preserve an enlightened American government.

The fledgling network pursued connections with British and Irish movements. Portland, the nation's northernmost significant harbor, in

---

[73] Sharp, *American*, 84.

[74] Foner, *Democratic-Republican*, 7; Sean Wilentz, *Chants Democratic: New York City & the Rise of the American Working Class, 1788–1850* (Oxford: Oxford University Press, 1984), 69.

[75] LC Samuel Adams Papers, Vol. 3.

[76] *Baltimore Daily Intelligencer*, March 7, 1794; *City Gazette*, March 26, 1794.

[77] Newman, *Parades*, 147.

[78] Foner, *Democratic-Republican*, 168, 73.

[79] *South-Carolina State-Gazette*, July 8, 1794.

[80] RIHS Ward Papers, MSS 11.

December 1793 sought correspondence with "all other Democratic and Republican Societies," either in "the United States or elsewhere," desiring an international alliance of organizations "supporting the general Rights of Man and the Liberties of their Country."[81] Radical British, Irish, and French refugees poured into the United States, founding immigrant associations, swelling the American press' ranks, and joining opposition politics.[82] Following movements abroad, the New York Democratic Society's banquet toasted "All true Republicans in Great-Britain and Ireland," desiring "their present venal and corrupt government be destroyed" in favor of "liberty established for ever."[83] Priestley's arrival in New York exile on June 4 brought deputations "from virtually all constituted groups – Governor Clinton, Dr. Prevost, bishop of New York, Mr. Osgood, late envoy to Great Britain, the heads of the college, most of the principal merchants, and deputations from the corporate body and other societies," including the Democratic Society, Tammany Society, and "British and Irish republican settlers," all desiring to associate with the liberal thinker. Priestley, however, having previously declined election to France's National Assembly, swore off all political activity, warning of the French government "degenerating into tyrannies."[84] Nevertheless, pursuing revolutionary universalism, the Democratic clubs continued seeking allies.

As clubs became more formidable, criticisms mounted. Newspaperman William Cobbett branded the Democratic-Republicans "butchers, tinkers, broken hucksters, and trans-Atlantic traitors," as the societies continued celebrating immigrants and foreign events.[85] Judge and future Vermont Senator Nathaniel Chipman in June 1794 asserted club power could reinstill "all the heat and ungovernable passions of a simple democracy" the Federalist system avoided by design. Instead of the slow, cool acquisition of knowledge, popular societies threatened "all the rashness of ignorance, passion and prejudice."[86] The prospect of open political disagreements worried many: "A House divided against itself cannot stand," the *Connecticut Journal* asserted.[87] Even among the elite Republican opposition, Kentucky Senator John Edwards fretted "two parties nearly equal," supporting "very opposite principles in Governt.," appeared the "fundamental cause of the Bloody war in Europe."[88]

---

[81] Maine Historical Society, Portland Republican Society Papers.
[82] Bradburn, *Citizenship*, 130, 211.
[83] Foner, *Democratic-Republican*, 168.
[84] Henry Wansey, *An Excursion to the United States of North America in the Summer of 1794* (Salisbury: Easton, 1796), 72; Foner, *Democratic-Republican*, 182–83; Tombs, *Sweet*, 198.
[85] Sean Wilentz, *The Rise of American Democracy: Jefferson to Lincoln* (New York: Norton, 2005), 61.
[86] Hamilton, *Papers*, Vol. 16, 1794.
[87] *Connecticut Journal*, June 25, 1794.
[88] LC Breckinridge Family Papers MSS 13698, Vol. 10.

As reports of French terror grew, politicians wondered what safeguards prevented similar American excesses.

Federalist counter-mobilizations, through town meetings and clubs, contested Democratic-Republicans claims to speak for the people. The government-sponsored *Gazette of the United States*, in a nod to the 1770s, argued that while "Nobody will deny the usefulness of popular Societies, in case of revolutions," nevertheless "the poison that killed tyranny is a bad diet for liberty."[89] Yet, many government supporters mobilized anyway. In Charleston, St. George's and St. Andrew's clubs toasted "the constitution of Great Britain" and improved Anglo-American relations.[90] John Adams wrote, "in New York and Philadelphia there is Meeting against Meeting and Clubb against Clubb, to the Utter Confusion of the Public Opinion."[91] Claiming to be the American Revolution's legitimate heirs, Federalists incited patriotic spirit in their own favor.

To celebrate July 4, 1794, Democratic Societies broke with tradition by holding partisan celebrations.[92] Baltimore's sponsored an abolitionist lecturer, while many others led Francophilic banquets. Philadelphia's toasted "the Jacobin Clubs of America," considering "vigilance is the only preservative of freedom," while "implicit confidence in public servants is a stride towards slavery."[93] New York festivities brought the Democratic, Mechanic, and Tammany societies (though not the Society of the Cincinnati) together, toasting "pure Philosophy," while wishing the French people a "free republican government" to ensure "political and individual happiness."[94] Across the country, popular toasts included to popular sovereignty, free speech, a free press, and an uncorrupted electorate. The Democratic Society of rural Wythe County, Virginia, asked, "If all tyrants unite against free people, should not all free people unite against tyrants?"[95] Portland two weeks later considered "the cause of France is our own" with both countries' future tied to combating the "Combined despots of Europe" leagued against liberty.[96] The republics appeared headed for a common Atlantic fate, while Federalists bore suspicious resemblance to Europe's counterrevolutionary combinations.

The new club model found its most aggressive applications west of the Appalachians. With resentment against East Coast elites already outstanding,

---

[89] Albrecht Koshnik, *"Let a Common Interest Bind Us Together": Associations, Partisanship, and Culture in Philadelphia, 1775-1840* (Charlottesville: University Press of Virginia, 2007), 631.

[90] Alderson, *Bright*, 62.

[91] *Adams Family*, Vol. 10, 112.

[92] Pasley, *First*, 78.

[93] Foner, *Democratic-Republican*, 338 and 107.

[94] *American Minerva*, July 5, 1794.

[95] Foner, *Democratic-Republican*, 22–23.

[96] Maine Historical Society, Portland Republican Society Papers.

club invitations spread quickly. Lexington's Democratic Society in February 1794 asked Western communities to "unite in a petition to Congress, to obtain the free navigation of the river Mississippi" and take a hard-line against Spain. Ominously, they added, "if the General Government refuses, they will not hold themselves answerable for any consequences, that may result from their own procurement of it."[97] Particularly given Genêt's attempt to capture Louisiana, any offensive could have led America into a general war. Washington required the forces of order "to prevent & suppress all such unlawful assemblages."[98] The thin connections between Eastern authorities and the frontier augured further trouble.

The French Revolution offered Americans inspiration and opportunity to undertake aggressive club organizing in ways they had previously not dared. The aggressive split between revolutionaries and counterrevolutionaries (whose coalition by 1793 included most of the British) mirrored the developing Federalist-Republican divide. The Democratic-Republican clubs sought to live up to their founding principles by keeping ordinary Americans politically mobilized but soon found they could not restrain enthusiasm along the Appalachian frontier.

The Whiskey Rebellion and Anti-Democratic Reaction

Long-festering antagonisms ignited the Whiskey Rebellion, opposing federal and local governance, Eastern and frontier priorities, and official authority with popular assemblies. The backcountry possessed an adversarial relationship with the seaboard, dodging taxes by passive and occasionally active means. Frontier military garrisons remained underfunded and undermanned by federal troops, encouraging a raucous militia culture, while federal laws enabled wealthy easterners' speculation in Western lands, making many frontiersmen tenant farmers. Yet Hamilton, to fund his banking schemes, ushered through the first federal whiskey excise tax (the frontier's most profitable commodity) in 1791. "Internal," as opposed to customs, taxes were detested across the eighteenth-century British World, with whiskey duties raising similar regional self-determination questions as the Stamp Act had. Hamilton designed the measure to fall disproportionately on small proprietors, instead of land taxes or tariffs targeting large landowners or merchants. Federalists made the tax a moral crusade, drawing the Philadelphia College of Physicians' endorsement, who claimed the tax would reform the "morals and manners" of rough frontiersmen.[99] With their interests underrepresented, Western residents mobilized.

---

[97] *American Minerva*, February 13, 1794.

[98] Hamilton, *Papers*, Vol. 16, 162.

[99] Thomas P. Slaughter, *The Whiskey Rebellion: Frontier Epilogue to the American Revolution* (Oxford: Oxford University Press, 1986), 12–27, 67, 95–100.

Antitax petitions proliferated, including from Western Pennsylvania militia-musters and Pittsburgh, Washington, and Brownsville mass meetings.[100] Pittsburgh argued in 1791 that, as they paid disproportionately, with funds earmarked for questionable uses, "the liberty, property, and even the morals of the people are sported with, to gratify particular men in their ambitions and interested motives."[101] Not waiting for a federal reply, crowds that autumn tarred and feathered two tax collectors. Another man met the same penalty for praising the excise law.[102] A Washington meeting resolved that citizens should treat "with contempt, and absolutely refuse all kind of communication" with excisemen.[103]

Amid Federal inaction, Western measures radicalized with an August 1792 Pittsburgh convention appointing county-level Committees of Correspondence, replicating the militant organizations that mobilized the American Revolution. The new organization pledged to communicate with "any committees of a similar nature" elsewhere and summon "general meetings of the people" as necessary.[104] Other organizations abetted their rise. Nearby Washington boasted a local Democratic-Republican chapter, while independent political societies existed nearby.[105] Rumors flew that, should the federal government call out the official militia, if it would "fight at all, it would be with the people."[106] Liberty poles rose across the region as potential rallying points for revolt should authorities try to force tax collection. The excise could only be imposed through outside coercion.

The spirit of discontent and insubordination grew. A Western Pennsylvania petition in late 1792 claimed excise enforcement demanded "perpetual inquisition" against consumers, though they claimed willingness to pay a federal "direct tax" (mostly impacting Eastern merchants) instead.[107] Genêt in spring 1793 attempted to mobilize his anti-Spanish scheme to assault Louisiana through the Western frontier and few thought settlers' American loyalties ran deep. As negotiations stalled, many in the backcountry radicalized, with an early 1794 Washington County petition asserting they would "never submit" to "all the burdens and enjoy none of the benefits" of the federal union.[108] The Democratic Society in Parkinson's Ferry called for a Committee of Public

---

[100] Leland D. Baldwin, *Whiskey Rebels: The Story of a Frontier Uprising* (Pittsburgh: University of Pittsburgh Press, 1939), 76–78.

[101] H. M. Brackenridge, *History of the Western Insurrection in Western Pennsylvania: Commonly Called the Whiskey Insurrection, 1794* (Pittsburgh: W.S. Haven, 1859), 36–37.

[102] Baldwin, 82–83; William Findley, *History of the Insurrection in the Four Western Counties of Pennsylvania in the Year M.D.CC.XCIV* (Philadelphia: Smith, 1796), 58.

[103] Elkins and McKitrick, *Age*, 462.

[104] Slaughter, *Whiskey*, 116.

[105] Link, *Democratic-Republican*, 145.

[106] Brackenridge, *History*, 54.

[107] NYHS Albert Gallatin Papers, reel 1.

[108] Slaughter, *Whiskey*, 164.

Safety to assume governing power.[109] Such rhetoric could only bring the region under Federal scrutiny. Back in Philadelphia, the Democratic Society adopted an anti-Excise resolution in spring 1794, while the German-Republicans' Independence Day banquet mockingly toasted "EXCISE, may this baneful exotic wither in the soil of freedom."[110] Frontier residents challenged each other, "Are you for Congress or Liberty?"[111] With Federal authority contested, elites observed resistance with trepidation. Although excise avoidance remained common along the Appalachians, with General "Mad" Anthony Wayne complaining of a "pervading spirit of Opposition" to federal measures in Kentucky as well, Western Pennsylvania's aggressiveness made it the Federal target.[112]

Federalist patience with Western resistance waned, particularly given broader "Jacobin" threats across America. On August 2, 1794, Washington, before his domestic cabinet officers, asserted the frontier proceedings "strike at the root of all law & order," while considering "the most spirited & firm measures" necessary to maintain authority.[113] Hamilton denounced the Western committees as "Armed Collections of men, with the avowed design of Opposing the execution of the laws" and demanded compliance.[114] The administration associated the growing resistance with the worst conspiracies imagined of their political opponents. On August 6, Washington privately described the agitation as "the first formidable fruit of the Democratic Societies": organizations "instituted by their father, Genêt" to "sow the Seeds of Jealousy & distrust among the people, of the government, by destroying all confidence in the Administration of it."[115] The triple threats of French, urban, and frontier uncertainty made all appear leagued against federal leadership.

On August 7, 1794, Washington declared a state of insurrection in four Western Pennsylvania counties. He denounced "the influence of certain irregular meetings" and attempts to subvert federal laws with attacks on revenue officials calling "the very existence of government" into question. All rebels needed to "retire peaceably" by September 1 or face suppression. Those taking loyalty oaths would be pardoned for past offenses.[116] Federal Commissioners traveled west to declare, "no indulgence would hereafter be

---

[109] "Resolutions proposed by Mr. Marshal at the Parkinson's Ferry Meeting of the 14th August, 1794," *Memoirs of the Historical Society of Pennsylvania* 6 (1858), 201.

[110] Roland M. Baumann, "Philadelphia's Manufacturers and the Excise Tax of 1794: The Forging of the Jeffersonian Coalition," in *The Whiskey Rebellion: Past and Present Perspectives*, Steven R. Boyd, ed. (Westport, CT: Greenwood Press, 1985), 146–47.

[111] LC Pennsylvania Whiskey Rebellion Collection MMC-1315.

[112] MHS Henry Knox Papers, Vol. 35.

[113] Hamilton, *Papers*, Vol. 17, 9.

[114] Ibid., Vol. 16, 461.

[115] Foner, *Democratic-Republican*, 30; Washington, *Papers*, Presidential Series, Vol. 16, 601–2.

[116] *Claypoole's Daily Advertiser*, August 11, 1794; Findley, *History*, 113.

given to any offence committed against the United States."[117] The weight of federal force and Washington's personal prestige sought to smother the resistance campaign.

Shortly after the president's proclamation arrived, rebel representatives met for an outdoor Parkinson's Ferry meeting on August 14. Drawn from across western Pennsylvania and cross-border Virginia counties, delegates gathered by a liberty pole reading "Liberty and no excise, and no asylum for cowards or traitors." Planners requested all eighty western townships send deputies (seventy-six complied), while inviting others to form a "Parisian gallery" to monitor proceedings. Though Federal commissioners had already arrived, the rebels tried to strengthen their negotiating position. While a rumored "declaration of independence" did not materialize, the meeting named a "committee of public safety" with members from each county to contest Federal forces.[118] The new organization, taking recognizably French forms, asserted command over thousands of militiamen to at least intimidate an end to the standoff.

Despite the Committee of Public Safety's creation, moderates at the Parkinson's Ferry meeting successfully urged compromise. Directly confronting federal forces augured probable bloodshed, repression, and political annihilation. Pennsylvania Congressman Albert Gallatin and other moderates convinced those assembled to rename the Committee of Public Safety the "standing committee" and appoint a new deputation to meet Federal peace commissioners. Following a parlay, where Washington's men demanded "Obedience to the National Will" and threatened to deploy armed forces against the backcountry, the deputation recommended submission. Though violent speeches from rebel militants followed, the sixty-member former Committee of Public Safety voted 34–23 on August 28 to accept the government's amnesty offer, pardoning all swearing loyalty.[119] No united uprising of the Western counties occurred.

Back on the East Coast, Federalists pressured the government to swiftly suppress the rebellion. Massachusetts Senator George Cabot in August declared "a wicked faction has triumphed over public liberty by assuming public names," finding the "general will" of voters "superseded," auguring "an end of that equality of rights which is the very essence of liberty."[120] East-west cultural and economic divides made denouncing frontier settlers easier with the *Gazette of the United States* considering, "the people of the back countries

---

[117] Bond, "Letters," 556.

[118] Findley, *History*, 114–15; Baldwin, *Whiskey*, 172; LC Pennsylvania Whiskey Rebellion Collection MMC-1315.

[119] Elkins and McKitrick, *Age*, 475–81; LC, Pennsylvania Whiskey Rebellion Collection MMC-1315.

[120] George Cabot, *Life and Letters of George Cabot* (Boston: Little, Brown, 1878), 79.

appear determined on war, within and without."[121] Sensing political advantage, the pro-government paper described the insurrection as "the natural fruit of their democratic clubs."[122] Even as insurrectionary threats lessened, the movement became symbolically important for Federalists to crush.

Washington seized the opportunity to condemn the Democratic-Republicans. Before Congress September 19, the president blamed the rebellion on "certain self-created societies," asking Americans to "determine whether it has not been fomented by combinations of men who, careless of consequence … have disseminated, from an ignorance or perversion of facts, suspicions, jealousies and accusations of the whole government."[123] Although multiple Democratic Societies denounced Pennsylvanian excesses, Washington used the rebellion to discredit their movement. As the government raised nearly thirteen thousand soldiers and militiamen against the rebels, the mood of militarist unanimity spread to settle politics on a Federalist paradigm.[124]

Ready to march on September 25, Washington issued his final warning to the rebels. Denouncing the Western counties for "propagating principles of anarchy" and violently contesting "every attempt to enforce the laws," the president asserted the "contest being whether a small portion of the United States shall dictate to the whole Union."[125] Randolph counseled that if "reconciliation is offered with one hand," there must be "terror borne in the other" for pacification.[126] The expedition aimed to demonstrate Federal supremacy by force. With Western Pennsylvania partisans (including much of the leadership) deserting in droves, Washington's army in October did not meet organized resistance. Though whiskey excise dodging persisted, with the federal government paying its Western Pennsylvania tax collectors more than they collected, organized rebellion ceased.[127]

Though Washington commanded consensus national support during the rebellion, his rhetoric against "self-created societies" raised widespread ire and suspicion. Several Democratic-Republican Societies responded, with New York's asserting the "unquestionable right of citizens, to associate, to speak and to publish their sentiments," while Philadelphia's German-Republicans suspiciously noted "patriotic societies were the objects of denunciation in the same year in Great Britain, France, and the United States of America!"[128] Even more detrimental for the president, his rhetoric worsened

[121] *Gazette of the United States*, August 9, 1794.
[122] Ibid., September 2, 1794.
[123] Foner, *Democratic-Republican*, 30.
[124] Slaughter, *Whiskey*, 212.
[125] H. M. Brackenridge, *History of the Western Insurrection in Western Pennsylvania Commonly Known as the Whiskey Insurrection* (Pittsburgh: Haven, 1859), 185.
[126] Elkins and McKitrick, *Age*, 480.
[127] Slaughter, *Whiskey*, 226.
[128] Foner, *Democratic-Republican*, 205; *Aurora General Advertiser*, December 27, 1794.

elite political divides, hastening the growth of party. Jefferson pronounced his horror that the president made "such an attack on the freedom of discussion, the freedom of writing, printing and publishing." Madison considered Washington's denunciation "the greatest error of his political life," orating in Congress that in the United States "the censorial power is in the people over the government, and not in the government over the people."[129] Not without reason, many Democratic-Republicans sensed Federalist inclinations toward an elected dictatorship.

Across the same months of 1794, the French model cratered as the Thermidorians took power and dismantled much of the preceding Jacobin regime. Between the Atlantic communication lag and political repressions on each side of the water, however, it was difficult for Americans in summer and autumn 1794 to divine the French Revolution's direction. Among the questions Jefferson, as Secretary of State, sent with new ambassador Monroe as he left for Paris in June 1794:

> Are there any of the old friends to the ancient regime remaining? Are any new friends created by the course of things? Are the Brissotines extinguished? Are the Dantonists overwhelmed? Is Robespierre's party firmly fixed? ... Is he friendly to the United States?[130]

Nevertheless, many still believed associations represented the political future, regardless of what extremities foreign war and domestic counterrevolutionaries drove French Revolutionaries to. The Duc de la Rochefoucauld, an *émigré* traveling the United States, found Americans ascribed the Revolution's excesses "to various factions, and carefully distinguish and separate them from the cause of liberty." Should French armies triumph, popular consensus went, the regime "will cease to be anarchy, and become true national freedom," whereas a counterrevolutionary coalition victory could "enslave the world."[131] Britain's intentions could be discerned through their alliances.

Even though the Democratic Societies never recovered from Washington's denunciation, their principles and potential endured. Joseph Fauchet, Genêt's successor as French ambassador, considered the club venture a success, believing through their influence "the patriotic party unite and connect themselves; they gain a formidable majority in the legislature."[132] Philadelphia's Democratic Society similarly considered, "Associations of citizens for political purposes keep a nation alive," while surveilling government conduct prevented

---

[129] Slaughter, *Whiskey*, 221; Ferling, *A Leap in the Dark: The Struggle to Create the American Republic* (Oxford: Oxford University Press, 2003), 374.

[130] Monroe, *Writings*, Vol. 2, 2.

[131] Duc de la Rochefoucauld, *Voyages dans les Etats-Unis d'Amérique, fait en 1795, 1796 et 1797* (Paris: du Pont, an VII), Vol. 1, 41.

[132] LC Edmund Randolph Papers MSS 1156.

abuses.[133] Washington's proclamations highlighted Federalist anti-democratic proclivities. "The game was," Madison wrote to Monroe, for the administration "to connect the Democratic Societies with the odium of the insurrection, to connect the Republicans in Cong[ress] with those Societies, to put the P. ostensibly at the head of the other party," thus reestablishing Federalist hegemony.[134] Gallatin asserted the Federalist furor was conducted "to carry on Electioneering plans."[135] While maintaining distance from the Whiskey rebels, Jefferson expressed his astonishment to Madison that Washington made "such an attack on the freedom of discussion, the freedom of writing, printing and publishing."[136] Fears grew of an effective Federalist dictatorship.

The fledgling political opposition party would prove stronger than the popular societies. A significant plurality of both American elites and voters disliked the Federalists' methods and ambitions. Though armed force on the Whiskey Rebellion model proved disastrous, new methods developed to promote political alternatives to the narrow regime. Regarding Federalists with growing suspicion, opposition organizers continued to creatively adapt the Democratic Societies' model to contest the Federalist consensus.

Jay's Treaty and the Revivification of Dissent

A Thermidorian mindset advanced in the United States and France across late 1794 and 1795. Many Federalists cheered the French Jacobins' fall and sought to restrict associational life in their own republic. Vice President John Adams opined to his wife, "Affiliations, Combinations, Correspondences, Corporate Acts of such societies must be prohibited."[137] His son John Quincy, diplomat to the Netherlands, considered, "Societies seem destined every where to grow as a monstrous wen upon the body of Liberty," asserting, "the reign of Robespierre has shewn what use they make of power when they obtain its exercise."[138] Many others believed such alliances destructive for American constitutional government, with Senator Cabot asking, "where is the boasted advantage of a representation system over the turbulent mobocracy of Athens, if the resort to popular meetings is necessary?"[139] Many Federalists, considering representative democracy an absolute, wanted to prevent Jacobin imitation. Yet a new diplomatic controversy rejuvenated dissent, with the political opposition enthusiastically taking the side of the French.

---

[133] *South-Carolina State-Gazette*, July 8, 1794.
[134] Cunningham, *Jeffersonian*, 66.
[135] Kenneth Owen, *Political Community in Revolutionary Pennsylvania, 1774–1800* (Oxford: Oxford University Press, 2018), 138.
[136] Jefferson, *Papers*, Vol. 28, 220, 228.
[137] *Adams Family*, Vol. 10, 335.
[138] John Quincy Adams, *Writings* (New York: Macmillan, 1913), Vol. 1, 331.
[139] Cabot, *Life*, 85.

Despite the Federalist leadership's French antipathy, with the bulk of Americans favoring the revolutionaries fighting against Britain, the government had limited diplomatic options in 1793–1794. As British depredations against neutral American commerce multiplied, surpassing four hundred American ships seized, in April 1794 Madison and the Republican opposition marshaled a nonimportation bill through the House of Representatives against British goods by 59–34, prohibiting "all articles of British or Irish production after the 1st. Novr. until the claims of the U.S. be adjusted and satisfied."[140] As with the 1770s boycotts, the measure sought to incite British domestic discontent: Jefferson argued to Washington, "nothing will force them to do justice" except "distressing their commerce."[141] Neither the Federalist-dominated Senate nor Washington, however, approved the measure. With popular support for economic warfare (likely to lead to an American recession) wanting, Boston and New York attempts to revivify nonconsumption of British goods fizzled. Alongside defense spending increases to further fortify American harbors, the Senate authorized Chief Justice Jay as special envoy to Great Britain to broker a new treaty.

British-American negotiations remained secret, and the resultant "Jay's Treaty" arrived in Philadelphia in March 1795 with its contents still unknown. Rather than release the document for public discussion, Washington sealed it until June's Senate debate. Such machinations raised suspicions about Federalist secrecy and unilateral decision-making. "If the people have the right and the capacity to govern themselves," one opposition paper complained, "they are certainly entitled to knowledge of their own affairs." Closed-door decisions seemed "practically monarchical."[142] Many feared influential "aristocratic" forces would decide the matter. "If it strengthens England," another newspaper considered, "it will not strengthen France."[143] With resentments growing and conspiracy fears abounding, the political opposition primed for a fight.

The treaty, whose contents became known only after Senate ratification (20–10 along party lines), created an uproar. "How does the secrecy of the Senate," asked one newspaper editorial, "comport with THE SOVEREIGNTY of the people?"[144] While the agreement secured British withdrawal from Western territory, compensation for naval seizures, and some additional trade with British colonies, it let Americans' impressment into the British Navy continue and restricted wartime trade with France. Rochefoucauld, still traveling, found Jay's Treaty "the universal subject of conversation" with the

---

[140] Jefferson, *Papers*, Vol. 28, 62–63; Ferling, *Leap*, 68.
[141] Jefferson, *Papers*, Vol. 28, 75.
[142] *Oracle of the Day*, June 16, 1795, Pasley, *First*, 108.
[143] *Aurora General Advertiser*, June 27, 1795.
[144] Elkins and McKitrick, *Age*, 418.

majority opposed. Each side called the other "jacobins" and "aristocrats," respectively, while "Those who do not admire the treaty with England are looked upon by the one party as guillotinists, whilst the opposers of the treaty, on the other hand, decry every man as an enemy of public liberty," cultivating political conflict in "all cities."[145] Democratic-Republican/Federalist debates advanced by proxy.

Senate approval came less than a week before Independence Day. Anti-treaty partisans organized opposition festivities. Tradesmen of Wilmington, Delaware, toasted "The virtuous and independent republican Minority of the Senate," while denouncing the "Coalition of Hypocritical Federalism and malignant Toryism" believed responsible.[146] New York's Tammany Society, at a Battery banquet, asked the United States, "never enter into any Alliance which may have a tendency to smother the flame of Liberty, or injure the Rights of Man," eliciting three cheers.[147] The *Philadelphia Minerva* concluded, "it appears that Lord Jay, prime minster of the union, has been most unmercifully toasted by a set of splenetic democrats."[148] Only a dozen years after the War of Independence's end, submitting to Britain remained anathema to many.

At Philadelphia, foregoing the usual Fourth of July celebrations, sailors, ship-carpenters, and other sympathizers from Northern Liberties mobilized a nighttime Independence Day demonstration to the center of the nation's capital. Authorities had blocked a daytime procession, keeping cavalry, infantry, militia, and police near the President's House and Independence Hall until 10 p.m. but then left for banquets. Reminiscent of the effigy processions against stamp collectors thirty years earlier, dissidents prepared a luminescent Jay caricature, holding a scale of justice reading "American liberty and independence" and "British gold" together in one hand, while clutching the treaty in the other. With Jay's image surrounded by grasping Senators, the caption read, "Come up to my price and I will sell you my country." At approximately 11 p.m., five hundred demonstrators descended through the Liberties, down Second to Market Street, marching in silence but with their message brightly lit. The cavalry, after banquet toasts, remounted and attacked the protesters, before retreating under a hail of stones and bottles. Only upon parading before Washington's residence and returning to the Liberties to burn the illumination was their silence broken, for three cheers.[149]

[145] Rochefoucauld, *Voyages,* Vol. 2, 78, 231–32.
[146] *Independent Gazetteer,* July 11, 1795.
[147] Foner, *Democratic-Republican,* 218.
[148] *Philadelphia Minerva,* July 18, 1795.
[149] *Greenleaf's New York Journal,* July 8, 10, 11, and 15, 1795; *The Daily Advertiser,* July 10, 1795; *Amherst Journal,* July 24, 1795.

As in 1765, copycat burnings followed up and down the East Coast. Over the following month, such demonstrations occurred in cities including Portsmouth, New York, Norfolk, Fredericksburg, and Charleston.[150] At the latter, a large crowd "paraded the streets in a most riotous manner," threatening to pull down the house of a Federalist Senator allegedly taking British bribes, before the public executioner committed Jay's figure and the hated treaty to the flames.[151] In some places, effigies of local Federalists and Jay allies suffered the same.[152] The violence was not only symbolic: opponents pelted Hamilton in New York with rocks after he harangued a crowd on the treaty's virtues – with the Federalist leader returning to challenge an opposing leader to a duel and lower-class protesters to fistfights. Frenchifying older traditions, the crowd guillotined Jay's effigy. In Philadelphia, protesters smashed British diplomats' windows, as well as a Federalist senator's.[153] Massachusetts Federalist Congressman Benjamin Goodhue, borrowing French Thermidorian language, denounced an "air of terrorism" present.[154] One Federalist publication conceded, "If we may judge of the public sentiment, from publications, mobile meetings, burning effigies, &c. &c. a large majority of the people are against the Treaty."[155] Such agitation suggested passing the accord could incite street-fighting or worse.

An anti-treaty petition campaign developed, pressuring Washington to reconsider. Boston's July 10 town meeting, numerically "unequalled since the memorable epoch of independence," unanimously approved a petition denouncing Jay's Treaty as "derogatory to their National Honour, and Independence," urging a presidential veto.[156] Portsmouth's July 17 meeting demanded "all the essential advantages" of 1783's Treaty of Paris, wanting Jay's renegotiated.[157] New York's meeting attracted five thousand, from "respectable mechanics" and laborers to "the ash men and the clam men," who shouted Hamilton down.[158] Philadelphia, holding an open-air mass-meeting drawing comparable numbers outside Independence Hall on July 25, asserted the treaty violated the "alliance with the republic of France," repudiating the people's will.[159] Norfolk considered the "Treaty is calculated to promote

---

[150] *Greenleaf's New York Journal*, July 25, 1795; *Aurora General Advertiser*, July 27, 1795; *Gazette of the United States*, July 28, 1795; *Albany Gazette*, August 3, 1795.

[151] *New-Jersey Journal*, August 5, 1795; SCHS Read Family Papers MSS 0267.00.

[152] *The Argus*, August 8, 1795; *Greenleaf's New York Journal*, July 25, 1795.

[153] Elkins and McKitrick, *Age*, 421; Nancy Isenberg, *Fallen Founder: The Life of Aaron Burr* (New York: Penguin, 2007), 140; *Massachusetts Spy*, July 29, 1795.

[154] Wolcott, *Memoirs*, Vol. 1, 221.

[155] *Federal Mirror*, August 14, 1795.

[156] *The Courier*, July 11, 1795.

[157] Washington, *Papers*, Presidential Series, Vol. 18, 355; *Eastern Herald*, July 20, 1795.

[158] Young, *Democratic*, 449; Octavius Pickering, *The Life of Timothy Pickering. By His Son, Octavius Pickering* (Boston: Little, Brown, 1867–1873), Vol. 3, 202.

[159] Washington, *Papers*, Presidential Series, Vol. 18, 418; VHS John Beckley Papers.

British influence in the United States, to divide the opinions of their citizens, and to afford an opportunity to the enemies of all free Government to subvert ours."[160] Lexington, Kentucky, found the treaty "submissive and humiliating."[161] Amid an unprecedentedly fierce war contrasting liberty and despotism, the treaty augured vast ramifications.

The Federalist leadership tried to weather the oppositional storm, while denouncing their opponents' tactics. Secretary of State Timothy Pickering considered such meetings "incapable of calm deliberation," believing "such bodies cannot possibly influence the opinion of any man of sense and experience, who gives the reins, not to his passions, but to his reason."[162] Treaty supporters attacked town meetings' composition: Jay himself considered agitation rooted among "Antifederalists, the debtors, and the French," associating with "Jacobin philosophers, the disorganizing politicians, and the malcontents of various descriptions."[163] New York Congressman Noah Webster proposed to "extinguish the evil" of "irregular town meetings" and accused Southern states of being "governed very much by the French Nation."[164] As party animosity rose to unprecedented heights, Federalists stuck by the treaty.

Federalists nevertheless borrowed their opponents' tactics to publicize their own popular supporters. Partisans argued the anti-Treaty meetings did not represent their communities and urged pro-Treaty petitions: Senator Cabot suggested "the propriety of a manly declaration of sentiments" to Boston merchants for the beleaguered Federalists. Senator Rufus King asserted "the friends of a fair Discussion" had not attended New York's municipal debates, while the city's merchant meeting assented (aware of the treaty's commercial advantages).[165] Economic divides became prominent: Federalist Congressman Chauncey Goodrich noted "strife between the opulent, and the discontented and factious at the head of the poor."[166] Federalists too worked to manipulate public opinion: Washington, after only sending pro-forma responses to anti-Treaty petitions, wrote Hamilton on July 29 that he would wait until "the paroxysm of the fever is a little abated," to see the people's "real temper," as "at present the cry against the Treaty is like that against a mad-dog; and every one, in a manner, seems engaged in running it down."[167] Whether the broader public would become content to live with the beast, however, remained uncertain.

[160] Washington, *Papers*, Presidential Series, Vol. 18, 509.
[161] Pickering, *Life*, Vol. 3, 202; LC Breckinridge Family Papers, Vol. 12.
[162] Pickering, *Life*, Vol. 3, 181.
[163] John Jay, *The Selected Papers of John Jay* (Charlottesville: University of Virginia Press, 2010–2017), Vol. 4, 193.
[164] NYPL Noah Webster Papers, reel 1.
[165] King, *Life*, Vol. 2, 20, 16.
[166] Wolcott, *Memoirs*, Vol. 1, 330.
[167] Washington, *Papers*, Vol. 18, 458.

On August 18, Washington signed Jay's Treaty. As during the Whiskey Rebellion, the president's personal prestige preserved order despite the political discord. Although rumors flew of Bostonians and Governor Samuel Adams "establishing committees of correspondence" across Massachusetts as in the 1770s "to gain a uniformity in the proceedings of opposition," no such confederacy revivified.[168] No organizations directly confronted the president. As seaborne incidents declined and Britain evacuated disputed territory, seaside and frontier communities both appreciated the agreement more. Federalists switched to accusing treaty opponents of politicizing discussions in a prelude to the 1796 election.[169]

The political battle over Jay's Treaty continued, however, moving into the House of Representatives. Opposition organizer Beckley wrote to Madison in September, "we have already dispersed in circular letters, all over the States, a petition to the H. of Represents" against the treaty.[170] Surviving Democratic-Republican societies that month began petitioning Congress to withhold funding for treaty enforcement. Initially, public opinion grew on the opposition's side, with petitions by December arriving from seemingly "every part of the Union" against procurement.[171] Beckley confidently predicted the treaty would remain an "unexecuted instrument."[172] Growing opposition led the House in spring 1796 to pass an anti-treaty resolution, requesting Washington release all documents relating to its negotiation.[173] Washington indignantly refused, implying the Republicans were grandstanding, while waiting for Federalists to come to his defense.

Treaty supporters sought to demonstrate their national influence. As both mercantile and frontier constituencies came to consider their interests aligned with the treaty, petition-campaigns gathered force from Massachusetts and New York City to (amazingly) Western Pennsylvania calling for enforcement.[174] Whereas considerations of national honor previously triumphed, economic factors now became paramount. Philadelphia's merchant association unanimously voted to petition the House to uphold the treaty and appointed a committee "to correspond with the Merchants in all the seaports" to do likewise.[175] Hamilton boasted New York's matching petition was "signed by almost every Merchant & Trader in the City," surpassing 3,200

---

[168] King, *Life*, Vol. 2, 31.
[169] Elkins and McKitrick, *Age*, 432; John E. Ferling, *Adams vs. Jefferson: The Tumultuous Election of 1800* (Oxford: Oxford University Press, 2004), 67; *Vermont Gazette*, September 18, 1795.
[170] VHS John Beckley Papers.
[171] Foner, *Democratic-Republican*, 83; UVSC James Maury Papers, Vol. 2.
[172] VHS John Beckley Papers.
[173] APS Filippo Mazzei Papers.
[174] Risjord, *Chesapeake*, 462–63; Elkins and McKitrick, *Age*, 446–47.
[175] *Adams Family*, Vol. 11, 251.

names.[176] Boston's town meeting reversed the previous year's anti-Treaty unanimity to oppose Congressional resistance. John Adams now touted the treaty as an "Example of Democratical Negotiation with foreign Nations."[177] Under growing pressure after "vast numbers of petitions from all parts of the country" were read, the House of Representatives' April 30 vote narrowly approved funding Jay's Treaty, concluding the long controversy.[178]

Though the opposition thought Jay's Treaty would give them a wedge into power – Beckley projected victory would bring "a republican president to succeed Mr. Washington" – the controversy concluded with the opposition weakened.[179] Madison complained to Jefferson that a "crisis which ought to have been so managed as to fortify the Republican cause, has left it in a very crippled condition," with state elections bringing Federalist gains. "Nothing but auspicious contingencies abroad or at home can regain the lost ground."[180] The opposition's popularity continued to rise or fall with public opinion about France's, Britain's, and America's place in the Atlantic world.

Resentments against Jay's Treaty remained strong into the 1796 election season. Jefferson, in an angry letter (leaked the following year) to Mazzei denounced how "an Anglican, monarchical and aristocratical party has sprung up, whose avowed object is to draw over us the substance as they have already done the forms of the British government." Only a change of ruling party could lead America away from neocolonial British subservience. Jefferson considered the "main body of our citizens however remain true to their republican principles, the whole landed interest is with them, and so is a great mass of talents."[181] To what extent mercantile interests represented their communities remained questionable.

Given the suspect machinations behind the treaty, older admonitions against party now appeared invalidated. Jay's Treaty gave the Democratic-Republican opposition the ability to fight domestic political battles by proxy, rallying popular discontent for demonstrations and petitions in ways that would have been deemed unsuitable for more mundane domestic issues. The passions the French Revolution engendered, against war's dramatic tableau, put Federalist/Democratic-Republican debates in sharper contrast and heightened stakes for the 1796 election season.

---

[176] Hamilton, *Papers*, Vol. 20, 121, 124, and 136.
[177] *Adams Family*, Vol. 11, 275, 308.
[178] Cunningham, *Jeffersonian*, 83; MDHS James Bayard Papers, Vol. 1.
[179] VHS John Beckley Papers.
[180] Dumas Malone, *Jefferson and the Ordeal of Liberty* (Boston: Little, Brown, 1962), 259.
[181] Jefferson, *Papers*, Vol. 29, 82.

Conclusion

Only through French inspiration, amid an Atlantic war, would the American political system definitively depart from Federalists' intended model of a faction-less, elite-directed republic to develop modern party politics. The rapid gains wrought for French liberty through popular mobilization, pushing many of the era's principles further than Americans had dared, made political quietism impossible. Genêt, by motivating the formation of and naming the Democratic societies created a new American political ideal of participatory democracy, in which "democratic" went from a term of disdain into an aspirational ideal. Federalists' extreme reaction against the early societies, meanwhile, demonstrated the influence even small political networks could attain. Using the French Revolution's worst excesses to dissuade popular mobilization, though most Democratic-Republican societies demobilized after the Whiskey Rebellion, did not deter the political opposition for long. Jay's Treaty exacerbated the continued divides in American politics. The country would never be without political parties again.

While the Genêt affair and the (often vague) influence of French revolutionary politics are mentioned in every survey of 1790s American politics, none have seen the Jacobins and their Atlantic brethren as having been central to the form American party politics took. Stanley Elkins and Eric McKittrick, despite devoting eight chapters to "The French Revolution in America" in their vast *The Age of Federalism*, found only an "erratic cycle of attraction and repulsion" between the two nations, leading to "nothing very cumulative" in their political relations.[182] Such a view, however, elides the importance of the exchanges that occurred: rather than modern political parties having been a uniquely American inspiration, opposition organizing instead adapted the international corresponding society model that had not been used for American general-interest organizing since the revolutionary Committees of Correspondence. Only through grappling with the revolutionary possibilities of the 1790s would the Democratic-Republicans take the form they did.

---

[182] Elkins and McKitrick, *Age*, 303–4.

15

From Revolutionary Committees to American Party Politics

A youthful British traveler, David Erskine, stepping ashore into the United States of October 1798, observed a dangerously politicized polity. The levels of "intolerance" seemed greater than in Britain, with American party men thinking "nothing of wishing each other destroyed." What's more, such feelings belonged not to a narrow political class, but the people at large: "Under one or other of these parties almost everybody ranks himself," making it "impossible for more heat & violence to be shewn than is most times the case when Politics are discussed."[1] The United States' developing political system seemed scarcely capable of controlling the passions it engendered.

Despite President Washington's efforts and the professed beliefs of most eighteenth-century revolutionaries, factionalization could not be prevented in the early Federal United States. Rather than being the Republic's downfall, and creating a Julius Caesar, Oliver Cromwell, or (by 1799) Napoleon Bonaparte figure, party politics offered Americans a political route forward. Whereas party organization remained weak in most areas during the mid-1790s controversies, and Jacobin-style popular Democratic-Republican Societies did not revive, across the elections of 1796 to 1800 local, regional, state, and federal-oriented committees of correspondence created durable political organizations permitting the rarest of feats in republics – peaceful transfers of power. The corresponding committee model survived the Age of Revolutions by turning into something else: durable political parties.

Party Mobilization in the Election of 1796

By mid-decade, Federalist-Republican divides grew irreconcilable. South Carolina Federalist Henry de Saussure, attending a Congressional session prior to his appointment as Director of the Mint noted, "warmth and dissension prevail on almost every question." Rather than a refuge for cool deliberation, the "Hall appears to be an arena where the Combatants descend to engage, not for persuasion, but for victory. No disciplined Prussians or

---

[1] D. M. Erskine: "Letters from America, 1798–1799," Patricia Holbert Menk, ed. *William and Mary Quarterly*, Vol. 6, no. 2 (April 1949), 257, 278.

enthusiastic French, adhere more firmly to their ranks" than party-mad congressmen."[2] Suspicions grew against those across the aisle: Connecticut Federalist Congressman Chauncey Goodrich, surveying Republican benches, considered, "No doubt a majority of the members owe their seats to clubs, factions, and the feverish state of things at the time of the election."[3] North/South divides worsened, with Treasury Secretary Oliver Wolcott denouncing Southern "Faction, dependence, pride and turbulence," believing "the effect of the slave system has been such that I fear our government will never operate with efficacy."[4] As political inhibitions weakened, many feared so too would the federal union.

Despite Democratic-Republican reversals over Jay's Treaty, the faction's future seemed promising going into the 1796 election. Jefferson considered that although "American merchants trading on British capital" were Federalists' natural constituency, a larger "Agricultural interest ... dispersed over a great extent of country" favored the opposition. Whereas rural inhabitants heretofore possessed "little means of intercommunication," allowing urban and elite networks hegemony, stronger party communications and rural outreach could "crush the machinations against their government."[5] Particularly given Northern factionalism, together with the three-fifths representation afforded the South per slave, Federalists' electoral position became assailable. With Democratic-Republican Societies dormant – the *Gazette of the United States* mid-campaign printing "the Demo societies are dead" without rebuttal – now congressional Republicans directed the opposition, adapting many popular society methods to electoral ends.[6]

French politics remained an enduring touchstone in the Federalist-Republican culture war, with reversals abroad in France and domestically over Jay's Treaty favoring America's governing party. The French Jacobins' downfall led Federalist newspapers to further smear the American opposition. *The Gazette of the United States* in early 1796 wished Democratic-Republicans the "fate of the Jacobinical croakers," hoping for an American Thermidor to "serve as a lesson to the future calumniators of the great and the good."[7] Federalists painted them as anarchists and nihilist wreckers importing the worst of Europe. Many considered the future with trepidation: John Quincy Adams in London noted, "the experience of the last four or five years has taught me to calculate a little upon the doctrine of reactions in popular Governments."[8] Yet revolutionary potential, in America as in France, remained unlimited.

[2] LC Richard Bland Lee Papers. MMC-3477.
[3] Wolcott, *Memoirs*, Vol. 1, 297.
[4] Ibid., 224.
[5] Sharp, *American*, 137.
[6] Wilentz, *Rise*, 69.
[7] *Gazette of the United States*, January 16, 1796.
[8] MHS Lee Family Papers.

The opposition, meanwhile, promoted the advantages of Jefferson's French relationships. To friends like Rush, Jefferson remained "a Citizen of the World and the friend of universal peace and happiness," while the Federalists became a close-minded "British Party."[9] In June 1796, Beckley believed "it morally certain that Mr. Jefferson and Col. Burr will be elected" president and vice-president, "as the Southern States will never consent to a War with France," which Federalists "believe to be inevitable." He predicted French victory, asserting the allied "Spanish, Dutch & French Marines will be extremely formidable, & most probably too powerful for England."[10] American interests could most benefit from a closer relationship with Europe's leading nation. Prospects of Britain's counterrevolutionary coalition triumphing on the continent, for the foreseeable future, appeared almost nil.

By autumn 1795, plans coalesced for the following year's elections. Madison and Virginia Representative William Giles ventured to Monticello to discuss strategy with Jefferson, while Burr visited separately amid a middle-states tour.[11] With Washington's retirement likely, ambitions ran high. "Electioneering" became part of an elected official's responsibilities, including coordinating with local party leaders, corresponding with constituents, and developing political platforms. Though party discipline in many areas remained lax, and no national committee existed (accentuating state and local variations), now virtually all areas acknowledged being part of a national campaign under Madison and Beckley's umbrella organization.[12]

Federalists attempted to match Republican electioneering tactics. New Hampshire state representative William Plumer on New Year's 1796 considered his party "ready to go any length that reason can justify" to oppose the "sons of anarchy" bent on takeover.[13] New York's Republican *Argus* newspaper criticized "the whole clan of stock-holders, land-jobbers, and speculating monopolizers, the fast friends of government, and the privileged citizens" conspiring to swing the election through hidden networks.[14] Each side believed factionalism unsustainable, given the new tactics' destructiveness. The Federalist Wolcott alleged that "calumny" typified the new politics: "Who, except the President, has not been assailed with

[9] Rush, *Letters,* Vol. 2, 779; Joanne B. Freeman, "The Presidential Election of 1796," in *John Adams and the Founding of the Republic,* Richard Alan Ryerson, ed. (Boston: Northeastern University Press, 2001), 143.

[10] VHS John Beckley Papers.

[11] Cunningham, *Pursuit,* 199; NYHS Aaron Burr Papers, reel 3 3518.

[12] William Nisbet Chambers, *Political Parties in a New Nation: The American Experience, 1776–1800* (Oxford: Oxford University Press, 1963), 82–83; Elkins and McKitrick, *Age,* 515; Ferling, *Election,* 87.

[13] LC William Plumer Papers MSS 36434, reel 2 262.

[14] *The Argus,* January 20, 1796.

success?"[15] Though the parties had significant policy differences, partisan rhetoric became baser.

In April, three weeks before the Jay Treaty's final vote, the Federalists suffered defeat in their Massachusetts stronghold, with Samuel Adams winning reelection as governor with nearly two-thirds the vote. The election seemed a referendum on both the Treaty and democratic organizing – with the Federalist candidate having "protested against the Anti Treaty meeting," and thus "the people were determined to shew him and his friends their marked disapprobation on that account." The right to assemble in party combinations seemed at stake, with one opposition paper hailing the victory as the "compleatest triumph" for "the cause of Democratic Republicanism" since Bostonians' spreading "the committee of Correspondence in 74."[16] The memory and personnel of earlier movements remained active, and new revolutions possible.

Party organizing developed furthest in New York City, where Burr's tactics drew Federalist opponents' envy. The Senator reputably had "an unequalled talent of attaching men to his views, and forming combinations of which he is always at the centre." Redeploying "thinking of a military cast" learnt in the War of Independence for political organizing, together with cultivated manners used to solve internal party disputes behind closed doors, Burr directed an ascendant popular party at the nation's electoral fulcrum.[17] If New York and Pennsylvania took the opposition's side, with the south they formed a ruling coalition.

The electoral map also altered in the opposition's favor through Tennessee's statehood. The Federalist Goodrich complained Tennesseans, having recently met the population requirement, had "cashiered the temporary government, self created themselves into a state, adopted a constitution" to join "the electioneering cabal for Mr. Jefferson." The frontier issues associated with the Whiskey Rebellion showed little sign of abating as states reached the international Mississippi River border, increasing foreign war's prospects. Rumors flew of France reacquiring Louisiana from Spain to create an American empire, and Wolcott worried that "in the event of a separation the western people ought to look to France as their natural ally and protector."[18] Distrust grew with the union.

A national strategy developed, and an electoral map with voting projections emerged. Beckley in mid-September predicted, "From Georgia, No. Carolina, South Carolina, Virginia, Kentucky & Tennessee we expect a unanimous vote – half Maryland & Delaware – some in New Jersey, and several to the

---

[15] Wolcott, *Memoirs*, Vol. 1, 351.
[16] *Argus*, April 15, 1796; *Aurora General Advertiser*, April 19, 1796.
[17] Wolcott, *Memoirs*, Vol. 1, 379; NYHS Aaron Burr Papers, reel 3 2433.
[18] Wolcott, *Memoirs*, Vol. 1, 338–39, 350.

Eastward – so that if Pennsylvania do well the Election is safe." By the month's end, he optimistically predicted: "Rhode Island will be with us – two in New Hampshire – three or 4 in Massachusetts, and one or two in Vermont and Connecticut."[19] Despite losing New York, a national majority remained attainable. Federalists, meanwhile, sought a solid New England front, with Ames that summer prognosticating the Virginian "in every event will fail of four" electoral votes.[20] Despite having only previously known unanimity in selecting a president, the Founders turned to vote-counting and partisan coalition-building.

Both sides encouraged partisan celebrations. Rather than arbitrating conciliation, Washington in May participated in the Federalist-dominated Society of the Cincinnati's elaborate festivities. The day after their annual meeting, members marched to the President's House near Independence Hall, where Washington greeted them "as old brother soldiers." The following night, the society held a banquet for the political elite. Far from republican simplicity, veteran and Connecticut Assemblyman Ephraim Kirby wrote to his wife, "the splendor of these dinners, the immense display of wealth and luxury is inconceivable to you."[21] Few could interpret such gatherings but as political organizing. Meanwhile, popular celebrations for French military victories favored by Democratic-Republicans continued. Charleston's William Read in August declared, "No news excites us now except the astonishing success of French arms," believing their triumphs "must to future generations when told in story seem like wild romance."[22] The opposition found little to celebrate with Federalists.

Washington only announced his retirement in late September by releasing his *Farewell Address*. Fearing political breakdown, Washington continued denouncing factionalism, though the address' language now seemed anachronistic. The "baneful effects of the spirit of party," he declared, marked by "alternate domination of one faction over another, sharpened by the spirit of revenge," could create "frightful despotism." The "constant danger of excess" would "distract the public councils and enfeeble the public administration," whereas consensus brought strength.[23] Washington did not say, however, how lessening party tensions could be accomplished. The president offered no workable vision for the Republic. The future would belong to party men.

Washington's theatrics changed nothing, as presidential campaigns were unleashed with pent-up energy. Though most predicted Washington's

---

[19] VHS John Beckley Papers.
[20] Wolcott, *Memoirs*, Vol. 1, 373.
[21] DUSC Ephraim Kirby Papers, Box 7, folder 1.
[22] SCHS Read Family Papers.
[23] George Washington, "Farewell Address," http://avalon.law.yale.edu/18th_century/wash ing.asp.

decision, the overt presidential campaign was brief: barely six weeks in many places. Beckley considered the short cycle "designed to prevent a fair election," favoring incumbents.[24] Wolcott too worried the situation had been mismanaged, fearing "the country is not sufficiently united to make a choice by the electors," which would throw the decision to the House of Representatives.[25] Nevertheless, canvassing advanced, with Beckley asserting, "a little exertion by a few good active republicans in each County would bring the people out" to vote. Ames, in a less-quoted ending to his famous observation that Washington's farewell "will serve as a signal, like dropping a hat, for the party racers to start," predicted "money, it is very probable, will be spent, some virtue and more tranquility lost" in hopes that "public order will be saved."[26] Few electoral machinations of later years were absent in 1796's presidential contest.

Party operatives diffused a wide variety of party material to publicize candidates, boost turnout, and win supporters. By Pennsylvania's election, Beckley wrote Madison that "30,000 tickets are gone thro' the State, by Express, into every county" – "tickets" being handbills listing the Republican candidates. This was especially useful since voters received blank ballots to write fifteen names for Electoral College delegates. The parties printed tickets and influential locals hand-copied many more for friends and neighbors. Beckley urged "getting all our friends to write as many tickets as they can," exercising personal connections.[27] Campaign literature, both issue and personality-based, proliferated: one Western Pennsylvania handbill endorsed Jefferson and fellow Republicans as "respectable yeomen, opposers of perverse systems of finance, enemies of monarchical trumpery and parade" while also "men of science and lovers of literature."[28] If still deferential to enlightened leadership, many increasingly considered the Republican opposition on their side.

County party organizations, connected statewide by committees of correspondence, spearheaded the campaign – vetting candidates and developing party unity. Minutes survive from one November Federalist meeting in a Palatine, New York home. Those assembled reached a consensus to nominate James Cochran (a lawyer and distant Hamilton in-law) for Congress and then appointed a "committee of Correspondence, to support the Election, of the

---

[24] VHS John Beckley Papers; Aaron Burr, *Political Correspondence and Public Papers of Aaron Burr*, Mary-Jo Kline and Joanne Wood Ryan, eds. (Princeton: Princeton University Press, 1984), Vol. 1, 265; Wolcott, *Memoirs*, Vol. 1, 382.

[25] Wolcott, *Memoirs*, Vol. 1, 382.

[26] Ibid., 384.

[27] John F. Hoadley, *Origins of American Political Parties, 1789–1803* (Lexington, KY: University Press of Kentucky, 1986), 43; Cunningham, *Jeffersonian*, 104–5; VHS John Beckley Papers.

[28] Malone, *Jefferson*, 284.

above Candidate." In publicizing their choice, they ordered their deliberations sent to three regional newspapers.[29] Cochran won. Organizers expected considerable conformity from Federalist candidates: South Carolina Congressman Robert Goodloe Harper complained to Hamilton that he found no one "however popular, had the least Chance of becoming an Elector if he was understood to be opposed to the old man."[30] Washington's shadow remained.

Active campaigning became an acceptable practice. Burr, in an innovation not regularly followed by national candidates until the twentieth century, took to the campaign trail. Seeking to break Federalists' New England stranglehold, Burr made his case for vice president (or, some suspected, president) in stops across Connecticut, Rhode Island, Massachusetts, and New York.[31] Other candidates' surrogates, meanwhile, remained busy. Even rural Vermont's *Rutland Herald* on October 17 ran a caricature of "The Electioneering Politician," marked by "Ambition, without principle; a zealous pursuit of wealth and power, by means of popularity; flattery, perfidy and deceit," with all the vices of politics displayed in an unprecedentedly intense campaign. *Andrews's Western Star* considered the "business of electioneering" a "practice from which every honest man must turn abhorrent."[32] Yet, coordination's utility in a close election accelerated such practices.

As the first contentious presidential election, risks beckoned as politicization intensified. Another *Western Star* editorial considered, "it is to be lamented that parties have risen to such a height," threatening to "destroy the freedom of elections, which constitute the vital principle of republican governments." Elections, rather than being determined by reason and dispassion, became "guided" by party leaders.[33] Employing venality and corruption, with wealthy candidates offering free rides to the polls and/or commandeering taverns to offer partisans free alcohol, parties cultivated seemingly undue influence.[34] Only pragmatic interests led many to conceal their distaste. With the example of French Jacobin excesses so fresh, factionalism and corruption, and then violence, civil war, and dictatorship became fearsome prospects.

The French foreign minister, Pierre Adet, sought to swing the election to the Republicans through diplomatic meddling nearly as offensive as Genet's. In late October, he announced the French would treat all American ships like enemy combatants, and in mid-November suspended his ministry over the

---

[29] *Ostego Herald*, November 2, 1796.
[30] Freeman, "Presidential," 146.
[31] VHS John Beckley Papers.
[32] *Andrews's Western Star*, October 24, 1796.
[33] Ibid., October 31, 1796.
[34] Alan Taylor, "The Art of Hook and Snivey: Political Culture in Upstate New York during the 1790s," *Journal of American History* 79, no. 4 (1993), 1387.

administration's pro-British policies, until the United States returned to "the alliance, and the sworn friendship between the two nations."[35] By implication, electing Jefferson would preserve peace. Federalists remained unimpressed, with Adams commenting privately he should "be mistaken, in my Guesses, if Americans in general are very servile."[36] Wolcott asserted French interference augured a showdown between systems: "if the elections are favourable, all will be safe; if infavourable, French democracy may prevail, in which case all will be lost." Together with their military conquests, he wondered if France would "dictate submission to the world."[37] Foreign interference in an American election remained too offensive to be effective.

The outcome remained uncertain approaching the election days (varying by state between October and December). Beckley considered Republicans "sanguine in our hopes" for Jefferson. "The other side are equally active and equally sanguine." Seeing a near split among eastern Pennsylvanians, Beckley hoped the recently insurgent Western counties would decide the race.[38] Misinformation abounded, with Burr asserting by late November that Adams "has no chance, the race will be between Jefferson and [Federalist running mate Thomas] Pinckney."[39] Adams, meanwhile, saw conspiracy behind the early returns, writing to Abigail, "French Maneuvers have gained the vote of Pennsylvania, and how many others is unknown," while Goodrich noted Jeffersonians going "to the polls with French cockades in their hats at Philadelphia."[40] None could assume a smooth outcome.

The final electoral tally was predictably close: Adams edged Jefferson by 71 to 68, via single Federalist votes in Pennsylvania, Virginia, and North Carolina.[41] New England unanimously sided with Adams. To the opposition, the lesson appeared that, rather than an excessive attachment to party, Republicans remained too lax, with Jefferson telling Madison the Northeast, "disciplined in the schools of their town meetings" for "operating in phalanx," understood unanimity's importance better than southerners.[42] Yet, Federalist unity did not extend into vice presidential voting. For "fear of making Pinckney president," Harper described, New England electors voted for obscure candidates, a "blamable policy" that worsened regional antagonisms and put the opposition next in line for the presidency.[43] Future electoral organizing would require greater stringency.

---

[35] Cunningham, *Pursuit*, 202.
[36] MHS John Adams Papers, reel 382.
[37] Wolcott, *Memoirs*, Vol. 1, 386.
[38] VHS John Beckley Papers.
[39] Burr, *Political*, Vol. 1, 275.
[40] MHS John Adams Papers, reel 382; Wolcott, *Memoirs*, Vol. 1, 394.
[41] Cunningham, *Pursuit*, 204.
[42] Jefferson, *Papers*, Vol. 29, 247.
[43] MDHS James Bayard Papers, Vol. 1.

The election's outcome augured more party feuding. With peaceful transfers of power still largely unknown, the Federalist order teetered. "The Adamites have at best but a poor triumph," Massachusetts observer Ezekiel Bacon considered, "& may almost say with the Carthaginian Commission, 'another such victory would ruin me.'"[44] Ames predicted Jefferson, with few vice presidential responsibilities, "may go on affecting zeal for the people; combining the antis, and standing at their head," so "Two Presidents, like two suns in the meridian, would meet and jostle for four years, and then Vice would be first."[45] No one projected an end to discord. The union's future remained uncertain. Wolcott worried a "phrenzy of the southern states" would consider secession should future elections bring further unfavorable results.[46]

The 1796 election subsequently appeared a transitional event presaging the more solid party structures to follow. Evolving beyond French Jacobin models, opposition Republicans found new utility in corresponding society models for electoral organizing – which Federalists quickly copied. The 1796 campaigns' successes and failures pushed organizing onward: indiscipline cost one party the presidency and the other the vice presidency, while growing partisanship led neither to expect political reconciliation. The future belonged to widespread, aggressive party organizing.

Party, Sedition, and Repression

Rather than appreciating their electoral victory, Federalists responded to the new party era with fear, inciting conflict with domestic rivals as well as the French. Foreign antagonisms provoked repressive measures against those domestic organizations long linked to the French Revolution. Democratic-Republicans, with political dissent's legitimacy questioned, were forced on the defensive in 1798 but emerged strengthened from their opponents' excesses.

Revolutionary France continued making the Democratic-Republicans' situation more difficult. America's oldest ally responded to Jay's Treaty by refusing to receive Federalist ambassador Charles Pinckney (sent to replace the Republican Monroe) in Paris and seizing American ships on the high seas.[47] Moreover, France's government in January 1798 published a letter from Jefferson to Mazzei, in which Jefferson described France as America's "real mother country because she assured their freedom and independence. As grateful children, far from forsaking her, they should have armed themselves for her defense." Jay's Treaty, however, "united them to Great Britain better

---

[44] DUSC Ephraim Kirby Papers, Box 7, folder 4.
[45] Malone, *Jefferson*, 317.
[46] Wolcott, *Memoirs*, Vol. 1, 409.
[47] John Chester Miller, *Crisis in Freedom: The Alien and Sedition Acts* (Boston: Little, Brown, 1951), 4.

than a treaty of alliance."[48] The French government paid no heed to the letter's American ramifications for Jefferson.

Despite Adams's service as an American diplomat in France, the president and his party turned against the sister republic. He wrote to Abigail in January, two months before taking office, "We have been opening our Arms wide to all Foreigners and placing them on a footing with Natives: and Now foreigners are dictating to us if not betraying us."[49] Though remaining skeptical toward both Anglophiles and Francophiles, Adams like many Federalists particularly feared France. As Federalist Elbridge Gerry wrote to Adams in April, should America fail to walk a thin line between the European powers, "our government would be overthrown, a new one would be formed on the french model, & we should hereafter be meer french colonies."[50] Given France's enormous expansion across neighboring Flemish, German, and Italian states – overthrowing republics in Switzerland, the Netherlands, and Venice as readily as monarchies elsewhere – many predicted French expansion in North America (into or beyond its former colonial possessions). Harper described in a public letter how the French military state became perpetual, "Resolved on a system of war and conquest, on which its own existence probably depends." Though stopping short of predicting an invasion, thinking France intimidating the United States into tribute payments more likely, he backed Federalists' hard-line in negotiations.[51]

Fear of French manipulations obsessed Adams's administration. The new president, in his inaugural address, inveighed against foreign electoral influence, considering "flattery or menaces, by fraud or violence, by terror, intrigue or venality" as possible vectors.[52] An Anglophile-Francophile brawl broke out on Philadelphia's streets that afternoon.[53] The president's cabinet went further with Wolcott (alongside fellow "High Federalist" Anglophiles including Secretary of State Timothy Pickering and Secretary of War James McHenry) considering Pinckney's French refusal "adds to other proofs that a party in this country act in conjunction with, and are devoted to the views of the government of France."[54] Adams, however, initially exercised restraint, avoiding repressive measures during his first year in office. The president accepted divisions more than Washington, arguing that as "France is divided," there "will ever be parties and divisions in all nations ... Not to expect divisions in a free country, would be an absurdity."[55] Such views did not endear him to

---

[48] APS Filippo Mazzei Papers.
[49] MHS John Adams Papers, reel 383.
[50] MHS John Adams Papers, reel 384.
[51] MDHS James Bayard Papers, Vol. 1.
[52] James D. Richardson, ed. *A Compilation of the Messages and Papers of the Presidents* (Washington, DC: United States Government Printing Office, 1896), 230.
[53] New Jersey Historical Society, Mahlon Dickerson Diary, Box 2.
[54] Wolcott, *Memoirs*, Vol. 1, 505.
[55] Adams, *Works*, Vol. 8, 548.

Federalist hardliners, however, who still considered the opposition a faction deserving annihilation.

Jefferson and fellow Republicans embraced party politics, seeing no end to ongoing differences of opinion. "It is now well understood," he wrote in February 1798, "that two political sects have arisen within the U.S. the one believing that the executive is the branch of our government which the most needs support; the other like that of the analogous branch in the English Government, it is already too strong for the republican parts of the constitution." Though using a British example perhaps to mollify his opponents, he added that Federalists still used as synonymous epithets "republicans, whigs, jacobins, disorganizers &c."[56] American political divisions, brought into dramatic relief by their Atlantic analogues, could not be ignored.

Despite the administration's early toleration of parties, Adams found little common ground with Congressional Republicans, who vetoed many of his 1797 proposals, including a military buildup. Federalists like Maryland Congressman William Hindman castigated France's "shameless Conduct" in seizing American shipping and called the opposition "high toned Jacobins."[57] Merchant pressure grew to stop French "piracys," but Republican towns petitioned against provocative measures.[58] Beckley asserted French affairs received "wicked misrepresentations," arguing American "interests and humanity" would profit from exhausting every diplomatic option.[59] Despite maritime incitements, Jefferson argued, "Our people must consent to small occasional sacrifices, to avoid the greater evil of war."[60] Despite rumors of a French offensive via the Mississippi, immediate invasion remained unlikely.[61] Nevertheless, "Congress will do no business of an important nature," Massachusetts Federalist Congressman Harrison Gray Otis predicted in December, preceding "the probable issue of the negociation with France."[62] Federalists needed further French provocations to decisively sway public opinion.

The Age of Revolution remained an open-ended phenomenon. Isolating America from Atlantic political developments seemed impossible, particularly as eighty thousand British, sixty thousand Irish, and thirty thousand French immigrated to America in the 1790s.[63] An American Society of United Irishmen formed in 1797, supporting radical Irish efforts back home, and

---

[56] Malone, *Jefferson*, 34.
[57] LC James McHenry Papers, Z999.P23.
[58] *Adams Family*, Vol. 11, 517 and Vol. 12, 150; MHS John Adams Papers, reel 388.
[59] LC James McHenry Papers, reel 2; VHS John Beckley Papers.
[60] Jefferson, *Papers*, Vol. 29, 431.
[61] Quincy Adams, *Writings*, Vol. 2, 156.
[62] LC Harrison Gray Otis Papers, MSS 59444, reel 2.
[63] Terri Diane Halperin, *The Alien and Sedition Acts of 1798: Testing the Constitution* (Baltimore: Johns Hopkins University Press, 2016), 35.

establishing corresponding clubs from New York to South Carolina.[64] The political equilibrium, however, remained uncertain. Adams discussed a potential alliance with the British crown, asserting, "In case of a revolution in England, a wild democracy will probably prevail for as long as it did in France" – "reviving and extending that delirium in America" the French Revolution unleashed.[65] Though sympathetic to the European counterrevolution, American Federalism found little international assurance.

In April 1798, Adams released correspondence outlining the "XYZ Affair," in which the corrupt French Directory demanded bribes and loans as preconditions for maritime agreements with the United States.[66] Opinions shifted across both regional and party lines. Philadelphia, which Adams previously considered "the center of foreign influence and Jacobinism," remained so united against the French that the President predicted, "the Hydra monster of Jacobinism is never to rise with such mischievous effects again."[67] Crowds roamed the streets sporting black cockades (the symbol of Europe's counter-revolutionary allies, used by the House of Habsburg, British Tories, and now the Federalists) calling for war and threatening anyone wearing French red, white, and blue.[68] Nationally, public support for France plummeted with a New Hampshire politician reporting the affair giving "new life & energy to the friends of the government."[69] Even along the Appalachian frontier, Secretary of State Pickering cited a "general change of sentiments among the people," as French "lust of universal dominion" led to "determination at every hazard to defend our country."[70] Rumors circulated of French plots to burn Philadelphia, assassinate political leaders, or start a bloody slave rebellion. Democratic-Republican congressmen, fearing electoral repercussions, lost their unity. Now a bellicose majority supported a hard-line against France, up to (and perhaps including) war.[71]

A massive petition campaign arose, encouraging the president to defend national honor. By May 1, Adams considered the affair's effects "wonderfull" and bragged of Philadelphia's petition attaining five thousand signatures, alongside others from New York, Baltimore, Boston, and Virginia. The petition wave grew across May and June, from cities and counties large and small.

[64] David A. Wilson, *United Irishmen, United States: Immigrant Radicals in the Early Republic* (Ithaca: Cornell University Press, 1998), 43.

[65] Wolcott, *Memoirs*, Vol. 2, 11.

[66] HL HM 64961, Thoreau and Sewall Papers, Vol. 2.

[67] MHS John Adams Papers, reel 388.

[68] Ferling, *John*, 356; Alexander DeConde, *The Quasi-War: The Politics and Diplomacy of the Undeclared War with France 1797–1801* (New York: Scribner's, 1966), 82.

[69] LC William Plumer Papers MSS 36434, reel 2, 394.

[70] Pickering, *Life*, Vol. 3, 380–81.

[71] Ferling, *John*, 356; MHS John Adams Papers, reel 388; Jules Witcover, *Party of the People: A History of the Democrats* (New York: Random House, 2003), 57; Elkins and McKitrick, *Age*, 588.

Albany pledged support against "all the machinations of its enemies, whether foreign or domestic." Even once-radical Charleston broadcast "preference of every Calamity, to a Servile Subjection to a foreign Yoke."[72] Federalist papers published over fifty addresses.[73] Adams responded to many, with similar bellicosity: "War" became "preferable to a surrender of national freedom," while if trends continued, "the French will become Enemies of the human Race against whom all Nations will have to Unite." The president believed Republicans were potentially treasonous, writing to Richmond that in civil wars "the Minority always resorts to foreign Influence for Support, and for assistance to overthrow, and take Vengeance on the Majority."[74] Amid the patriotic upsurge, Adams gained authority to counter French threats with ready rationales for measures against Francophiles at home.

Many Federalists believed Democratic-Republicans needed to be coerced into line. Hamilton wrote Washington in May, as they prepared to command the new Congressionally approved army of ten thousand, that the opposition would not stop until they "new model our constitution under the influence or coercion of France." Despite many patriotic addresses from the South, he argued dissent took a "Geographical complexion," where "from the South of Maryland nothing has been heared but accents of disapprobation of our Government and approbation or apology for France." Washington agreed, predicting that the French would "commence in the Southern" states, "because they will expect, from the tenor of debates in Congress, to find more friends there."[75] Reestablishing domestic order and reducing the opposition appeared imperative.

Bellicose measures multiplied. Commercial relations with France ceased on July 1. Congress commissioned new naval frigates and created the Marine Corps to serve as infantry units aboard Naval vessels for anti-French actions. Between 1796 and 1799 the federal budget, due to rising military expenditures, more than doubled. 1778's Perpetual Alliance treaty was repealed, leading to a quasi-war. Only a handful of small engagements against the French on the high seas followed, however, with most efforts contesting privateers sailing under the French flag. The Navy recommissioned their first prize, the French privateer *Croyable*, as *Retaliation*.[76] With French military attention focused in Europe, American naval power rapidly expanded its purview.

Federalists passed repressive domestic legislation, the Alien and Sedition Acts, in June and July 1798. The drafting committee explicitly sought to tame American politics, emphasizing "cooperation" with the government, while

---

[72] MHS John Adams Papers, reel 388.
[73] Newman, *Parades*, 77.
[74] MHS John Adams Papers, reel 389.
[75] Washington, *Papers*, Retirement Series, Vol. 2, 279, 397.
[76] Deconde, *Quasi-War*, 191, 126.

asserting their domestic opponents followed "the principles of that exotic system which convulses the civilized world."[77] The ironically named Alien Friends Act (alongside a nearly identical Alien Enemies Act in case of war) aimed to reduce undesirable immigration, especially from France and Ireland, by detaining and/or deporting noncitizens deemed "dangerous to the peace and safety of the United States." Cosmopolitanism came under attack, with Otis denouncing before Congress the "French apostles of sedition" who weakened neighboring lands before revolutionary armies arrived.[78] Only a measure to deny all foreign-born citizens' political office failed.[79] The right to free political speech had already been abrogated during the Adams administration, with Congressman Samuel Cabell indicted in May 1797 for "unfounded calumnies" against the government in a letter to his constituents.[80] Now, with the Sedition Act of July 14, passed the ninth anniversary of the Bastille's fall, the attack on political dissent widened. Though references to France and treason were struck from the original draft, the final law made it illegal to "conspire together with intent to oppose any measure or measures of the government of the United States," with a minimum six-month prison sentence, which if fully enforced could have strangled party politics. The press, however, was the principal target with the second clause declaring, "if any person shall write, print, utter or publish . . . with intent to defame" the government, conviction carried a $2,000 fine and up to two years in prison. The law was not permanent but expired on March 3, 1801 – conveniently, sunsetting with the president's term.[81]

In 1798's Fourth of July celebrations, partisan contestations became little short of open battle. Already that spring, Philadelphian Federalist-favoring youths twice attacked the house and presses of Republican printer Benjamin Franklin Bache (his grandfather's namesake).[82] In Baltimore, sailors declared they would march "with the French national cockade," prompting locals' warning that if they "raise the banners of a foe, they will be treated as an open enemy, according to the rules of war."[83] In opposition areas, banquet toasts celebrated, "Our Sovereign, the People – May their voice and their will be one, in defence of their Liberties," naming Jefferson and Monroe their defenders.[84] Virginian military officers toasted: "The Sedition Bill – may it

[77] Wolcott, *Memoirs*, Vol. 2, 84.
[78] DeConde, *Quasi-War*, 98.
[79] Elkins and McKitrick, *Age*, 590.
[80] Malone, *Jefferson*, 334.
[81] *A Century of Lawmaking for a New Nation: U.S. Congressional Documents and Debates, 1774–1875* (Washington, DC: Library of Congress, 1998), 596–97; Elkins and McKitrick, *Age*, 592.
[82] Halperin, *Alien*, 1–3.
[83] *Carey's United States Recorder*, July 5, 1798.
[84] *Time Piece*, July 13, 1798.

never be known in America; and may the name of it moreover be remembered with detestation."[85] Pro-government areas, meanwhile, drank to "The American Eagle: May it take the Gallic Cock by the Gills" and, curiously, "Adams and Liberty."[86] The president exulted in his rare popularity, sending his son in Europe newspaper clippings of crowds parroting Federalist slogans like "millions for defence, but not a cent for tribute."[87] For perhaps the only time, the Federalists excelled at popular politics.

Despite years of criticizing a "Jacobin" opposition, Federalists used coercion for partisan purposes. Governmental power, many declared, ought to strengthen the federal order against those seeking to undermine it. Boston's *Columbian Centinel* considered, "Whatever American opposes the Administration is an Anarchist, a Jacobin, and a Traitor."[88] *The Gazette of the United States* that summer adopted the slogan "He that is not for us is against us," adding, "it is patriotism to write in favor of our government – it is sedition to write against it."[89] Though the Alien Act remained little used, prosecutors the next two years indicted seventeen newspapermen (including a Congressman) under the Sedition Act, with almost every leading opposition paper facing charges.[90]

The opposition's regional Southern and frontier strength prevented its outright suppression. Secretary of War McHenry in August criticized Federalist colleagues who "imagine, that nothing was left to be done, but to exterminate every one who had been of the Democratic side," considering such thinking "a delightful way to introduce a civil war."[91] Almost all Sedition Act prosecutions occurred in northern states with neither southern judges nor juries inclined to enforce it. In retribution, the *New York Gazette* called for new Committees of Safety, "associations to prosecute the enemies of your country," believing popular force might be necessary against "The long knives of Kentucky, the whiskey boys of the woods of Pennsylvania, the United Irishmen of Virginia" sowing "insurrection and confusion."[92] Military annihilation threatened, but so did protracted rebellion across vast regions.

Through a mixture of national fervor and bullying, Federalists gained significant momentum heading into autumn 1798's elections. Federalist John Hopkins reported the "opposition is certainly much lessened and silenced,"

[85] *Aurora General Advertiser*, July 20, 1798.
[86] Miller, *Crisis*, 7–9.
[87] MHS Adams Family Papers, reel 390.
[88] James Morton Smith, *Freedom's Fetters: The Alien and Sedition Laws and American Civil Liberties* (Ithaca: Cornell University Press, 1956), 178.
[89] Malone, *Jefferson*, 397.
[90] Sharp, *The Deadlocked Election of 1800: Jefferson, Burr and the Union in the Balance* (Lawrence: University Press of Kansas, 2010), 42; Smith, *Freedom's*, 186.
[91] LC James McHenry Papers, reel 2.
[92] Smith, *Freedom's*, 186–87, 180.

even in Richmond.[93] Given the increased repression, Portland's *Eastern Herald* prognosticated with the campaign underway, "the future house of representatives will consist of a much greater proportion of federal characters than the former."[94] If unable to defeat the opposition outright, Federalists successfully marginalized their electoral appeal.

Democratic-Republicans remained besieged throughout election season. Some, like organizers in New Jersey's Eastern District, sought to deflect attention onto their opponents' rhetorical excesses: "those who will not vote for a certain ticket, are all branded with the opprobrious names of 'foreign jacobins, French democrats, and anti-federalists.'"[95] On the defensive, Jefferson became reduced to hoping the "reign of witches pass over" and "the people, recovering their true sight, restore their government to its true principles." Internationally, Jefferson declared his desire for France to invade Britain and permanently end the international rivalry.[96]

In the mid-term elections, Democratic-Republicans suffered predictable reversals: Federalist New York newspaper editor Noah Webster noted that after recent events, "opposers were silenced or became moderate & neutral," while Federalists gained "boldness & confidence."[97] Cabot hoped in Massachusetts, "we should have no more Jacobin votes after the present Congress."[98] But even with Federalists sweeping Congressional elections in the Carolinas, the triumph remained partial. Federalist William Smith reported mixed outcomes in other swing-states: New York's "majority of the new members to Congress will be in opposition," New Jersey's returns "unfavourable," Tennessee's "divided," and Kentucky's "opposed to the measures of the government."[99] Federalist party strength broadened but remained shallow. When Congressional Federalists held a secret war caucus in December 1798, the majority opposed pursuing conflict with France.[100]

Formal opposition to Federalist measures followed in Kentucky and Virginia. On August 29 in the symbolic town of Paris in Bourbon County, Kentucky (eighteen miles northeast of Lexington), four to five thousand citizens met under the constitutionally protected occasion of drawing a petition to assert their right "of peaceably assembling together to deliberate upon the propriety or impropriety of public measures and of expressing and publishing our opinions of the same." By "the law of nature" and "federal & state constitutions," they proclaimed their right to resist "any law to the

---

[93] Wolcott, *Memoirs*, Vol. 2, 108.

[94] *Eastern Herald*, October 15, 1798.

[95] *New-Jersey Journal*, October 2, 1798.

[96] Elkins and McKitrick, *Age*, 566.

[97] NYPL Noah Webster Papers, reel 1.

[98] Wolcott, *Memoirs*, Vol. 2, 111.

[99] LC William Smith Papers, 45.

[100] Manning J. Dauer, *The Adams Federalists* (Baltimore: Johns Hopkins Press, 1953), 225.

contrary." They asserted the Alien Acts gave the president "arbitrary, dangerous and despotic powers."[101] Four other Kentucky counties held similar mass
meetings that summer, urging legislative action and organizing militias. On
November 10, the state legislature (consulting Jefferson) passed resolutions
that the states are "not united on the principle of unlimited submission to their
General Government," and as the Bill of Rights protected freedoms of speech
and press from Federal limits, the Sedition Act was unconstitutional.[102]
Organized Democratic-Republican opposition to the Acts took shape.

Madison and Jefferson lent their pens and covert support to the 'Virginia
Resolves' that their state senate passed on Christmas Eve 1798. Denouncing the
"dangerous exercise" of federal power, the resolves asserted the central government had usurped powers not constitutionally granted to them. Railing
against the Alien and Sedition Acts, the resolves asserted such measures would
"transform the present republican system of the United States, into an absolute, or at best a mixed monarchy."[103] With fears rising of disunion or even
secession, no additional states passed matching resolutions and ten of the
fourteen others disavowed them.[104] Still, the controversy continued. Adams
wrote to Abigail, complaining Congress "will dispute about the Alien and
Sedition Laws all winter I suppose."[105] The summer's anti-French upsurge
ebbed.

The Alien and Sedition Acts barely survived the popular reaction.
Reportedly, the "table of congress has been loaded with memorials and remonstrances against these odious acts" from across the country.[106] Angry
Federalists alleged French and opposition subterfuge with Jay claiming "the
Jacobins are still more numerous, more desperate, and more active in this
country than is generally supposed."[107] The legislation barely survived: repeal
failed narrowly in February 1799 and then passed the House in early 1800
before being ignored by the Federalist Senate.[108] As summer 1798's war threats
and passions faded, the bill's partisan ambitions became starker.

Democratic-Republican identity remained entwined with support for
France. Madison worried "loss of liberty at home" would follow "danger real
or pretended from abroad."[109] The French Revolution divided Americans

[101] *Universal Gazette*, October 4, 1798; *Claypoole's American Daily Advertiser*,
September 28, 1798.
[102] *The Virginia and Kentucky Resolutions of 1798 and 1799* (Washington: Elliot, 1832),
15–17.
[103] Ibid., 6.
[104] Elkins and McKitrick, *Age*, 720.
[105] MHS John Adams Papers, reel 392.
[106] LC John Breckinridge Papers, Vol. 17.
[107] Jay, *Selected*, Vol. 4, 253.
[108] Miller, *Crisis*, 180; Cunningham, *Circular*, 158.
[109] Ketcham, *James*, 393.

"into such violent parties, that nothing depending on opinion, nor much even on facts, is received without a strong tincture from the channel through which it passes."[110] Yet the Alien and Sedition Acts were not enforced aggressively enough to effect a full American Thermidor and suppress the opposition. Rather than solidifying public support, Federalists' self-interested persecution of opponents alienated many moderates. Soon, the Democratic-Republican opposition re-commandeered the cause of liberty.

Republican Recovery and the Election of 1800

The "Revolution of 1800" represented as profound a regime change as any of its eighteenth-century predecessors. Despite the potential for disunion or violence in the factionalized United States, across 1799 and 1800 opposition Democratic-Republicans regained American electoral graces and won control of the Federal government. In so doing, they adapted earlier corresponding society models to create a new paradigm as a coordinated political party.

Facing Federalist repression, opposition protesters redeployed older methods. Dissidents erected liberty poles (including several around Philadelphia) covered with seditious graffiti. The pole in Dedham, Massachusetts, featured old and new slogans: "Liberty and Equality – No Stamp Act – No Sedition – No Alien Bills – No Land Tax – Downfall to the Tyrants of America," which soon incited a brawl between the town's Federalist and opposition partisans.[111] Democratic-Republican supporters revivified public banquets, adopting many themes of 1793's societies. New York City's Tammany Society in April 1799 toasted "Freedom of Speech and the Press," the "Marseillais Hymn on the Irish Harp," and their wish "the torch of freedom be carried through the universe to enlighten mankind" while destroying "Thrones of Tyrants."[112] A Pennsylvania banquet celebrated "The Republican cause throughout the world," before publicizing the fall gubernatorial election and their "Republican Corresponding Committee."[113] With the opposition tarred as "Jacobins" regardless their French connections' extent, Republicans remobilized earlier campaigning spirit.

Jefferson asserted that Federalist repression would subside. Already in February 1799, he wrote to Madison of "public sentiment" changing, asserting, "The engine is the press." Jefferson authored numerous anonymous tracts, revivified Republicans' correspondence networks, and circulated clippings with his letters. Only through reasoned debate, Jefferson argued, could Federalists be defeated: should Republicans avoid "show of force," operatives

---

[110] James Madison, *The Papers of James Madison*, William T. Hutchinson et. al., eds. (Charlottesville: University Press of Virginia, 1956-), Vol. 17, 237.

[111] Chambers, *Political*, 140; MHS John Adams Papers, reel 393; Miller, *Crisis*, 114–15.

[112] NYPL Tammany Society Papers.

[113] *Aurora General Advertiser*, May 6, 1799.

could "bear down the evil propensities of the government, by the constitutional means of election and petition."[114] Federalist centralization made the committee model more attractive, as it embodied Democratic-Republicans' ideal of distributing power more broadly. "Power is in its nature the enemy of liberty," wrote Virginia state congressman John Taylor.[115] To the opposition, a mass movement became necessary to prevent a narrow Federalist governing monopoly.

Rebellion flared again, this time not far outside Philadelphia. Reacting against recent property tax-hikes to pay for the Quasi-War's military expenditures, seditious assemblies formed. After several months without making political headway, covert rebel bands began moving from town to town on horseback harassing and threatening taxmen. When authorities arrested and detained eighteen men, local auctioneer John Fries mobilized 140 others to liberate them from the jail in Bethlehem, Pennsylvania. Adams deployed troops for "dispersing all unlawful combinations" opposing the tax.[116] Fries was arrested and convicted.

Fries' Rebellion did not dampen mainstream opposition as the Whiskey Rebellion had five years earlier. By springtime, the opposition's growing energy became apparent to their opponents. Ames wrote in the *Boston Gazette*, "The jacobins have at last made their own discipline perfect: they are trained, officered, regimented and formed to subordination, in a manner that our militia have never yet equaled." New converts were sought among "every class of men," with party operatives infiltrating "Every threshing floor, every husking, every party at work on a house-frame or raising a building, the very funerals are infected with bawlers or whisperers against government."[117] Though the Sedition Act applied to speech as well as print, dissidents quickly realized the small American judicial system could only process a limited number of cases.[118]

The international situation improved. French authorities withdrew prior bribery demands, promising Adams's new American envoy would "be treated with the respect due to the representative of a free, independent, and powerful country."[119] Adams reopened negotiations. The Federalist naval buildup influenced changes at sea. Harper in February 1799 noted that with increased patrols, "privateers have wholly disappeared from our coasts" and shipping

---

[114] Malone, *Jefferson*, 414; Cunningham, *Jeffersonian*, 129–30.
[115] LC Henry Innes Papers MSS 24201, Vol. 1, 75.
[116] Paul Douglas Newman, *Fries's Rebellion: The Enduring Struggle for the American Revolution* (Philadelphia: University of Pennsylvania Press, 2004); MHS John Adams Papers, reel 394.
[117] Cunningham, *Jeffersonian*, 202.
[118] Miller, *Crisis*, 138.
[119] Ferling, *John*, 375.

insurance fell 50 percent.[120] Prospects of peace and economic recovery lessened the fears behind 1798's saber-rattling.

In Pennsylvania, the autumn 1799 gubernatorial election became a proxy for the next year's presidential battle. Each side mobilized behind correspondence committees with Democratic-Republicans running the state's Chief Justice Thomas McKean. Mobilization spread across county and town levels – one September Bucks County meeting (north of Philadelphia) drew 350 party activists, who organized ten simultaneous town meetings three weeks later at precisely 2 p.m. to support a common program and fixed slate of candidates. Fearing new restrictions, Bucks County's committee (in Fries' Rebellion territory) asserted that as "freedom of election remains unimpaired," patriots needed "to avail themselves of it, to procure a change of men and a change of measures."[121] Democratic-Republicans published their structure and plans. Despite potential sedition charges, grassroots excitement bolstered the campaign with partisans distributing letters and handbills. Corresponding club life developed on a scale unseen since 1775.

Once Federalists demurred from directly attacking the party organizations, even when publicizing via the press, the opposition's resolve grew bolder. Over eighty-five recognizably partisan pro-Republican newspapers circulated by the election, a two-third increase from before the Sedition Act.[122] Yet Federalist lassitude did not lessen Republican ire: a suburban Philadelphia meeting at Passyunk denounced British influence's "banefull effects" considering Federalist "principles in direct opposition to the spirit of Republican Government" and "subversive of that freedom and Independence" at the American system's heart.[123] Only by out-mobilizing opponents could Democratic-Republicans right the system. Another Bucks County committee meeting considered that "if a party, by the influence of wealth, office, and various other means, can keep themselves continually in power," then popular sovereignty became endangered.[124] The committees focused not just on publicizing candidates, but surveilling the elections. Philadelphia's Corresponding Committee asked anyone witnessing "irregularities" to report them to their local committees.[125] The opposition asserted it would no longer be intimidated.

Pennsylvania's Federalist gubernatorial candidate, James Ross, ran on a law-and-order platform. The *Philadelphia Gazette* printed a circular calling for those wanting to "suppress the spirit of anarchy and insurrection" to vote for him. Only thereby could "the original spirit of American liberty" not be "adulterated by the new and dangerous tenets that divide or desolate the

---

[120] MDHS James Bayard Papers, Vol. 1.
[121] *Claypoole's American Daily Advertiser*, September 21, 1799.
[122] Pasley, *Tyranny*, 126.
[123] *Herald of Liberty*, September 2, 1799.
[124] *Claypoole's American Daily Advertiser*, September 7, 1799.
[125] *Aurora General Advertiser*, April 16, 1799.

greatest portion of Europe."[126] Atlantic analogies remained the most effective rhetorical strategy for rousing support. Concurrently, Federalists tried to match Republicans' organization, attempting to bring townships into their committee network, and – fostering the appearance of widespread consensus – publicizing their resolutions in handbills and newspaper notices.[127] Winning an election without party mobilization now appeared virtually impossible.

The Republican McKean won Pennsylvania's election. The groundswell caught Federalists by surprise, as Adams received word that even in former strongholds they had miscalculated their strength "by some hundreds of votes."[128] The election proved a bellwether. In New Jersey, where opposition representatives had unsuccessfully introduced amended versions of the Virginia and Kentucky resolves, Republicans won legislative control. Also by November, sixteen hundred signatures were collected statewide calling for "the people's choosing the Electors" for president instead of the state legislature.[129] A Vermont Congressman (and newspaperman), Matthew Lyon, won reelection while imprisoned under the Sedition Act for anti-Federalist writings.[130] From Federalist Massachusetts, Ames prophesized "the great states leaguing together under democratic governors" into a muscular coalition.[131]

As democracy developed in America, it entered its death throes in France with Napoleon Bonaparte's 18 Brumaire coup in November 1799. "I will never believe that man is incapable of self-government," Jefferson responded, opining, "this last revolution is an additional lesson against a standing army," as Bonaparte could have come to power no other way.[132] The Federalist Harper, meanwhile, celebrated the death of a Revolution featuring "ten years of agitation, anarchy, proscription, murder, pillage and crimes of every kind," and now a dictator "invested with a power more absolute in effect than any King of France ever enjoyed."[133] Abigail Adams mocked her husband's opponents, writing to John Quincy, "The Jacobins in this Country have never been so completely foild, they know not what to say, to execrate Bunaparte they dare not."[134] John Quincy blamed "That hideous monster of democracy" creating unintended consequences.[135] French regime change, however, benefitted

[126] *Philadelphia Gazette*, August 9, 1799.
[127] *Claypoole's American Daily Advertiser*, September 3, 1799.
[128] MHS John Adams Papers, reel 396.
[129] NJHS Mahlon Dickerson Letterbook, Box 3.
[130] Carl E. Prince, *New Jersey's Jeffersonian Republicans: The Genesis of an Early Party Machine* (Chapel Hill: University of North Carolina Press, 1967), 33; Ferling, *Leap*, 452.
[131] Wolcott, *Memoirs*, Vol. 2, 319.
[132] Jefferson, *Papers*, Vol. 31, 488.
[133] MDHS James Bayard Papers, Vol. 1.
[134] MHS John Adams Papers, reel 397.
[135] John Quincy Adams, *Writings* (New York: Greenwood Press, 1968), Vol. 2, 457.

American negotiations, as President Adams found a more pragmatic ruler willing to settle differences. The Quasi-War faded away.

With the Republicans having regained momentum, each party contested the Election of 1800 in an unprecedentedly heated and well-organized manner. Committees of Correspondence spread across the nation. Virginia Republicans set up a Richmond central committee to "communicate useful information to the people relative to the election" in every county. Expecting a tough contest, the committee sought "to repel every effort which may be made to injure the ticket" by opponents.[136] The five-man committee possessed ninety satellites. New Jersey, despite little prior Republican organizing, now boasted committees in every county and most towns.[137] Maryland Republican committees innovated their own publicity practices, appointing speakers to "canvass" for candidates at public gatherings from church services to sporting events.[138]

Grassroots Republican support grew stronger. Traveling across Pennsylvania, Federalist Connecticut Senator Uriah Tracy wrote from Pittsburgh that partisans "are establishing Democratic presses and newspapers in almost every town," while "Federal presses are failing for want of support." Immigrants disproportionately joined the opposition: Tracy described "many Irishmen, and with a few exceptions they are United Irishmen, Free Masons, and the most God-provoking Democrats on this side of Hell."[139] Abigail Adams considered the opposition unstoppable, as "No jury would be returned to convict them" under the Sedition law.[140] The extent of disobedience created powerful momentum against the Federalists.

At the moment Federalists needed greater unity than ever, their party splintered. As Adams's popularity waned, Wolcott (serving as Treasury Secretary) in 1799 already complained, "a want of concert is visible among the friends of government." By June 1800, he predicted "no administration of the government by President Adams can be successful," as his "prejudices are too violent, and the resentments of men of influence are too keen."[141] Hamilton broke with Adams, alleging the president "alluded" to him heading a "British faction" undermining the government.[142] Adams, now believing French peace on the horizon, adopted a centrist course, refusing to indulge Anglophiles with anti-French proclamations.

Presidential voting in 1800 remained a complex and lengthy process with Electoral College members chosen by different methods. Indeed, the process

[136] Sharp, *Deadlocked*, 120; Cunningham, *Jeffersonian*, 151.
[137] Ferling, *Adams*, 144; Cunningham, *Jeffersonian*, 154; *Centinel of Freedom*, April 1, 1800.
[138] Witcover, *Party*, 68.
[139] Wolcott, *Memoirs*, Vol. 2, 398.
[140] MHS John Adams Papers, reel 397.
[141] Wolcott, *Memoirs*, Vol. 2, 299 and 371.
[142] Ibid., Vol. 2, 376.

had become less democratic since 1796, with Federalists pushing to have electoral votes decided by state legislatures instead of popular voting. Four of nine states allowing direct popular voting in 1796 now empowered legislatures to select delegates.[143] Elsewhere, the party in power enacted regional delegate selection, hoping to divide southern and swing states. Federalist North Carolina Congressman William Barry Grove argued, "Faction & party have a greater field to display itself" without elite safeguards.[144] Republicans needed to control state legislatures to gain electoral votes, as capturing the presidency required triumphing in an array of contests.

Republican momentum built with New York's May 5 election. Under the rules in place, the party winning the state legislative majority controlled the twelve presidential electoral votes. Burr's aggressive organizing, motivated by an expected vice presidential nomination, inspired new "ward committees" mobilizing New York City neighborhoods. Burr directed events from a central tavern headquarters open *en permanence*, whose partisans were encouraged to frequent with free drinks and complementary mattresses upstairs. All sorts were welcomed to join the campaign. Whereas Federalists built a nativist reputation, Burr sought ethnic minority votes, employing German-speaking operatives. Burr also excelled at closed-door politics, entertaining at his estate north of the city (future Greenwich Village). Equally important, he recruited candidates with name recognition, "men likely to run well," including General Horatio Gates and former Governor Clinton, while Federalists ran little-known nominees. Hamilton, belatedly following Burr's innovations and riding between polling stations on Election Day on a white horse, could not stem the electoral tide.[145] With the presidential election poised to determine "our future destiny," one New York politician wrote, "The management and industry of Col. Burr has effected all that the friends Civil Liberty could possibly desire."[146] Republicans won the state legislature, and the presidential electoral map became favorable. Although Hamilton urged Governor Jay to violate the state constitution by appointing presidential electors himself, arguing the voting results would "sacrifice the substantial interests of society," the outcome stood.[147] Electioneering became expected – with its efficacy all too apparent.

---

[143] Sharp, *Deadlocked*, 116.

[144] University of North Carolina Special Collections, William Barry Grove Papers.

[145] Ferling, *Leap*, 454; Ferling, *Adams*, 130; Isenberg, *Fallen* 196–200; Freeman, "Corruption and Compromise in the Election of 1800: The Process of Politics on the National Stage," in *The Revolution of 1800: Democracy, Race & the New Republic*, James Horn, Jan Ellen Lewis, and Peter S. Onouf, eds. (Charlottesville: University of Virginia, 2002), 98; Rosemarie Zagarri, "Gender and the First Party System," in *Federalists Reconsidered*, Doron Ben-Atar and Barbara B. Oberg, eds. (Charlottesville: University Press of Virginia, 1998), 124.

[146] NYHS Albert Gallatin Papers, reel 4.

[147] Jay, *Selected*, Vol. 4, 271.

The July 4, 1800 celebrations evinced an accelerating Democratic-Republican movement on the precipice of power. In Pennsylvania, a Jefferson toast led to a sixteen-gun salute, followed by wishes for "A speedy and honorable termination of all existing differences, between the United States and the French Republic," and celebrating "The friends of Liberty throughout the world." In New Jersey, a toast to the "Federal Constitution" called for protecting it against "all assaults, foreign and domestic," while supporting "law, not tyranny."[148] Denouncing the Alien & Sedition Acts, Democratic-Republicans became a confident movement facing down their retreating opponents.

The contrast between parties – one surging and the other fracturing – heightened by late summer. Congressman Harper, surveying electoral projections, spread alarm: "Mr. Adams cannot be elected without either getting two votes at least from South Carolina, or seven from North Carolina instead of five, or nine from Maryland instead of seven."[149] Yet the Federalists increasingly fractured. Ames complained, "federalists scarcely deserve the name of party," being "shaken by every prospect of labour or hazard."[150] Viewing the opposition, "The Jacobins appear to be completely organized throughout the United States," Massachusetts lawyer Theophilus Parsons wrote to Jay with "agents dispersed in every direction."[151] Concurrently, Federalist friends faded, avoiding growing dysfunction. Pennsylvania's Federalist nominating assembly was "very thinly attended" with a "want of influential characters" seeking election.[152]

The Sedition Act, no longer effectively muzzling dissent, hindered the Federalist ticket. Many indictments came to trial during the campaign, and the near-ubiquity of convictions in northern states heightened opposition distaste for Federalist-appointed judges. Democratic-Republican newspapers continued under new editors with only two folding after prosecution. Over the Adams administration's last two and a half years, opposition newspapers doubled.[153] Republicans denounced the government's tactics with Kentucky Congressman John Fowler condemning the Sedition Act, as "an engine in the hand of the Executive administration to oppress the printers of patriotic newspapers" with "almost every Republican press north of the Potomack" facing charges.[154] Opposition papers nevertheless became more vocal. New York's *American Citizen* heralded the "increase of republican sentiment, the diffusion of knowledge, and the gradual decay of that unreasonable

[148] *Aurora General Advertiser*, July 25, 1800.
[149] LC Harrison Gray Otis Papers, reel 3.
[150] Wolcott, *Memoirs*, Vol. 2, 396.
[151] Witcover, *Party*, 70.
[152] HSP Tench Coxe Papers MICRO 18,376, reel 71.
[153] Halperin, *Alien*, 73, 99.
[154] Cunningham, *Circular*, 212.

attachment of stupid adherence to monarchy" with the "liberty of the press" triumphant.[155] Freedom became associated with the political opposition.

With electoral projections turning in their favor, Republicans grew emboldened. "If the republicans are only vigilant there can be no doubt of their success," wrote New Jersey organizer Mahlon Dickerson after the New York victory.[156] The Federalist Goodrich, meanwhile, complained from Hartford, that since the New York election, "Democrats have taken courage to come out into open day" and campaign vigorously.[157] Beckley, updating his strategic map in August, with New York in hand, expected several Connecticut electoral votes, significant Maryland and Carolina majorities, the "moral certainty of success" in New Jersey and Delaware, and electoral sweeps in Georgia, Kentucky, Tennessee, Pennsylvania, and Virginia.[158] Federalists, meanwhile, displayed internal distrust, with Adams alleging, "Hamilton has been on a tour through New England to persuade the people to choose electors who will give a unanimous vote for Gen. Pinckney," but not Adams himself.[159] Hamilton did author a pamphlet denouncing Adams for lacking "talents adapted to the administration of Government," blaming him for having "sown the seeds of discord at home, and lowered the reputation of the Government abroad."[160] Interest in Adams's reelection faltered, with Cabot dangerously arguing "Jefferson's election would tend to reunite the federal party" in opposition thereafter.[161] Only fear of annihilation rallied Federalists as each party's electoral momentum became apparent.

Down-ballot, campaign events, debates, and popular street politics proliferated. Adams's son Thomas described "Electioneering warfare" intensifying as elections approached.[162] Both parties' candidates in Maryland embarked on speaking tours. A traveler in the new Federal City, renamed Washington that November, noted "Shouting matches" common between supporters and even politicians themselves. In one event, the two candidates running for the nearby Prince George's County seat in the Maryland assembly each spoke for an hour, while in the crowd, after "Brandy, Cider & whisky were dealt out with a liberal hand ... Cursing, Fighting &c." ensued. The Republicans subdued their opponents to "close the whole with 3 Huzzas for Jefferson."[163] Far from the

[155] *American Citizen*, April 17, 1800.
[156] NJHS Mahlon Dickerson Letterbook, Box 3.
[157] Wolcott, *Memoirs*, Vol. 2, 411.
[158] VHS John Beckley Papers.
[159] MHS John Adams Papers, reel 120, 188.
[160] Hamilton, *Letter from Alexander Hamilton, Concerning the Public Conduct and Character of John Adams, Esq. President of the United States* (New York: Lang, 1800), 4, 23.
[161] Hamilton, *Papers*, Vol. 25, 63.
[162] MHS John Adams Papers, reel 398.
[163] HSP MSS 39, Louis Beebe Journal, Vol. 3, 8; Cunningham, *Jeffersonian*, 191.

Federal founders' ideal of independent men dispassionately evaluating candidates, politics verged on a brawl.

Sensing victory near, Democratic-Republican rhetoric radicalized as they attempted to rout the opposition. New York's *American Citizen* newspaper already in April considered the moment to augur a democratic revolution:

> The election approaches, and now is the time to display that democratic energy, that patriotic firmness and that love of liberty, which generated the revolution of the western world, and astonished the corrupt court of the ancient hemisphere, by unfurling successfully the banners of freedom, and restoring to the lost character of man its true dignity and civil excellence.[164]

American and Atlantic revolutions appeared to near fruition. Democratic-Republican committee of Essex County, New Jersey, in late August asserted the election would "fix our national character, determine whether republicanism, or aristocracy, is to prevail," urging supporters to mobilize against those possessing "an irreconcilable hatred against the sovereignty of the people, under the name of democracy." Given the "madness of the aristocratic faction," the committee asked partisans to "seal your political salvation, and entitle you to the thanks of the whole human race."[165] Still, democratic rhetorical excesses could backfire: Gabriel's Rebellion, a late August slave uprising in Richmond planning to set fires, kidnap Governor Monroe, and seize the state arsenal and treasury, led Federalists (with little precise justification) to present it as an outgrowth of Republicans' heated rhetoric on liberty.[166] Many feared heated political battles could lead to social degeneration.

Although rumors of ruptured French negotiations continued through the summer, potentially aiding the Federalists, a peace settlement arrived in October. The Treaty of Môrtefontaine recognized America's right to trade most items with belligerents. Though not compensating American merchants for past seizures, the agreement met general acquiescence, removing French relations as a campaign issue.[167] Bonaparte, as an anti-Jacobin centrist, now seemed a potential administration ally: Federalist Oliver Ellsworth, Envoy Extraordinary to France, declared, "the reign of Jacobinism is over in France," and peace at hand.[168] The French rivalry ended – ironically, just as the Francophile party was poised to take power.

---

[164] *American Citizen*, April 26, 1800.
[165] *Constitutional Telegraphe*, August 30, 1800; *Herald of Liberty*, September 29, 1800.
[166] Taylor, *American*, 422.
[167] LC Ebenezer Foote Papers MSS 20941, reel 1; Marshall, *Papers*, Vol. 4, 240; Lawrence S. Kaplan, *Jefferson and France: An Essay on Politics and Political Ideas* (New Haven: Yale University Press, 1967), 86; Ferling, *John Adams*, 408.
[168] Wolcott, *Memoirs*, Vol. 2, 434.

The election turned to the Republicans in October voting, with Maryland and soon almost the entire South and West siding with Jefferson and Burr. Pennsylvania official Andrew Ellicott enthused to Jefferson that "this will be distinguished as an epoch in which republicanism not only became triumphant, but be too firmly established ever again to be shaken by the advocates for Monarchy."[169] A revolutionary shift loomed: Jefferson himself declared the Maryland victory a renaissance of "the spirit of 76."[170] Although in some respects Democratic-Republicans' victory remained partial – indeed, without the southern electoral votes being weighted to include three-fifths slave representation, or several hundred more votes in New York City, Adams would have triumphed – Republicans successfully built an electoral coalition.[171]

Due to the election's undifferentiated double-voting, requiring two choices for president, with the second-place finisher winning the vice presidency, resulting in equal votes for Jefferson and Burr, the Electoral College descended into confusion. Many expected South Carolina to decide the election, but the state united for both Republicans instead of native son and Federalist vice presidential Candidate Charles Pinckney. Alongside Democratic-Republican party discipline elsewhere, the Electoral College ended in a tie. Few predicted this: only four years earlier, electoral votes went to thirteen candidates with Jefferson besting the second Federalist candidate by nine votes. The House of Representatives would decide the election in February. The crisis created opportunities for either a Federalist coalition with Burr or negotiating concessions with the Jeffersonians. Backroom betrayals threatened: Wolcott on November 28 optimistically asserted, "If the democrats are certain that Mr. Jefferson cannot be elected, they will support Mr. Adams; not from personal attachment, or confidence, but with the view of fostering, and increasing the divisions among the federalists."[172] Possibilities abounded in the uncertain atmosphere.

Burr's ambitions were checked only through a combination of Hamilton's influence among Federalists and fellow Republicans' intimidation. Already in August, Hamilton denounced his future dueling mate as a man who would "attempt to reform the Government a la Buonaparte. He is as unprincipled & dangerous a man as any country can boast; as true a Cataline as ever met in midnight conclave."[173] Democratic-Republicans resorted to threats: Maryland Congressman Samuel Smith wrote to Burr in January, "the Feds will attempt to disunite us," and should he attempt a new coalition, Jefferson-supporting states would consider it "an usurpation and will I am inclined to think and

[169] Jefferson, *Papers*, Vol. 32, 224.
[170] Ibid., 227.
[171] Gary Wills, *Negro President: Jefferson and the Slave Power* (Boston: Houghton Mifflin, 2003).
[172] Wolcott, *Memoirs*, Vol. 2, 449.
[173] Hamilton, *Papers*, Vol. 25, 57.

act accordingly."[174] Jefferson himself cautioned of an "abyss at which every sincere patriot must shudder" and prophesized a new Constitutional Convention should Federalists maneuver for a different candidate.[175]

Though Jefferson, almost two decades later in retirement, referred to the events as "the revolution of 1800," the proceedings could have followed their bloodier eighteenth-century predecessors had Jefferson's faction been out-maneuvered. Burr refused to withdraw from presidential consideration, and conspiracy fears multiplied. Gallatin believed that with "desperate" Federalists working to prevent Jefferson's election, "either dissolution of the Union if that usurpation should be supported by New England, or a punishment of the usurpers" would follow.[176] Republicans asserted they would "riske all" to effectuate regime change. Rumors spread around Washington, DC., in mid-February of Federalist rebels seizing the federal arsenal at Philadelphia.[177] Political passions remained too high and regional divisions too great to allow Federalists into a coalition government.

Jefferson's election on the thirty-sixth Congressional ballot on February 17, after a Delaware Federalist abstention broke the tie, enabled peaceful regime change. Celebrations followed through much of the country, as bells rang in Philadelphia for two days.[178] A North Carolina celebration toasted the "Tree of Liberty Moistened by the tears of Aristocracy," and in Kentucky a partisan exulted how his compatriots, "termed a faction, the enemies of the Constitution" became "the majority, the friends of the constitution."[179] While Jefferson, in his inaugural address, famously declared, "We are all republicans: we are all federalists," while proclaiming an end to "political intolerance," the Federalists once deprived of power receded into regional, and eventually total, insignificance.[180]

Though more uprisings and battles around the Atlantic basin were still to come – as Napoleon's regime expanded (and then retracted) across Europe, Haitians expelled the French, and Latin Americans rose against Spain – the great wave of Atlantic Revolutions receded. The American Ambassador soon reported from Paris that the "Terrorist Party" were "completely down and will not probably rise again," while in America conventional wisdom came to

[174] LC Samuel Smith Papers MSS 40469, reel 1.

[175] Merill D. Peterson, *Thomas Jefferson and the New Nation: A Biography* (Oxford: Oxford University Press, 1970), 644; Freeman, "Corruption," 90.

[176] NYHS Albert Gallatin Papers, reel 4.

[177] NJHS Mahlon Dickerson Papers, Box 1, folder 11; VHS, John Beckley Papers.

[178] NJHS Mahlon Dickerson Diary, Box 2.

[179] Delbert Harold Gilpatrick, *Jeffersonian Democracy in North Carolina, 1789–1816* (New York: Columbia University Press, 1931), 124; David Waldstreicher, *In the Midst of Perpetual Fetes: The Making of American Nationalism, 1776–1820* (Chapel Hill: University of North Carolina Press, 1997), 189.

[180] Jefferson, *Papers*, Vol. 33, 149.

disdain foreign examples and focus on the developing of what they increasingly considered a distinctly "American" political system.[181] Though little resembling the ideals of organizers in 1765, 1775, 1787, or 1793, a party claiming "Democratic" principles solidified power.

Conclusion

The new Democratic-Republican order took power only after a decade of party organizing, French interactions, and electoral contests. Though French influence became more symbolic than direct after 1794, the Jacobin model deeply influenced the form the Democratic Party took. The Age of Revolutions' most durable progeny adapted the era's central social movement model, committees of correspondence, into a party organization – aspects of which continued operating continuously, while others revivified during election campaigns – that could regularize the republic's political process. Though more elite-directed than most 1790s corresponding societies, parties proved more successful at integrating popular input (particularly from voting adult white males) into the governing system. Whereas corresponding society models elsewhere met suppression, in America they survived the Atlantic Thermidor by developing a new paradigm to capture control of government, in ways that would slowly be adapted by Britain and other nineteenth-century emerging representative governments.

Much was lost in the transition from popular associations to parties. The new Democratic Party remained dominated by its elite, elected beneficiaries and slave to southern interests that left the abolitionist and egalitarian ideals of many of its preceding social movements behind. Nevertheless, party formation – for all its messiness during election cycles – provided a venue and process for working through political debates more effectively (over the long term) than the intimidation of the Sons of Liberty, Jacobins, or United Irishmen.

---

[181] LC Robert R. Livingston Papers MSS 60194; Cotlar, *Tom*, 111.

~

Conclusion

John Adams, fourteen years into retirement at Peacefield in the Massachusetts countryside, looked back on the initial Boston Committee of Correspondence and remarked,

> What an engine! France imitated it, and produced a revolution. England and Scotland were upon the point of imitating it, in order to produce another revolution, and all Europe was inclined to imitate it for the same revolutionary purposes.
> The history of the world for the last thirty years is a sufficient commentary upon it.

Though still considering "committees of secret correspondence are dangerous machines," the revolutionary motor of his lifetime was apparent.[1]

The predominantly nation-based histories of the Age of Revolutions have obscured how the actors themselves understood the tide of events. Rather than a fragmented Atlantic basin focused on separate national progressions, which have often been further fragmented by particularlist historiographies, this study instead chronicles an unbroken chain of movements creatively adapting organizing tactics to their own advantage. Each movement examined here explicitly borrowed from their predecessors as they built their campaigns as "Friends of Freedom," creatively adapting rhetoric, models, and strategy from their predecessors to pursue their own visions of liberty.

American innovations created this new model with the Sons of Liberty affiliating British-style clubs to mobilize an unprecedentedly unified response to the hated Stamp Act. The similarity of grievances and protest tactics across the colonies – spread by newspaper accounts and letters – motivated colonists to combine their efforts, sacrificing autonomy for solidarity. The new organization helped enforce nonimportation, led militia organizing, and engaged in political lobbying. While the Sons of Liberty declined after the Stamp Act's repeal, and merchant associations failed to successfully galvanize boycotting efforts against the Townshend Acts, Committees of Correspondence arose between 1772 and 1775, extending the affiliated club model into becoming

---

[1] Adams, *Works*, Vol. 10, 197.

an alternative government for the colonies. Rather than deferring to the mysteries of ancient government, American Patriots rapidly developed the infrastructure to overthrow British rule and institute a new regime incorporating unprecedented degrees of democratic participation and liberty.

British and Irish reformers of the 1760s to 1780s, having joined the colonists in agitating against the Stamp Act, soon applied the new American model to their own campaigns. John Wilkes' Society of Supporters of the Bill of Rights, with a Virginia planter as its secretary, constructed the first comparable British network, albeit on a smaller scale, to seek expanded political liberties. While internal divisions and Wilkes's greed undermined the campaign, such tactics grew in popularity during the American War of Independence. Disgusted with the ruling ministry's corruption and incompetence, an Association movement rose among British voters for Parliamentary Reform and, more dramatically, the Irish Volunteer militia movement armed tens of thousands, nominally to fend off a possible Franco-Spanish invasion, but soon turning its attention to Irish political autonomy and potential structural changes to its Parliament. Amid the common imperial crisis of the late 1770s and early 1780s, activists across the Isles borrowed American tactics to contest the closed and corrupt ways of the British Parliament.

Movements for religious liberty in Britain and America soon adapted such campaigns for liberty to push for new standards of toleration and religious freedom. Although British Dissenters had previously used their congregational networks to lobby Parliament to repeal the Test and Corporation Act restrictions, they had remained silent for decades before several prominent ministers became involved in the American prerevolutionary controversies. In 1772–1773, active organizing and lobbying recommenced, bringing their cause (unsuccessfully) before Parliament. In America, Dissenters used the American Revolution to fulfill their long-standing grievances against established churches, developing alliances and in most areas successfully agitating for disestablishment and broad religious freedom. In the aftermath of American independence, British Dissenters corresponded with Americans and increasingly allied with Parliamentary reformers, revivifying their campaign to come within twenty House of Commons votes of passing repeal. Moreover, their campaign stalwarts soon played integral roles in radicalizing abolitionist and political movements.

Modern abolitionism developed from the transatlantic political fervor of the 1770s. Quakers, a dissenting sect influential across Britain's empire, contested traditional Christian justifications of slavery over the seventeenth and eighteenth centuries. By the time Quakers withdrew into neutrality for America's revolutionary war, many increasingly questioned the place of slavery within a new regime based on natural rights. The Continental Congress banned the slave trade during the Revolutionary War and motivated states thereafter to abolish trafficking and begin eliminating slavery itself. After Britain's parliamentary reform efforts failed under the Younger Pitt's administration, reformers used political corresponding society models for an antislavery effort that became the era's largest campaign, drawing hundreds of thousands of petition-signatures. Already versed in empathizing with claimants across the oceans, British and American friends of freedom now sought to improve conditions for the Atlantic's most oppressed peoples.

French Revolutionaries quickly understood, empathized with, and incorporated Anglo-American practices into their budding revolution. The French began antislavery organizing soon after the British, sought overseas models as they refounded their government, and in late 1789 organized the Jacobin Club network on the inspiration of London's Revolution Society. Over the next four years, the Jacobin Club network developed into the most powerful force in French politics, with more than six thousand locals and a central Paris branch that served as the National Assembly's radical caucus. By the war's advent in April 1792, the Jacobins aggressively endorsed internationalizing the revolution, spreading their Rights of Man and endorsing universal rights for all peoples. Pushing further, faster than their Anglo-American brethren, the Terror of 1793–1794, followed by the Jacobins' suppression over the following year, served as a cautionary tale – but the near-utopian hopes revolutionaries spread set off a second, radicalizing wave of movement organizing around the Atlantic basin.

Men of color in Saint-Domingue adapted French-style organizations to lobby the French to enforce their revolutionary principles. The rise of the abolitionist Friends of the Blacks in France inspired the creation of an aggressive anti-abolitionist network, the Club Massiac, attempting to win colonial autonomy amid France's political disorder. The arrival of news of the Bastille's fall in Saint-Domingue led Free Men of Color to organize in pursuit of civil and voting rights, developing transatlantic networks to lobby for the National Assembly's intervention. The democratizing order in Saint-Domingue splintered under the antagonisms of race, region, and faction, leading to near-civil war conditions even among the whites as all sides sought to utilize French associational models to their advantage. The colony was further destabilized by Vincent Ogé, a mixed-race colonist and abolitionist Friend of the Blacks, who returned from Bordeaux and Paris via antislavery circles in London to start an uprising for racially equal rights. Amid this ferment, in August 1791 slaves organized their own surreptitious networks along the colony's northern plain and started the Haitian Revolution.

British and Irish reformers each sought to use the French Revolution to spread and radicalize campaigns in their own countries. With Britain surpassed as Europe's freest country, in 1792 the London Corresponding Society, featuring multinational French radicals and abolitionist stalwarts including Equiano, attempted to bring a Jacobin-style associational network to Britain. Their efforts were overshadowed, however, by a loyalist organization borrowing their tactics, the Society for the Preservation of Liberty and Property from Republicans and Levellers. In Ireland, the Society of United Irishmen formed in 1791, seeking to unite Catholics and Protestants in pursuit of Irish democratization and self-determination. The Irishmen moved underground after the beginning of war with France in 1793, becoming a conspiratorial organization seeking to win French assistance for an anti-British uprising. After a failed 1796 French expedition, the Irishmen rose with disastrous results in 1798.

American Democratic-Republicans adapted Jacobin-style clubs to disrupt the Federalist consensus, enabling the rise of party politics. Founded with the help of the Girondin ambassador Genêt, Democratic-Republicans embraced French Revolutionary ardor and sought to bring similar levels of democratic political engagement to the United States. The society's marginal role in helping create a "Committee of Public Safety" amid the 1794 Whiskey Rebellion in Western Pennsylvania, followed by Washington's denunciation of opposition societies, gravely injured the organization. The opposition's shift into electoral political organizing amid the Jay's Treaty controversy in 1795 allowed the cause to escape the "Atlantic Thermidor" that suppressed its brethren in Europe. With French issues a national litmus (with Federalists backing the British), the Democratic-Republicans coordinated a national network through state and county-level correspondence committees to strongly contest the election of 1796 and capture power in 1800. Francophile American clubs spurred the creation of modern political parties, which together with continued dissident social movements provided the chief organizing models for modern democratic politics.

More than nationally contained political progressions, we see a series of interconnected campaigns around the Revolutionary Atlantic, seeking greater liberty through associating together. In each of the cases studied, international examples prompted activists to adopt methods foreign to their national political traditions in pursuit of bringing home changes occurring elsewhere. Rather than "Atlantic" events being marginal to national histories of the Revolutionary Era, we instead find international ideas and methods circulating to inspire ambitious movements for freedom.

Understanding the development of the modern democratic tradition requires tolerance for the many partial, incomplete solutions achieved (or sometimes even sought) as activists worked to implement changes to the inegalitarian societies of the late eighteenth century. Activists struggled with the uncertainties of revolutionary change, while simultaneously not knowing if more moderate and incrementalist approaches had a greater probability of success. Yet their movements' broad inclusivity (and often-universalistic rhetoric) made virtually anything seem possible. Old barriers of race, class, gender, and nationality became assailable, though many proved too sturdy to be quickly overthrown. Clubs spread ideals of fraternity, displaying the power of an assembled people and their potential to effect major changes. If the radical changes debated by these movements necessarily remained an uncompleted project in their era, the fundamental challenges of liberty and inclusion they posed often remain ours too.

What struck contemporaries most was not these movements' limitations, but rather their audacity. The cosmopolitanism of the Enlightenment era, with writers regularly seeking global precedents to justify their philosophies of politics and human nature, furthered an urge to emulate alluring, distant exemplars. As the Age of Revolution unfolded, international movements recurrently inspired reformers and revolutionaries to seek radical new possibilities lying outside their domestic political traditions and local experience. Belief in the possibilities of freedom and universally applicable models led radicals to believe faraway examples could fuel change at home.

Demonstrating the historical genealogy of social movements to be wider than Charles Tilly's Anglocentric conception allows us to see them as consubstantial with the development of democratic politics.[2] The diversity of eighteenth-century actors, using such methods to push for greater rights and participation in government, made such campaigns one of the chief motors for expanding democratic politics. The methods the Sons of Liberty pioneered proved readily comprehensible and adaptable by a great variety of actors over the course of the revolutionary era. Subsequently, social movement organizing has remained foundational for advancing and maintaining democracies.

Transnational affinities between social movements should not be seen as an eighteenth-century exception, but rather have proved a rule among many of modern history's most influential movements for political and social change. The underground Carbonari network opposing the early nineteenth-century Restoration governments centered in Italy (some branches with names like "Universal Republic" and "Liberty or Death") stretched from Russia to France and Spain, while more moderate liberal clubs organized for constitutional government.[3] The French Revolution of 1830 gave rise to a new *Société des amis du peuple* contesting the rightward plunge of the July Monarchy and a *Société des Droits de l'Homme et du Citoyen* that plotted the failed June 1834 uprising. In the regime's later years, banquets drawing tens of thousands sparked the regime's fall.[4] During the revolutionary wave of 1848, proponents and opponents alike agreed with the Austrian archconservative Clemens von Metternich: "When Paris sneezes, Europe catches cold." Clubs again organized around similar ideals of liberty – Parisians alone founding more than two hundred clubs, three of which took the Jacobins' name – while insurgents in

---

[2] Tilly, *Social Movements*.

[3] Richard Stites, *The Four Horsemen: Riding to Liberty in Post-Napoleonic Europe* (Oxford: Oxford University Press, 2014), esp. 138.

[4] Jill Harsin, *Barricades: The War of the Streets in Revolutionary Paris, 1830–1848* (New York: Palgrave, 2002), 49–51, 84; John J. Baughman, "The French Banquet Campaign of 1847–48," *Journal of Modern History* 31, no. 1 (1959), 1–15.

Vienna founded a Committee of Public Safety and a Democratic Congress club network across the German states developed 950 locals with half a million members.[5] Modern socialism spread through a series of three International Workingmen's Associations. The *Inaugural Address* of the first, cowritten by Karl Marx in 1869, not only urged "Proletarians of all countries, unite!" but argued worker "numbers weigh only in the balance, if united by combination and led by knowledge."[6] The local workers councils named Soviets that were supposed to govern revolutionary Russia sought to expand the Revolutionary Era's emphasis on self-government into labor.

Contemporary history has been marked by waves of change in common moments of revolution and revolt – most prominently, those centered in 1968, 1989, and 2011 – in which the power of international examples emboldened many to act as they had not dared before. These often took the forms of groups daring to gather and discuss subversive ideas – whether French, American, or Mexican students in 1968, the Civic Forum in Czechoslovakia or the Citizens Movement of East Germany in 1989, or the public rallies in Tunis, Cairo, and so many Arab cities in 2011. New exemplars can trigger rapid "learning processes," as sociologist Donatella della Porta describes, in which foreign events motivate new forms of action.[7] In established democracies, more formal networks have often dominated the social movement scene: nongovernmental organizations (NGOs), typically led by those Sidney Tarrow terms "rooted cosmopolitans," able to speak to both local and global concerns, have become considered the lifeblood of the contemporary "social movement society."[8] The rise of online social networks over the last two decades, meanwhile, both imitates and advances centuries of collective organizing as they develop new platforms giving previously marginal voices greater reach. Utilized across the political spectrum, the campaigns leading to Brexit and Donald Trump's

---

[5] Peter H. Amann, *Revolution and Mass Democracy: The Paris Club Movement in 1848* (Princeton: Princeton University Press, 1975), 33–38; Martin Kitchen, *A History of Modern Germany, 1800–2000* (New York: Blackwell, 2006), 75–76; David Blackbourn, *The Long Nineteenth Century: A History of Germany, 1780–1918* (Oxford: Oxford University Press, 1998), 158.

[6] Karl Marx, "Inaugural Address and Provisional Rules of the International Working Men's Association," in *The Marx-Engels Reader*, Robert C. Tucker, ed. 2nd ed. (New York: Norton, 1978), 518.

[7] Donatella della Porta, "Riding the Wave: Protest Cascades, and What We Can Learn from Them," in *Global Diffusion of Protest: Riding the Protest Wave in the Neoliberal Crisis,* della Porta, ed. (Amsterdam: Amsterdam University Press, 2017), 25.

[8] David S. Meyer and Sidney Tarrow, eds. *The Social Movement Society: Contentious Politics for a New Century* (New York: Rowan & Littlefield, 1998); Sidney Tarrow, *The New Transnational Activism* (Cambridge: Cambridge University Press, 2005), esp. 40–42; J. Craig Jenkins, Michael Wallace and Andrew S. Fullerton, "A Social Movement Society? A Cross-National Analysis of Protest Potential," *International Journal of Sociology* 38, no. 3 (2014), 12–35.

election in 2016 followed increasingly effective alt-right networking, foreign influencing, and online popular outreach. Today, both the promise and challenges posed by social movements have never been greater.

The continued prevalence of international inspirations in sparking mass movements shows the allure of distant examples (sometimes in part because of their distance) when speaking to commonly shared beliefs and aspirations. Amid domestic political impasses, international examples recurrently give hope and courage to activists as they seek political solutions. Particularly as global networks grow still more complex, transnational diversities of experience and ranges of possibilities provide beacons for innovative reformers and revolutionaries. Eighteenth-century activists, inventing the archetypal movements fueling modern democracy, presaged the forms and tensions of our own contentious era.

The era's friends of freedom recognized their international brethren to be part of a common cause, using shared rhetoric of liberty to mobilize broad social movements through a corresponding society model readapted for each campaign. Arguments over freedom's boundaries and applications convulsed every undertaking. Nevertheless, as liberty's offspring, each movement sought to advance their vision of what a new order of freedom could be.

BIBLIOGRAPHY

Archives

Archives des affaires étrangères (La Courneuve, France) – P4666, P5984

Archives départementales de la Charente-Maritime (La Rochelle, France) – 41 ETP 69, 41 ETP 175

Archives départementales de la Côte-d'Or (Dijon, France) – L 3024

Archives départementales de la Gironde (Bordeaux, France) – 61 J 71, 12 L 207, 12 L 209, C 4364, C 4368, C 4369, C 4371

Archives départementales de l'Hérault (Montpellier, France) – L 5527, L 5532, L 5539, L 5542, L 5543, L 5545

Archives départementales de l'Ille-et-Vilaine (Rennes, France) – L 1557

Archives départementales de l'Indre (Châteauroux, France) – L 110

Archives départementales de la Loire-Atlantique (Nantes, France) – 1 ET A 28, C 626, C 627, C 628, E 691

Archives départementales de la Sarthe (Le Mans, France) – L 270

Archives départementales de la Seine-Maritime (Rouen, France) – L 828

Archives départementales de la Tarn-et-Garonne (Montauban, France) – L 236, L 388, L 402

Archives départmentales de Puy-de-Dôme (Clermont-Ferrand, France) – L 388, L 657, L 6372, L 6374, L 6375

Archives départementales des Bouches du Rhône (Marseille, France) – L 1971, L 2075, L 2076

Archives départementales du Haute-Vienne (Limoges, France) – L 822

Archives départementales du Morbihan (Vannes, France) – L 1530, L 2000

Archives départementales du Nord (Lille, France) – L 10248

Archives municipales de Besançon (Besançon, France) – AA 36

Archives municipales de Bordeaux (Bordeaux, France) – I 79

Archives municipales de Cherbourg (Cherbourg, France) – 2 1 112, 2 1 124

Archives municipales de Lorient (Lorient, France) – BB 14

Archives municipales de Marseille (Marseille, France) – 4 D 43

Archives municipales de Nantes (Nantes, France) – I2 C2

Archives municipales de Reims (Reims, France) – FR 1110, FR 2I102, FR 2I108, FR 2I113

Archives municipales de Rennes (Rennes, France) – I 74

Archives municipales du Havre (Le Havre, France) – D(3) 41, F(2) 10, F(2) 11, K 45

Archives nationales (Paris and Pierrefitte-sur-Seine, France) – 251 MI 1, 252 MI 28, AD XVIIIc 116, AD XVIIIc 117, AF ET B(I) 372, D XXV 59, D XXV 78, D XXV 85, D XXV 86, D XXV 89, D XXV 90, D XXV 110, D XXV 824, AF ET B(I) 372, W 14

Archives nationales d'outre-mer (Aix-en-Provence, France) – 213 MIOM 134, 213 MIOM 138

Bristol Archives (Bristol, UK) – 08527847, SMV/7/2/1/15, SMV/8/3/2/5

Kent Archives (Maidstone, UK) – Pratt Papers, U840/C112, U840/O160, U840/ 071, U840/O136, U840/0143, U840/0146, U840/0147, U840/0156A, U840/ 0165A, U840/0173, U840/0177

Liverpool Record Office (Liverpool, UK) – 920 CUR/108, 920 ROS/247, 920 ROS/ 252, 920 ROS/253, 920 ROS/257

National Archives (London, UK) – CO 5/116, CO 5/117, CO 5/217, CO 5/218, CO 5/219, CO 5/396, CO 5/756, CO 5/757, 5/760, CO 5/763, CO 5/769, CO 5/891, CO 5/934, CO 5/939, CO 5/1098, CO 5/1139, FO 91/1, HO 55/11, PRO 30/8/97, PRO 30/8/121, PRO 30/8/329, PRO 30/8/331, TS 11/952, TS 11/959

National Archives of Scotland (Edinburgh, UK) – Home GD 267/1/16, RH2/4

York County Archives (York, UK) – M 25

Manuscript Collections

American Antiquarian Society (Worcester, MA)
   United States Revolution Collection
   Priscilla Holyoke Diary
   Jonathan Sayward Diary
American Philosophical Society (Philadelphia, PA)
   Filippo Mazzei Papers Mss.Ms.Coll.47
   Pennsylvania Stamp Act and Non-Importation Resolutions Collection Mss. 973.2.M31
   Benjamin Vaughan Papers Mss.B.V46p
Bibliothèque de l'Assemblée nationale (Paris, France)
   Affiches révolutionnaires C5, Ch5, 34
Bibliothèque de l'Institut de France (Paris, France)
   Papiers de Condorcet MS 857
Bibliothèque historique de la ville de Paris (Paris, France)
   Evénements révolutionnaires DP 306
Bibliothèque municipale de Clermont-Ferrand (Clermont-Ferrand, France)
   Lettres de Jean-Henri Bancal MSS 348
Bibliothèque municipale de Nantes (Nantes, France)
   Correspondance d'Etienne Chatillon Mic B 48/44
   Fonds Dugast-Matifeux D-M 21 6
   Lettre sur les désordres de Port-au-Prince (4 mars 1791) MS 1810

Bibliothèque municipale de Poitiers (Poitiers, France)
  Lettres reçues par la Société des amis de la Constitution 142/1, S/26 146, S/26
    147, S/26 148, S/26 149, S/26 150
Bibliothèque nationale – Richelieu (Paris, France)
  Journal des événements survenus à Paris, du 2 avril au 8 octobre 1789 FF 13713
  Mathurin de Lescure, Correspondence secrète NAF 13278
Birmingham Public Library (Birmingham, UK)
  James Watt, Jr. Correspondence MS 3219/4
Bodleian Library (Oxford, UK)
  MS Wilberforce c.46
British Library (London, UK)
  Crown & Anchor Association Papers ADD MS 16919, 16920, 16922, 16929
  Edgerton Papers ADD MS 3711
  Henry Flood Papers ADD MS 22930
  Charles James Fox Papers ADD MS 47567
  Hardwicke Papers ADD MS 35911
  Thomas Hardy Papers ADD MS 27808
  Letters to Rev. W. Butler ADD MS 27578
  Minute Books of the London Abolition Committee ADD MS 21254, 21255
  Henry Moore Papers ADD MS 22679
  John Wilkes Papers ADD MS 30875
  Westminster Politics ADD MS 27849
Connecticut Historical Society (Hartford, CT)
  American Revolution Collection
Duke University Special Collections (Durham, NC)
  Ephraim Kirby Papers
  John Rutledge, Jr. Papers
Gloucestershire Record Office (Gloucester, UK)
  Granville Sharp Papers D 3549
Harvard Business School Library (Cambridge, MA)
  William Lloyd Letterbook
Haverford College (Haverford, PA)
  Anthony Benezet Papers MSS 852
  Letters from British Friends MSS 681
  Quaker MS MICRO BX 7619
  Robert Pleasants Collection MSS 1116/168
  Virginia Meeting Correspondence MSS 1116/159
Historical Society of Pennsylvania (Philadelphia, PA)
  Clifford Correspondence MSS 0136
  Tench Coxe Papers MICRO 18,376
  Louis Beebe Journal MSS 39
  James & Drinker Papers MSS 30795
  James Marshall Papers MSS 0395
  Pennsylvania Abolition Society Papers MICRO 572

Huntington Library (San Marino, CA)
    Untitled handbill Rare Books 281258
    Clarkson-Mirabeau Letters HM CN 53
    Clarkson-Wilberforce Letters HM 813
    Thoreau and Sewall Papers HM 64961
    W Hutton, A Narrative of the Dreadful Riots in Birmingham, July 14, 1791 HM
        847
John Rylands Library (Manchester, UK)
    Gazettes manuscrites sent to Breton René le Pretre de Châteaurgiron,
        1775–1793, French MSS 51
Library of Congress (Washington, DC)
    Samuel Adams Papers MSS 10223
    Breckinridge Family Papers MSS 13698
    Dennys de Berdt Papers MMC-0298
    Stephen Collins Records MSS 16436
    Silas Deane Papers MSS 23655
    Ebenezer Foote Papers MSS 20941
    Peter Force Papers MSS 20990
        American Stamp Act Papers
        Massachusetts Town Records
        New York Committee of Observation Papers
        Norwich Town Papers
        Thomas Penn Correspondence
        Ezra Stiles Diary
        Ezra Stiles Papers
        Virginia Reports to British Secretary of State
        Woolsey and Salmon Letterbook
    Galloway-Maxcy-Markoe Papers MSS 21857
    James Grant of Balindalloch Papers MSS 89460
    Great Britain Colonial Office Class 5, Vol. 40
    John Hancock Papers MMC-3655
    Henry Innes Papers MSS 24201
    Richard Bland Lee Papers MMC-3477
    Robert R. Livingston Papers MSS 60194
    James McHenry Papers Z999.P23
    New York Committee of Observation Papers MSS 85783
    Harrison Gray Otis Papers MSS 59444
    Pennsylvania Whiskey Rebellion Collection MMC-1315
    Pinckney Family Papers MSS 59840
    William Plumer Papers MSS 36434
    Edmund Randolph Papers MSS 1156
    Horatio Sharpe Papers MSS 1722
    Samuel Smith Papers MSS 40469
    William Loughton Smith Papers MSS 40483

Charles Thomson Papers MSS 42861
Peter Van Schaack Papers MSS 4918
Library of the Society of Friends (London, UK)
    Mathews Papers MSS A 1/5
    Minute Book of the Meeting for Sufferings Committee on the Slave Trade MSS
        F 1/7
London Metropolitan Archives (London, UK)
    English Liberty MS 3332
Maine Historical Society (Portland, ME)
    Portland Republican Society Papers
Maryland Historical Society (Baltimore, MD)
    James Bayard Papers MSS 109
    Revolutionary War Collection MSS 1814
    Purviance Papers MSS 1394
Massachusetts Historical Society (Boston, MA)
    John Adams Papers
    Jeremy Belknap Diaries
    James Freeman Letterbook
    Thomas Hollis Papers
    Henry Knox Papers
    Lee Family Papers
    Samuel Mather Papers
    James Murray Papers
    Diary of Thomas Newell
    Portsmouth Sons of Liberty Papers
    Ezekiel Price Papers
    Tea Party Meeting Minutes
    John Tudor Papers
National Archives of Ireland (Dublin, Ireland)
    Francis Dobbs Papers 2551
    Joseph Haughton Papers 1576
    Rebellion Papers 620/15, 620/18, 620/19, 620/20, 620/21, 620/22, 620/24, 620/
        25, 620/26, 620/28, 620/29, 620/31, 620/35
    Westmoreland Papers PRIV 1258
National Library of Ireland (Dublin, Ireland)
    Ennis Volunteers Records and Accounts MS 838
National Library of Scotland (Edinburgh, Scotland)
    Henry Dundas Papers MS 16
New Jersey Historical Society (Newark, NJ)
    Mahlon Dickerson Diary
    Mahlon Dickerson Letterbook
    Mahlon Dickerson Papers
New York Public Library (New York, NY)
    Bancroft Collection

Connecticut Papers
Letters to Burke
Lexington Town Meeting
Tammany Society Papers
Noah Webster Papers
New-York Historical Society (New York, NY)
Aaron Burr Papers
Albert Gallatin Papers
Genet Family Papers
John Lamb Papers
Alexander McDougall Papers
Public Record Office of Northern Ireland (Belfast, UK)
Minute Book of the First Newry Volunteers T/3202
Grand National Convention, 1783 T/2541
Rhode Island Historical Society (Providence, RI)
Sons of Liberty Papers MSS 9005
Ward Papers MSS 11
Senate House Library, University College of London (London, UK)
West India Committee Papers M915 reel 3
South Carolina Historical Society (Charleston, SC)
Committee of Correspondence Papers 1034.00
Richard Hutson Papers 34/0559
Robert Raper Papers 34/0511
Read Family Papers 0267.00
St John's College Library (Cambridge, UK)
Thomas Clarkson Papers
Swarthmore College (Swarthmore, PA)
Philadelphia Meeting for Sufferings MR-PH507, MR-PH508
Trinity College (Dublin, Ireland)
Prior Notebooks MSS 3365
Virginia Historical Society (Richmond, VA)
Mercier Correspondence MSS 5345
John Beckley Papers MSS B3886
University of Liverpool Sydney Jones Library Special Collections (Liverpool, UK)
Rathbone Family Papers RP IV 1.1A
University of North Carolina Special Collections (Chapel Hill, NC)
William Barry Grove Papers
University of Reading Special Collections (Reading, UK)
Turner Collection 263
University of Virginia Special Collections (Charlottesville, VA)
Berkeley Family Papers
William Lee Papers
James Maury Papers

Newspapers

Affiches américaines
Albany Gazette
American Citizen
American Mercury
American Minerva
Amherst Journal
Analyse des papiers anglois
Andrews's Western Star
Annales de la République française
Annales patriotiques et littéraires
Argus
Aurora General Advertiser
Baltimore Daily Intelligencer
Bath Chronicle
Boston Evening Gazette
Boston Evening-Post
Boston Gazette
Boston Post-Boy
Bristol Journal
Bulletin de Bordeaux
Carey's United States Recorder
Carlisle Journal
Centinel of Freedom
Chronique de Strasbourg
City Gazette
Claypoole's Daily Advertiser
Club des impartiaux
Connecticut Courant
Connecticut Gazette
Connecticut Journal
Constitutional Telegraphe
Courier
Courier of New Hampshire
Courrier politique et littéraire du Cap-Français
Courrier républicain
The Crisis
Cumberland Gazette
Daily Advertiser
Dunlap's American Daily Advertiser
Eastern Herald
English Chronicle
Evening Mail

Federal Gazette
Federal Mirror
Freeman's Journal
Gazette de France
Gazette de Saint-Domingue
Gazette du jour
Gazette of the United States
Gazetteer
General Advertiser
General Evening Post
Georgia Gazette
Greenleaf's New York Journal
Herald of Liberty
Hibernian Chronicle
Hibernian Journal
Independent Chronicle
Independent Gazetteer
Independent Journal
Journal de Bordeaux
Journal de correspondence de Paris à Nantes et du department de la Loire inférieure
Journal de Perlet
Journal de la Montagne
*Journal de la municipalité, du Département, des Districts & des Sections de Paris, et
     correspondance des départemens & des principales Municipalités du Royaume*
Journal de la Société de 1789
Journal de la Société des amis de la constitution monarchique
Journal des amis de la constitution
Journal des clubs
Journal des débats de la société des amis de la constitution
Journal des décrets de l'Assemblée nationale
Journal des sociétés-patriotiques françaises
Leeds Mercury
Liberty and Property Preserved against Republicans and Levellers
Litchfield Monitor
Lloyd's Evening Post
London Chronicle
London Courant
London Evening Post
London Packet
Massachusetts Centinel
Massachusetts Gazette
Massachusetts Sentinel
Massachusetts Spy
Maryland Gazette

Mercure universel
Middlesex Journal
Moniteur colonial
Moniteur universel
Morning Chronicle
Morning Post
National Gazette
New Daily Advertiser
New-Hampshire Gazette
New London Gazette
New-Jersey Journal
New-York Daily Gazette
New-York Gazette
New-York Journal
New-York Mercury
New-York Packet
Newport Herald
Newport Mercury
Northern Star
Nouvelles de Saint-Domingue
Nouvelliste national
Observateur provincial
Oracle
Oracle of the Day
Owen's Weekly Chronicle
Patriote français
Pennsylvania Gazette
Pennsylvania Journal
Pennsylvania Mercury
Philadelphia Gazette
Philadelphia Minerva
Providence Gazette
Pennsylvania Packet
Porcupine's Gazette
Public Advertiser
Public Ledger
Révolutions de Paris
Salem Mercury
South-Carolina Gazette
South-Carolina State-Gazette
St. James's Chronicle
Star
Sun
Thermomètre du jour

Time Piece
The Times
True Briton
United States Chronicle
Universal Advertiser
Universal Gazette
Vermont Gazette
Virginia Gazette
Washington Spy
Westminster Journal
Whitehall Evening Post
Woodfall's Register
World
York Courant
Yorkshire Freeholder

Primary

An Act for Securing the Dependency of His Majesty's Dominions in America upon the Crown and Parliament of Great-Britain. London, 1766.

Adams Family Correspondence, L. H. Butterfield, ed. Cambridge, MA: Harvard University Press, 1963–2015. 12 vols.

An Address from the Committee of Association of the County of York, to the Electors of Great-Britain. York: Blanchard, 1781.

An Address to the Dissidents of England on Their Late Defeat. London, 1790.

An Address to the Public from the Society for Constitutional Information. London, 1780.

Adresse à l'assemblée-nationale, pour les citoyens-libres de couleur, des isles & colonies françoises. 12 octobre 1789. Paris, 1789.

Adresse au roi et discours à Sa Majesté par les colons français de Saint-Domingue réunis à Paris. Paris, 1791.

Adresse de la Société des amis de la constitution à Caen, à l'assemblée nationale. S.l., 1791.

Adresse de la société des amis de la constitution du Mans, à toutes les sociétés patriotiques du royaume. Le Mans, 6 mars 1791. Le Mans: Pivron, 1791.

Adresse de la société des amis des noirs, à l'Assemblée nationale, à toutes les Villes du Commerce, à toutes les Manufactures, aux Colonies, à toutes les Sociétés des Amis de la Constitution. Paris, 1791.

Adresse de la Société républicaine de Saint-marcellin, Département de l'Isère, à la Convention Nationale. Saint-Marcellin: Beaumont, 1793.

Adresse des sociétés des amis de la Constitution, établies en France, aux peuples voisins. Paris: Imprimerie nationale, 1791.

Adresses, &c., &c., &c. London, 1792.

Advice to the Patriot Club of the County of Antrim on the Present State of Affairs in Ireland, and Some Late Changes in the Administration of That Kingdom. Dublin, 1756.

An Alarm to Dissenters and Methodists. London: Keith, 1769.

Anniversary of the Revolution in France. London, 1790.

The Appendix: Or, Some Observations on the Expediency of the Petitions of the Africans, Living in Boston, &c. Boston: Russell, 1773.

An Argument on Behalf of the Catholics of Ireland. Belfast, 1791.

Association for Preserving Property against Republicans and Levelers / Crown and Anchor Tavern, Strand. November 10, 1795. London, 1795.

Association Papers. Part 1. London, 1793.

At a Meeting of Officers Present at the Newry Review, on the 21st and 22nd of August. S.l., 1780.

Avis aux français sur les clubs. Paris, 1791.

A Brief Account of the General Meeting of the Catholic Delegates Held in Dublin, December 1792. Dublin: Fitzpatrick, 1792.

Bute County Committee of Safety Minutes, 1775–1776. Warrenton, NC: Bicentennial Committee, 1977.

By His Excellency Francis Bernard, Esq. A Proclamation. Boston, 1765.

Cahier contenant les plaintes, doléances, & réclamations des citoyens-libres & propriétaires de couleur des isles & colonies françaises. S.l., s.d.

Calendar of Historical Manuscripts Relating to the War of the Revolution in the Office of the Secretary of State. Albany, NY: Weed, Parsons & Co., 1868.

The Case of Our Fellow-Creatures, the Oppressed Africans, Respectfully Recommended to the Serious Consideration of the Legislature of Great Britain, by the People Called Quakers. London: Phillips, 1784.

The Case of the Dissenters of England, and of the Presbyterians of Scotland: Considr'd in a True and Fair Light. London: Farmer, 1738.

A Century of Lawmaking for a New Nation: U.S. Congressional Documents and Debates, 1774–1875. Washington, DC: Library of Congress, 1998.

A Collection of Addresses Transmitted by Certain English Clubs and Societies to the National Convention of France. London: Debrett, 1793.

A Collection of the Resolutions Passed at the Meetings of the Clergy of the Church of England, of the Counties, Corporations, Cities, and Towns, and of the Society for Promoting Christian Knowledge, Assembled to Take into Consideration the Late Application of the Dissenters to Parliament, for the Repeal of the Corporation and Test Acts. London: Rivington, 1790.

"Constitution of Vermont – July 8, 1777," http://avalon.law.yale.edu/18th_cen tury/vt01.asp.

Copie de la lettre de M. Nicoleau, habitant de Saint-Domingue. Au Cap, le 3 septembre 1791. S. l., 1791.

Corporation and Test Acts, December 30, 1789. By the Committee of Protestant Dissenting Laymen and Ministers of the Three Denominations for the West-Riding of the County of York. Wakefield, 1790.

Correspondance secrète des colons députés à l'Assemblée constituante: servant à faire connaitre l'esprit des colons en général, sur la Révolution. Paris: Anjubault, s.d.

"Correspondence of Clark and Genet," *Report of the Historical Manuscripts Commission of the American Historical Association* (1898), 930–1110.

"Correspondence of the French Ministers to the United States, 1791–1797," Frederick Jackson Turner, ed. *Annual Report of the American Historical Association* 7 (1904).

The Correspondence of the London Revolution Society in London, with the National Assembly, with Various Societies of the Friends of Liberty in France and England. London, 1792.

The Debate in the House of Commons, on the Repeal of the Corporation and Test Acts: March 2, 1790. London: Stockdale, 1790.

The Declaration, Resolutions and Constitution of the Societies of United Irishmen. S. l., s.d.

"Députation de la part de la Société constitutionnelle de Londres, admise à la Convention nationale de France, le 28ieme novembre, 1792," *A Collection of Addresses by Certain English Clubs and Societies to the National Convention of France.* London, 1793.

Discours de MM. Cooper et Watt, Députés de la société constitutionnelle de Manchester, prononcé à la société des amis de la Constitution, séante à Paris, le 13 avril 1792. Paris, 1792.

Discours sur la nécessité d'établir à Paris une Société pour concourir, avec celle de Londres, à l'abolition de la traite & de l'esclavage des Nègres. Paris, 1788.

Exposé historique des motifs qui ont amené la rupture entre la République française et S.M. Britannique. Paris, 1793.

Extrait de la délibération de la société des amis de la constitution à Rouen, du 18 décembre 1790. Rouen, 1790.

Facts, Reflections and Queries, Submitted to the Consideration of the Associated Friends of the People. Edinburgh, 1792.

General Observations on the State of Affairs in Ireland, and Its Defence against an Invasion. By a Country Gentleman. Dublin: Johnson, 1797.

The History of the Proceedings and Debates of the Volunteer Delegates of Ireland, on the Subject of a Parliamentary Reform. Dublin: Porter, 1784.

"An Impartial Relation of the First Rise and Cause of the Recent Differences in Publick Affairs, in the Province of North Carolina; and the Past Tumults and Riots That Happened in the Province," *in Some Eighteenth-Century Tracts on North Carolina*, William K. Boyd, ed. (Raleigh, NC: Edwards & Broughton, 1927), 253–334.

An Inquiry into the Causes of the Insurrection of the Negroes in the Island of St. Domingo. London: Johnson, 1792.

"Journal of a French Traveler in the Colonies, 1765," *American Historical Review* 27, no. 1 (1921), 70–89.

Journals of the House of Burgesses of Virginia, 1773–1776, Including the Records of the Committee of Correspondence, John Pendleton Kennedy, ed. Richmond, 1905.

Journals of the House of Commons of the Kingdom of Ireland. Dublin: Grierson, 1796.

A Letter to the Right Honourable Edmund Burke, in Reply to His "Reflections on the Revolution in France, etc.," by a Member of the Revolution Society. London, s.d.

Letters of an Impartial Observer, on the Affairs of Ireland. Dublin: Clarke, 1793.

The Letters of Junius, John Cannon, ed. Oxford: Oxford University Press, 1978.

Letters on Political Liberty and the Principles of the English and Irish Projects of Reform; Addressed to a Member of the English House of Commons. London: Ridgeway, 1789.

Lettre de la Société des amis des noirs à M. Necker, avec la réponse de ce Ministre. Paris, 1789.

Lettre de la Société des Whigs constitutionnels à l'Assemblée nationale avec la réponse de M. le Président. Paris: Imprimerie nationale, 1791.

Lettre des députés de Saint-Domingue à leurs commettans, en date du 12 aout 1789, intercepté par un mulâtre. Paris, 1790.

Memoire, or Detailed Statement of the Origin and Progress of the Irish Union: Delivered to the Irish Government, by Messrs. Emmett, O'Connor and McNevin. London: Robinson, 1802.

"Minute Book of the Catholic Committee, 1773–1792," *Archivium Hibernicum* 9 (1942), 2–172.

Minutes of the Albany Committee of Correspondence, 1775–1778, vol. 1. Albany: University of the State of New York, 1923.

"The Olive Branch Petition," http://ahp.gatech.edu/olive_branch_1775.html.

Parliamentary History of England: From the Norman Conquest, in 1066, to the Year 1803. London: Bagshaw, 1806–20. 36 vols.

The Parliamentary Register, or History of the Proceedings and Debates of the House of Commons of Ireland. (Dublin: Byrne and Porter, 1784), 15 vols.

Pendez les Jacobins, ce sont des scélérats. S.l., 1794.

"Petition from Pennsylvania Abolition Society to Congress (1790)," in Nash, *Race*, 144–45.

A Petition of the Freeholders of the County of Middlesex, Presented to His Majesty, the May 24, 1769. London: Fenwick, 1769.

The Principles of Government, in a Dialogue between a Scholar and a Peasant. Written by a Member of the Society for Constitutional Information. London, 1782.

Proceedings of the Committees of Safety of Cumberland and Isle of Wight Counties, Virginia, 1775–1776. Richmond: Bottom, 1919.

Proceedings of the Society of United Irishmen, of Dublin. Philadelphia: Stephens, 1795.

Proceedings Relative to the Ulster Assembly of Volunteer Delegates: On the Subject of a More Equal Representation of the People in the Parliament of Ireland. Belfast: Joy, 1783.

Procès-verbal de la séance de la Société des amis de la constitution de Vitry-le-François. S.l., 1790.

Procès-verbal des séances de l'assemblée des colons électeurs de La Martinique, tenue à Paris. Paris: Demonville, 1789.

Procès-verbal des séances et délibérations de l'assemblée générale des électeurs de Paris, réunis à l'Hôtel de Ville le 14 juillet 1789. Paris: Baudouin, 1790.

Public Documents Declaratory of the Principles of the Protestant Dissenters, and Proving That the Repeal of the Corporation and Test Acts, Was Earnestly Desired by King William III and King George I. Birmingham, 1790.

Qu'est-ce que les Cloubs, ou exposé simple & fidelle des principes & de la conduite de la Société des Amis de la Constitution établie à Tulle. Brive, 1790.

Réclamations adressées à l'Assemblée nationale, par les personnes de Couleur, Propriétaires & Cultivateurs de la Colonie Françoise de Saint-Domingue. Paris, 1789.

Règlement pour la Société des amis de la Constitution, établie dans la ville de Vire le 6 juin 1790. S.l., 1790.

Relation authentique de tout ce qui s'est passé à Saint-Domingue avant et après le départ forcé de l'Assemblée coloniale. Paris, s.d.

Rélation exacte des troubles de S. Domingue et les attentats commis par les agens du pouvoir exécutif, dans la nuit du 29 au 30 juillet 1790. Paris: Caillot, 1790.

Réponse à l'écrit de M. Malouet, sur l'esclavage des nègres, dans lequel est exprimé le voeu formé par les colons d'avoir des représentants aux Etats-Généraux: Par un membre de la Société des amis des noirs. S.l., 1789.

The Report from the Secret Committee of the House of Commons. Dublin: King, 1798.

"Report: The Fifteenth March 1799," *in Reports of the Committees of the House of Commons.* S.l., 1803.

"Resolutions proposed by Mr. Marshal at the Parkinson's Ferry Meeting of the 14th August, 1794," *Memoirs of the Historical Society of Pennsylvania* 6 (1858), 201.

The Right of British Subjects to Petition and Apply to Their Representatives, Asserted and Vindicated. London: Smith, 1733.

The Right of Protestant Dissenters to a Compleat Toleration Asserted. London: Johnson, 1787.

The Rights of the People to Petition, and the Reasonableness of Complying with Such Petitions: In a Letter to a Leading Great Man. London: Williams, 1769.

A Second Address from the Committee of Association of the County of York, to the Electors of the Counties, Cities, and Boroughs within the Kingdom of Great Britain. York: Blanchard, 1781.

Second Report of the Committee of Secrecy. London: Debrett, 1794.

"Seditious Meetings Act," *English Historical Documents, 1783–1832,* David C. Douglas, ed. Oxford, UK: Oxford University Press, 1959.

A Sketch of the History and Proceedings of the Deputies Appointed to Protect the Civil Rights of the Protestant Dissenters. London: Burton, 1813.

La Société populaire de Limoges, à la société populaire de Paris, dite des Jacobins. Paris, 1793.

Suffolk Resolves, http://www.masshist.org/database/viewer.php?item_id=696&pid=2.

Suite de la découverte d'une conspiration contre les intérêts de la France. S.l., 1790.

Supplique et pétition des citoyens de couleur des isles et colonies françoises. Paris, 1789.

Thoughts on the Conduct and Continuation of the Volunteers of Ireland. Dublin: Williams, 1783.

The Virginia and Kentucky Resolutions of 1798 and '99. Washington: Elliot, 1832.

Adams, John. *Papers of John Adams,* Robert J. Taylor, ed. Cambridge, MA: Belknap Press, 1977–. 13 vols.

Adams, John. *The Works of John Adams.* Boston: Little, Brown & Co., 1852–1865. 10 vols.

Adams, John Quincy. *Writings.* New York: Macmillan, 1913. 7 vols.

Adams, Samuel. *The Writings of Samuel Adams,* Henry Alonzo Cushing, ed. (New York: Putnam's, 1904–1908). 4 vols.

Agnew, Jean, ed. *The Drennan-McTier Letters, 1776–1793.* Belfast: Irish Manuscripts Collection, 1998.

Albemarle, George. *Memoirs of the Marquis of Rockingham and His Contemporaries.* London: Bentley, 1852. 2 vols.

Almon, John. *Memoirs of a Late Eminent Bookseller.* London, 1790.

Appleton, Nathaniel. *Considerations on Slavery.* Boston: Edes and Gill, 1767.

Auckland, Lord. *The Journal and Correspondence of William Eden, Lord Auckland.* London: Bentley, 1861. 3 vols.

Aulard, Alphonse, ed. *La Société des Jacobins: recueil de documents pour l'histoire du club des Jacobins de Paris.* Paris, 1889–1897. 6 vols.

Barbé-Marbois, Marquis de. *Réflexions sur la colonie de Saint-Domingue, ou, Examen approfondi des causes de sa ruine, et des mesures adoptées pour la rétablir.* Paris: Garnery, 1796.

Barskett, James. *History of the Island of St. Domingo: From Its First Discovery by Columbus to the Present.* S.l., 1818.

Barthel, *Les Jacobins assassins du peuple.* Paris: Bonnes Gens, 1794.

Beatty, John D. ed. *Protestant Women's Narratives of the Irish Rebellion of 1798.* Dublin: Four Courts Press, 2001.

Benezet, Anthony. *A Caution and Warning to Great Britain and Her Colonies in a Short Representation of the Calamitous State of the Enslaved Negroes in the British Dominions.* Philadelphia: Miller, 1766.

Beresford, John. *The Correspondence of the Right Hon. John Beresford.* London: Woodfall and Kinder, 1854. 2 vols.

Bernadau, Pierre. *Les débuts de la Révolution à Bordeaux, d'après les tablettes manuscrites de Pierre Bernadau.* Paris: Alcan, 1919.

Biard, Michel, ed. *Procès-verbaux de la société populaire de Honfleur (Calvados) (janvier 1791-février 1795).* Paris: Éditions CTHS, 2011.

Blanchelande, Filbert-François de. *Supplément au Mémoire de M. Blanchelande, sur son administration à Saint-Domingue.* Paris, s.d.

Boissonnade, Pierre. *Saint-Domingue à la veille de la revolution et la question de la représentation coloniale aux États generaux.* Paris: Geuthner, 1906.

Bond, Phineas. "Letters of Phineas Bond, British Consul at Philadelphia, to the Foreign Office of Great Britain, 1790–1794," J. Franklin Jameson, ed. *Annual Report of the American Historical Association,* 11 (1898), 1–143.

Boyd, William K. *Some Eighteenth-Century Tracts Concerning North Carolina.* Raleigh: Edwards & Broughton, 1927.

Bradburn, Samuel. *An Address to the People Called Methodists; Concerning the Evil of Encouraging the Slave Trade.* Manchester: Harper, 1792.

Brissot, Jacques-Pierre. *Correspondance et papiers.* Paris: Picard, 1912.

Brissot, Jacques-Pierre. *Discours sur l'utilité des sociétés patriotiques et populaires, sur la nécessité de les maintenir et de les multiplier par-tout.* Paris, 1791.

Brissot, Jacques-Pierre. *Exposé de la conduite de la nation française, envers le peuple anglais, et des motifs qui ont amené la rupture entre la République française & le Roi d'Angleterre.* Paris, 1793.

Brissot, Jacques-Pierre. *Mémoire sur les noirs de l'amérique septenrionale.* Paris, 1789.

Brissot, Jacques-Pierre. *Nouveau voyage dans les Etats-Unis de l'Amérique Septentrionale, fait en 1788.* Paris: Buisson 1791.

Brown, Jonathan. *The History and Present Condition of St. Domingo.* Philadelphia: Marshall, 1837.

Browning, Oscar, ed. *Despatches from Paris, 1784–1790.* London: The Society, 1910.

Burgh, James. *Political Disquisitions: Or, an Inquiry into Public Errors, Defects and Abuses.* London: Dilly, 1774. 3 vols.

Burke, Edmund, *Correspondence.* Chicago: University of Chicago Press, 1958–1978. 10 vols.

Burke, Edmund. *Thoughts on the Present Discontents.* London: Dodsley, 1770.

Burke, Edmund. *The Writings and Speeches of Edmund Burke,* Peter James Marshall, ed. Oxford: Oxford University Press, 2015. 8 vols.

Burr, Aaron. *Political Correspondence and Public Papers of Aaron Burr,* Mary-Jo Kline and Joanne Wood Ryan, eds. (Princeton: Princeton University Press, 1984). 2 vols.

Cabot, George. *Life and Letters of George Cabot.* Boston: Little, Brown & Co., 1878.

Carroll, Charles. *Dear Papa, Dear Charley: The Peregrinations of a Revolutionary Aristocrat.* Chapel Hill: University of North Carolina Press, 2001.

Carteau, Félix. *Soirées bermudiennes, ou Entretiens sur les événemens qui ont opéré la ruine de la partie française de l'Isle Saint-Domingue.* Bordeaux: Pellier, 1802.

Cartwright, John. *An Address to the Gentlemen, Forming the Several Committees of the Associated Counties, Cities, and Towns, for Supporting the Petitions for Redress of Grievances, and against the Unconstitutional Influence of the Crown over Parliament.* London, 1780.

Cartwright, John. *American Independence the Glory and Interest of Britain.* London: Woodfall, 1774.

Cartwright, John. *The Life and Correspondence of Major Cartwright.* New York: AMS Press, 1969. 2 vols.

Cartwright, John. *The People's Barrier against Undue Influence and Corruption.* London, 1780.

Cartwright, John. *Take Your Choice!* London: Almon, 1776.

Champion, Richard. *The American Correspondence of a Bristol Merchant, 1766–1776.* Berkeley: University of California Press, 1934.

Charlemont, *Earl of. The Manuscripts and Correspondence of James, First Earl of Charlemont.* London Eyre and Spottiswoode, 1891. 2 vols.

Clarkson, Thomas. *The History of the Rise, Progress, and Accomplishment of the Abolition of the Slave Trade.* London: Longman, 1808. 2 vols.

Clavière, Étienne and Jacques-Pierre Brissot, *De la France et des Etats-Unis.* London, 1787.

Combes de Patris, Bernard, ed. *Procès-verbaux des séances de la Société populaire de Rodez.* Rodez: Carrère, 1912.

Condorcet, Marquis de. *Lettres d'un citoyen des Etats-Unis à un Français, sur les affaires presents, par Mr. le M** de C*.* S.l., s.d.

Cooper, George. *Letters on the Irish Nation, Written during a Visit to That Kingdom, in the Autumn of 1799.* London, 1800.

Cooper, Thomas. *Letters on the Slave Trade.* Manchester: Wheeler, 1787.

Cornwallis, Charles. *Correspondence of Charles, First Marquis of Cornwallis.* London: Murray, 1859. 3 vols.

Couthon, Georges. *Correspondance de Georges Couthon, député de Puy-de-Dôme à l'assemblée législative et à la Convention nationale (1791–1794).* Paris: Aubry, 1872.

Crèvecoeur, Hector Saint-Jean de. *Letters from an American Farmer and Sketches of Eighteenth-Century America.* New York: Penguin, 1986.

Crombie, James. *A Sermon Preached before the United Companies of the Belfast Volunteers, on Sunday the First of August, 1779, in the Old Dissenting Meeting-House.* Belfast: Magee, 1779.

Cuguano, Quobna Ottobah. *Thoughts and Sentiments on the Evils of Slavery.* New York: Penguin, 1999.

Cunningham, Jr., Noble E., ed. *Circular Letters of Congressmen to Their Constituents, 1789–1829.* Chapel Hill: University of North Carolina Press, 1978. 3 vols.

Dalmas, Antoine. *Histoire de la revolution de Saint-Domingue: depuis le commencement des troubles jusqu'à la prise de Jérémie et du Môle par les Anglais.* Paris: Mame, 1814.

Davis, Thomas W, ed. *Committees for the Repeal of the Test and Corporation Acts: Minutes 1786–1790 and 1827–1828.* London: London Record Society, 1978.

Descourtliz, Michel-Etienne. *Histoire des désastres de Saint-Domingue.* Paris: Gernery, 1795.

Dillon, Arthur. *Progrès de la Révolution française en Angleterre.* Paris: Gattey, 1792.

Dobbs, Francis. *A History of Irish Affairs, from the 12th of October, 1779, to the 15th September, 1782, the Day of Lord Temple's Arrival.* Dublin: Mills, 1782.

Dobbs, Francis. *Thoughts on Volunteers*. Dublin: Mills, 1781.

Dorigny, Marcel and Bernard Gainot, eds. *La Societe des amis des noirs, 1788–1799: contribution à l'histoire de l'abolition de l'esclavage*. Paris: UNESCO, 1998.

Drennan, William. *The Drennan Letters, 1776–1819*, D. A. Chart, ed. Belfast: HMSO, 1931.

Drought, Thomas. *Letters on Subjects Interesting to Ireland, and Addressed to the Irish Volunteers*. Dublin: Coles, 1783.

Dupont de Nemours, Pierre-Samuel. *Avant-dernière chapitre de l'histoire du jacobinisme*. S.l.: Dupont, s.d.

Duval de Sanadon, David. *Tableau de la situation actuelle des colonies, présenté à l'assemblée nationale*. S.l., 1789.

Edwards, Bryan. *The History, Civil and Commercial, of the British Colonies in the West Indies*. London: Stockdale, 1793.

Elliot, Gilbert. *Life and Letters of Sir Gilbert Elliot*. London: Longmans, 1874.

Equiano, Olaudah. *The Interesting Narrative of the Life of Olaudah Equiano, or Gustavus Vasa, Told by Himself*. London, 1790.

Erskine, D. M. "Letters from America, 1798–1799," Patricia Holbert Menk, ed. *William and Mary Quarterly*, vol. 6, no. 2 (April 1949), 251–84.

Escherny, François-Louis de. *Correspondance d'un habitant de Paris aver see amis en Suisse*. Paris: Gattey, 1791.

Fell, Ralph. *Memoirs of the Public Life of the Late Rt. Hon. Charles James Fox*. London: Hughes, 1808. 2 vols.

Ferguson, Adam. *An Essay on the History of Civil Society*. Edinburgh, 1767.

Findley, William. *History of the Insurrection in the Four Western Counties of Pennsylvania in the Year M.D.CC.XCIV*. Philadelphia: Smith, 1796.

Foner, Eric. *The Story of American Freedom*. New York: Norton, 1999.

Foner, Phillip S. *The Democratic-Republican Societies, 1790–1800: A Documentary Sourcebook of Constitutions, Declarations, Addresses, Resolutions and Toasts*. Westport, CT: Greenwood Press, 1976.

Ford, Worthington C., ed. *Journals of the Continental Congress*. Washington: Government Printing Office, 1905. 34 vols.

Fortescue, J. B. *The Manuscripts of J.B. Fortescue, Esq., Preserved at Dropmore*, William Windham, ed. London: Stationary Office, 1892.

Fox, Charles James. *Memorials and Correspondence*. London: Bentley, 1853–1857. 4 vols.

Fox, William. *An Address to the People of Great Britain, on the Propriety of Abstaining from West India Sugar and Rum*. London: Gurney, 1791.

Franklin, Benjamin. The *Papers of Benjamin Franklin*, Leonard W. Labaree et. al., eds. New Haven: Yale University Press, 1959–. 42 vols.

Franklin, James. *The Present State of Hayti*. London: Murray, 1828.

Fray-Fournier, A., ed. *Le club des Jacobins de Limoges (1790–1795), d'après ses deliberations, sa correspondence et ses journaux*. Limoges: Charles-Lavauzelle, 1903.

Frossard, Benjamin-Sigismond. *La cause des esclaves nègres, et habitans de la Guinée, porté au tribunal de la justice, de la religion et de la politique.* Lyon: Roche, 1789. 2 vols.

Gage, Thomas. *The Correspondence of General Gage.* New Haven: Yale University Press, 1931.

Garran de Coulon, Jean-Philippe. *An Inquiry into the Causes of the Insurrection of the Negroes in the Island of Santo Domingo.* London, 1792.

Garran de Coulon, Jean-Philippe. *Rapport sur les troubles de Saint-Domingue, fait au nom de la Commission des Colonies, des Comités de Salut public, de Législation et de Marine, réunis.* Paris, 1797. 2 vols.

Geggus, David. *The Haitian Revolution: A Documentary History.* Indianapolis: Hackett, 2014.

Gilbert, John Thomas. *Documents Relating to Ireland, 1795–1804.* Shannon: Irish University Press, 1970.

Girod-Chantrans, Justin. *Voyage d'un Suisse dans différentes colonies d'Amérique pendant la dernière guerre, avec une table d'observations météorologiques faites à Saint-Domingue.* Neuchâtel: Imprimerie de la Société typographique, 1785.

Gordon, James. *History of the Rebellion in Ireland, in the Year 1798.* Dublin: Porter, 1801.

Gordon, William. *The History of the Rise, Progress and Establishment of the Independence of the United States of America.* London, 1788. 3 vols.

Gower, Earl. *The Despatches of Earl Gower.* Cambridge: Cambridge University Press, 1885.

Grattan, Henry. *The Life and Times of the Right Honourable Henry Grattan.* London: Colborn, 1839. 5 vols.

Grattan, Henry. *The Speeches of the Right Honourable Henry Grattan.* London: Longman, 1822. 4 vols.

Grimouard, Henri de. *L'amiral de Grimouard au Port-au-Prince: d'après sa correspondance et son journal de bord (mars 1791-juillet 1792).* Paris: Larose, 1937.

Gouy d'Arsy, Louis-Marthe de. *Confession d'un député dans ses dernier momens, ou liste des péchés politiques.* S.l., 1791.

Gouy d'Arsy, Louis-Marthe de. *Précis sur la position actuelle de la députation de Saint-Domingue, aux Etats-Généraux. Versailles, le 20 juin 1789.* Versailles, 1789.

Grosley, Pierre-Jean. *A Tour of London, or New Observations on England and Its Inhabitants.* London: Lockyer Davis, 1772. 2 vols.

Hamilton, Alexander, John Jay, and James Madison, *The Federalist.* New York: Co-Operative Publishing Company, 1901.

Hamilton, Alexander. *Letter from Alexander Hamilton, Concerning the Public Conduct and Character of John Adams, Esq. President of the United States.* New York: Lang, 1800.

Hamilton, Alexander. *The Papers of Alexander Hamilton,* Harold C. Syrett, ed. New York: Columbia University Press, 1961–1987. 27 vols.

Harrison, Walter. *A New and Universal History, Description and Survey of the Boroughs of London and Westminster, the Borough of Southwark, and Their Adjacent Parts.* London: Cooke, 1775.

Hartley, David. *Letters on the American War*, 6th ed. London: Almon, 1779.

Heitz, Friedrich Karl. *Les sociétés politiques de Strasbourg pendant les années 1790 à 1795 : extraits de leurs procès-verbaux.* Strasbourg: Heitz, 1863.

Henry, Patrick. *Life, Correspondence and Speeches.* New York: Scribner's, 1891. 3 vols.

Higgins, Francis. *Revolutionary Dublin, 1795–1801: The Letters of Francis Higgins to Dublin Castle*, Thomas Bartlett, ed. Dublin: Four Courts Press, 2004.

Higginson, Stephen. "Letters of Stephen Higginson, 1783–1804," in *Annual Report of the American Historical Association* (1897), 704–841.

Hofstadter, Richard. *The Idea of a Party System: The Rise of Legitimate Opposition in the United States, 1780–1840.* Berkeley, CA: University of California Press, 1969.

Holcroft, Thomas. *A Plain and Succinct Narrative of the Late Riots and Disturbances in the Cities of London and Westminster and in the Borough of Southwark.* London: Fielding and Walker, 1780.

Holt, Joseph. *Memoirs of Joseph Holt, General of the Irish Rebels, in 1798.* London: Colburn, 1838.

Hopkins, Samuel. *A Dialogue Concerning the Slavery of the Africans*, in Nash, ed. *Race*, 100–111.

Horsley, Samuel. *A Review of the Case of the Protestant Dissenters.* London: Robson, 1790.

Hunter, Alexander, and Christopher Wyvill, *Original Letters.* York, 1780.

Huntingford, George Isaac. *Letter the First Addressed to the Delegates from the Several Congregations of Protestant Dissenters Who Met at Devizes on September 14, 1789.* 2nd ed. Salisbury: Easton, 1790.

Huntingford, George Isaac. *A Second Letter Addressed to the Delegates from the Several Congregations of Protestant Dissenters Who Met at Devizes on September 14, 1789.* Salisbury: Easton, 1789.

James, Charles Fenlon. *Documentary History of the Struggle for Religious Liberty in Virginia.* Lynchburg, VA: Bell, 1900.

Jay, John. *The Life of John Jay: With Selections from His Correspondence and Miscellaneous Papers.* New York: Harper, 1833. 2 vols.

Jay, John. *The Selected Papers of John Jay*, Elizabeth Miles Nuxoll et. al., eds. Charlottesville: University of Virginia Press, 2010–2017. 5 vols.

Jebb, John. *An Address to the Freeholders of Middlesex, Assembled at Free Mason's Tavern, in Great Queen Street, Upon Monday the 20th of December 1779.* London: Dixwell, 1779.

Jefferson, Thomas. *Autobiography.* New York: Putnam, 1821.

Jefferson, Thomas. *Papers*, Julian P. Boyd, ed. Princeton: Princeton University Press, 1957–2017. 43 vols.

Johnson, Samuel. *Taxation no Tyranny: An Answer to the Resolutions and Address of the American Congress.* London: Cadell, 1775.

Joly, Étienne de. *Adresse des citoyens de couleur des Isles & colonies françoises; à l'Assemblée générale des représentans de la Commune de Paris, prononcée le premier Février 1790*. Paris, 1790.

Jovy, Ernest. *Documents sur la Société populaire de Vitry-le-François pendant la Révolution*. Vitry-le-François, Denis, 1892.

Joy, Henry. *Belfast Politics: Or, a Collection of the Debates, Resolutions, and Other Proceedings of That Town*. Belfast: Joy, 1794.

Joy, Henry. *Historical Collections Relative to the Town of Belfast: From the Earliest Period to the Union with Great Britain*. Belfast, 1817.

King, Rufus. *The Life and Correspondence of Rufus King*. New York: Putnam's Sons, 1894.

Knox, Alexander. *Essay on the Political Circumstances of Ireland*. London: Plymsell, 1798.

Knox, Vicesimus. *Personal Nobility: Or, Letters to a Young Nobleman, on the Conduct of His Studies, and the Dignity of the Peerage*. London: Dilly, 1793.

Laborie, P. J. *Réflexions sommaires adressées à la France et à la colonie de S. Domingue*. Paris: Chardon, 1789.

Lacaste, M. L. et. al., eds., *Les archives parlementaires: recueil complet des débats législatifs et politiques des chambres françaises* (Paris, 1867-). Série 1, 82 vols.

Lacroix, Pamphile. *Mémoires pour server à l'histoire de la révolution de Saint-Domingue*. Paris: Pilles, 1819.

Lacroix, Sigismond, ed. *Actes de la Commune de Paris pendant la Révolution*. Paris: Cerf, 1894-1942. 17 vols.

Laffon de Ladebat, André-Daniel. *Discours sur la nécessité et les moyens de détruire l'esclavage dans les colonies*. Bordeaux: Racli, 1788.

Lameth, Alexandre de. *Histoire de l'assemblée constituante*. Paris: Moutardier, 1828. 2 vols.

Lee, Arthur. *An Essay in Vindication of the Continental Colonies of America, from a Censure of Mr. Adam Smith, in His Theory of Moral Sentiments*. London: Becket, 1764.

Lee, Richard Henry. *Life of Arthur Lee*. Boston: Wells and Lilly, 1829.

Lescallier, David. *Réflexions sur le sort des nègres de nos colonies*. S.l., 1789.

Lindsey, Theophilus. *The Letters of Theophilus Lindsey*, G.M. Ditchfield, ed. Woodbridge, UK: Boydell Press, 2007.

Louis XVI, *Déclaration du roi, à tous les François, à sa sortie de Paris*. Paris: Baudouin, 1791.

Luzerne, Comte de. *Mémoire envoyé le 18 juin 1790, au Comité des rapports de l'Assemblée nationale*. Paris: Imprimerie royale, 1790.

McCahill, Michael W. *The Correspondence of Stephen Fuller, 1788-1795: Jamaica, the West India Interest, and the Campaign to Preserve the Slave Trade*. London: Wiley-Blackwell, 2014.

McSkimin, Samuel. *Annals of Ulster, from 1790-1798*. Belfast: Cleeland, 1906.

Madiou, Thomas. *Histoire d'Haiti*. Port-au-Prince, 1847. 3 vols.

Madison, James. *The Papers of James Madison*, William T. Hutchinson et. al., eds. (Chicago: University of Chicago Press and Charlottesville: University Press of Virginia, 1956-), 43 vols.

Malmesbury, Earl of. *Diary and Correspondence of James Harris, First Earl of Malmesbury*. London: Bentley, 1844.

Marshall, John. *The Papers of John Marshall*, Charles T. Cullen et. al., eds. Chapel Hill: University of North Carolina Press, 1974-, 10 vols.

Marx, Karl. "Inaugural Address and Provisional Rules of the International Working Men's Association," *in The Marx-Engels Reader*, Robert C. Tucker, ed. 2nd ed. (New York: Norton, 1978), 512–19.

Mason, George. *The Papers of George Mason, 1725–1792*, Robert A. Rutland, ed. Chapel Hill: University of North Carolina Press, 1970. 3 vols.

Mauger, Auguste. *Discours prononcé dans la Société des amis de la Liberté et de l'Egalité de Metz, le 23 septembre 1792*. Metz: C. Lamort, 1792.

Mazzei, Phillip. *My Life & Wanderings*, S. Eugene Scalia, trans. Morristown, NJ: American Institute of Italian Studies, 1980.

Métral, Antoine. *Histoire de l'insurrection des esclaves dans le nord de Saint-Domingue*. Paris: Scherff, 1818.

Mirabeau, Comte de. *Discours du comte de Mirabeau, dans la séance du 11 juin, sur la mort de Benjamin Francklin*. Paris, 1790.

Monroe, James. *The Writings of James Monroe*, Stanislaus Murray Hamilton, ed. New York: Putnam's Sons, 1898. 7 vols.

Mons, B. de. *Reflections on the Causes and Probable Consequences of the Late Revolution in France with a View of the Ecclesiastical and Civil Constitution of Scotland*. Edinburgh: Hill and Cadell, 1790.

Moore, John. *The Diary of John Moore*. London, 1904.

Moreau de Saint-Méry, Médéric. *Considérations présentées aux vrais amis de repos et du Bonheur de la France, à l'occasion des nouveaux mouvemens de quelques soi-disant Amis-des-noirs*. Paris, 1791.

Morgan, Edmund S. *Prologue to Revolution: Sources and Documents on the Stamp Act Crisis, 1764–1766*. Chapel Hill: University of North Carolina Press, 1959.

Morris, Gouverneur. *A Diary of the French Revolution, 1752–1816*, Beatrix Cory Davenport, ed. Boston: Houghton-Mifflin, 1939. 2 vols.

Musgrave, Richard. *Memoirs of the Different Rebellions in Ireland from the Arrival of the English*. Dublin: Marchbank, 1802.

O'Bryen, Denis. *A View of the Present State of Ireland*. London: Jordon, 1797.

O'Conor, Charles. *The Letters of Charles O'Conor of Belanagare*. Ann Arbor, MI: Irish American Cultural Institute, 1980. 2 vols.

Ogé, Vincent. *Motion faite par M. Vincent Ogé, jeune, à l'assemblée des colons, habitans de S-Domingue, à l'hôtel de Massiac*. Paris, 1789.

Pache, Jean-Nicolas. *Observations sur les sociétés patriotiques*. S.l., 1790.

Paine, Thomas. *Address and Declaration to the Friends of Universal Peace and Liberty*. London, s.d.

Paine, Thomas. *Common Sense*. New York: Eckler, 1918.

Paine, Thomas. *Rights of Man: Being an Answer to Mr. Burke's Attack on the French Revolution*. London: Jordan, 1791–1792. 2 vols.

Pickering, Octavius. *The Life of Timothy Pickering. By His Son, Octavius Pickering*. Boston: Little, Brown & Co., 1867–1873. 4 vols.

Pitt, William. *Correspondence of William Pitt, Earl of Chatham*. London: Murray, 1840. 4 vols.

Pitt, William. *The Speeches of the Honourable William Pitt in the House of Commons*. London: Longman, 1806. 3 vols.

Pitt, William and Christopher Wyvill, *The Correspondence of the Rev. C. Wyvill and the Right Honourable William Pitt*. London: Todd, 1796. 2 vols.

Plowden, Francis. *An Historical Review of the State of Ireland*. London: Roworth, 1803.

Pons, François-Raymond de. *Observations sur la situation politique de Saint-Domingue*. Paris: Quillau, 1790.

Price, Richard. *The Correspondence of Richard Price*, W. Bernard Peach and D. O. Thomas, eds. Durham: Duke University Press, 1981–1992. 3 vols.

Price, Richard. *A Discourse on the Love of Our Country*. London: Cadell, 1789.

Price, Richard. *Observations on the Importance of the American Revolution: And the Means of Making It a Benefit to the World*. London: Johnson, 1785.

Price, Richard. *Observations on the Nature of Civil Liberty, the Principles of Government, and the Justice and Policy of the War with America*. London: Cadell, 1776.

Priestley, Joseph. *An Address to Protestant Dissenters of All Denominations, on the Approaching Election of Members of Parliament, with Respect to the State of Public Liberty in General, and of American Affairs in Particular*. London: Johnson, 1774.

Priestley, Joseph. *Autobiography of Joseph Priestley*. Teaneck, NJ: Dickinson University Press, 1970.

Priestley, Joseph. *The Conduct to be Observed by Dissenters in Order to Procure the Repeal of the Corporation and Test Acts*. Birmingham: Thompson, 1789.

Priestley, Joseph. *An Essay on the First Principles of Government, and on the Nature of Political, Civil, and Religious Liberty*. 2nd ed. London: Johnson, 1771.

Priestley, Joseph. *A Letter to the Right Honourable William Pitt, First Lord of the Treasury, and Chancellor of the Exchequer; on the Subject of Toleration and Church Establishment*. London: Debrett, 1787.

Priestley, Joseph. *Letters to the Right Honourable Edmund Burke, Occasioned by His Reflections on the Revolution in France*. Birmingham: Pearson, 1791.

Priestley, Joseph. *A Sermon on the Subject of the Slave Trade, Delivered to a Society of Protestant Dissenters, at the New Meeting, in Birmingham, and Published at Their Request*. Birmingham: Pearson and Rollasson, 1788.

Priestley, Joseph. *A View of the Principles and Conduct of the Protestant Dissenters*. S.l., 1769.

Rabaut de St. Etienne, J. P. *Address to the English Nation*. London: Johnson, 1791.

Raimond, Julien. *Correspondance de Julien Raimond avec ses frères de Saint-Domingue*. Paris: Cercle sociale, 1793.

Ramsay, David. *History of the American Revolution*. Philadelphia: Aitken, 1789. 2 vols.

Ramsay, James. *An Essay on the Treatment and Conversion of African Slaves in the British Colonies*. London: Phillips, 1784.

Raylet, Abbé. "Procès-verbaux de la société des amis de la constitution de St. Affrique," *Mémoires de la société des lettres de l'Aveyron* (1942), 297–515.

Raynal, Abbé. *Histoire philosophique et politique des établissemens & du commerce des Européens dans les deux Indes*. La Haye, 1774. 10 vols.

Richardson, James D., ed. *A Compilation of the Messages and Papers of the Presidents*. Washington, DC: United States Government Printing Office, 1896.

Robespierre, Maximilien. *Oeuvres complètes*. Paris: Leroux, 1912–2007. 11 vols.

Robespierre, Maximilien and Augustin Robespierre. *Correspondance de Maximilien et Augustin Robespierre*, Georges Michon, ed. Paris: Société des études robespierristes, 1924–6. 2 vols.

Rochefoucauld, Duc de la. *Voyages dans les Etats-Unis d'Amérique, fait en 1795, 1796 et 1797*. Paris: du Pont, an VII.

Romilly, Samuel. *The Life of Sir Samuel Romilly*. London: Murray, 1842.

Rowe, John. *Letters and Diary of John Rowe, Boston Merchant, 1759–1762, 1764–1779*. Boston: Clarke, 1903.

Rush, Benjamin. "The Correspondence of Benjamin Rush and Granville Sharp, 1773–1809," John A. Woods, ed. *Journal of American Studies* 1, no. 1 (1967), 1–38.

Rush, Benjamin. *Letters of Benjamin Rush*. Philadelphia: American Philosophical Society, 1951. 2 vols.

Saint-Just, Louis-Antoine de. *Oeuvres completes*. Paris: Gallimard, 2004.

Sharp, Granville. *A Declaration of the People's Right to a Share in the Legislature: Which Is the Fundamental Principle of the British Constitution of State*. London: White, 1775.

Sharp, Granville. *Memoirs of Granville Sharp*. London: Colburn, 1820.

Sharp, Granville. *A Representation of the Injustice and Dangerous Tendency of Tolerating Slavery in England*. London: White, 1769.

Sharp, Granville. *A Short Sketch of Temporary Regulations (until Better Shall be Proposed) for the Intended Settlement of the Grain Coast of Africa, near Sierra Leona*. London: Baldwin, 1788.

Smith, Adam. *An Inquiry into the Nature and Causes of the Wealth of Nations*. Edinburgh: Nelson, 1843.

Somerville, Thomas. *The Effects of the French Revolution, with Respect to the Interests of Humanity, Liberty, Etc.* Edinburgh, 1793.

Sparks, Jared. *The Life of Gouverneur Morris*. Boston: Grey & Bowen, 1832.

Stephens, Alexander. *Memoirs of John Horne Tooke: Interspersed with Original Documents*. London: Johnson, 1813.

Strahan, William and Hall, David. "Correspondence between William Strahan and David Hall, 1763–1777," *Pennsylvania Magazine of History and Biography* 11, no. 1 (1887), 86–99.

Tarbé, Charles. *Rapport sur les troubles de Saint-Domingue*. Paris: Imprimerie nationale, 1791.

Thrale, Hester Lynch. *Thraliana: The Diary of Mrs. Hester Lynch Thrale (Later Mrs. Piozzi), 1776–1809*. Oxford: Clarendon Press, 1951. 2 vols.

Thale, Mary, ed., *Selections from the Papers of the London Corresponding Society, 1792–1799*. Cambridge: Cambridge University Press, 1983.

Teeling, Charles Hamilton. *Personal Narrative of the "Irish Rebellion" of 1798*. London: Teeling, 1828.

Tooke, John Horne. *A Letter on Parliamentary Reform: Containing the Sketch of a Plan*. London: Ridgway, 1782.

Tooke, John Horne and Richard Price. *Facts: Addressed to the Landholders, Stockholders, Merchants, Farmers, Manufacturers, Tradesmen, Proprietors of Every Description, and Generally to All the Subjects of Great Britain and Ireland*. London: Johnson, 1780.

Vaux, Robert. *Memoirs of the Life of Anthony Benezet*. Philadelphia: Parke, 1817.

Viefville des Essarts, Jean-Louis de. *Discours et projet de loi pour l'affranchissement des nègres, ou l'adoucissement de leur régime, et réponse aux objections des colons*. Paris: Imprimerie nationale, 1791.

Voltaire, *Letters Concerning the English Nation*. London: Davis, 1733.

Walker, Thomas. *A Review of Some of the Political Events Which Have Occurred in Manchester, during the Last Five Years*. London: Boden, 1794.

Walpole, Horace. *Memoirs of the Reign of George III*. London: Lawrence and Bullen, 1894.

Warren, Mercy Otis. *History of the Rise, Progress and Termination of the American Revolution*. Boston: Larkin, 1805.

Washington, George. "Farewell Address," http://avalon.law.yale.edu/18th_century/washing.asp.

Washington, George. *The Papers of George Washington*, W. W. Abbot, ed. Charlottesville: University of Virginia Press, 1983–1999). Colonial Series. 10 vols. and Presidential Series. 19 vols.

Weslager, C. A. *The Stamp Act Congress*. Newark, DE: University of Delaware Press, 1976.

Wesley, John. *Thoughts Upon Slavery*, 4th ed. Dublin: Whitestone, 1775.

Wilberforce, William. *The Correspondence of William Wilberforce*. London: Murray, 1840. 2 vols.

Wilkes, John. *The Correspondence of the Late John Wilkes, with His Friends*. London: Phillips, 1805. 5 vols.

Wilkes, John. *English Liberty: Being a Collection of Interesting Tracts, from the Year 1762 to 1769*. London: Baldwin, 1769.

Williams, Helen Maria. *Letters on the French Revolution: Written in France, in the Summer of 1790, to a Friend in England*. London: Cadell, 1790.

Wimpffen, Baron von. *A Voyage to Saint Domingo, in the Years 1788, 1789 and 1790*. London: Cadell, 1797.

Wolcott, Jr., Oliver. *Memoirs of the Administrations of George Washington and John Adams*, George Gibbs, ed. New York: Van Norden, 1846.

Wolfe Tone, Theobald. *Life and Adventures of Theobald Wolfe Tone*. Glasgow: Cameron, 1898.

Wolfe Tone, Theobald. *The Writings of Theobald Wolfe Tone, 1763–1798*, T. W. Moody, R. B. McDowell and C. J. Woods, eds. Oxford: Clarendon, 2009. 2 vols.

Wyvill, Christopher. *Political Papers*. York: Blanchard, 1794.

Young, Arthur. *Travels during the Years 1787, 1788, & 1789*. London: Richardson, 1794.

Zinn, Howard and Anthony, Arnove, eds. *Voices from a People's History of the United States*, 2nd ed. New York: Seven Stories Press, 2014.

Secondary

Adams, Catherine and Elizabeth H. Pleck, *Love of Freedom: Black Women in Colonial and Revolutionary New England*. Oxford: Oxford University Press, 2010.

Adelman, Jeremy. "The Age of Imperial Revolutions," *American Historical Review* 113, no. 2 (2008), 319–40.

Ahlstrom, Sydney E. *A Religious History of the American People*, 2nd ed. New Haven: Yale University Press, 2004.

Alderson, Robert J. *This Bright Era of Happy Revolutions: French Consul Michel-Ange-Bernard Mangourit and International Republicanism in Charleston, 1792–1794*. Columbia, SC: University of South Carolina Press, 2008.

Alexander, John K. *Samuel Adams: The Life of an American Revolutionary*. Lanham, MD: Rowan & Littlefield, 2011.

Alpaugh, Micah. *Non-Violence and the French Revolution: Political Demonstrations in Paris, 1787–1795*. Cambridge: Cambridge University Press, 2015.

Alpaugh, Micah. "The Right of Resistance to Oppression: Protest and Authority in the French Revolutionary World," *French Historical Studies* 39, no. 3 (2016), 567–98.

Alpaugh, Micah. "A Self-Defining Bourgeoisie in the Early French Revolution: The *Milice Bourgeoise*, the Bastille Days of 1789, and Their Aftermath," *Journal of Social History* 47, no. 3 (2014), 696–720.

Ammerman, David. *In the Common Cause: American Response to the Coercive Acts of 1774*. Charlottesville: University Press of Virginia, 1974.

Ammon, Henry. *The Genet Mission*. New York: Norton, 1973.

Andress, David. *1789: The Threshold of the Modern Age*. New York: Farrar, Straus & Giroux, 2008.

Andress, David. *The Terror: The Merciless War for Freedom in Revolutionary France*. New York: Farrar, Straus & Giroux, 2006.

Andrew, Donna T. "Popular Culture and Public Debate: London 1780," *Historical Journal* 39, no. 2 (1996), 405–23.

Andrews, Charles McLean. *The Boston Merchants and the Non-importation Movement*. Cambridge, MA: John Wilson & Son, 1917.

Andrews, Dee E. *The Methodists and Revolutionary America, 1760–1800: The Shaping of an Evangelical Culture*. Princeton: Princeton University Press, 2000.

Andrews, Stuart. *Unitarian Radicalism: Political Rhetoric, 1770–1814*. New York: Palgrave Macmillan, 2003.

Anstey, Roger. *The Atlantic Slave Trade and British Abolition, 1760–1810*. Atlantic Highlands, NJ: Humanities Press, 1975.

Armitage, David. "Three Concepts of Atlantic History," in *The British Atlantic World, 1500–1800*, David Armitage and Michael J. Braddick, eds. *The British Atlantic World, 1500–1800*. New York: Palgrave Macmillan, 2002.

Auricchio, Laura. *The Marquis: Lafayette Reconsidered*. New York: Knopf, 2014.

Bailyn, Bernard. *Atlantic History: Concepts and Contours*. Cambridge, MA: Harvard University Press, 2005.

Bailyn, Bernard. *The Ideological Origins of the American Revolution*. Cambridge: Harvard University Press, 1967.

Baer, Marc. "Political Dinners in Radical, Whig and Tory Westminster," *Parliamentary History* 24, no. 1 (2005), 183–206.

Baer, Marc. *The Rise and Fall of Radical Westminster, 1780–1890*. London: Palgrave, 2012.

Baker, Keith Michael and Dan Edelstein, *Scripting Revolution: A Historical Approach to the Comparative Study of Revolutions*. Stanford: Stanford University Press, 2015.

Baldwin, Leland D. *Whiskey Rebels: The Story of a Frontier Uprising*. Pittsburgh: University of Pittsburgh Press, 1939.

Banks, Bryan A. "Real and Imaginary Friends in Revolutionary France: Quakers, Political Culture and the Atlantic World," *Eighteenth-Century Studies* 50, no. 4 (2017), 361–79.

Barlow, Richard Burgess. *Citizenship and Conscience: A Study in the Theory and Practice of Religious Toleration in England during the Eighteenth Century*. Philadelphia: University of Pennsylvania Press, 1962.

Barrell, John. *The Spirit of Despotism: Invasions of Privacy in the 1790s*. Oxford: Oxford University Press, 2006.

Bartlett, Thomas. "Clemency and Compensation: The Treatment of Defeated Rebels and Suffering Loyalists after the 1798 Rebellion," in *Revolution, Counterrevolution and Union*, Jim Smyth, ed. (Cambridge: Cambridge University Press, 2000), 99–127.

Bartlett, Thomas. *Ireland: A History*. Cambridge: Cambridge University Press, 2010.

Baughman, John J. "The French Banquet Campaign of 1847–48," *Journal of Modern History* 31, no. 1 (1959), 1–15.

Baumann, Roland M. "Philadelphia's Manufacturers and the Excise Tax of 1794: The Forging of the Jeffersonian Coalition," in *The Whiskey Rebellion: Past and Present Perspectives*, Steven R. Boyd, ed. (Westport, CT: Greenwood Press, 1985), 135–64.

Becker, Carl. *The History of Political Parties in the State of New York, 1760–1776*. Madison: University of Wisconsin, 1909.

Beeman, Richard R. *Our Lives, Our Fortunes, and Our Sacred Honor: The Forging of American Independence, 1774–1776*. New York: Basic Books, 2013.

Belissa, Marc. *Fraternité universelle et intérêt national (1713–1795): Les cosmopolitiques de droit des gens*. Paris: Kimé, 1998.

Bell, David A. *The First Total War: Napoleon's Europe and the Birth of War as We Know It*. Boston: Houghton Mifflin, 2007.

Bell, David A. "Questioning the Global Turn: The Case of the French Revolution," *French Historical Studies* 37, no. 1 (2014), 1–24.

Bell, James B. *A War of Religion: Dissenters, Anglicans and the American Revolution*. New York: Palgrave Macmillan, 2008.

Bell, Madison Smartt. *Toussaint Louverture: A Biography*. New York: Pantheon, 2007.

Beneke, Chris. *Beyond Toleration: The Religious Origins of American Pluralism*. Oxford: Oxford University Press, 2006.

Benot, Yves. "The Insurgents of 1791, Their Leaders, and the Concept of Independence," in *The World of the Haitian Revolution*, David Patrick Geggus and Norman Fiering, eds. (Bloomington: Indiana University Press, 2009), 99–110.

Bernasconi, Robin and Anika Maaza Mann, "The Contradictions of Racism: Locke, Slavery and the Two Treatises," in *Race and Racism in Modern Philosophy*, Andrew Valls, ed. (Ithaca: Cornell University Press, 2005), 89–107.

Bewley, Christina and David. *Gentleman Radical: A Life of John Horne Tooke, 1736–1812*. London: Tauris, 1998.

Blackbourn, David. *The Long Nineteenth Century: A History of Germany, 1780–1918*. Oxford: Oxford University Press, 1998.

Blackburn, Robin. *The American Crucible: Slavery, Emancipation and Human Rights*. London: Verso, 2013.

Blackburn, Robin. *The Overthrow of Colonial Slavery, 1776–1848*. London: Verso, 1988.

Blacker, William, and Robert H. Wallace, *The Formation of the Orange Order, 1795–1798*. Belfast: Grand Orange Lodge of Ireland, 1994.

Blackman, Robert H. *1789: The Revolution Begins*. Cambridge: Cambridge University Press, 2019.

Blackstock, Alan. *Loyalism in Ireland, 1789–1829*. Woodbridge, UK: Boydell Press, 2007.

Blanning, T. C. W. *The French Revolution in Germany: Occupation and Resistance in the Rhineland, 1792–1802*. Oxford: Clarendon, 1983.

Bleackley, Horace. *Life of John Wilkes*. New York: Lane, 1917.

Bonin, Serge, Jean Boutier, Philippe Boudry, and Claude Langlois, eds. *Atlas de la Révolution française, Vol. 6: Les sociétés politiques*. Paris: EHESS, 1992.

Bonomi, Patricia U. "Religious Dissent and the Case for American Exceptionalism," in *Religion in a Revolutionary Age*, Ronald Hoffman and Peter J. Albert, eds. (Charlottesville: University Press of Virginia, 1994), 31–51.

Bonomi, Patricia U. *Under the Cope of Heaven: Religion, Society and Politics in Colonial America.* Oxford: Oxford University Press, 1986.

Booth, Alan. "Popular Loyalism and Public Violence in the North-West of England, 1790-1800," *Social History* 8, no. 3 (1983), 295-313.

Borden, Morton. *Parties and Politics in the Early Republic, 1789-1815.* Arlington Heights, IL: Harlan Davidson, 1967.

Bourke, Richard. *Empire & Revolution: The Political Life of Edmund Burke.* Princeton: Princeton University Press, 2015.

Bouton, Terry. *Taming Democracy: "The People," the Founders, and the Troubled Ending of the American Revolution.* Oxford: Oxford University Press, 2009.

Brackenridge, H. M. *History of the Western Insurrection in Western Pennsylvania: Commonly Called the Whiskey Insurrection, 1794.* Pittsburgh: W.S. Haven, 1859.

Bradburn, Douglas. *The Citizenship Revolution: Politics and the Creation of the American Union, 1774-1804.* Charlottesville: University of Virginia Press, 2009.

Bradley, James E. "The British Public and the American Revolution," *in Britain and the American Revolution*, H. T. Dickinson, ed. (London: Longman, 1998), 124-54.

Bradley, James E. *Popular Politics and the American Revolution in England: Petitions, the Crown and Public Opinion.* Macon, GA: Mercer University Press, 1986.

Bradley, James E. *Religion, Revolution and English Radicalism: Nonconformity in Eighteenth-Century Politics and Society.* Cambridge: Cambridge University Press, 1990.

Bradley, James E. "The Religious Origins of Radical Politics," *in Religion and Politics in Enlightenment Europe*, Bradley and Dale K. Van Kley, eds. (Notre Dame: Notre Dame University Press, 2001), 187-253.

Branson, Susan. *These Fiery Frenchified Dames: Women and Political Culture in Early National Philadelphia.* Philadelphia: University of Pennsylvania Press, 2001.

Breen, T. H. *American Insurgents, American Patriots: The Revolution of the People.* New York: Hill and Wang 2010.

Breen, T. H. *The Marketplace of Revolution: How Consumer Politics Shaped American Independence.* Oxford: Oxford University Press, 2004.

Brekus, Catherine A. "The Revolution in the Churches: Women's Religious Activism in the Early American Republic," *in Religion and the New Republic: Faith in the Founding of America*, James H. Hutson, ed. (Lanham, MD: Rowan & Littlefield, 2000), 115-36.

Brette, Armand de. "Les gens de couleur libres et leurs deputes en 1789," *Révolution française* 29 (1895), 326-45, 385-407.

Brewer, John, *Party Ideology and Popular Politics at the Accession of George III.* Cambridge: Cambridge University Press, 1976.

Brewer, John. *The Pleasures of the Imagination: English Culture in the Eighteenth Century.* Chicago: University of Chicago Press, 2000.

Brewer, John. *The Sinews of Power; War, Money and the English State, 1688–1783.* London: Routledge, 1989.

Bric, Maurice J. "Ireland and the Atlantic World, 1690–1840," in *The Oxford Handbook of Modern Irish History*, Alvin Jackson, ed. (Oxford: Oxford University Press, 2014), 462–78.

Brims, John D. "The Scottish Democratic Movement in the Age of the French Revolution." PhD thesis, University of Edinburgh, 1983.

Bromwich, David. *The Intellectual Life of Edmund Burke: From the Sublime and Beautiful to American Independence.* Cambridge, MA: Harvard University Press, 2014.

Brown, Christopher Leslie. *Moral Capital: Foundations of British Abolitionism.* Chapel Hill: University of North Carolina Press, 2006.

Brown, Gordon S. *Toussaint's Clause: The Founding Fathers and the Haitian Revolution.* Jackson, MS: University Press of Mississippi, 2005.

Brown, Peter. *The Chathamites: A Study in the Relationship between Personalities and Ideas in the Second Half of the Eighteenth Century.* London: Macmillan, 1967.

Bryant, Irving. *James Madison: Father of the Constitution, 1787–1800.* Indianapolis: Bobbs-Merrill, 1950.

Buckley, Thomas E. *Establishing Religious Freedom: Jefferson's Statute in Virginia.* Charlottesville: University of Virginia Press, 2013.

Bullion, John L. *A Great and Necessary Measure: George Grenville and the Genesis of the Stamp Act, 1763–1765.* Columbia: University of Missouri Press, 1982.

Bullock, F. W. B. *Voluntary Religious Societies, 1520–1799.* St. Leonard's on Sea: Budd & Gilatt, 1963.

Burke, Edmund. *Reflections on the Revolution in France, and On the Proceedings of Certain Societies in London Relative to That Event.* London: Dodsley, 1790.

Butler, Jon. "Coercion, Miracle, Reason: Rethinking the American Religious Experience in the Revolutionary Age," in *Religion in a Revolutionary Age*, Ronald Hoffman and Peter J. Albert, eds. 1–30.

Butterfield, Herbert. *George III, Lord North, and the People, 1779–1780.* London: Bell, 1949.

Cardenal, Louis de. *La Province pendant la Révolution: histoire des clubs jacobins, 1789–1795.* Paris: Payot, 1929.

Carey, Bryychan and Geoffrey Plank, "Introduction," in *Quakers and Abolition*, Carey and Plank, eds. (Urbana, IL: University of Illinois Press, 2014), 1–14.

Carp, Benjamin L. *Defiance of the Patriots: The Boston Tea Party and the Making of America.* New Haven: Yale University Press, 2010.

Carretta, Vincent. *Equiano, The African: Biography of a Self-Made Man.* New York: Penguin, 2005.

Cash, Arthur. *John Wilkes: The Scandalous Father of Civil Liberty.* New Haven: Yale University Press, 2006.

Chambers, William Nisbet. *Political Parties in a New Nation: The American Experience, 1776–1800*. Oxford: Oxford University Press, 1963.

Champion, Richard. *The American Correspondence of a Bristol Merchant, 1766–1776*. Berkeley: University of California Press, 1964.

Cheney, Paul. "French Revolution's Global Turn and Capitalism's Spatial Fixes," *Journal of Social History* 52, no. 3 (2018), 575–83.

Christie, Ian. *Crisis of Empire: Great Britain and the American Colonies, 1754–1783*. New York: Norton, 1966.

Christie, Ian. *The End of North's Ministry, 1780–1782*. London: Macmillan, 1958.

Christie, William. *An Essay, on Ecclesiastical Establishments in Religion*. Montrose, 1791.

Clark, Dora Mae. *British Opinion and the American Revolution*. New Haven: Yale University Press, 1930.

Clark, J. C. D. *English Society, 1660–1832*, 2nd ed. Cambridge: Cambridge University Press, 2000.

Clark, J. C. D. *The Language of Liberty, 1660–1832: Political Discourse and Social Dynamics in the Anglo-American World*. Cambridge: Cambridge University Press, 1994.

Clark, Peter. *British Clubs and Societies, 1580–1800: The Origins of an Associational World*. Oxford: Oxford University Press, 2000.

Clifford, Mary Louise. *From Slavery to Freetown: Black Loyalists after the American Revolution*. Jefferson, NC: McFarland, 2006.

Coclanis, Peter A. ed. *The Atlantic Economy during the Seventeenth and Eighteenth Centuries: Organization, Operation, Practice and Personnel*. Columbia, SC: University of South Carolina Press, 2005.

Colley, Linda. *Britons: Forging the Nation, 1707–1837*, 3rd ed. New Haven: Yale University Press, 2009.

Conkin, Paul. "The Church Establishment in North Carolina, 1765–1776," *North Carolina Historical Review* 32 (1955), 1–30.

Connolly, S. J. *Divided Kingdom: Ireland, 1630–1800*. Oxford: Oxford University Press, 2008.

Conser, Walter H., Jr. "Stamp Act Resistance," in *Resistance, Politics, and the American Struggle for Independence, 1765–1775*, Conser, Ronald M. McCarthy, David J. Toscano, and Gene Sharp, eds. Boulder, CO: Lynne Reinner, 1986.

Conway, Stephen. *The British Isles and the War of American Independence*. New York: Oxford University Press, 2002.

Cookson, J. E. *The Friends of Peace: Anti-War Liberalism in England, 1793–1815*. Cambridge: Cambridge University Press, 1982.

Cornell, Saul. *The Other Founders: Anti-Federalism & the Dissenting Tradition in America, 1788–1828*. Chapel Hill: University of North Carolina Press, 1999.

Cotlar, Seth. *Tom Paine's America: The Rise and Fall of Transatlantic Radicalism in the Early Republic*. Charlottesville: University of Virginia Press, 2011.

Countryman, Edward. *The American Revolution*. New York: Hill and Wang, 1985.

Countryman, Edward. *The American Revolution*, rev. ed. New York: Hill and Wang, 2003.

Countryman, Edward. *A People in Revolution: The American Revolution and Political Society in New York, 1760-1790*. Baltimore: Johns Hopkins University Press, 1981.

Crane, Verner W. "The Club of Honest Whigs: Friends of Science and Liberty," *William and Mary Quarterly* 23, no. 2 (1966), 210–33.

Cunningham, Noble E., Jr. *The Jeffersonian Republicans: The Formation of Party Organization, 1789-1791*. Chapel Hill: University of North Carolina Press, 1957.

Cunningham, Noble E., Jr. *In Pursuit of Reason: The Life of Thomas Jefferson*. Baton Rouge: Louisiana State University Press, 1987.

Curry, Thomas J. *The First Freedoms: Church and State in America to the Passage the First Amendment*. Oxford: Oxford University Press, 1986.

Curtin, Nancy. "Symbols and Rituals of United Irish Mobilization," in *Ireland and the French Revolution*, Hugh Gough and Dickson, eds. (Dublin: Irish Academic Press, 1990), 68–82.

Curtin, Nancy. "The United Irish Organization in Ulster: 1795-1798," in *The United Irishmen: Republicanism, Radicalism and Rebellion*, Dickson, Kogh, and Whelan, eds. (Dublin: Lilliput Press, 1993), 209–21.

Curtin, Nancy. *The United Irishmen: Popular Politics in Ulster and Dublin, 1791-1798*. Oxford: Oxford University Press, 1998.

Dauer, Manning J. *The Adams Federalists*. Baltimore: Johns Hopkins Press, 1953.

Davis, David Brion. *The Problem of Slavery in the Age of Revolution, 1770-1823*. Ithaca: Cornell University Press, 1975.

Davis, David Brion. *The Problem of Slavery in Western Culture*. Ithaca: Cornell University Press, 1966.

Davis, Michael T. "The Mob Club? The London Corresponding Society and the Politics of Civility in the 1790s," in *Unrespectable Radicals? Popular Politics in the Age of Reform*, Davis and Paul A. Pickering, eds. (London: Ashgate, 2008), 21–40.

Dawson, Henry. *The Sons of Liberty in New York*. Poughkeepsie: Platt & Schram, 1859.

Debien, Gabriel. *Les colons de Saint-Domingue et la Révolution*. Paris: Armand Colin, 1953.

DeConde, Alexander. *The Quasi-War: The Politics and Diplomacy of the Undeclared War with France 1797-1801*. New York: Scribner's, 1966.

della Porta, Donatella. "Riding the Wave: Protest Cascades, and What We Can Learn from Them," in *Global Diffusion of Protest: Riding the Protest Wave in the Neoliberal Crisis*, della Porta, ed. (Amsterdam: Amsterdam University Press, 2017), 9–30.

Derry, John. *English Politics and the American Revolution*. New York: St. Martin's Press, 1976.

Desan, Suzanne, Lynn Hunt, and William Max Nelson, "Introduction," in *The French Revolution in Global Perspective*, Desan, Hunt and Nelson, eds. Ithaca: Cornell University Press, 2013.

Deschamps, Léon. *La constituante et les colonies: la réforme colonial*. Paris: Perrin, 1898.

Dickson, David. *Dublin: The Making of a Capital City*. Cambridge, MA: Harvard University Press, 2014.

Dickson, David. *New Foundations: Ireland, 1660-1800*. Dublin: Irish Academic Press, 2000.

Dickson, David. "The State of Ireland before 1798," in *The Great Irish Rebellion of 1798*, Cathal Póirtéir, ed. (Boulder, CO: Mercier Press, 1998), 15-26.

Dickinson, H. T. *British Radicalism and the French Revolution, 1789-1815*. Oxford: Blackwell, 1985.

Dijn, Annelin de. *Freedom: An Unruly History*. Cambridge, MA: Harvard University Press, 2020.

Ditchfield, G. M. "The Parliamentary Struggle over the Repeal of the Test and Corporation Acts, 1787-1790," *English Historical Review* 89, no. 1 (1974), 551-77.

Dreisbach, Daniel. "Church-State Debate in the Virginia Legislature: From the Declaration of Rights to the Statute for Establishing Religious Freedom," in *Religion and Political Culture in Jefferson's Virginia*, Garrett Ward Sheldon and Daniel Dreisbach, eds. (Lanham, MD: Rowan and Littlefield, 2000), 135-66.

Drescher, Seymour. *Abolition: A History of Slavery and Antislavery*. Cambridge: Cambridge University Press, 2009.

Dorigny, Marcel. "Mirabeau and the Société des Amis des Noirs: Which Way to Abolish Slavery?" in *The Abolitions of Slavery: From L.F. Sonthonax to Victor Schoelcher, 1793, 1794, 1848* (Oxford: Berghahn, 2003), 121-32.

Dorigny, Marcel. "Le movement abolitionniste français face à l'insurrection de Saint- Domingue ou la fin du mythe de l'abolition graduelle," in *L'insurrection des esclaves de Saint-Domingue (22-3 août 1791)*, Laennec Hurbon, ed. (Paris: Karthala, 2000), 29-40.

Dorsey, Peter A. *Common Bondage: Slavery as Metaphor in Revolutionary America* Knoxville: University of Tennessee Press, 2009.

Dozier, Robert J. *For King, Constitution and Country: The English Loyalists and the French Revolution*. Lexington: University of Kentucky Press, 1983.

Dubois, Laurent. "An Atlantic Revolution," *French Historical Studies* 32, no. 4 (2009), 655-61.

Dubois, Laurent. *Avengers of the New World: The Story of the Haitian Revolution*. Cambridge, MA: Harvard University Press, 2004.

Dubois, Laurent. *A Colony of Citizens: Revolution and Slave Emancipation in the French Caribbean, 1787-1804*. Chapel Hill: University of North Carolina Press, 2004.

Duffy, Michael. *The Younger Pitt*. Harlow, England: Longman, 2000.

Duffy, Michael. "William Pitt and the Origins of the Loyalist Association Movement of 1792," *Historical Journal* 39, no. 4 (1996), 943-62.

Dun, James Alexander. *Dangerous Neighbors: Making the Haitian Revolution in Early America*. Philadelphia: University of Pennsylvania Press, 2016.

Dunn, Susan. *Sister Revolutions: French Lightning, American Light*. New York: Faber & Faber, 1999.

Eastwood, David. "Patriotism and the English State in the 1790s," in *The French Revolution and British Popular Politics*, Mark Philp, ed. (Cambridge: Cambridge University Press, 1991), 146–68.

Eberly, Wayne J. "The Pennsylvania Abolition Society, 1775–1830." PhD thesis, Pennsylvania State University, 1973.

Edelstein, Dan and Bilana Kassabova, "How England Fell off the Map of Voltaire's Enlightenment," *Modern Intellectual History* 17, no. 1 (2020), 29–53.

Edelstein, Dan. *The Terror of Natural Right: Republicanism, the Cult of Nature & the French Revolution*. Chicago: University of Chicago Press, 2009.

Egerton, Douglas R. *Death or Liberty: African Americans and Revolutionary America*. Oxford: Oxford University Press, 2009.

Ekirch, A. Roger. *"Poor Carolina": Politics and Society in Colonial North Carolina*. Chapel Hill: University of North Carolina Press, 1981.

Elkins, Stanley and Eric McKitrick, *The Age of Federalism: The Early American Republic, 1788–1800*. Oxford: Oxford University Press, 1993.

Ellery, Eloise. *Brissot de Warville: A Study in the History of the French Revolution*. Boston: Houghton Mifflin, 1915.

Elliott, J. H. *Empires of the Atlantic World: Britain and Spain in America, 1492–1830*. New Haven: Yale University Press, 2006.

Elliott, Marianne. *Partners in Revolution: The United Irishmen and France*. New Haven: Yale University Press, 1982.

Elliott, Marianne. *Wolfe Tone: Prophet of Irish Independence*. New Haven: Yale University Press, 1989.

Elofson, W. M. *The Rockingham Connection and the Second Founding of the Whig Party, 1768–1773*. Montreal: McGill, 1996.

Eltis, David. "Was Abolition of the U.S. and British Slave Trade Significant in Broader Atlantic Context?" *William and Mary Quarterly* 66, no. 4 (2009), 717–36.

Emsley, Clive. "An Aspect of Pitt's 'Terror': Prosecutions for Sedition during the 1790s," *Social History* 6, no. 2 (1981), 155–84.

Emsley, Clive. *Britain and the French Revolution*. London: Pearson, 2000.

Emsley, Clive. "Repression, 'Terror' and the Rule of Law in England during the Decade of the French Revolution," *English Historical Review* 100, no. 397 (1985), 801–25.

Esbeck, Carl H. and Jonathan J. Den Hartog, eds. *Disestablishment and Religious Dissent: Church-State Relations in the New American States, 1776–1833*. Columbia: University of Missouri Press, 2019.

Evans, Chris. *Debating the Revolution: Britain in the 1790s*. London: I.B. Tauris, 2006.

Evans, Howard V. "The Nootka Sound Controversy in Anglo-French Diplomacy," *Journal of Modern History* 46 (1974), 609–40.

Eze, Emmanuel Chukwudi, ed. *Race and the Enlightenment: A Reader*. Oxford: Blackwell, 1997.

Farrell, Sean. *Rituals and Riots; Sectarian Violence and Political Culture in Ulster, 1784–1886*. Lexington: University Press of Kentucky, 2000.

Featherstone, David. "Contested Relationalities of Political Activism: The Democratic Spatial Practices of the London Corresponding Society," *Cultural Dynamics* 22, no. 2 (2010), 87–104.

Fehrenbacher, Don E. *The Slaveholding Republic: An Account of the United States Government's Relations to Slavery*. Oxford: Oxford University Press, 2001.

Ferguson, Niall. *The Square and the Tower: Networks and Power, from the Freemasons to Facebook*. New York: Random House, 2018.

Ferguson, Robert A. *The American Enlightenment, 1750–1820*. Cambridge, MA: Harvard University Press, 1994.

Ferling, John. *Adams vs. Jefferson: The Tumultuous Election of 1800*. Oxford: Oxford University Press, 2004.

Ferling, John. *Almost a Miracle: The American Victory in the War of Independence*, Oxford: Oxford University Press, 2007.

Ferling, John. *Jefferson and Hamilton: The Rivalry That Forged a Nation*. New York: Bloomsbury, 2013.

Ferling, John. *John Adams: A Life*. Knoxville: University of Tennessee Press, 1992.

Ferling, John. *A Leap in the Dark: The Struggle to Create the American Republic*. Oxford: Oxford University Press, 2003.

Fick, Carolyn E. *The Making of Haiti: The Saint Domingue Revolution from Below*. Knoxville: University of Tennessee Press, 1990.

Finkelman, Paul. *Slavery and the Founders: Dilemmas of Jefferson and His Contemporaries*. New York: Routledge, 1995.

Fischer, David Hackett. *The Revolution of American Conservatism: The Federalist Party in the Era of Jeffersonian Democracy*. New York: Harper & Row, 1965.

Fladeland, Betty. *Men and Brothers: Anglo-American Antislavery Cooperation*. Urbana, IL: University of Illinois Press, 1973.

Flavell, Julie. *When London Was Capital of America*. New Haven: Yale University Press, 2010.

Forrest, Alan. *The Death of the French Atlantic: Trade, War and Slavery in the Age of Revolution*. Oxford: Oxford University Press, 2020.

Foster, R. F. *Modern Ireland, 1700–1972*. New York: Penguin, 1989.

Freeman, Joanne B. "Corruption and Compromise in the Election of 1800: The Process of Politics on the National Stage," in *The Revolution of 1800: Democracy, Race & the New Republic*, James Horn, Jan Ellen Lewis, and Peter S. Onouf, eds. (Charlottesville: University of Virginia, 2002), 87–120.

Freeman, Joanne B. "The Presidential Election of 1796," in *John Adams and the Founding of the Republic*, Richard Alan Ryerson, ed. (Boston: Northeastern University Press, 2001), 142–67.

Froude, James Anthony. *The English in Ireland in the Eighteenth Century*. London: Longmans, 1895. 3 vols.

Fruchtman Jack, Jr. *Atlantic Cousins: Benjamin Franklin and His Visionary Friends*. New York: Thunder's Mouth Press, 2005.

Furet, François. *Interpreting the French Revolution*, Elborg Foster, trans. Cambridge: Cambridge University Press, 1981.

Furstenberg, François. "Beyond Freedom and Slavery: Autonomy, Virtue, and Resistance in Early American Political Discourse," *Journal of American History* 89 (2003), 1295–1330.

Furstenberg, François. *When the United States Spoke French: Five Refugees Who Shaped a Nation*. New York: Penguin, 2015.

Galabert, François. "Le Club Jacobin de Montauban," *Revue d'histoire modern et contemporaine* 1 (1899–1900), 457–74.

Garnham, Neil. *The Militia in Eighteenth-Century Ireland: In Defence of the Protestant Interest*. Woodbridge, UK: Boydell & Brewer, 2012.

Garrett, Mitchell B. *The French Colonial Question, 1789–1791: Dealings of the Constituent Assembly with Problems Arising from the Revolution in the West Indies*. New York: Negro Universities Press, 1916.

Garrigus, John D. *Before Haiti: Race and Citizenship in French Saint-Domingue*. New York: Palgrave Macmillan, 2006.

Garrigus, John D. "Saint Domingue's Free People of Color and the Tools of Revolution," in Geggus and Fiering, *World*, 49–64.

Garrioch, David. "'Man Is Born for Society': Confraternities and Civil Society in Eighteenth-Century Paris and Milan," *Social Science History* 41, no. 1 (2017), 103–19.

Gaustad Edwin S. and Leigh E. Schmidt, *The Religious History of America*, rev. ed. New York: HarperOne, 2002.

Gaustad, Edwin S. "Religious Tests, Constitutions, and 'Christian Nation,'" in Hoffman and Albert, *Religion*, 218–35.

Gauthier, Florence. *L'aristocratie de l'épiderme: Le combat de la Société des citoyens de Couleur, 1789–1791*. Paris: CNRS, 2007.

Gay, Peter. *The Enlightenment: An Interpretation: The Science of Freedom*. New York: Norton, 1969.

Gee, Austin. *The British Volunteer Movement, 1794–1814*. Oxford: Clarendon Press, 2003.

Geggus, David and Norman Fiering, eds. *Haitian Revolutionary Studies*. Bloomington: Indiana University Press, 2002.

Geggus, David. "Racial Equality, Slavery, and Colonial Secession during the Constituent Assembly," *American Historical Review* 94, no. 5 (1989), 1290–1308.

Gellman, David N. *Emancipating New York: The Politics of Slavery and Freedom, 1777–1827*. Baton Rouge: Louisiana State University Press, 2006.

Genet, George Clinton. *Washington, Jefferson and "Citizen" Genet, 1793*. New York, 1899.

Gerlach, Larry R. *Prologue to Independence: New Jersey in the Coming of the American Revolution*. New Brunswick, NJ: Rutgers University Press, 1976.

Gigantino II, James J. *The Ragged Road to Abolition: Slavery and Freedom in New Jersey, 1775–1865*. Philadelphia: University of Pennsylvania Press, 2015.

Gilmartin, Kevin. "In the Theater of Counterrevolution: Loyalist Association and Conservative Association in the 1790s," *Journal of British Studies* 41, no. 3 (2002), 291–328.

Gilpatrick, Delbert Harold. *Jeffersonian Democracy in North Carolina, 1789–1816.* New York: Columbia University Press, 1931.

Gilroy, Paul. *The Black Atlantic: Modernity and Double Consciousness.* Cambridge, MA: Harvard University Press, 1993.

Ginter, Donald E. "The Financing of the Whig Party Organization, 1783–1793," *American Historical Review* 71, no. 2 (1966), 421–40.

Ginter, Donald E. "The Loyalist Association Movement of 1792–1793 and British Public Opinion," *Historical Journal* 9, no. 2 (1966), 179–90.

Godineau, Dominique. *The Women of Paris and Their French Revolution,* Katherine Streip, trans. Berkeley: University of California Press, 1998.

Goode, Michael and John Smolenski, eds. *The Specter of Peace: Rethinking Violence and Power in the Colonial Atlantic.* Leiden: Brill, 2018.

Goodman, Dena. *The Republic of Letters: A Cultural History of the French Enlightenment.* Ithaca: Cornell University Press, 1993.

Goodwin, Albert. *The Friends of the People: The English Democratic Movement in the Age of the French Revolution.* London: Hutchinson, 1979.

Goodwin, George. *Benjamin Franklin in London: The British Life of America's Founding Father.* New Haven: Yale University Press, 2016.

Gough, Hugh. "France and the 1798 Rebellion," in Póirtéir, 37–49.

Gould, Eliga H. *The Persistence of Empire: British Political Culture in the Age of the American Revolution.* Chapel Hill: North Carolina University Press, 2000.

Gould, Eliga H. and Peter S. Onuf, eds. *Empire and Nation: The American Revolution in the Atlantic World.* Baltimore: Johns Hopkins University Press, 2005.

Graham, Thomas. "'A Union of Power'? The United Irish Organization: 1795–1798," in Dickson, Keogh, and Whelan, *United,* 197–208.

Green, Steven K. *The Second Disestablishment: Church and State in Nineteenth-Century America.* Oxford: Oxford University Press, 2010.

Greene, Jack P. "Bridge to Revolution: The Wilkes Fund Controversy in South Carolina, 1769–1775," *Journal of Southern History* 29, no. 1 (1963), 19–52.

Greene, Jack P. *The Quest for Power: The Lower Houses of Assembly in the Southern Royal Colonies, 1689–1776.* Chapel Hill: University of North Carolina Press, 1963.

Grieder, Josephine. *Anglomania in France, 1740–1789: Fact, Fiction and Political Discourse.* Geneva: Droz, 1985.

Griffin, Patrick. *America's Revolution.* Oxford: Oxford University Press, 2013.

Griffin, Patrick. *The Townshend Moment: The Making of Empire and Revolution in the Eighteenth Century.* New Haven: Yale University Press, 2017.

Guyatt, Nicholas. *Bind Us Apart: How Enlightened Americans Invented Racial Segregation.* New York: Basic Books, 2016.

Gwynn, Stephen. *Henry Grattan and His Times.* London: Harrap, 1939.

Hague, William. *William Pitt the Younger.* New York: Knopf, 2005.

Hague, William. *William Wilberforce: The Life of the Great Anti-Slave Trade Campaigner.* Boston: Harcourt, 2007.

Hale, Mathew Rainbow. "Regenerating the World: The French Revolution, Civic Festivals, and the Forging of Modern American Democracy, 1793–1795," *Journal of American History* 103, no. 4 (2017), 891–920.

Hall, Walter Phelps. *British Radicalism, 1791–1797.* New York: Columbia University Press, 1912.

Halperin, Terri Diane. *The Alien and Sedition Acts of 1798: Testing the Constitution.* Baltimore: Johns Hopkins University Press, 2016.

Hammersley, Rachel. *The English Republican Tradition and Eighteenth-Century France: Between the Ancients and Moderns.* Manchester: Manchester University Press, 2010.

Hancock, David. *Citizens of the World: London Merchants and the Integration of the Atlantic Community, 1735–1785.* Cambridge: Cambridge University Press, 1995.

Hanson, Paul R. *The Jacobin Republic under Fire: The Federalist Revolt in the French Revolution.* University Park, PA: Penn State University Press, 2003.

Hanson, Paul R. "The Monarchist Clubs and the Pamphlet Debate over Political Legitimacy in the Early Years of the French Revolution," *French Historical Studies* 21, no. 2 (1998), 299–324.

Hardman, John. *The Life of Louis XVI.* New Haven: Yale University Press, 2017.

Harris, Bob. "The Patriot Clubs of the 1750s," in *Clubs and Societies in Eighteenth-Century Ireland*, James Kelly and Martyn J. Powell, eds. (Dublin: Four Courts Press, 2010), 224–43.

Harris, Bob. "Political Protests in the Year of Liberty, 1792," in *Scotland in the Age of the French Revolution*, Bob Harris, ed. (Edinburgh: Donald, 2005), 49–78.

Harris, Bob. *The Scottish People and the French Revolution.* London: Pickering & Chatto, 2008.

Harsin, Jill. *Barricades: The War of the Streets in Revolutionary Paris, 1830–1848.* New York: Palgrave, 2002.

Hay, Carla H. "The Making of a Radical: The Case of James Burgh," *Journal of British Studies* 18, no. 2 (1979), 90–117.

Hay, Edward. *History of the Insurrection of the County of Wexford, A.D. 1798.* Dublin: Stockdale, 1803.

Haydon, Colin. *John Henry Williams (1747–1829), "Political Clergyman": War, the French Revolution and Church of England.* Woodbridge, Suffolk: Boydell, 2007.

Hazan, Eric. *A People's History of the French Revolution.* London: Verso, 2014.

Hemmings, Ray. *Liberty or Death: Early Struggles for Parliamentary Democracy.* London: Lawrence and Wishart, 2000.

Hempton, David. *Methodism in British Politics, 1750–1850.* Stanford: Stanford University Press, 1984.

Henriot, Marcel. *Le club des jacobins de Semur*. Dijon: Rebourseau, 1933.

Henriques, Ursula. *Religious Toleration in England, 1787–1833*. London: Routledge, 1961.

Higgins, Padhraig. *A Nation of Politicians: Gender, Patriotism and Political Culture in Late Eighteenth-Century Ireland*. Madison: University of Wisconsin Press, 2010.

Higonnet, Patrice. *Goodness beyond Virtue: Jacobins during the French Revolution*. Harvard: Harvard University Press, 1998.

Hilton, Boyd. *A Mad, Bad and Dangerous People? England 1783–1846*. Oxford: Oxford University Press, 2006.

Himmelfarb, Gertrude. *The Roads to Modernity: The British, French and American Enlightenments*. New York: Knopf, 2004.

Hinderaker, Eric. *Boston's Massacre*. Cambridge, MA: Cambridge University Press, 2017.

Hoadley, John F. *Origins of American Political Parties, 1789–1803*. Lexington: University Press of Kentucky, 1986.

Hochschild, Adam. *Bury the Chains: Prophets and Rebels in the Fight to Free an Empire's Slaves*. New York: Mariner, 2005.

Hoerder, Dirk. *Crowd Action in Revolutionary Massachusetts, 1765–1780*. New York: Academic Press, 1977.

Holt, Mack P. *The French Wars of Religion, 1562–1629*. 2nd ed. Cambridge: Cambridge University Press, 2005.

Holton, Woody. *Forced Founders: Indians, Debtors, Slaves and the Making of the American Revolution in Virginia*. Chapel Hill: University of North Carolina Press, 1999.

Hoock, Holger. *Scars of Independence: America's Violent Birth*. New York: Crown, 2017.

Horne, Gerald. *The Counter-Revolution of 1776: Slave Resistance and the Origins of the United States of America*. New York: New York University Press, 2014.

Horton, James Oliver and Lois E. Horton, *Slavery and the Making of America*. Oxford: Oxford University Press, 2005.

Hudson, Nicholas. "'Britons Never Will Be Slaves': National Myth, Conservatism, and the Beginnings of British Antislavery," *Eighteenth-Century Studies* 34, no. 4 (2001), 559–76.

Hunt, Lynn. *Inventing Human Rights: A History*. New York: Norton, 2008.

Hunt, Lynn. *Writing History in the Global Era*. New York: Norton, 2015.

Innes, Joanna. "'Reform' in English Public Life: The Functions of a Word," in *Rethinking the Age of Reform: Britain 1780–1850*, Arthur Burns and Innes, eds. (Cambridge: Cambridge University Press, 2007) 71–97.

Innes, Joanna and Mark Philp, eds. *Re-Imagining Democracy in the Age of Revolutions: America, France, Britain, Ireland, 1750–1850*. Oxford: Oxford University Press, 2015.

Irvin, Benjamin H. *Samuel Adams: Son of Liberty, Father of Revolution*. Oxford: Oxford University Press, 2002.

Irvin, Benjamin H. "Tar, Feathers and the Enemies of American Liberties, 1768–1776," *New England Quarterly* 76, no. 2 (2003), 197–238.

Isaac, Rhys. "Evangelical Revolt: The Nature of the Baptists' Challenge to the Traditional Order in Virginia, 1765 to 1775," *William and Mary Quarterly* 3rd Series, 31 (1974), 345–68.

Isaac, Rhys. *The Transformation of Virginia, 1740–1790*. New York: Norton, 1988.

Isenberg, Nancy. *Fallen Founder: The Life of Aaron Burr*. New York: Penguin, 2007.

Israel, Jonathan. *Democratic Enlightenment: Philosophy, Revolution, and Human Rights, 1750–1790*. Oxford: Oxford University Press, 2011.

Israel, Jonathan. *Revolutionary Ideas: An Intellectual History of the French Revolution from the Rights of Man to Robespierre*. Princeton: Princeton University Press, 2014.

Jackson, Alvin. *Ireland 1798–1998: Politics and War*. London: Blackwell, 1999.

Jackson, Maurice. "Anthony Benezet and the Dream of Freedom: Then and Now," in *The Atlantic World of Anthony Benezet (1713–1784): From French Reformation to North American Quaker Antislavery Activism*, Marie-Jeanne Rossignol and Bertrand Van Ruymbeke, eds. (Leiden: Brill, 2017), vii–xxii.

Jackson, Maurice. *Let This Voice Be Heard: Anthony Benezet, Father of American Abolitionism*. Philadelphia: University of Pennsylvania Press, 2009.

Jacob, Margaret. *Living the Enlightenment: Freemasonry and Politics in Eighteenth-Century Europe*. Oxford: Oxford University Press, 1991.

Jacob, Margaret. *Strangers Nowhere in the World: The Rise of Cosmopolitanism in Early Modern Europe*. Philadelphia: University of Pennsylvania Press, 2006.

Jacob, Rosamond. *The Rise of the United Irishmen*. London: Harrap, 1937.

Jameson, J. Franklin. *The American Revolution Considered as a Social Movement*. Boston: Beacon Press, 1956.

Jarvis, Katie. *Politics in the Marketplace: Work, Gender, and Citizenship in Revolutionary France*. Oxford: Oxford University Press, 2019.

Johnson, Erica R. *Philanthropy and Race in the Haitian Revolution*. New York: Palgrave Macmillan, 2018.

Johnson, Thomas Cary. *Virginia Presbyterianism and Religious Liberty in Colonial and Revolutionary Times*. Richmond: Presbyterian Committee of Publication, 1907.

Johnston, Kenneth R. "The First and Last British Convention," *Romanticism* 13, no. 2 (2007), 99–132.

Jones, Colin. "The Overthrow of Maximilien Robespierre and the 'Indifference' of the People," *American Historical Review* 119, no. 3 (2014), 689–713.

Jordan, David P. *The Revolutionary Career of Maximilien Robespierre*. New York: Free Press, 1985.

Jourdan, Annie. *La Révolution: une exception française?* Paris: Flammarion, 2004.

Juster, Susan. "The Evangelical Ascendency in Revolutionary America," in Gray and Kamensky, *Oxford Handbook of the American Revolution*, 407–26.

Kammen, Michael G. *A Rope of Sand: The Colonial Agents, British Politics and the American Revolution*. Ithaca: Cornell University Press, 1968.

Kaplan, Lawrence S. *Jefferson and France: An Essay on Politics and Political Ideas.* New Haven: Yale University Press, 1967.

Kars, Marjolene. *Breaking Loose Together: The Regulator Rebellion in Pre-Revolutionary North Carolina.* Chapel Hill: University of North Carolina Press, 2002.

Kates, Gary. *The Cercle Social, the Girondins, and the French Revolution.* Princeton: Princeton University Press, 1985.

Kelly, James. *Henry Flood: Patriots and Politics in Eighteenth-Century Ireland.* Notre Dame: University of Notre Dame Press, 1998.

Kelly, James. *Prelude to Union: Anglo-Irish Politics in the 1780s.* Cork: Cork University Press, 1992.

Kennedy, Michael L. *The Jacobin Clubs in the French Revolution: The Early Years.* Princeton: Princeton University Press, 1982.

Kennedy, Michael L. *The Jacobin Clubs in the French Revolution: The Middle Years.* Princeton: Princeton University Press, 1988.

Kennedy, Michael L. *The Jacobin Clubs in the French Revolution, 1793–1795.* New York: Berghahn, 2000.

Ketcham, Ralph. *James Madison: A Biography.* New York: Macmillan, 1971.

Kidd, Thomas S. *God of Liberty: A Religious History of the American Revolution.* New York: Basic Books, 2010.

Kidd, Thomas S. *The Great Awakening: The Roots of Evangelical Christianity in Colonial America.* New Haven: Yale University Press, 2007.

King, Stuart R. *Blue Coat or Powdered Whig: Free People of Color in Pre-Revolutionary Saint-Domingue.* Athens: University of Georgia Press, 2001.

Kirk, Russell. *Edmund Burke: A Genius Reconsidered.* Peru, IL: Sugden, 1988.

Kitchen, Martin. *A History of Modern Germany, 1800–2000.* New York: Blackwell, 2006.

Knights, Mark. "The 1780 Protestant Petitions and the Culture of Petitioning," in *The Gordon Riots: Politics, Culture and Insurrection in Late Eighteenth-Century Britain*, Ian Haywood and John Seed, eds. (Cambridge: Cambridge University Press, 2012), 46–68.

Knott, Sarah. "Narrating the Age of Revolution," *William and Mary Quarterly* 73, no. 1 (2016), 3–36.

Kooster, Wim. *Revolutions in the Atlantic World: A Comparative History.* New York: NYU Press, 2009.

Koschnik, Albrecht. "The Democratic Societies of Philadelphia and the Limits of the American Public Sphere, circa 1793–1795," *William and Mary Quarterly* 58, no. 3 (2001), 615–36.

Koshnik, Albrecht. *"Let a Common Interest Bind Us Together": Associations, Partisanship, and Culture in Philadelphia, 1775-1840.* Charlottesville: University Press of Virginia, 2007.

Labaree, Benjamin Woods. *The Boston Tea Party.* New York: Oxford University Press, 1964.

Labroue, Henri. *La société populaire de Bergerac pendant la Révolution.* Paris: Au siège de la Société, 1915.

Lacorne, Denis. *L'invention de la République: Le modele américaine*. Paris: Hachette, 1991.

Lambert, Frank. *The Founding Fathers and the Place of Religion in America*. Princeton: Princeton University Press, 2003.

Lambert, Frank. *"Pedlar in Divinity": George Whitefield and the Transatlantic Revivals, 1737–1770*. Princeton: Princeton University Press, 1994.

Lammey, David. "The Free Trade Crisis: A Reappraisal," in *Parliament, Politics and People: Essays in Eighteenth-Century Irish History*, Gerard O'Brien, ed. (Dublin: Irish Academic Press, 1989), 141–70.

Landers, Jane G. *Atlantic Creoles in the Age of Revolutions*. Cambridge, MA: Harvard University Press, 2010.

Landes, David. *The Wealth and Poverty of Nations: Why Some Are So Rich and Some So Poor*. New York: Norton, 1998.

Langley, Lester D. *The Americas in the Age of Revolution, 1750–1850*. New Haven: Yale University Press, 1998.

Laprade, W. T. *England and the French Revolution, 1789–1797*. Baltimore: Johns Hopkins University Press, 1909.

Law, Robin. "La cérémonie du Bois Caiman et le 'pacte de sang' dahoméen," in *L'Insurrection des esclaves de Saint-Domingue (22-23 août 1791): actes de la table ronde internationale de Port-au-Prince, 8 au 10 décembre 1997*, Lannec Hurbon, ed. (Paris: Karthala, 2000), 131–47.

Lecky, William Edward Hartpole. *England in the Eighteenth Century*. London: Longman's, 1879. 7 vols.

Lecky, William Edward Hartpole, *A History of Ireland in the Eighteenth Century*. London: Longmans, 1892. 5 vols.

Leclerc, Lucien. "La politique et l'influence du club de l'hôtel Massiac," *Annales historiques de la Révolution française* 14 (1937), 342–63.

Lee, Wayne E. *Crowds and Soldiers in Revolutionary North Carolina: The Culture of Violence in Riot and War*. Gainesville: University Press of Florida, 2001.

Lefebvre, Georges. *The French Revolution, Volume II: From 1793 to 1799*. New York: Columbia University Press, 1964.

Lemisch, Jesse. *Jack Tar vs. John Bull: The Role of New York's Seamen in Precipitating the Revolution*. New York: Garland, 1997.

Leutscher, George D. *Early Political Machinery in the United States*. New York: Da Capo Press, 1971.

Liébart, Déborah. "Un groupe de pression contre-révolutionnaire: le Club Massiac sous la Constituante," *Annales historiques de la Révolution française* 354 (2009), 29–50.

Lilti, Antoine. *Le monde des salons: sociabilité et mondanité à Paris au XVIIIe siècle*. Paris: Fayard, 2005.

Linebaugh, Peter and Marcus Rediker, *The Many-Headed Hydra: Sailors, Slaves and the Hidden History of the Revolutionary Atlantic*. Boston: Beacon, 2000.

Link, Eugene Perry. *Democratic-Republican Societies, 1790-1800*. New York: Columbia University Press, 1942.

Linton, Marisa. *Choosing Terror: Virtue, Friendship, and Authenticity in the French Revolution*. Oxford: Oxford University Press, 2013.

Linton, Marisa and Mette Harder, "'Come and Dine': The Dangers of Conspicuous Consumption in French Revolutionary Politics, 1789–1795," *European History Quarterly* 45, no. 4 (2015), 615–37.

Livesey, James. *Civil Society and Empire: Ireland and Scotland in the Eighteenth-Century Atlantic World*. New Haven: Yale University Press, 2009.

Loiselle, Kenneth. *Brotherly Love: Freemasonry and Male Friendship in Enlightenment France*. Ithaca: Cornell University Press, 2016.

Lougue, Kenneth J. *Popular Disturbances in Scotland, 1780–1815*. Edinburgh: John Donald Publishers, 1979.

Lounissi, Carine. *Thomas Paine and the French Revolution*. New York: Palgrave Macmillan, 2018.

Lovat-Fraser, J. A. *Henry Dundas, Viscount Melville*. Cambridge: Cambridge University Press, 1916.

Lutnick, Solomon. *The American Revolution and the British Press, 1775–1784*. Columbia: University of Missouri Press, 1967.

Lyon, Eileen Groth. *Politicians in the Pulpit: Christian Radicalism in Britain from the Fall of the Bastille to the Disintegration of Chartism*. London: Ashgate, 1999.

McBride, I. R. *Scripture Politics: Ulster Presbyterians and Irish Radicalism in the Late Eighteenth Century*. Oxford: Clarendon, 1998.

McBride, Spencer W. *Pulpit and Nation: Clergymen and the Politics of Revolutionary America*. Charlottesville: University of Virginia Press, 2016.

McCalman, Iain. *Radical Underworld: Prophets, Revolutionaries and Pornographers in London, 1795–1840*. Cambridge: Cambridge University Press, 1988.

McCormack, Matthew. *Embodying the Militia in Georgian England*. Oxford: Oxford University Press, 2015.

McDonnell, Michael A. *The Politics of War: Race, Class and Conflict in Revolutionary Virginia*. Chapel Hill: University of North Carolina Press, 2007.

McDowell, R. B. *Ireland in the Age of Imperialism and Revolution, 1760–1801*. Oxford: Clarendon Press, 1979.

McFarland, E. W. *Ireland and Scotland in the Age of Revolution: Planting the Green Bough*. Edinburgh: Edinburgh University Press, 1994.

McGaughy, J. Kent. *Richard Henry Lee of Virginia*. London: Rowan & Littlefield, 2004.

McNeill, William H. "Transatlantic History in World Perspective," in *Transatlantic History*, Steven G. Reinhardt and Dennis Reinhartz, eds. (College Station: Texas A&M University Press, 2006), 3–40.

McPhee, Peter. *Robespierre: A Revolutionary Life*. New Haven: Yale University Press, 2012.

Mackenzie, Peter. *The Life of Thomas Muir, Esq*. London: Simpkin & Marshall, 1831.

Madden, Richard Robert. *The United Irishmen: Their Lives and Times*. London: Madden, 1842–1846. 12 vols.

Maier, Pauline. *From Resistance to Revolution: Colonial Radicals and the Development of American Opposition to Britain, 1765–1776*. New York: Knopf, 1972.

Maier, Pauline. "John Wilkes and American Disillusionment with Britain," *William and Mary Quarterly* 20, no. 3 (1963), 373–95.

Malone, Dumas. *Jefferson and the Ordeal of Liberty*. Boston: Little, Brown & Co., 1962.

Mansergh, Danny. *Grattan's Failure: Parliamentary Opposition and the People of Ireland, 1779–1800*. Dublin: Irish Academic Press, 2005.

Marini, Stephen A. *Radical Sects of Revolutionary New England*. Cambridge, MA: Harvard University Press, 1982.

Mark, Irving. *Agrarian Conflicts in Colonial New York, 1711–1775*. New York: Columbia University Press, 1965.

Martin, Fernand. *La Révolution en Province: les Jacobins au village*. Clermont-Ferrand, 1902.

Mason, Bernard. *The Road to Independence: The Revolutionary Movement in New York, 1773–1777*. Lexington: University Press of Kentucky, 2014.

Mason, Matthew. *Slavery and Politics in the Early American Republic*. Chapel Hill: University of North Carolina Press, 2006.

Mathieson, William. *The Awakening of Scotland: A History from 1747 to 1797*. Glasgow: Maclehose, 1910.

Mathiez, Albert. *Le Club des Cordeliers pendant la crise de Varennes et le massacre du Champ de Mars*. Genève: Slatkine-Megariotis Reprints, 1975.

Mathiez, Albert. *La Révolution et les étrangers: cosmopolitisme et defense nationale*. Paris: Renaissance du livre, 1918.

Mayo, Lawrence Shaw. *John Langdon of New Hampshire*. Port Washington, NY: Kennikat Press, 1937.

Meilke, H. W. *Scotland and the Age of Revolution*. Glasgow, Maclehose, 1912.

Menschel, David. "Abolition without Deliverance: The Law of Connecticut Slavery, 1784–1848," *Yale Law Journal* 111 (2001), 183–222.

Meyer, David S. and Sidney Tarrow, eds. *The Social Movement Society: Contentious Politics for a New Century*. New York: Rowan & Littlefield, 1998.

Middlekauff, Robert. *The Glorious Cause: The American Revolution, 1763–1789*. Oxford: Oxford University Press, 1982.

Midgley, Claire. *Women against Slavery: The British Campaigns, 1780–1870*. New York: Routledge, 1992.

Miller, John Chester. *Crisis in Freedom: The Alien and Sedition Acts*. Boston: Little, Brown & Co., 1951.

Miller, John C. *Origins of the American Revolution*. Stanford: Stanford University Press, 1943.

Miller, William Lee. *The First Liberty: Religion and the American Republic*. New York: Knopf, 1986.

Mills, H. E. *The Early Years of the French Revolution in Santo Domingo*. Poughkeepsie, NY: Haight, 1892.

Mitchell, Austin. "The Association Movement of 1792–1793," *Historical Journal* 4, no. 1 (1961), 56–77.

Mitchell, L. G. *Charles James Fox*. Oxford: Oxford University Press, 1992.

Morgan, Edmund S. and Helen M. Morgan, *The Stamp Act Crisis: Prologue to Revolution*. Chapel Hill: University of North Carolina Press, 1953.

Morgan, Kenneth. "Liverpool's Dominance in the British Slave Trade, 1740–1807," in *Liverpool and Transatlantic Slavery*, David Richardson, Suzanne Schwarz and Anthony Tibbles, eds. (Liverpool: Liverpool University Press, 2007), 14–42.

Morgan, Phillip D. and Jack P. Greene, "Introduction: The Present State of Atlantic History," in *Atlantic History: A Critical Appraisal*, Greene and Morgan, eds. (Oxford: Oxford University Press, 2009), 3–34.

Mori, Jennifer. *Britain in the Age of the French Revolution*. London: Longman, 2000.

Morley, Vincent. *Irish Opinion and the American Revolution, 1760–1783*. Cambridge: Cambridge University Press, 2002.

Mugnier, François. *La Société populaire ou Club des Jacobins de Thonon*. Paris: Champion, 1898.

Muthu, Sankar. *Enlightenment Against Empire*. Princeton: Princeton University Press, 2003.

Namier, Lewis. *England in the Age of the American Revolution*. London: Macmillan, 1963.

Namier, Lewis. *The Structure of Politics at the Accession of George III*. London: Macmillan, 1929.

Nash, Gary B. "The African Americans' Revolution," in *The Oxford Handbook of the American Revolution*, Edward G. Gray and Jane Kamensky, eds. (Oxford: Oxford University Press, 2013), 250–72.

Nash, Gary B. *Race and Revolution*. Madison: Madison House, 1980.

Nash, Gary B. *The Unknown American Revolution: The Unruly Birth of Democracy and the Struggle to Create America*. New York: Viking, 2005.

Nash Gary B. and Jean R. Soderlund. *Freedom by Degrees: Emancipation in Pennsylvania and Its Aftermath*. Oxford: Oxford University Press, 1991.

Navickas, Katrina. *Protest and the Politics of Space and Place, 1789–1848*. Manchester: Manchester University Press, 2016.

Newman, Paul Douglas. *Fries's Rebellion: The Enduring Struggle for the American Revolution*. Philadelphia: University of Pennsylvania Press, 2004.

Newman, Richard S. *Freedom's Prophet: Bishop Richard Allen, the AME Church, and the Black Founding Fathers*. New York: New York University Press, 2008.

Newman, Richard S. "The Pennsylvania Abolition Society and the Struggle for Racial Justice," in *Antislavery and Abolition in Philadelphia: Emancipation and the Long Struggle for Racial Justice in the City of Brotherly Love*, Newman and James Meuller, eds. (Baton Rouge: Louisiana State University Press, 2011), 118–48.

Newman, Richard S. *The Transformation of American Abolitionism: Fighting Slavery in the Early Republic*. Chapel Hill: University of North Carolina Press, 2002.

Newman, Simon P. *Parades and the Politics of the Street: Festive Culture in the Early American Republic.* Philadelphia: University of Pennsylvania Press, 1997.

Norris, John M. *Shelburne and Reform.* New York: St. Martin's, 1963.

Norton, Mary Beth. *1774: The Long Year of Revolution.* New York: Knopf, 2020.

Norton, Mary Beth. *Liberty's Daughters: The Revolutionary Experience of American Women, 1750–1850.* Boston: Little, Brown & Co., 1980.

O'Brien, Conor Cruise. *The Long Affair: Thomas Jefferson and the French Revolution, 1785–1800.* Chicago: University of Chicago Press, 1996.

O'Connell, Maurice. *Irish Politics and Social Conflict in the Age of the American Revolution.* Philadelphia: University of Pennsylvania, 1965.

O'Donnell, Ruán, *The Rebellion in Wicklow, 1798.* Dublin: Irish Academic Press, 1998.

O'Gorman, Frank. "Campaign Rituals and Ceremonies: The Social Meaning of Elections in England, 1780–1860," *Past & Present* 135 (1992), 79–115.

O'Gorman, Frank. "The Paine Burnings of 1792–1793," *Past & Present* 193 (2006), 111–55.

O'Gorman, Frank. *The Rise of Party in England: The Rockingham Whigs, 1760–1782.* London: George Allen, 1975.

O'Gorman, Frank. *The Whig Party and the French Revolution.* London: Macmillan, 1967.

O'Shaughnessy, Andrew Jackson. *An Empire Divided: The American Revolution in the British Caribbean.* Philadelphia: University of Pennsylvania Press, 2000.

Ohline, Howard A. "Slavery, Economics and Congressional Politics, 1790," *Journal of Southern History* 46, no. 3 (1980), 335–60.

Oldfield, J. R. "The London Committee and Mobilization of Public Opinion against the Slave Trade," *Historical Journal* 35, no. 2 (1992), 331–43.

Oldfield, J. R. *Popular Politics and British Anti-Slavery: The Mobilization of Public Opinion against the Slave Trade, 1787–1807.* Manchester: Manchester University Press, 1995.

Oldfield, J. R. *Transatlantic Abolitionism in the Age of Revolution: An International History of Anti-Slavery, c. 1787–1820.* Cambridge: Cambridge University Press, 2013.

Oliver, Bette W. *Jacques Pierre Brissot in America and France, 1788–1793: In Search of Better Worlds.* Lanham, MD: Lexington Books, 2016.

Olson, Alison Gilbert. *Anglo-American Politics, 1660–1775: The Relationship between Parties in England and Colonial America.* Oxford: Clarendon Press, 1973.

Olson, Alison Gilbert. *Making the Empire Work: London and American Interest Groups, 1690–1790.* Cambridge, MA: Harvard University Press, 1992.

Olson, Alison Gilbert. *The Radical Duke: The Career and Correspondence of Charles Lennox, Third Duke of Richmond.* Oxford: Oxford University Press, 1961.

Orihel, Michelle. "'Mississippi Mad': The Democratic Society of Kentucky and the Sectional Politics of Navigation Rights," *Register of the Kentucky Historical Society* 114, nos. 3–4 (2016), 399–430.

Osborne, John W. *John Cartwright*. Cambridge: Cambridge University Press, 1972.

Ott, Thomas O. *The Haitian Revolution, 1789-1804*. Knoxville: University of Tennessee Press, 1973.

Owen, Kenneth. *Political Community in Revolutionary Pennsylvania, 1774-1800*. Oxford: Oxford University Press, 2018.

Page, Anthony. "Rational Dissent, Enlightenment, and the Abolition of the British Slave Trade," *Historical Journal* 54, 3 (2011), 741-72.

Palmer, R. R. *The Age of the Democratic Revolution: A Political History of Europe and America, 1760-1800*. Princeton: Princeton University Press, 1959-1964. 2 vols.

Parkenham, Thomas. *The Year of Liberty: The Story of the Great Irish Rebellion of 1798*. London: Thomas & Parkenham, 1969.

Parkinson, Robert G. *The Common Cause: Creating Race and Nation in the American Revolution*. Chapel Hill: University of North Carolina Press, 2016.

Parolin, Christina. *Radical Spaces: Venues of Popular Politics in London, 1790-c.1845*. Canberra: Australian National University Press, 2010.

Parssinen, T. M. "Association, Convention and Anti-Parliament in British Radical Politics, 1771-1848," *English Historical Review* 88, no. 348 (1973), 504-33.

Pasley, Jeffrey L. *The First Presidential Contest: 1796 and the Founding of American Democracy*. Lawrence: University of Kansas Press, 2013.

Pasley, Jeffrey L. *"The Tyranny of Printers": Newspaper Politics in the Early American Republic*. Charlottesville: University Press of Virginia, 2001.

Patrick, Allison. *The Men of the First French Republic: Political Alignments in the National Convention of 1792*. Baltimore: Johns Hopkins University Press, 1972.

Patterson, James G. *In the Wake of the Great Rebellion: Republicanism, Agrarianism and Banditry in Ireland after 1798*. Manchester: Manchester University Press, 2008.

Perkins, Samuel G. *"On the Margin of Vesuvius": Sketches of St. Domingo, 1785-1793*. Lawrence, KS: Institute of Haitian Studies, 1995.

Perl-Rosenthal, Nathan. "Atlantic Cultures and the Age of Revolution," *William and Mary Quarterly* 74, no. 4 (2017), 667-96.

Perl-Rosenthal, Nathan. "Corresponding Republics: Letter Writing and Patriot Organizing in the Atlantic Revolutions, circa 1760-1792." PhD dissertation: Columbia University, 2011.

Pestana, Carla Gardina. *Protestant Empire: Religion and the Making of the British Atlantic World*. Philadelphia: University of Pennsylvania Press, 2009.

Peterson, Mark A. *The City-State of Boston: The Rise and Fall of an Atlantic Power, 1630-1865*. Princeton: Princeton University Press, 2019.

Peterson, Merill D. *Thomas Jefferson and the New Nation: A Biography*. Oxford: Oxford University Press, 1970.

Peterson, Merill D. and Robert C. Vaughan, eds. *The Virginia Statute for Religious Freedom: Its Evolution and Consequences in American History*. Cambridge: Cambridge University Press, 1988.

Peyrard, Christine. *Les Jacobins de l'Ouest: sociabilité révolutionnaire et forms de politisation dans le Maine et la Basse-Normandie (1789–1799)*. Paris: Sorbonne, 1996.

Philp, Mark. *Reforming Ideas in Britain: Politics and Language in the Shadow of the French Revolution, 1789–1815*. Cambridge: Cambridge University Press, 2014.

Philp, Mark. "Vulgar Conservatism, 1792–1793," *English Historical Review* 110, no. 435 (1995), 42–69.

Phillips, Kevin. *1775: A Good Year for Revolution*. New York: Viking, 2012.

Phillips, N. C. "Edmund Burke and the County Movement," *English Historical Review* 76, no. 299 (1961), 254–78.

Pigott, Charles. *The Whig Club, or a Sketch of the Manners of the Age*. London, 1794.

Pingué, Danièle. *Les mouvements jacobins en Normandie orientale: Les sociétés politiques dans l'Eure et la Seine-Inférieure, 1790–1795*. Paris: Editions CTHS, 2001.

Planté, Adrien. *Les Jacobins d'Orthez: la société populaire et le comité de surveillance: procès-verbaux*. Pau: Garet, 1903.

Polasky, Janet L. *Revolution in Brussels, 1787–1793*. Brussels: Académie royale de Belgique, 1987.

Polasky, Janet L. *Revolutions without Borders: The Call to Liberty in the Atlantic World*. New Haven: Yale University Press, 2015.

Pomeranz, Kenneth. *The Great Divergence: China, Europe and the Making of the Modern World Economy*. Princeton: Princeton University Press, 2000.

Popkin, Jeremy D. "A Colonial Media Revolution: The Press in Saint-Domingue, 1789–1793," *The Americas* 75, no. 1 (2018), 3–25.

Popkin, Jeremy D. *A Concise History of the Haitian Revolution*. Chichester, MA: Wiley-Blackwell, 2012.

Popkin, Jeremy D. "Saint-Domingue, Slavery and the Origins of the Haitian Revolution," in *From Deficit to Deluge: The Origins of the French Revolution*, Thomas E. Kaiser and Van Kley, eds. (Stanford, CA: Stanford University Press, 2011), 220–48.

Popkin, Jeremy D. *You Are All Free: The Haitian Revolution and the Abolition of Slavery*. Cambridge, UK: Cambridge University Press, 2010.

Porritt, Edward. *The Unreformed House of Commons: Parliamentary Representation before 1832*. Cambridge: Cambridge University Press, 1909. 2 vols.

Porter, Dale H. *The Abolition of the Slave Trade in England, 1784–1807*. Hamden, CT: Archon, 1970.

Porter, Roy. *The Creation of the Modern World: The Untold Story of the British Enlightenment*. New York: Norton, 2001.

Potts, Louis W. *Arthur Lee: A Virtuous Revolutionary*. Baton Rouge: Louisiana State University Press, 1981.

Powell, Martin J. *The Politics of Consumption in Eighteenth-Century Ireland*. London: Palgrave, 2005.

Powell, Martin J. "The Society of Free Citizens and Other Popular Political Clubs, 1749–1789," in Kelly and Powell, *Clubs and Societies*, 203–23.

Prince, Carl E. *New Jersey's Jeffersonian Republicans: The Genesis of an Early Party Machine*. Chapel Hill: University of North Carolina Press, 1967.

Quarles, Benjamin. *The Negro in the American Revolution*. Chapel Hill: University of North Carolina Press, 1961.

Ragosta, John A. *Wellspring of Liberty: How Virginia's Religious Dissenters Helped Win the American Revolution and Secured Religious Liberty*. Oxford: Oxford University Press, 2010.

Ragsdale, Bruce A. *A Planters' Republic: The Search for Economic Independence in Revolutionary Virginia*. Madison, WI: Madison House, 1996.

Randall, Adrian. *Riotous Assemblies: Popular Protest in Hanoverian England*. Oxford: Oxford University Press, 2006.

Raphael, Ray. *The First American Revolution: Before Lexington and Concord*. New York: New Press, 2002.

Rappelye, Charles. *Sons of Providence: The Brown Brothers, the Slave Trade, and the American Revolution*. New York: Simon and Schuster, 2006.

Rapport, Michael. *Nationality and Citizenship in Revolutionary France: The Treatment of Foreigners, 1789–1799*. Oxford: Clarendon Press, 2000.

Rapport, Mike. *The Unruly City: Paris, London and New York in the Age of Revolution*. New York: Basic Books, 2017.

Rawley, James A. and Stephen D. Behrendt, *The Transatlantic Slave Trade: A History*, rev. ed. Lincoln: University of Nebraska Press, 2005.

Rediker, Marcus. *The Fearless Benjamin Lay: The Quaker Dwarf Who Became the First Revolutionary Abolitionist*. Boston: Beacon Press, 2017.

Reid, Loren. *Charles James Fox: A Man for the People*. London: Longmans, 1969.

Reilly, Robin. *Pitt the Younger, 1759–1806*. London: Cassell, 1978.

Reinhard, Marcel. Review of Robert R. Palmer, *The Age of the Democratic Revolution*, in *Annales historiques de la Révolution française* 32 (1960) 220–23.

Reynolds, Sian. *Marriage and Revolution: Monsieur and Madame Roland*. Oxford: Oxford University Press, 2012.

Richter, Daniel K. *Facing East from Indian Country: A Native History of Early America*. Cambridge, MA: Harvard University Press, 2001.

Risjord, Norman K. *Chesapeake Politics, 1781–1800*. New York: Columbia University Press, 1978.

Rivage, Justin du. *Revolution against Empire: Taxes, Politics and the Origins of American Independence*. New Haven: Yale University Press, 2017.

Robin, Corey. *The Reactionary Mind: Conservatism from Edmund Burke to Donald Trump*. 2nd ed. Oxford: Oxford University Press, 2017.

Rodgers, Nini. *Ireland, Slavery, and Anti-Slavery, 1612–1865*. New York: Palgrave, 2007.

Rogers, George C., Jr. *Evolution of a Federalist: William Loughton Smith of Charleston, 1758–1812*. Columbia, SC: University of South Carolina Press, 1962.

Rogers, Nicholas. "Burning Tom Paine: Loyalism and Counter-Revolution in Britain, 1792–1793," *Histoire sociale / Social History* 32, no. 64 (1999) 139–71.

Rogers, Nicholas. *Crowds, Culture, and Politics in Georgian Britain*. Oxford: Clarendon Press, 1998.

Rogers, Nicholas. "The Gordon Riots and the Politics of War," in *The Gordon Riots*, Haywood and Seed, eds., 23–45.

Rogers, Rachel. "The Society of the Friends of the Rights of Man, 1792–1794: British and Irish Radical Conjunctions in Republican Paris," *Révolution française* 11 (2016), 1–26.

Roney, Jessica C. *Governed by a Spirit of Opposition: The Origins of American Political Practice in Colonial Philadelphia*. Baltimore: Johns Hopkins University Press, 2014.

Rose, Lisle A. *Prologue to Democracy: The Federalists in the South, 1789–1800*. Lexington: University of Kentucky Press, 1968.

Rosenfeld, Sophia A. *Common Sense: A Political History*. Cambridge, MA: Harvard University Press, 2011.

Rosman, Doreen. *The Evolution of the English Churches, 1500–2000*. Cambridge: Cambridge University Press, 2003.

Rudé, George. "The Middlesex Electors of 1768–1769," *English Historical Review* 75, no. 297 (1960), 601–17.

Rudé, George. *Wilkes and Liberty*. Oxford: Oxford University Press, 1962.

Russell, David Lee. *The American Revolution in the Southern Colonies*. Jefferson, NC: Macfarland, 2000.

Ryerson, Richard Alan. "Leadership in Crisis: The Radical Committees of Philadelphia and the Coming of the Revolution in Pennsylvania, 1765–1776. A Study in the Revolutionary Process." PhD thesis, Johns Hopkins University, 1973.

Ryerson, Richard Alan. *The Revolution Is Now Begun: The Radical Committees of Philadelphia, 1765–1776*. Philadelphia: University of Pennsylvania Press, 1978.

Sainsbury, John. *Disaffected Patriots: London Supporters of Revolutionary America, 1769-1782*. Montreal: McGill-Queen's University Press, 1987.

Saint-Louis, Vertus. *Mer et liberté: Haiti (1492–1794)*. Port au Prince: Bibliothèque nationale de Haiti, 2008.

Schama, Simon. *Patriots & Liberators: Revolution in the Netherlands, 1780–1813*. New York: Collins, 1977.

Schama, Simon. *Rough Crossings: Britain, the Slaves, and the American Revolution*. New York: Ecco, 2006.

Scott, Julius. *The Common Wind: Afro-American Currents in the Age of the Haitian Revolution*. London: Verso, 2018.

Seed, John. "Gentleman Dissenters: The Social and Political Meanings of Rational Dissent in the 1770s and 1780s," *Historical Journal* 28, no. 2 (1985), 299–325.

Semmel, Bernard. *The Methodist Revolution*. New York: Basic Books, 1973.

Seymour, Joseph. *The Pennsylvania Associators, 1747–1777.* Yardley, PA: Westholme, 2012.

Sharp, James Roger. *American Politics in the Early Republic: The New Nation in Crisis.* New Haven: Yale University Press, 1993.

Sharp, James Roger. *The Deadlocked Election of 1800: Jefferson, Burr and the Union in the Balance.* Lawrence: University Press of Kansas, 2010.

Shoemaker, Robert. *The London Mob: Violence and Disorder in Eighteenth-Century England.* London: Hambleton, 2004.

Shusterman, Noah C. "All His Power Lies in the Distaff: Robespierre, Women and the French Revolution," *Past & Present* 223, no. 1 (2014), 129–60.

Sinha, Manisha. *The Slave's Cause: A History of Abolition.* New Haven: Yale University Press, 2016.

Skeats, Herbert S. *History of the Free Churches of England, 1688–1891.* London: Alexander & Shepherd, 1891.

Slaughter, Thomas P. *Independence: The Tangled Roots of the American Revolution.* New York: Hill and Wang, 2014.

Slaughter, Thomas P. *The Whiskey Rebellion: Frontier Epilogue to the American Revolution.* Oxford: Oxford University Press, 1986.

Slavin, Morris. *The Hébertistes to the Guillotine: Anatomy of a Conspiracy in Revolutionary France.* Baton Rouge: Louisiana State University Press, 1994.

Small, Stephen. *Political Thought in Ireland, 1776–1798: Republicanism, Patriotism, and Radicalism.* Oxford: Clarendon Press, 2002.

Smith, James Morton. *Freedom's Fetters: The Alien and Sedition Laws and American Civil Liberties.* Ithaca: Cornell University Press, 1956.

Smyth, David. "The Volunteer Movement in Ulster: Background and Development 1745–1785." PhD thesis, Queen's University Belfast, 1974.

Soderlund, Jean R. *Quakers & Slavery: A Divided Spirit.* Princeton: Princeton University Press, 1985.

Sorel, Albert. *L'Europe et la Révolution française.* Paris: Plon, 1885. 8 vols.

Sosin, Jack M. *Agents and Merchants: British Colonial Policy and the Origins of the American Revolution.* Lincoln: University of Nebraska Press, 1965.

Spangler, Jewel L. *Virginians Reborn: Anglican Monopoly, Evangelical Dissent, and the Rise of the Baptists in the Late Eighteenth Century.* Charlottesville: University of Virginia Press, 2008.

Standiford, Les. *Desperate Sons: Samuel Adams, Patrick Henry, John Hancock, and the Secret Bands of Radicals Who Led the Colonies to War.* New York: Harper, 2012.

Stanhope, Earl. *Life of the Right Honourable William Pitt.* London: Murray, 1861. 4 vols.

Stites, Richard. *The Four Horsemen: Riding to Liberty in Post-Napoleonic Europe.* Oxford: Oxford University Press, 2014.

Stoddard, Lothrop. *The French Revolution in San Domingo.* Boston: Houghton Mifflin, 1914.

Stuart, Daniel. *Peace and Reform, against War and Corruption.* London, 1794.

Sydenham, M. J. *The Girondins*. London: Athlone Press, 1961.

Tackett, Timothy. *Becoming a Revolutionary: The Deputies of the First French National Assembly and the Emergence of a Revolutionary Culture (1789–1790)*. Princeton: Princeton University Press, 1996.

Tackett, Timothy. *The Coming of the Terror in the French Revolution*. Cambridge, MA: Harvard University Press, 2015.

Tarrow, Sidney. *The Language of Contention: Revolutions in Words, 1688–2012*. Cambridge: Cambridge University Press, 2013.

Tarrow, Sidney. *The New Transnational Activism*. Cambridge: Cambridge University Press, 2005.

Taylor, Alan. "The Art of Hook and Snivey: Political Culture in Upstate New York during the 1790s," *Journal of American History* 79, no. 4 (1993), 1371–96.

Taylor, Alan. *The Internal Enemy: Slavery and War in Virginia, 1772–1832*. New York: Norton, 2013.

Tenbus, Eric G. "Crisis in Ireland: The Tenure of Lord Fitzwilliam, 1794–1795," *The Consortium on the Revolutionary Era: Selected Papers, 1998* (1999), 47–56.

Thackeray, Francis. *A History of the Right Hon. William Pitt*. London: Rivington, 1826. 2 vols.

Thiot, Léonard. *Les sociétés populaires du Beauvais, 1793-1794*. Beauvais: Imprimerie départementale de l'Oise, 1910.

Thomas, Leslie J. "The Nonconsumption and Nonimportation Movement against the Townshend Acts, 1767–1770," in Cosner, McCarthy, Toscano, and Sharp, eds. *Resistance*, 137–92.

Thomas, Peter D. G. *British Politics and the Stamp Act Crisis: The First Phase of the American Revolution, 1763–1767*. Oxford: Clarendon Press, 1975.

Thomas, Peter D. G. *George III: King and Politicians, 1760–1770*. Manchester: Manchester University Press, 2002.

Thomas, Peter D. G. *Tea Party to Independence: The Third Stage of the American Revolution*. Oxford: Oxford University Press, 1991.

Thomas, Peter D. G. *The Townshend Duties Crisis: The Second Phase of the American Revolution, 1767–1773*. Oxford: Clarendon Press, 1987.

Thompson, E. P. *The Making of the English Working Class*. New York: Pantheon, 1964.

Thornton, John K. "I Am the Subject of the King of Congo," African Political Ideology and the Haitian Revolution," *Journal of World History* 4, no. 2 (1993) 181–214.

Tiedemann, Joseph S. *Reluctant Revolutionaries: New York City and the Road to Independence, 1763–1776*. Ithaca: Cornell University Press, 1997.

Tilly, Charles. "Britain Creates the Social Movement," CRSO Working Paper No. 232. Ann Arbor, 1981.

Tilly, Charles. *Popular Contention in Great Britain, 1758–1834*. Cambridge, MA: Harvard University Press, 1995.

Tilly, Charles. *Social Movements, 1768–2004*. Boulder, CO: Paradigm Press, 2004.

Tombs, Robert. *The English and Their History*. New York: Vintage, 2014.

Tombs, Robert and Isabelle. *That Sweet Enemy: Britain and France: History of a Love-Hate Relationship*. New York: Vintage, 2006.

Toohey, Robert E. *Liberty and Empire: British Radical Solutions to the American Problem, 1774–1776*. Lexington: University Press of Kentucky, 1978.

Tozzi, Christopher. *Nationalizing France's Army: Foreign, Black, and Jewish Troops in the French Military, 1715–1831*. Charlottesville: University of Virginia Press, 2016.

Turley, David. *The Culture of English Antislavery, 1780–1860*. London: Routledge, 1991.

Turner, Frederick Jackson. "The Origin of Genet's Projected Attack on Louisiana and the Floridas," *American Historical Review* 3, no. 4 (1898), 650–71.

Turner, Michael J. *Pitt the Younger: A Life*. London: Hambledon, 2003.

Tyler, John W. *Smugglers and Patriots: Boston Merchants and the Advent of the American Revolution*. Boston: Northeastern University Press, 1986.

Ulrich, Laurel Thatcher. "Political Protest and the World of Goods," in Gray and Kamensky, eds. *The Oxford Handbook of the American Revolution*, 64–84.

Valentine, Alan. *Lord North*. Norman: University of Oklahoma Press, 1967. 2 vols.

Vaudry, Richard W. *Anglicans and the Atlantic World: High Churchmen, Evangelicals, and the Quebec Connection*. Montreal: McGill-Queen's University Press, 2003.

Veitch, George Stead. *The Genesis of Parliamentary Reform*. Hamden, CT: Archon, 1965.

Verhoeven, Wil. *Americomania and the French Revolution Debate in Britain, 1789–1802*. Cambridge: Cambridge University Press, 2013.

Vincent, Emma. "The Responses of Scottish Churchmen to the French Revolution, 1789–1802," *Scottish Historical Review* 73, no. 2 (1994), 191–215.

Wahnich, Sophie. *L'impossible citoyen: L'étranger dans le discours de la Révolution française*. Paris: Albin Michel, 1997.

Waldman, Steven. *Founding Faith: Providence, Politics, and the Birth of Religious Freedom in America*. New York: Random House, 2008.

Waldstreicher, David. *In the Midst of Perpetual Fetes: The Making of American Nationalism, 1776–1820*. Chapel Hill: University of North Carolina Press, 1997.

Waldstreicher, David. *Runaway America: Benjamin Franklin, Slavery and the American Revolution*. New York: Hill and Wang, 2004.

Waldstreicher, David. *Slavery's Constitution: From Revolution to Ratification*. New York: Hill and Wang, 2009.

Walter, Gérard. *Histoire des Jacobins*. Paris, 1946.

Walvin, James. *An African's Life: The Life and Times of Olaudah Equiano, 1745–1797*. London: Cassell, 1998.

Walvin, James. *Black and White: The Negro in English Society, 1555–1945*. London: Allen Lane, 1973.

Walvin, James. *England, Slaves and Freedom, 1776–1838*. Jackson, MS: University Press of Mississippi, 1986.

Walvin, James. "The Slave Trade, Quakers, and British Abolition," in *Quakers & Abolition,* Brycchan Carey and Geoffrey Plank, eds. (Urbana: University of Illinois Press, 2014), 165–79.

Walvin, James. *The Zong: A Massacre, the Law, and the End of Slavery.* New Haven: Yale University Press, 2011.

Wansey, Henry. *An Excursion to the United States of North America in the Summer of 1794.* Salisbury: Easton, 1796.

Ward, Harry M. *The War of Independence and the Transformation of American Society.* London: UCL Press, 1999.

Ward, W. R. *Religion and Society in England, 1790–1850.* London: Batsford, 1972.

Warner, William B. *Protocols of Liberty: Communication Innovation & the American Revolution.* Chicago: University of Chicago Press, 2014.

Wells, William V. *The Life and Public Services of Samuel Adams, Being a Narrative of His Acts and Opinions.* Boston: Little, Brown & Co., 1865–1866. 3 vols.

Werkmeister, Lucyle Thomas. *A Newspaper History of England, 1792–1793.* Lincoln: University of Nebraska Press, 1967.

Westerkamp, Marilyn J. *Women and Religion in Early America, 1600–1850.* New York: Routledge, 1999.

Whelan, Kevin. *The Tree of Liberty: Radicalism, Catholicism and the Construction of Irish Identity, 1760–1830.* Notre Dame: University of Notre Dame Press, 1996.

White, Ashli. *Encountering Revolution: Haiti and the Early Republic.* Baltimore: Johns Hopkins University Press, 2010.

Whiteman, Jeremy J. *Reform, Revolution and French Global Policy, 1787–1791.* London: Ashgate, 2003.

Whyte, Iain. *Scotland and the Abolition of Black Slavery, 1756–1838.* Edinburgh: Edinburgh University Press, 2006.

Wick, Daniel L. *A Conspiracy of Well-Intentioned Men: The Society of Thirty and the French Revolution.* New York: Garland, 1987.

Wilentz, Sean. *Chants Democratic: New York City & the Rise of the American Working Class, 1788–1850.* Oxford: Oxford University Press, 1984.

Wilentz, Sean. *No Property in Man: Slavery and Antislavery at the Nation's Founding.* Cambridge, MA: Harvard University Press, 2018.

Wilentz, Sean. *The Rise of American Democracy: Jefferson to Lincoln.* New York: Norton, 2005.

Williams, Basil. *The Life of William Pitt, Earl of Chatham.* New York: Longmans, 1913.

Williams, Gwyn A. *Artisans and Sans-Culottes: Popular Movements in France and Britain during the French Revolution.* New York: Norton, 1969.

Wills, Gary. *Negro President: Jefferson and the Slave Power.* Boston: Houghton Mifflin, 2003.

Wilson, David A. *United Irishmen, United States: Immigrant Radicals in the Early Republic.* Ithaca: Cornell University Press, 1998.

Wise, Steven M. *Though the Heavens May Fall: The Landmark Trial That Led to the End of Human Slavery.* Cambridge, MA: Da Capo Press, 2005.

Witcover, Jules. *Party of the People: A History of the Democrats.* New York: Random House, 2003.

Withrow, Bryce E. "A Biographical Study of Barlow Trecothick, 1720–1775." Master's thesis, Emporia State University, 1979.

Wold, Alte L. *Scotland and the French Revolutionary War, 1792–1802.* Edinburgh: Edinburgh University Press, 2015.

Woloch, Isser. *Jacobin Legacy: The Democratic Movement under the Directory.* Princeton: Princeton University Press, 1970.

Woodcock, George. "The Meaning of Revolution in Britain," in *The French Revolution and British Culture*, Ceri Crossley and Ian Small, eds. (Oxford: Oxford University Press, 1989), 1–30.

Yates, Nigel. *Eighteenth-Century Britain: Religion and Politics, 1714–1815.* London: Pearson, 2008.

York, Neil Longley. *Neither Kingdom nor Nation: The Irish Quest for Constitutional Rights, 1698–1800.* Washington, DC: Catholic University of America Press, 1995.

Young, Alfred E. *The Democratic-Republicans of New York: The Origins, 1763–1797.* Chapel Hill: University of North Carolina Press, 1967.

Young, Christopher J. "Connecting the President and the People: Washington's Neutrality, Genet's Challenge, and Hamilton's Fight for Public Support," *Journal of the Early Republic* 31, no. 3 (2011), 435–66.

Zagarri, Rosemary. "Gender and the First Party System," in *Federalists Reconsidered*, Doron Ben-Atar and Barbara B. Oberg, eds. (Charlottesville: University Press of Virginia, 1998), 118–34.

Zagarri, Rosemary. *Revolutionary Backlash: Women and Politics in the Early American Republic.* Philadelphia: University of Pennsylvania Press, 2011.

Zilversmit, Arthur. *The First Emancipation: The Abolition of Slavery in the North.* Chicago: University of Chicago Press, 1967.

CPSIA information can be obtained
at www.ICGtesting.com
Printed in the USA
LVHW011503270723
753506LV00006B/211